Studying and Describing
Unwritten Languages

Studying and Describing Unwritten Languages

by Luc Bouquiaux
and Jacqueline M. C. Thomas

translated by
James Roberts

A Publication of
SIL International
1992

Originally published in 1976 by Société d'Etudes Linguistiques et Anthropologiques de France as *Enquête et description des langues à tradition orale. L'enquête de terrain et l'analyse grammaticale, 1. Approche linguistique, 2. Approche thématique, 3.*

English translation © 1992 by SIL International
New Impression 2006
Library of Congress Catalog No: 92–80686
ISBN: 0–88312–814–4

All Rights Reserved

No part of this publication may be reproduced, stored in a retrieval system, or transmitted in any form or by any means—electronic, mechanical, photocopy, recording, or otherwise—without the express permission of the SIL International, with the exception of brief excerpts in journal articles or reviews.

Copies of this and other publications of SIL International may be obtained from

International Academic Bookstore
SIL International
7500 W. Camp Wisdom Road
Dallas, TX 75236-5699

Voice: 972-708-7404
Fax: 972-708-7363
Email: academic_books@sil.org
Internet: http://www.ethnologue.com

Contents

Foreword vii

Preface ix

Translator's Preface xi

1 Fieldwork and Grammatical Analysis 1
   Part I – Introduction to Fieldwork 3
      1. General problems 5
      2. Material aspects of the study 9
      3. Gathering data 27
      4. Using the questionnaires 39
      5. Processing the data 71
   Part II – Concepts of Linguistic Analysis 95
      1. Phonology 97
      2. Morphology 103
      3. Word-level analysis 113
      4. Grammatical categories 115
      5. Phrase-level analysis 125
      6. The level of grammatical functions 135
      7. Utterance level (enoncematic, clausematic) 143
      8. Recapitulation 153
         Bibliography 159

2 Linguistic Approach—Questionnaires 175

1. Instructions for the recording of linguistic data 177
2. Linguistic inventory questionnaire 183
3. Questionnaire for an extensive survey 199
4. Phonological guide 231
5. Morphology: derivation and compounding 239
6. Verb phrase 257
7. The noun and the noun phrase 275
8. Sentence types 303
9. Sentence questionnaire 309

3 Thematic Approach—Questionnaires 399

10. Traditional technologies 401
11. Ethnobotany 513
12. Ethnozoology 521
13. Anatomy and physiology, animals and plants 557
14. Instructions for collecting zoological and botanical specimens 641
15. Sociological phenomena 653
16. Psychological phenomena 665
17. Names, measurement, and time 673
18. Oral tradition 689
19. Language contact 715
20. Sociolinguistic questionnaire 723

Foreword to the Second Edition (1976)

by Luc Bouquiaux

The first edition of these questionnaires was exhausted within three years. This is surprisingly quick for a work of this type, given the rate of sale of descriptive monographs of unwritten languages, whose study is meant to be facilitated by these questionnaires. This indicates that they responded to a real need. The authors, Africanists for the most part, were able to envision the problems posed by research and description in a sufficiently general way, so that workers in other areas—specialists in Oceanic, American, Oriental, and even European languages—could use them profitably. The questionnaires were intended to be an indispensable working tool of field research, the only book needed together with notebooks, especially in out-of-the-way places where luggage must be kept to a minimum.

In order to complete the resources of the ethnolinguist, one last working tool was still lacking (the only one that could not be dispensed with at the beginning, if we intend to do scientific work), that is, a practical manual of phonetics. This void has now been filled. Three among the authors of this work have put together an *Introduction to Phonetics (articulatory and distinctive)*, published by the Presses Universitaires de France. The book comes with a record of the sounds described. The authors showed the same care as in the compilation of the questionnaires in making a practical manual which allows for resolution of notation problems and which opens onto phonological analysis, a preliminary indispensable to any description. While generativists have come to think that the phonemic level is not useful in passing from a more or less abstract syntactic form to the full phonetic realization, it is good to reiterate that the authors, in contrast, feel that the phonemic system does correspond to a reality for the speakers of a given language. Especially the introduction, which has only been modified slightly, sets forth a strongly structuralist position, in which the phonological model is extended to the totality of the linguistic facts. This viewpoint is particularly evident in the Part 2 of this first volume, entitled *Concepts of Linguistic Analysis*. Although the generative outlook is original in some respects and places great importance on the form of rules, it has hardly reflected on the problem of the categories and units of language. For us this is the central problem, the pivotal point of all description. We feel that grammatical categories, far from being identical from one language to another, must be redefined in a given frame for each language, following methods similar to those used for determining phonemes. Apart from the method presented in the introduction, it is envisioned that this book would be as complete a collection of documentation as possible, whatever theoretical use is ultimately made of it.

Readers' comments and personal experience with using the questionnaires led us to correct most of the spelling and typing mistakes, to modify several inappropriate utterances in the sentence questionnaire, to transfer or develop certain points, notably in the questionnaires dealing with phonological research and problems of derivation and inflection. Ethnologist colleagues also criticized, sometimes sharply, the questionnaires of family relationships, but since they had nothing better to suggest, nothing was changed in them; we felt that something that existed, though not faultless, was inappreciably better than nothing. Besides, these questionnaires are not aimed at a study of the family, but at an exhaustive coverage of terminology.

The bibliography was redone to include the most recent publications in the field of unwritten languages.

This new edition was also expanded with several new questionnaires, including a questionnaire on linguistic inventory. We thank our colleagues of ERA 246, among whom I especially want to mention Pierre-Francis Lacroix, Geneviève Calame-Griaule and Suzanne Platiel, for adding their questionnaires on time expressions, currency, the oral style of traditional storytellers, and the research matrix on measures and accounts.

Jacques Barrau pointed us to Pierre Boiteau's questionnaires on the study of medicines, as well as R. N. H. Bulmer's field methods in ethnozoology.

Also appearing here are the originals of Claudine Friedberg-Berthe's questionnaires on ethnobotany. These questionnaires are not as foreign to language study as it might seem, if you accept our point of view which is expressed throughout the work, namely that the language is equally an instrument of communication and an expression of a social reality. One cannot stand without the other, and neither of these two aspects may be neglected.

This work was realized with the technical collaboration of Annette François, Françoise Leduc, Charlotte Levantal, and Jacques Silly. Drawings and their labellings are by Corinne Venot, for the first edition (1971); and with Colette Chaumet, Anne du Parc, Françoise Landau, Micheline Lebarbier, Anne-Marie Renaud, Jacqueline Vallet, for the second edition (1976).

Preface

The principal part of this volume consists of documents resulting from work carried out by a team of researchers. Formed in 1966, this team consisted at first of a dozen researchers, linguists, ethnologists, and naturalists (these latter concerned principally with ethnobotany and ethnozoology) under Cooperative Research Program No. 121, The Central African Plateau, of the Centre National de Recherche Scientifique (CNRS). Occasionally the group profited from the collaboration of an ethnomusicologist. In 1968 the ethnologists left this program to form another group, while the other researchers regrouped within the Research Team 74 (ER 74), following the collaboration begun three years earlier. This gave the group a more specifically linguistic orientation.

The territory where the members of ER 74 worked stretches from northern Nigeria to the farther reaches of the Central African Republic and the Sudan, including Cameroon and Chad and portions of Congo and Zaire. This area encompasses many languages, genetically and typologically very diverse; in fact, the three main families of African languages described by Greenberg converge here: the Congo-Kordofanian, the Nilo-Saharan, and the Afro-Asiatic. We find both languages with noun classes and languages with gender categories; both monosyllabic and polysyllabic (even agglutinating) languages. The diversity in the phonologies, both segmental and tonal, is just as great. Thus, the scholars of ER 74 had a great wealth of varied materials from their very first meetings. They customarily met every other week, except during sessions on the field, to share their data, problems, and experiences. Other researchers with the same concerns, although not Africanists, joined them from time to time.

Young researchers, doing fieldwork for the first time, thus came into contact with the experience of older scholars—experience gained with much difficulty by a series of trials and errors. The struggles of the younger workers made most of us realize how necessary it is to have some research techniques available at the outset.

Each one had, no doubt, received a solid linguistic training. However, theoretical university courses, even with some practical exercises, do not fill certain gaps. One becomes aware of these, sometimes with bitterness and discouragement, when in an isolated area, perhaps in difficult physical conditions, faced with the fleeting reality of a language, which at first seems bristling with insurmountable difficulties and seems impossible to write down. Such things must be drawn out of language helpers, no doubt well-meaning and well-intentioned, but who also must have some training before they can set forth their extensive knowledge in an orderly and systematic manner.

The questions of the younger researchers and the experiences of the older ones, and the exchanges between the two, led first to a progressive elaboration of linguistic research questionnaires. Founded on proven methodological bases, these materials include very simple techniques and practical, even mundane, details of the conditions of fieldwork. Workers who already have some field experience will realize that this is not an inconsequential matter, but that organizational details, the manner of collecting data, along with its classification and documentation, although they seem banal, determine to a fair extent the quality of the research, its speed and efficiency.

The emphasis placed on methodology throughout this work will therefore not be surprising. But our ambitions, of course, are not limited to linguistic research alone; sooner or later, this must lead to a description whose principles are seen in the background of even the first research questionnaires.

While older members of the ER have published complete language descriptions, younger workers have not had to wait to finish their fieldwork (if indeed it is ever finished) before publishing their first results. The Bulletin de la SELAF *(Société pour l'Etude des Langues Africaines)*, since its creation in 1967, has afforded them the opportunity of publishing their studies.

Since the primary purpose of this volume is to offer a group of varied questionnaires for our colleagues to evaluate, we will not linger on questions directly relevant to linguistic description. Several years of collaboration between the various members of the team has given rise, not to a single doctrine nor to a school, but to a certain community of views and ideas. Accordingly, there is a noticeable relationship between different works already published, a clear resemblance in the way of approaching a problem or of reacting to a proposal. Thus we have devoted an exposé to the principles of description that we recommend. These principles could no doubt be improved, but we do not claim to have arrived at the end of our examination, and the advice and criticism that we will receive will permit us to progress in our study. At least it will be agreed that for comparative purposes, it is valuable to have descriptive grammars of a large number of languages that follow a single set of principles, and (if possible) a single model.

The introduction which follows this preface takes up and develops the main points of a course given by Luc Bouquiaux at the Session of African Linguistics organized by *Afrique et Langage* in July 1969 at the Faculté des Lettres of Aix-en-Provence. This course was aimed at providing a method of linguistic research for the participants, who were already involved or about to be involved with the description of an African language. For the purposes of publication and in the perspective of the Colloquium that we organized on this subject, we enlarged its scope; this was done without difficulty, for while the ER 74 was essentially concerned with Africa, we were made sensitive to problems common to all working with unwritten languages. Meetings with Oceanist and Americanist colleagues, among others, made us feel how much they shared our concerns and how much their studies had in common with ours; above all, the sharing of our respective experiences allowed each of us to enlarge our horizons.

Translator's Preface

We felt in questionnaire 9 (Sentences), the exemplifying sentences in French were translated and realphabetized according to the key word in English. Choosing a key word for the English rendering was not always easy, especially when an idiomatic expression was involved. We did attempt, however, to choose a variety of expressions and key words whenever possible. The reader will notice also that the list does not exhaust the English lexicon, although it still covers the same semantic ground as the French original. For example, only one use is given for the word *about* (sentence #3), although several other usages could be exemplified for this English word. Other meanings of *about* are exemplified under the key words *around, almost, close,* etc. Browsing through an English dictionary revealed other lexical items that might have been included: between *abandon* (#1,2) and *about* (#3) come the words *abide* and *able/ability*. Although these latter words do not appear, the semantically-related items *stay* (for *abide*) and *capable* (for *able*) are exemplified elsewhere among the sentences. The authors themselves emphasize that the questionnaires are to be used mainly as a guide. If a researcher wishes to add more words and sentences to the list, he should feel free to do so. We felt, however, that it would not be worthwhile to add a significant number of new examples simply to yield a more complete coverage of the English lexicon. The sentences are to be used, after all, to exploit the lexicon of the language under study, not of some western language. The authors point out (p.78) that the speaker should be guided by the spirit of his language, not by the English sentences he is to translate. It is important that he understand this; he should feel free to write down any additional vernacular words that occur to him while he is working on the sentences, even if they do not fit into one of the sentences in the list.

1
Fieldwork and Grammatical Analysis

Part I
Introduction to Fieldwork

Most of the authors of this work have been influenced to some extent by the teaching of André Martinet. In the course of our studies, we have become familiar with his theories and his terminology, which we have adopted for the most part. However, since Martinet is not specifically concerned with the complete description of a given language (of an African language in particular, or of any exotic language in general), we were led to reconsider many of the problems that he treats in his works from a new perspective, and to treat them differently. Some of his postulates, sketched roughly in his *Elements of General Linguistics,* have been greatly developed and reinterpreted, especially those which deal with exploiting the minimum utterance.

The teaching of André G. Haudricourt and his working methods have likewise influenced most of us profoundly; this is particularly evident in phonology. It was Haudricourt who also drew our attention to the related fields of ethnobotany, ethnozoology, and technology, and to the contribution that research in these areas could make to our studies, and in a general way, to the total human context of linguistic study.

Finally, the thought of Emile Benveniste provided fruitful reflections on particularly sticky aspects of grammar. The keen interest that he showed for our work, particularly for our methodological research, and the encouragement he lavished on us from the beginning, have prompted us to dedicate this book to him.

The theoretical bases of our research and descriptions are thus traceable to these three masters of French linguistics.

1
General Problems

1.1 Goal of the study

Field research in unwritten languages might have several quite different goals. It may focus on the scientific description of the grammar of a language, for example. Or, beyond the strictly linguistic aspects, it may focus on the ethnological background, or on ways of thinking that underlie linguistic expression (for example, the way that reality is divided up by tense and aspect categories). The goal might be the compilation of a normative grammar, especially if the language is to be taught. Again, the thrust may be toward the problems of translation, as in the case of missionary linguists and Bible societies. Finally, it may be limited to the collection of documents for comparative or typological studies.

1.2 Working conditions

As indicated in the preface, most of the authors work basically in central Africa. Some Africanists working in West Africa also participated in the development of the questionnaires, as well as one Americanist, three Oceanists, and one Southeast Asian specialist. These scholars from diverse backgrounds, in sharing their personal experiences, became keenly aware that the problems of linguistic description often differ widely by locality and geographic environment, even within the same continent.

Geographic considerations

Africa. Almost everywhere there is a major common European language (English, French, Portuguese). All peoples were colonized to some extent, but colonization did not destroy the existing social structures. In spite of the noticeable influence of the colonial European language, especially evident in loanwords, there has not in general been any drastic decline of the local languages. In addition, there are trade languages in many places, and most speakers are bilingual.

All, or almost all, of these peoples are accessible, although certain obstacles, make some groups difficult to reach mainly due to the nature of the terrain. As elsewhere, peoples of the forest, of the mountains, or even of the river, are often harder to contact than those on the savannahs.

Even if in-depth studies are not numerous, sufficient information is still available on linguistic and cultural ties, and placing the ethnic groups does not cause any difficulty. Even the smallest languages can be fit into the larger picture.

Oceania. The population here have been strongly acculturated, and greatly repressed by the colonizers. In some areas, this has resulted in the loss of the mother tongue. Linguistically, we find very small groups which are greatly differentiated.

America. Many places are almost inaccessible. The major languages of civilization have not reached them, and there are very few trade languages. This situation makes the beginning research particularly difficult, since the researcher and the language speaker do not share a common language. Almost everywhere we find very small groups in the process of disappearing, and our knowledge about linguistic and cultural affinities is sketchy.

Asia. Here also, many places are difficult to reach. Alongside widespread languages that have served as the vehicle of great and venerable civilizations, we find many small languages and cultural minorities, still poorly known and localized today.

These geographical conditions determine the working conditions. If the field is accessible by car, a lot of material can be taken along, and the work will of course be quite different than when long journeys must be made on foot, with luggage kept to a minimum.

Similarly, the investigation will be done differently, depending on whether a major European language or a trade language is used. When no common language exists, a different procedure will be required from the start, since the linguist will first have to gain a practical knowledge of the language he is studying.

Sociological conditions

The sociological conditions of the project are equally important. The language studied will vary according to whether the community is urban or rural, whether the people are farmers or fishermen, or whether the religion is Christian, Muslim, or animist. In a patriarchal or matriarchal society, the position of the woman will vary, and will influence the course of the study. In a closed society the researcher may have great difficulty in making contacts. In some communities he will have to live in a communal dwelling, while in others, he may be obliged to live isolated.

Personal factors

Similarly, characteristics of the worker himself will determine differences in the working situation. His personality, age, sex, social position, and physical appearance are all factors which affect his relationships with the people, and thus the particular form of the research, and even its results.

General Problems

The working conditions will also vary according to the techniques used (study of the total population; sampling; use of a single speaker with surveys; etc.).

In light of these considerations, it does not seem possible to propose a single method which will meet all possible situations. The questionnaires, whether presented here or still being developed, take into account the experiences of the different participants, of course. However, the questionnaires are only good insofar as they are sufficiently flexible and adaptable to the needs and circumstances. The ones presented here are more a guide for thought, and an orientation for suggested research; they are not strict instructions or rigid principles to be applied without adaptation or reinterpretation.

1.3 Principles of investigation

Regardless of the working conditions and the goal of the study, the collection of data will be done either directly, or by means of questionnaires. Our approach combines these two methods. The use of questionnaires is clearly more fruitful for extensive surveys, the establishment of the phonology, collection of specialized vocabulary (techniques, anatomy, social structures, etc.), problems of language contact and dialectology, in fact everything that is more strictly linguistic. On the other hand, some data will have to be collected almost entirely by the direct method, such as that concerned with the oral literature. And some data will be advantageously collected by a combination of these two methods, as for some grammatical questionnaires, the sentence questionnaire, the questionnaire on sentence structure, and especially for that which concerns thematic studies (vocabulary of objects and technical activities, ethnozoology, ethnobotany, etc.).

1.4 Objectives of the study

The objectives of the study justify the method used, and provide guidance and orientation for the study. In extensive surveys for comparative purposes, it is clear that the first two or three of our questionnaires will be enough to supply the needed material, since this study is of a distinct character once the elementary data is collected. However, in an intensive investigation intended for a monograph, greater use of our questionnaires can be made; as a whole, they provide the material for an in-depth study. In intensive research, most of the documents collected must be combined with an in-depth ethnological study, to be truly valuable. This is not always possible, because many linguists have no ethnological training. Thus, we have sought to provide for the reader a great number of explanatory notes. These notes are fundamental from the ethnological standpoint, but are not intended for specialized ethnological studies.

From our perspective, a minimum of basic intensive research must be done for each group. This will facilitate research with neighbors within the same group, and gives a fullness and depth to an extensive survey of these people that would be impossible without the knowledge gained through the beginning intensive study. Proceeding in this way allows us to deepen comparison and to push it farther than if the study had been exclusively extensive. On the other hand, it seems preferable for beginners to begin with intensive study which will allow them to perfect and test their training. Extensive research alone will always be superficial, and should preferably be left for the experienced worker.

Finally, we propose as a postulate of our own research that a study of the culture must accompany the study of an unwritten language. A narrowly linguistic study of the languages of well-known civilizations may be possible (although the notable works of E. Benveniste, for one, dispute this claim); however, this is unthinkable in the study of unwritten languages, of whose civilizations we know little or nothing. Otherwise, linguistic study remains an empty shell, a skeleton without flesh. Analyzing the grammatical structures of a language with no idea of the realities that they serve to express seems quite futile. Even though carefully thought out, such an undertaking is at least partially destined to failure, for we cannot dissociate a language from the society which uses it as a means of communication. The converse also seems true: the study of the structure of a society, independent of that of its language, can likewise have only limited value.

2
Material Aspects of the Study

The problems discussed here are mundane, certainly, but very important; knowing them will make work easier and will direct beginning efforts. This section is especially addressed to new workers and nonspecialists. We do not claim to exhaust the subject, but simply to share the results of our own experiences.

2.1 Setting up the project

This is determined by certain general problems already considered in the preceding chapter. We will not dwell on happenstances which are often quite far from linguistic considerations, but which turn the worker toward the choice of one language rather than another. Assuming these points have been settled, we will consider here only the technical aspect of establishing the project.

The type of study, whether intensive or extensive, determines the length of stay on the field. For collecting basic information and thematic research materials, the worker must be present on location, along with all necessary equipment (vehicles for transportation, camping equipment, manpower, etc.). On the other hand, for working on questionnaires for analysis, making revisions, and preparing for field research, a permanent base is necessary, complete with laboratory equipment and reliable speakers. This base will be established on the territory of the project, since the principal speakers must stay, as much as possible, in their local context. Moreover, most of the material preparation of an expedition can only be done on location.

2.2 Recording techniques

Since the recording of the data determines everything else, we will pay particular attention to this aspect, which constitutes the very foundation of the research.

2.2.1 Sound recording

What to record and why. We record in order to keep evidence and to have a means of control. Mistakes can be made; especially for beginners, it is good to allow others with more experience and a better ear to do checking. We can also review fragments where the transcription does not seem satisfactory (especially in materials collected at the beginning of the project), sometimes to furnish an illustration for publications, etc.

This method is useful both for phonology (e.g., recording lists of words in pairs) and for some grammatical studies (lists of noun phrases or verb phrases).

But the most important material to record is in fact spontaneous material which cannot be recorded by writing directly. Oral literature and the collection of texts (stories, conversations, speeches, proverbs, etc.) thus constitute the privileged domain of sound recording.

When to record. We do not record indiscriminately without first having a knowledge of the language and its problems. For phonology or grammatical examples, we make controlled recordings that are carefully prepared.

Even in collecting spontaneous documents, we do not record indiscriminately. We do not start the tape recorder as soon as someone opens his mouth. A bit of preparation is needed, to know what is worthwhile. Thus, some knowledge of the situation is desirable; we want to know who speaks well, who knows the stories, who is a good orator, what are the interesting ceremonies, the animated and instructive discourses, what are the conversation subjects to keep.

Identifying the recording. It is essential that the recording be precisely identified. The identification should appear first on the tape itself. The necessary information should be recorded at the beginning of the tape; briefly and clearly summarized on a label on the cartridge; and also indicated on the storage box. A separate card should be prepared with more precise identifications.

For recording texts, a questionnaire card has been provided (cf. Questionnaire 18.1, Text collection). Similar information should be collected, regardless of the type of material recorded (phonological, grammatical, etc.).

The technical instructions on recording are given in Questionnaire 1 (Instructions on recording). They may seem onerous sometimes, but are in fact very profitable, for penny-pinching economizations (recording at slow speed, on several tracks, making no copies of unique documents) often ends in disaster (loss of original documents, deterioration, erasure, impossibility of accurate monitoring, echo, bleeding when the speed is too slow, interferences, poor restoration).

The precautions on the quality of the recording are necessary because the documents collected will be submitted to authorized persons for advice. In addition, in order to be publishable, the recordings must be of sufficient technical quality.

The importance of preparation for strictly linguistic recordings may seem exaggerated, in that such documents are somewhat artificial with respect to the everyday current language. We ask for careful enunciation, and whistling for the tones; we make the speaker learn lists of words; we make him read (to avoid interruptions and repetitions); but we must remember that we are dealing in such cases with working documents. Spontaneity is not at issue.

In any case, whatever the type of documents collected, there must never be recording without transcription. Neither may there be transcription without translation,

Material Aspects of the Study

in both word-for-word and freer renderings. In fact, unless the language is well-known, the word-for-word translation is not only desirable, but essential. Conversely, it is not enough to give a simple word-for-word translation, which is sometimes almost incomprehensible. A free translation is necessary to grasp the general sense of the text. What seems obvious at the moment of recording during the research is not obvious two months later.

The recording instructions take into account the quality of the tape, but say nothing about the machine itself. The linguist's work is not that of a reporter; thus, small machines of the Mini 7 type are not recommended. On the other hand, those such as Nagra are not needed unless we are recording music at high fidelity. For speech, an intermediate machine (such as Uher, Philips, Gründig, even Sharp), simple to operate, and which will work both on batteries or from the main lines, will give excellent results.

While the recording machine can properly be chosen in a medium range, the quality of the microphone is essential, and one should not be stingy about its price. The primary criterion for the tape recorder used by a linguist is its handling for monitoring; that is, it must have a flexible and sturdy system, allowing frequent, numerous, and instantaneous rewinding that is necessary for transcription. The Nagra, for example, is particularly poorly adapted for this, while the touch system of the Uher is satisfactory, although somewhat fragile.

For one's first field project in language research, a dozen tapes will be sufficient; these will be pressed into service immediately.

The limitations of the machine. As valuable as the tape recorder's help can be, it is dangerous to rely on it too heavily. Linguistic research does not consist of gathering hours of recordings that can be worked through later at leisure. A recording is only useful if it is examined in detail immediately afterward with the speaker, to transcribe and translate it carefully.

The working method of some linguists is to record systematically, and only later to make a narrow phonetic transcription with a statistical and mechanical analysis of the data obtained. We find this largely a waste of time, an expenditure of effort disproportionate with respect to the results obtained. Above all, it exhibits a disdainful attitude toward the language and its speakers, treating them simply as passive objects.

No matter what recording machine is used, whether simple or more sophisticated for phonetic and acoustic analysis (kymograph, sonograph, etc.), it should be clear that no machine can replace the analysis done by the researcher. It is futile to imagine that it is enough to make a recording and then to put it through some laboratory instruments to produce a ready-made phonology, a succinct analysis of the tone system, etc. This work is up to the worker on the field. The machines are primarily means of control and verification of data; they cannot elaborate on them, nor give answers apart from precise questions. They can neither state problems nor resolve them.

The work of the linguist and the heart of data recording, then, is work with written records.

2.2.2 Written records

Two essential points must be covered: on one hand, the material used, and on the other hand, the use made of it.

A. The materials to use. In general, we recommend writing in pencil, using an eraser without crossing out. A relatively soft lead is recommended because it lasts better than a hard pencil. Never use water-soluble ink: dirty documents, stained with rain and mud, are still usable, but washed-out, obliterated documents are irretrievably lost.

We use ordinary notebooks, preferably with lined paper, and not loose sheets: sewn notebooks or stapled pads are better than glue or clips, because glues, even plastic ones, do not hold up in tropical climates, and metal clips rust and spoil the neighboring material. The notebooks must also have a firm cover.

In addition, we will need cards of a rather large size (5" x 8") whose use will be explained later, with wooden file boxes to hold 1000 cards. Wood is preferable, because iron rusts, is heavy, and is more expensive; cardboard boxes crush easily and do not hold up well in transport.

We also use notebooks for transcribing texts: manifolds (8½" x 11") with the necessary carbons for making duplicates.

Finally, we use manifold-type sheets (5" x 7" lined, with two copies) for the development of the dictionary.

For research by questionnaires, we provide a sufficient quantity of duplicating paper and stencils.

B. Use of the materials. This depends on the type of work involved:

(1) For DIRECT RESEARCH, research notebooks must be used for all first-draft notes. It is advantageous to use one notebook per subject: one for the techniques, one for animal names, one for plant names, etc. This method facilitates finding things later in the study, as well as working with them.

Even while on the field, the data must be put on cards to break down the documentation and to plan the research. As soon as a hundred words have been collected, this is indispensable, so that the same information is not collected several times, and so that the data may be checked, compared, and classified. To do this, we write each word, with its translation, explanations, and related examples, on two-copy manifold sheets. Thus, by writing it only once, we get three different cards, each to be classified as follows:

    1. Vernacular - English file (in phonological order)
    2. English - Vernacular file (in alphabetical order)
    3. Subject file

The Vernacular-English file enables us to develop the phonology quickly, to find forms easily that must be checked or compared with others, and to evaluate our progress in the study of the lexicon. The English-Vernacular file is more for semantics than for form: it facilitates finding equivalents and allows a better narrowing of the sense of the terms collected. The third file, arranged by subject, allows us to see how well a subject has been covered and what are the gaps in our information.

This type of organization constitutes the beginnings of a dictionary, although it will not be prepared for publication until much later.

(2) For RESEARCH BY QUESTIONNAIRE, especially those on personal names, lineages, domestic animals (Questionnaire 17), text collection (Questionnaire 18), language contact (Questionnaire 19), etc., a large number of copies must be reproduced in advance, so that they can be filled out directly. For useful results, a minimum of a hundred copies of each form must be provided.

Material Aspects of the Study

(3) For GATHERING TEXTS, we use notebooks. As soon as the text is recorded, we must proceed to transcription, either by the method with two tape recorders, or by simple dictation by the reference speaker. It will be beneficial to prepare beforehand a manifold notebook with two copies, using the top margin for indications relative to the text (title, name of speaker, page, etc.). In the left margin, we mark off every fifth line to indicate the place for the transcription. The line above is for transcribing tones, and the line below for the word-for-word gloss; two lines below the word-for-word gloss will be the free translation. From the beginning, the text will be transcribed, sentence by sentence, divided into segments as short as possible (for an example, see the reproduction of a handwritten text from *Contes Ngbaka-ma'bo (Ngbaka-ma'bo Stories)* in section 5.2.1).

C. Notational conventions. Since we are dealing with the transcription of unwritten languages, the problem of traditional orthography does not usually arise, even if for certain languages attempts have been made for administrative or missionary purposes. These attempts have rarely been felicitous, and it is not good to rely on them.

The linguist can draw on several notation systems devised since the end of the 19th century. Of the different proposed systems, it is now customary to use the IPA (International Phonetic Alphabet), modified to the needs of specific groups of languages (e.g., the languages of Africa). The IAI (International African Institute) has kept the IPA notation for the most part (see the table below), but replaces [j] with [y] for the palatal fricative, since few African languages have [ü], indicated in IPA as [y]. Again, the IAI uses [c] and [j] to represent palatal stops (more or less affricated), very frequent in many African languages.

The two tables shown here can be compared. It is apparent that, in dealing with other languages, even the general IPA conventions could be modified differently. What is essential is that the conventions be absolutely coherent and remain consistent throughout the transcription, so that another reader will be alerted from the start. It is good for the worker to indicate any ad hoc conventions that he finds useful, manageable, and appropriate to the language being studied. Research notes must always be written out as if they were going to be picked up and used by another worker. It is essential for work in a team that one person's work be accessible and usable by all; if for any reason he is interrupted, a colleague must be able to take it up and continue.

The first notations are done in scrupulous phonetic transcription; phonological reduction will come later. Even in later stages of research, different phonetic realizations or variants should be indicated without erasing the first transcription. A certain familiarity permits a rather rapid approach to the phonological level. From that point, the phonetic notation is all the more important, and greater care should be taken with it despite the temptation to neglect it. Accurate phonetic notations can furnish extremely valuable information whose importance is not apparent at the beginning.

The phonetic notation system can be made more precise with the use of diacritics. For example, a hook underneath a vowel indicates an intermediate degree of openness: [o̧] represents a vowel more open than [o] but more closed than [ɔ], etc. For all transcription questions, refer to *La notation des langues* by A. G. Haudricourt and J. M. C. Thomas (cf. Bibliography).

An extremely troublesome problem is that of transcribing tone, which we will now treat in some detail.

D. Tone. Tone presents one of the greatest difficulties for the study of African languages, indeed for the majority of unwritten languages.

We distinguish two principal types of notation: one for melodic or contour tone languages, such as most Far Eastern languages, and one for level or register tone languages, as for most languages of Africa and Oceania. For the contour tone languages, there is already a well-established orthographic tradition. The problems to which we devote most attention concern African languages, since our research team worked essentially with them. We will give some suggestions to facilitate handling the problem of tone, based on our experiences thus far.

Finding a frame. We cannot usually conclude anything about tone from a word in isolation, especially at the beginning of study and if the word is a monosyllable. For example, in Birom (a Nigerian language that we will use often for examples), what tone does the word *da* 'father' have? From a simple sequence of words in a list, we get some indication: when followed by *gwà* 'brother', *dá* seems to have a higher tone. But already we must beware: the speaker may have formed the phrase 'the father of the brother' *dá gwà*, where a tonal scheme due to the syntax comes in. The addition of a third word *hwā* 'wife' reveals a third level, higher than that of *gwà*, but lower than that of *dá*. It seems then that we have three register tones, three significant levels. But this must be checked in a frame, to confirm the existence of three levels, and to see if the tone is a property of the words themselves, or due to contextual modifications, whether morphological or syntactic.

To settle these different problems, we must first find a simple identical environment that can be used with all the words. In Birom, we find that the possessive [hɔŋ] 'my', following the noun, always has the same tone. After several tries, it is identified as mid tone. Thus:

    da hɔŋ   [¯ -]   HM   'my father'
    gwa hɔŋ   [. -]   LM   'my brother'
    hwa hɔŋ   [- -]   MM   'my wife'

The reference word (the frame) must remain strictly identical in all cases; we must be sure that the context does not modify it, for whatever reason. Here *hɔŋ* keeps the same tone regardless of the preceding or following word. (This is not the case in Isongo, as we shall see later.) A frame with mid tone is advantageous, at least for languages with three levels, because it is between the two extremes, and it allows us to hear better the difference in levels. If we had used a frame with low tone, the distinction between H-L (high-low) and H-M (high-mid) would be harder to hear.

For two-syllable words the method is the same, but the frame must surround the beginning and end of the word, so that the tone of both the first and second syllable may be tested. In the word *bɔnō* 'dog' from Ngbaka-ma'bo (Central African Republic), we notice first that the first syllable is higher than the second. But since we know that the language has three levels, three interpretations are possible without a frame:

    High-Low   High-Mid   Mid-Low
    [¯ .]   [¯ -]   [- .]

For an environment preceding the noun, we can use the presentational *ʔá* 'it is' or 'there is', whose tone has been identified, after several tries, as high. This environment is useful, for it can precede any noun. Thus:

    ʔá bɔ́nō   'It's a dog.'

Material Aspects of the Study

The syllable *bɔ́* appears clearly as the same level as *ʔá*. Hypothesis c) Mid-Low can thus be excluded for the tonal pattern of *bɔnō*. Now we need to see if the second syllable *nō* has mid or low tone. To do this, we complete the environment after the noun by adding the negation *lē*, found to have invariable mid tone which does not modify a noun in its environment. Thus we have:

    ʔá bɔ́nō lē   'It's not a dog.'

This sequence shows clearly that the syllable *nō* is on the same level as *lē*. Hypothesis b) High-Mid [⁻ -] thus turns out to be correct.

We could also find a frame with other elements, for example numerals which can be used with all the nouns.

A list of reference words. After we are sure of the tone of some words, we can classify new words by listing them with others of the same tone pattern, under a reference word. Thus we establish a list of all possible tone patterns for one-syllable, two-syllable, three-syllable words, etc.

For example, in Sango (CAR) we have the following patterns:

One syllable:

H		M		L	
wá	'fire'	zī	'to dig'	zè	'panther'
yé	'thing'	pē	'to winnow'	zò	'human'
		kā	'wound'	tè	'to eat'

Two syllables:

LH		LM		LL	
gàlá	'market'	ngàngū	'strength'	nyàmà	'animal, meat'
bàdá	'squirrel'	vùrū	'white'	gòzò	'manioc'
		bòngō	'garment'	tòtò	'noise'
		pèkē	'bamboo wine'	tàbà	'sheep'

MH		MM		ML	
yāngá	'mouth'	kōtā	'big'	wōmbà	'paternal aunt'
tōndá	'to begin'	yākā	'field'		
		pōtō	'Europe'		

HH		HM		HL	
lélé	'donkey'	ngbándā	'thread'	sárà	'to make'
pápá	'sandal'	várā	'shield'	úrù	'to blow'
pókó	'Mpoko river'	légē	'road'	túkù	'to throw'
póngó	'struggle'	kɔ́lī	'man'	tágbà	'antelope'
				pásì	'misery'

Three syllables:

HHH		HLM		HLL		
mbálátá	'horse'	wógàrā	'daughter-in-law,'	bágàrà	'ox/beef'	
úlúlú	'quarrel'		'mother-in-law'	wɔ́tɔ̀rɔ̀	'bee'	
tíndání	'soon'					
pélélé	'morning'					
MHM		MMM		MLL		
pāpáyē	'papaya'	kɔ̄dɔ̄rɔ̄	'village'	tōngànà	'as, like'	
		pīndīrī	'charcoal'			
LHL		LMM		LLL		
pàlábà	'palaver'	tàtārā	'mirror'	tòngòlò	'star'	
tàmbúlà	'to walk'			àràrà	'umbrella'	
LLH						
lìkɔ̀ngɔ́	'spear'					

There are numerous advantages of this method. First, it can reduce effort for the researcher, especially if he has trouble hearing tone. After establishing a list of reference words with great care, he need only accustom his speaker to indicating the tones on newly encountered words by reference to this list. Thus, the speaker will say:

yé	'thing'	is like	wá	'fire'
várā	'shield'	is like	ngbándā	'thread' etc.

In addition, this system may clarify rather quickly some features of the phonology or morphology:

Revealing preferred patterns. In Sango, for example, we find that most verbs have the tone pattern HL or LL. When we find a different pattern, it is usually a loan word.

Revealing missing patterns. In Banda-Linda, for example, it seems that sequences of extreme tones are impossible within the word. This means that we cannot have words with the patterns HL or LH.

Revealing minimal pairs. In Manza (CAR), when we compare the syllable [yi] with the reference words, we find three possibilities:

yì	like gɔ̀	'panther'	means	'water'
yī	like kō	'hand'	means	'eye'
yí	like kú	'leg'	means	'face'

Thus we have discovered an example of minimal pairs, giving evidence of the three levels used in the language.

Revealing evidence of morphological phenomena. In Birom, an attempt to compare the syllable [rum] with the reference words reveals that two are possible:

rūm	like *hwā*	'wife'	means	'the tails'
rùm	like *gwà*	'brother'	means	'the tail'

Similarly, we find:

cóŋōt	'chickens'	like *súrū*	'ladder'
còŋōt	'chicken'	like *nyàmā*	'animal'

Thus the singular/plural distinction is marked by the opposition of low tone in the singular to high or mid tone for the plural.

Some techniques for mastering tone. The procedures discussed above are best for transcribing individual words inserted into a given context which does not change. For morphological or syntactic tone changes, or for transcribing the tones of a connected text, other practical procedures are necessary. Some of these techniques are particularly useful at the beginning of the study, when one is not very familiar with the language; others, like whistling, are good to fall back on throughout the project.

Whistling. Of all possible techniques, this is by far the simplest and most efficient, and thus the most recommended, except where whistling is taboo, as it is with the Dendi of Niger who believe that the act of whistling attracts demons. There may also be difficulties in populations which have a (more or less esoteric) whistled language. But in general, the speaker of a tone language will understand very readily why he is being asked to whistle, and very few are incapable of doing it. In normal speech, the researcher must pay attention both to the articulations and to the melody; with whistling, however, he can direct all his attention to the musical levels often so unfamiliar to him. The musician may have particular difficulties, since his specially trained ear will lead him to perceive more distinctions in levels than the language uses distinctively.

Glasses of water. When whistling the tones is not possible, a relatively practical method consists of filling glasses with different levels of water, one for each register tone of the language (2, 3, or 4): the speaker then taps the glass corresponding to the tone being pronounced. This method can help a beginner to train his ear and become aware of the different levels used in the language, but it is evident that it cannot be continued for the whole length of the study. This procedure works well for level tones, but falls short for contour or modulated tones. Most of the time, even a very adept speaker will refuse to decompose them into a sequence of level tones.

Flute or whistle. A similar technique to that of the glasses involves playing 2, 3, or 4 notes (according to the tone) on a flute or whistle. These instruments are more suitable than glasses for executing modulated tones, but the method is still a slow one. It must proceed by trial and error, as the worker proposes a suggested melody to the speaker each time; otherwise he must teach the speaker to use the instrument, which requires a minimum of musical knowledge for both the speaker and the researcher. This method, like that with the glasses, has the advantage of supplementing possible auditory deficiencies with visual impressions. The glass with the least water gives the lowest tone, allowing us to identify the tone when we see the glass tapped, even if we cannot distinguish it auditorily; the same goes for the holes of the flute.

Speaking with the mouth closed. Even if he cannot or will not whistle, the speaker may consent to pronouncing the words or sentences with his mouth closed, which leaves little but the tones. This method is not nearly as good as whistling, though, since the tones are less clear, and there are more chances of confusion.

Shouting. Finally, if none of the other methods can be used, hearing tone can be facilitated by having the speaker shout, as if he were addressing someone far away or at least away from the workplace. In these conditions, the respective differences between tones are greatly amplified and become more clearly perceptible. Public speeches are thus excellent for spotting tones.

Other difficulties in tone languages. Tone presents a few special problems of analysis and description.

Unexpected change of level. Even when we have gained some mastery in distinguishing the two or three levels that may exist in a given language, the problems are not over yet. We may in fact find some discourse phenomena that are very confusing, even (or especially) for a worker with a trained musical ear. Thus we may have a sequence of tones such as:

$$[\_ - \_ ^{-} - -] \qquad [\_ - \_ ^{\overline{-}} - -]$$

where the speaker suddenly changes to a higher register when going from one sentence or phrase to the next. In such a case, a strictly musically oriented ear will hear the notes in some absolute sense, and will be baffled. The linguist, on the contrary, must get used to hearing the relevant differences to analyze the phonology of the tones, as he does with the consonants and vowels.

E.g., Ngbaka-ma'bo (J. M. C. Thomas, *Ngbaka-ma'bo stories*, 25.20).

'She says:
"So those who eat the livers of my husband's game, it's you, then"' *ʔé ɓō :
sákàdē wà-ndɔ́ ʔā-hō̄ kɔ́ndè-sɔ́-kā-kɔ̄-ɲā nò̰ ʔā-dó ʔā ʔìũ*

which can be realized phonetically as:

1. [¯ _ - ¯ _ ¯ - ¯ _ ¯ ¯ ¯ _ -] [- ¯ - _ ¯ _]

2. [¯ _ - ¯ _ ¯ - _ ¯ - - - - _] [- ¯ - _ ¯ _]

or on the same level, depending on the stylistic fancy or mood of the speaker. Still, nothing has changed in the relative differences that serve to distinguish one tone from another. The differences of register between a man's low voice and a woman's or child's high voice likewise do not affect the relevance of the tone. When such differences occur in the speech of a single speaker, it is more troublesome, though.

Interference of intonation in the tone pattern. This phenomenon occurs in Hausa, where a sentence such as:

táá tàfì bàakín kòògíí
'She went to the river.'

has the following phonetic realization:

[¯ ¯ _ - _ _ _ _ ¯ ¯]

Material Aspects of the Study

The constant falling intonation causes the second high tone to be lower than the first high tone; the level of the third high is lower than that of the second, and so on. On the purely phonetic level, we would end up with 5, 6, or x different tone levels, and wonder why a sentence-initial word with low tone has a higher pitch than a word with high tone at the end of the sentence. This is explained by the interference of a falling intonation which always raises the beginning of the sentence to a very high level in this language. For Hausa, we will end up keeping only two significant tone levels, high and low. This example is typical as we move from the tone to toneme, or from phonetic tone to phonological tone.

Downstep. This is a common phenomenon in certain Bantu languages such as Lega (Eastern Zaire):

bùùsị́ búmòzị̀ ángà èèndà kùtégá ↓ mátégá mágé
'one day, he went to set his nets'

Here the contrastive high and low tones are constant in register up to the downstep, indicated by the arrow, where the sequence high-low is shifted to a slightly lower level. The fall, which was gradual in Hausa, occurs here at a specific point. Here the explanation is that this language does not allow three high tones in a row at the same level: the third high is always slightly lowered, indicated also by a vertical stroke: [‴] or [‴']. The rest of the utterance continues at a lower level, taking the lowered tone as a new reference point. Must we indicate the downstep in this case? It is not strictly necessary if we know the rules of its occurrence and/or if it is purely phonetic. However, transcribing it may keep us from forgetting the rule. To indicate it, use either an exclamation point *(kùtégá ꜝmátégà)* or a vertical stroke on the first syllable after the drop *(kùtégá mȧtégà)*.

When the downstep is unpredictable and has distinctive value, it must be indicated. This is the case in Bafia, Balom (Fà?), Mangisa, and other Bantu languages of Cameroon (Guarisma 1975). In these languages, morphological analysis reveals the existence of an intervening low tone, not represented on the phonological level, which causes the lowering of the following tone:

Bafia
ɓóó mʌ́ ꜝnú	'great nights'
ɓóó´ mʌ̀-nú	/ great | nights /
ŋúáp ú kúí ꜝté	'the branch of the tree'
ŋù-áp ú-ǿ kì-té	/ branch | of | tree /

Note that the difficulties in tonal analysis posed by downstep, intonation interferences, and register changes do not appear while we deal solely with words in isolation. A number of phenomena may be missed entirely in this way. For this reason, we cannot emphasize too much the necessity of a two-sided phonological analysis, both with and without the context.

Modulated tones. We mentioned that languages with register tones may also exhibit modulated tonal realizations. Some languages make distinctive use of these modulations. This may cause trouble for the researcher in hearing and identifying them, even if he is aware of them. Several situations are possible:

(a) The modulation is accompanied by a slight nondistinctive lengthening of the vowel. This case is the most favorable for the researcher.

Birom
  yùú   [yùū:]   'spider (spec.)'
  nèéy   [nèē:y]   'oil'

(b) The modulation is not accompanied by greater length, and the vowel must remain short. This is the case in Yakoma (Boyeldieu 1973). Often, when we notice the modulation, we tend to lengthen the vowel excessively, which may lead to confusion. The speaker refuses the form put to him, not because there is anything wrong with the modulation itself, but because he is shocked at the importance placed on the length.

(c) The oppositions of modulation combine with oppositions of length; this is the most troublesome case.

Zarma (Tersis, 1972):
  one mora - short vowel   *hábú*   'market'
  one mora - long vowel   *kù:nú*   'hedgehog'
  two morae - short vowel   *fùúndì*   'life'
  two morae - long vowel   *máà:rí*   'pimento (spec.)'

When the modulations correspond to morphological or syntactic phenomena, they are rather easily accounted for. Thus, in Birom:

  (1) *syáp*   'basket'
      syààáp   'baskets'
  (2) *syààáp bíàyàbà* 'a basket of bananas'

In the first case *syáp* / *syààáp*, the opposition high tone/rising tone distinguishes the plural form from the singular. In the second, the connective *à* is fused with the head of the phrase, producing on it a modulated rising-falling tone (without noticeable lengthening; the repetition of the vowel is a simple written convention—see below).

It is much more difficult to pin down the modulated tones in a language where tone is used lexically:

Ngbaka-ma'bo
  tòó   'fruit of Landolphia'
  mbɔ̀ɔ́ɔ̀   'mongoose'
  kpáā   'leaf'
  ɓáà   'plank'
  kpáàá   'one'

Another difficulty in analyzing the modulated tones lies in identifying the levels of their realization. It is customary to represent them as a combination of level tones, using the beginning and ending points. Thus, low-high is a tone moving from low register to high register; high-mid is a modulation starting at the high register and ending at the medium register. Given the rapidity of execution, the placement of the starting and ending points is often very difficult to hear in languages with more than two levels. In Vute, for example, a language with three levels, several combinations for rising tones (LH, LM, MH) and for falling tones (HL, HM, ML) are all realized:

  rising tones
    kòó   'bed'
    sòō   'squirrel'
    wōó   1. 'red' 2. 'ripe'

Material Aspects of the Study   21

>   falling tones
>   *ɓììn*   'knoll'
>   *mīīn*   'cheap'
>   *bììn*   'heart'

In other cases, all combinations are not found. Thus in Ngbaka-ma'bo we have only:

>   high-falling   [HM]   *káā* [káā]   'only'
>   low-falling   [HL] or [ML]   *káà* [káà ~ kāà]   'again'
>   and
>   high-rising   [LH] or [MH]   *màá* [màá ~ māá]   'I'
>   low-rising   [LM]   *màā* [màā]   'me'

Finally, certain relevant modulations may not correspond to distinctive tone registers in the language. Monzombo distinguishes four registers (extra high, high, mid, low), but uses the following modulated tones:

>   extra high-falling   [XH-M : ″ ˗]
>   high-falling   [H-L :   ´ `]
>   extra low-falling   [M-XL : ˗ ͵͵]

The extra low tone level has no distinctive function in the language.

We have dealt with the question of contour tones at length because of the difficulties they present which often baffle the researcher. Their importance in languages that use them is absolutely fundamental. We have already seen the role they can play in morphology. In the Birom example, the word 'father' occurs in two forms:

>   *dáà gōy*   'the father of the sun'
>   *dá gōy*   'Father Sun (similar to the Mother Earth)'

In the first form, we find the connective morpheme *à* fused with the head noun *dá*, yielding the falling modulated tone *dáà*.

It is clear that if we had not discovered the modulated tone, we might have missed an important element of the morphological description.

Similarly, in the verbal conjugation, aspectual forms may be marked only by changes in level or modulated tones. Ngbaka-ma'bo offers a striking example of this phenomenon (cf. J. M. C. Thomas in J. Derive, *Collecte et traduction des littératures orales,* 114–19). We cannot emphasize the issue of tone notation too strongly, since it has repercussions on all levels of linguistic analysis.

Notation of tones. All tones must be indicated everywhere. In a publication, a more economical notation system is permissible. One need only indicate, in a language with two registers, the less frequent tone; the other tone would be indicated by the absence of a mark. In a language with three registers, the mid tone would be the unmarked one. This economy is not recommended for research, though. The absence of tone indication can result from hesitation or oversight; it would be unfortunate if this were interpreted as a mark. The marking of all tones must thus be kept as a principle at the research stage.

Not simply must all tones be indicated, but they must be indicated clearly. To avoid mistakes and loss of time due to faulty notation, a completely clear notation system is essential. A recommended system for register tone languages consists in working on narrow-lined paper, using the different lines in the following way:

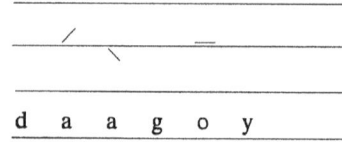

High tone, indicated by an acute accent, starts on the line and goes up; low tone, indicated by the grave accent, starts on the line and goes down; mid tone appears directly on the line as a horizontal dash. In a language with four levels, the highest tone can be represented by a double acute accent, which is preferable in handwriting:

Monzombo
    ndőngóātì   'pepper'

Typesetting, however, uses different conventions, extra high tone being represented by the acute accent, and high tone by a vertical stroke:

    ndóngóātì

Modulated tones may be indicated differently, depending on whether the language has two or more than two contours. When there are only two modulated tones, we use the circumflex and inverted circumflex to indicate falling and rising tones, respectively. Once we find more distinctions among the contours, the use of repeated vowels with the level tone marks is preferable to complex marks on a single vowel. Complex marks are hard to read and reread, may be easily confused, and are almost impossible for typesetting.

Thus, indications of rising and falling tones such as:

LH	ǎ	HL	â
LM	ǎ	HM	â̄
MH	ā́	ML	ā̀

are better replaced by:

LH	àá	HL	áà
LM	àā	HM	áā
MH	āá	ML	āà

This latter system generally corresponds to the analysis of modulated tones into morae, and is often justified by morphological analysis. Even when morphological justification is lacking, simple practical considerations are enough to recommend this usage.

Other systems of tone notation are mentioned in Tucker (n.d.), and Haudricourt and Thomas (1967). These include the use of melodic lines on top of the text, numbers, melodic patterns in parentheses following the word or sentence, etc. From experience, we find the system presented here the simplest, and the most common besides.

Tonetics and tonology. Phonological analysis is necessary for tones, just as for vowels and consonants, in order to identify what is actually distinctive and relevant and to eliminate what is conditioned. We sometimes use the term toneme as the tone equivalent of the phoneme.

Consider the following example, taken from Birom:

[é gbín áà ~ áā]	'Is it an elephant?'
[é mwāt āà]	'Is it a person?'
[é syàāp āà]	'Is it a basket?'
[é bībàk àà̀]	'Are they sesames?'

([é] is a presentative 'it is', 'there is'.)

In this data, is there truly an opposition between the falling tones H-L, H-M, M-L, and L-XL? As elsewhere, we look for minimal pairs (proving the existence of distinct phonemes) and examine the environment (which may be responsible for phonetic, nondistinctive differences in the realization of a single phoneme). In the present case, we notice that the contour tone on the interrogative morpheme *aa* always begins on the same level as the tone of the preceding syllable. We conclude that it is characterized phonologically by a falling tone (without further specification), written / áà /; its realization is predictable and determined by the environment.

A more complex phenomenon is seen in Isongo (a Bantu language of CAR), where a list of isolated words before pause shows the following:

à	'he'	dĩ	'eats'	fá	'knife'
				mɔ̀lɔ̀	'pap'
				mɔ̀fɔ̀	'corn'
				ɓòĩ	'village'
				fō	'mouse'
				mbá	'hut'
				mbálátá	'horse'
				gɔ̀gìlà	'manioc'

With these, we get utterances such as:[1]

à dĩ	'he ate'
à dĩ mɔ̀lɔ̀	'he ate pap'
à dĩ mɔ̀lɔ̀ gɔ́gìlà	'he ate cassava pap'
à dĩ mɔ̀lɔ̄ mɔ́fɔ́	'he ate corn pap'

This is a particularly complex case; the tone of a word is modified both by what precedes and by what follows. To determine the rule for the modification, we systematically vary only a single element at a time:

(1) 'manioc pap'
    'corn pap'
    etc.

(2) 'I ate pap'
    'I ate cassava'
    'I ate corn'
    etc.

(3) 'I ate cassava pap'
    'I ate the corn pap'
    etc.

In general, we choose frames for analysis that allow as many differences as possible. Thus, in studying conjugation, we must choose a verbal form whose tone differences

---

[1] ´ extra high tone, ' high tone, ¯ mid tone, ` low tone.

are part of the lexical form, and not an aspectual form where the tone required by the aspect covers up the lexical tone.

Thus, in Ngbaka-ma'bo, the verbs 'to fill' and 'to light' have lexically distinct forms in the completive: *màá sī* 'I have filled', *màá sì* 'I have lit'. This distinction is concealed in the incompletive because the high tone of the verbal form dominates: *mā sí* 'I fill' ~ 'I light'.

Problem of tone-bearing consonants. Certain sounds, usually classified as consonants, may actually carry tone. Most often, it is the nasals, sometimes the liquids *l* or *r*, and in a few cases the sibilants *s* or *z*.

This raises a question of phonological interpretation. In Sara (Chad), do we interpret the mid tone of *màān* 'water' as on the vowel or on the nasal consonant (and thus write: [màñ])? Phonetically, an acoustic study shows that the tone may very well be realized on the nasal, but phonological analysis is necessary to determine the most economical and coherent interpretation within the system in question. Whatever may be the phonological conclusions, it seems most convenient, for writing purposes, to indicate tone on the vowel rather than on the consonant.

2.2.3 Pictorial recording

An indispensable complement to linguistic fieldwork is the pictorial illustration of the physical objects collected. Even the best descriptions and most detailed explanations can hardly substitute for simple sketches, drawings, or photographs of objects, apparatus, special gestures, etc., for which we are collecting vocabulary. Besides, these can be an invaluable tool for research itself, as we study with the speaker sketches or photos of a technique recorded at several stages, considering its different parts. It will be good to set up a separate pictorial file with cross-references to the files on linguistics proper and to the collection of recorded texts. A careful examination of these documents will prompt the speakers to reflect, comment, and possibly to recall additional texts, techniques, or other things. Later, it can afford an excellent basis for comparative work with other ethnic groups. Finally, it is almost indispensable as a method of illustration when publishing dictionaries and texts.

Similarly, ethnozoological research will benefit greatly from a collection of slides of animals. However, we must be aware of the limits of this technique. Although it will surely yield an abundant vocabulary, the precise identification of the species pictured may leave something to be desired: the recognition of drawn or photographed specimens is often problematical, because size, proportion, color, and behavior often play an important part. The speaker may be confused or mistaken. Further checking will be necessary, but at least we will know that such an animal exists.

2.3 Collections

Related to the use of pictorial documents for ethnozoological research is the more general issue of collections for research. We distinguish two types of collection according to their nature and use.

Material Aspects of the Study 25

2.3.1 Permanent collections

Permanent collections, once assembled, can be reused in each new project within certain regional limits. A whole team of workers in a specific region can use them with various ethnic groups.

Pictorial collections. These cover different topic areas of the study, such as slides of animals (as discussed above), or characteristic plants, and photos or sketches of technical objects, possibly of ceremonies or rituals. They are not used for getting precise identification as much as for making comparisons, bringing back memories, and prompting stories or comments. For animals, we mentioned that identification may be difficult and risky. For techniques, rituals and ceremonies, etc., it may not be a question of identification as we pass from one group to another, but a means of recall which often spares us from long and wearisome research or from serious gaps.

This type of collection requires some equipment besides the photos and sketches themselves and their files and filing boxes or folders. Using slides necessitates a projector and an electric generator to run it; a slide viewer may be enough, but by reducing the audience, we reduce the information obtained.

Zoological collections. These include a variety of zoological specimens: mounted insects, fish, reptiles, amphibians in formaldehyde, birds, pelts of small mammals, heads of large game animals, flat skins of large animals (antelopes, wild cats, crocodiles), etc.

These specimens are good for wide climatic and ecological areas, and are presented for identification right on the field. We thus not only get the word that designates them, but also interesting tales and comments about their ways, beliefs involving them, myths and stories in which they play a part. They provide an incredible wealth of information, and help to speed and expand the research, as well as making contacts easier with the people being studied.

The use of this type of collection requires a significant amount of equipment, including materials and containers: classification cases, plastic bags, preservatives, etc.

Zoological collections, as well as the pictorial collections above, should never be considered complete. On the contrary, each worker should continue to build them up and add to them as he is using them for each new project. This also requires quite a bit of equipment: hunting instruments, containers, preparations and preservatives, etc.; photographic and drawing equipment for the pictorial collections (which are indispensable to complement the collection of zoological specimens, in addition to their own function).

2.3.2 Occasional collections

These collections by nature are not reusable, and must be completely redone in each field situation. Their impermanence results either from their specific nature, like the technical collections, or from the conditions of their preservation, like botanical collections.

Technical collections. Although the techniques themselves are very general, their procedures and especially their products are usually very specific to a given group. Showing photographs, sketches, or examples of one group's techniques in another group may be good to stimulate discussion, but not for precise identification. A scientific identification, whether of a technique, an animal, or a plant, must be absolutely precise. It is not enough to say that one group's basket-making technique is similar to some other type in a neighboring group. A simple description is quite insufficient, especially without the technical knowledge necessary for isolating the distinctive characteristics. Pictures are better, but not perfect. A characteristic detail may not even show up on the photo or sketch; besides, the owner of an object may not allow it to be photographed, or no sample may be available for the photo.

Here again, collection is the best way to ensure incontestable identification. Besides, it is often possible to obtain objects for the collection that would not get photographed. An artisan will work more eagerly if he knows he will be able to sell his product than if he is simply photographed during the activity, even though he gets some present for his good will.

This type of collection does not require a great deal of equipment at the outset. However, materials for arranging, classifying, and transporting the collection must be provided as it becomes sizable.

Botanical collections. The flora, even more than the fauna, are usually distributed widely throughout a region such as equatorial or tropical Africa, so that the same species are used by several ethnic groups. Thus it is not the nature of this collection which is in question, the diffuculty here lies rather in the means of preservation. The only method known and used to date is by drying and pressing. Although plants prepared and stored in good condition can be kept indefinitely, such specimens have only a vague and distant resemblance to the living plant. The botanist may find this method good for identifications, but speakers cannot at all recognize a dried plant in a book. The bearing, color, size, smell, and even the environment of the plant, are all important criteria for its identification, but these cannot be preserved in drying.

Thus it is impossible to put together a permanent reference collection, in this particular case. For each term on the field, we must make a new collection with the speakers themselves, which will subsequently be submitted to a botanist for scientific identification.

For this type of collection, some significant equipment is necessary, on one hand at the field base where the preservation will be done (drying oven, presses, etc.), and on the other hand right on the field location for collecting undried or dried plants (plastic bags, papers, presses, preservatives, pruning-scissors, machetes, shovels, knives, pruning-shears, etc.).

The research collections, both permanent and occasional, involve a significant amount of material to store and move. First, the reference collections must first be taken along to the field location, and after they are augmented by the technical and botanical collections, they must be taken back, and all the collections must finally be carried home either for identification or for preservation. It is rarely possible to leave the reference collections in the country, even with adequate security; tropical climates, where most of our studies take place, spawn mildews and parasites. With this type of fieldwork, then, adequate means of transportation and considerable freight expenses must be provided for.

3
Gathering Data

3.1 General questions

The research techniques used depend on certain preliminary issues.

3.1.1 The problem of a common language

Do the researcher and the people being studied have a common language? It may be the language of a major civilization, usually that of the colonizer—French, English, Spanish, or Portuguese—or a local trade language (Swahili, Hausa, Lingala, Sango, dialectal Arabic) by means of which the beginnings of the study can be carried out. If the people being studied know no language but their own, the research will proceed very differently.

The most favorable case, of course, is when the people speak the researcher's native language. In this case, there is only one hurdle to cross, from the language studied to the researcher's language. Mistakes and confusion are kept to a minimum, and the speed and efficiency of the study are optimal. The questionnaires presented here have been composed essentially for this type of study, since these are the conditions in most of black French-speaking Africa where our team works. Still, the proposed procedures are perfectly adaptable to the less favorable situation where the common language is not the mother tongue of the researcher, e.g., English for a French researcher in English-speaking Africa, or French for a Spanish-speaking worker in francophone Africa. In that case, the risk of errors is multiplied in the double passage from one language to another.

The same is true if a trade language must be used. The researcher must devote considerable additional time to learning this language, although there may be advantages insofar as it is closer to the language to be studied than to a European language. This is not always so, however, and the impoverishment of many trade languages in comparison to vernacular languages may make them a less appropriate research instrument than a European language that is less similar.

The most troublesome situation is where the researcher and the people have no language in common. This is rare in Africa or Oceania, but is still quite frequent with small minorities in America or Asia. There, it is mandatory that the worker gain a working knowledge of the language he intends to describe before proceeding with his studies, which may cause long delays in getting started with systematic research. Some techniques proposed here, such as the use of grammatical and certain thematic questionnaires, will have to be modified; others may not be usable, such as those that require active participation and assistance on the part of the speaker (questionnaires on names of persons, lineages, domestic animals, sentences, etc.).

The problem of the common language comes up at different points of the study in different ways. Linguistic or thematic ethnolinguistic questionnaires require a speaker/helper who knows the common language, and a western language is almost indispensable for that; on the other hand, some parts of the research, such as text collection, can be accomplished apart from any shared language. Text collection requires speakers having almost no knowledge of the common language; it is most often done with older storytellers, who are often the only ones who know the tradition perfectly. Besides, a more familiar trade language may have to be used for some aspects of the study, even if the speaker knows French or English well. In Birom, fruitful ethnozoological and ethnobotanical study had to be conducted through the medium of Hausa. Although the speaker with whom we were working was an old schoolteacher and knew English well, these aspects of the study were more stimulating for him through his knowledge of Hausa.

3.1.2 Idiolect or language of a group

The difficulties of variation among individuals, as well as dialect differences, often tempt the researcher to limit his study to the speech of a single speaker. This procedure must be rejected, even on the linguistic level, because it results in the description of an idiolect, as well as limiting the study considerably. A phonological description done with a single speaker before going to the field is a good training exercise for a beginning worker, but this procedure must not be systematized as a research method. We will see, though, that the linguistic study of a group will be much easier, more profitable, and more economical if we use the services of one reference speaker, with whom the various information collected in the group can be compared. Thus we end up by systematizing the individual idiosyncratic within a homogeneous group, or dialectal variants within several subgroups. The information must be collected from the group as a whole, even if some aspects of the study are covered with the reference speaker alone. It is even advantageous to make a sociological and demographic sampling (of age, sex, profession, etc.), to obtain a truly representative picture of the language in question.

3.1.3 Dialectology or standard language

In only exceptional cases is there a standard language or even a prestige dialect recognized as a norm. Usually, each community considers its own speech patterns the best, and all others to be DIALECTAL. For linguistic study, it is best at first not to deal with all the dialectal forms found, but to choose one, preferably not marginal, and to study it thoroughly. Other dialectal forms will then be studied with reference to the one chosen first. Any other procedure complicates the research and inevitably leads to confusion. In the extreme case, the researcher may end up describing a nonexistent

Gathering Data

language, which he has stuck together from different dialects. Once the first basic study has been carried out, dialectological investigation is done like any other study of the same type elsewhere.

3.1.4 Previous works

Even in the most remote region where work is being considered, there are usually some works by laymen (missionaries, administrators, travelers) that can be consulted before undertaking the fieldwork. Before doing anything else, we must compile an exhaustive bibliography of the ethnic group we will be studying; insofar as possible, we obtain these books and articles, or photocopies of them if they are not otherwise available. Even the works of nonspecialists can furnish very fruitful bases for work, giving a point of departure for the study of certain techniques, plants, rituals, etc. The works of Vergiat on the Mandja of the Central African Republic, for example, allowed us to establish a file on the names of plants used in medicine, in rituals, and in magic. Later, we were able to check and perfect the transcriptions of these with speakers (phonemes and tones). When works such as these are illustrated, it may be worthwhile to keep some of the illustrations for the pictorial collections.

If a dictionary already exists, prepared by a nonlinguist independently of his own investigations, we must review it systematically with our speakers to redo the transcription and indicate tone, as well as to clarify vague parts. The principal use of older works, even if their linguistic descriptions are inadequate, is to provide some perspective in studying these civilizations, of whose history we know little or nothing. They offer a wealth of material for comparison, showing earlier phenomena and events which have since disappeared as a result of contact with western civilizations. This was the case with the Banda dictionary by F. C. Tisserant; its linguistic notation was quite faulty, but it contained remarkable items of information on the Banda. Similarly, the *Vocabulaire français-gmbwaga-gbanziri / monjombo* of J. Calloc'h, almost unusable for linguistic study, provided an excellent base of information, once we knew these languages well enough to make some hypotheses. Specifically, we found a number of terms and expressions that have now disappeared from the language and civilization, but which stirred the memory of the older people, allowing us to enrich our knowledge of the pre-colonization period.

It may also be possible to consult general works, such as the *Handbook of African Languages* series, which place one language relative to others, indicating that a certain language belongs to the Teke group, that another language has certain dialects and seems to have three tone registers, etc.

We must always remember, however, that the transcriptions in most of these works are inadequate. Therefore, if a manual or grammar of the language already exists, it is unwise to consult it before working out the phonology and much of the grammatical systems separately. The danger, especially in our first project, is in being influenced by the written word. Once we have established our system, though, it is useful to look at these works; even a CLASSICAL grammar, which improperly treats the structure of the language studied as identical to that of the author, may give a rather complete summary of existing forms.

3.2 The research

We consider here only those problems dealing specifically with the data in the research situation, that is, what type of information is obtained and by what methods. The methods themselves, and what is involved in these different parts of the research, will be considered later.

3.2.1 Research by questionnaire

This work can be carried out with a single reference speaker; it concerns principally the strictly linguistic and analytic aspects of the study of an unwritten language. It requires tranquility and working facilities, and can be done on the base, or in a small town, but not away from the country, where the speaker would be cut off from his environment.

3.2.2 Preparation for the field and review

In both cases, the work is carried out with the reference speaker. He participates in planning and preparation for intensive research within the group, where everyone in the chosen village will contribute information in differing degrees. Such preparation includes both the physical conditions of the stay and the various aspects of the study to be investigated (for example, vocabulary of a given technique, ethnobotanical or ethnozoological study, text collection, etc.). After the return from the field, the equally important job of review (refining the translations, going over the data, classifying) must be done, again in close collaboration with the reference speaker. Like the work on questionnaires, these activities must be done in a relatively peaceful atmosphere, with suitable physical conditions (sufficient space and light, appropriate scientific equipment in good working order, etc.). This type of activity is also done on the base.

3.2.3 Field research proper

By this term we mean a term of residence of active research in a completely traditional setting, as little urbanized and acculturated as possible. In Africa, the village provides an environment where the alienating urban influence and the languages of trade and civilization are felt least.

The most profitable term of field research proper, for a young researcher on his first in-depth linguistic project, must be relatively long. At the base camp, an additional period of preliminary preparation will be necessary, as well as a period afterward for clarification and analysis with the reference speaker. At least four months at the outset are imperative; six months are preferable, and an expedition of 12 to 18 months, broken up by several periods of review at the field base, will be the most fruitful for an in-depth study.

A veteran researcher, once familiar with the field he is to study, will be able to work with more or less related groups nearby in much less time. Often several short periods on the field, rather than a long stay, will allow him to conduct profitable and developed research.

Familiarity with a given region allows more specific preparation for research, immediate attention to the richest and most original subjects, and rapid discovery of the best speakers and the most eloquent and esteemed storytellers. Thanks to previous knowledge of the area and through comparison with neighboring groups, information

Gathering Data

can be elicited that would otherwise only be obtained after a long initial stay on the field in a completely new region.

What aspects of the research come out of fieldwork proper? Some aspects of the study of a society and its language cannot be treated in any other way, such as the relationship of man to his natural environment; plants and animals and the related activities of fishing, hunting, food-gathering, agriculture, animal husbandry, and related techniques; economic and living conditions. Social organization likewise can only be studied in person; text collection, either of oral tradition proper or of other types, such as technical accounts, and extensive survey work, are inconceivable apart from work on the field.

3.3 The speaker

The situation is different if we are dealing with the reference speaker or occasional speakers, and whether or not the study is carried out by means of a common language. Since most of our experiences involved research through a common language, this is the case we will consider principally.

3.3.1 Choosing speakers If one dialect of the language being studied has acquired prestige status, providing some sort of linguistic norm, it could be troublesome and regrettable to choose a marginal dialect, and is thus not recommended. Apart from this case, however, the choice of language is not important, and the question of the number of its speakers is irrelevant from a linguistic viewpoint.

The essential thing is to find speakers representative of the language or dialect under consideration.

3.3.2 The reference speaker

Reasons for this type of speaker. One or two reference speakers are of prime importance to the whole research task. With him we confront, analyze, explain, and comment on all the material gathered from other speakers of the language. If we choose and train the reference speaker with care, he will in good circumstances become more than just a translator and commentator that we need at the beginning. He must be able to participate in the research and become a true assistant. He has an intimate knowledge of his environment that the researcher could not share; he also can carry out parts of the research that would be impossible or very difficult for the researcher to gain access to. This is the case in a closed circle of membership to which the speaker belongs, but to which the researcher would not be allowed. If the researcher is a woman, this is true of all that pertains to the society of the men. Again, it is possible that speakers would refrain from making certain observations that they considered too daring in front of the researcher (man or woman), while they would not hesitate to share them in front of one of their own.

In addition to these advantages, reviewing all documentation with a reference speaker allows us to avoid the common mistake of mixing dialects. Especially at the early stages of working out the phonology, the researcher is not in a position to identify the speech of different speakers precisely or to make a comparative study of several dialects; it would thus be dangerous for him to take all data without discrimination. It would be very difficult to pull together a coherent phonology in this situation; we are tempted to resort to diachronic arguments to explain the apparent inconsistencies in the system as due to ARCHAIC or PROGRESSIVE forms. This approach is valid in a careful comparative study, but has no place in the phonological analysis of a language which should be strictly synchronic and monographic. It does not matter if the reference speaker belongs to a numerically unimportant group. Extensive studies can be carried out later and more quickly by placing other dialects with respect to the reference language. In general, a reference speaker is used to avoid the generalizing excesses which aim to establish a standard language, but which neglect a whole range of characteristics specific to the language in question.

On the other hand, we must avoid describing an idiolect, that of the reference speaker. We take his pronunciation habits as general, but from the very beginning, we compare the forms he gives with those given by other speakers of the language, in order to avoid his idiosyncrasies.

Choosing the reference speaker. Several factors come into play, including the social situation and personality of the reference speaker. One of the first and most important is his rapport with the researcher. Such close and long-term work as is involved is hardly possible unless there is a degree of congeniality between the two. Other personal qualities are equally important. The speaker must be patient and calm; the researcher will be putting him through the mill by having him repeat the same things countless times (words difficult to transcribe, explanations poorly understood, translations he finds unclear). Similarly, the reference speaker will have to keep explaining to other occasional speakers what the researcher wants and why. The reference speaker must also be interested in the job he is undertaking so that he will participate actively and intelligently, and not as under obligation. He must be attentive and curious, for he will be led to ask himself questions about his environment, culture, and language that he never considered before; he must pay attention to the explanations and questions of the researcher, and also to what goes on around him in his society. Finally, he must prove himself scrupulous and careful in his work, always giving all the information he can furnish, recording it exactly and completely faithfully when he is not the source of the information.

Availability is a necessity that depends less on his personality than on circumstance. Preferably, the reference speaker will be free of employment obligations or practices a trade which allows him enough leisure and freedom of movement, for he must provide the researcher daily service at the base and move about with him on the field. A city-dweller, unless he is unemployed, will generally be less free than a country-dweller. This issue is often related to age; young people are more easily available than older men. It is true that the older people are better repositories of tradition than the young and must be consulted for information, but an older person is not essential as the reference speaker. The opposite may even be preferable; even a teenager may make an excellent speaker, if he knows his language well, and if he has not been separated from his family and environment for a long time (for schooling, for example). The young are easier to train for their new function than older people.

Besides age, another issue is education. Should the speaker be literate? A completely illiterate reference speaker may be difficult to train and may never become the assistant researcher that we need to train. On the other hand, a speaker with too much education or specialized training may become a veritable nuisance. The schoolteacher-speaker, who is always trying to fit his language into the framework of French or English grammar and burden the researcher with superfluous explanations, is this type of feared speaker. The best subject, we feel, would have an education roughly equivalent to that of the French CEP

Gathering Data 33

(Certificate of Primary Studies) or better yet, corresponding to the 4th or 5th level of high school. Preferably, he should not have finished his studies a very long time ago, and he may be asked to take them up again to improve his knowledge of the common language. Still, it is possible to find an excellent speaker without such formal education, whose open intelligence makes up for the lack.

Before hiring the reference speaker, we must test him. One day of work with the candidate will be enough for this purpose. We ask him first for a rather short list of about 50 words; from his reactions, we can judge his patience, interest, curiosity, openness, knowledge of the language, attention to detail, etc. His answers to questions about the techniques and customs of his people, whether straightforward or hesitating, clear or confused, will indicate his abilities. Finally, it is important to find out his motivations for wanting this work, whether he is likely to take an interest in the study or whether he just wants the money. Although a choice of candidates is of course desirable, we are sometimes glad to find one available speaker, whatever his aptitudes, qualities, or faults. One situation not yet considered is working with a woman reference speaker. In some societies this is not an issue; the women are rarely available, being occupied from a very young age with household and subsistence duties and caring for the children. In addition, they rarely have any formal education, and most do not know the common language at all. Finally, even among occasional speakers, we have never found women who seem willing to do the job, even though they sometimes show great interest in our work.

Finally, how do we choose a reference speaker, whether man or woman, when there is no common language? In this area, our experiences are rather limited, but we feel that his qualities and aptitudes should be the same, although the issues of translation and formal education will be irrelevant. The methods, type of work, and its conditions will be different.

Information about the reference speaker. In order to place the reference speaker with respect to his society and his language, we need to know his civil status, his environment, his origins, his curriculum vitae, and his education.

His civil status: his name, other given names (with meaning, if any), age, place of birth, places of residence through the age of 15 (where, between what ages, and in what ethnic and linguistic environment).

His environment: his ethnic group, his clan and his lineage; his dialect, possibly subdialect; the number of speakers of his language; linguistic geography of his language; distribution of the dialects, limits of mutual intelligibility; name of the language and of the ethnic group to which it belongs (names given by the people themselves, by neighboring groups, by the government as the official name); his religion and that of his family.

His origins: the places of residence and original language of his parents, grandparents, and spouse(s); their ages, professions, and educational levels; the languages they use beside their native language.

His education and curriculum vitae: was he raised using the speech of his father or of his mother, if they are different; has he travelled away from his people and linguistic environment; what neighboring languages does he know (understand or speak); how does he use the trade language and the common language; what is the length and highest level of his education; what profession(s) has he worked in (length, linguistic circumstances, etc.)?

Training the reference speaker. Once the reference speaker has been chosen, we can proceed to train him. If he is gifted, this may not take long. We must realize that the speaker does not know at the start what is expected of him, nor what linguistic work entails. For continued and fruitful collaboration, the researcher must make the effort to explain simply and clearly his intentions, aims, and working methods, so that the speaker is aware of the problems of interest to him and the importance of his study. It is of fundamental importance that the speaker see the value of his culture and language, especially in a colonized country where traditional values are often belittled, ridiculed, or even condemned by the colonizers.

This psychological training is essential, but it must be supplemented with technical training. First, the reference speaker must be able to write his language. In the least favorable situation, an orthography (from missionaries or others) already exists, which is probably poor or at least incomplete. Such orthographies generally leave out the indication of tone and precise distinctions between vowels, and often confuse similarly articulated consonants. They often use more or less complicated graphic devices. For example, [ɔ] is transcribed *ho* in Sango; thus [sangɔ] is written *sangho*. If the speaker knows this orthography of his language and cannot quickly become accustomed to phonological notation, it may be useful for him to jot down for himself in his orthography the information he gives or reviews with the researcher. Even if such transcription is faulty, it will allow the speaker to reread to himself correctly most of the time; at least he is used to it, and the language is his mother tongue. Especially when recording linguistic reference data, the speaker should have a list, established beforehand, where he has indicated the words or phrases he is to say. With this method he need not memorize a list of examples, and the researcher will not have to interrupt him continually. At a more advanced stage of the research, he may himself collect information, or items of oral literature (stories, proverbs, riddles, etc.). This material will then be retranscribed and analyzed with the linguist, sentence by sentence. At least this is the solution we must resort to if the speaker cannot manage to learn a phonetic or phonological transcription of his language.

The best situation, of course, is where the speaker learns and masters a scientific transcription system. We do not teach him the International Phonetic Alphabet, but introduce him to a systematic transcription of his own language; a phonological transcription, if it has been established, is better than a phonetic one. Even some excellent speakers are stubborn on this point; questions of age and previous education are important factors. Others, once they see the usefulness of the linguist's notation, learn it very quickly. They may pride themselves on using it, since they realize that transcription makes the language available to all, just like a prestige language; even a stranger can immediately pronounce any word of the language in an intelligible way. The speaker now becomes a true collaborator. At the outset, this training is often tedious, as we take pains to explain how to write each word, the value of the consonants and vowels, the importance of tone and its transcription. A speaker already conditioned by previous orthographic habits may have as much trouble getting rid of these habits as the beginning linguist has getting rid of the articulatory habits of his native language. In any case, we do not want to impose a system on the speaker; we want him to adopt it as we explain it to him, but not to force him if he is averse to it.

In transcription, the speaker must get used to certain writing habits essential for making good documents. These are equally important for the researcher himself. Transcriptions must be printed, since cursive writing is too personal and often difficult to decipher. It is very important that words be separated clearly and arranged as shown for the transcription notebooks. The speaker must also learn methods of translation, and how to break up the text, at least into lexical units, with the interlinear word-for-word notation.

The reference speaker must also be taught recording techniques. He should know how to operate the tape recorder, and how to monitor and rewind the tape for the direct transcription of documents, so that he can collect, record, transcribe, and translate texts himself. In addition, he will be very helpful to the linguist during the research once he has mastered the transcription notation and can correct it. For the researcher, each new word requires an effort to identify the phonemes, tones, and meaning completely. For the speaker identification is automatic, once he knows the transcription system, since the language is his own; his only effort involves finding semantic equivalents.

Finally, we must teach the speaker to use the questionnaires. We first explain why we use them, what they are good for, and what their limitations are. Then we show him how to use each one—whether he is to use it by himself or whether he is simply to participate. Thus, the speaker can see to the sentence questionnaire (No. 9) on his own, after being given the necessary explanations. The researcher will be leading most of the topical questionnaires, and only the participation of the speaker is needed there.

In general, we need to make the speaker understand that we want to see him master the working techniques we are teaching him, but that we do not expect him to know everything about his culture. We want him to realize quickly what he does not know, without judging him, and to show him the need to consult the older people, women, artisans, or those who know for sure. We must train him for the work, call on his critical powers, develop his powers of observation and objectivity, arouse his curiosity, and develop a professional conscience in him.

Attitudes and working methods. What has been stated above shows the principles of a positive and fruitful attitude toward the speaker. To arouse interest and scientific motivation in the speaker, to give him a solid technical training, and to have him participate in the researcher's work is infinitely more pleasant and profitable to both parties, than simply to use the speaker passively.

Negative attitudes must be avoided. A common attitude among enlightened amateurs, sometimes recently introduced to linguistics, is the old missionary attitude:

"How do you say that?"
" ... " (response of the speaker)
"No, that's not it," responds the researcher.
"Yes it is!" the speaker insists.
"No, it's not! Anyway, I ought to know. I've been here 30 years, and you are only 20. I remember when you were born!"

A faulty interpretation of scientific objectivity is likewise excluded. A researcher with this attitude never intervenes in any way: he never has the speaker repeat (claiming that only the first form given is valid), makes many recordings, but never asks questions or seeks for clarification. He treats the speaker as an object, never allowing his active participation in the study. He is waiting until afterwards to do his own analysis, to put together the system of the language by himself. Unfortunately, under these circumstances, such a system is likely to be very idiosyncratic.

There are also erroneously positive attitudes. Thus, we do not ask the speaker strictly linguistic questions about his language, such as "Does this word have 2 or 3 syllables?" He can only answer that sort of question with a personal opinion which has no scientific basis. His response may reveal his own orthographic conditioning more than any real distinction in the language. And then we remember the beginner who asked his speaker if there was a voiced/voiceless opposition in his language .... There is of course a way of asking such questions. Instead of "Are there 2 or 3 syllables in this word?", we ask, "Is this word broken like that one?", giving for reference a word whose number of syllables has been firmly established. If a voiced/voiceless distinction is not apparent in the language at first, we may make up possible pairs based on words already collected, and ask if the made-up words exist and are distinguished in the language. Assuming we have found that voiceless stops predominate, we give the speaker a list to try to isolate the voiced stops. If the words [pi, pingi, pü, pama, pongo,] etc. already exist, we might suggest the words [bi, bingi, bü, bama, bongo,] etc. The speaker can then tell us if these exist in the language and if their meaning is different from the first words. In any case, we must not burden the speaker with the technical aspect of the linguist's work.

The researcher must know how to accept correction. Although he is a linguist, he must be humble, realizing always that it is the speaker who speaks and knows the language. At the outset, the speaker will undoubtedly have a preconception of the stranger as one who will always be massacring the language; "I must accept the inevitable ... and be polite," he thinks. Even if (maybe especially if) he is used to working with the language (for example, with missionaries), he may not be inclined to correct the researcher. To counteract this, we test him by trying to make conscious mistakes. After mispronouncing words that we are sure of, we look for his reaction. If he corrects them, we can trust him for the rest; if not, we need to teach him to correct. The one remaining difficulty is that we don't always know why a form has been rejected. Was it the rhythm, the tone, the vowel, the consonant, or an inappropriate semantic context that made the speaker say: "No, you can't say that!" The work of correcting must be done carefully. We must educate the speaker, leading him gradually to specify why something is unacceptable and to indicate what he thinks is the necessary correction.

Finally, in the work schedule imposed on the speaker, certain rules must be observed, which depend on the type of research. Research on the field proper can progress at a more rapid and intensive rate, for much longer periods of time, since it involves a variety of interesting and entertaining jobs for the speaker. Systematic research (such as research by questionnaire) or transcription of texts, on the other hand, is very tedious and monotonous because of the countless repetitions. Therefore, despite the eagerness of the researcher, the work must be broken up. One hour at a stretch seems to be a maximum, and it may be good to have a break after half an hour. Anyway, the point at which attention begins to fade will be readily apparent.

Remuneration of the speaker. This is a delicate problem, for which we have no general rule, unless previous researchers have instituted customs which we are more or less obligated to respect. In countries where we are sent to work, there may be other regulations that must be followed.

Gathering Data

There are two main possibilities: payment of a salary (by the hour, day, or month), or payment of gifts or services. Although the first solution may seem the simplest, it may become very troublesome.

It is always difficult to establish a fixed contract at the outset, since we want to remain flexible in case the speaker is unsuitable. At the beginning, payment by the hour or by the day is preferable, and can be adjusted based on the speaker's qualifications, whether he is a farmer, cook, teacher, clerk, etc. When the speaker has been proved, monthly payment may be in order, since this means higher status for him. However, the researcher must realize that at this point he is taking on a moral obligation that he must consider seriously beforehand. The salary question is always sticky; in this situation, it is difficult to maintain a balanced relationship between the speaker and researcher that does not become simply that of employee to employer.

When payment is by means of gifts or services, the equal status that is essential to the smooth conduct of the research is easier to maintain. However, this is a more complicated system, and a balance satisfactory to both parties is not always easy to achieve.

At any rate, one point is clear: the speaker must be remunerated in some way or other.

3.3.3 Occasional speakers

There is no fixed number of occasional speakers; they will choose you more than you will choose them. They may be men, women, or children; young or old; illiterates or scholars. All this is irrelevant if they are part of the group being studied, know their language well, and have something to say, some information to relate, or some story to tell. We certainly prefer to seek a polished speaker or an older person who is the keeper of a long tradition. It would be wrong to suppose, however, that their contribution was the only valuable one. Children and young people are often excellent speakers for things concerning small animals, whereas experienced hunters would only be familiar with big game animals; women are the experts in many techniques. On the purely linguistic level, there may be speech styles specific to certain segments of the society based on sex or age. It would indeed be surprising, even in societies with specialists in the oral tradition, if others did not have traditional knowledge in other fields or current narratives which are relevant to the linguist.

Occasional speakers, even if they seem permanent, are indeed occasional, for they provide the basic information, the raw material which will be reworked later with the reference speaker. Usually, they are all the people of the village where the fieldwork is conducted. They may be easy to situate in this way, but it is still good to take down certain information, at least for those who contribute most actively (harvesters, hunters, storytellers, artisans, etc.). Certain peculiarities of speech may show up (pronunciation, vocabulary, etc.) that can be explained by travels abroad, parents from a different area, etc. Anonymous data has little value.

Remuneration poses less of a problem for occasional speakers than for the reference speaker. Whether payment is in kind or in currency, it should be, when appropriate, in the form of a gift or an exchange, so that neither party's dignity is offended. Still, it is important to be well informed about the lifestyle of the village where you will stay for fieldwork, so that the researcher does not overpay; this would only hurt everyone concerned, as well as the researcher's budget.

3.3.4 Type of research according to type of speaker

This point seems to flow naturally from the preceding remarks about speakers. We will review only the essential points:

(a) On-site fieldwork and the gathering of raw data (collection of plants, ethnozoology, study of techniques, information on social structures, collection of texts, etc.) are done with the help of the occasional speakers.

(b) Analysis of documents, the use of some questionnaires, and systematic linguistic research are done in collaboration with the reference speaker(s). Control checking will still be done with occasional speakers for the use of the questionnaires and systematic linguistic research.

3.3.5 When there is no common language

We will not dwell on this point, since we have not had sufficient experience with it. It would be useful to study with workers who have developed research methods for this special situation. However, it is likely that this situation will become rarer and rarer.

In any case, though, the problems are not fundamentally different. Apart from translation and the use of certain questionnaires, the roles of the different types of speakers will be about the same. The researcher, though, will be forced to do a number of the routine jobs himself. The study will proceed more slowly, and besides, the researcher will have to learn to speak the language he is studying. This is usually repugnant to a true linguist, but will be all the more worthwhile.

4
Using the Questionnaires

The questionnaires and guides for research and description have been developed along specific theoretical and methodological lines, which explain their organization and order of presentation. Thus, the strictly linguistic matters come first—the establishment of an alphabet and a grammar (Questionnaires 2–8). Secondly, we treat questions relating to the physical culture and civilization (Questionnaires 9–17), which provide the basic material for a dictionary; then, we consider everything included in the rather vague and paradoxical term oral literature (Questionnaire 18); and finally, we make a brief foray into the marginal realm of sociolinguistics (Questionnaires 19–20). The order of presentation is that which we have adopted in our own descriptive works: in each sphere, we move from the simplest to the more complex, from the more linguistic to the less linguistic, and from the most concrete to the more abstract. It is relatively arbitrary and by no means imperative. Nor must it be considered a straitjacket, an obligatory order for research and analysis. However, we feel that these research procedures can be used, in whole or in part, by any type of researcher, despite the diverse considerations necessary for developing any working method.

By proposing subjects and outlines, we hope to facilitate and expedite the project. With such methods and framework for investigation and description, the comparison stage can be reached as soon as possible. This was essentially the objective of the authors' research group.

Almost all these questionnaires are intended simply to be suggestive. When they present a vocabulary to investigate, it is not intended to be exhaustive, but only to provide direction to the investigation. In the midst of fieldwork, even experienced researchers fail to consider a problem from all angles; the questionnaires thus serve as a reminder.

Some aspects of the vocabulary are difficult to explore because the specificity of the subject area would necessitate a new study for each ethnic group. In this case it is better to collect an explanatory text on the subject spoken by the speaker in his language. The text is then translated as usual with the speaker (word-for-word and free translation), but also commented upon and explained by him. This procedure allows us to collect a substantial vocabulary unattainable by the questionnaires. As an example, consider Questionnaire 13.2 (Animal and plant anatomy and physiology), §1.2 (Giving birth): the phrases 'care for the mother' and 'care for the newborn' do not indicate so much translation of the terms as subjects for explanatory narratives to be elicited from the speakers.

In a linguistic investigation, we must always remember to collect terms related to each concept systematically (as in a vocabulary list on a topical questionnaire), so that all lexical categories of the language are covered: nouns and/or nominals (words designating beings, things, actions, states, concepts, etc.), verbs and/or verbals (terms expressing processes), adverbs (which qualify processes), and various qualifiers (which qualify nouns and nominals), as appropriate. This principle is valid for all questionnaires, although it is not always indicated at the top of each one.

The order of presentation of the questionnaires does not imply anything about the sequence or the manner of their use. In the explanations and justifications which follow, we have rearranged the order to make working with them easier, whether during the fieldwork or during analysis.

4.1 Questionnaires and research guides

Many of the questionnaires can be used as guides either for fieldwork or for analysis. Some, however, are oriented more than others toward a specific goal; we present them here with that in mind. Regardless of whether they are strictly for fieldwork, or whether they are guides for research and analysis, the questionnaires may be grouped by the degree to which the reference speaker is involved in their use.

4.1.1 Questionnaires used by the reference speaker alone

Clearly, this does not mean that the researcher simply gives the reference speaker a packet of these questionnaires, asking him to fill them out as soon as possible. For each one, the researcher must show him its importance and explain its purpose, giving necessary instructions for its use. He should start doing it with the speaker, guiding and checking his first attempts. He must be sure that the speaker understands the questionnaire's significance and handling before he leaves it with him, and must still make periodic checks.

This does not mean that the speaker is now forced to work in isolation. He must be willing to work alone, but know that he can ask the investigator as soon as any difficulty arises. His knowledge of English may be limited, and certain terms may require explanation. A small English dictionary may be provided to make the job easier; however, the investigator's explanations will be more helpful, since he is already somewhat familiar with the new language, and knows how well the speaker can handle English.

Questionnaire 9: Sentences. This questionnaire includes more than six thousand sentences, arranged in English alphabetical order according to the key word being illustrated in each sentence:

Using the Questionnaires

   2. They *abandoned* their village.
   7. I have an *abscess* on my thigh.
  10. I have an *abscess*.

  347. *Bees* sting a lot.   etc.

We have tried to include most current, nontechnical English words that we suppose can be translated. The main objective of this questionnaire was to compile the basis for an English-Vernacular dictionary and to highlight problems of equivalence for translating into the vernacular. It can be used from the very beginning as a means of eliciting very short texts, which give a better feel for the language than isolated words, and are simple enough to transcribe and analyze in the early stages of study.

In use, this questionnaire has been found extremely fruitful in many ways. In particular, it covers aspects of the vocabulary otherwise unexplored elsewhere in the investigation. It also provides simple examples for grammatical analysis which do not often appear in connected narrative texts.

This type of study is a long-term project, requiring about four to five months of diligent work, as only about fifty sentences can be translated at one sitting. In fact, it is best to spread the task out over the entire investigation, rather than trying to finish this questionnaire before starting another. Although the exercise generally interests the speaker, it is advisable to distribute it in small doses, so that it does not become a drudgery or simply a mechanical activity done without thinking. This will also hold true for the investigator if the speaker cannot write his own language and the two have to work together on it.

Even though a list of sentences is proposed, this questionnaire should be regarded above all as a guide. Absolutely exact translations are not required. The speaker should be reflective and creative; whenever he deems it appropriate, he should transform the sentence according to the spirit of the language as much as to the characteristics of the civilization. We simply ask him in this case to give a new rendering in English.

Optimally, the transcription of the sentences should be done on sheets with carbon(s) (8½" x 11"), yielding at least one or two additional copies. The number of the sentence should appear first, followed by the transcription in the language with the interlinear word-for-word translation.

```
(Ngbaka)
 10. ʔé        hā       sɔ̄       ɓō       bɔ́nɔ̄
      he   /   gave  /  meat  /  to    |   dog //
 24. nzóì -   lɔ́   -   ō        bɔ́lɔ̀             pā
      bee  |  this  |  s     /  make honey  /   a lot //
```

The reason for making copies is not only to protect against the loss of the original, but also to allow the same sentence to be classified under a number of different headings. For example, 2996 'The canoe landed' could be classified both under 'land' and 'canoe' because both terms are very specific. In sentence 5717, 'he gave meat to the dog', the headings 'give' and 'to' could be illustrated, rather than 'meat' and 'dog', which could appear in any context. Care should be taken that the speaker is not so impressed by the questionnaire that he simply produces mirror-image forms of the English rather than a true translation into his own language. This will be all the more difficult if his formal education is limited. We have observed that a poor knowledge of English often leads to carbon copy translations which do injustice both to the English and to the vernacular. It will therefore be advisable to check the speaker's translations from time to time with other speakers of the language.

Questionnaire 13.1: Anatomy (illustrations and vocabulary). The vocabulary list is illustrated by a series of sketches which permit a more precise definition than that provided by a verbal description. There is also not always a precise correspondence between languages; hence, certain body parts or postures could be defined by one language but not by another. The sketches help to determine the exact locations, and to pinpoint the semantic fields of terms which are often fairly general for the body.

Thus 'leg' in English and *jambe* in French indicate both the entire lower limb as well as the section from the knee to the foot. 'He broke his leg' signifies that the lower limb was broken without giving the exact location. However, in French, *il s'est fait une fracture à la jambe* indicates that the fracture was located between the knee and the foot. In another language the term for the lower limb would not necessarily indicate the identical part of the body. Examining the sketch can also help the speaker to recall other expressions not included in the list, which is obviously not exhaustive. It may be useful to have a number of copies of each sketch and to use colored pencils to show the area that each term may designate, which is obviously not possible with the numbering system used on the questionnaire.

The investigator should initially work with the reference language speaker until he is thoroughly familiar with handling the questionnaire. The speaker can then work with the drawings on his own. For best results, though, the investigator should review the trickier parts with him and with some occasional speakers (e.g., in studying general terms: members ≠ arms + legs; in studying specific terms in detail: limb ≠ arm; etc.).

The questionnaire treats human anatomy first, and then specific items of animal anatomy that are different. Terms such as 'head', 'eyes', 'mouth', etc. will probably be identical for both humans and animals, but specific terms will likely be used for animal parts such as 'cock's comb', 'fin', 'scale', and perhaps even for 'paw', 'back', etc. It is particularly interesting to identify equivalent terms: is the 'knee' of an animal the same as the 'knee' of a person, and if not, what are the criteria for identifying this part of the body that suggested the parallel? Plant anatomy is considered last, being generally the least anthropomorphic, and containing the greatest number of specific terms. The investigation of animal and plant anatomy is an essential complement to the ethnobotanical and ethnozoological investigation.

Questionnaire 17: Appendices: Names of persons, lineages, and domestic animals.

These three questionnaires address a single topic, and were designed for collecting information which is both linguistic and ethnological. It was inspired by a study of the peoples of Central Africa, and may well be of only limited interest outside this area. Nevertheless it will take only a short time to try it out, and if it proves relevant, it will be very profitable. The study will be extremely interesting and rewarding in societies where a name indicates a specific stage of life, or is used as a means of appeasement, commemoration, or protection from evil spirits.

Names consisting of a short sentence in the form of a maxim or motto present interesting linguistic constructions, and may furnish instances of archaic vocabulary or of revealing examples of syntactic behavior and other phenomena. They also provide much important ethnological information related to the social structure and its organization (familial, political, religious, economic, judicial, etc.).

For good results, this investigation should be carried out on a relatively large scale with at least one hundred or more forms. Interesting points will appear from the

Using the Questionnaires 43

comparison and cross-checking of the information. It is essential that the information be gathered from people not simply from the same ethnic group and language, but specifically from the same dialect and preferable from the same village.

4.1.2 Questionnaires guided by the investigator

The questionnaires covered in this section are only slightly different from those in the preceding section, but require somewhat closer supervision on the investigator's part because they require a greater knowledge of linguistics and ethnolinguistics. The degree of the investigator's involvement will also depend upon the aptitude and disposition of the reference language speaker, rather than solely upon the nature of the questionnaire.

Questionnaire 5.1: Morphology (topical). To explore the phenomena of derivation and compounding, we provide lists of semantically related words involving derivation, and of words commonly used as bases for compounding. These lists are based upon the authors' field experience and knowledge of similar phenomena in other languages.

This study can be started with the speaker, so that he can grasp the nature of the relationship sought and demonstrate it if it exists in his language. Later, when he has thoroughly understood the process under investigation, he can continue on his own to find lists of examples illustrating the types of derivation and compounding isolated with the investigator.

Questionnaire 6.1: Verb phrase (topical). In this questionnaire English examples are presented containing tense forms or paraphrases which could be translated by a specific verbal form (of mood, aspect, etc.) in the vernacular, if such forms exist in the language.

One should take particular care to ensure that the speaker does not literally translate the paraphrase which had to be used in English to express an aspect or mood, when his language has a special form for it. He must learn to make a dynamic transfer into his language, not to passively accept the English rendering as inflexible. It is also possible that, because of his limited knowledge of English, he will not grasp some nuance which would be expressed by a specific verbal form in his language. For example, Gbanzili has a specific dual subject pronoun *yóōté* 'they-two'. The speaker, however, seeing the English rendering 'they two', translated it literally into the phrase *yóō ɓīsì*.

What is gained from this questionnaire varies greatly, and depends essentially upon the ability of the speaker and his knowledge of English, upon the properties of the vernacular, and upon the skill of the investigator.

The questionnaire needs to be explained very carefully to produce valid results. For example, it is essential that the pronominal forms listed as §1.1 to §1.10 be accurately determined before investigating later stages; and in §7, the speaker must understand clearly the distinctions required: in 7.7, $S_i = S_j$ means 'He$_i$ said that he$_j$ (himself) would come', and in §7.8, $S_i \neq S_j$ means 'He said that he (someone else) would come'.

When the English example brings a certain form to light, first examine all its possibilities before proceeding. Try it with the different pronouns of the language, in positive and negative forms, and in contexts with subjects and object forms of the various categories and classes already found. For a tonal language, check the behavior of tone with the subject and object complements (direct, indirect, locative, temporal, etc.) for each verbal form. For example, in Ngbaka, which has three register tones, we examine in turn the tonal behavior where the subject and complements have high, mid, and low tone.

with Subjects: *hō̄-* 'to eat' *hố* 'to eat'
(COMPLETIVE)   (INCOMPLETIVE)

bó	'crocodile'	bó	hō̄	bó	hố
vō	'man'	vó	hō̄	vō	hố
mbù	'sorcerer'	mbù	hō̄	mbù	hố

with Object complements (here, direct object and locative):
  sī   'fish'   ʔé hō̄ sī ʔé hō̄ sī   'He is eating/ate fish'
  bēlē 'forest' ʔé hố bēlē ʔé hố bēlē 'He is eating/ate in the forest'

The schematic verbal questionnaire will help the investigator to complete and systematize the information discovered through the topical questionnaire.

If the speaker cannot use this questionnaire to maximum advantage by himself, he can at least be taught to take the forms isolated and analyzed with the investigator, and provide a complete series of examples for each in context, with the first one given as a model.

Questionnaire 7: Noun phrase. This questionnaire is easier to use than the one on the verb phrase, as it is based on lists. After the investigator explains each list to the reference speaker and does the first three or four examples with him, the speaker can continue alone. It will nevertheless be advisable to check the work in general with various occasional speakers to ensure the acceptability of the translations provided. A questionnaire of this nature can distort the speaker's judgment, so that he may accept inadmissible or less accurate forms, or exceed the normal limits for a sequence of modifiers.

Questionnaire 19: Language contact. The investigator's first step in using this questionnaire is to fill it out with the reference speaker as the first interviewee. He can explain it thoroughly and in detail to the speaker as they proceed, showing him how to do it and what is significant about it. One should not hesitate to spend a lot of time on this, so that the speaker will thereafter be able to continue on his own, acting as an assistant investigator.

Numerous responses to this questionnaire are needed to obtain useful results, so we suggest that 100 copies of it be made. It is advisable to have answers recorded on the questionnaire form itself to make processing easier. The sample given in this book, which allows little space for this purpose because of publication constraints, should thus be retyped before duplication.

The two parts of the questionnaire provide a shorter and longer version of the same study. The first part can be used complete in itself, while the second part is an extension of the first, and must be used in conjunction with it. The sociolinguistic interest of this study can be enhanced by expanding the linguistic aspect of either the shorter or the longer form. A sampling of those interviewed must be made, representative as to age, sex, ethnic group, profession, educational level, and languages spoken. Each subject is then to record a short narrative in each of the languages he speaks (e.g., vernacular, trade language, language of colonization or of education, etc.). It is best for comparison purposes if all tell the same story, such as a well-known fable of the region. In Central Africa, the tale of the race between the snail (or tortoise) and the antelope is sufficiently universal for this purpose.

4.1.3 Questionnaires used by the investigator alone

The series of questionnaires falling under this heading include practical guides on topics such as instructions for recording (Questionnaire 1) and instructions for the collection of botanical and zoological samples (Questionnaire 14), as well as strictly linguistic and ethnolinguistic research guides.

Little comment is required on the practical guides. They are necessary, for the investigator does need some technical knowledge, notably to operate a tape recorder (or to use a camera, to drive various vehicles, etc.) and to collect ethnoscientific samples. In fact he could use an entire brochure of technical advice and detailed instructions for the nonspecialist in the preparation of pictorial, ethnozoological, and technical collections. However, we will limit the discussion to the areas where we ourselves had the most difficulty.

The other questionnaires are principally guides for both research and analysis. As research guides they suggest possible options on linguistic questions, or offer the choice between various formal hypotheses. For ethnolinguistic investigation, they present various options to remind the investigator of areas which he may not have considered.

Questionnaire 3: Extensive survey. This type of questionnaire has numerous objectives. It may serve simply as a point of departure for a linguistic survey. Because of the scope of its data, though, it may also be used to work out a suitable phonology, or even a brief linguistic description. In the survey of a given area for comparative purposes, it can provide quick and brief analyses of languages, which are more useful in comparisons than simple word lists.

In dialect survey work, the questionnaire as given here provides for collecting the basic data needed. It will be advisable to adapt the questionnaire to the characteristics of the group being studied, insofar as these have already been identified for at least one dialect.

Questionnaire 4: Phonology. Questionnaire 4 was planned especially for the nonlinguist or for the beginning investigator, and reviews the different operations necessary in establishing a working alphabet. It was not designed as an introduction to phonology and should not be regarded as such.

Questionnaire 5.2: Morphology (schematic). This questionnaire covers systematically the different morphological phenomena known to us, which either contribute to word formation, such as derivation and compounding, or account for the morpheme variants, such as the fused forms found in some verb conjugations.

This guide obviously does not claim to be exhaustive, since it is based on the authors' experience with the languages of Africa (specifically central Africa), and it will no doubt be all the more valuable if the language studied is similar to one of these. Nevertheless the questionnaire is included to remind the linguist of these problems which are sometimes not obvious and hence may be neglected. In the study of a Bantu language, or one with noun classes, a great deal of attention (perhaps too much) is typically devoted to morphology; in a language with little morphology, though, these issues risk being ignored.

Questionnaire 6.2: Verb phrase (schematic). This questionnaire is different from the preceding questionnaires in that an investigation cannot begin with it. A certain number of forms is required, perhaps obtained through the topical verb phrase questionnaire; from these all the forms used in the verbal paradigm can be systematically explored. This questionnaire will be used alternatively as a guide for analysis, then for investigation, then for several more rounds of analysis and investigation, until the subject has been thoroughly explored.

Thus, at one point, we might find the following forms:

Ngbaka
a ʔé hō̄   'he eats'
b ʔé pá   'he passes'
c ʔé dù   'he thrusts'

Several questions arise from these forms. The English equivalents are not very meaningful; we can not usually expect to base a serious analysis of the verbal paradigm on the translations of a speaker who has a limited knowledge of English. Based only on the lexical differences of these three forms, several hypotheses are possible. It may be that the forms cited are the lexical forms: they have the same verbal form, and differences in consonants, vowels, and tones. It may also be, however, that they are different grammatical forms, due to a change of tone, vowels, or possibly consonants. Now we proceed to the investigation stage, considering the various formal possibilities. After ruling out any grammatical effect from changing the consonants and vowels, we find that changing the tone is of interest:

(a) ʔé hō̄   'he has eaten'   ʔé hó   'he eats'
                (COMPLETIVE)   (INCOMPLETIVE)
                                   ʔé hò̌   'he ate'
                                          (COMPLETIVE)

(b) ʔé pá   'he passes'   ʔé pā   'he has passed'
                (INCOMPLETIVE)   (COMPLETIVE)
                                   ʔé pà   'he passed'
                                          (COMPLETIVE)

(c) ʔé dù   'he has thrust'   ʔé dú   'he is thrusting'
                (COMPLETIVE)   (INCOMPLETIVE)
            = 'he thrust'   = 'he is returning'
                (EXISTENTIAL)   (INCOMPLETIVE)
            = 'he returned'   ʔé dū   'he returned'
                (EXISTENTIAL)   (COMPLETIVE)

From these forms, we observe:

(1) Change in tone with grammatical effect: each verb in (a) and (b) has three forms [CV̄ (COMPLETIVE), CV́ (INCOMPLETIVE), and CV̀ (COMPLETIVE)], corresponding to three different forms in its conjugation.

(2) Change in tone with both grammatical and lexical effect: in (c) the situation is more complex—CV̀ corresponds to two different forms of the same verb root (dù 'to thrust') which are not distinguishable here, whereas CV̄ corresponds to another verb root (dū 'to return').

Thus this language uses tone to indicate both lexical and grammatical distinctions:

lexical: ʔé dù   'he thrust'   (COMPLETIVE)
            ʔè dū   'he returned' (COMPLETIVE)

grammatical: ʔé hō̄ (COMPLETIVE)
ʔé hố (INCOMPLETIVE)
ʔé hò̗ (COMPLETIVE)

And some forms fall together:

ʔé dù permits
- two grammatical forms
  - COMPLETIVE of dù
  - COMPLETIVE of dù and dū
- two lexical forms
  - 'to thrust' (COMPLETIVE and COMPLETIVE)
  - 'to return' (COMPLETIVE)

This example shows the amount of information which can be obtained from the questionnaire, and its function in both analysis and research.

Questionnaire 8: Sentence types. Questionnaire 8 is based on the same principles as the previous one and is used in the same way. It is not intended for use at the beginning of the investigation, for it presupposes some knowledge about the language. It is designed to systematize the investigation of information about the language already obtained empirically.

Of all the working guides, this one is the most closely associated with, and oriented toward, analysis.

Questionnaires 10–16: Topical questionnaires. These questionnaires concern ethnolinguistics, and investigate aspects of the social and material culture from various angles. Some are forms to be filled out, such as Questionnaires 11 (Plant names), 12 (Animal names), and 15.2 (Kinship terms).

The questionnaire on plant names, for example, includes as complete information as possible for identification purposes. As it is not possible to obtain such detailed information for each plant, only the relevant features should be recorded; nevertheless the questionnaire is useful in that it reminds the investigator of the areas to explore if he wants to continue with a serious ethnobotanical study. The same observations apply to the questionnaire on animal names.

One may question the emphasis placed on ethnobotanical and ethnozoological studies in a linguistic investigation. In a nonindustrialized and nonurban society, the natural surroundings occupy a prominent place in man's conception of the universe, especially the plants and animals which provide him with the greatest part of his sustenance. A study of the language immediately reveals how extensive this vocabulary is, with important ramifications in all aspects of life. A botanical and zoological file can provide a variety of information. For example, ethnological and historical information about the Ngbaka came to light from some of their animal names. Although they are a forest people, they have their own names for the rhinoceros *(kpáàkɔ́.dì.gbā̄)* and the giraffe *(ngɔ̀lù)*, both of which live only on the savannah. It is therefore likely that before migrating, the Ngbaka too came from the savannah. They themselves say that they came from the east by the river; linguistic comparisons place them in the Upper Nile area possibly one millenium ago. On the other hand, their name for the hippopotamus *(ngùbú)* is a Bantu loan word and it appears that they encountered this animal relatively late at the Ubangi or Congo river. A network of such information can provide evidence about ethnic migrations and relationships between languages.

This part of the vocabulary can even make a valuable contribution to the study of certain linguistic phenomena such as compounding, since many plant and animal names are compounds.

The questionnaire on techniques (No. 10) is organized as a research guide, examining in turn each aspect of physical activity in a nonindustrialized society. It does not claim to be universal, based as it is on Africa, and specifically central Africa. For each subject or technique to be investigated, it explains what must be found out: the raw materials involved, the tools and the manufacturing process, and the finished products. Numerous terms are presented and illustrated so that both the investigator and the speaker can understand the exact meaning; the terms are also found in short sentences that show how they are used. This questionnaire should not simply be regarded as a form to fill out, but the investigator should use it as a guide to investigate each technique as fully and accurately as possible with each artisan. The artisans interviewed may weary quickly of this type of questioning, which shows only too clearly the investigator's ignorance; often they do not wish to, or know how to, give the desired explanations on their own. Although the linguist's aim is not to conduct a technical investigation, the gathering of vocabulary and assembling of good documentation are indeed a part of his work. To do this he will have to go beyond the strictly linguistic concerns. It is important for the linguist to know, for example, that the language distinguishes a variety of types of baskets (carried on the back, held in the hand, used for storage), distinguished according to their shape and/or function. Or again there may be a dozen terms which all seem to signify 'to tap, hit, knock', whereas in reality the language uses them to distinguish between hitting with the flat of the hand, with the fist, with the foot, with a blunt instrument, with a cutting instrument, from the bottom to the top, from the top to the bottom, with an instrument held vertically, with an instrument held horizontally, etc.

When using the twelve kinship charts (Questionnaire 15.2), one should start with unlabeled charts where the relationships are indicated by position alone. The charts use simple terminology, with paraphrases to indicate the relationships rather than terms which are specific to our own kinship system, and which may be completely different from those of the society being investigated. In addition, certain of our kinship terms 'cousin', 'uncle', 'little brother', or 'father' may be used in the locally spoken English with a completely new meaning, so that using them would be even more confusing. One should also be careful that the speaker does not translate the paraphrase literally if his language has a specific term for the relationship. The best way to ensure this is to build up one or more actual genealogies and then to examine the relationships by citing specific individuals in them. The information should also be checked several times, with a variety of speakers. Certain kinship terms may be reciprocal, often for maternal uncle and nephew, or for grandparent and grandchild; it would be most unfortunate to accuse a speaker of ignorance in such a case.

Questionnaire 15.1 (Family, political, and social organization) complements the kinship charts, clarifying and extending certain points, especially for relationships which are hard to express in chart form (special cases, adoption, residence), as well as ways of forming and breaking alliances. It also investigates various aspects of social and political organization. It must not be used as a simple list of terms to be translated; the investigator must have some basic knowledge of ethnology so that he can formulate appropriate questions. Its role is principally to remind him of the different possibilities he must explore.

Hence, in §2.1, the joking relationships indicate that we want to find out whether such an institution exists in the society, not simply to ask for the translation of the words. The investigator should first ask the speaker whether there are people in his society with whom he can or must exchange jokes or insults when they meet. If this does not apply to him personally, might it apply to others? If so, what is this behavior called; who practices it; how do these people refer to and address each other; what are their reciprocal obligations; how did they enter into this relationship; what forms does the institution take? etc. The speaker should explain these things in his own language, as he will be much more at ease in speaking about something specific to his own culture that does not exist in that of the language of communication (English, French, etc.). Also, all related vocabulary will be obtained, which would otherwise be lost in translation.

Anatomical and physiological questionnaires (No. 13.2) are used in much the same way as Questionnaire 15.1. They extend the investigation which was started using drawings, to abstract aspects of physiology and pathology which can not easily be illustrated. Again it should not be forgotten that the principal objective is a linguistic study. So, starting from a term such as *fever* (§1.4), one should investigate all the different ways to express the state (nouns), the process (verbs), and modifications (adverbs and qualifiers)—'fever', 'to have a fever', 'feverishly', 'feverish', etc.—if these possibilities exist in the language. Numerous terms will be discovered which were not anticipated in the questionnaire, and these should be followed up. With *fever,* for example, specific expressions meaning 'recurring fever', 'latent fever', etc. might be found.

Questionnaire 16 (Psychological phenomena) was certainly the most difficult to develop because of its abstract nature. The questionnaire does not claim to be exhaustive or flawless, but was designed to give direction to the investigation. It overlaps with several other questionnaires (botanical, zoological, sociological) on various points, but it is not a duplication of effort because the approaches are different and hence complementary. The questionnaire may seem rather cursory in areas which belong uniquely to it (sensations, emotions and feelings, language and thought, the perception of space and time, and symbolic systems), but diversity among civilizations is extremely great in this sphere. This area is also the least understood and the least studied until now. Very few rigorous research methods have been established, so we have to proceed by trial and error, using models either of our own culture, which are not very appropriate, or else those based on our own previous experiences, which are less well studied.

Included in this questionnaire are certain aspects of the understanding and perception of the exterior world, and of oneself within that world. Some difficult aspects have only been lightly touched on and really require a specific questionnaire themselves. The notion of color, for example, is particularly difficult to explore. It has often been stated that African languages distinguish only three colors, and even that the people do not perceive more than these three, a theory now abandoned. The equivalents to these colors, given in English as 'black', 'white', and 'red', are misleading. It would be much preferable to say 'dark', 'light', and 'bright': 'dark' includes dark blue, indigo, dark green, brown, black, ... ; 'light' includes yellow, light green, sky blue, white, ... ; and 'bright' includes bright yellow, orange, red, ochre, ... In fact most languages express color by analogy, as we in fact do in English when speaking of hazel or chestnut eyes, a lemon or lilac dress, etc. In an African language, one would in the same way say '(like) manioc leaves' for a shade of green, '(like) soup made from palm nut pulp' for a dark golden yellow, or '(like) lime' for white. Much can be added to this investigation by using a color chart.

It should not be surprising to find that the senses are divided up differently in other languages. For instance, the senses of hearing and smell are often combined into the same semantic class, so that one hears (perceives) an odor in the same way as a sound.

Similarly, the delineation of physical space is frequently ethnocentric. For the Ngbaka, *ɓàlè* indicates the Ubangi River, the greatest of rivers to the exclusion of all others. Cardinal points may be expressed in relation to the location of the ethnic group. This is the case among the Birom, south being designated as the direction of the Angass people, their southern neighbors. Vocabulary will almost always be related to the group's immediate environment. Among the Banda, a people of the plain, there is no term to precisely indicate plain or valley, but even the slightest elevation will be termed 'mound', 'hillock', 'hill', or 'mountain'.

Forest dwellers generally have little interest in the constellations. On the other hand, people of the savannah have a rich vocabulary relating to the stars and constellations, as they can contemplate the full beauty of the starry sky, and often have important mythologies about them. Across tropical Africa, for example, Orion is the shepherd or hero who courts the Pleiades. A star chart from the equator to the tropics is useful for such an investigation (cf. *Atlas du Ciel,* published by Gauthier-Villard, which shows maps of the constellations at different times of the year).

Questionnaire 18: Oral tradition. This questionnaire consists of two parts. Part 1 concerns text collection, and is presented as a form to fill out in classifying and identifying each text. This subject does not lend itself to a true questionnaire approach; discussion of problems and techniques for guiding and orienting the investigation will be deferred to the detailed treatment in §4.3.5.

The second part of the questionnaire (18.2) handles ethnomusicological issues, which are closely connected with numerous forms of spoken expression in a society without a written tradition. Singing, of course, touches on both musicology and linguistics, and is used in different types of traditional and nontraditional texts. Beyond this is the study of the music itself, including first the study of musical instruments, a technology not covered in the questionnaire on techniques. Ethnomusicology problems are also treated more fully in §4.3.5. Given the various technical and sociological implications of this subject, the questionnaire is itself quite a detailed guide into these areas. It seeks to provide not only lists of specialized terms for which equivalents are sought, but also indications of subjects for research.

4.2 Guides for analysis and description

Some of the strictly linguistic questionnaires were designed to meet the needs of both research and analysis, and consequently of description as well. For us, language description involves giving an account first of the process of analysis, and then of its results, at each successive stage.

This is especially true for the phonological questionnaire (No. 4), which indicates the areas to be investigated, the technical methods for discovering phonological phenomena, and the analytical procedures for isolating functional units. It presents the topic as a progressive plan, like that used by the authors in most of their works.

For the systematic investigation of morphemes, Questionnaire 5.D.2 (Morphology: schematic) offers both a procedure for research and a method for analysis, which are equally profitable. It seeks to give the most objective and complete view of the facts possible, and its presentation is easily grasped, because it is based on form without neglecting either meaning or function.

The schematic verbal questionnaire (6.B) is similar, but is much shorter. As an illustration of this model, as well as its method of presentation, the reader is referred to J. M. C. Thomas' *Le syntagme verbal*. This series of lectures was given at a session of the Initiation à la Linguistique Africaine *(Afrique et Langage)* at Aix-en-Provence, July 1969. *La langue. Encyclopédie des Pygmées Aka I.4. La civilisation.* SELAF 50:I.2 Paris: Peeters, 1991.

The study of the noun phrase (No. 7) is based on form, consisting here of the order, number, and type of components of the phrase, for both the head and its modifiers. This method of presentation, which is good for both research and analysis at different points of the study, is useful, objective, and clear. Several works by our team members follow this model.

Of all the questionnaires, the one on sentence types (No. 8) is the most oriented to analysis and description. The process uses a finite number of functional units, and investigates their possible combinations and structures by starting with the simplest arrangement, and moves progressively toward the most complex. This guide, more than any other, assumes familiarity with certain theoretical concepts and vocabulary, which are explained in the second part of this volume.

The structure of some of the topical questionnaires may provide an outline for the exposition of the subject treated, such as in a dictionary arranged by topic. Questionnaire No. 10 on techniques, and Nos. 11 and 12 concerning the names of plants and animals are especially of this type.

4.3 Principal aspects of the study of a language accessible through questionnaires

It is obviously not possible to include all aspects of the study of a language in a work such as this, however great our ambitions or methods. Even if we had sufficient experience and research workers, our undertaking would be limited to the problems that we are most concerned with at present.

Although we seek to know as much as possible about the languages and cultures we are studying, the urgency of the task and the feebleness of our efforts do not allow us to devote many years, let alone a whole lifetime, to each one. As a result, we must skip over some areas which seem less essential.

4.3.1 Comparison

Language comparison is one of our principal aims, both in the development of certain questionnaires (such as the extensive survey), and in the overall methods and procedures of investigation, analysis, and description proposed here. We hope, by generalizing our techniques, at least within our own research group, to arrive at the comparison stage as quickly and efficiently as possible.

The specialized questionnaire will be used for a systematic study of the dialects of each language studied. It allows for precise definition of the dialect boundaries, as well as the limits of extension of the language itself. This approach also avoids the unfortunate muddle found in many works, wherein the language as described, being a mixture of several dialects, is spoken by no one.

The same questionnaire can be used effectively on a larger scale, and in some depth, for the comparison of languages within the same language family. An intensive investigation of at least one language, based upon a common model for which the questionnaires are proposed, in combination with an extensive survey of the other languages and dialects of the same family, will rapidly open onto a comparative study of some magnitude.

This aspect of the linguistic study is mentioned first because of its importance; however, in practice, it is a final stage rather than a beginning one.

4.3.2 Phonology

The phonology is in fact the first step in the systematic analysis of a language, as the establishment of an alphabet for transcription is fundamental to all subsequent studies. A good phonetic transcription is certainly preferable to some arbitrary notation, but only a phonological transcription is truly profitable, and satisfactory also for morphological and grammatical analysis. One can never spend too much time on this aspect of research and analysis. The phonology of the language is also an extremely important aspect for comparison purposes.

One question that arises concerns the type and quantity of data required for this analysis. The answer depends on the language under scrutiny, of course, but experience leads us to believe that a list of 500 words will be sufficient to make a plausible analysis on the level of the word. For a refined analysis, at least 1000–1500 words will be needed. A serious study must not stop with the phonology of the word in isolation, however, but continue on to an analysis of connected speech. This stage requires a number of short utterances and connected texts for studying the behavior of the phonemes: their phonetic realizations, variants, distributions, neutralizations, frequencies, combinations, etc. We suggest a minimum of 100 sentences and 10–15 pages of texts for this purpose.

For gathering the data and then for analyzing and testing it, Questionnaires No. 3 (Extensive survey) and No. 4 (Phonology) are particularly relevant, and should be sufficient.

Another important consideration involves the type of speaker used for the analysis, and whether to begin with the phonology of the group or of the individual. The beginning investigation of an unknown language is always difficult, and working with several speakers at this stage only makes it harder. It will thus be advisable to determine the main outlines of the phonology from a single speaker's speech. Then this analysis can be tested with other speakers of the group, carefully chosen as those having the same speech style and dialect. Dialectal comparisons will be made at a more advanced stage of the study.

In the second part of this volume, we will discuss a number of important principles relevant to this analysis and description.

4.3.3 Grammar

Phonological analysis is an indispensable first step for any study of a civilization without a written tradition, whether of its culture or of its language. For the ethnologist, the study of the language may end there, but for the linguist, phonology is simply a start, providing a specialized tool for use in the heart of his study—the grammar.

Half of the linguistic questionnaires (Nos. 5–9) aim at gathering data specifically for grammatical analysis, which includes morphology and both phrase-level and sentence-level syntax. We will return to these points in the second part of this work, which is devoted specifically to grammatical analysis.

For the purposes of the investigation itself, we will consider only the corpus of data needed for establishing the grammar. For such a study we cannot rely on the questionnaires alone, of course, but they do allow us to complete and systematize our information. Spontaneous, connected discourse is clearly the basis for serious analysis of the grammar of a language. To this end, we will need a collection of diverse texts (about 200 handwritten pages), from extended conversations to traditional narratives of stories and myths. This variety is necessary in an in-depth study, allowing access to different levels of the language. Traditional texts often use an affected, even archaic, form of the language, while conversation (even at a fairly formal level) uses a more relaxed form, noticeably different from that of a sustained discourse. It is therefore essential to make a careful sampling of all the various styles.

Grammatical analysis must be based on spontaneous text, it is true, but working with texts alone to develop a grammar will not provide comprehensive coverage. To find all possible structures of the language, we would need such a large corpus that gathering, examining, and analyzing the texts would be impossible. Since we approach the study of these languages from the outside, and consequently do not have a native speaker's linguistic intuitions, we cannot by ourselves fill in the gaps in an analysis based on texts. Besides, this procedure requires two stages: first, collecting, organizing, and analyzing the texts, then developing grammatical hypotheses; and secondly, testing the hypotheses and progressively eliminating the gaps. Such a procedure is not practical for unwritten languages when a second field trip cannot be guaranteed. Thus, we must start putting together the basic material necessary for our work from the very beginning. This is where the use of questionnaires is indispensable, since they were designed specifically for this purpose. They offer a maximum number of logical, formal, thematic, and combinatory hypotheses, and permit the investigation of a language of which one has only a superficial knowledge (from the questionnaire on extensive surveys, for example). All the hypotheses are obviously not applicable to every language, nor do they exhaust all issues encountered, but they do provide avenues of research to follow up when a phenomenon exists in the language. In systematizing the investigation, the questionnaires thus serve to anticipate the second stage of analysis by taking the place of the hypothetical inspection of an impossibly large corpus of spontaneous texts. The main drawback of the questionnaires is that they rely heavily on the linguistic awareness of the assistant, which in some cases gives doubtful results.

From a practical point of view, Questionnaires No. 6 (Verb phrase), No. 7 (Noun phrase), and No. 8 (Sentence types) seem essential. Questionnaire No. 5 (Morphology: derivation and compounding) provides the clarifications needed for understanding the greater part of the structure of the phrase in some languages with a rich morphology. Problems of derivation and compounding, which are word-level phenomena, are rather marginal at this level of analysis, though, and are more relevant to the study of the lexicon (cf. §4.3.4). Finally, a minimum of 1000–1500 sentences from Questionnaire 9 (Sentences) will be necessary to the analysis. Their use will bring to the grammatical study some rich and varied material to exploit, since the topical questionnaires are designed basically for developing and deepening the study of the lexicon.

The corpus should always remain open for the inclusion of additional material, unless circumstances prevent it (e.g., the impossibility of returning to the field, or the loss of the last speaker of the language). The analysis, as we see it, must be able to account for all real or hypothetical possibilities of the language.

4.3.4 Lexicography and semantics

The myth of the pure linguist is unfortunately still very much alive, and some will consider the linguist's task finished at this point. For the authors, however, grammatical analysis is just one stage in the study of a language, especially one with no written tradition which is doomed to disappear with its last speakers.

Equivalences and semantic fields. The fundamental problem in lexicography, and thus in the compilation of a dictionary, is that of finding equivalences. This is the purpose of several of the questionnaires, as we have seen. For techniques, plants, and animals, satisfying results can be obtained even though a long and specialized investigation is necessary to study them: plants and animals are scientifically identified; and tools, technical processes, and artisanal products are clearly defined. As the degree of abstraction increases, precise definitions (let alone equivalences) become more difficult. The semantic fields of words are always difficult to delimit precisely; the numerous cross-checks in the questionnaires are designed for researching them. And the problem can be almost insoluble if one takes up specific aspects of a culture without questionnaires to direct the investigation toward a study of the structures appropriate to the society concerned. Again, we reiterate that we are not making a sociological study, but are exploring how a society's language expresses its awareness of its organization and also its understanding of the physical and spiritual world in which man lives.

In compiling a dictionary, the greatest effort will no doubt be expended in searching for equivalences for the Vernacular-to-English (or French) part. However, the work should not stop there, for it is just as important to consider the converse equivalences, English (or French)-to-Vernacular, at least for languages in areas where an international language (English, French, etc.) is used as the language of education, and where part of the population is bilingual. Thus, the English-Vernacular dictionary will not be simply a reference index (as is generally the case), but rather the result of a real investigation, which joins the field of sociolinguistics here in the issue of language contact (cf. §4.3.6). This was our main goal as we developed the sentence questionnaire.

The study of semantic fields is too vast to be limited to the work on the dictionary. This study can be accomplished easily in more than usual depth; the questionnaires were designed to facilitate the research as much as possible. For example, let us take the Ngbaka word $mò$-, obtained from Questionnaire 13 on human anatomy. Glossed as 'mouth', it can mean both 'opening' and 'oral cavity'. A study of animal anatomy later shows the same uses. Moving on to the technological questionnaire, we find the semantic range of $mò$- extended in several directions: on an iron tool (knife, hook, axe, hoe, etc.), it means the active, piercing, or cutting part of the blade, i.e., the 'point' of the spear, and the 'blade' of the hoe; on a container (basket, pot, house), $mò$- means both the 'opening' and 'closing': for a house it is the 'door' and its 'frame', for the pot it is the 'opening' and its 'lid'; for a long object (stick, beam, rope, etc.), $mò$- is the 'end' or 'extremity', and if relevant, the end closest to the speaker or hearer, depending on the case. When we come to the questionnaire on psychological phenomena, we find that $mò$- means 'language', 'speech', and 'word' in the abstract sense (word of honor, giving one's word). Finally, in relation to space and time, $mò$- signifies 'beginning' (e.g., of a path, of a season). A dictionary should account for such facts as much as possible.

Synthematic formation and categorial organization of the lexicon. A dictionary should not simply be an inventory or catalogue of a language's lexical units. Developing one requires active research, like that in grammar, not just passive recording. The analysis of word formation, whereby the lexicon is enriched, adapted, and renewed, will be important in this perspective, so that a dictionary must include a rather complete study of the processes of derivation, compounding, and even of loan words.

Questionnaire 5 (Morphology: derivation and compounding) was intended for this purpose, although its particular aim is to systematize research. The material itself will be furnished by topical questionnaires such as those on Techniques, Names of plants and animals, and Anatomy and physiology of plants and animals, all spheres in which lexical creations are abundant.

It will also be of interest for the dictionary to show how the lexical apparatus integrates with syntactic function, and consequently what type of operational unit each lexeme belongs to. This aspect of the study is valuable enough for simple lexemes, but is all the more important for formations where the processes for converting from one grammatical category to another must be analyzed.

This study proceeds from the analysis rather than from the fieldwork, but some grammatical questionnaires touch on it. In any case, it will be the first step in the grammatical study, so that developing the dictionary can begin as soon as this problem is worked out.

A three-part dictionary and the structure of the lexicon. The first two parts of the dictionary, English-Vernacular and Vernacular-English, have been mentioned above, and already imply certain theoretical and methodological stands. The third section, which we call simply subject classification, also rests on assumptions about research and description, and carries a conception of linguistics and ethnolinguistics that is not necessarily universal.

The primary purpose of this type of lexical study is to reach a certain degree of exhaustiveness. Most dictionaries betray the interests, ties, and background of their authors more than they reveal the language and culture under study. While showing great richness and precision in areas such as plant names, for example, they may ignore sociological vocabulary almost completely, and manifest an impressionistic vagueness in technical definitions. Our questionnaires which deal with the principal areas of human thought and activity seek to avoid these dangers by suggesting the threads of a course for a rather comprehensive investigation.

Organizing the lexicon in this way also attempts to bring out the indigenous classifications found in some domains. In botanical or zoological studies, for example, we must not necessarily expect to find some great hierarchical system similar to our scientific classifications, although we tend to look for them, more or less consciously. If such classifications exist, the questionnaires ought to allow us to isolate them. Rather, though, we are likely to find a series of small systems or subsystems which overlap or interact with each other. Although preference is given to these areas (perhaps because of our own predispositions toward scientific classifications), they are not the only ones where classification systems may be found. Techniques and social organization (by its very nature) have comparable systems, but are not always examined in this way. There is also structure to psychological phenomena, in the perception of time, space, feelings, colors, etc. To be used effectively, a dictionary organized in this way must present both the INDIGENOUS classification and the LOGICAL classification (i.e., the arbitrary system of our culture), when these are different.

A more linguistic aspect of indigenous classifications concerns the analogies and contrasts brought out through the language's use of synonyms and antonyms within a single semantic domain. Certain questionnaires anticipate the systematic investigation of spheres that lend themselves easily to this method (physiology and pathology, social and political organization, psychological phenomena). However, they cannot fully capture the reality of the new language, since they are based on English. This study depends on the language and its own modes of expression, and must be carried out in the course of the fieldwork.

4.3.5 Oral Tradition

A. Text Collection
(by Jean-Claude Rivierre)

The gathering of vernacular texts must be a part of the total program of any linguistic research. Even though the oral traditions of many ethnic groups are in danger of disappearing, such literature is not always collected. From a linguistic point of view, it is truly authentic, conceived in the language and not the product of translation or interpretation. As in general linguistic research, text collection requires some ethnographic knowledge and interest in the group being studied.

Oral literature. We will consider this topic in the wider sense of oral tradition, which includes:

- the major traditional genres: historical narratives, myths, stories, poems, ...
- the minor genres: proverbs, riddles or puzzles, short stories, lullabies, nursery rhymes, ...
- songs

This list is not exhaustive, and each group develops its own specialties. Also included here is any verbal expression associated with special events in social or religious life, such as ritual formulas, songs, and customary discourses (given at festivals, births, marriages, funerals, etc.).

Even apart from any oral tradition, the researcher can still collect anecdotes, biographies, conversations, or explanations of various techniques in the vernacular, so that more will eventually survive than just catechisms or the responses to a questionnaire. Linguistic research requires a variety of texts, including narratives of the oral tradition with their careful, affected, and often even archaic style, as well as more spontaneous texts, such as explanations of techniques, biographical accounts and anecdotes, or conversations, in a quite different style which is often neglected.

Difficulties of the investigation. Sizable populations which have largely escaped domination or colonization by another civilization have generally preserved, almost intact, a tradition that needs to be collected. Such research is much more arduous in small groups who have long ago been colonized or invaded by more powerful neighbors. There, the people may well have forgotten much of the oral tradition. But when someone says "No one knows any more" or "You came too late", we must remember how important a faithful retelling may be to the speaker. He may refuse simply because he has forgotten some details or names, although much may still remain of the tradition.

A group which has been colonized or christianized may refuse to admit that oral traditions still exist. A speaker may be afraid or inhibited with a stranger who is not likely to understand the language or appreciate the content of the story; or, he may be afraid to speak into a microphone. Besides, certain literary genres may be restricted to specific times and places.

Even if the tradition has been preserved in the most favorable conditions, its very nature may cause other problems for the elicitation. The role and significance of certain narratives must be taken account of, for their explicit or symbolic content may have important social implications, such as: the claim or affirmation of land ownership rights; the acknowledgment or challenge of a social rank or allegiance; the evocation of specific historical events or secret knowledge; etc. In such cases, reluctance, downright hostility, or a conscious deceit may conceal a rich part of the traditional oral literature.

A bigger problem is the interpretation that the speaker gives to his text. Many narratives carry a double meaning, an obvious one for the general audience and another reserved for the initiated. Such language devices as double meanings and plays on words are often used for this, and are of particular interest to the linguist. It is usually long and laborious work to discover the hidden side of a narrative, and a good knowledge of the society in question will be of help in solving the problem.

Traditional narratives, then, do not come naturally; nor are they necessarily produced on request. The group may try to satisfy the investigator with a few short stories, apparently known by everyone and supposed to represent the entire heritage, or that which remains of an almost extinct tradition. Text gathering usually requires much time, attention, patience, and prudence.

Gathering texts. The vocabulary of a language will give a good idea of the different genres extant. Since there may be several words for myth, historical narrative, or poetry, a systematic investigation of such terms is necessary.

For eliciting and transcribing, it is good to be already familiar with the people, the language, and its phonology.

The tape recorder will be necessary, since oral literature by definition must be spoken, and the way in which it is spoken is important linguistically, socially, psychologically, and esthetically. Because cultures without a written tradition are disappearing so quickly in the modern world, this literature must be transcribed, and as much as possible preserved in sound recordings. The tape recorder is very convenient for transcribing texts; besides, the speaker will enjoy hearing his own voice. On the other hand, though, he may fear being laughed at, or fear that too many people might hear him talk, so the method of elicitation must be adapted to the situation. Besides, we must not make tape recording the only means of collecting texts, although it should be used as often as possible to get spontaneous discourse.

Who knows the stories? Conditions vary widely. In some societies, story-telling is the occupation of specialists, for instance the griots of West Africa. Even in societies where everyone participates in it, certain individuals may be considered better story-tellers, or have a larger and more varied repertoire. In Melanesia, each family and clan will have its own collection of stories and each must be investigated; however, but some clans are more productive than others. The elders and highly respected members of the society usually know the stories, and the good story-tellers are usually known by everyone. In any case, inquiries must be made; many nonspecialists also have interesting things to say.

Taping. Depending on the time and circumstances, the researcher may either organize taping sessions and invite everyone, or contact people individually for taping.

The researcher should make an effort to be at every public meeting and to request permission to record. The participants should be informed of this, and should be given enough time to think about it. Taping should not be done too hurriedly, but every chance should be seized immediately, for it may never be repeated. The good story-tellers must be observed several times, in different styles of expression: in public, at a festival, or at home.

To encourage participation or to overcome reservations, the researcher must use what he already knows. For example, he may show that he knows the history of the people or the major subjects of its myths by asking about specific points. He may also use what he has gleaned from neighboring villages or dialects. Rivalries, local antagonisms, or a spirit of competition among the narrators may be helpful, too.

The investigator should not hesitate to record several versions of the same story, for the differences, through space and time, are very interesting both linguistically and ethnologically.

Questionnaire No. 1 (Instructions for recording linguistic documents) gives specific advice on the taping itself. The investigator must never forget to identify the text at the beginning of the recording, before the speaker starts: Story of . . . ; as told by . . . ; dialect and language . . . ; place . . . ; date . . . .

Text transcription. It is beneficial to be able to transcribe with the narrator himself; however, this is not always possible. For many a storyteller, having to repeat a tale in a slow and deliberate style may be repulsive and risks drying up the stories at the source. He must be allowed to think and to speak at leisure, without worrying about dictating. Transcription and word-for-word translation will be done as soon as possible afterwards with another speaker. The narrator should stay nearby so that he can be consulted for explanation of obscurities in the translation, or information about persons, places, or bygone customs. It is good to draw up maps and, if possible, to retrace on foot the routes described. Any plants or animals mentioned must also be identified.

At least a rough word-for-word translation must be done immediately, along with a free translation. The memory cannot be trusted: what seems obvious at the moment and ought to be remembered later may be quickly and completely forgotten in even a few days.

Finally, it is very important to note the circumstances of the recording, the behavior of the narrator and audience, the reactions and comments on the text, the value and credence attached to it, the interpretation made of it, and any other relevant information. For example: The speaker got this text from such-and-such a relative; it was given by the war chief at the last meeting before the battle.

Putting off the transcription may spare the narrator's patience, but also has drawbacks. Experience has shown that if the recording is of mediocre quality, even native speakers of the language may hardly understand it. In addition, some traditional texts such as poetry are often difficult and obscure, even to the narrator himself. Transcribing such texts with a third person may yield numerous errors and misinterpretations.

Research of this type will often spark the people's interest in their literature and history. Among literate peoples, the investigator may leave copies of his transcribed texts and distribute notebooks or tape recorders, since some speakers would rather write than record. Realizing that this literature is being passed down less and less, the investigator may decide to record as much as possible. Especially if his time is short

Using the Questionnaires 59

and if the people are agreeable, the recording can be carried out even if the transcription must wait until much later.

Finally, some practical suggestions. Medium-length tapes are best for recording. Immediately after recording, the titles of the texts should be entered on the cassette case and on the tape itself. The tape should be wound tightly and evenly. A hermetically sealed case will be needed, and if possible, a copy of the tape should be made and sent to a safe place, along with a copy of the transcription.

Examples of useful categories. Instead of making the study of ORAL TEXTS a separate and independent issue, one can start collecting them while developing the lexicon, proceeding by means of categories. The categories may be complementary or overlapping, but all can be made to relate to the traditional literature. In this case, rather than eliciting what is already known, the researcher should gather material with linguistic and ethnographic interest by asking for comments, explanations, recollections, etc.

Locations and geographical and social environment. The themes of the oral tradition take place in specific locations. A list might be compiled of the places within and surrounding the village community, in occupied or familiar territories (inhabited areas, hunting or fishing grounds), and along traditional routes used for contacting or traveling to neighboring tribes.

Observations about geographic landmarks (such as caves, springs, wells, crags, mountains, etc.), or the list of places, including comments and meanings attached to them, may remind the speaker of many mythical or historical events.

Some places may call forth anecdotes, memories, or past events. Others (such as fortified areas, shelters, observation points, meeting places, marketplaces, etc.) provide opportunities to ask about near or distant neighbors, relatives, allies and enemies, how they are perceived, and the history of relations with these groups.

Special natural features (crags, mountains, enclosed valleys, rivers, springs, etc.) may be the physical form of mythical beings, or may be places of worship, cemeteries, or sacred, forbidden or haunted places. From these, the investigator can learn the names of supernatural beings, demons, spirits of the mountains or the bush, and the stories, myths, taboos, and rituals involving them.

Astrological notions should not be neglected, either. Included with this will be the magic or myths concerning the rain, sun, wind, day, night, heat, fire, etc.

Plants and animals. In the ethnobotanical or ethnozoological investigation, certain plants and animals will bring many things to the speaker's mind. Some recollections may concern the possible uses of these plants and animals, others the knowledge or beliefs about their physiology, behavior, or origin. Often, traditional narratives involving them will be suggested; Questionnaires 11 and 12 are designed for the systematic investigation of this aspect of the study.

Similarly, in collecting samples of oral literature, special attention should be paid to plants or animals cited in the texts. A deeper study of these may draw out other narratives. For example, many peoples have cycles of stories revolving around a single plant or animal character.

Social organization. Besides lists of clans and lineages, other possible social subdivisions, and kinship terms, other materials can be collected which give justification of the organization and present establishment of groups, their hierarchy, alliances, allegiances, enmities, etc. This includes genealogies and totems; myths of the origin of the world, of the community, or of different clans or lineages; and narratives, myths, or epics about ancient migrations and wars. The traditional literature will reveal information on the religious and juridical foundations of the community, its cosmology, gods, cultural heroes, ancestors, protective spirits, totems, cults, sects, incantations, taboos, rituals, prayers, etc. Expressions of rights may also be found in proverbs, etiquette formulas, fables, myths, collected from genealogists, seers, elders, dignitaries, etc.

Seasonal and nonseasonal activities. Another possible source for eliciting texts begins with the names of the parts of the year and corresponding community activities, such as work and ceremonies that occur on specific dates.

For a farming people, we collect narratives telling about the technological, magical, and ritual aspects of the growing cycle (clearing the ground, tilling, planting or sowing, putting in stakes, germinating, ripening, harvesting, the firstfruits, etc.). Other narratives may deal with rites concerning winds, rain, or sun, or else taboos or games connected with the agricultural calendar. Many other activities are also associated with the different phases of the calendar (fishing, gathering food, hunting, dances, initiation festivals, festival of the return of the dead, etc.), which provide valuable documentation both for the linguist and for the ethnologist.

Other notable events which do not occur regularly (great festivals, commercial expeditions, marriages, funerals, wars, epidemics, famines) may provide important text materials. Relative to war, for example, the investigator may collect (besides warrior's accounts) speeches, exhortations, dances, sacrifices, divination rites; narratives about the warring party and its training and preparation for battle, taboos, alliances, conducting war, making peace, reparations; songs celebrating alliances or victories, etc.

Life of the individual. Certain genres of oral tradition are learned or recited in connection with particular stages of life, and so these stages must be followed: birth, name-giving, circumcision, age classes, rites of passage and puberty, betrothal, marriage, changes of status or rank, old age, sickness, and death. Most of these events call for festivities, gift giving, speeches, songs, poetry, and rituals connected with the mythology.

Concerning birth, there may be myths or rites concerning fertility, sterility, prediction of the sex of a child, delivery, twins, or name-giving.

As to children's (and also adult's) amusements there will be stories, riddles, songs, verses, ditties to accompany rounds, dances, games of skill or chance, walking, bathing, musical games, games of imitating adults, string games, etc.

Education and the different stages of teaching can be considered, including precepts and didactic stories. This aspect touches on the age groups, their knowledge, dances, myths, emblems, tests, amusements, totemic images, masks, etc. Attention should be paid to the initiation rites themselves: the seclusion, bodily mutilation, taboos, testings.

Coverage of adolescence, betrothal, and marriage will include the traditional opportunities and methods of courting, love songs, issues related to the choice of the spouse or the reservation of the wife, rules for preferred marriage, betrothal and marriage ceremonies, the exchange of gifts.

After a death, texts can be collected on the announcement of death, lamentations, funeral wakes, reflections about death, words of consolation, and speeches to the relatives of the deceased. Also, matters concerning the belongings of the deceased, the funeral ceremony, the taboos, or the end of the mourning period will yield narratives, as will anecdotes about accidental deaths, or laments or tragic poems on the death of a close relative or chief. Myths about the life beyond, the journey of the soul, the abode of the dead, return from the dead, the cult of the dead, and reincarnation must also be investigated.

Finally, individuals could be asked to write biographies.

Technology. The gathering of technological vocabulary will also lead to the collection of some very significant texts. Concerning instruments and tools, the investigator will ask about the materials used, how they are made, myths about their origin, etc. Concerning fire, metals, and alloys, there may be rituals, myths about their origin (possibly involving a cultural hero), taboos for individuals or classes.

Other aspects must similarly be considered and explained, for example the symbolism of decoration, the religious significance of ornamentation, written symbols (on pottery, emblems on weapons, etc.). This may be done through a study of furniture, houses, masks, statuettes, etc.

Of special interest are narratives about the use of these tools, and the industries of acquisition or production. The investigator should investigate myths about origins, and elicit descriptions and commentaries. For example, consider the technical and social aspect of canoe-making: composition of the work party and prestations, cutting down and exorcizing the tree, maneuvering and transporting the trunk; mythology about the canoe, its decoration, ceremonial rites for binding it, putting it into the water; then, things related to navigation, fishermen's or ferrymen's songs, etc. Again, for hunting: songs of leaving for the hunt, techniques and ceremonies used, call to the hunters, celebration of the catch, ritual distribution, return from the hunt; songs, dances, narratives of the hunt, of brush fires, myths of the origins of the hunt or of the animals, stories about animals, animal imitation, etc.

Similarly, the researcher may consider the construction of a house, cooking, medicine, pottery, metal-working, and so on. Each skill and athletic, technological, martial, or artistic specialization (songs, elocution, creation, memorization) may in principle involve the use of magic techniques and the invocation of mythical characters or spirits.

Literary genres. Investigation of the different existing or possible genres may progress by the following classification:

Texts requested or suggested by the investigator. This category includes technological accounts (iron-working, farming, basketry, medicine), definitions, explanations and commentaries about certain terms, conversations, palavers, narratives, descriptions, anecdotes, autobiographies, etc.

Fixed content texts, passed down and recited in everyday speech (with different styles possible). These could be:

– historical accounts: wars, migrations, origins of social groups, contact with other civilizations (e.g., the arrival of the white man, missions), etc.

– myths: origins of cultivated plants or domestic animals, of human races, of the universe, of techniques, etc.

– fables, ballads, stories, legends: traditional characters, cycles, etc.

- minor genres: mottoes, proverbs, adages, sayings, morals, riddles, puzzles, nursery rhymes, ditties to accompany rounds, ritornellos, lullabies, satirical songs, funny stories, obscene stories, scatological jokes, insults, joking relationships, etc.

Special usages, poetic or sung.

- poetry: several different genres according to subject or (metrical) form; may involve poetry of a specific caste, or popular poetry.
- declaimed texts: eulogies, ceremonial speeches, oratorical contests, ...
- chanted or mumbled: rites, prayers, ...
- acted out: comical or dramatical scenes, satires, pantomimes and incidents from everyday life, ...
- danced: for amusement, war, funerals; dances specific to sects, age classes, sex classes, ...
- sung: solos, duets, choirs, singing tournaments, singing with or without musical accompaniment (different instruments) ...
- special cases: whistled speech, drummed speech (indicating its significance), language of etiquette, aristocratic speech, women's speech; secret or esoteric forms (for the initiated), language of the spirits, deformed speech (Javanese); archaisms, borrowed forms, extinct languages, parody of foreign languages, plays on words, tongue twisters, etc.

Using Questionnaire 18.1 on the gathering of texts. This may be more a research guide than a true questionnaire. It was conceived as a file slip which must accompany each recording, constituting a type of identification card to allow precise identification and rapid classification even during the field research. It thus becomes possible to expand the collection and explore more intensively some aspects of the oral literature covered poorly or insufficiently, if need be.

Proposals for publishing texts for comparative study. This format for text publication was proposed at the Congrès des Africanistes de Yaoundé in 1966. The following should be presented:

- transcription of the text in the original language (preferably phonological, but possibly phonetic);
- literal and interlinear translation;
- free translation;
- a general introduction;
- linguistic, ethnographic, and stylistic comments on each text which also take into account the sociological and historical context.

As for the arrangement of the material, the text is divided into phrases as short as possible which are then numbered and presented, text and translation side by side, in the following manner:

Using the Questionnaires

Left page	Right page
free translation, numbered	vernacular text, numbered, with interlinear translation
1.	1. text word-for-word translation
2.	2. text word-for-word translation
3.	3. text word-for-word translation

Linguistic notes

Ethnological and miscellaneous notes

Several works have already been published in this format, such as Luc Bouquiaux's *Textes Birom,* or Jacqueline Thomas' *Contes Ngbaka-ma'bo.* A page of the latter work is shown here as an example.

Tô and the Chickens

1. (One day), Tô went to exchange[1] with Gbaso
2. and found him building a chicken house[2];
3. then, taking a stick covered with white mushrooms[3], Gbaso thrust stuck it inside the house
4. and there, it turned into a large number of chickens, all white.[4]
5. He took some of them and killed them for Tô
6. who ate all of them.
7. He told him (Tô) that he would give him some others to take along.
8. Tô refused, saying he already had some chicks at home.
9. He left. Upon arriving home, he asked his mother
10. if she had seen anywhere a stick covered with white mushrooms.

LINGUISTIC NOTES

[1] *ló-ngándá*, modified noun phrase without a determiner morpheme preceding the modifier; the order is head-modifier of the type *nō̄-só* 'a pot of meat', i.e. 'a pot containing meat'; here, 'a stick carrying bearing mushrooms'.

[2] *pīkì*, verb derived with *-kV̌* from *pī* 'to divide, split, separate'.

[3] *bùbùnzú*, noun derived from the adjective *bùnzú* (cf. JMCT, 5, 124) (10.1-10).

MISCELLANEOUS NOTES

[1] The *yèlè* is a system of reciprocal gift-giving which originally permitted the establishment of contacts outside the circle of alliances, thus enlarging the area of security in which the individual could develop (cf. JMCT 6, 110–113).

[2] It is not customary to build a special shelter for domestic animals, who take advantage more or less of human dwellings: the goats sleep in the shelter of the veranda while the cats, dogs, and poultry sleep in a corner of the house. However, if the fowl are rather numerous, a chicken coop may be built for them: a small hut on piles, with an opening just wide enough to allow the chickens to enter with the help of a branch serving as a staircase ladder. However, this solution is often not used because of the numerous bold predators.

[3] *ngándá* is a type of white mushroom which grows on wood; it is edible and is eaten with meat. (The collected samples have not yet been identified.)

[4] All-white chickens are rare and in earlier times were used as a sacrifice to the ancestral spirits or in other circumstances which demanded a blood offering, such as the opening inauguration of a new dwelling. The story is really about this rather than the construction of a chicken house. In fact, the first five sentences may be a play on words in the dialect of B. B. L. where the determiner of the noun phrase is *-ngā-* instead of *-kā-*, and similarly for the possessives. One can thus create an ambiguity between *tē-ngō̄* 'chicken house' / hut | chickens / and *té-ngóō̄* 'their hut' / hut | their /. The text would then read, 'Tô went to exchange with Gbaso and Gbaso went to build their house. He took a stick covered with white mushrooms and thrust it inside where it turned into chickens, all white. He took some which he killed for Tô ....'

Tô and the Chickens

1. tò nő yèlé ngā-gbàsɔ̀
   Tô / goes + to / exchange + to / by | Gbaso #

2. ʔɛ̀ gbàsɔ̀ nɔ̄-mɔ́ tē-ngɔ̄
   then / Gbaso / goes | constructs / hut | chickens

3. gbàsɔ̀ nɔ̄-hā ló-ngándá,[1]
   Gbaso / comes | takes / wood | white mushroom #
   dɔ̄-dùú tē-ngɔ̄-ʔàɓō
   comes | thrusts + into / hut | chickens | this //

4. ʔé pīkì[2] ngɔ̄-ō káà.bīā.ɓō bùbùnzú[3]
   he / transforms # chicken | s / nothing but | white //

5. ʔé hā-mōlò ɓō tò
   he / takes | kills / for | Tô //

6. tò hɔ̄ gbó
   Tô / eats / all //

7. ʔé ɓō : ʔī há ɓéè gà, ʔé gɔ̄-té
   he / (says) that # he / gives / to him / other # he / leaves | with //

8. tò ɓō ʔī há dē, ʔī té ngɔ́-kā.ʔī-ō
   Tô / (says) that # he / takes / not # him / with | chicken | his
   | s //

9. tò pā-gɔ̄-nɔ̄-bū, nɔ̄-hīngà kánà-ngéè ɓō :
   Tô / passes | leaves | goes | arrives # goes | asks / mother | his | that #

10. ʔī mú gà-ló-ngándá síó wā
    she / sees / another | wood | white mushrooms / not / INTERR // (10.1–10)

B. Ethnomusicology
(by Simha Arom)

Ethnomusicology is a two-sided discipline, as the name suggests. On the one hand, it concerns ethnology, and on the other, musicology in the narrow sense. We will leave this latter aspect aside, considering music only as a social phenomenon, and the instruments (in the fundamental sense of the term) with which it is made. Thus, we consider in our study all forms of expression where music, words, and gestures are integrated, mutually affecting, interdependent, and sometimes inseparable.

Linguistics and Musicology. The integration and correlation between musical and linguistic forms of expression are particularly noticeable in the music-text relationship in tonal languages, where musical instruments are used to transmit linguistic messages. This is also true for a number of forms of oral literature in which the text is accompanied by a musical instrument from beginning to end, even though it is not completely sung. In much the same way, the spoken and sung parts of the chantefable form various links in a single chain.

An ethnomusicologist doing the study must have a basic knowledge of the techniques of linguistic research. Similarly, it is useful for a linguist to be able, with specifically linguistic techniques, to conduct a study of the musical instrument or music itself, with its meaning and socio-cultural context.

The aim of Questionnaire 18.2 is to provide the linguist with the elements for such an investigation. One part is devoted to instruments, and the other to songs. These questionnaires are intended for the nonmusician, and therefore do not contain questions requiring musical or musicological knowledge on the part of the linguist.

Objectives of the ethnomusicology questionnaires. This questionnaire has many purposes:

(1) To encourage the gathering on the field of a maximum of relevant information about the role of music in the society, when it is used, etc., through a specialized and relatively quick study conducted empirically around a characteristic instrument or musical piece.

(2) To enable the field linguist to collect sound recordings of music which is doomed to disappear sooner or later. Unfortunately, the nonspecialist often tends to neglect this aspect of the investigation, through an otherwise commendable scientific humility about an unfamiliar field. Such documents, however, will not only enrich the existing data, but will also furnish valuable elements to competent specialists (musicologists) who do not have the chance to go to the field themselves. For optimum usefulness, such documents should include information collected by the field worker at the time of recording.

(3) To draw the attention of the linguist to a number of ramifications and implications that an ethnomusicological study can lead to in further research in his own discipline, through and beyond the actual questions asked and the content of certain responses given.

Using the Questionnaires

(4) Further, to show the great interest it can stimulate in areas where linguistics and musicology overlap.

Overlap of musicology and linguistics: Topics to investigate. Here are some typical examples of this interaction:

(1) From a consideration of song taken by itself, the investigator will discover the rites, religious ceremonies, and formalities with which it is connected. This allows related ethnolinguistic study, the collection of the text(s) constituting its context, and the fitting together of the whole.

(2) The musical instrument assumes a functional and symbolic role. It is one of the most stable aids to many means of social expression, especially in much of the oral literature (myths and stories, legends, epics, which are accompanied by an instrument or which retell its origin, often supernatural, or its establishment in the society which uses it). The study of the different parts of the instrument and their names may reveal a whole realm of symbolism previously unknown. The making of the instrument may lead to the discovery of new technological aspects, specific tools, customs related to an unexpected social stratification, etc. Often, the instrument is the only remaining vestige of an obsolete cult.

(3) The study of tone can be facilitated when musical instruments are used to transmit linguistic messages. By using these instruments, a concrete check of the relevance of tone can be made. It must be pointed out that the tone system places constraints on the melodic structure of songs; consequently, all such information is valuable to the musicologist.

(4) Purely instrumental music is often simply a transposition of a song; the words are thus understood. This phenomenon is fascinating for the musicologist as he compares the played and sung versions, and examines the processes involved in this type of orchestration. A summary of the complete range of instruments of an ethnic group, with their vernacular names and the way they are classified by the people, will provide a linguistic, ethnolinguistic, and musicological dimension. Are there types of rhythms used for certain instruments and/or in particular situations? Ascertaining their vernacular names with literal translations will interest both the linguist and the musicologist.

(5) A study of groups of similar wind instruments (e.g., horn bands or ensembles of whistles) which only produce one sound each may be very revealing. In this type of ensemble, each performer often has fragments of linguistic utterances as models of his part, which he executes, not verbally, but instrumentally. The fragments may be taken from a corresponding song, or specially composed for this purpose. In the latter case, do the linguistic models have an immediate or symbolic meaning, or are they simply mnemonic formulas? So many of these aspects and questions can expand the linguist's field of investigation. Therefore, the piece should be recorded in its entirety, and then each instrument's part separately, immediately followed or preceded by the corresponding linguistic model.

The use of questionnaires. One of the questionnaires deals with the study of a musical instrument, and the other of a piece sung with or without instrumental accompaniment.

For the investigation of an instrumental piece, a cross-section of questions from both questionnaires should be drawn up. It is very difficult to isolate those elements that are always considered closely connected by those that use them. For the same reason, certain questions, asked from different angles, may overlap in the same questionnaire.

We have endeavored to make these questionnaires as useful as possible. They are not exhaustive, and cannot accommodate all situations where they can be used. Thus, the user must use common sense to avoid questions that are irrelevant in his situation, and also to add ones he feels are necessary. We have tried to outline a memory aid to keep items essential to this type of study from being missed.

Technical advice. The electronic recording of data will be facilitated by observing the following practices:

Recording tape. For recording music, it is preferable to use new tapes, because reusing old ones may run the risk of incomplete erasure, leaving echoes, ringing, or residues from the previous recording. Low noise tapes will minimize background noise. Although the long play tapes (90 and 120 minute ones) are more economical, their thinness makes them much more fragile than those of medium (standard) thickness; they are more likely to break, stretch, or get caught in the machine. They might be used for a long musical performance, where time for changing tapes would be saved (loading and unloading the machine), and the continuity of the recording would not be interrupted.

Recording on one or more tracks. Recording on two tracks also seems more economical than on only one track. However, the latter is recommended, for it facilitates locating items and especially splicing. The pieces (or texts) may thus be cut apart and separated with colored markers. This is obviously impossible if there is another recording on the other side.

Recording speed. In a similar vein, a slow recording speed (4.75 cm/sec or 9.5 cm/sec) allows recordings twice or four times as long on a single tape or track. Nevertheless, a speed of 19 cm/sec or greater is preferred, being satisfactory from a professional standpoint for possible publication (phonographic records, illustrations of lectures or courses, etc.). This is true for linguistic documents to be analyzed phonologically (including tone), and particularly for any musical recordings. The slower the speed, the narrower is the acoustic spectrum of the sound recorded, and the poorer is the reproduction of the characteristic timbre of the voices and instruments.

Recording various versions. The importance of making several recordings of each musical piece cannot be overstated. The greater the number of versions of a piece, the more interesting will be the subsequent study of the material, and the more conclusive will be its results. The repetitions may be by the same musician after the space of several minutes, hours, or days; or it may be by several musicians, of different generations and sex, if possible. The form, structure, and cohesion of a piece can only be determined through a comparison of the constants and the variables of the different versions; examination of a single specimen for this type of analysis is almost always insufficient.

Recording in entirety. Songs with several verses or developments must be recorded entirely. Some songs, especially in Africa, appear at first to be series of identical repetitions of a single melodic theme, indefinitely long. However, in most cases, these repetitions involve variants related to one of the previous ones. These variants are relevant to the musical organization and structure as well as to the language. Therefore, the recording should be continued long enough to get an overview of the character of these variants and their position within the cycle, insofar as new material makes a contribution to it. The investigator should thus listen carefully while he is recording, even if he is not a qualified musicologist.

Stimulation of the participants. Playing the recording for the performers stimulates a certain rivalry among them. This may bring out other documents that can be recorded which might otherwise be missed.

4.3.6 Sociolinguistic problems

The field of sociolinguistics is often considered marginal in relation to pure linguistics. Its definition is still very imprecise and varies according to the school of thought. Some feel that everything related to language as a means of communication, which is justified only by its social nature, is sociolinguistic. Others consider only problems of language contact to be included in this discipline. We are not seeking to settle this debate. Let us simply say that the study of language in oral societies is so closely linked to the culture that when we speak of sociolinguistic problems, we are using the term in its narrowest sense.

Admittedly, a linguistic study as much may not devote a special part to such questions as these. However, most of our team have worked in areas where there has been considerable intermingling and migrations of populations for two centuries. The influence of colonization here has been felt keenly in all spheres, especially in the language, so that a part of the population is at least bilingual. The women generally remain monolingual, but the men (especially in Central Africa) know, besides their own vernacular language, one or several trade languages (Sango, Lingala). Some even speak several vernacular languages. The educated and many city-dwellers know French and sometimes English (at least a book knowledge). In these conditions, all our linguistic investigation constantly opens onto sociolinguistic problems: adaptation of vocabulary to the demands of integration into a modern economy; concurrent but specialized usage of three languages–the vernacular (familial and rural), the trade language (interethnic, urban, and commercial), and French (language of education and politics)—and the inevitable interferences that result. All linguistic study should account for borrowings, their formation, and interferences on different levels, from phonology to syntax.

The Sentence Questionnaire (No. 9) is specifically geared to the study of the problem of equivalents from English. In the Technological Questionnaire (No. 10), the particular aspect of adaptation to the demands of modern technology is often considered. Certain topics in Questionnaire 15 (Sociological phenomena) which deal with the issues of colonization or of economy (a special questionnaire will be published later on this latter subject) cannot avoid sociolinguistic problems.

We do provide a specific questionnaire on certain problems of particular interest to us in the area of knowledge, use, and attitudes toward the three languages (vernacular, trade language, and French) as to their ethnic origin, and their place in urbanization, education, and occupation.

5
Processing the Data

The systematic processing of collected data is just as problematical for the analysis of an unwritten language as the investigation itself, and perhaps even more important.

Materials gathered during a well-done investigation are very often underexploited. Unfortunately, the means and necessary technical assistance are not usually available on the field. This is not critical, however. From our perspective, all possible materials must be recorded while this is still possible; analysis will come in due time. On the other hand, poor processing of the data results not only in an avoidable underutilization of the documentation, but also in the possibility of errors, both in fact and in interpretations.

For clarity of exposition, we have first presented the problems of research on the field, and now turn to those of the processing. In reality, an efficient investigation does not proceed just so. The gathering and exploiting of the data must be effected somewhat simultaneously, at least for the beginning of the processing, which involves several successive stages.

Unprocessed notebooks, questionnaires, and texts should definitely not be left to accumulate. Reserving all exploitation until the return from the field is as ineffective as expecting to do all language analysis on the spot.

As we see it, processing should be progressive, and depends on the subject matter and the opportunity. The filling out of file cards for vocabulary gathered from data notebooks, questionnaires, and texts commences at the very beginning of the fieldwork. It is good to make a review at the end of each day, to recall the information that has been collected, and to note the gaps in the information, which can then be filled in the following day. It is not a waste of time to spend an hour or two each day updating the file, as many novices may think. The discipline of filing familiarizes the worker with the language and his data, so that he does not repeat the same questions after several days' interval, which irritates the speakers and gives them a poor opinion of the investigator. Hence the card file constitutes a remarkably useful working tool: an outline of phonological analysis, a research guide, and a memory aid. The file is of course only a rough skeleton of the work that will eventually be produced. Most of these field file cards will have to be recopied once or several times while the vocabulary is being worked out, to add supplementary information, to make various modifications, to reorganize, and finally to prepare it for publication. Similarly, part of the time spent at the field base should be spent in making a brief but complete scrutiny of all the grammatical documentation, to ensure that essential elements are not found missing after the fieldwork has been completed.

Most of the processing will take place after the return from the field, though, since it requires more tranquillity and privacy than can be found in even the best conditions on the field.

Processing involves three different phases: examination, classification, and reproduction. These phases may proceed in successive cycles, or in some cases may be done simultaneously, but we must obviously consider them one at a time.

5.1 Examination of the data

Principal distinctions in types of data must be recognized from the start. Data which is strictly linguistic is treated differently from that which comes from related fields (e.g., language contact), but there will be numerous interrelationships in the ethnolinguistic documentation (techniques, ethnobotany, ethnozoology, etc.).

5.1.1 Examining the vocabulary

From field research documents, there is a mass of information spread throughout different notebooks, questionnaires, and file cards, all of which must be systematically organized. As noted earlier, it is preferable to put all the vocabulary on cards as they are encountered all through the course of the investigation. Some of these file cards may not have to be recopied or even completed, notably those dealing with rare words. For all others, the definitive version will be made up at the second or third stage as we seek to give the lexicon a truly coherent presentation. A particular type of file card is recommended; in this section we show how it is to be set up and why.

Materials and notational conventions are discussed in §2.2.2, Written Documentation. If the method is formalized from the very beginning of the investigation, the first notations will be usable for the entire length of the study, and the work of recopying is limited as much as possible.

The initial field file slips are made in triplicate on carbon paper sets (3" x 5" lined grid paper) which are then separated and glued onto stiff card (Bristol board, size 5" x 8").[2] The pasting job can be done by a helper, either the speaker outside of his time working on linguistics, or a temporary clerical worker. In this way one obtains three copies for each item, which are classified in the three files mentioned above (Vernacular-English, English-Vernacular, and Subject files).

The use of punch cards, which are not recommended for the lexical study as a whole, may be valuable at a more advanced stage of the research. They can be used for a systematic analysis (of phonology, for example), or for an exhaustive study of a specific subject (thus Samarin, in *Field Linguistics,* shows their use in the study of ideophones) or again in the study of verb derivation (cf. Questionnaire 5 on the morphological phenomena of derivation and compounding). Using them at the

---

[2]If possible with dry glue or with that used to stick photographs. The advantage of these glues is that they do not make the paper buckle. [The Limpidol brand is recommended.]

Processing the Data 73

beginning of the investigation will not be very profitable, and would even be wasteful as they are relatively expensive.

The preparation of more elaborate and complex research file cards will require a systematic review of the data, but will in general be subject to the same rules. Below we give instructions for the preparation of different types of file cards.

Vernacular-English file. At the top left-hand side of the card, enter the vernacular word in phonological transcription, accompanied by phonetic transcription(s) if necessary. In parentheses, add the initials of the speaker, as there may be several, thus avoiding possible dialect confusion. It is useful also to indicate the year, as a linguistic study pursued over several years reveals variations which are interesting to situate in time.

On the upper right hand side, enter synonyms and dialectal variations, spaced evenly and preceded by the necessary symbols and followed by the initials of the speaker(s), as well as doublets and variations in information (differing opinions of two equally sure speakers), etc.

If the word is a compound, enter the literal translation beneath the phonological transcription. On the line below that, indicate the abbreviation for its grammatical category. For a derived form, indicate the root and its grammatical category, if different. A little below, reserve at least one line and preferably two for meanings, given the vast semantic domain of certain terms and their numerous equivalents in English. Number each different meaning separately, and indicate in parentheses the initials of the speaker and the reference; give the number of the sentence if referring to the sentence questionnaire, or the number of the text and the sentence within it if referring to an oral text. After these notes give examples illustrating the different meanings. Example sentences should be accompanied by a word for word interlinear translation and a free translation. Note the reference here, too.

When one side of a card is full, it is advisable to continue on a new card. Using the reverse side, for reasons of economy, makes handling of the file so awkward that it is not advisable.

Below are examples of file cards drawn up according to these principles.

In practice, the file cards will be drawn up somewhat differently according to the information being handled, whether general, technical, or ethnoscientific. The above description is for a card of a general nature. A technical card would have a detailed explanatory paragraph immediately after the English equivalent, and a sketch if the object is small. For a larger object or apparatus, the drawing should be on a second card, with the name in the upper left hand corner. Linguistic examples will appear on a separate card. Finally, for ethnoscientific cards concerning the names of plants and animals, immediately after the English equivalent, if this exists, enter the initials of the collector and the number of the botanical or zoological sample. This will be followed by the scientific identification when it can be obtained, giving the name of the genus, species, author, and family. Immediately afterward, indicate the name of the identifier or his initials. The different uses of the specimen and other information concerning it will be recorded on the same card, in the order in which they appear in the questionnaire. Strictly linguistic information concerning the item (occurrence in a proverb, play on words, etc.) would appear on a different card.

A certain number of general rules should be observed for drawing up all cards. For each new term, make a new card, and each time that a term already known is encountered with a new sense, add this on the existing card together with an example to illustrate its use. In their final, definitive version, cards should list meanings in a

PREPARATION OF FILE CARDS

Gbandili Bulaka example
General file card

bɔ̄tɔ́   (T₆₇) (D₆₈)

v.

——— 1. to take off 2. to disrobe, to undress (T.) 3. to unbutton (D.) 4. to open (T.) 5. to deliver, to loosen, to liberate (D.) 6. to take off the handle (D.) 7. to remove (D.) 8. to put off mourning (D.) 9. to unearth (D.)

+ wo bɔ́tɔ́ nɔ̀bɔ̀. kàlà tɔ̄ sa̋-ngɔ dèkè, wo gɔ̀ — They raised the anchor yesterday (P₂₄₁)
  ‖ they / took up / anchor / to | under | water/ yesterday‡ they / left ‖

+ ʔa bɔ̀tɔ́ ɓɔ́ngɔ sɔ — he did not undress (Yar)
  ‖ he / take off / clothes / not ‖

+ bɔ̀tɔ́ bìtóo tɔ̀-mó-ɓɔ̀ngɔ̀ — unbutton your clothes
  ‖ take off / button / to | mouth | clothes ‖

+ ʔa bɔ̀tɔ́ mòngè-tètè — he opens the door

+ ʔa bɔ̀tɔ́ mòngè-tètè tɛ̀ nó-ɛ — he opens the door with his foot
  ‖ he / open / door | house / with | foot | his ‖

+ ʔa bɔ̀tɔ́ kàkpè — one liberated the slave
  ‖ one / liberated / slave ‖

bɔ́tɔ̄ 2

+ ʔa bɔ́tɔ̀ kpe-kongó — he took off the handle of the hoe
  // he / take off / sleeve | hoe //

+ ʔa bɔ́tɔ̀ ma miná — he removed something of mine
  // he / take off / to my / thing //

  bɔ́tɔ̀ tɛ-mu — Remove yourself from there!
  // take off / body | your //

+ ʔa bɔ́tɔ̀ bilí — he put off mourning (P478)
  // he / take off / mourning //

+ ʔa bɔ́tɔ̀ kó tɔ-tó — he unearthed the body
  // he / take off / dead body / to | earth //

derived

pètèkèlè̀ (T67) [pētèkɛ́[ɛ] = pétékèné (G68)

V. ← pētèkè ← pèté ← pḕ (v.)
1. to spread out (P568) 2. to flatten, to be flattened, to be flat-nosed (P302)

+ ʔa pētèkèlè̀ nza - tóɓo - he spread out the clay (to stop up the holes in the canoe).
‖ he /spread out/ inside /clay ‖

+ ʔo - e ʔa pétèkèlè̀ - his nose is very flattened, flat (P302)
‖ nose ‖ his ‖ it / is flattened ‖

compound

$$\overline{\underset{\text{/person}}{\underset{|}{\text{bo.}\acute{\text{ʔa}}}}\;\underset{\text{| DET | broken |foot/}}{\underset{|}{\text{gɔmɔ.nu}}}}\quad (\text{T}_{67})$$

N. comp. (N + DET + Q + ND)

— crippled, lame person (N.)

$+\;\underset{\text{// villagers || they / mock / lame man //}}{\underset{|}{\text{bo.ngba}}\;\;\underset{|}{\text{ʔo}}\;\;\underset{|}{\text{mɔ}}\;\;\underset{|}{\text{bo.ʔá.}}\;\underset{|}{\text{gɔmɔ.nu}}}$ — the villagers mock the lame man

technical

lúsu (P₆₉)

— calabash-gourd, calabash-bottle

usage - in the form of a bottle, one keeps all sorts of precious liquids: wine, fine oil, prepared drinks...

mò ↓
ngɔ̂ ↓

↓ bū

↙ kpátā

ethnoscience card

mbìlì gùmà (M)(Je)
            CB 68

1. _Morinda lucida_   2. _Lindackeria dentata_ Oliv.
   HB – Rubiaceae (M)   HB – Flacourtiaceae (Je)

+ _technical_ – body paint: the fruit gives an "ink" which is painted on the forehead and cheeks of men and women for the dancing at various ceremonies (funeral, end of circumcision, etc.) (M.)

  – same: the sap which comes out of the cut trunk is used to the same end (Je)

fixed order, always proceeding from the most concrete to the most abstract. Examples are arranged in the same order as the meanings.

This presentation is good for the reference and working files. It is equally desirable for the publication of the dictionary, with the restriction that when a term has several English equivalents, the illustrative examples of each meaning should appear immediately after it; this is not practical for the everyday use of the card file, though. And certain information (names of speakers, date, varying phonetic transcriptions) will obviously not appear in the dictionary. These modifications will result in the following type of presentation:

term / word-for-word gloss / DN ← $k\mathfrak{o}$- (V)
  1. first meaning
      e.g.,
  2. second meaning
      e.g.,
  3. third meaning
      e.g.,
  +   synonym
  =   dialectal variant
  ≡   doublet
  ~   another speaker

English-Vernacular file. The general principles for making up these cards are much the same as for those described above, but with the opposite orientation. The English-Vernacular file is like an inverse dictionary of the former; permitting an easy cross-referencing from one to the other is its most traditional use. As we are trying to add a different dimension to it, more extensive research will be needed. These cards carry the various terms corresponding to the English terms found in the Vernacular-English file. Here, however, we pay special attention to the English-Vernacular equivalents.

For the field file cards, the first copy of the Vernacular-English file slip will be glued onto a stiff card, which can be smaller (4" x 6") than those used in the preceding file. As these copies have the vernacular word in the upper left-hand corner with the translation further down, it would be useful to rewrite the translation in the upper right-hand corner to facilitate reference.

In preparing file cards for processing, a new format is necessary. The English term must appear in the upper left-hand corner, and the various equivalents in the vernacular are arranged in a specified order (from the most concrete to the most abstract, for example), each illustrated by one or more sentences showing the respective uses of the term. Synonyms or terms related to the English are indicated in the upper right-hand corner.

Subject file. The subject file cards do not differ appreciably from the others. They contain concurrently the term in the vernacular and the English equivalent, both of which may be used for classification. Any difference in the making of these cards would be essentially in the greater amount of information which they contain: more detailed technical descriptions, greater precision on uses for ethnoscientific specimens, more detailed and more extensive information concerning terms having to do with societal institutions and various sociological phenomena. On the other hand, linguistic examples will not usually be found here.

5.1.2 Processing of materials for the development of the grammar

For the elaboration of the grammar, a substantial part of the data needs to be entered onto cards, taken either from the lexicon, as for the analysis of compounding and derivation, or from the questionnaires and texts (for drawing up file cards of utterances illustrating either syntagmatic phrase-level or sentence-level relationships. These cards will be substantially smaller than those used for the lexicon. The standard 3" x 5" card size is quite satisfactory, although one might like to have a slightly larger size (4" x 6") for the study of derivation.

The cards for derived words are based on the root, either actual or hypothetical. A list of derived forms is presented, showing each affix or inflectional modification in turn. The meaning is given opposite each item (see the sample card below).

The preparation of the cards for compounds depends upon the numerous angles from which one can view this phenomenon. Multiple copies of the same file cards can be used, or else punch cards. The card will have the term in the vernacular, its word-for-word gloss and its free translation on the left-hand side. On the right-hand side appear the indications of the grammatical categories of the compound and of its constituent parts, the syntactic or nonsyntactic nature of the compound, the stem of the compound, etc.

Finally, in drawing up file cards for phrase-level and sentence-level utterances, the vernacular should appear in the center of the card followed by its word-for-word and free translations, together with the reference. The top half of the card is reserved for working out and symbolizing the structure represented by the example (see the sample card below).

5.1.3 Processing of texts

The final processing of the texts requires a careful revision of the texts gathered on the field. The first operation is to make a thorough division of the text into more balanced sentences (or phrases) than had been possible when gathering the data. For each text the sentences will be numbered from 1 to n. The final numbering of the texts themselves cannot be made until after they have been classified. This poses a general problem for referencing during the compilation of the lexicon or of grammatical file cards. After this first stage of dividing and recopying the sentences comes the word by word structuring, which implies that the grammatical analysis has already been done. The arrangement of the word-by-word gloss will indicate the grammatical divisions of the sentence. A certain number of key morphemes are designated by the category or series to which they belong.[3] Thus for the Ngbaka *ʔé dɔ́-nũ̄*, instead of 'he will come (perhaps)' one indicates // he / come + INCOMPLETIVE |FUTURE // '. The entire form indicates the hypothetical future. Such a notation system for grammatical structure has already been used in several works (see especially articles on the Central African Plateau languages in *Les langues du monde*; J. M. C. Thomas' *Contes ngbaka*; L. Bouquiaux' *Textes birom*; S. Arom's *Conte et chantefables ngbaka*). A full-length reproduction of this system is given below.

For publication purposes, the first approximation of a free translation, based on the speaker's translation at the time of the elicitation, must be reviewed and expanded.

---

[3]By CATEGORY, we mean the grammatical category to which the (grammatical) morpheme belongs; by SERIES we mean the sub-category, generally of a semantic nature, into which it fits within the category.

GRAMMATICAL ANALYSIS CARDS

Ngbaka example

Derivation

yɛ̀ / yɛ̀yɛ́ɛ̀ - to deviate (from his path), to prepare for oneself a path (in a crowd))

-lì		yɛ́lì / yɛ̀yɛ́lì	1. to meet, to go meet someone
			2. to slip, to slip between the fingers (BBL)
	-kì	yɛ́lɛ̀kɛ̀ / yɛ̀yɛ́lɛ̀kɛ̀	to slip (Bok+)
		→ yɛ́lɛ̀kɛ́	polished, smooth
	-kpì	→ yɛ́lɛ̀kpɛ́ . yɛ́lɛ̀kpɛ̀	sticky, viscous
-ngv̀		yɛ̄ngɛ̀ / yɛ̀yɛ̄ngɛ̀	to sift
	-lì	yɛ̄ngɛ̀lɛ̀ / yɛ̀yɛ̄ngɛ̀lɛ̀	to strain, to swing, to threaten (with a finger)
	-sì	→ yɛ̄nçɛ̀sɛ̀ ~ yɛ̀kɛ̀sɛ̀	strainer (Bob.)

relative structure

N B C₃
[+ n b c₅ +]

-(ʔo) dɔ-nɔ-gbɛ̀gbɛ́nɛ́kɛ̀ sìndì -nɛ̀ lìndóngà
// they / come | go | group together around / sesame | that # bird lindonga /
dɔ́lɔ̀-ʔá-mbú kótó nɛ̀
peck | DET | throw + to/on the ground / m.p. //
- They came and gathered around the sesame which the bird had thrown to the ground while pecking.

Text Analysis
(Structure in the word-for-word glosses)

Symbol	Meaning
//	separates independent utterances; this is the boundary of a sentence or utterance (in the terminology used in this work).
#	separates clauses in a relation of dependence; this is a clause (or clauseme) boundary.
#	indicates the boundaries of a clause modifying a non-verbal term of the utterance, such as the relative clause; i.e. a dependent clause included within another clause; this is also a clause boundary (clausal secondary expansion).
/	separates the primary elements of the utterance from one another; this is a functioneme boundary, which may consist of a single term, as well as a complex phrase.
||	separates elements within a phrase which are in a relationship of coordination, of juxtaposition, or of double determination; determination of the second degree.
|	separates the terms of a phrase, in a determinative relation one to another, i.e. the elements of the secondary expansion.
|/ /|	indicates a discontinuity in a phrase.
+	indicates a portmanteau or fused form.
.	separates the constituents of a compound, or possibly of a derived form.

This provides a more careful expression in a more refined English style, and takes into account the finer points and subtleties of the vernacular text. Indeed, the first rendering will especially miss verbal nuances brought to light by grammatical analysis.

At this point, finally, a close analysis of the text permits us to prepare notes on it. Linguistic notes, on the one hand, explain certain difficulties of the word-by-word gloss and certain rare forms. Ethnological notes, gathered from comments by the storyteller and the reference speaker and from analysis of the topical questionnaires, clarify certain otherwise unintelligible points, give the identification of plants and animals, technical explanations, etc.

5.2 Classification of data

It is evident here, as in the analysis of the documentation, that the procedure will differ for the lexicon (and different types of lexicons), for the grammar, and for texts.

5.2.1 Classification of the lexicon

Vernacular-English file. The usual method, although not the best, is to use alphabetical order, new phonemes being included after those which they more or less resemble. For example: a, b, ɓ, c, d, ɗ, e, ɛ, f, g, gb, h, i, j, k, kp, l, m, mb, etc.

The only advantage of this arrangement is to avoid an effort of memory and concentration, as everyone is supposed to know the order of the letters of the alphabet. However, it will be agreed that this is hardly scientific, referring implicitly to one or another European language. The fundamental rule of structuralism is to describe a language without referring to a pre-established framework. Thus, the phonological system of the language itself must provide the criteria for classification. However unfamiliar the investigator may be with the placement of sounds in a phonetic chart (with points of articulation from the lips to the back of the mouth, arranged from left to right), he will be able to find information just as easily with this sequence as with the traditional alphabetical order. This proposal is not original. For thousands of years Indian grammarians have been classifying the phonemes of Sanskrit in this way, and their dictionaries, even though published in the West, have always respected this arrangement. Such a classification immediately accounts for the general organization of the language, and provides a direct, immediately accessible phonological chart. A dictionary designed for specialists (linguists, ethnologists) will follow the same order as that of this file. However, in a dictionary for the general public, as that of a widely used trade language, it would be better to retain the traditional alphabetical order, which is more immediately accessible.

The vowels will be classified first, and then the consonants, in the following manner:

1. Vowels. Their arrangement follows the vowel triangle, from the most closed to the most open. Different possibilities exist:

(a) systems of 5, 7, 9, or 10 oral vowels, especially common in African languages:

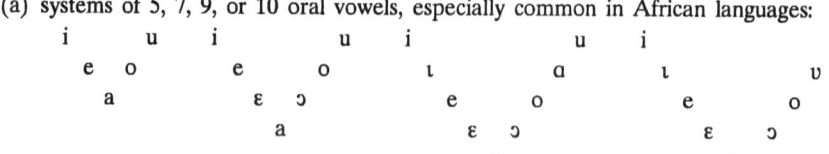

Processing the Data

The following order will be used: i, e, a, o, u or i, ɪ, e, ɛ, a, ɑ, ɔ, o, ʊ, u, taking the two extreme examples.
(b) systems with oral and nasal vowels, the latter generally fewer in number:

```
   i        u            ĩ        ũ
    e      o              ẽ      õ
     ɛ    ɔ                  ã
       a
```

Each nasal vowel is placed immediately after the corresponding oral vowel, according to the order indicated above, viz.: i, ĩ, e, ẽ, ɛ, a ...
(c) systems with central or back unrounded or front rounded vowels:

```
        i      ɯ      u
        e      ɤ      o
        ɛ      ʌ      ɔ
        a             ɑ
```

The vowels will be arranged in series of the same degree of aperture, from the most closed to the most open: i, ɯ, u; e, ɤ o; ɛ, ʌ, ɔ; a, ɑ.
(d) systems with tense and lax vowels:

```
       tense            lax
     i      u        ɪ      ʊ
      e    o          ɛ    ɔ
        a               ə
```

The vowels will be arranged according to their degree of aperture, with the tense vowel first and then the lax, as follows: i, ɪ, e, ɛ, a, ə, o, ɔ, u, ʊ.
(e) systems with long vowels:

```
    short              long
   i      u       ii      uu       i:      u:
    e    o         ee    oo         e:    o:
      a               aa               a:
```

Two systems of transcription are possible, depending on whether or not a language with more than two tone levels has distinctions in both length and tone glides. For a language with two level tones and gliding tones, one could use accent marks to indicate tone contours and double vowels to indicate length.

short vowels with gliding tones: ê, ě
long vowels with gliding tones: èé, éè

On the other hand, for a language with three or more tone levels, we have seen that it is impractical to use angled accent marks as a notation for tone glides (as above). Since double vowels must then be used for indicating contour tones, they cannot be used to indicate length. In this case a colon could be used for length.

short vowels with gliding tones: ēé, éè, éē
long vowels with gliding tones: ēé:, éè:, éē:

Long vowels will appear immediately after the corresponding short vowels, as follows: i, i: or ii, e, e: or ee, etc.[4]

2. *Tones.* Each vowel will be classified according to its tone, from lowest to highest, and for glides starting with the rising tone, in the following order:

1. low tone, then those derived from low: low-mid, low-high;
2. mid tone, then those derived from mid: mid-high, mid-low;
3. high tone, then those derived from high: high-mid, high-low.

Thus: ì, ìī, ìí, ī, īí, īì, í, íī, íì, è, èē, èé, ē, ...

3. *Consonants.* They will be arranged first by point of articulation, and then by manner of articulation within the same point. For example, consider the consonant system for Manza of Dekoa, Central African Republic:

	bilabial	labio-dental	apical	central	back	labio-velar
voiceless	p	f	t	s	k	kp
voiced	b	v	d	z	g	gb
implosive	ɓ		ɗ			
prenasal	mb	mv	nd	nz	ng	ngb
nasal	m		n	ɲ	ŋ	ŋm
continuant			l	y	h	w
vibrant		v̂	r			

The order will be: p, b, ɓ, mb, m, f, v, mv, v̂, t, d, ɗ, nd, ... When there is a series of implosives, as in this case, they may also be placed before the voiceless counterparts: ɓ, p, b, mb, m, f, v, mv, v̂, ɗ, t, d, nd, ... However this is not the best arrangement, as it is often difficult, especially at the beginning of study, to distinguish b-ɓ and d-ɗ with certainty, since implosives in some languages are not pronounced very prominently. For later checking it may then be inconvenient to have the voiceless consonants between the implosives and the voiced consonants. In either case, the index tabs of the card file should be arranged so that, with each point of articulation done in consistent fashion, a single series (e.g., implosives) is kept lined up together (see diagram).

The advantages of this arrangement are many and varied. It allows classification of data from the very beginning, so that patterns emerge. It permits a quick assessment of the relative frequency of phonemes. It points up phonemes that occur only in initial, medial, or final position. A quick check of the file shows whether all vowel phonemes may be followed by all consonantal phonemes and vice versa, making neutralization phenomena readily apparent. In Birom, for example, one sees immediately that of the seven vowels i, e, ɛ, a, ɔ, o, u which appear in final and interconsonantal positions, only e, a, and o are found initially. In Banda one sees that the two central vowels ɨ and ə do not appear after any of the palatal consonants ʃ, ʒ, c, j, nj, ɲ, and y.

---

[4]It follows that after consonants, vowels will likewise appear in the recommended order; for example, after p one would have, in a language with seven oral vowels: pi, pe, pɛ, pa, pɔ, po, pu.

Processing the Data

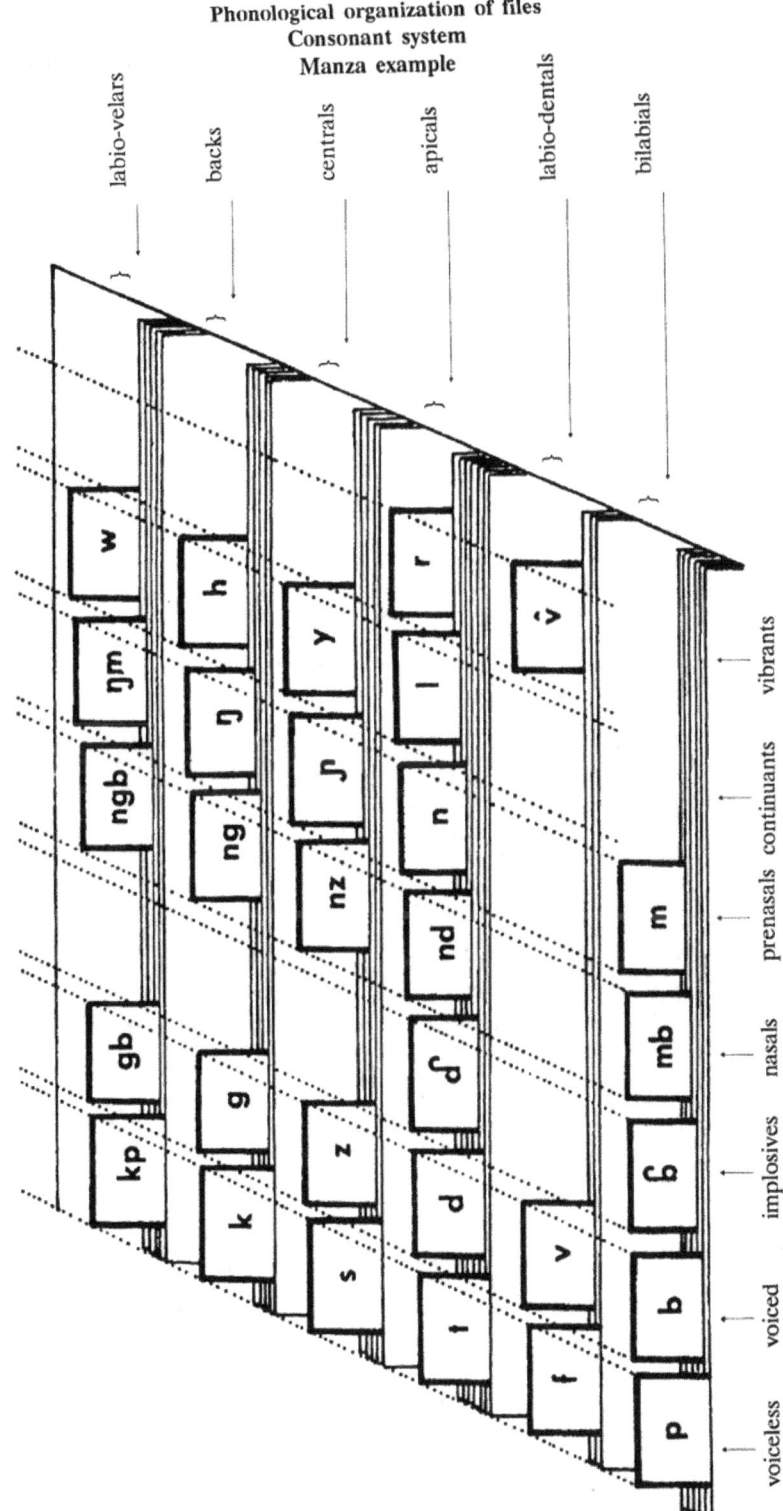

Introduction to Fieldwork

Collection of Texts
(example of a page of manuscript from Ngbaku-ma'bo Folktales)

29	Louis MBOKA 54 years TO and GBASƆ : for pounding nuts III
	Ngbaka – Bokua 29 April 1966
	FOLKTALES I – Recording 205-255 19 cm/s ⌀ 13 cm.

1 – gà ʔelè vo ʔe ʔa tò ʔe ʔotɛ gbasɔ ʔe
   other|name|person /it is/ TƆ | and | Gbaso //
   One was Tɔ, the other Gbaso.

2 – gà ʔelè vo ʔe ʔa gbasɔ ʔe ʔotɛ tò ʔe
   other|name|person /it is/ Gbaso | and | Tɔ //
   One was Gbaso, the other Tɔ.

3 – tò no ʔe, no- yèlè nga gbasɔ ʔe, no- bu ʔe
   Tɔ / goes # goes + to /change + to/ house of |Gbaso # goes |arrive //
   Tɔ left; he went to trade at Gbaso's house, and arrived.

4 – gbasɔ 'bo ʔe : ʔosu ʔi..na-o, ʔi..na-o, ʔi ha 'buka-
   Gbaso / say that # you all || fathers|my|-s || mothers|my|-s|| you/take/mortars
   Gbaso said: You all, my fathers, my mothers, take your mortars.

5 – kā- ʔi-lɔ-o, [ʔi] ʔɔ gbo tè
   you |these|-s # you/ put + to / inside | house //
   and put them in the house.

6 – [gà] 'bukà -na 'bo, ʔe mɛnɛ 'bu ma ha mi, ʔi 'bu-tè mbia
   other|mortar|my + to /there // he / do # before that / I /give/to you# you/pound| with
   I have a mortar, I will give it to you for pounding your nuts.   nuts//

7 – ndakpa kanà gbasɔ 'bo : gbasɔ ʔelè, gbasɔ, lɛ-kia, ʔelè-
   then/mother| Gbaso / say that # Gbaso/ look // Gbaso || child |my / name|
   Then Gbaso's mother said: Let's see Gbaso, my child, what is

1	• = of the respondent (MM.)	5	[ ] omitted by the translator (MM) said
2	yèlé = yèlè ʔèè		by the teller, appears on the re-
3	ʔosu – you all (address)		cording.
4	ʔi ha... ʔi ʔɔ (+ ʔèè)		

Conversely after s and z, i and ə are found, but not i or e. Thus one can quickly locate problem areas and consequently plan later stages of the research.

Arrangement for publication will be the same as for the working file. In both cases there are certain problems which cannot be resolved through phonological classification alone. Thus the classification of derivatives and compounds is a particular problem. Although they must evidently appear in the appropriate place in the phonological classification, we feel it indispensable that they also be entered by their root. This shows up the productivity of the root, and the processes it undergoes.

Another problem is that of homonymy, which is found in most languages. In which order should the homonyms appear? Clearly, we cannot use sometimes one order, and sometimes another. It is essential to maintain the same policy throughout the file, which requires classification in terms of a single criterion. We ourselves have chosen the criterion of category; for grammatical categories we use the following fixed and arbitrary order: first lexical categories (verbs, nouns, nominoids, numerals, adjectives, qualifiers, adverbs, etc.), and then, (person markers, clause level particles, noun phrase modifiers, verbal affixes, nominal affixes, etc.).

For a simple working file, certain specific classifications are recommended, especially a classification by endings, which is extremely interesting for phonological and comparative analysis.

English-Vernacular file. The arrangement here is by English alphabetical order, but there are still two possibilities: either to give a vernacular equivalent for each English word, which would necessitate a certain amount of duplication, or to group the different equivalents under one English key term, with other related English expressions having a cross reference to the key term. In reality, there is never an exact correspondence between two languages, either in grammatical categories or in meanings, so that equivalents are not word for word, but rather idea for idea; the key term presentation seems to reflect this better.

Subject file. This third area of lexical analysis is certainly the most troublesome. The decimal system of classification, used in many libraries, might have offered an interesting basis for the classification of data. Unfortunately, it is too closely oriented to Western culture. Because it is poorly suited to the realities of the languages which we are studying, we have had to look for other criteria for classification. The system we are proposing here fits fairly well the characteristics of the societies familiar to us, although we do not claim that it is the only one for subject classification. It divides linguistic reality into five principal parts:

I. Techniques. This includes all that concerns man's control of matter and his ways of adapting the environment to his needs. Alongside an objective classification according to the broad outlines of Questionnaire 10 (Techniques), which allows comparisons, one establishes a subjective classification based on the language and the indigenous classifications discovered, which points out its specific features.

II. Plants. This covers data concerning the relationship of man to the plant world around him, and his conception of it. The first part concerns general ideas about plants—their anatomy, physiology, and possibly pathology. The plants themselves are classified according to the two main criteria used throughout the subject file. Firstly, the objective classification will be a scientific classification by families in alphabetical order (separating Phanerogams and Cryptogams, however): Acanthaceae,

Amarantaceae, Anonaceae, Apocynaceae, then within each family the names of the genera and species in alphabetical order: Solonaceae—Capsicum annuum, C. frutescens; Solanum anomalum, S. melongena, S. torvum, S. welwitschii. Secondly, the subjective classification will itself have two parts. One is based on ethnological information collected, by methods of production (cultivation, domestication, gathering), uses (technological, nutritional, medicinal, magical, social) and the different images that they evoke (beliefs, place in literature, in naming, symbolism). The other will show the vernacular taxonomies according to the different systems found: explicit classifications of plants (male/female; forest/savannah; water/land; etc.) or implicit classifications (relationships: families, fathers, mothers, etc.; or types: grasses, vines, trees, etc.).

We propose essentially the same principles of presentation for the publication of an ethnobotanical lexicon, taking into account certain questions of particular interest to naturalists, whose requirements are different and often divergent from those of linguists. For this type of lexicon, after a section of generalities identical to that for the card file, we adopt a five-part scheme:

(1) List of scientific names by family: Latin name, vernacular name (there may be several vernacular names for one Latin name, and vice versa; it is good to be aware of the fact that the criteria for identification do not always coincide and that a distinction made in one system may not be made in another).

(2) Criteria of vernacular classification: by sex (male, female); by production (cultivated, protected, wild); by habitat (savannah, domestic forest, deep forest, land or water); by shape (small leaves, big leaves; small fruit, large fruit); by color (white, yellow, red, etc.).

(3) List of vernacular names in phonological order: vernacular name, Latin name, then linguistic notes about the name of the plant (derived forms, compounds, folk etymology, etc.) and about the method of production, uses and images it evokes.

(4) Classification by uses and types of representations, using the file classification proposed for this subject (cf. above).

(5) Finally, an alphabetical index of the genera of the scientific classifications will facilitate reference to the work, as much for the naturalist as for the linguist and ethnologist.

III. Animals. This includes data relevant to man's relationship to the animal kingdom and his conception of it, including man himself as a species. The first part is devoted to general ideas about the existence, anatomy, and physiology (including pathology) of animals and humans. In the second part, animals are classified according to the same two criteria used in the other domains: logical or objective, and subjective. The objective classification coincides with the scientific classification organized by phylum, class, order, family, genus, and species, as follows:

Vertebrates - Mammals - Insectivores
- Chiroptera
- Primates
- Pholidota
- Rodents
- Carnivores - Canines
- Mustelidae
- Viverridae - *Herpestes paludinosus*
- *Ichneumia albicauda*
- Birds
- Amphibians
- Reptiles
- Fish

Invertebrates - Arachnida   etc.

The subjective classification will have essentially the same organization as that for plants, divided into two parts: one based on ethnological information collected, the other on vernacular taxonomies.

For the publication of an ethnozoological lexicon we will maintain the same principles of presentation as for plants.

IV. Sociological. This covers all the vocabulary concerning the relationship of man with man, whether familial, political, or social organization, the systems established, and the place of the individual within these systems. The objective classification, following in general the plan of Questionnaire 15 (Sociological phenomena) coincides in most cases with the subjective classification. Here in fact there is no a priori, arbitrary classification, but the organization of the data is itself a function of the organization of the facts. In order to facilitate comparison, it is advisable to maintain a fixed order of presentation into which the data fit according to their internal organization.

V. Psychological. This concerns the part of the lexicon dealing with the relationship of man with the outside world and with himself, his perception of them and how he conceives of them. Even though strongly socialized, the perception and conception are treated separately, reserving for the sociological category that which properly belongs to it. Here objective and subjective classifications again diverge if we adopt on the one hand a scientific classification of perceptions, sensations, etc., and on the other hand the vernacular structures which emerge from the study of the lexicon.

Certain parts of this five-point classification necessarily overlap. We do not think that this generally represents a duplication of effort. If a term occurs in several areas of the lexicon, it is because it has multiple meanings with various facets that are best to consider from different viewpoints.

It is more difficult to know where to classify certain terms which do not seem to fall completely within any of the divisions, but rather partially within several. Thus, should the abstract ideas about man's perception and conception of society and social relations be placed in subdivision IV or V? The same problem arises for symbolic systems (arts, games, divination; ways of classifying, counting, measuring) which are all equally socialized, and touch more or less on the realm of thought.

5.2.2 Grammatical classification

The grammar file cards drawn up as described above (§5.1.2) must be classified; the grammatical analysis will fall out naturally from this classification. On the other hand, certain types of classification for grammar do not require special file cards; the cards needed can be taken directly from the lexicon. This is perhaps one case where punch cards would be useful. However, using this type of card requires so much effort to reorganize the file into specific classifications that we usually prefer the lazy solution, i.e., copying the file cards as many times as necessary for the different classifications. Furthermore, this solution permits immediate access to any type of classification needed during the work, which is not possible with selective classifications on punch cards.

In working up the grammatical files, we distinguish the word level (synthematic), the phrase level (syntagmatic), and the clause level (énoncematic, clausematic).

Word level (synthematic). This concerns the classification of derived forms and of compounds. At least one file is necessary for each.

Derived forms will be classified either by the root, on file cards prepared specifically for this purpose (see §5.1.2), or by element (e.g., affix) or word-forming process (e.g., inflection), working directly from the lexical file cards. One could also consider the semantic or grammatical function of each type of word formation.

Compounds offer more possibilities for classification (cf. Questionnaire 4):

(a) Combination of elements of the compound: number of parts of the compound; grammatical or lexical character of the components; grammatical categories of the parts of the compound; the grammatical category of the compound as a whole;

(b) Identification of the elements of the compound: compounds completely identified, those partially identified; probable compounds; compounding stems;

(c) Degree of integration within the grammatical structures: syntactic compounds; asyntactic compounds (asyntactic combinations; formal modifications).

Phrase level (syntagmatic). This type of classification divides into two major parts: the noun phrase and the verb phrase.

For the noun phrase, different types of phrases, arranged on file cards prepared for this purpose (see §5.1.2), are classified according to their function and form: attributive noun phrases (with or without attributive marker; marked by affix or inflection), relative noun phrases, coordinate phrases, etc. On the other hand, for certain particular cases such as that of languages with noun classes, a file must be set up for nouns by class marker (prefix, infix, or suffix), based on the lexical file. In tone languages, one could check if there are grammatical noun classes distinguished by tone, although this has not yet been attested.

For the verb phrase, the file cards (see §5.1.2) are organized according to verb form: simple inflectional forms, reduplications, repetitions; affixed forms (prefix, infix, suffix); forms with auxiliaries; and finally, combinations of the preceding types. Also one will see whether a classification is possible by formal categories (verb classes functioning according to tone, or vowel, or consonant) or by semantic categories (transitive, intransitive, optional etc.).

Clause level (clausematic). Finally, the file cards of utterances will also be divided into two classes. The first, analyzing simple clauses, will file different types of functions (subject, predicate, complement; the latter also subdivided into various types, etc.).

Processing the Data 93

The second will classify simple clauses, from simplest to most developed; then the complex utterances from least complex to most complex, arranged into several categories according to form: with or without clause level markers (negative, interrogative, etc.); with or without conjunctions (juxtaposed, coordinate, subordinate); clause modification affecting either one constituent (relative clause) or the whole of the sentence (subordinate clause).

5.2.3 Classification of texts

Here again there are numerous possibilities. To proceed easily to the different possible classifications, one obviously does not work with the texts themselves, but with the identifying file cards drawn up while eliciting the texts and completed later during their processing.

The principal classification will be by genre (elicited texts: technical descriptions, biographies, descriptions, etc.; nontraditional spontaneous texts: speeches, conversations, ... ; traditional texts in everyday language: stories, myths, legends, proverbs, ... ; traditional texts in specialized language: poetry, songs, ...). Within each genre will be a classification by subject matter, for example for stories: narratives about animals, about humans, in a cycle, about a hero, etc.; stories for the layman, for the initiated; moral, didactic, or recreational; etc.

Classification by the circumstances of delivery—concerning the ways and means of narration, as well as the speaker (age, sex, social situation)—will yield very interesting sociolinguistic analyses.

5.3 Reproduction of documents

We have mentioned the problem of the multiple reproduction of file slips, both for processing and classifying data. Producing the field file cards initially in triplicate will allow an initial organization for the lexicon. However, the numerous classifications leading to the analysis of the language will require many recopyings of a great number of file cards, unless punch cards are used, whose great disadvantages have already been mentioned.

Mechanical reproduction is possible. Carbon paper may be used, but scarcely more than five copies can be made per set. Photocopying or duplication by stencils is also possible; apart from the burdensome nature of these processes, their major drawback is that making x number of copies of the same file card does not fill the requirement of the different types of desirable classification.

In fact, in moving from the Vernacular-English file to the English-Vernacular file, for example, a single word in the vernacular may have several English equivalents. In the English lexicon, however, the cards will not have to show the same entries as the vernacular lexicon. Thus, in Ngbaka-ma'bo:

kɔ́lɔ̀ / kɔ̀kɔ́lɔ̀
    V ← *kɔ́* ('gather, slice')
    1. to cut - *màá kɔ́lɔ̀ kú* 'I cut the cord' // I / + ACCOMPL + cut / cord //
    2. to slice - *ʔé kɔ́lɔ̀ lé.náā* 'he slices the fruit' // he / + ACCOMPL + cut / fruit //
    3. to cross - *vó kɔ́lɔ̀ ngó* 'the people cross the river' // people / + ACCOMPL + cut / water //
    4. to dance (the belly dance) *ʔé kɔ́lɔ̀ lúùdú* 'she dances the belly dance' // she / + ACCOMPL + cut / belly dance //
    5. to decide (a matter), to settle (a discussion)—*mòkònzì kɔ́lɔ̀ wō* 'the chief decided the matter' // chief / + ACCOMPL + cut / word //

The Ngbaka term will therefore require five English-Ngbaka file cards, but they cannot simply be duplications of the one above:

    TO CUT   + to slice + to gather + to whittle + to cut down
    1. *kɔ́lɔ̀ / kɔ̀kɔ́lɔ̀* 'to cut, slice'
    -*ʔé kɔ́lɔ̀ kú-bélē* 'he cut the kid's cord'
    2. *kɔ́lɔ́kɔ̀ / kɔ̀kɔ́lɔ́kɔ̀* 'to cut several times, into several pieces (FREQ)'
    -*ʔé kɔ́lɔ́kɔ̀ mápà* 'he cuts the bread into pieces'
    3. *dē / dèdéè* 'to cut, cut down'
    -*ʔé dē náā* 'he cuts down the tree'
    etc.

The same holds true for the subject file cards for the lexicon.

On the other hand, sentences from the sentence questionnaire and utterances taken from texts can be mechanically reproduced in several copies. The sentences from the questionnaire will be entered on the appropriate lexical file cards. For utterances from texts, a file card will likewise be added under each of the classifications that might be concerned, with highlighting of the aspect relevant to the particular classification.

Ngbaka
    lèsè.wōlōsè-ná-gbā̄-ō-gbó pā-kā-gɔ́ɔ̀gɔ́ bēlē-sī
    // child.woman | DET | village | -s | all / ACCOMPL + past | DET | to leave + to / forest | fish //
    'All the little girls of the village have prepared to go fishing.' (57.1)

This sentence will be classified respectively under:

(a) noun phrase
    attributive
        without marker   *bēlē-sī*
        with marker   *lèsè.wōlōsè-ná-gbā̄*
        with grammatical modifiers   *lèsè.wōlōsè-ná-gbā̄-ō-gbó*
        with lexical modifiers   *bēlē-sī*
                                        lèsè.wēlōsè-ná-gbá
        with function word   *-bēlē-sī (= ʔěě bēlē-sī)*

(b) verb phrase
    affixed + inflected
        infixed   *pā-kā-gɔ́ɔ̀gɔ́ɔ̀*

Part II
Concepts of Linguistic Analysis

In the first part of this Introduction to the Questionnaires, we gave information on the practical aspects of field work and language description. In this second section, we clarify the theoretical and methodological bases which led us to propose the particular steps, order, and interpretation given for the analysis.

We cover the principal classic divisions of linguistic description, i.e., phonology and grammar, where grammar includes morphology, word-level (synthematic) analysis, phrase-level (syntagmatic) analysis, and syntax. This outline constitutes a program in itself, in that it presents an order of analysis that does not necessarily correspond to that used by other linguists.

1
Phonology

The first step in studying a language is the establishment of its phonology. As mentioned above, we see linguistic analysis as a study progressing from the simple to the complex. In this perspective, then, finding the operational units in phonology (i.e., the minimal distinctive units) is basic. This type of phonological analysis is in large measure that recommended by Martinet in his works (1956, 1960). A number of descriptions based on these principles as applied to exotic languages have already appeared (J. Thomas, 1963; L. Bouquiaux, 1970; SELAF Bibl. 1, 2, 3, 4, 5, 8, 9, 10, 11, 14, 15, 17, 18, 25, 27, 31, 33, 38, 49, 63–64, 66, 68, 71, 75–76; Tradition Orale 4, 16, 17, 20, 24, 28; and unpublished works).

Some are surprised at how wide-ranging and important we make this aspect of the analysis, which is often considered minor. Many studies show only a table summarizing the phonemes of the language with a few supplementary remarks. For us, defining each phoneme is a small problem to be resolved. Data must be presented and a solution proposed. This is the only scientifically valid procedure, we feel, since it allows the reader to verify the results. Some arbitrariness is unavoidable, but at least we limit it to the selection of data. A linguist who simply gives a list of phonemes adds the arbitrariness of his interpretations, which are not open to evaluation.

Specific points of view

Several considerations based on our experiences (with African languages, primarily) have led us to take certain positions especially suited to our studies.

1 Paradigmatic vs. syntagmatic analysis of the phoneme

In the controversy between those who insist on analysis of the segments in the speech stream and those who favor paradigmatic considerations, we take an intermediate stand. Analysis must proceed along both fronts, paradigmatic and syntagmatic. Both paradigmatic and syntagmatic approaches are important. In paradigmatic analysis, substitution (commutation) procedures are first used to isolate the forms from the lexicon to be submitted to analysis. This is a purely theoretical view, in actual fact, for it is quite possible to obtain a sufficient number of units through a lexical investigation, without having to undertake the long and detailed steps involved in substitution. To satisfy the most rigorous, we could settle on the frame used for studying tone as a sufficient environment for performing substitution. Whatever the case, we prefer to start looking for phonemes within the lexical unit for several reasons. Phonemes usually appear in this context in their most characteristic form; it is also the simplest to analyze. In this way, we obtain a definite unit, a sort of fixed standard against which to compare its different realizations in the speech stream. Then we put the isolated unit back into the sequence, and consider all its possible realizations, the modifications it undergoes through contact with other units, etc.

2 Position of the phoneme within the lexical item

Defining the phoneme requires a systematic examination of each possible position it may occupy in the word—generally speaking, the initial, medial, and final positions. This does not mean that we will end up with three different phonological systems, even if we examine each position separately for ease of exposition. Rather, the same system is balanced differently according to the environment. This is shown best be basing the analysis on the positions. We examine successively the phonemes in initial position, then in medial position, and lastly in final position. This procedure allows us to highlight the neutralizations within the system (reduction of a correlation, e.g., of voicing; or a reduction of two orders, e.g., labial and labio-dental, etc.). If we examine each phoneme, on the other hand, in its several positions, we risk viewing the phenomena of neutralization, distribution, etc. as specific to the individual phoneme, even though they are relevant to the entire system.

3 Defining the phoneme

One requirement of a description is that it clearly separate phonetics and phonology. To distinguish these two aspects clearly, it is essential when identifying a phoneme to give both a narrow phonetic description and its phonological definition. The latter includes only the relevant features that give a phoneme its distinctive character in the language, in opposition to other phonemes. The phonetic description will include all the articulatory features that characterize the phoneme in its realization(s). Thus, the French *p* is phonetically a voiceless bilabial oral stop; as a phoneme, it is defined as **voiceless** in contrast to *b,* **oral** in contrast to *m,* and **bilabial** in contrast to *f.* In French, the stop feature is not opposed to the fricative feature, and is not relevant phonologically, since *p* is distinguished from *f* by the point of articulation, and not by the manner; both are involved in a voicing opposition. To use another example from French, *m* is phonetically a bilabial nasal stop, sometimes voiceless, sometimes voiced, depending on the environment (voiced in initial, intervocalic, and final positions; voiceless after a voiceless consonant in a final consonant cluster: asthme [asm̥], rythme [ritm̥]).

We reiterate that it is absolutely necessary to give a precise phonetic description, for several reasons. First, the search for the operational units must not obscure the concrete reality of its fluctuations and uncertainties, but must account for them faithfully. Secondly, the phonological system, as we present it, is the expression of an

Phonology

abstract reality on a strictly synchronic level. As a result, it does not give any indication of its possible evolution in the past or future. A careful phonetic description, though, gives the elements necessary for a diachronic analysis. It is good at least to present both a phonetic chart and a phonological chart, since modifications of the system in the evolution of the language are conditioned both by the necessity of equilibrium within the system and by the weakening of the phonemes as they are used in discourse.

4 The system

From this viewpoint, the phonological systems presented are decidedly synchronic and leave no possibility of a diachronic interpretation (such as with empty slots to be filled or recently vacated). It seems to us that the system in a given state of the language achieves balance without appealing to potential elements, past or future. If we find a different system in another state of the language, discovered diachronically or comparatively (another dialect), we need not consider one to be based on the other. This would imply a value judgment, one being considered incomplete with respect to the other (shown by empty slots, for example). Rather, each system is considered on its own; it has its own equilibrium at any given stage. We then study the transformations the system has undergone to account for its (diachronic) reorganization. Moreover, in presenting the phonological system of a language, we consider each phoneme as part of the whole; it only exists in the system in relation to the other phonemes. This implies that no phoneme(s) may be outside the system. Since we are presenting language as a structure within which a structured phonological system of distinctive units can be isolated, it seems inconsistent to exclude some units from the system because their phonological status is more difficult to define than their phonetic status. Such a procedure is a solution of convenience, but unfortunately results in denying the concept of a system.

In this perspective, the consonant system of Ngbaka-ma'bo would be presented as in (1), rather than as a truncated system with a more phonetic interpretation, as in (2). This second chart excludes from the system the lateral *l*, the two semivowels (palatal *y* and labiovelar *w*), and the glottal phonemes (the bilabial ɓ and the laryngeal ʔ with its laryngeal continuant counterpart *h*).

(1)	bilabial	labio-dental	apical	central	back	labio-velar
glottalized	ɓ				ʔ	
voiceless	p	f	t	s	k	kp
voiced	b	v	d	z	g	gb
prenasalized	mb		nd	nz	ng	ngb
nasals	m		n	ɲ		
continuants			l	y	h	w

(2)

	bilabial	labio-dental	apico-alveolar	pre-palatal	palatal	velar	labio-velar
voiceless	p	f	t	s		k	kp
voiced	b	v	d	z		g	gb
prenasalized	mb		nd	nz		ng	ngb
nasals	m		n		ɲ		

Similarly, we chart the consonant system of French as in (3) rather than as in (4), where *r* and *l* do not fit in, and *w, ɥ* and *y* are left out too.

(3)

	bilabial	labio-dental	apical	alveolar	central	back
voiceless	p	f	t	s	ʃ	k
voiced	b	v	d	z	3	g
nasals	m		n		ɲ	
continuant	w		l	y	ɥ	r

(4)

	bilabial	labio-dental	apical	sibilant	palato-alveolar	palatal	velar
voiceless	p	f	t	s	ʃ		k
voiced	b	v	d	z	3		g
nasals	m		n			ɲ	

5 Tone

In our works, we present the vowel phonemes by specifying their degree of openness (e.g., by minimal pairs opposing *o* to *ɔ*), frontness or backness *(ü/u)*, whether they are rounded or unrounded *(ü/i)*, and oral or nasal *(a/ã)*. In the same way, we define their pitch register, or tone *(ú/ù, á/ā)*, since this also is a distinctive feature. This position, while valid for the languages that we study, should not be taken as a universal. Tone, like all other features considered, is completely dependent on the language being described and its system. It would be quite inappropriate to describe contour tones in the same way. In Vietnamese, for example, the tone affects not only the vowel, but the entire syllable, and is a strictly suprasegmental phenomenon. This is even more evident in a language such as Tamang (a Tibeto-Burmese language of Nepal), where the tone affects not only the syllable, but the entire lexical item, regardless of the number of syllables.

When dealing with a language where tone is a distinctive feature of the vowel, we examine it separately in the description for reasons of economy. It may be possible to integrate tone into the description of each vowel if the language has only five vowels and two tones, as in Mbum (a language of the Adamawa group); in a language such as Ngbaka, though, with twelve vowels and nine tones, this method becomes tedious. It would be just as profitable to apply the procedure to define sound qualities, and to classify the distinctive features, thus presenting oppositions of openness, then of point of articulation, of nasality, etc.

Other topics included in phonology

We could leave the study of phonology once the phonemes have been defined. However, we prefer to expand it in certain ways, considering problems of distribution, phoneme combinations, frequency, demarcation phenomena, and prosody. By distribution, we mean the behavior of phonemes in the speech stream, i.e., their phonetic realization, and the phenomena of neutralization and complementary distribution. In studying combinations, we consider consonant clusters (which must be carefully distinguished from articulatorily complex unit phonemes), vowel clusters, vowel and consonant harmony, tone sequences, consonant-vowel and vowel-consonant sequences in different possible positions (initial, medial, and final position in the moneme or in the phrase). Syllabification will also be considered under this heading. Frequency will be examined in the lexicon and in the speech chain, also in different positions. Demarcation phenomena include all phonological and phonetic features that indicate the boundaries of a lexical, phrasal, or clausal unit. Finally, prosody includes tone (considered as a suprasegmental phenomenon), intonation, and accent, whether phonetic or phonological.

The study of all these phenomena, so often neglected or insufficiently treated, is indispensable, in view of their repercussions in the later study of morphological and syntactic phenomena.

2
Morphology

2.1 The distinction between phonology and morphology and their respective roles

The methodology being outlined here starts with the identification of phonemes and finishes with the syntax. Thus, once the phonology of the language has been established, we turn to the study of the morphology. Morphology can be defined as the study of the formal variation within a paradigm, whether the verbal conjugation paradigm or the nominal paradigm. It is these variations which need to be defined. Some languages have a rich morphology, such as the Bantu languages, and others are relatively lacking in morphology, such as the lingua franca Sango. The main problem for the analyst is defining precisely the part which belongs to morphology; morphological phenomena must be clearly distinguished from phonological phenomena, and their description must not encroach upon the domain of syntax.

Thus, a study of the phonology of Birom reveals a regular alternation of consonants and vowels CVCV(C) ... However, the sequences CwV or CyV are also permitted, as in the following examples:

pyàk	'many'
mwīn	'really'
tyèŋ	'similar'
rwās	'man, male'
dwā	'horse'
rwéy	'beautiful (class 1)'
nyàmā	'animal' etc.

A superficial examination of these data, based purely on similarity of form, might lead us to analyze all cases of this type within the phonology. However, there is a fundamental distinction here. Forms such as *pyàk, mwīn, tyèŋ* appear totally isolated in the language, and as such, are unanalyzable. They do not fit into a paradigm, and are considered monomonematic, whether or not they are the results of reduplication. On the other hand, forms such as *rwās, dwā, nyàmā,* etc. have a certain number of specific characteristics in common: they form part of a paradigm, they have variant forms, and they can be shown through analysis to be composed of two morphemes. In fact *rwās* contrasts with a plural *bīrās, dwā* with a plural *bīdwā, rwéy* with a plural *bīréy,* or with *éréy, bìrèéy, bāréy,* etc. according to the noun which it modifies; *nyàmā* contrasts with a plural *nyāmā,* or in another paradigm, with *ēnāmā / bānāmā* 'meat'. In these cases therefore, *-w-* and *-y-* constitute morphemes with well-defined functions as class markers.

The careful examination of this data leads us to consider them in two different ways. CwV and CyV sequences will as a whole be treated in the phonology, but the specifically morphological role of *-w-* and *-y-* will be examined in the morphology.

Great care should be taken to avoid giving a phonological interpretation of morphological phenomena, such as for *fwā / bìtà* 'stone' (compared with *rwās / bīrās* 'male') considering *f* as the realization of *t* before *w*.

In Bafia, there are three (phonetic and phonological) tone registers with downstep, which can be reduced to two when final position is excluded. At the morphological level, we can settle on two basic registers, all of the tones can be represented by a combination of these two in the structural forms.

2.2 Morphophonemics

A strictly synchronic description, which is our objective in the analysis of unwritten languages, inevitably encounters a number of complex problems that could largely be elucidated if it were possible to view them from a diachronic perspective. This is the essential difficulty in morphological analysis. Once the domain of morphology has been clearly defined, the first step is to establish an inventory of forms which can be analyzed in paradigms. It is generally not very difficult to tabulate the different conjugation forms or, in a language with noun classes, all the elements modifying the noun which can undergo formal modification. However, beside the phenomena that are easy to interpret and fit well into a system with clear rules of application, there will always be exceptions and irregularities which cannot be assimilated and defy all attempts at interpretation. It is here that we use a technique which has been especially developed to take account of these formal variations without resorting to historical explanation in a strictly synchronic analysis—cases traditionally described as elision, contraction, and consonantal alternation. This connecting link between phonology and morphology proper is morphophonemics.

Morphophonemics postulates that, in addition to the phonetic and phonological levels, a third level must be distinguished, the structural (grammatical or morphophonemic) level, where monemes are analyzed into morphophonemes, i.e., operational units chosen to reveal the characteristics of each morpheme, especially those which are independent of their environment. Realization rules show the correspondences between morphophonemes and phonemes, accounting for characteristics due to the environment. Just as a sound is the (phonetic) realization of a phoneme, so a phoneme can be thought of as the realization of a morphophoneme.

We thus have the following three levels, which must be carefully distinguished in notation, along with their corresponding units:

Morphology

phonetic	sound	tone	[ ]
phonemic	phoneme	toneme	/ /
morphophonemic	morphophoneme	morphotoneme	| |
(or ° preceding the structural form)			

It is important to define precisely what is meant by variations of the same morpheme. Consider the forms of the irregular French verb *aller* 'to go': *je vais* 'I am going', *j'allais* 'I was going', *j'irai* 'I will go'. Similar differences are not found in the conjugation of other French verbs. Hence this is a subsystem which does not constitute a paradigm except in the conjugation of the single verb *aller*. We cannot speak of morphological variants in this case; in order to appeal to morphophonemic reasoning, there must be some complementarity of distribution to ensure that one is dealing with the same unit.

2.2.1 The role of morphophonemics with respect to phonology

Consider the following examples from Sotho, a Bantu language of South Africa (A. E. Meeussen, *Morfotonologie van de vervoeging in het Suthu*, in *Zaire*, vol. XII, no. 4 (A. E. Meeussen, 1958), pp. 383–392):

mmatlį   'a searcher'
ríbátle   'let us search'
hubatla   'to search'

Here there is only one root, although it appears phonologically in three different forms: -*matl*-, -*bátl*-, -*batl*-. It is evident that we cannot speak here of phonological alternation; the conditioning which determines the variation in the root is morphological. Each time we want to refer to this verb root in putting together a description and lexicon of Sotho, we must choose one of the morphs at random (e.g., *matl*- or *bátl*-), if we don't want to mention all three. However, with morphophonemics the choice of the citation form is not left to chance. We choose the morph which permits the simplest formalization of the relationships between the morphs, or between the word as a grammatical structure and the word as a sequence of phonemes. We must not choose a morph which appears in a phonologically restricted position. Hence in Sotho, we would choose -*batl*- rather than -*bátl*- because the morph -*bátl*- appears in *ríbátle* 'let us search', a verbal form where all roots have high tone; here a restriction overrides the phonological distinction of high or low tone in the root. On the other hand, the morph -*batl*- is found in positions such as infinitive (*hubatla* 'to search'), where approximately half of all roots have a low tone and the other half have high tone. In this position, the distinction between high and low tone in the root is possible. (The case of *mmatlį* will be handled later.)

In referring to a moneme, then, we represent it as much as possible with the morph which shows best its intrinsic characteristics, considering the internal cohesion we are trying to bring out in the language.

A more difficult and confusing case for beginners is that in which the characteristics of one moneme are distributed throughout different allomorphs, but are not all present in any one. This frequently occurs in a conjugation when the combination of the tones and vowels of the pronouns, affixes, and root make it impossible to isolate each of these elements. We must then set up as the structural form a simple and objective representation which shows what is particular to the moneme as a general and abstract unit in as economical a way as possible.

Seen in this light, monemes are composed not of phonemes (phonological units), but of units of a different sort, called morphophonemes. Even if phonemes and morphophonemes are very similar units, they must be distinguished in certain cases. Consider, for example, the following Latin forms:

	(a) *canto*	*cantamus*	*cantare*
	'I sing'	'we sing'	'to sing'
compared to:			
	(b) *venio*	*venimus*	*venire*
	'I come'	'we come'	'to come'

There is no difficulty in identifying in (b) a moneme *veni-*, used with *-o*, *-mus*, and *-re*, while in (a) we might posit a form *canta-* with *-o*, *-mus*, and *-re*. However, if we consider that we are dealing here with phonemes and a case of elision or fusion *(canta-o > canto)*, we must carefully distinguish this case from all others where the phenomenon does not operate to fuse the two morphemes together. It is also better to have a different term for these units when we are making explicit reference to their grammatical role.

Representation rules. Compare the following four forms of the infinitive found in the Bantu language Rwaanda (according to A. Coupez):

/ kùrè:bà /	'to look at'
/ kwà:mbàrà /	'to wear a garment'
/ kó:gà /	'to be in water, to bathe'
/ gùkórà /	'to make, to work'

The characteristic class prefix is found in four different forms: *kù-*, *kw-*, *k-*, and *gù-*. The complementarity of the distribution permits us to say that we have here a single morphemic unit represented by four different (allo)morphs. The problem is to choose the morph which permits the simplest and most economical formalization of the relationship between them. In this case, let us say that the infinitive prefix in Rwaanda is represented by |kù-|. Now we must justify this choice and formulate the realization rules. Why choose a morphophoneme |k-| rather than a morphophoneme |g-|? Because the correspondence rule is simpler, and can be formulated as follows: the morphophoneme |k-| is represented by /k-/ unless the following consonant is a voiceless stop (as in /gùkórà/).

Similarly for the vowel, we can state the following rule: the morphophoneme |u| is generally represented as /u/, but (1) it is realized as /w/ before the vowels *a, e, i;* and (2) it is not represented between a palatal stop *(g* or *k)* and a back vowel (i.e., *u* or *o*).

As for the tone of the prefix, we state that it is dominated by that of the verb root if the root begins with a vowel and has high tone (as in *kó:gà*).

We have thus established the following correspondences between the phonological and morphophonemic forms:

/ kùrè:bà /		kù-rè:bà	
/ kwà:mbàrà /		kù-à:mbàrà	
/ kó:gà /		kù-ó:gà	
/ gùkórà /		kù-kórà	

Any other formulation would be more complex.

Morphology

Consider the structural or morphophonemic forms resulting from our analysis. On the whole they are formulae which indicate only the intrinsic characteristics and the position of each individual morpheme. The formulae are incomplete until we have determined what allomorphs each moneme has, and which allomorph appears in a given position on the phonological level. The realization rules are specifically intended to permit a generalization of the relationships between morphemes and allomorphs, and hence to simplify them by expressing them in terms of morphophonemes and phonemes.

Returning to the case of *mmatlį* 'searcher', cited above, we were led to choose *-batl-* as the structural form, since it permitted the simplest formalization of the relationships between the different morphs observed. An examination of the nominal prefixes of the language, on the other hand, led us to posit the form *mu-* for the same reasons. Now we need only state at this point that the monemes *mu-* and *-batl-* in the structural or morphological form | mu-batl- | are represented by their allomorphs *m-* and *-matl-* in / mmatlį / 'searcher' (-į is an agentive noun suffix). Other cases of the same type, such as *mu-* and *-búp-* in / mmúpį / 'creator', will be handled similarly. Hence, we are able to formulate a REALIZATION RULE which will tell us that the sequence of morphophonemes *mu-b-,* in such a position, is realized by the phonemes / mm- /. Expressed in this way, our rule does not stray from the framework of a synchronic analysis. This would have been the case had we appealed to explanations of contraction or assimilation phenomena, which almost always imply a reference to diachrony.

Let us consider a different problem. What form shall we use to represent the root of the following verbal forms in Rwaanda?

/ kù:zà /	'to come'
/ ǹjè /	'I come'
/ bà:jè /	'they come'

The root is represented by | -ːz- |, with the following realization rule: the morphophoneme of length is realized as vowel length, when it is in contact with a vowel (as in *kù:zà* and *bà:jè*); otherwise it is not realized (as in *ǹjè*). Thus we have the following correspondence between the phonological and structural forms:

/ kù:zà /	| kù-ːz-à |
/ ǹjè /	| ǹ-ːz-yè |
/ bà:jè /	| bà-ːz-yè |

These examples, and those which we considered above regarding the infinitive prefix, reveal that once the realization rules have been formulated, there is a perfect regularity in the alternations at the morphophonemic level, although not at the phonological level.

The correspondence between phonemes and morphophonemes: the word as a sequence of phonemes and as a grammatical structure. In general, each phoneme corresponds to an identical morphophoneme, except in specific well-defined cases. Sometimes, however, to show the particularities of a moneme, we need fewer morphophonemes than phonemes. Thus, a language may often have *i* and *y* (or *u* and *w*) as separate phonemes, but only needs one of these as a morphophoneme. Similarly, for suprasegmental units such as tone, we may well find that a language has three distinctive phonemic register tones and downsteps on the phonological level, whereas two levels are sufficient in the structural analysis. This seems to be the case in Bafia, a Bantu language of Cameroon.

On the other hand, the facts may lead us to posit a morphophoneme which does not correspond to any phoneme. An example is the mute h of French, which is not pronounced, but blocks the elision of a preceding vowel. In the structural analysis, one would be led to represent it in one way or another to explain these facts, especially in words which have never had an *h*, such as *le onzième* 'the eleventh', but which behave exactly the same as *la hache* 'the axe' or *le hêtre* 'the beech tree'.

Sometimes it is necessary to pass through a series of strata and to set up two, three, or four levels of morphophonemes. As we have seen, a morphophoneme can be realized by different phonemes, or may not be realized at all. Compare the following examples from Rwaanda:

/ twá:tò /	| tù-átò |	'small canoes'
/ ùmùhùtú /	| ù-mù-hùtú |	'a Hutu'
/ àrà:jè /	| à-rà-ːz-yè |	'he is coming'

In the utterance / ùmùhùt àrà:jè / 'the Hutu is coming', |u| is not represented by /w/ (as in the earlier case of | kù-à:mbàrà | / kwà:mbàrà /). In fact it is not realized at all. Hence the rules are different once the words combine with each other.

Possible combinations. When showing the correspondences between morphophonemes and phonemes, a number of combinations are possible:

Complete correspondence between morphophoneme and phoneme.:

| Rwaanda | / ùmùhùtú / | \| ù-mù-hùtú \| | 'a Hutu' |

Nonrepresentation of a morphophoneme (elision):

Rwaanda	/ ùmùhùt àrà:jè /	| ù-mù-hùtú à-rà-ːz-yè |	'the Hutu is coming'
	/ kó:gà /	| kù-ó:gà |	'to bathe'
Birom	/ yéy /	| r-ȳ-éy |	'beautiful (CLASS 10)'

Nonrepresentation is frequent when tone is concerned. Neither the morphophoneme |y| nor the mid morphotoneme class marker are realized in the following phonological form.

| Birom | / yúmúŋ / | \| ȳ-yúmúŋ \| | 'spitting cobra' |

Contraction. This is the simultaneous representation of two (or more) morphophonemes by one phoneme which corresponds to neither of them.

Sanga (Bantu language of Shaba)
| \| má-ìmá \| | > | / mêmá / | 'water' |
| \| tú-ìmá \| | > | / twîmá / | 'a little water' |

In these examples, a mid-vowel phoneme is the representation of a high-vowel morphophoneme plus a low-vowel morphophoneme.

Representation of a morphophoneme by a different phoneme. Refer to the example above from Rwaanda where |u| is represented by /w/, and to the following forms:

Morphology 109

| / àràmèɲè / | | à-rà-mèɲ-yè | | 'he knows' |
| / àrà:mèɲè / | | à-rà-n-mèɲ-yè | | 'he knows me' |

The representation rule would be stated as follows: a nasal morphophoneme preceding a nasal is represented as vowel length. A rule formulated in this way is much more explicit than an explanation appealing to the phenomena of dissimilation or assimilation.

Displaced realization. A morphotoneme is represented on a morpheme to which it does not belong.

the demonstrative *-nò* in Rwaanda
| / bánò / | | bá-nò | | (CLASS 2) |
| / ùnó / | | ú-nò | | (CLASS 1) |

The rule is stated as follows: a morphotoneme that belongs to a morpheme of one phoneme is realized on the following syllable (as with |ú-| in *ùnó*). The low tone on *ù* in / ùnó / is therefore considered here as the unmarked term of the tone opposition.

2.2.2 Morphophonemics brings morphological units to light

The use of morphophonemic techniques is particularly relevant when morphological units need to be brought out in a given paradigm.

In a language with noun classes such as Birom, the class markers generally appear phonologically as prefixes or infixes, readily identifiable in most cases:

1. *mwāt*   2. *bīmāt*   'man, human being'
   marker for class 1:   -w-
   marker for class 2:   bī-

5. *ēnāmā*   6^B. *bānāmā*   'meat'
   marker for class 5:   ē-
   marker for class 6^B: bā-

On the other hand, the differences between classes 9 and 10 show up only as tone contrasts of different types on the phonological level:

SINGULAR (CLASS 9)		PLURAL (CLASS 10)		
còy	(low tone)	cōy	(mid tone)	'panther'
yààŋ	(rising tone)	yáŋ	(high tone)	'wild cat'
nyàmā	(low-mid tone)	nyāmā	(mid-mid tone)	'animal'
yùmúŋ	(low-high tone)	yúmúŋ	(high-high tone)	'spitting cobra'

In the description of the classes, it would hardly be economical to subdivide classes 9 and 10 into four subclasses, since the other classes 1, 2, 5, and 6 were not divided in this way. Consequently we need to find a realization rule which will allow us to account for these four subclasses. If we examine the nouns appearing in classes 9 and 10, we find that they all begin either with a *y* or with a palatalized consonant. This is particularly clear when we compare *ē-nāmā* 'meat' (class 5) and *n-y-àmā* 'animal' (class 9). Here we evidently have the same root *-nāmā* which can belong either to the class of objects or of animals, depending on the marker; the class marker here functions also as a derivational affix. It can therefore be claimed that the nouns of classes 9 and 10 all have a class marker which could be represented by the morphophoneme |y-|, as long as we can formulate a simple and functional rule at the structural level.

On the other hand, if we consider the tone pattern of the nouns, we can state that the tone is always higher in the plural than in the singular. Hence we can formulate the following rule: class 9 is characterized by a morphophoneme |ỳ-| with a low morphotoneme, class 10 by a morphophoneme |ȳ-| with a mid morphotoneme which is always dominated (or never represented) in combination. Consequently the root form of the nouns will be that of the plural, with the following tone realizations:

| v̀ + v̀ | >   / v̀ /
| v̄ + v̄ | >   / v̄ /
| v̀ + v́ | >   / v̌ /   word finally
| v̀ + v́ | >   / v̀ /   word internally (as in *yùmúŋ*)

It will also be noted that the rising tone, in addition to its own value, has a demarcative function, so that if we had **yùúmúŋ*, we would be dealing with a compound whose first element would be **yùú*.

The correspondence between phonological and morphophonemic forms will be as follows:

SINGULAR (CLASS 9)		PLURAL (CLASS 10)	
còy	| ỳ-cōy |	cōy	| ȳ-cōy |
yàáŋ	| ỳ-yáŋ |	yáŋ	| ȳ-yáŋ |
nyàmā	| ỳ-nāmā |	nyāmā	| ȳ-nāmā |
yùmúŋ	| ỳ-yúmúŋ |	yúmúŋ	| ȳ-yúmúŋ |

Once defined, the representation rules considerably simplify the analysis of morphological phenomena. These rules constitute an explicit formulation of the unconscious automatisms of the speaker, and bring out a great underlying regularity to a surface structure which, at the phonemic level, appears to lack any system and to be unanalyzable. The morphophonemic forms are unpronounceable, and are simply intended to account explicitly for the phonological forms; they should not influence the phonemic notation. Hence at the structural level, we represent the class markers by a morphotoneme without a vowel, or by a low trailing morphotoneme, whose existence is proposed for reasons of convenience if we would be consistent in the application of the rules. Consider, for example, an illustration from a paradigm of the adjective *-réy* 'beautiful', for different classes in Birom:

1.	/ rwéy /	| w-réy |
2.	/ bīréy /	| bī-réy |
3.	/ rwéy /	| w-réy |
4a.	/ rèéy /	| `-réy |
b.	/ bìrèéy /	| bì`-réy |
5a.	/ réy /	| ∅-réy |
b.	/ ēréy /	| ē-réy |
c.	/ rīréy /	| rī-réy |
6^B.	/ bāréy /	| bā-réy |
6^N.	/ ǹrèéy /	| ǹ`-réy |
7.	/ gòrwèéy /	| gò`w-réy |
8.	/ bìrèéy /	| bì`-réy |
9.	/ yèéy /	| ỳ-réy |
10.	/ yéy /	| ȳ-réy |
11.	/ kìrèéy /	| kì`-réy |

Comparing the two columns, a number of interesting facts emerge. First, the structural forms show all the class markers as prefixes, whereas at the phonemic level some are infixed (classes 1, 3, 7); some are represented formally by a tone (4a, 9, 10), or even zero (5a). The structural forms of some prefixes (classes 4b, 6^N, 7, 8, 11) have an additional low morphotoneme which, in combination with the high tone of the root, explains the rising tone in these classes. This is not an artificial ad hoc procedure, for the rules which produce the rising tone are exactly those which were formulated above in connection with the identification of classes 9 and 10. If morphophonemics is to be established as a technique which does not introduce new complications to replace existing ones, the representation rules which it proposes must be relatively few in number, reasonably simple, and as general as possible. That is, one rule should apply to as many different cases as possible. This is exactly the aim of our presentation of prefixes with the sequence of low morphotonemes in the example above. This avoids, among other things, positing the existence of two adjectival stems: *-réy* for classes 1, 2, 3, 5, 6^B and *-rèéy* elsewhere. Morphophonemics, in effect, should enable us to represent each morphological element with a single, fixed form.

We must also emphasize that one of the advantages of this technique is to allow a clear presentation of elements inextricably interwoven on the phonological level. As we will see when determining grammatical categories based on the minimum utterance, this method is only profitable if it enables us to identify precisely the sequence of meaningful forms isolated by substitution. In languages with a complicated morphology, the identification of these terms is often difficult, but it must be done accurately or it will distort the remainder of the description. The paradigm of the adjective *-réy* illustrates this quite clearly. A class prefix may be represented by just a tone (class 4a), or even by a zero moneme (class 5a), but the presentation shows clearly that in this language an adjective always consists of two terms (here, identical with the monemes). We will become more aware of the importance of this technique while establishing the grammatical categories, where our heuristic approach demands a precise account of the elements constituting the utterance being analyzed.

3
Word-Level Analysis (Synthematic)

The questionnaire on the morphological phenomena of derivation and compounding (No. 5) covers the formal processes and parts of speech involved, and gives a list of expressions to help draw out these phenomena. While the study of morphology naturally follows that of the phonology, the study of derivation and compounding is more difficult to place. (Martinet groups these two processes together under the term SYNTHEMATICS.) Such word-level analysis could come either immediately before or after the study of grammatical categories and before that of the noun and verb phrase. Since it is not easy to draw a clear line between derivation and compounding, it is natural to study these phenomena together. Wherever it is decided to treat them in the description, frequent references will still be necessary to the sections dealing with grammatical categories, phrase-level (syntagmatic) analysis, and even clause-level (clausematic) analysis.

We might consider a derived form to be the result of adding to one moneme another morpheme which does not belong to a grammatical category and is not a free form in the language. This definition implies, however, that we already know exactly what the grammatical categories of the language are, especially since the function of certain types of derivation is to change a form from one grammatical category to another. These reservations would thus lead us to discuss derivation after establishing the inventory of categories.

On the other hand, certain problems in the study of compounding might prescribe that compounding be treated before the grammatical categories. For example, a syntactic compound, such as English *bull's-eye* or Ngbaka *tɔ̄.kpé* 'morning' (lit. /new.day/) (cf. Questionnaire 5), is only defined as a compound because it fits into the paradigm of some grammatical category (here, that of the noun), shown by its possibilities of combination and use. Thus it would be necessary to have the inventory of compounds established first and to show how they fit into a particular grammatical category whose behavior they adopt.

Again, these same compounds of a syntactic or endocentric nature have by definition the same syntagmatic structure as attributive or relative noun phrases. We would therefore be justified in studying these compounds after having studied the phrase.

Finally, other types of compounds are not formally distinct from whole utterances in the language, e.g., English *forget-me-not,* Ngbaka *mā.hō̄.má.gɔ̄* 'type of plantain banana' (lit. / (that) I.eat. (and) I.leave/). These should therefore only be studied together with or after the study of the utterances, which normally falls within the syntax.

These reservations, it will be agreed, should not lead us to scatter the treatment of word-level processes throughout the write-up, in a series of paragraphs spread between the study of grammatical categories and that of grammatical functions. For clarity's sake, we devote a separate section to this topic, but make frequent references to other sections (e.g., grammatical categories, secondary expansions, grammatical functions and relations) that bear directly.

The preparation of the section on word-level analysis will be greatly facilitated by the use of the classification proposed for the processing of the data (§I-5.1.2, §I-5.2.2). In a way, this classification will constitute the complete analysis of the topic. We should point out that this aspect of the linguistic study is more relevant to the elaboration of the lexicon; as far as the grammar is concerned, all we need to consider is how they are formed.

4
Grammatical Categories (Syntaxemes)

Before beginning phrase-level analysis, we first need to find the operational units necessary on that level of analysis, just as we did in phonology.

We have already treated the question of determining grammatical categories in an article entitled *La détermination des catégories grammaticales dans une langue à classes* (J. Thomas and L. Bouquiaux, 1967). We thought it wise to include some of that material in this context in order to make the article easier to consult. In the current presentation we will only dwell on a few points where our outlook has changed slightly, and on questions which have been reconsidered, either to refine certain aspects or to add another dimension to the procedure.

4.1 Determining grammatical categories (1967)

Determining grammatical categories (syntaxemes) is the basis for all syntactic analysis. Otherwise, the researcher will sooner or later end up confusing the grammatical categories of the language being described with those of his own language. Or he may overgeneralize about phenomena specific to a given language, if he has wider experience with languages.

We hold therefore that the determination of grammatical categories (syntaxemes) is a preliminary to any syntactic analysis. This procedure must be rigorous and objective, not subjectively based on the categories of the describer's language, nor on semantic definitions. To achieve this objectivity, we rely on formal criteria for determining the categories, such as are valid for any language. First we consider the series of criteria that make up the method, clarifying those points that need more precise definition. Then we will look at particular problems posed by languages with noun classes.

4.1.1 Criteria for identification

A series of five criteria or groups of hierarchized criteria will be used in defining the grammatical categories (syntaxemes):
1. the type of utterance;
2. the position(s) within the utterance type;
3. the possibilities of substitution, of cooccurrence, and mutual exclusion in an utterance type, or within a single utterance of that type;
4. the combinatory possibilities;
5. the membership in a class of a particular type.

Because of the hierarchical nature of these criteria, some categories can be determined by using fewer criteria than others. All the criteria, however, can be used systematically for determining each category.

Each criterion requires certain comments, explanations, and definitions; we will try to provide them here. The first point, the one which seems essential to ensure the rigor necessary to the analysis, is to define at the outset the framework in which it takes place. This framework constitutes the first criterion.

1. Type of utterance. The first distinction made is that between marked and/or incomplete utterances and unmarked and complete utterances, the former being excluded from the first phase of analysis. The following are considered marked and/or incomplete utterances:

(a) the interrogative utterance, which is marked as a question (in whatever way), and/or which is incomplete because it implies a response;

(b) the response utterance, which is marked as a response (in whatever way), and/or which is incomplete because it implies a question;

(c) the imperative utterance, which is marked as a command (in whatever way), and/or which is incomplete because it implies a response (compliance or refusal);

(d) the exclamatory utterance, which is marked as an exclamation (in whatever way), and/or which is incomplete because the context (linguistic or nonlinguistic) is required to understand it.

In a previous work *(J. Thomas, 1963:69–70)*, first and second person pronoun forms are excluded from the minimum utterance, because they are only completely identified because we know who is speaking and who is being spoken to, that is, in context. We will not exclude them here, however, because the notion of context seems extralinguistic, indeterminate, and more psychological. Besides, the personal pronouns are perfectly identified, not by reference to the context, but by reference to their semantic value. The first person *I* is always identified as the 'speaker', whoever that may be, and the second person *you* is always identified as the 'addressee,' whoever that may be. In the same way, neither more nor less, the third person *he* is identified as 'the one spoken about.' The fact that the speaker or the addressee is Peter, Paul, or James is neither more nor less important than when it concerns the one spoken about. The essential thing is to know that one is dealing with the speaker, addressee, or one spoken of; the personal pronouns are sufficient to express this.

The analysis will therefore start with unmarked and complete utterances, beginning with the smallest utterance possible in the given language. This minimum utterance is

Grammatical Categories

defined as the combination of the smallest number of terms which, in a given language, is able to form a complete, unmarked utterance. Each language has a certain number of utterance types which differ in their constituents, and which satisfy this definition. However, the rest of the analysis, using the other criteria, requires that the minimum utterance include only those utterances having exactly the same number of terms. Of course, this number will vary according to the language. For some, it may be two terms, as in Ngbaka (e.g., *yìà hō̄* 'the elephant is eating'). For other languages, there will be three terms, as in Birom (e.g., *yèn ā-rū* 'they are hitting'). There may be languages whose minimum utterance has only one term, or others with at least four. Within one language, though, the important thing is always to treat as minimum utterances only those with the same number of terms. After all categories that can appear in the minimum utterance have been dealt with, we can move on to analyze utterance types with an additional term.

The minimum utterance is always the smallest possible complete utterance having the smallest number of terms. Ngbaka is a language where this type of utterance has two terms:

	A	B	
1.	mòkònzì	hō̄	'the chief is eating'
2.	ʔé	hō̄	'he is eating'
3.	mòkònzì	kpáàkɔ́	'there is only one chief'
4.	hòhóò̯	zūlù	'the food burned'
5.	ʔá	mòkònzì	'this is a chief'
6.	ʔá	hòhóò̯	'this is food'
7.	ʔé	mòkònzì	'he is the chief'
8.	ʔé	kɔ̀ɔ́	'it's like that'
9.	mòkònzì	kɔ̀ɔ́	'the chief is like that'

An utterance with three terms, such as:

10. *vō ɓàá bɔ́nō̄* 'man is like a dog' (lit. / man / like | dog /)

cannot therefore be considered, according to our definition, as a minimum utterance. It is perfectly original, since it is not an expansion of the previous ones, and it is the smallest possible utterance of this type, but it must be considered with utterances of three terms. Therefore, it will be necessary to distinguish clearly between original utterances and minimum utterances, both of which are irreducible. A minimum utterance is always original. However, an original utterance, although irreducible, can have more terms than a minimum utterance, which must adhere strictly to the definition given above. An original utterance with three terms will be analyzed with other utterances with three terms, which will be referred to as expanded. We thus have:

MINIMUM UTTERANCE: smallest possible utterance, irreducible, distinctive
ORIGINAL UTTERANCE: varying number of terms, irreducible
EXPANDED UTTERANCE: varying number of terms, reducible

After exhausting all the categories which can appear in one utterance type, we move on to the next utterance type (defined, as indicated above, as an utterance with one more term than the preceding one). We again consider all categories that appear in this type; we continue similarly until we have exhausted all the categories of the language. In this way, the analysis, based on utterance type, progresses from the minimum utterance to the sequence of clauses of the complex utterance. Certain categories in fact appear only in utterances with clausal expansion (i.e., in the dependent clause).

When all possibilities for the unmarked and complete utterances have been covered, we can analyze categories which appear only in marked and/or incomplete utterances, as defined above, if such categories exist in this type of utterance. We can already see that a category may be characterized as belonging to a particular utterance type. Membership in an utterance type can be symbolized by using special characters: upper case letters for the minimum utterance, lower case letters for the next type, then italics, Greek letters, etc. However, belonging to a particular type of utterance is not sufficient in most cases to define the categories. Thus we use a second criterion, which complements the first. And of course, we want to exhaust the series of criteria for determining the categories in one type of utterance before continuing to the next type.

2. Position(s) within the utterance type. Obviously, the use of this criterion presupposes that the position within an utterance is relevant to the language being studied. In English, for example, *the hunter killed the panther* and *the panther killed the hunter* are two different utterances determined by the position of terms in the utterance. In a language where position is not relevant, like Latin *(librum Paulo do, Paulo do librum, do Paulo librum, ...)*, the very absence of this criterion is an important characteristic for comparison with other languages.

To use this criterion, the utterance types must be determined with complete rigor and consistency; otherwise the criterion of position is worthless. Also, the definition of position will always be within the framework of a given utterance type, since each utterance type has a specific number of terms. A category can thus be characterized by its position in the utterance type that it appears in. In a language whose minimum utterance has two terms, the category (or categories) appearing only in the first position of an utterance of this type is distinguished from the category or categories which appear only in the second position of an utterance of this type. Likewise, these categories can be distinguished from the category or categories which can appear in either of the two positions.

In the Ngbaka examples cited above, the position of terms gives us the following three possibilities:

Group A: words found only in the first position: ex. 2, 5, 6, 7, 8 - *ʔé* (ex 2, 7, 8), *ʔá* (e.g., 5, 6)

Group B: words found only in the second position: ex. 1, 2, 3, 8, 9 - *hō̄* (e.g., 1, 2), *kpáàkɔ́* (e.g., 3), *kɔ́ɔ́* (e.g., 8, 9)

Group AB: words found in either first or second position (with a variable frequency in one or the other): *mòkònzì* (e.g., 1, 3, 9 in first position; e.g., 5, 7 in second position) *hȍhőȍ* (e.g., 4 in first position; e.g., 6 in second position)

Here again, a category may be definable by position. Nevertheless, this criterion is not always sufficient either, since several categories can occur in the same position(s) in the same utterance type. A third criterion is therefore necessary. Membership in a position can be symbolized by using successive letters of the alphabet, the case of the letters corresponding to the utterance type. For example, A = first position in the minimum utterance, ab = first and second position in the next utterance type, etc.

Grammatical Categories

3. Possibilities of substitution, of cooccurrence, and of mutual exclusion in an utterance type, or within a single utterance of that type. Using the previous two criteria, we have isolated a group of categories which share the characteristic of occupying the same position with the same utterance type. The third set of criteria allows us to determine each of the categories in this group.

The first possibility is that substitution is impossible. Category A^1 is distinguished from category A^2 because they cannot be interchanged; for example, A^2 cannot appear in utterances 1 and 3, where A^1 appears. The following utterances from Birom:

	A	B	C	
1.	é	bā	-mōs	'they are hammers'
3.	é	bā	-mén	'they are theirs'
2.	yèn	ā	-rū	'they are hitting'
5.	yèn	ā	-sé	'they exist'

can be symbolized as:

1.	A^1	AB^1	C^1
3.	A^1	AB^1	C^3
2.	A^2	B	C^2
5.	A^2	B	C^4

Because A^1 and A^2 cannot be interchanged, utterances such as *é ā-rū, *é ā-sé, *yèn bā-mōs, *yèn bā-mén are impossible.

In this case, there could be a combining criterion, which states that A^1 cannot occur in utterance 2 because it cannot cooccur with C^2, though alternatively, the A^2 does occur in utterance 2.

The second possibility is that substitution is possible: categories d^6 and d^7 can be interchanged; each can appear equally well in utterances 1 and 2, for example. The possibility of substitution does not mean they are mutually exclusive, however, for they may both occur together in the same utterance. Thus, in Birom:

1.	é	bā-mōs	wēt		'they are not hammers'
	A^1	$AB^1\ C^1$	d^6		
2.	yèn	ā-rū	wēt		'they are not hitting'
	A^2	B C^2	d^6		
1.	é	bā-mōs	pyàk		'they are many hammers'
	A^1	$AB^1\ C^1$	d^7		
2.	yèn	ā-rū	pyàk		'they are many to hit'
	A^2	B C^2	d^7		
1.	é	bā-mōs	pyàk	wēt	'they are not many hammers'
	A^1	$AB^1\ C^1$	d^7	d^6	
2.	yèn	ā-rū	pyàk	wēt	'they are not many to hit'
	A^2	B C^2	d^7	d^6	

The possibilities of substitution thus provide a criterion for identifying categories. If substitution is impossible, we can distinguish two groups as separate categories. Likewise, if substitution is possible, and there is no obligatory mutual exclusion, we can distinguish two categories. In the latter case, though, identifying a distinct category is often premature, so we must resort to an additional criterion, as we must when there is mutual exclusion.

4. Combinatory possibilities. In most languages, there are impossible, possible, or even necessary combinations of certain categories with one another. When combination is possible, the order of the elements may be distinctive, so that a given category may precede another category, but may only follow a third category. These key categories may differ across languages, but usually include the personal pronouns, modals, and the plural marker, notably. Thus, we distinguish category C^1 from category C^2 in that C^1 can combine with AB^1, while C^2 never can. Similarly, we distinguish categories d^2, d^4, d^3, and d^5 from each other based on combinations with another category d^8: d^8 may follow d^2, while it may only precede d^4; d^8 may either precede or follow d^3, but may never occur with d^5, either before or after. This is the case in Birom:

1. é bā -mōs ó mó   'they are these hammers in question'
   A^1 AB^1 C^1 d^2 d^8
2. é bā -mōs nèŋ-néŋ mó   'they are these thin hammers'
   A^1 AB^1 C^1 d^3 d^8

or

3. é bā -mōs mó néŋ-néŋ
   A^1 AB^1 C^1 d^8 d^3
4. yèn ā -rū mó ānó   'they are hitting this so'
   A^2 B C^2 d^8 d^4
5. yèn ā -rū mé   'they are hitting me'
   A^2 B C^2 d^5

But *yèn ā-rū mó mé and *yèn ā-rū mé mó are impossible. So we see that:

d^8 mó can follow d^2 ó;
d^8 mó can precede d^4 ānó;
d^8 mó can precede or follow d^3 néŋ-néŋ;
d^8 mó can neither precede nor follow d^5 mé,

which enables us to distinguish categories d^2, d^3, d^4, and d^5, by their possibilities of combining with d^8 mó.

Depending on the case, one or several of the criteria of this set may be necessary to define a category.

Supplementary criterion. Actually, the sequence of these four series of criteria should allow for the identification and definition of all grammatical categories of the language being described. However, it will be helpful to characterize each category by one additional identifying criterion: 5. membership either in a limited class (i.e., the class can be enumerated easily) or an unlimited class (i.e., virtually nonenumerable).

4.1.2 Application to a language with noun classes

Discontinuous forms. The most important problem in applying this analytic method to languages with noun classes is the use of the term and notion MONEME in the analysis. The moneme is a minimal meaningful unit (of the first articulation) with two facets: the signifié and the signifiant (cf. A. Martinet, 1960, pp. 97–98). In most African languages without noun classes and with little morphology, there may be a nearly perfect one-to-one correspondence between the moneme and each of the constituent elements of the minimum utterance and successive utterance types. The same is not

Grammatical Categories

true in languages with noun classes, however, where we find discontinuous forms. As a result, a single moneme may correspond to several forms or terms of a given utterance. We cannot then identify each form as one moneme. In the part of the analysis in which we determine the categories by the position of the terms, it is not only useless to speak of the moneme, but confusing to use the term, since it is not appropriate here. It is unwise to speak of a five-morpheme utterance in the case of an utterance type with five terms, if some of these five-term utterances have only four monemes. These Birom utterances have five terms:

yèn ā-rū ná mé   'they hit with me'
é bā-mōs bā-rāt   'they are beautiful hammers'

The first of these does have five monemes, but the second has only four: the discontinuous marker bā- ... bā- represents only one moneme. Besides, if we hold to the definition of moneme given above, it is clear that we cannot identify the morpheme with the grammatical category. Unless we change the definition, we would be forced to exclude compounds and derived forms. Thus, in Ngbaka, kpé 'day' and wóndó 'noon' are single-moneme nouns; tɔ́-kpé (lit. /new.day/), on the other hand, means 'morning', and contrasts as a whole with wóndó 'noon' and mɔ̀kɔ̀lɔ̀ 'evening', just as wóndó contrasts with kpé, all belonging to the noun 'paradigm'. In the same way kpà 'to shave' and sīā̀ 'to tear' are one-moneme verbs, and contrast with kpākà 'to scrape, grate' and sīā̄kā̀ 'to tear to pieces' taken as wholes. At any rate, in determining the grammatical categories that we have just discussed, it is best to choose simple forms; compounds and derived forms belong to another level of analysis of the language.

Zero forms. Other difficulties may arise in the case of categories filled by zero forms, on one hand, or portmanteau forms on the other hand. Both types of problems arise when we start analyzing categories by the method where the number of terms and their position within the utterance are significant. The solution to this double problem is to choose for the paradigm a representative form, i.e., one where the different terms, *signifié* and *signifiant*, are actually represented. Thus, in the Birom noun paradigm, we choose a form like ē-mōs 'hammer' / bā-mōs 'hammers' where the class marker ē- / bā- is formally represented and autonomous, rather than the form yīs 'eye' / bā-yīs 'eyes' where the class marker is not formally represented in the singular (thus, singular: class marker ∅; plural: bā-). The form nyàmā 'animal' / nyāmā 'animals' will not suit, either, because the class marker is represented by the infix -y- with low tone in the singular, and with mid tone in the plural. The formal existence of the marker is undeniable, but is hard to exploit in the analysis, for it is fused and can only be detected through a study of the noun paradigm, which is a separate phase of the analysis.

ē-mōs   'hammer'   /   bā-mōs   'hammers'
ē-gì   'egg'   /   bā-gì   'eggs'

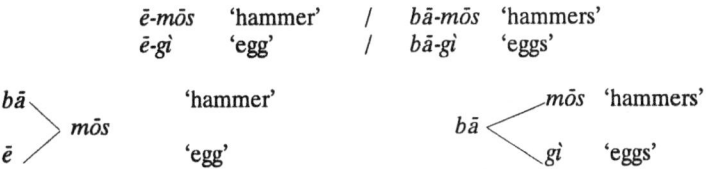

Autonomous contrasts in this context with independent. The class marker is considered autonomous because it fits into the paradigm and always constitutes a choice relative to other elements of the paradigm. In the same way, the noun -*mōs* is considered autonomous because it fits into the paradigm and always constitutes a choice relative to other elements of the paradigm. But neither the class marker nor the noun is independent; an item from one category cannot occur without an item from the other category:

Likewise, in the verb paradigm, we use the form:

    yèn ā-rū   'they hit' (REALIS AORIST)

where the verbal aspect category *ā-* is actually represented, signifié and signifiant, and is autonomous. Other forms are unsuitable. In:

    yèn rū   'let them hit' (VIRTUAL AORIST)

the verbal aspect has a zero form; and in:

    bā-rū   'they (the hammers) hit' (REALIS AORIST) (1)
               'let them (the hammers) hit' (VIRTUAL AORIST) (2)

two forms converge: in (1) it is the fusion of verbal aspect *ā-* of the realis aorist with the class marker *bā-* | bā ā-rū |, and in (2) the virtual aorist has a zero-form verbal aspect.

Distinctives of this method. In the determination of grammatical categories, the most troublesome problems, especially for languages with noun classes, should thus be resolved both by a very careful choice of the utterances used for the analysis, and by eliminating the notion and term moneme from this level of analysis. We speak instead of the term (or possibly form, component, or element). In all cases we are referring to successive meaningful forms isolated through substitution, whether or not they correspond to monemes.

Despite the formal character of this method of analysis, it is clear that meaning can in no case be disregarded. Neither is this procedure to be used without some familiarity with the language to be described; it requires a rather thorough knowledge of the paradigms appropriate to certain grammatical categories or groups of categories. It also requires a particular type of investigation to find the minimum utterances and utterance types necessary to the analysis. The goal of this analytic procedure is a more rigorous and objective determination of the grammatical categories of the languages being described. To us it seems applicable to any language, and suitable for making comparisons between languages.

4.2 Our current position (1971)

Revision of the identification of categories. At the current stage of our research, we retain the first four criteria for identifying and defining grammatical categories, as proposed in the preceding article. These criteria, or groups of hierarchized criteria, are:

Grammatical Categories

1. the type of utterance;
2. the position(s) within the utterance type;
3. the possibilities of substitution, of cooccurrence, and of mutual exclusion in an utterance type, or within a single utterance of that type;
4. the combinatory possibilities.

The fifth criterion presented in the article was of a different nature. It can be kept as a feature characterizing one category with respect to another, we feel, but not as a criterion of identification. From the work that we have done to this point, it also seems that the formal characteristics of a grammatical category may be of the same order of importance. Thus, in examining categories, we will keep the following two characteristics, in addition to the four criteria listed above:

1. membership in an inventory type (= the old criterion 5)
2. formal characteristics: possibilities of affixation

By the latter we mean the possibilities of formal modification characteristic of a grammatical category. The Ngbaka noun, for example, cannot undergo any formal modification. In contrast, the verb may include numerous affixed modifications (tone changes, reduplication). The verb-noun category, which does not allow of formal modification, is made up entirely of derived forms resulting from a formal modification (reduplication with tone change). In Birom, the entire verb-noun category is made up of derived forms which may not undergo formal derivation, but which are themselves the result of a derivation of this type (tone change).

Finally, we insist strongly that the criteria be used hierarchically, in order to preserve the effectiveness of the method.

Key categories in combinations. Another question that is important from our comparativist perspective is the choosing of key categories in examining the possibilities of combining grammatical categories. This criterion (#4) presents the greatest differences across languages. After conducting several different analyses by this method, it would no doubt be good to select a certain number of these key categories found regularly on a recurring basis.

Hierarchy of the terms of the utterance. With respect to this method of enumerating and identifying the terms of the minimum utterance, some are surprised at our indifferent attitude toward the hierarchy between the terms of these utterances, because they feel that the establishment of the hierarchy must precede the analysis and definition of the terms of the utterance. We do not ignore this hierarchy, but our type of analysis allows us to consider it after enumerating and categorizing the terms rather than before. Our procedure discovers, then specifies exactly, the order of the hierarchy. In fact, once the grammatical categories have been identified, we can determine the level of analysis to which they are relevant in the structuring of the categories that make up the utterance. Our main concern is to arrange in a hierarchical order the levels for each phase of the grammatical analysis and to define the operational units appropriate to each level. As we shall see later, this matter is of concern in the rest of the description as well as in the search for the grammatical categories.

Morpheme/term relationship. The problem of the moneme/term relationship comes up at several junctures. For us, the moneme is a lexical or semantic unit. Using it while determining grammatical categories is not necessary, and at times may pose a serious difficulty at this level of analysis.

Thus, the moneme(s)/term(s) relationship would hardly come up, since we propose to simply eliminate the notion and the use of the moneme from this phase of the study. In fact, though, since our type of analysis does not allow meaning to be sacrificed at the expense of the form, the question is always relevant.

This relationship seems to vary according to the language. In Ngbaka, for example, it is hardly a problem, for the two coincide almost completely. In a language with noun classes such as Birom, however, it is clearly necessary to use an operational unit different from the semantic unit for determining the grammatical categories; the term and the moneme do not coincide here.

We can schematize and generalize the term/moneme relationship by the following representation:

moneme $\quad\dfrac{\text{signifié}}{\text{signifiant}} \quad \dfrac{\text{signifié}}{\text{signi ... fiant}}$

term $\quad\dfrac{\text{signifié}}{\text{signifiant}} \quad \dfrac{(\text{signifié})_n}{\text{signifiant}} \quad \dfrac{\text{signifié}}{(\text{signifiant})_n}$

Term must no longer be identified with grammatical category. It is a simple operational unit useful only at the level of analysis where it permits the definition of another unit, the grammatical category. Since this latter is a syntactic unit, it can no longer be identified with the moneme.

An utterance is thus seen as a succession of terms, which may or may not coincide on the one hand with the monemes, or on the other hand with the grammatical categories. Similarly, the utterance can be seen as a sequence of monemes which may or may not coincide with the terms or the grammatical categories. Or, the utterance is seen as an arrangement in linear order of grammatical categories, whether or not they coincide with the terms or the monemes.

These, then, are different levels of the analysis. Confusing them, we find, is the source of all kinds of problems.

Syntaxeme. Each level of analysis discussed to this point has its own type of operational unit. First we saw how the phonemes, the distinctive units in phonology, were isolated. The moneme was the significant unit for the elaboration of the lexicon on the word level (synthematic). The grammatical category as defined above could be called the syntaxeme, and is a syntactic unit whose role we are now going to examine in phrase-level (syntagmatic) analysis.

5
Phrase-level Analysis (Syntagmatic)

This aspect of the analysis includes essentially the study of syntactic constructions on the secondary level. In this section, we will study first the secondary expansion of the noun and its substitutes, and then the secondary expansion of the verb.

5.1 Noun phrase

Studying the constructions found in the noun phrase presupposes that we have already defined the category of the noun and the categories that may possibly substitute for it. These make up the basis of phrase-level constructions. A rigorous consideration of the constructions studies each type of form in turn, and shows also its role in communication. Thus, we will present the noun phrase according to a scheme almost identical to the classification used for organizing the data, as seen in §I-5.2.2 (Grammatical classification). With form as the basis, we first consider phrases with the simplest make-up (combination of two lexemes without, and then with, modification; lexeme-grammatical morpheme combination without, and then with, modification; finally combination of more than two lexemes and/or grammatical morphemes–three, four, etc.), and end up with the most complex forms. We will examine three formal types.

5.1.1 The determinative noun phrase

A whole series of combinations is possible depending on the language. We will consider first the following possibilities of form:

A. Presence or absence of a determining morpheme (grammatical moneme). This determiner may be affixed to the modifier or to the head or to both. The fact that it is preposed to the modifier, for example, may be characteristic; it may also be postposed to the modifier, or preposed or postposed to the head. These variations will be specific to the language in question. Finally, the language may not use a determiner at all, but simply juxtapose the elements. Let us consider the two cases:

Without a determining grammatical morpheme. Since the relation of modification is not expressed with a mark, we must show what characterizes it:
  (a) Order of the two elements. The sequential order of the elements of the phrase is a first characteristic. It may be:

>   modifier–head
>   head–modifier

Most languages use only one of these possibilities. In Birom or Bafia, only the order head-modifier is possible. Samo (Mande group) allows only the order modifier-head. Some languages have a special use for each of the possibilities; thus, Ngbaka uses the order modifier-head (*zókò-bónō* 'a lovely dog') for an adjectival modifier, and the order head-modifier (*nō-só* 'pot of meat') for a noun modifier. In French, the two combinations are grammatically possible, but often have particular semantic or stylistic uses (e.g., *bonnet blanc = blanc bonnet, un gros homme ~ un homme gros, un grand homme ≠ un homme grand*).
  (b) Grammatical or lexical character of the components. The lexical or grammatical character of the modifier and/or the head, considered successively, may constitute another characteristic:
    –the head is grammatical or lexical
    –the modifier is grammatical or lexical
The head is always the noun or its substitute.

With modification marker. Here the relation of determination is expressed by a mark, the modification marker or determiner. This mark may have different formal manifestations, affixation or inflection. Affixation may take the form C, CV, CVC, ... or V, VV, VC ...

Hausa:	*sár(í)kí-n gàríí*	'the chief of the village'
Ngbaka:	*vō ná gbā̄*	'the people of the village'
Birom:	*vū à gɔ̀m*	'the dog of the chief'

An inflection, when used, may be vocalic, consonantal, or tonal:

Manza:	*tōā tòlō*	'the dog's house'
		(*tòà* 'hut'; *tòlō* 'dog')
Isongo:	*mòndó ɓóī*	'someone from the village'
		(*mòndò* 'person'; *ɓòī* 'village')

The order of the elements is also characteristic. It may be:

>   head + *determiner* + modifier
>   modifier + *determiner* + head

or

>   *determiner* + head + modifier
>   *determiner* + modifier + head

or

>   head + modifier + *determiner*
>   modifier + head + *determiner*

Some languages have only one of these possibilities; others have several.

We follow the same course here that we used for the phrase without determining grammatical morpheme: grammatical or lexical character of the modifier and of the head. As before, the head is always the noun or its substitute; if a substitute, then the head is a grammatical morpheme (personal or demonstrative pronoun, etc.).

B. Simple or complex character of the modification. This is a different division of the preceding material, and should be examined in the same way (without, then with, determining grammatical morpheme). In the case of simple modification, there is only one modifier. In composite or complex modification, there are several. The occurrences of two, three, and four modifiers should be considered successively, and whether the modifiers are lexical, grammatical, or mixed (one grammatical modifier + one lexical modifier, etc.).

C. Categorial composition of the phrase. From an examination of this type of phrase, we determine which grammatical categories can fill the respective roles of head, modifier, and determiner:

as HEAD, the categories:	as MODIFIER, the categories:	as DETERMINER, the categories:
noun	noun	relator
verb-noun	adjective	conjoiner
deictic	numeral	
personal pronoun	deictic	

5.1.2 The appositive noun phrase

As for the determinative noun phrase without determining grammatical morpheme, the formal structure of the appositive noun phrase is a juxtaposition of the elements that make it up. This type of phrase, though, is marked by a pause which justifies a separate treatment, rather than fitting into the determinative noun phrase. Besides, this type of phrase does not necessarily produce a determining relationship.

When it exists as such, its main role is to simplify a complex modification, when the sequence of modifiers has reached the saturation point. One of the stages in the sequence of modification is replaced by a juxtaposition:

Ngbaka   nzò-   bɔ́nɔ́-   kā-   wálá-   kàmá-   mòkònzì
/ head | dog | DET | wife of | brother | chief /
'the head of the dog of the wife of the brother of the chief'

may be changed to:

     wálá-   kàmá-   mòkònzì,   nzò-   bɔ́nɔ́-   kéè
     / wife of | brother | chief || head | dog | her /
     'the wife of the brother of the chief, the head of her dog'

     kàmá-   mòkònzì,   nzò -   bɔ́nɔ́-   kā-   wóló-   ngéè
     / brother | chief || head | dog | DET | wife | his /
     'the brother of the chief, the head of the dog of his wife'

Here we see both a simplification of the modification and a highlighting of one element of the phrase.

This highlighting role may be the only function of the appositive form in the noun phrase. The expansion is then no longer of the determinative type. This is seen in the following examples:

>   *moi, je m'en vais*   'I, I go away'

>   *ʔó hā yéè, mbéèmbé*
>   // one / ACCOMPL + catch / him || snail //
>   'Someone caught him, the snail'

>   *mbòkò, kàmá-ɲā, mò̰ hí nó̰ dē*
>   // cephalophus ||sister | my || you / know / walk / not //
>   'Duiker, my sister, you really don't know how to walk.'

5.1.3 The relative noun phrase

A special point in the analysis of the noun phrase involves the relative noun phrase. As a secondary expansion of a nonverbal primary element of the utterance, it belongs to the study of the noun phrase. However, it most often involves a clausal expansion, which must be examined also in the study of utterance types.

All sorts of forms may be affected. To characterize it, we must define the determiner (which may be a relative pronoun here) and the modifier (which may go from a single word to a complete clause). The head may be grammatical or lexical, agent or patient. Our example is from Ngbaka, where we have two types of relative noun phrase. The order of the terms in both cases is:

>   head + (determiner) + modifier

First type:

>   the head is agent:
>   *mɔ́kɔ̄sè ʔà-nɔ̀*
>   / man # REL | dances #
>   'the man who dances'

>   the head is patient:
>   *nzènzè ʔà-dè-té yàá*
>   / machete # REL / cuts | with / thing #
>   'the machete with which one cuts'

Second type. This type does not take into account the patient or agent nature of the head, and the clausal expansion makes a special use of the demonstratives as markers to delimit it. This is the structure specific to this type of relative noun phrase.

>   *nū-lɔ́, ʔó hà-lī béké lɔ́ nò̰, wūlù*
>   // bird | this # one / CMPLM + take | DISTANT PAST | yesterday / this | CLAUSE MARKER # CMPL + fly away //
>   'the bird that someone had taken yesterday flew away'

5.2 The verb phrase

As for the noun phrase, we now examine syntagmatic constructions whose base is a verb. We go through the use of the different modalities (aspects, tenses, etc.) modifying the verb, and which, through the various possibilities of affixation (prefixation, infixation, suffixation), constitute the verb phrase. Forms with auxiliaries are considered as a specific case of affixation, whether discontinuous or not.

The most objective way of presenting the different formulas used by a language in forming the verb phrase is based on form: the forms obtained are not prejudged, and reminiscences of the conjugation paradigm of the analyst's language are not projected.

Thus, we will examine successively:

    verb phrase with prefixed modalities
    verb phrase with infixed modalities
    verb phrase with suffixed modalities

Prefixations and suffixations are easily interpretable:

Ngbaka   *vō dɔ̀-lī*   'people had come.'
           // people | CMPL + come | DISTANT PAST //

           mɔ̀ gbɔ̀-lɛ́   'you had hit him'
           // you | CMPL + hit | RECENT PAST //

           ʔé kó-há yéè   'he is going to catch him'
           // he / ASP | take / him //

Infixes sometimes allow different interpretations which must be considered. They involve either two verbal forms, or the repetition of the verbal form:

Ngbaka   *ʔé nō̄-ʔā-gbɔ́ vō*   'he left to fight with the people'
           // he / goes | DET | strike / people //

           ʔé pā-kā-páàpáà   'he started on the way'
           // he / passes | DET | put to pass //

Of course, we consider also the possibilities of combining the modalities with each other.

To complement this first distinction based on the position of verbal modifiers, we consider a second distinction among different sorts of verb phrases based on the identity of the modifiers, i.e., the grammatical categories that they belong to. The combination of these two criteria allows us to define the different types of verb phrases:

    VP of temporal modality
        ʔé gbɔ̀-lī
        ʔé gbɔ̀-lɛ́   } postposition + temporal modality
        ʔé gbɔ̀-nṹ

    referential VP
        ʔé gbɔ̄-káà   } postposition + relator
        ʔé gbɔ̄-tɛ́

aspectual VP
ʔé máā-gbɔ́
ʔé kó-gbɔ́   } preposition + aspect marker
ʔé kā-gbɔ́

neo-aspectual VP
ʔé nō-gbɔ̄
ʔé dɔ̄-gbɔ̄   } preposition + verb (of movement)

The verb phrase will have to be presented in two stages. We begin with verb phrase analysis proper, as described above; then, to facilitate reading, we recapitulate the whole conjugation paradigm, including first the inflectional forms which do not come under the phrase level, and have already been covered in the morphology. Then we take up affixed forms and forms with auxiliaries as well as the different possible combinations of them. We have already considered the main points of the study of the verb and its secondary expansion in the presentation of phrase level classification (cf. §I-5.2.2).

To illustrate this method of description for both the noun phrase and the verb phrase, the reader is referred to some previous studies (J. Thomas, L. Bouquiaux, J.-P. Caprile, C. Hagège, F. Cloarec-Heiss, G. Guarisma-Popineau).

5.3 Special problems in phrase-level analysis

When we look into the noun phrase and verb phrase, certain questions arise at different levels concerning problems which are strictly semantic (ambiguity, saturation, acceptability) as well as more properly grammatical ones (the place of certain types of phrases within our framework of the phrase level).

5.3.1 Ambiguity, saturation, acceptability

All languages, of course, have certain cases of ambiguity. Thus, a certain type of determinative noun phrase with determiner (or other marker) may semantically be either attributive or predicative. For example, *a Dalmatian jacket* may be either 'a jacket for a Dalmatian' or 'a jacket of Dalmatian skin'. This type of ambiguity is easily resolved by substitution: 'a Dalmatian jacket like a woman's jacket', and 'a Dalmatian jacket like a leather jacket'. Similarly, it is difficult to tell which phrase type the following phrases belong to:

English: *this rascal of a child*
Birom: *gògwáráp à gòdàm gòmó*
       'this naughty sorcerer of a nightjar'

Here we need only substitute another type of phrase with the same meaning but where the type of modification is unambiguous; here we go from a determinative noun phrase to a relative noun phrase:

this child ⌐who is a rascal⌐

gòdàm gòmó ⌐dè ā-sé gògwáráp⌐

'this nightjar which is a naughty sorcerer'

Phrase-Level Analysis

Now it is clear that we have the sequence modifier-head:

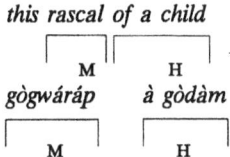

this rascal of a child

M H
gògwáráp à gòdàm

M H

Saturation is a problem we already mentioned in connection with the noun phrase (in the Ngbaka example, 'the head of the dog of the wife of the brother of the chief'). This phenomenon is common to all types of phrase, occurring in the verb phrase as well. In each language there is a point beyond which further expansion is not allowed, whether in the sequence of modifiers or in the sequence of modifying phrases. Although we realize the difficulties involved, we attempt to identify the saturation point in the language. Statistical study is more revealing and is clearly more objective than direct investigation in this case. The closer the frequency is to zero, the closer we are to the saturation point.

Acceptability is a related problem. Even though a certain sequence of modifiers may be grammatically possible, it may be considered unacceptable or "unsayable" by the speakers; saturation, then, is a case of unacceptability. Other cases may involve semantic impossibilities or idioms. Thus, the following determinative noun phrases, while grammatically possible, must be rejected because they are meaningless: a corrupt pole, an emotional tree, a grassy thought, a masterful pebble. Only a poetic style might possibly use them.

These three aspects of the study of a language pertain more to semantics than to a strictly grammatical study. In the search for the basic mechanisms permitting linguistic communication, which is our principal concern here, they occupy only a marginal place, and should be the object of a special, more detailed study in another framework.

5.3.2 Phrase-level phenomena not related to secondary expansion

In studying the noun phrase or the verb phrase, we are led to consider certain phrase-level constructions which are not really concerned with the determinative secondary expansion treated above. We are thinking notably of the relator noun phrase and coordinate noun and verb phrases.

A. The relator noun phrase. This cannot objectively be considered a type of secondary expansion of the phrase. Usually it consists of a single word or some noun phrase which constitutes the governed element, and a governor that we call a relator because it gives the phrase a sort of autonomy and indicates generally its function:

English *with*   *him*
        governor (relator) + governed element (personal pronoun)
        like   *his brother*
        governor (relator) + governed element (determinative NP:
                                        possessive determiner
                                        +
                                        head noun)

With the governing term there may be a whole series of governed elements with the same characteristics as the different types of noun phrases allowed in the language. If there are restrictions, those of a grammatical nature, which will be considered here, must be carefully distinguished from those of a semantic nature, which will not be part of this study. All grammatical categories which may appear as the governed elements are considered.

This type of phrase may not be represented in some languages which do not use relators, however. This relation of government is realized as a simple relation of determination:

Monzombo ʔá ʔɔ́ gbè gbó-nō̄
// he / puts / Gambian rat / interior | pot //
'he puts the rat into the pot'

This is one of the reasons we include the relator noun phrase in the study of the noun phrase. In this perspective, the relator noun phrase may be considered (however the language may use it) a particular type of determinative noun phrase where the governor (relator) is the head and the governed element (grammatical category or phrase) is the modifier. In this type of phrase, the relationship of determination is obligatory (in many languages, at least).

This obligatory relationship is not restricted just to this one category of heads (the relators). Numerous languages have various types of obligatory relationships on the phrase level. Thus, Ngbaka has a category of dependent nouns or nominoids which in their simple form may only occur with a modifier on the phrase level:

mò-vō̄ ʔó   'the mouth of the man opens'
└──┘
H M

This utterance is irreducible, since the head of the phrase mò-vō̄ cannot appear without a modifier.

Similarly, in the Birom utterance, the categories noun and verb exist only in an obligatory determinative relation on the phrase level:

é bā-mōs   'they're hammers'
└────┘
M   H

This utterance is irreducible, since the head (noun) of the phrase bā-mōs cannot occur without its obligatory modifier (class marker).

Similarly, in the English utterance, the category noun only exists in an obligatory relationship with its determiner on the phrase level:

ðə dɔg ɪz sliːpiŋ   'the dog is sleeping'
└────┘
M H

This utterance is irreducible, since the head (noun) of the phrase ðə dɔg cannot occur without its obligatory determiner (ðə, ə, ðɪs, etc.).

Let us now reconsider the question of the relator noun phrase from the same perspective:

hi kʌmz wɪθ hɪm   'he comes with him'
         └────┘
          H M

The phrase *wɪθ hɪm* is irreducible, since the head (relator) *wɪθ* cannot occur without the obligatory modifier.
This is true for English; Ngbaka, however, is different:
 ?é dɔ́ té-vō   'he came with someone'
 ?é dɔ́ té   'he came along' ('he came with')
A dialectal usage in English may present a comparable phenomenon.

It seems that it is always a characteristic of a given category (nominoid in Ngbaka, noun and verb in Birom, noun and relator in English) to occur in the utterance only in an obligatory determinative relation on the phrase level. But the type of obligatory determiner varies:

- In Ngbaka, the obligatory modifier of the nominoid is lexical or grammatical, and may belong to several possible grammatical categories (noun, possessive pronoun, demonstrative);
- In Birom, the obligatory modifier of the noun is grammatical and comes only from a single category (class marker);
- In English, the obligatory modifier of the noun is grammatical and may come from several categories (articles, demonstratives, possessive pronouns)

It is evident that, we are not concerned with secondary expansions here, since there is no expansion, but rather with irreducible constructions, so it is not right to use the term expansion. It is a phrase-level problem, however, albeit of the second degree, on the level of the secondary structures of the utterance.

When we state that certain determinative relations are obligatory at this level, while others are only optional or complementary, we are aware of the hierarchy among the relations of the terms of the utterance. This hierarchy materializes not only between the primary and secondary levels of structure, but also within each level by the existence of this obligatory or optional (or complementary) determinative relation.

B. Coordination. Finally, the problem of coordination in the noun phrase and the verb phrase undoubtedly belongs in the framework of the phrase level, although it is not a secondary type of expansion. However, even if the second element of the coordination is not to be considered secondary on the semantic level, it seems possible on the syntactic level that coordination places the second (and following) element(s) on a secondary plane.

Ngbaka *bɔ́nō hɔ́*
 'the dog eats'

 bɔ́nō-té-ngō hɔ́
 // dog | with | hen / eat //
 'the dog and the hen eat'

The primary structure of the utterance here is not affected by the presence or absence of the expansion due to coordination; only the meaning of the utterance is changed. The situation is just the same as in the determinative noun phrase, where the presence or absence of the modifier changes only the structure of the phrase, and not of the utterance. From a strictly syntactic perspective, we could consider that we have a relation of determination in both cases, differentiated semantically as subordinating (usually called determinative) or coordinating (coordination).

In some languages, such as English, the use of coordination is highly developed:

the dog and the cat or the hen and the rabbit

Coordination may or may not have a mark just like the determinative phrase:

the dog, the cat, the hen, the rabbit ...
the dog, the cat, the hen, and the rabbit ...

In other languages, coordination is related to a form of determinative phrase:

Ngbaka *kánà-ngéè-té-kàmá-ɲā*
// mother | his | with | brother | my /
'his mother and my brother'

In addition, *té*, translated here as 'with', is a dependent noun which literally means 'body' and figuratively means 'belonging' or 'accompaniment'. Thus we have here a sequence of determinative phrases.

5.3.3 Complex syntactic units: syntagmemes

The main reason for including the relator noun phrase with the noun phrase and the phenomena of coordination with the noun phrase or verb phrase is that both are complex syntactic units, just as the grammatical categories are simple syntactic units. Thus the relationship of the phrase level to grammatical categories (syntaxemes) is the same as the relationship of the word level to the morphemes. Here, the categories are arranged to make up syntactic units of the same type as the categories themselves, but of a complex nature. They function at the same operational level where syntaxemes and syntagmemes are units whose role we will examine on the level of grammatical functions.

6

The Level of Grammatical Functions (Functionematic)

In this aspect of the analysis, we tackle the primary structures of the utterance in the first degree of determination, just as we considered the secondary structures of the utterance in the second degree of determination.

6.1 The two degrees of determination

Two degrees of determination are distinguished in the hierarchy of the terms of an utterance. The first is on the level of grammatical functions and the second on the phrase level.

For the first degree, the units of the determination are essential; the presence or absence of such a relation of determination will change or even destroy the structure of the utterance.

For the second degree, the presence or absence of the relation of determination does not affect the structure of the utterance, but only its meaning. The internal structure of the phrase is affected and may even be eliminated if just the base syntaxeme is left; beyond this, the structure of the utterance would be changed.

Ngbaka *bɔ́nō̃ hɔ́ sɔ́*   // dog / eats / meat //
'the dog eats the meat'

This may be illustrated in the following way. Let us take an utterance showing the first degree of the relation of determination, on the level of grammatical functions:

Suppressing one of the determination relations changes the structure of the sentence as well as the meaning:

bɔ́nō̄ hɔ́   'the dog eats'
  └─┘
  M H

If the other relation of determination is now suppressed, there is more than just a change in structure; the utterance itself is destroyed:

*hɔ́ (no longer a complete utterance)

On the other hand, let us consider an utterance which shows in addition the second degree of the determinative relation, on the phrase level:

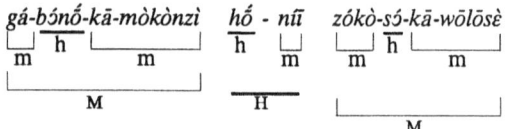

// big | dog | DET | chief / eats | FUT / good | meat | DET | woman //
'the chief's big dog eats the woman's good meat'

Without changing the functional structure, we can suppress one or the other (or both) of the determinative relations on the phrase level; only the phrase level structure and the meaning are affected:

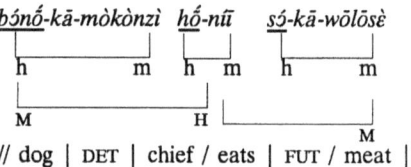

// dog | DET | chief / eats | FUT / meat | DET | woman //
'the dog of the chief will eat the meat of the woman'

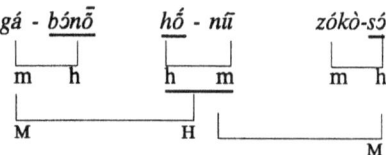

// big | dog / eats | FUT / good | meat //
'the big dog will eat the good meat'

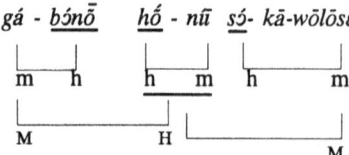

// big | dog / eats | FUT / meat | DET | woman //
'the big dog will eat the meat of the woman'

The Level of Grammatical Functions

We could even suppress all the phrase-level modifiers (mod.); the basic syntaxemes continue to maintain the relation of determination on the level of the grammatical functions (Mod.):

```
bɔ́nō    hɔ́    sɔ́
└──┬──┘  └─┬─┘
  M    H └──┬──┘
            M
```

In this perspective, we see that syntaxemes (or grammatical categories), which are simple units, and syntagmemes (or phrases), which are complex units, make up the functionemes (or functions) which are the operational units on the level of grammataical relations or functions. Here we find the first degree of determination (primary structures) that we are now going to study under the heading of grammatical functions.

6.2 Hierarchy in the relation of determination

At this level of grammatical analysis, where we study the grammatical functions, the hierarchy between the different types of determinative relations soon becomes obvious. The same hierarchy is also found on the phrase level; but we rarely treat it with the same rigor there because it is less apparent. Before continuing with a detailed study of the functionemes and their organization in the determinative relations, we will place them within the hierarchy of these relations. The following table sets up the parallel with the phrase level.

	Relation of determination		
	Obligatory		Complementary
Primary level = functionematic grammatical relation/function ↓ UTTERANCE	Subject obligatory obligatory ðə dɔg 'the dog	Predicate base functioneme i:ts eats	Complement complementary complementary (ðə-mit) the meat'
Secondary level = syntagmatic phrase level ↓ PHRASE	obligatory functioneme ðə 'the	base syntaxeme dɔg dog	complementary functioneme awtsayd outside'

6.3 Functionemes

In the first stage of the study, we define the functionemes and consider their composition; definition and composition relate to their place in the foregoing hierarchy. This hierarchy is evident if we base the definition of the functioneme on the minimum utterance. The complement functioneme does not generally occur in the minimum utterance, but only in the expansion of it. The minimum utterance includes, with rare exceptions, the base functioneme and the obligatory functioneme, and sometimes only the base functioneme.

Definition. In most languages, the criterion of the utterance type and the position in the utterance type are enough to define the functioneme formally:

Ngbaka-ma'bo

A	B
mòkònzì	hō̄
ʔé	hō̄
hòhóò	zūlù
mòkònzì	kpáàkɔ́
ʔá	mòkònzì

The base functioneme and obligatory functioneme appear in the minimum utterance; the base functioneme can only appear in the second position, and the obligatory functioneme only in first position. Inversion of the order of the terms invalidates the utterance.

The complement functioneme appears in the expansion of the (two-term) minimum utterance; it likewise is characterized by its position in the three-term utterance:

    mòkònzì hō̄ sɔ́   'the chief ate the meat'

The complement functioneme can only occur in the third position. Inverting the order of the terms would not make the utterance ungrammatical, at least in certain cases, but would change it semantically, so that we end up with a different utterance:

    sɔ́ hō̄ mòkònzì   'the animal ate the chief'
    sɔ́-mòkònzì hō̄   'the flesh of the chief is eaten'
                        (at the limit of comprehensibility)

**hō̄ mòkònzì sɔ́* is no longer either an intelligible or grammatical utterance.

More generally, apart from any individual language, the functionemes seem to be characterized by their place in the relation of determination in the following way:

Base functioneme	always head never modifier
Obligatory functioneme	modifier of the base functioneme never head
Complement functioneme	possible modifier of the base functioneme never head

These are the subject (or, more generally, actualizer), predicate, and complement of standard terminology (which we are not challenging, by the way).

Composition. Once we have made a formal definition, which is not the most important problem at this level of analysis anyway, it is now critical to examine the composition of the different types of functioneme. This composition which is peculiar to each language, may be considered a third criterion of identification, so that the type of functioneme is only considered to be defined when its composition has been examined.

The Level of Grammatical Functions   139

The composition of a functioneme type is constituted by the set of syntaxemes (grammatical categories = simple syntactic units) and/or syntagmemes (phrases = complex syntactic units) corresponding to this type of functioneme.

Thus we have, in a given language:

Ngbaka-ma'bo

Base functioneme = (Predicate)
- Syntaxemes
  - Verb
  - Noun
  - Numeral
  - Adverb
- Syntagmemes
  - Verb phrase with modality
  - Aspectual verb phrase
  - Neo-aspectual verb phrase, etc.
  - Determinative noun phrase
  - Relative noun phrase
  - Relator noun phrase

Obligatory functioneme = (Predicate)
- Syntaxemes
  - Noun
  - Verb-noun
  - Actualizer
  - PM_1
- Syntagmemes
  - Determinative noun phrase
  - Appositive noun phrase
  - Relative noun phrase

Complement functioneme = (Complement)
- Syntaxemes
  - Noun
  - Verb-noun
  - PM_2
  - Numeral
  - Adverb
- Syntagmemes
  - Determinative noun phrase
  - Appositive noun phrase
  - Relative noun phrase
  - Relator noun phrase
- Clausemes
  - Subordinate modifying clause
  - Coordinate modifying clause

We can state immediately, for example, that only the base functioneme (predicate) includes the syntaxeme Verb, while the obligatory functioneme (subject) does not include the syntaxemes Numeral and Adverb that are found in the composition of the other functionemes.

Combinations. This enumeration of the components, while it must be exhaustive, is clearly not sufficient. It is not enough to consider the functionemes in themselves; we must also study how they are arranged together to make up the utterance. This is the domain specific to the grammatical function level. Thus, for each component of the base functioneme, we will consider what are the possible components of the obligatory functioneme (i.e., for a given predicate, what are the possible subjects). In Ngbaka, for example:

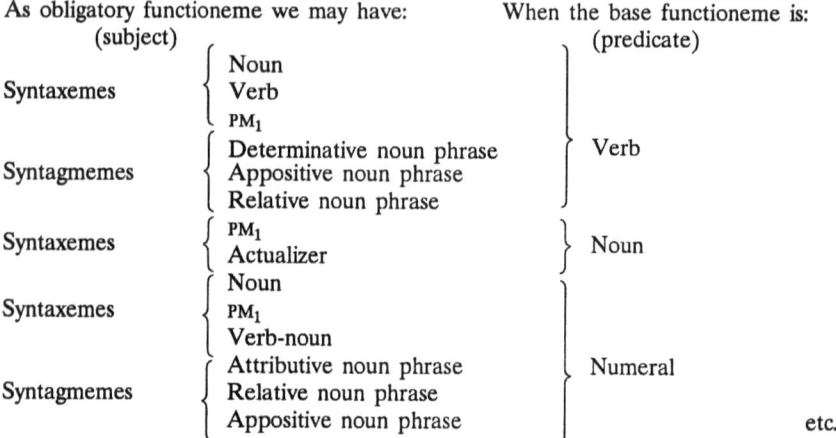

As obligatory functioneme we may have:
(subject)

		When the base functioneme is: (predicate)
Syntaxemes	{ Noun, Verb, PM_1 }	Verb
Syntagmemes	{ Determinative noun phrase, Appositive noun phrase, Relative noun phrase }	Verb
Syntaxemes	{ PM_1, Actualizer }	Noun
Syntaxemes	{ Noun, PM_1, Verb-noun }	Numeral
Syntagmemes	{ Attributive noun phrase, Relative noun phrase, Appositive noun phrase }	etc.

Then, we review the co-occurrence of the base functioneme with the complement functionemes (such as: with this predicate, these complements are possible ...):

Ngbaka-ma'bo (cont'd)

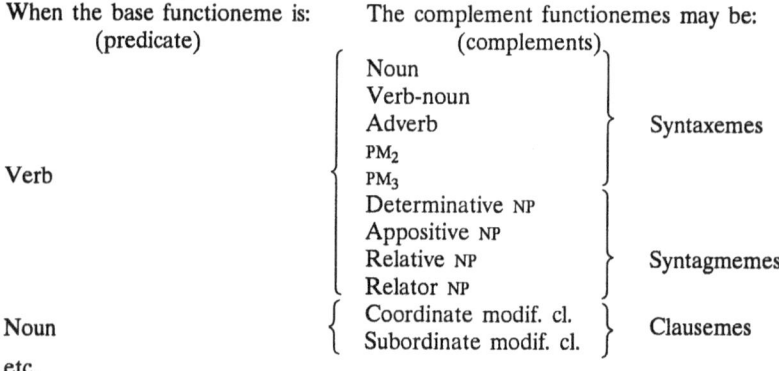

When the base functioneme is: (predicate)	The complement functionemes may be: (complements)	
Verb	{ Noun, Verb-noun, Adverb, PM_2, PM_3 }	Syntaxemes
	{ Determinative NP, Appositive NP, Relative NP, Relator NP }	Syntagmemes
Noun	{ Coordinate modif. cl., Subordinate modif. cl. }	Clausemes
etc.		

This phase is more complex than the previous ones, for we must analyze what are the possible complement functionemes, not only for each type of base functioneme, but also for each combination of base functioneme with obligatory functioneme.

In addition, the complement functionemes, which show more specialization and variety in composition than the other two types of functioneme, may also be combined. Some peculiarities may accompany this possibility: certain types of complement functionemes may be mutually exclusive; or there may be a hierarchy between the different types, manifested by their sequential order in the utterance or by some other formal means.

Thus, we must show the compatibilities, incompatibilities, and any such hierarchy. For example, we may have a hierarchy such as:

C_1	C_2	C_3	C_4	C_5	C_6
PM_2 +	PM_3 +	Noun Verb-noun Determinative NP Appositive NP Relative NP	+ Relator NP (nonlocative)	+ Relator NP (locative)	+ Adverb

	C_7	C_8	C_9
+	Juxt. mod. clause	+ Coord. mod. clause	+ Subord. mod. clause

But we may also state that C_1 and C_3 are incompatible, being mutually exclusive.

Frequency. Finally, our study is not complete and does not give an accurate picture of the language without a study of frequencies. In fact, after showing the different possible combinations of the functionemes, we are presented with a typology of the possibilities of each allowed in the language; but this gives no idea of their respective productivity in discourse. This productivity is just as characteristic of the language as a listing of the types, if not more so.

Thus, it will be more interesting and representative to know that in a given language we find as base functioneme: verb (90%), noun (7%), numeral (1%), etc., than to have only the indication that the base functioneme = verb, noun, numeral, ...

The indications of frequency may be more or less involved, depending on whether they are considered only for the composition of the type of functioneme or also for combinations of functionemes. Similarly, frequencies based on the type of discourse (conversation, formal speech, traditional narrative) could be checked.

6.4 Grammatical functions and the clause

The study of grammatical functions does not coincide with that of the utterance (or more precisely, the simple clause), contrary to what one might think.

As we see it, the goal of studying grammatical functions is to pick out and then to identify the functionemes, which are the primary determinative units whose arrangement constitutes the clause. After these units have been identified, we examine their combinatory possibilities. But once we find that certain units (functionemes) may themselves be made up of clausemes, i.e., units more complex than the functioneme and with a structure identical to that of a clause, it is clear that the study of grammatical functions has not exhausted the problem of the make-up of the utterance.

7
Utterance Level (Enoncematic, clausematic)

This aspect of the linguistic analysis deals with the study of the make-up of the utterance, which is considered the final product.

On the grammatical function level, we studied how certain units, the functionemes, are arranged to produce a larger unit, the clauseme. This clauseme may in some cases stand on its own, and coincide, with the utterance; or it may represent only a complex form of a functioneme, just as the syntagmeme represents the complex form of a syntaxeme.

7.1 The simple utterance

This is defined as utterance composed of simple functionemes. Only in this case does the clauseme coincide with the utterance. There is no need to repeat the entire discussion of the previous chapter, where we already saw how the simple utterance is made up of a combination of functionemes.

On this level of analysis, on the contrary, we must choose and highlight what is specific to this type of clause, in the choice of the combinations as well as in the hierarchy of complement functionemes and the study of frequencies. In addition, we complete the analysis of the formation of this type of clause by trying to determine the limits of saturation, as we saw earlier on the phrase level.

Likewise on this level, we consider the possibility of resolving ambiguities by substituting complex utterances to simple ones, whose structures we are now going to look at.

7.2 Complex utterances

An utterance becomes complex once the clauseme no longer corresponds exactly to a simple utterance, i.e., an utterance composed of simple functionemes.

7.2.1 The modal utterance

This issue actually belongs to the grammatical function level. In many African languages, notably, one or several grammatical categories may modify the whole of the utterance, and not just one or another of its terms. These categories are situated among the determinative Relations at a level not yet considered:

Ngbaka-ma'bo

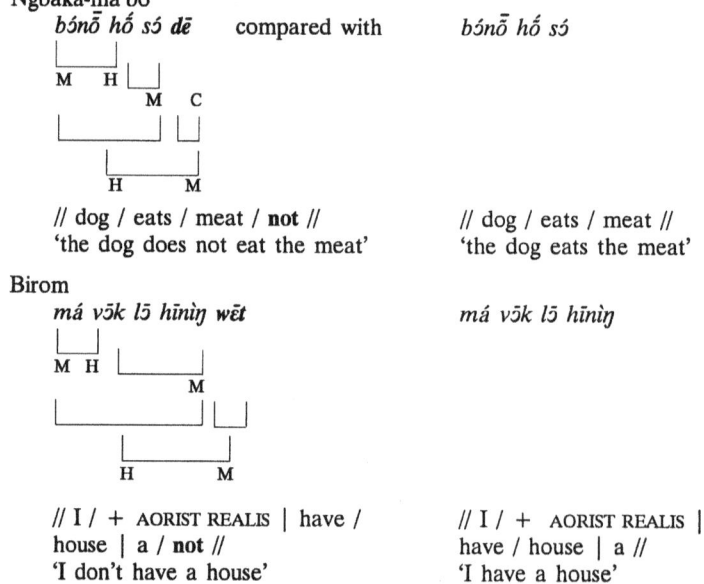

Birom

má vɔ̄k lɔ̄ hīnìŋ wēt   compared with   *má vɔ̄k lɔ̄ hīnìŋ*

// I / + AORIST REALIS | have / house | a / **not** //
'I don't have a house'

// I / + AORIST REALIS | have / house | a //
'I have a house'

However, we could just as well consider these clausal modalities as a type of functioneme (supplementary functioneme) which, as we saw above, is hierarchically placed with respect to the others. That is, it is in a supplementary relation of determination, but always in reference to the base functioneme, the head par excellence.

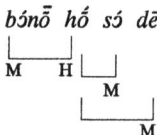

'the dog does not eat the meat'

When presented with such a case, we may hesitate to consider the use of clausal modalities as supplementary functionemes which fit into the utterance normally, because this type of functioneme may affect the simple utterance and/or the complex utterance and/or the different clausemes of a complex utterance:

Ngbaka

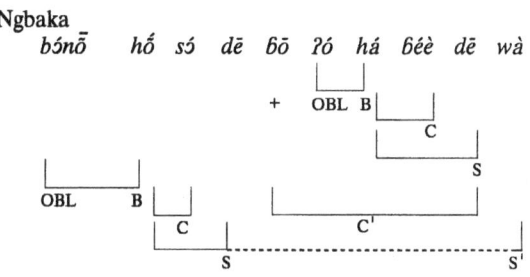

// dog / eats / meat / NEG CL MOD # because / one / gives /
to him / NEG CL MOD # DUB CL MOD //
'the dog may not be eating the meat because he wasn't given any'

Birom

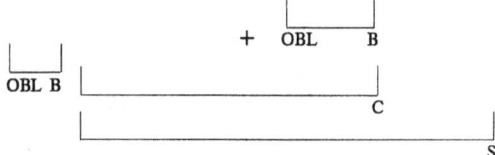

// I / + AORIST REALIS MOD | have / house | a # that / I /
+ INCOM VIRT MOD | NEO-AUX "go" | give birth # not //
'I have no house where I can go to give birth'

In the Ngbaka example, the sequences of complement functionemes and of supplemental functionemes are discontinuous. Such a discontinuity has already been found at other stages of the analysis (word-level: verb phrase, noun phrase, etc.) and does not seem to be a major obstacle to such an interpretation. If need be, we can settle this problem within the study of hierarchies internal to the functioneme types. Another possibility is to treat the clausal modalities as a particular type of complement functioneme, thus removing the problem of discontinuity. This solution, however, would not account for the specific character of the determinative relation seen in this case.

If this question is treated by using the supplementary functioneme, the analysis and description of the modal utterance will then belong within the treatment of the simple utterance. However, when discussing each type of complex utterance, we must not forget to consider combinations that include the use of supplementary functionemes.

Because the different types of complex utterances overlap systematically with the structure of clauses with the supplementary functioneme, it may be better for clarity of exposition to treat the issue separately. A special heading would be devoted to the modal utterance, when it exists. Whatever viewpoint is taken, it is likely that a distinction among utterance types, when relevant, would divide them in such a way as:

–declarative modal utterance (negative, positive, affirmative, dubitative, etc.)
–interrogative modal utterance
–exclamatory modal utterance

Clearly, this is neither limiting nor generalizable. Certain languages may have modal utterances only of the declarative type or interrogative type or some other kind.

7.2.2 Utterance with determinative clauseme

This type of utterance includes in its composition one functioneme (or possible several) which itself contains a clauseme. There are two different cases: in one, the obligatory or complementary functionemes correspond to a relative noun phrase; in the other, the different complementary functionemes are formed from a clauseme.

A. The relative. This case was already considered on the phrase level, but must be reconsidered on the utterance level as a specific type of clauseme. On this level, we study its structure (combinations, composition, etc.) and its formal behavior (formal modifications of the verb(al) form, for example). We also consider its different modes of use: frequencies, possible equivalents, etc.

B. Determinative clauseme. We are still dealing with a complement functioneme formed from a clauseme. The simplest procedure for analysis and description is to consider the facts, first according to form, and then according to meaning. The following three divisions combine these two criteria:

Juxtaposed determinative clauseme. Although logical subordination is often involved, this clauseme is not formally marked with the use of a syntaxeme, which would be a clause-level relator like a conjunction:

Ngbaka

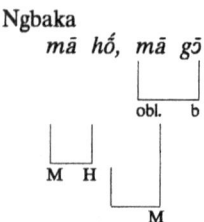

// I / eat # (so that) I / leave //
'I eat in order to leave'

This juxtaposition rarely expresses subordination by itself. Formal procedures less obvious than the use of a conjunction will have to be studied. These will be procedures that are used for focusing, for example, on a particular verb form or a certain type of agreement.

This question concerns the whole of the complex utterance, and we will return to it later.

Coordinating determinative clauseme. Logical coordination (or weak subordination) is involved in this case; the clauseme is formally marked by the use of a clause-level conjunction:

clauseme + coordinating conjunction

In many languages, this type is difficult, if not impossible, to distinguish in practice from the subordinated type (below). Because logical coordination is semantic and more cultural than real, it often corresponds to a distinction in the analyst's language rather than a distinction in the language under study.

As on all levels of the analysis, the analyst must be keenly aware of the need for objectivity in his outlook. This is undoubtedly more difficult to attain as the complexity of the structures increases. If we are not careful, the influence of the meaning becomes more and more formative and tends to shift our thinking toward a parallel restructuring based on our own language.

If this type of clauseme does truly exist, clearly marked formally by the use of specific coordinating conjunctions, the analysis and description will present the different characteristics of the functional clauseme (composition, combinations, formal modifications, position in the structure of the utterance, etc.).

Subordinate determinative clauseme. Here we have logical subordination formally marked by the use of a clause-level conjunction:

clauseme + subordinating conjunction

In this type of clauseme, we usually consider subdivisions according to the clause-markers, or the formal structure, or both. Those most frequently found are:

(a) indirect discourse, which often involves specific formal modifications:

Ngbaka
ʔé kò ɓō ʔé dɔ́   'he says that he (someone else) came'
ʔé kò ɓō ʔī dɔ́   'he says that he (himself) came'

(b) circumstantial, which on the clause level corresponds exactly to the relator noun phrase on the phrase level:

English
he came after the train arrived
he came after the thunderstorm

(c) conditional, which has not only a clause-level conjunction (or several), but also specific formal modifications:

Here we see the use of conjunctions and a verbal form specific to the conditional, as well as the relevant sequence of clausemes.

Ngbaka

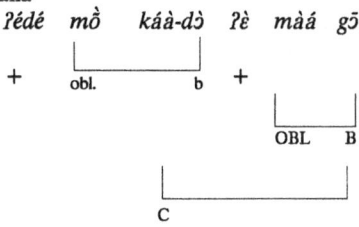

// if / you / ASP | DISTANT + come # COND SUB CM / I / COMPL + leave //
'When you come, I will have left'

In all cases, the analysis and description must point out first the different types that exist; then, the different characteristics for each, as mentioned above. The study of frequencies, saturation, and equivalent clause types, while less basic, is often revealing and must not be forgotten.

7.3 Characteristics of utterance-level analysis

Whatever type of utterance is being examined, it is advisable to conduct the analysis by studying the phenomenon from different angles, but always the same ones, in order to show what is characteristic of each clause type considered.

Formal modifications. In the structure of a complex utterance, for example, we must always pay close attention to modifications or formal characteristics of the different elements of the utterance, notably the clause type of complement functioneme. Thus, in Ngbaka, there is a specific verbal form in the clauseme serving as the complement functioneme (sequential purposive $\bar{:}V$).

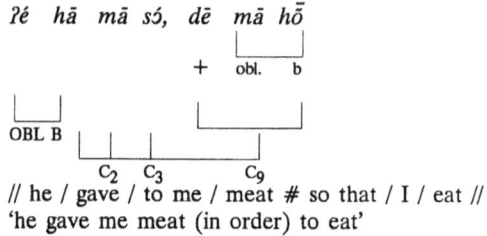

// he / gave / to me / meat # so that / I / eat //
'he gave me meat (in order) to eat'

The same thing is true of the subjunctive forms of French or English:

French: *il lui ouvre la porte pour qu'il parte*
English: I would banish him if I **were** king

Sometimes, this study will enable us to discover an agreement phenomenon among verbal forms; that is, when one verbal form occurs in the base of the utterance, the clausal complement functioneme will obligatorily have some other verbal form:

Ngbaka

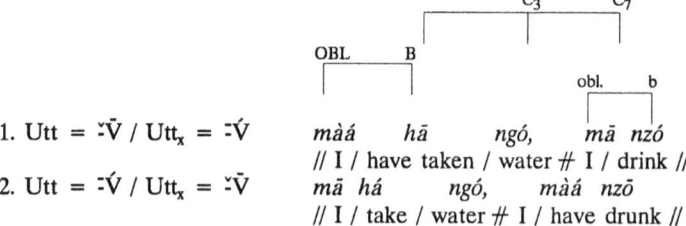

1. Utt = $\bar{:}V$ / Utt$_x$ = $:\acute{V}$ *màá hā ngó, mā nzó*
   // I / have taken / water # I / drink //
2. Utt = $:\acute{V}$ / Utt$_x$ = $\bar{:}V$ *mā há ngó, màá nzō*
   // I / take / water # I / have drunk //

This agreement is significant:

in (1), we have a sequence: 'I take the water, and then I drink'

in (2), we have a consequence: 'I take the water that I drink'

These formal modifications are of great interest in complex utterances. They are of relevance to other sentence types too, though, and we must note the characteristics of modal clauses carefully in this regard. We must not forget the simple utterance, either, although we have already studied these phenomena in morphology to begin with, and then from another angle on the phrase level. On the utterance level, the problem is different yet, related to the possible combinations and the sentence type, notably.

Utterance Level

Thus, in the repertoire of verbal forms, it seems that some can never occur in certain utterance types. The conditional *káà-V̀* never appears in the simple utterance type in Ngbaka, for example:

?é káà-dɔ̀, ?è ?ó mólò   yéè
// he / COND ASP | comes # COND SUB CM
/ one / INCOM / kills / him //
'when he comes, they will kill him'

Thus, for each utterance type, we must take note of all the possibilities, for verbal forms especially.

Composition. The problem of composition is the same here as before. On the level of grammatical functions, we considered the composition of different types of functionemes. In that context, however, we were interested in a general inventory. Here, on the utterance level, we must check what part of the inventory is appropriate to each utterance type. But more than that, it is important on this level to study what characterizes its units. We will pay special attention to the composition of the clauseme (complement functioneme) and of the complete utterance. In Ngbaka, for example, we find that reported discourse may only contain a limited number of nonclausal complement functionemes (composed simply of certain grammatical categories):

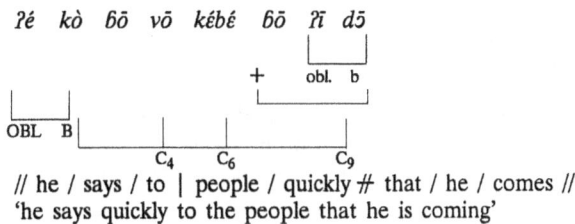

// he / says / to | people / quickly # that / he / comes //
'he says quickly to the people that he is coming'

As BASE, we may have only a verb or verb phrase (expressing a feeling or communication), and as COMP most often we have C_9 alone, sometimes accompanied by C_3; less frequently C_4, C_5, or C_6 in some cases; but never C_1, C_2, C_7 nor C_8 (cf. 6.3).

Combinations and structures. This question must be dealt with on different levels, for we must be concerned with the combinations within the clauseme (complement functioneme), and in the whole of the simple or complex utterance. The possible sequential order of the functionemes in the utterance is of particular interest. In French, the interrogative utterance is characterized notably by a sequence BASE OBL (COMP), which is different from the sequence OBL BASE (COMP) of the noninterrogative utterance:

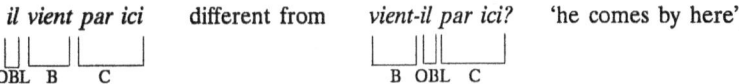

In Ngbaka, the order OBLIG-BASE-(COMPL$_x$)-COMPL$_9$ or COMPL$_9$-OBLIG-BASE-(COMPL$_x$) is relevant in the conditional. In the first case, below, the order expresses a real condition, but a hypothetical condition in the second.

```
ʔédé    mɔ̀     dɔ́,    mā     gɔ́-nū̃
 +      obl.    b
 └──────C₉──────┘      └OBL┘  └─B─┘
```
// if / you / INCOM + come ≠ I / INCOM + leave | FUT //
'when you come, I will leave'

```
mā     gɔ́-nū̃,   ʔédé   mɔ̀     dɔ́
                 +      obl.    b
└OBL┘  └─B─┘    └──────C₉──────┘
```
// I / INCOM + leave | FUT # if / you / INCOM + come //
'I will leave, if you come'

Frequency, saturation, and substitution. While examining each type of utterance, we consider the question of frequency of use, both in the absolute and according to the different types of discourse. The frequencies of certain utterance types will no doubt be rather general in most languages: questions and exclamations are mostly a matter of the style of conversation, for example. But others will be characteristic of the type of discourse of the language being studied. These are clearly the most interesting for our purposes.

Saturation must likewise be defined, as much as possible, both for each type of clauseme and for each type of utterance. The limits of expansion will be studied, for each utterance type; we will also try to determine the limits on the combinations of clausemes that make it up:

English

    the man ⌜who is eating the soup⌝ is quite happy

    the man ⌜who is eating the soup ⌜that his wife made for him⌝⌝ is quite happy

    the man ⌜who is eating the soup ⌜that the woman ⌜that he married⌝ made for him⌝⌝ is quite happy
        etc.,
  but
    the man who is eating the soup that the woman he married one
    day when the sun was shining made for him is quite happy

is an impossible sentence, having exceeded the limits of saturation.

Even so, English has a much higher limit for saturation than Ngbaka, where a maximum of only two successive clausemes is allowable.

Utterance Level

mɔ́kɔ̄sè - | lɔ́ ʔé hō̄ sɔ́ lɔ́ nɔ̀ | té zúzúkò
// man | THIS # he / eats / meat / THIS / CL MOD # with | happiness //
'the man who eats the meat is happy'

mɔ́kɔ̄sè - | lɔ́ ʔé hō̄ sɔ́-lɔ́ wólό-kéè̩ zūlù lɔ́ nɔ̀ || té zúzúkò
// man | THIS # he / eats / meat | THIS # wife | his / grill / THIS / CL MOD # with | happiness //
'the man who eats the meat that his wife grilled for him is happy'

Finally, in studying these cases of saturation, ambiguities, or the types of utterances with clausal functionemes, we seek to define equivalents by substitution, as we did on the phrase level:

ʔé hā sɔ́ dē̄ vō hō̄
└─┘ └─┘ └─┘ └──────┘
OBL B C$_3$ C$_9$

// he / gives / meat # COND SUB CL-M / people / eat //
'he gives meat for (so that) the people to eat'

ʔé hā sɔ́ ná-hɔ̀hɔ́-kā-vō
└─┘ └─┘ └─┘ └──────────┘
OBL B C$_3$ C$_4$

// he / gives / meat / for | the food | DET | people //
'he gives meat for the people's food'

Here, we state that the complex utterance with the structure OBL-B-(C$_x$)-C$_9$ (where C$_9$ = circumstantial subordinate determinative clauseme) corresponds to OBL-B-(C$_x$)-C$_4$, where C$_4$ = relator noun phrase. We must ascertain whether this is a general rule or a particular case, and seek to define the rules.

8
Recapitulation

In the preceding account, we have tried through grammatical analysis to bring to light the structures and mechanisms which allow for linguistic expression. The investigation of these structures revealed a series of levels; on each level we can study the mechanisms that organize units of the same type. Beginning on the simplest level, the investigation of mechanisms enables us to determine the unit on the next higher level; we then study the possible constructions at that level in turn, which allows the definition of new units again. Continuing thus from stage to stage, we end up with the most complex complete utterance.

The use of special terminology may surprise or even shock the reader. This use does not come from a desire for originality at all cost, but corresponds exactly to the perspective for analysis proposed here. It is not our wish to create new terms, but to suggest some expressions that are immediately interpretable, on the model of existing and familiar terminology, given that:

(a) the suffix *-eme* designates a simple or complex unit functioning on a given level:

    syntaxeme—simple syntactic unit
    syntagmeme—complex syntactic unit

(b) the suffix *-matic* designates the level of analysis:

    syntagmatic—formation of the phrase (secondary determination); the constituent units are syntaxemes, the resulting units are syntagmemes.

Below is a table recapitulating the different terms used and showing the different levels with their units, illustrated with several examples (see Table 1).

If we now apply this type of analysis to a Ngbaka or Birom sentence, we see the systematic structure of the utterance from the phonetic level upward.

Table 1

			distinctive unit	/o/
phonology		phoneme		
monematic	phoneme = or ≠	moneme →	simple meaningful unit	*o* 'oh' *to* 'toe'
synthematic	+	syntheme →	complex meaningful unit	bull's-eye
grammatical categories (syntaxematic)	moneme = or ≠	syntaxeme →	simple syntactic unit	pig piglet
phrase level (syntagmatic, phrasematic)	+	phrase(me) syntagmeme →	complex syntactic unit	my brother's pig
grammatical (functionematic) functions	syntaxeme = or ≠	functioneme →	simple functional unit	pig my brother's pig
clause level (énoncematic, clausematic)	+	clause(me) →	complex functional unit	the pig is eating
	clauseme = or ≠	utterance	finished product	the pig comes as soon as you call him

Recapitulation 155

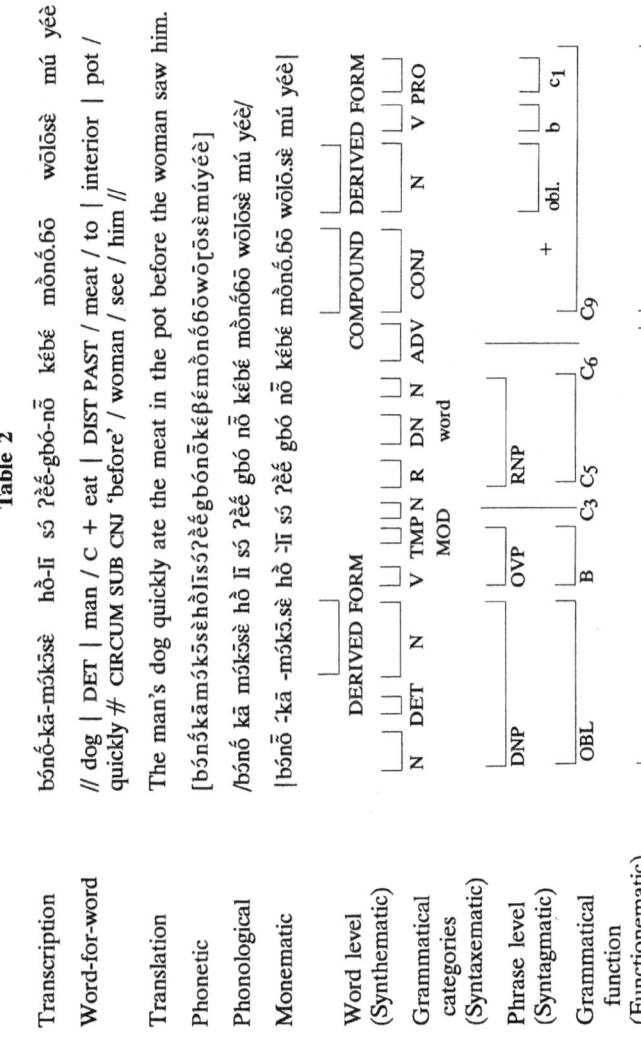

Table 2

Ngbaka (Notes on Table II)

On the phonetic level, we note the presence of the fricatives [χ] and [β] and the single-flap lateral [ɽ].

On the phonological level, it seems that these consonants are not phonemic, but the respective realizations of the back voiceless stop /k/, the voiced bilabial stop /b/, and the apical continuant /l/, in intervocalic position. The demarcative character of the occlusion of the velars is seen in *kā* and *kébé*.

Passing to the moneme level allows us to see the strict vowel harmony found in the language. Also, we note that the moneme division does not correspond to the phonematic structure; notably, the determiner morpheme -́*kā* is accompanied by a preceding high tone which affects the head.

On the word level (synthematic), we discover that certain terms in the utterance are composed of two monemes. These are derived forms *(mɔ́kɔ́.sè, wōlō.sè)* or compounds *(mɔ̀nɔ́.ɓō)*.

On the level of the syntaxemes, we can see that each syntaxeme corresponds either to a moneme or to a complex word (derived or compound).

We next jump to the phrase level, where we see the make-up of noun phrases and verb phrases. On the grammatical function level, these phrases correspond to functionemes. The functionemes may be represented by syntaxemes or even by a group of functionemes making up a larger unit, the clauseme.

On the utterance level, we have two clausemes, one of which is embedded in the other; the whole makes up the utterance.

We might mention that the transcription of Ngbaka that we customarily use and which appears in texts already published (Thomas, 1970) corresponds to the level of grammatical functions, strictly observed (without taking into account clausemes as complement functionemes).

Recapitulation

Table 3

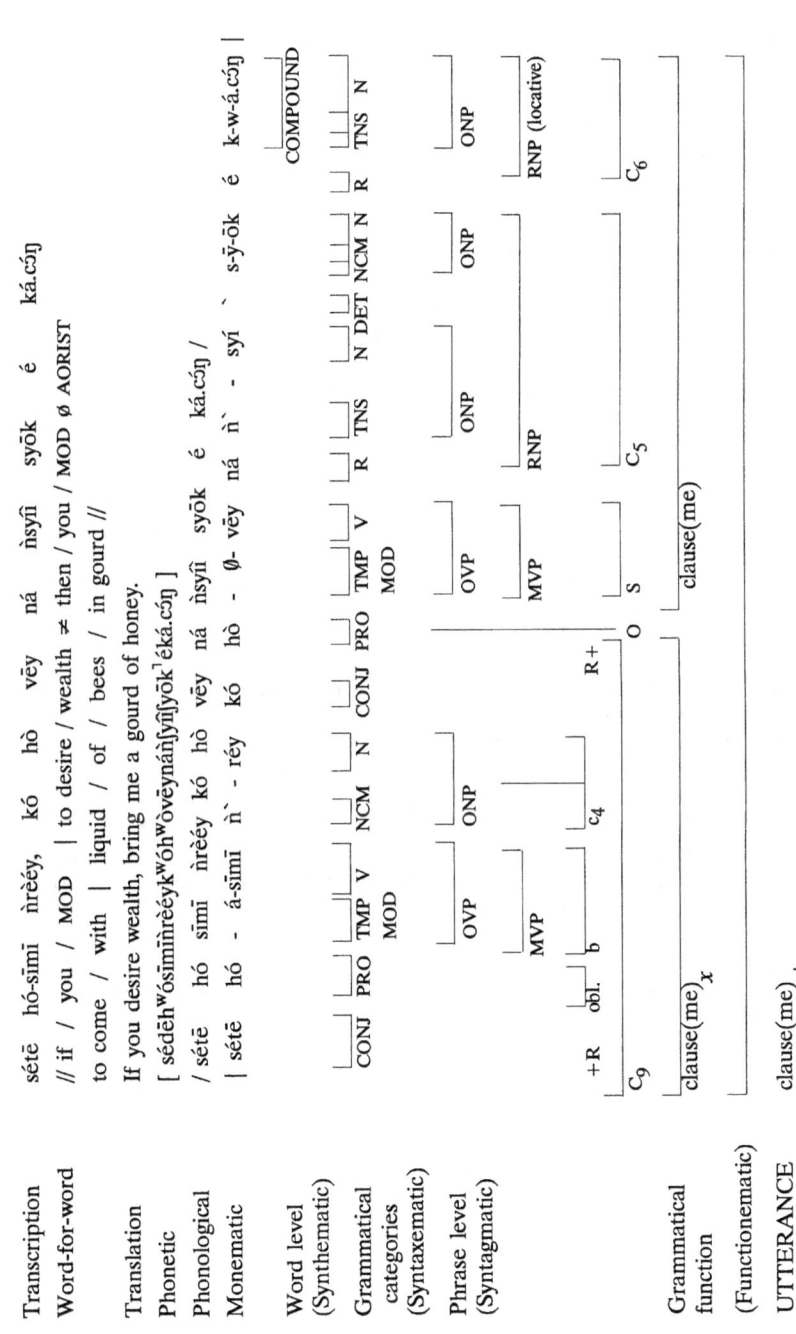

Birom (Notes on Table III)

On the phonetic level, it is not difficult to cut the string into meaningful elements because there are a number of demarcative signs, notably vowel harmony *(sédē, sīmī;* the sequence *a.ɔ* in *ká.cɔ́ŋ* indicates a compound). Also, certain phonemes may only occur initially *(h, ǹ, v)*, while other realizations are only possible in final position (e.g., the unreleased *[k¹]*, rising tones as in *ǹrèéy* or falling tones as in *ǹsyîi)*.

Continuing on to the phonological level, we note that the oral stops are generally voiced in medial position *[sédē]; k, g,* and *h* are labialized before *o* and *ɔ* *(hʷo, kʷo)*; *s* is palatalized before *y (ǹſyí, ſyōk¹);* the rising toneme is realized as rising from low to mid; and final consonants are not released: *ſyōk¹*.

As we pass to the moneme level, a series of fused forms appear: the subject pronoun and the verbal modality in | hò-á-sīmī | → *hó-sīmī;* the class marker with the noun: *ǹ`* (with low tone following) as in | ǹ` - réy | → *ǹrèéy*, | ǹ` syí | → *ǹsyí;* -w- in | k-w-á.cɔ́ŋ | → *ká.cɔ́ŋ;* the determiner with its head: | ǹ` syí ` s-ȳ-ōk | → *ǹsyîi syōk*.

On the word level (synthematic), the obligatory noun phrases characteristic of languages with noun classes appear. One of these, *ká.cɔ́ŋ,* has already been identified as a compound for phonological reasons: *c* may only occur at the beginning of a morpheme and the sequence *a.ɔ* is incompatible within a single morpheme.

On the higher levels, we can make the same observations as for Ngbaka.

The obligatory noun phrase is considered an indivisible unit, except on the level of morphological analysis, and is thus transcribed without a break. A hyphen joins the elements of a verbal form when they are fused (cf. *hó-sīmī*), or the elements of a compound when each is identifiable; otherwise, they are separated with a period (as in *ká.cɔ́ŋ*) (cf. Bouquiaux 1970b).

We conclude with some comments about the relationships between meaning, mechanism, and structure, as we see them. We trust that it is sufficiently clear from our remarks that all our formal and structural work could not be done without taking meaning into account. Our work centered basically on highlighting the fundamental processes that lead to communication, i.e., to the expression and to the apprehension of meaning. Meaning is involved in the functioning of the mechanisms, but the research procedure defining the operational units and levels of analysis transcends it.

Meaning is a fundamental issue of which we must be clearly aware in communication. While the utterance is seen as a sequence or interweaving of dependencies operating at different levels, the base of the utterance is the place where the grammatical base (the head par excellence) and the semantic foundation of the utterance coincide. The analysis pivots upon this indissociable grammatical/semantic base, whether directed toward functional research, which we have attempted, or toward semantic study.

Bibliography

This bibliography is not exhaustive. On the one hand, it lists theoretical or methodological works that inspired the present authors (sometimes through reaction) with a basis for their personal experiences. On the other hand, it gives works produced within the research framework, using the proposed methods and following the directions and theoretical options chosen, in order to test their efficacy and appropriateness, to refine them, to improve them, and if necessary to modify them.

Alvarez-Pereyre, Frank. 1982. Ethnolinguistique. Contributions théoriques et méthodologiques. Actes du Colloque d'Ivry, CNRS, 1979. LACITO–Documents, Eurasie 5. Paris: SELAF.

———, ed. 1979. Aspects de l'espace en Europe (Étude interdisciplinaire). Langues et civilisations à tradition orale 33. Paris: SELAF.

———, ed. 1982. Ethnolinguistique: contributions théoriques et méthodologiques. LACITO–Documents, Eurasie 5. Paris: SELAF.

Arom, Simha. 1969. Essai d'une notation des monodies à des fins d'analyse. Revue de Musicologie 55(2):172–216.

———. 1970a. Conte et chantefables ngbaka-ma'bo (République Centrafricaine). Bibliothèque 21–22. Paris: SELAF.

———. 1970b. Guide d'enquête pour la collecte d'instruments de musique. Ethnic Music Instruments. London: International Council of Museums.

———. 1972. Normes de catalogage: la fiche synoptique à codage visuel et l'analyse de collections d'instruments de musique. Copenhagen International Association of Musical Instruments–Conseil International des Musées.

———. 1973a. L'ethnomusicologie africaine. L'Afrique au sud du Sahara. Coll. Guides de Recherche, FNSP. Paris: Armand Colin.

———. 1973b. Esquisse d'une méthode de transcription de polyphonies et de polyrythmies de tradition orale. Musique en Jeu 13.

———. 1973c. La vie musicale en République Centrafricaine. Die Musik Geschichte in Bilder 2. Leipzig: Deutscher Verlag für Musik.

———. 1973d. La musique en Afrique, expression du 'sacré'? Axes Recherches pour un Dialogue entre Christianisme et Religiones 6(2):28–33.

———. 1974. Une méthode pour la transcription de polyphonies et de polyrythmies de tradition orale. Revue de Musicologie 59(2):165–90.

———. 1975a. Eléments pour une analyse fonctionnelle des monodies vocales. Les langues sans tradition écrite: enquête et description, 391–416. Colloques Internationaux du Centre National de la Recherche Scientifique, Nice, 28 June–2 July, 1971. NS 3. Paris: SELAF.

———. 1975b. Folk music of Central African Republic. Grove's dictionary of music and musicians. 6th ed. London.

———. 1975c. Afrique noire. Dictionnaire de la musique 3. Paris: Bordas (in collaboration with B. Lortat-Jacob).

———. 1975d. La situation de la musique en République Centrafricaine. Sohlmans Musiklexicon. Stockholm.

———. 1985. Polyphonies et polyrythmies instrumentales d'Afrique Centrale. Structure et méthodologie. Ethnomusicologie 1. Paris: SELAF.

——— and France Cloarec-Heiss. 1974. Rondes et jeux chantés banda-linda (République Centrafricaine). Paris: SELAF-ORSTOM (CETO).

——— and ———. 1975. Le langage tambouriné des Banda-Linda: morphologie et sémantique. In Luc Bouquiaux (ed.), Théories et méthodes en linguistique africaine. Paris: SELAF.

——— and Jacqueline Thomas. 1974. Les Mimbo, génies du piégeage et le monde surnaturel des Ngbaka-ma'bo (République Centrafricaine). Bibliothèque 44–45. Paris: SELAF.

Aubaile-Sallenave, Françoise. 1987. Bois et bateaux du Viêtnam. Ethnosciences 3. Paris: SELAF.

Bahuchet, Serge. 1985. Les pygmées aka et la forêt centrafricaine. Ethnologie écologique. Ethnosciences 1. Paris: SELAF.

———, ed. 1979. Pygmées de Centrafrique. Études historiques, ethnologiques et linguistiques sur les Pygmées 'Ba-Mbenga' (Aka/Baka) du Nord-Ouest du Bassin Congolais. Bibliothèque 73–74. Paris: SELAF.

Bensa, Alban and Jean-Claude Rivierre. 1982. Les chemins de l'Alliance. L'organisation sociale et ses représentations en Nouvelle-Calédonie. Langues et cultures du Pacifique 1. Paris: SELAF.

Benveniste, Emile. 1966. Problèmes de linguistique générale. Paris: Gallimard.

——— 1974. Problèmes de linguistique générale 2. Paris: Gallimard.

Bernot, Denis. 1978–1992. Dictionnaire birman–français (15 fascicules). Asie du sud-est et monde insulindien 3. Paris: Peeters–SELAF.

Bouquiaux, Luc. 1964. A propos de la phonologie du sara. Journal of African Languages 3(3):260–72.

———. 1967. Le système des classes nominales dans quelques langues (birom, ganawuri, anaguta, irigwe, kaje, rukuba) appartenant au groupe 'Plateau' (Nigéria Central) de la sous-famille bénoué-congo. La classification nominale dans les langues négro-africaines, 133–56. Paris: Centre National de la Recherche Scientifique.

———. 1969. La créolisation du français par le sango véhiculaire, phénomène réciproque. Annales de la F.L.S.H. de Nice 7:57–70.

———. 1970a. La langue birom (Nigéria septentrional): phonologie–morphologie–syntaxe. Paris: Belles Lettres.

———. 1970b. Textes birom (Nigéria septentrional) avec traduction et commentaires. Paris: Belles Lettres.

———. 1973. Quelques réflexions sur le système phonologique du rundi. Problèmes de phonologie, 113–19. Bibliothèque 38. Paris: SELAF.

———. 1974. Langues et cultures en République Centrafricaine. Cahiers du Centre Protestant pour la Jeunesse 15. Bangui.

———. 1975. Le travail en équipe: méthodes d'enquête et de description des langues à tradition orale: expériences de 1ER 74 du Centre National de la Recherche Scientifique. Les langues sans tradition écrite: enquête et description, 525–36. NS 3. Paris: SELAF.

———. 1976. Contes de Tôlé vu les avatars de l'aragne (Centrafrique). Paris: CILF.

———. 1977. L'arbre ngbè et les relations amoureuses chez les Ngbaka-ma'bo (République Centrafricaine). In G. Calame-Griaule (ed.), Ethno-linguistique africaine, 103–14. Paris: Maspero.

———. 1978. Recherche fondamentale et enseignement des langues africaines. Recherche, Pédagogie et Culture 34.

———. 1983. Sango, Lexicon der Afrikanistik. In H. Jungraithmayr and W. J. G. Möhlig (eds.), Afrikanische Sprachen und ihre Erforschung. Berlin: D. Reimer.

———. 1985. Syntaxématique: définition et classement des unités syntaxiques ou catégories grammaticales ou parties du discours. Actes du XIe Colloque International de Linguistique Fonctionnelle, Bologne, 2–7 July, 1984. Rapport de l'atelier 2: phonologie–morphonologie–morphologie. Padoue: CLESP.

———. 1986. Syntaxématique: définition et classement des unités syntaxiques ou catégories grammaticales ou parties du discours. Modèles Linguistiques 8(1).

———. 1987a. Les problèmes théoriques de la description des langues d'Afrique. Diogène 137.

———. 1987b. Theoretical problems in the description of African languages. Diogenes 137.

———. 1989. Les développements récents de la grammaire comparée et des classifications linguistiques en Afrique sub-saharienne. Linguistique aréale et recherches comparatives. Mémoires de la Société de Linguistique de Paris, Nouvelle Série 1.

———, ed. 1979. Multilinguisme dans les domaines bantou de nord-ouest et tchadique. Le point de la question en 1977 (ATP 'Internationale du CNRS'). LACITO–Documents, Afrique 3. Paris: SELAF.

———, Daniel Barreteau, Raymond Boyd, Gladys Guarisma, Patrick Renaud, Michka Sachnine, and Jacqueline Thomas. 1974. Questionnaire d'inventaire linguistique–QIL. 2nd ed. Yaoundé and Paris: SLA and SELAF.

———, France Cloarec-Heiss, and Jacqueline Thomas. 1976. Initiation à la phonétique: phonétique articulatoire et distinctive. Le linguiste. Paris: Presses Universitaires de France.

———, Gladys Guarisma, and Gabriel Manessy, eds. 1980. Problèmes de comparatisme et de dialectologie dans les langues africaines. Bibliothèque 83. Paris: SELAF.

———, Jean-Marie Kobozo, and Marcel Diki-Kidiri. 1978. Dictionnaire sango–français et lexique français–sango. Langues et civilisations à tradition orale 29. Paris: SELAF.

———, Gabriel Manessy, and Jan Voorhoeve, eds. 1980. L'expansion bantoue. Actes du Colloque International du CNRS, Viviers, April 1977. NS 9. Paris: SELAF.

―――― and Serge Sauvageot. 1989. De quelques indices d'influences aréales dans le domaine négro-africain. Linguistique aréale et recherches comparatives. Mémoires de la Société de Linguistique de Paris, Nouvelle Série 1.

―――― and Jacqueline Thomas. 1975. Une aire de génération de tons en Afrique Centrale: problèmes tonaux dans quelques langues oubanguiennes et bantoues périphériques. IIe Congrès de Linguistique Fonctionnelle, Clermont-Ferrand, July 1975.

Boyd, Raymond. 1974. Étude comparative dans le groupe Adamawa. Bibliothèque 46. Paris: SELAF.

―――― and France Cloarec-Heiss. 1978. Études comparatives. Oubanguien et Niger-Congo–Nilo-Saharien. Bibliothèque 65. Paris: SELAF.

Boyeldieu, Pascal. 1973. Phonologie du yakoma. Problèmes de phonologie, 11–72. Bibliothèque 38. Paris: SELAF.

――――. 1975a. Études yakoma, langue du groupe oubangien (République Centrafricaine): morphologie–synthématique. Bibliothèque 47–48. Paris: SELAF.

――――. 1975b. Esquisse phonologique du lua ou 'niellim'. Phonologies des langues bua. Études et documents tchadiens, série C, Linguistique 2. Ndjamena: INSH.

――――. 1985. La langue lua (niellim) (groupe Boua-Moyen Chari, Tchad): phonologie–morphologie–dérivation verbale. Description de langues et monographies ethnolinguistiques 1. Paris: SELAF.

――――, ed. 1987. La maison du chef et la tête du cabri. Des degrés de détermination nominale dans les langues d'Afrique Centrale. LACITO. Paris: Geuthner.

―――― and Marcel Diki-Kidiri. 1982. Le domaine ngbandi (Centrafrique). Bibliothèque 93. Paris: SELAF.

―――― and Christian Seignobos. 1974. Contribution à l'étude du pays niellim (Moyen-Chari-Tchad): géographie humaine–linguistique–socio-linguistique. Ndjamena: INSH.

Calame-Griaule, Geneviève. 1967. Essai d'étude stylistique d'un texte dogon. Journal of West African Languages 4:15–24.

――――. 1969–1974. Le thème de l'arbre dans les contes 1, 2, et 3. Bibliothèque 16, 20, 42–43. Paris: SELAF.

――――. 1970. Pour une étude ethnolinguistique des littératures orales africaines. Langages 18:22–47.

――――. 1971. Étude stylistique d'un conte dogon. Afrikanische Sprachen and Kulturen, 266–78. Hamburg: Deutsches Institut für Afrika-Forschung.

――――. 1975. Pour une étude des gestes narratifs. In G. Calame-Griaule (ed.), Langages et cultures africaines, essais d'ethnolinguistique. Paris: Maspéro.

Canu, Gaston. 1976. La langue mò:rē, dialecte de Ouagadougou: description synchronique (Haute-Volta). Langues et civilisations à tradition orale 16. Paris: SELAF.

Caprile, Jean-Pierre. 1968. Essai de phonologie d'un parler mbay. Les emprunts arabes en mbay. Bibliothèque 8. Paris: SELAF.

――――. 1969. Lexique mbay–français. Lyons Afrique et Langage (Documents 2).

――――. 1971. La dénomination des couleurs chez les Mbay de Moïssala (une ethnie sara du sud du Tchad). Bibliothèque 26. Paris: SELAF.

――――. 1973a. Lexique toumak–français et index français–toumak. Marburg: Institut d'Études Africaines de l'Université de Marburg.

――――. 1973b. Les langues africaines et la situation linguistique au Tchad. Revue Pédagogique Tchadienne 10:75–84.

———. 1973c. Étude contrastive du phonisme des parlers du groupe 'sara' et du français. Ndjamena: Université du Tchad.

———. 1973d. Quelques particularismes du français parlé dans le sud du Tchad, petit vocabulaire du frandien. Revue Pédagogique Tchadienne 10:85–99.

———. 1975a. La dénomination des couleurs en mbay: problèmes d'enquête. Les langues sans tradition écrite: enquête et description. NS 3. Paris: SELAF.

———. 1975b. Inventaire des langues du Tchad. In J. Cabot (ed.), Atlas du Tchad.

———. 1975c. Étude comparative sur les langues de la famille tchadique parlées entre le Chari et le Logone dans le sud du Tchad. Africana Marburgensia.

———. 1976a. The languages of Chad. Chicago: Encyclopaedia Britannica.

———. 1976b. La situation socio-linguistique du français au Tchad, au Niger et en République Centrafricaine. In G. Manessy (ed.), Le français hors de France: L'Afrique au sud du Sahara.

———. 1978a. Contacts de langues en Afrique 1. Démographie linguistique: approche quantitative. LACITO–Documents, Afrique 4. Paris: SELAF.

———. 1978b. Contacts de langues en Afrique 2. La situation au Tchad: approache globale au niveau national. LACITO–Documents, Afrique 5. Paris: SELAF.

———. 1978c. Contacts de langues en Afrique 3. La création lexicale spontanée en Afrique Centrale par emprunt au français. LACITO–Documents, Afrique 6. Paris: SELAF.

———. 1981. Les langues bongo–baguirmiennes et leur classification. In G. Manessy (ed.), Description des langues du monde 1: Afrique. Paris: Centre National de la Recherche Scientifique.

———. 1982. Contacts de langues et contacts de cultures 4. L'expansion des langues africaines: peul, sango, kikongo, ciluba, swahili. LACITO–Documents, Afrique 8. Paris: SELAF.

———, ed. 1977. Études phonologiques tchadiennes. Bibliothèque 63–64. Paris: SELAF.

——— and Christian Bouquet. 1976. Quelques aspects démographiques de l'extinction d'une langue: le cas du babalia au Tchad. Théories et méthodes en linguistique africaine. Bibliothèque 54–55. Paris: SELAF.

——— and Jacques Fedry. 1969. Le groupe des langues 'sara' (République du Tchad). Archives linguistiques 1. Lyons: Afrique et Langage.

——— and Claude Gadbin. 1972. Remarques sur les insectes ravageurs du mil et sur les dénominations des papillons chez les Mbay (République du Tchad). Paris: JATBA: 572–74.

——— and Hermann Jungraithmayr. 1973. Inventaire provisoire des langues 'tchadiques', parlées sur le territoire de la République du Tchad. Africana Marburgensia 6:231–48.

——— and ———, eds. 1978. Préalables à la reconstruction du Proto-Tchadique. LACITO–Documents, Afrique 2. Paris: SELAF.

——— and Christian Seignobos. 1974. Esquisse de présentation du pays tobanga ou 'gabri-nord' (Préfecture de la Tandjilé et du Mayo-Kebi, Tchad). Ndjamena: Université du Tchad.

Charpentier, Jean-Michel. 1979a. La langue de Port-Sandwich (Nouvelles-Hébrides). Introduction phonologique et grammaire. Langues et civilisations à tradition orale 34. Paris: SELAF.

———. 1979b. Le pidgin bislama(n) et le multilinguisme aux Nouvelles-Hébrides. Langues et civilisations à tradition orale 35. Paris: SELAF.

———. 1983. Atlas linguistique du Sud-Malakula–Linguistic atlas of south Malakula (Vanuatu). Langues et cultures du Pacifique 2. Paris: SELAF.

Clément-Charpentier, Sophie and Pierre Clément. 1990. L'habitation lao dans les régions de Vientiane et de Louang-Prabang. Asie et monde insulindien 18, 21. Paris: Peeters–SELAF.

Cloarec-Heiss, France. 1967. Essai de phonologie du parler banda-linda de Ippy (République Centrafricaine). Bibliothèque 3. Paris: SELAF.

———. 1969. Banda-linda de Ippy. Phonologie, dérivation et composition 1. Les modalités personnelles dans quelques langues oubanguiennes 2. Bibliothèque 14. Paris: SELAF.

———. 1972. Le verbe banda: étude du syntagme verbal dans une langue oubanguienne de République Centrafricaine. Langues et civilisations à tradition orale 3. Paris: SELAF.

———. 1986. Dynamique et équilibre d'une syntaxe: le banda-linda de Centrafrique. Description de langues et monographies ethnolinguistiques 2. Paris: SELAF.

——— and Jacqueline Thomas. 1978. L'aka, langue bantoue des Pygmées de Mongoumba (République Centrafricaine): phonologie. Introduction à l'étude linguistique. Langues et civilisations à tradition orale 28. Paris: SELAF.

Cohen, Marcel. 1950. Instructions pour les voyageurs: instructions d'enquête linguistique. 2nd ed. Paris: Institut d'Ethnologie.

———. 1950–51. Questionnaire linguistique. Comité International Permanent de Linguistes, Commission d'Enquête Linguistique. Republished. Netherlands: Nimeguen.

Colombel, Véronique de. 1986a. Phonologie quantitative et synthématique. Propositions méthodologiques et théoriques avec application à l'ouldémé (langue tchadique du Nord-Cameroun). Introduction géographique, historique et ethnologique. Langues et cultures africaines 7. Paris: SELAF.

———. 1986b. Structure et quantification. Propositions méthodologiques en phonologie. Usage de la quantification. Bulletin de la Société de Linguistique de Paris: 53–69.

Dehoux, Vincent. 1986. Chants à penser gbaya de Centrafrique. Ethnomusicologie 2. Paris: SELAF.

Delobeau, Jean-Michel. 1983. Yamonzombo et Yandenga. Relations entre villages monzombo et campements pygmées aka (sous-préfecture de Mongoumba, Centrafrique). Bibliothèque 97–98. Paris: SELAF.

Demesse, Lucien. 1978. Changements techno-économiques et sociaux chez les Pygmées babinga (Nord-Congo et Sud-Centrafrique). Langues et civilisations à tradition orale 26. Paris: SELAF.

———. 1980. Techniques et économie des Pygmées babinga. Paris: Institut d'Ethnologie.

Derive, Jean. 1976a. Collecte et traduction des littératures orales: un exemple négro-africain, les contes ngbaka-ma'bo (République Centrafricaine). Langues et civilisations à tradition orale 18. Paris: SELAF.

———. 1976b. La pluralité des versions et l'analyse des oeuvres du genre narratif oral: d'après un exemple ngbaka-ma'bo (République Centrafricaine). In G. Calame-Griaule (ed.), Langages et cultures africaines, essais d'ethnolinguistique, 265–302. Paris: Maspéro.

Derive, Marie-Jo. 1990. Étude dialectologique de l'aire manding de Côte-d'Ivoire. Langues et cultures africaines 11. Paris: Peeters–SELAF.

———, Jean Derive, and Jacqueline M. C. Thomas. 1975. La crotte tenace et autres contes ngbaka-ma'bo de République Centrafricaine. Langues et civilisations à tradition orale 13. Paris: SELAF.

Deschamps-Wenezoui, Mattine. 1981. Le français, le sango et les autres langues centrafricaines. Enquête sociolinguistique au quartier Boy-Rabe (Bangui, Centrafrique). Langues et civilisations à tradition orale 49. Paris: SELAF.

Dieu, Michel. 1975. Première esquisse phonologique du lobiri. Notes Voltaïques.

———, Patrick Renaud, and Michka Sachnine. 1976. Étude de la situation sociolinguistique du Cameroun: programme et méthodes. Théories et méthodes en linguistique africaine. Bibliothèque 54–55. Paris: SELAF.

Diki-Kidiri, Marcel. 1977. Le sango s'écrit aussi: esquisse linguistique du sango, langue nationale de l'Empire Centrafricain. Langues et civilisations à tradition orale 24. Paris: SELAF.

Doneux, Jean. 1966. Introduction pratique à l'étude et à la description des langues africaines. Dakar: Fraternité Saint-Dominique.

———. 1967. Questionnaires d'enquête linguistique destinés aux langues négro-africaines (Greenberg–Tervuren–Welmers). Documents linguistiques 9. Dakar: Université-Faculté des Lettres et Sciences Humaines.

Drettas, Georges. 1980. La mère et l'outil. Contribution à l'étude sémantique du tissage rural dans la Bulgarie actuelle. Langues et civilisations à tradition orale 39. Paris: SELAF.

Ducos, Gisèle. 1971. Structure du badiaranke de Guinée et du Sénégal: phonologie-syntaxe. Bibliothèque 27, 28. Paris: SELAF.

Ferry, Marie-Paule. 1968. Deux langues tenda du Sénégal Oriental, basari et bedik. Bibliothèque 7. Paris: SELAF.

———. 1991. Thesaurus tenda. Dictionnaire ethnolinguistique de langues sénégalo-guinéennes (bassari–bedik–konyagi). Langues et cultures africaines 15. Paris: Peeters–SELAF.

François, Frédéric. 1968. La description linguistique. Le langage. Encyclopédie de la Pléiade 25:171–282.

Frimigacci, Daniel. 1990. Aux temps de la terre noire. Ethnoarchéologie des Iles Futuna et Alofi. Langues et cultures du Pacifique 7. Paris: Peeters–SELAF.

Greenberg, Joseph H. 1963. The languages of Africa. The Hague: Mouton.

Grenand, Françoise. 1981. La langue wayãpi: phonologie-grammaire (Guyane française). Langues et civilisations à tradition orale 41. Paris: SELAF.

———. 1989. Dictionnaire wayãpi-français. Lexique français-wayãpi (Guyane française). Langues et sociétés d'Amérique traditionnelle 1. Paris: Peeters–SELAF.

Grenand, Pierre. 1980. Introduction à l'étude de l'univers wayãpi. Ethnoécologie des Indiens du Haut-Oyapock (Guyane française). Langues et civilisations à tradition orale 40. Paris: SELAF.

Guarisma, Gladys. 1967. Esquisse phonologique du bafia. Bibliothèque 1. Paris: SELAF.

———. 1969. Études bafia: phonologie, classes d'accord et lexique bafia–français. Bibliothèque 15. Paris: SELAF.

———. 1972a. Sur la détermination des catégories grammaticales en bafia par la méthode de l'énoncé minimum. Notes linguistiques. Bibliothèque 32. Paris: SELAF.

———. 1972b. Notes sur la phonologie du vuté (Cameroun). Bibliothèque 32. Paris: SELAF.

———. 1973. Le nom en bafia: étude du syntagme nominal d'une langue bantoue du Cameroun. Bibliothèque 36–37. Paris: SELAF.

———. 1978. Études vute (langue bantoïde du Cameroun): phonologie et alphabet pratique, synthématique, lexique vouté–français. Bibliothèque 66–67. Paris: SELAF.

———, ed. 1981. Tons et accents dans les langues africaines. LACITO–Documents, Afrique 7. Paris: SELAF.

——— and Suzy Platiel, eds. 1980. Dialectologie et comparatisme en Afrique Noire. Oralité–Documents 2. Paris: SELAF.

———, Gabriel Nissim, and Jan Voorhoeve, eds. 1982. Le verbe bantou. Oralité–Documents 4. Paris: SELAF.

Guédou, Georges A. G. 1985. Xó et gbè. Langage et culture chez les Fon (Bénin). Langues et cultures africaines 4. Paris: SELAF.

Guthrie, Malcolm. n.d. Bantu questionnaire.

Hagège, Claude. 1968. Description phonologique du mbum. Bibliothèque 5. Paris: SELAF.

———. 1969. Esquisse linguistique du tikar (Cameroun). Bibliothèque 11. Paris: SELAF.

———. 1970. La langue mbum de Nganha (Cameroun): phonologie–grammaire. Bibliothèque 18–19. Paris: SELAF.

———. 1972. On system constraints in the presentation of the phonemes of Mundang (Lere, Chad). Fourth Conference on African Linguistics. Indiana University, Bloomington.

———. 1974a. Profil d'un parler arabe du Tchad. Comptes rendus du Groupe Linguistique d'Études Chamito-Sémitiques, supplément 2: Atlas linguistique du monde arabe, Matériaux 1. Paris: Geuthner.

———. 1974b. La 'ponctuation' dans quelques langues de l'oralité (mbum, mundang, tuburi, guidar et tera). Mélanges offerts à Emile Benvéniste. Paris: Société de Linguistique.

———. 1975a. Les pronoms logophoriques. Bulletin de la Société de Linguistique de Paris 69(1):287–310.

———. 1975b. The 'adjective' in some Central African languages. Fifth Congress of American Africanists, Stanford.

———. 1976a. La grammaire générative. Réflexions critiques. Le linguiste 17. Paris: Presses Universitaires de France.

———. 1976b. Notes sur la situation linguistique dans le Cameroun central. Contribution de la recherche ethnologique à l'histoire des civilisations du Cameroun. Paris: Centre National de la Recherche Scientifique.

———. 1981. Les langues de l'Adamawa et leur classification. In G. Manessy (ed.), Description des langues du monde 1: Afrique. Paris: Centre National de la Recherche Scientifique.

———. 1982. La structure des langues. Que sais-je? Paris: Presses Universitaires de France.

——— and André G. Haudricourt. 1978. La phonologie panchronique. Le linguiste. Paris: Presses Universitaires de France.

Haudricourt, André G. 1971. See bibliography of André G. Haudricourt, Langues et techniques. Nature et société (Hommage à André G. Haudricourt). Paris: Klincksieck.

———. 1972. Problèmes de phonologie diachronique. Langues et civilisations à tradition orale 1. Paris: SELAF.

——— and Louis Hédin. 1987. L'homme et les plantes cultivées. 2nd ed. Paris: Métailié.

——— and Françoise Ozanne-Rivierre. 1982. Dictionnaire thématique des langues de la région de Hienghène (Nouvelle-Calédonie). LACITO–Documents, Asie–Austronésie 4. Paris: SELAF.

——— and Jacqueline Thomas. 1967. La notation des langues: phonétique et phonologie. Paris: Institut Géographique National and Institut d'Ethnologie.

Houis, Maurice. 1967. Aperçu sur les structures grammaticales des langues négro-africaines. Réflexions sur le langage en Afrique noire. Lyon: Faculté de Théologie.

Jungraithmayr, Herrmann, ed. 1986. Langues tchadiques et langues non tchadiques en contact en Afrique Centrale. Actes de la Table Ronde franco-allemande, Ivry, France, 8–12 December, 1978. LACITO–Documents, Afrique 10. Paris: SELAF.

Lacroix, Pierre-Francis, ed. 1972. L'expression du temps dans quelques langues de l'ouest africain: études lexicales. Bibliothèque 29. Paris: SELAF.

———. 1975. Quelques réflexions sur les questionnaires d'enquête et l'usage qui peut en être fait. Les langues sans tradition écrite: méthodes d'enquête et de description. NS 3. Paris: SELAF.

——— and Suzanne Platiel. 1975. Questionnaires d'enquête de l'ERA 246 du Centre National de la Recherche Scientifique. Les langues sans tradition écrite: méthodes d'enquête et de description. NS 3. Paris: SELAF.

Ladefoged, Peter. 1964. A phonetic study of West African languages: An auditory-instrumental survey. West African Languages monograph 1. London: Cambridge University Press.

La Fontinelle, Jacqueline de. 1976. La langue de Houaïlou, Nouvelle Calédonie: description phonologique et description syntaxique. Langues et civilisations à tradition orale 17. Paris: SELAF.

Latouche, Jean-Paul. 1984. Mythistoire tungaru. Cosmologies et généalogies aux Iles Gilbert. Langues et cultures du Pacifique 5. Paris: SELAF.

Leiderer, Rosmarie and Gladys Guarisma. 1982. La médecine traditionnelle chez les Bekpak (Bafia) du Cameroun. Collectanea Instituti Anthropos 26–27. Sankt Augustin: Haus Völker und Kulturen.

Leroi-Gourhan, André. 1943. L'homme et la matière. Paris: Albin Michel.

———. 1945. Milieu et technique. Paris: Albin Michel.

———. 1947. Le geste et la parole. Paris: Albin Michel.

Lortat-Jacob, Bernard. 1987. L'improvisation dans les musiques de tradition orale. Ethnomusicologie 4. Paris: Peeters–SELAF.

Manessy, Gabriel. 1960a. La morphologie du nom en bwamu (bobo-oulé), dialecte de Bondoukuy. Publications de la section des langues et littératures 4. Dakar: Faculté des Lettres et Sciences Humaines.

———. 1960b. Tâches quotidiennes et travaux saisonniers en pays bwa. Publications de la section des langues et littératures 5. Dakar: Faculté des Lettres et Sciences Humaines.

———. 1969. Les langues gurunsi: essai d'application de la méthode comparative à un groupe de langues voltaïques 1 et 2. Bibliothèque 12–13. Paris: SELAF.

———. 1971. Les langues gurma. Bulletin de l'IFAN 23(1):117–246, Series B.

———. 1975. Les langues oti-volta: classification généalogique d'un groupe de langues voltaïques. Langues et civilisations à tradition orale 15. Paris: SELAF.

———. 1979. Contribution à la classification généalogique des langues voltaïques: le proto-central. Langues et civilisations à tradition orale 37. Paris: SELAF.

——— and Maurice Houis, eds. 1967. La classification nominale dans les langues négro-africaines. Paris: Centre National de la Recherche Scientifique.

——— and Jacqueline Thomas, eds. 1975. Les langues sans tradition écrite: méthodes d'enquête et de description. NS 3. Paris: SELAF.

Martin, Pierre. 1991. Le montagnais. Langue algonquienne du Québec. Langues et sociétés d'Amérique traditionnelle 3. Paris: Peeters–SELAF.

Martinet, André. 1956. La description phonologique, avec application au parler franco-provençal d'Hauteville. Paris: Droz–Minard.
———. 1961. A functional view of language. Oxford: Clarendon.
———. 1965. La linguistique synchronique. Le linguiste 1. Paris: Presses Universitaires de France.
———. 1967. Eléments de linguistique générale. 2nd ed. Paris: Armand Colin.
———. 1969a. La linguistique: guide alphabétique. Paris: Denoël.
———. 1969b. Elements of general linguistics. London: Faber & Faber.
———. 1985. Syntaxe générale. Coll. 'U'. Paris: A. Colin.
Mazaudon, Martine. 1973. Phonologie tamang: étude phonologique du dialecte tamang de Risiangku (langue tibéto-birmane du Népal). Langues et civilisations à tradition orale 4. Paris: SELAF.
Meeussen, Achiel E. 1962. L'informateur en linguistique africaine. Aequatoria 25(3):92–94.
Moïnfar, Djafar. 1974. L'accentuation dans les parlers arabes du Tchad. Mélanges linguistiques offerts à Emile Benvéniste. Paris: Société de Linguistique.
Moñino, Yves. 1970. Dérivation, composition et emprunt dans le vocabulaire des techniques ngbaka-ma'bo (République Centrafricaine). La linguistique 6:117–46.
———. 1972. Comparaison de quatre parlers gbaya-manza. Bibliothèque 32. Paris: SELAF.
———. 1977. Conceptions du monde et langue d'initiation l'á6ì des Gbaya-Kara (République Centrafricaine). In G. Calame-Griaule (ed.), Langage et cultures africaines, essais d'ethnolinguistique, 115–47. Paris: Maspéro.
———, ed. 1988. Lexique comparatif des langues oubanguiennes. Paris: Geuthner.
——— and Paulette Roulon. 1972. Phonologie du gbaya kara 6odoe de Ndongué Bongowen (région de Bouar, République Centrafricaine). Bibliothèque 31. Paris: SELAF.
Monod-Becquelin, Aurore. 1975a. La pratique linguistique des indiens Trumai (Haut-Xingu, Mato Grosso, Brésil). Langues et civilisations à tradition orale 9. Paris: SELAF.
———. 1975b. Mythes trumai (Haut-Xingu, Mato Grosso, Brésil). Langues et civilisations à tradition orale 10. Paris: SELAF.
Motte, Elisabeth. 1980. Les plantes chez les Pygmées aka et les Monzomno de la Lobaye (Centrafrique). Contribution à une étude ethnobotanique comparative chez des chasseurs-cueilleurs et des pêcheurs-cultivateurs vivant dans un même milieu végétal. Bibliothèque 80–82. Paris: SELAF.
Moyse-Faurie, Claire. 1983. Le drehu, langue de Lifou (Iles Loyauté). Phonologie, morphologie, syntaxe. Langues et cultures du Pacifique 3. Paris: SELAF.
Ndïaye-Correard, Geneviève. 1970. Études fca ou balante (dialecte ganja). Bibliothèque 17. Paris: SELAF.
Nida, Eugene A. 1946. Syntax: A descriptive analysis. Glendale, CA: Summer Institute of Linguistics.
———. 1947. Field techniques in descriptive linguistics. International Journal of American Linguistics 13:138–46.
———. 1949. Morphology: The descriptive analysis of words. Ann Arbor: University of Michigan Press.
Nissim, Gabriel. 1981. Le bamileke gomala' (parler de Bandjoun, Cameroun). Phonologie, morphologie nominale, comparaison avec des parlers voisins. Langues et civilisations à tradition orale 45. Paris: SELAF.

Nougayrol, Pierre. 1979. Le day de Bouna (Tchad). Eléments de description linguistique: phonologie–syntagmatique nominale–synthématique, 1. Bibliothèque 71–72. Paris: SELAF.

———. 1980. Le day de Bouna (Tchad). Lexique day–français–day, 2. Bibliothèque 77–78. Paris: SELAF.

———. 1989. La langue des Aiki dits Rounga (Tchad–République Centrafricaine). Esquisse descriptive et lexique. Paris: Geuthner.

Ozanne-Rivierre, Françoise. 1976. Le iaai (langue mélanésienne d'Ouvéa), Nouvelle Calédonie: phonologie–morphologie–esquisse syntaxique. Langues et civilisations à tradition orale 20. Paris: SELAF.

———. 1979. Textes nemi (Nouvelle-Calédonie). Katvatch et Tendo 1. Bas-Coulna et Haut-Coulna 2. Lexique nemi–français. Langues et civilisations à tradition orale 31–32. Paris: SELAF.

———. 1984. Dictionnaire iaai (Ouvéa, Nouvelle-Calédonie). Langues et cultures du Pacifique 6. Paris: SELAF.

Paulian, Christiane. 1971. Esquisse phonologique du duala (Cameroun). Études bantoues 2. Bibliothèque 25. Paris: SELAF.

———. 1975. Le kukuya, langue teke du Congo: phonologie–classes nominales. Bibliothèque 49–50. Paris: SELAF.

Platiel, Suzanne. 1972. Esquisse d'une étude du musey. Bibliothèque 6. Paris: SELAF.

Randa, Vladimir. 1986. L'ours polaire et les Inuit. Ethnosciences 2. Paris: SELAF.

Renaud, Patrick. 1976. Description phonologique et éléments de morphologie nominale d'une langue pygmée du Sud-Cameroun: la langue des Bagyeli (Bipindi). Les dossiers de l'ALCAM 1–2. Yaoundé: ONAREST.

Revel, Nicole. 1990a. Fleurs de paroles. Histoire naturelle palawan 1. Les dons de Nägsalad. Ethnosciences 5. Paris: Peeters–SELAF.

———. 1990b. Fleurs de paroles. Histoire naturelle palawan 2. La maîtrise d'un savoir et l'art d'une relation. Ethnosciences 6. Paris: Peeters–SELAF.

———. 1992. Fleurs de paroles. Histoire naturelle palawan 3. Chants d'amour–chants d'oiseaux. Ethnosciences 7. Paris: Peeters–SELAF.

Revel-Macdonald, Nicole. 1979. Le palawan (Philippines): phonologie–catégories–morphologie. Asie du sud-est et monde insulindien 4. Paris: SELAF.

Rivierre, Jean-Claude. 1973. Phonologie comparée des dialectes de l'extrême-sud de la Nouvelle-Calédonie. Langues et civilisations à tradition orale 5. Paris: SELAF.

———. 1980. La langue de Touho: phonologie et grammaire du cèmuhî (Nouvelle-Calédonie). Langues et civilisations à tradition orale 38. Paris: SELAF.

———. 1983. Dictionnaire paici–français, suivi d'un lexique français–paici. Langues et cultures du Pacifique 4. Paris: SELAF.

———, Ozanne-Rivierre Françoise, and Claire Moyse-Faurie. 1980. Mythes et contes de la Grande-Terre et des Iles Loyauté (Nouvelle-Calédonie). LACITO–Documents, Asie–Austronésie 3. Paris: SELAF.

Rombi, Marie-Françoise. 1984. Le shimaore (Ile de Mayotte, Comores). Première approche d'un parler de la langue comorienne. Langues et cultures africaines 3. Paris: SELAF.

———, ed. 1982. Études sur le bantou oriental (Comores, Tanzanie, Somalie et Kenya). Dialectologie et classification. LACITO–Documents, Afrique 9. Paris: SELAF.

Roulon, Paulette. 1968. Essai pour une phonologie du tyembara, dialecte sénoufo parlé à Korhogo (Côte d'Ivoire). Bibliothèque 9. Paris: SELAF.

———. 1972. Étude du français et du sango parlés par les Ngbaka-ma'bo (République Centrafricaine). Ethnies 2.

———. 1975. Le verbe en gbáyá: étude syntaxique et sémantique du syntagme verbal en gbáyá kàrá ɓòdòè, République Centrafricaine. Bibliothèque 51–52. Paris: SELAF.
———. 1977. Classifications gbaya des animaux. In G. Calame-Griaule (ed.), Langage et cultures africaines, essais d'ethnolinguistique. Paris: Maspéro.
Ruelland, Suzanne. 1973. La fille sans mains: analyse de dix-neuf versions du conte type 706. Bibliothèque 39–40. Paris: SELAF.
———. 1988. Dictionnaire tupuri–français–anglais (région de Mindaoré, Tchad). Langues et cultures africaines 10. Paris: Peeters–SELAF.
Sachnine, Michka. 1976. Esquisse phonologique et morphologique du lame (langue tchadique du Cameroun). Africana Marburgensia.
———. 1982. Le lamé. Un parler Zime du Nord-Cameroun: phonologie–dictionnaire. Langues et cultures africaines 1. Paris: SELAF.
Samarin, William J. 1967. Field linguistics: A guide to linguistic field work. New York: Holt, Rinehart and Winston.
Sebeok, Thomas A., ed. 1967–1971. Current trends in linguistics. Linguistics in East Asia and South East Asia 2; Linguistics in South Asia 5; Linguistics in South West Asia and North Africa 6; Linguistics in Sub-Saharan Africa 7; Linguistics in Oceania 8. The Hague: Mouton.
Sivers, Fanny de. 1978. Structuration de l'espace dans les langues de la Baltique orientale. LACITO–Documents, Eurasie 1. Paris: SELAF.
———. 1979. La main et les doigts dans l'expression linguistique, 1. LACITO–Documents, Eurasie 4. Paris: SELAF.
———. 1980. La main et les doigts dans l'expression linguistique, 2. LACITO–Documents, Eurasie 6. Paris: SELAF.
———. 1984. Structuration de l'espace dans les langues de la Baltique orientale 2. Organisation de l'espace habité. LACITO–Documents, Eurasie 7. Paris: SELAF.
———. 1989. Questions d'identité. Sociolinguistique 4. Paris: Peeters–SELAF.
Surugue, Bernard. 1972. Contribution à l'étude de la musique sacrée zarma-songhay. Niamey: Études Nigériennes.
———. 1979. Études gulmance Niger: phonologie–classes nominales–lexique. Bibliothèque 75–76. Paris: SELAF.
Tersis, Nicole. 1967. Essai pour une phonologie du gurma parlé à Kpana (Nord-Togo) et lexique gurma–français. Bibliothèque 4. Paris: SELAF.
———. 1968. Le dendi (Niger). Phonologie. Lexique dendi–français. Emprunts (arabe, hausa, français, anglais). Bibliothèque 10. Paris: SELAF.
———. 1972. Le zarma (République de Niger): étude du parler djerma de Dosso. Bibliothèque 33–34. Paris: SELAF.
———. 1976. La mare de la vérité: contes et musique zarma (Niger). Langues et civilisations à tradition orale 19. Paris: SELAF–ORSTOM.
——— and Alan Kihm, eds. 1988. Temps et aspects. Actes du Colloque CNRS, Paris, 24–25 October, 1985. NS 19. Paris: Peeters–SELAF.
Tersis-Surugue, Nicole. 1981. Economie d'un sysème: unités et relations syntaxiques en zarma (Niger). Bibliothèque 87–88. Paris: SELAF.
Therrien, Michèle. 1987. Le corps inuit (Québec arctique). Arctique 1. Paris: SELAF.
Thomas, Jacqueline M. C. 1959. Notes d'ethnobotanique africaine: plantes utilisées dans la région de la Lobaye (Afrique centrale). JATBA 6(8,9):353–90.
———. 1960a. Quelques plantes connues des Ngbaka de la Lobaye. Journal de la Société des Africanistes 30:75–93.

———. 1960b. Sur quelques plantes cultivées chez les Ngbaka de la Lobaye (République Centrafricaine). Bulletin de l'Institut d'Études Centrafricaines (Brazzaville). NS 19–20:5–43.

———. 1963. Le parler ngbaka de Bokanga: phonologie–morphologie–syntaxe. Le Monde d'outre-mer, passé et présent. Series 1. Études 22. The Hague: Mouton.

———. 1965. Considérations sur le système des tons en twi. La linguistique 2:123–28. Paris: Presses Universitaires de France.

———. 1967. Linguistique et ethnologie. Revue de l'Enseignement Supérieur 1–2:73–79. Paris.

———. 1970. Contes, proverbes, devinettes ou énigmes, chants et prières ngbaka-ma'bo (République Centrafricaine). Langues et littératures de l'Afrique noire 6. Paris: Klincksieck.

———. 1971. Esquisse linguistique du monzombo. Bibliothèque 26:109–16. Paris: SELAF.

———. 1972a. Problèmes de dérivation verbale en ngbaka et comparaison avec le gbandili. Bibliothèque 26:118–20. Paris: SELAF.

———. 1972b. Aires de phonèmes et aires de tons dans les langues d'Afrique Centrale. Langues et techniques. In Lucien Bernot and Jacqueline M. C. Thomas (eds.), Nature et société, 111–19. Paris: Klincksieck

———. 1977. A propos de la structure du vocabulaire botanique en ngbaka-ma'bo (République Centrafricaine). In G. Calame-Griaule (ed.), Langage et cultures africaines, essais d'ethnolinguistique, 37–51. Paris: Maspéro.

———. 1980. Adaptation de la littérature orale à l'enseignement. Pourquoi? Pour qui? Comment? 'De l'éducation. Orgueil et préjugés'. Recherche, Pédagogie et Culture 8(46). Paris: AUDECAM.

———. 1987a. Des goûts et dégoûts chez les Aka, Ngbaka et autres. De la voûte céleste au terroir, du jardin au foyer. In Bernard Koechlin, François Sigaut, Jacqueline M. C. Thomas, and Gérard Toffin (eds.), Mosaïques sociographiques. Paris: EHESS.

———. 1987b. Relations sociales et projections idéologiques. Exemple des Ngbaka-ma'bo et des Pygmées aka d'Afrique Centrale. Cahiers du LACITO 2. Paris.

———. 1987c. D'autres propos sur l'ethnolinguistique. Ethnologiques (Hommages à Marcel Griaule). Paris: Hermann.

———. 1988. Du ngbaka à l'aka: enquête des catégories grammaticales. La linguistique 24(2). Paris: PUF.

———. 1989. Des noms et des couleurs. Graines de parole (Écrits pour Geneviève Calame-Griaule). Paris: Ed. du CNRS.

———, ed. 1985. Linguistique, ethnologie, ethnolinguistique. NS 17. Paris: SELAF.

——— and Serge Bahuchet. 1981. Encyclopédie des Pygmées aka. Techniques, langage et société d'une population forestière de chasseurs-cueilleurs d'Afrique Centrale 2. Dictionnaire ethnographique 1. Langues et civilisations à tradition orale 50. Paris: SELAF.

——— and ———. 1983. Encyclopédie des Pygmées aka. Techniques, langage et société d'une population forestière de chasseurs-cueilleurs d'Afrique Centrale 1. Introduction. Langues et civilisations à tradition orale 50. Paris: SELAF.

——— and ———. 1985. Conservation des ressources alimentaires en forêt tropicale humide: chasseurs-cueilleurs et proto-agriculteurs d'Afrique Centrale. Les techniques de conservation des grains à long terme 3(1). Paris: Ed. du CNRS.

——— and ———. 1986. Linguistique et histoire des Pygmées de l'ouest du Bassin congolais. Actes du Colloque 'Chasseurs–cueilleurs d'Afrique', St. Augustin, 2–6 January, 1985. SUGIA 7(2).

—— and ——. 1987. Pygmy religions. In M. Eliade, et al. (eds.), The encyclopedia of religions 12. New York: Macmillan.

—— and ——. 1988. La littérature orale pour l'histoire de l'Afrique Centrale forestière. La littérature orale en Afrique comme source pour la découverte des cultures traditionnelles. In W. J. G. Möhlig, H. Jungraithmayr, and J. F. Thiel (eds.), Table Ronde franco-allemande, St. Augustin, 18–20 February, 1985. Anthropos 36.

—— and ——. 1991a. Encyclopédie des Pygmées aka. Techniques, langage et société d'une population forestière de chasseurs-cueilleurs d'Afrique Centrale 1. Les Pygmées aka: 2. Le monde des Aka: 1. Ethnoécologie 2. Conception du monde. Langues et civilisations à tradition orale 50. Paris: Peeters–SELAF.

—— and ——. 1991b. Encyclopédie des Pygmées aka. Techniques, langage et société d'une population forestière de chasseurs-cueilleurs d'Afrique Centrale 1. Les Pygmées aka: La société 3. Langues et civilisations à tradition orale 50. Paris: Peeters–SELAF.

—— and ——. 1992. Encyclopédie des Pygmées aka. Techniques, langage et société d'une population forestière de chasseurs-cueilleurs d'Afrique Centrale 1. Les Pygmées aka: La langue 4. Langues et civilisations à tradition orale 50. Paris: Peeters–SELAF.

—— and Luc Bouquiaux. 1967. La détermination des catégories grammaticales dans une langue à classes. In G. Manessy and M. Houis (eds.), La classification nominale dans les langues négro-africaines, 27–44. Paris: Centre National de la Recherche Scientifique.

——, ——, Jean-Pierre Caprile, France Cloarec-Heiss, Claude Hagège, and Yves Moñino. 1981a. Langues des plateaux d'Afrique Centrale. In Gabriel Manessy (ed.), Les langues de l'Afrique subsaharienne. In Jean Perrot (ed.), Les langues dans le monde ancien et moderne. Paris: Ed. du CNRS.

——, ——, ——, ——, ——, and ——. 1981b. Langues des Plateaux d'Afrique Centrale (Bénoué-Congo et Adamawa-oubanguien de Niger-Congo; Soudanais Central de Nilo-Saharien). In G. Manessy (ed.), Description des langues du monde 1: Afrique. Paris: Centre National de la Recherche Scientifique.

Thomas,-Fattier, Dominique. 1982. Le dialecte sakalava du nord-ouest de Madagascar. Phonologie, grammaire, lexique. Asie du sud-est et monde insulindien 10. Paris: SELAF.

Tourneux, Henry. 1978. Le mulwi ou vulum de Mogroum (Tchad): phonologie-éléments de grammaire. Bibliothèque 68–70. Paris: SELAF.

——, Christian Seignobos, and Francine Lafarge. 1986. Les Mbara et leur langue (Tchad). Langues et cultures africaines 6. Paris: SELAF.

Troubetzkoy, Nicolas S. 1949 [1939]. Principes de phonologie (tr. by J. Cantineau). Paris: Klincksieck.

Tsoungui, Françoise. 1986. Clés pour le conte africain et créole. Paris: Conseil Intrnational de la Langue Française.

Tucker, A. N. n.d. Systems of tone-marking. Bulletin of the School of Oriental and African Studies.

Van Spaandonck, Marcel. 1970. L'analyse morphotonologique dans les langues bantoues: identification des morphotonèmes et description de leur représentations tonologiques. Bibliothèque 23–24. Paris: SELAF.

Vincent, Jeanne-Françoise and Luc Bouquiaux. 1985. Mille et un proverbes beti recueillis par Théodore Tasala. Langues et cultures africaines 5. Paris: SELAF.

Voorhoeve, Jan and Larry M. Hyman, eds. 1980. Les classes nominales dans le bantou des Grassfields (Cameroun). In L. Bouquiaux (ed.), L'expansion bantoue. NS 9(1). Paris: SELAF.

Welmers, William E. 1959?. Questionnaire. List of words, phrases and sentences for a survey of African languages.

Westermann, Dietrich and Ida C. Ward. 1933. Practical phonetics for students of African languages. London: Oxford University Press for I.A.I.

Wolfe, Alvin. 1959. Field guide to west and central Africa. Field guide series 2. Committee on International Anthropology of the Division of Anthropology and Psychology. Washington: National Academy of Sciences and National Research Council.

2
Linguistic Approach Questionnaires

Questionnaire 1
Instructions for the Recording of Linguistic Data

by Jacqueline M. C. Thomas

A. General Instructions

1 Recording techniques

a) Record on one side of the tape only.

b) Make a preliminary trial recording to check for quality: avoid buzzing caused by a microphone too close to the speaker, hums and whines due to mis-setting of the recording or volume levels, intrusive background noises, etc.

c) Recording speed: 19 cm (7½") or, if necessary, 9.5 cm (3¾"), never lower.

d) Tapes to use: not longer than extended play; avoid double length.

e) Place the microphone on a stable support (preferably on a table stand or tripod, or, failing these, on some kind of support). As a precaution, place a cloth between the support and microphone to avoid vibrations. Do not hold the microphone or have it held by anybody else, and prevent the language helper from touching either the microphone itself or its cord. If possible, suspend the microphone on a strong cord in the form of a V.

f) See that the speaker is sitting comfortably, so that he will not be constantly fidgeting and making extraneous noises. Beware of creaky or wobbly chairs and stools, small objects that might be fiddled with unconciously, paper that might be rustled or simply moved around near the microphone, etc.

g) Outdoors, use the microphone windshield.

h) Eliminate extraneous noises as much as possible: laughs, coughs, animal noises, simultaneous conversations.

2 Preparing to record

a) Prepare for the recording with the speaker and practice at least once before recording.

b) Make a numbered list (1, 2, 3, ...) of the words and phrases to be recorded with their translations.

Example:
1. *pā* / *kpā* - to pass / to shave, to scratch
2. *kpà* / *gbà* - to embrace / to cover
3. *gbà* / *ɓà* - bundle / adze, etc.

Example:
1. *pì* - to split
2. *bì* - celebration for a valiant warrior
3. *ɓì* - to clothe, to gird
4. *mbì* - to push, to move apart
5. *mì* - to swallow

c) Have the speaker speak alone; do not interrupt him to give the number on the list or the translation of the word or phrase cited. To ensure this:
   - if he can read, give him the list prepared beforehand with him;
   - if not, have him memorize sets of about ten terms (less or more, according to his ability), and make the recording in sections.

d) On each page of text, indicate the number of the tape position counter corresponding to the material being recorded. If the recorder has no counter, make a mark on the reel with red pencil.

e) Interrupt the recording as many times as necessary: to allow the speaker to rest (keep the recording homogenous); to turn a page (avoid noises made by the paper); to erase or simply record over a slip, etc.

3 Identifying the recording

Since it is essential to be able to identify the recording, the investigator must give the following information very clearly at the beginning of the tape: date and place of the investigation; ethnic group; language, name, and place of birth of the speaker.

This information must also appear on the written text accompanying the recording, and it must be supplemented by the following: ethnic and linguistic affiliations of the father and mother of the speaker, his or her place of residence up to the age of fifteen years, length of time at present place of residence, level of education, occupation, age, and sex.

B. Instructions For Various Types Of Documents

1 Recording words

    a) Ask the speaker to say the word, or pair of words with similar pronunciation, three times: once carefully but at normal speed, and twice slowly.

    b) Have him take a breath before each repetition of the word.

    c) Have him whistle each word three times by itself, then speak and whistle it in a brief context (always the same context for all the words recorded).

Example:	it is a dog	ʔá bɔ́nō̄
	it is a fish	ʔá sī
	it is an animal	ʔá sɔ́
	it is a panther	ʔá sùà
	etc.	
or:	it is not a dog	ʔá bɔ́nō̄ lē
	it is not a fish	ʔá sī lē
	etc.	
or	I see a dog	màá mū bɔ́nō̄
	I see a fish	màá mū sī
	etc.	

Example:	now he is coming	or	he is coming quickly
	now he is leaving		he is leaving quickly
	now he is running		he is running quickly
	now he is eating		he is eating quickly
	etc.		etc.

2 Recording short sentences

These are recorded with substitutions.

Examples:
1. I am eating rice   2. I am eating rice   3. I am eating rice
    you are eating rice   I ate rice   I am eating manioc
    he is eating rice   I will eat rice   I am eating meat
    etc.

    a) Have the set said once at a careful but normal speed (not more than three or four short sentences at a time; for a longer set, it is better to break it into two or three groups).

    b) Have it said a second time, very slowly.

    c) Have it whistled slowly (for tone languages).

3 Recording phrases

The procedure is the same as for short sentences.

Types of phrases to collect:

1. the fine dog
   the fine hut
   the fine field   etc.
2. the fine dog
   the ugly dog
   the big dog
   the fine hut
   the ugly hut
   the big hut   etc.
3. the fine, big dog
   the fine, big, black dog
   the fine, big, black and white dog   etc.
4. the child's head
   the child's foot
   the child's mother
   the child's uncle
   the child's dog
   the child's hut   etc.
5. the child's mother's head
   the child's dog's head
   the child's mother's dog's head
   the child's mother's hut
   the child's mother's uncle
   the child's mother's big hut
   the child's big dog's head   etc.
6. a dog   / the dog   / this dog   / that dog   / my dog/   etc.
   a hut   / the hut   / this hut   / that hut   / my hut /   etc.
   a field   / the field   / this field   / that field   / my field /   etc.
7. I am eating now
   I ate yesterday
   I will eat this evening   etc.
8. I eat alone
   I eat with my brother
   I eat heartily   etc.

Try to consider as many combinations as possible in the language concerned.

4 Recording texts

a) Make an initial spontaneous recording of the narrator, who is allowed to speak in a normal manner for a limited time (15–20 minutes at most).

b) Go over this spontaneous recording, either with the narrator himself or with a qualified speaker, in order to have it repeated sentence by sentence, in a careful, relatively slow, yet normal manner, and to have it whistled (tone languages).

c) With this recording you should provide:
   – a transcription
   – a word-for-word translation (as close as possible)
   – a free translation

d) To obtain (b) (a careful sentence-by-sentence recording, and a whistled rendering of each sentence) there are two possible procedures, according to the means available:

- using two tape recorders:
  - on the first recorder, place the tape recorded by the narrator; he then listens to it one sentence at a time;
  - on the second recorder, the informant rerecords the sentences, one by one, in the way explained in (b).
- using only one tape recorder:
  - the speaker listens to the spontaneous recording, sentence by sentence, and repeats each sentence fairly slowly, so that it can be transcribed as he dictates;
  - afterwards, the speaker rerecords this transcription (in the way explained in (b)).

5 Choosing the type of documents to record

The recording should not be long, but of good quality. It should not consist of all the documentation gathered, but give an representative sample of it. The examples chosen should cover both the most basic and most troublesome aspects of the linguistic analysis, namely:

1. phonology—pairs or series of words (A.2.b) and words in context (B.1.c).

2. morphology—short substitution frames (B.2), phrases (B.3), verbal conjugation paradigms.

3. texts—an initial, spontaneous recording must first be made of all texts, especially narratives (stories, legends, myths, etc.), speeches and pleas, or conversations and discussions. This raw research material is almost unusable, though, unless it has been gone over slowly and carefully (B.4.b and c). The examples chosen for rerecording for study purposes should therefore be fairly short, complete texts or passages from texts, especially narratives that will supply information to supplement the phonological and morphological recordings.

Questionnaire 2
Linguistic Inventory Questionnaire

by Daniel Barreteau, Luc Bouquiaux, Raymond Boyd,
Michel Dieu, Gladys Guarisma, Patrick Renaud,
Paulette Roulon, Michka Sachnine, Jacqueline Thomas,
and Corinne Venot

Introduction

The Linguistic Inventory Questionnaire (LIQ) is in two complementary parts, one sociolinguistic and the other specifically linguistic. The first part is subdivided into three questionnaires which concern, respectively, the speaker, the language, and the ethnic group involved. This data will enable us to make up indexes and maps of languages, ethnic groups, and villages, transcribed as accurately as possible. The second part contains phonetic and phonological information, a questionnaire of words and sentences, and additional morphological information. It should therefore provide representative samples of the languages surveyed, so that lexical, phonological, morphological, and syntactic comparisons can then be studied. This questionnaire is based on Swadesh's two hundred word list; our main contribution is the addition of illustrative sentences in which each entry word is used in at least one sentence. Traditional English word classes are represented as follows: 98 nouns (including three at the end of the questionnaire), 37 adjectives (including 13 numerals), 57 verbs, and 29 pronouns, prepositions and conjunctions, making a total of 221 entries with 255 accompanying sentences.

Although the LIQ was originally intended for linguistic surveys in Central Africa, it can easily be adapted for use in other areas.

The questionnaire was drawn up in several stages and revised after it had been tested by researchers from the University of Yaoundé, from Group 32 of the CNRS and from the ORSTOM.

It has proven more practical to use duplicated questionnaires with enough room left for filling in the required information, rather than to collect the information on a blank writing pad. However, it has not been possible to present the LIQ in its more developed form here. Persons or institutions wishing to acquaint themselves with this method for extensive surveys may direct requests to PEETERS, 52 Boulevard St. Michel, 75005 Paris.

We will indicate, though, that the first pages on sociolinguistic information have scarcely been modified, although they appear here without extra blank space. The phonetic and phonological information may take up a whole page. In the vocabulary questionnaire, we put only five or six sentences on a page, and on one side only, with enough room to write the phonetic transcriptions and a word-for-word translation underneath. For each noun entry, both the singular and the plural form should be given if the language makes a distinction. Here is an example from Mà tá cùvŏk (North Cameroon):

...	...	...
11. arm SG χà PL χà hāy	27, 73ab, 164	He has blood on his arm. bámbèʒ fà χà tá-tā // blood / on | arm | of . him //
...	...	...

Although the additional morphological information appended to the questionnaire proper can be partially deduced from the latter, it should also be researched and checked separately in order to be sufficiently informative. Its being presented in appendixes does not mean that it is less important. On the contrary, because of its importance it is considered an essential part of the linguistic sketch provided by the type of inventory considered here.

Note Concerning the Linguistic Inventory Questionnaire. Researchers are requested to fill in Parts 1, 2, and 3 of the questionnaire very carefully. The information obtained should make it possible to draw up a card file of villages with their alternative name(s), a file of languages and dialects, and a file of ethnic groups with their variant name(s), by the source of the designation (from the people themselves, their neighbors, the government, etc.).

It is preferable to use the phonetic alphabet of the International African Institute or IPA (International Phonetic Alphabet) as much as possible, insofar as the linguist's custom does not interfere. Wherever the transcription differs from this, it is important to indicate your conventions on the page reserved for that purpose (Part 4: Phonetics and Phonology).

In Part 5 (Words and Sentences), it is absolutely essential to write below the translation of the sentence an exact word-for-word rendering in English, giving the specific sense of the lexemes and morphemes of the languages. Here are two examples from Màfà (North Cameroon):

82. bird SG *dîyàk* PL *dîyákì hí*	28, 120, 139	The birds are eating the millet seeds. *dîyákì hí tá ndí tsɔ̀r dàw* // birds + PL | they / eat / seed | millet //
92. root SG *ɓɔ́ɓɔ̀r wáf* PL *ɓɔ́ɓɔ̀r wúf hî*		Those trees over there have long roots. *wúf hì ùtá ɓɔ́ɓɔ̀r tá jíkjík-ʔéʔé* // trees + PL | those ... there / root | their / long . participle //

Very often, one English word has several possible translations in an African language. In such cases, one entry will have several illustrative sentences designed to bring out the specific meaning of the different words in the African language. Thus, when a comparative study is made, it will be possible to compare words that are semantically related (e.g., 57. sand).

Similarly, we have grouped together words which, although different in English, may be the same in some African languages (e.g., 149. to take vs. to give).

The figures appearing in the second column of Part 5 and in the appended tables refer to other sentences in which the entry word appears. For example, the word 'head' appears in sentences 147a and 180. See:

3. head	147a, 180	....

Do not forget the last pages of the questionnaire; they constitute an essential morphological supplement for the investigation.

Part 1. The Survey

1. Researcher
   Name
   Address
   Professional
       affiliation

2. Language variety
   surveyed

3. Place and date
   of the survey

4. Informant
   Surname
   Forename
   Age
   Sex
   Father's ethnic
       group
   Father's language

   Place of birth
   Place of residence
   Level of education
   Languages spoken
   Mother's ethnic
       group
   Mother's language

5. Remarks

Part 2. The Language

1. Administrative (or common) name of the language variety surveyed
2. Other names (with origins)
3. Name(s) given by the speakers to their own language variety
    Translate: 'I speak ... (name of language)'

4. Area in which the language variety surveyed is spoken:
   Department or prefecture / political subdivision or district or sub-prefecture / canton(s) or military district(s) / villages[5] in phonetic transcription

5. Other idioms (variants of the same dialect) with which there is mutual intelligibility, and places where these idioms are spoken

Part 3. The Ethnic Group

1. Informant's ethnic group

   –Administrative (or common) name

   –Name that the group gives to itself

   Translate: 'I am ... ' / 'We are ... (name of the ethnic group).'

2. Name(s) given to neighboring groups by the speaker's ethnic group: administrative name / name given by the speaker's ethnic group

Part 4. Phonetics and Phonology

Indicate here your conventions of notation where different from those of the phonetic alphabet of the International African Institute or IPA, as well as any phonological observations.

Part 5. Words and Sentences[6]

1. mouth		She has a small mouth.
2. eye		They were rubbing their eyes.
3. head	86, 147a, 180	He has a big head and a long neck.
4. a) hair (human)	153, 86	She has long hair.
b) hair, fur (animal's)		This animal's fur is black.
5. tooth		These are dogs' teeth.
6. tongue		He bit his tongue.
7. nose		He is scratching his nose.
8. ear		He is scratching behind his ear.
9. neck (specify whether the throat or the nape of the neck if there is no general term)	3	His neck is swollen.
10. breast		She is washing her breasts.
11. arm	27, 73ab, 164	He has blood on his arm.
12. claw		I am afraid of panthers' claws.

[5]Refer to maps on a scale of 1 / 200,000.
[6]For items 1–95, collect both singular and plural forms.

Linguistic Inventory Questionnaire

13. a) leg b) thigh c) hip	145, 164	a) The skin on your leg is white. b) He hit him on the thigh. c) He is scratching his hip.
14. foot	26, 148, 183c	He has big feet.
15. penis		He is washing his penis.
16. vagina		She is washing her vagina.
17. buttocks, bottom		She is washing her child's bottom.
18. abdomen, belly		Your belly is swollen.
19. navel		I see the woman's navel.
20. liver		Did he eat the animal's liver?
21. guts, intestines		We could see all the animal's guts (intestines).
22. blood	11, 119	There is blood on your spear.
23. urine		There is urine on his clothes.
24. excrement, dung		I found some elephant's dung.
25. bone	161	This animal has large bones.
26. skin	13a	He is scratching the skin on his feet.
27. wound		He has a wound on his arm.
28. wing		That bird's wings are red.
29. feather		This feather is long.
30. horn		That animal had only one horn.
31. tail		He pulled our dog's tail.
32. person, human being, people	158, 170, 188	People sleep at night.
33. man	73, 110b, 111b, 114b, 121, 127, 137, 176	One man danced, the other sang.
34. woman	19, 35, 40, 65b, 121, 129, 140, 175, 182b, 186	That woman is my mother.
35. wife	41, 156	My father has three wives.
36. husband		I don't know her husband.
37. father	34, 78, 181, 183a, 185a	Your father killed a snake.
38. mother	34, 43, 55, 165, 179	Their mother died four years ago.
39. child	17, 86, 114a, 116, 122, 128, 134, 136, 142 143, 177, 182c	Your children cry a lot.
40. brother		We saw that woman's brother.
41. sister	153, 209	That is my wife's sister.
42. maternal uncle		I saw my maternal uncle.
43. name		He does not know my mother's name.
44. sky		There are many stars in the sky.
45. night	32, 47, 175, 176	We are afraid of the night.
46. moon		When there are clouds, we cannot see the moon.
47. star	44	Tonight there are a lot of stars.

48. day		
a) period of time		a) He slept for two days.
b) daylight		b) It is daylight.
49. sun	51	We can see the sun.
50. wind		The wind is blowing.
51. cloud	46	The sun is behind a big cloud.
52. dew		There is dew on the grass.
53. rain	54	The rain washes the leaves.
54. a) rainy season		a) It has rained a lot this rainy season.
b) dry season	56	b) He will come in the dry season.
55. year	38	Their mother died four years ago.
56. ground	108, 144, 162, 166b	The ground is dry during the dry season.
57. sand		a) He is lying on the sand bank.
		b) He is getting sand out of the water.
		c) There is sand on the road.
58. stone	99a, 100, 106, 123	There are stones on the path.
59. hill	77a, 117	The lake is behind this hill.
60. road	57c, 58, 93, 101, 102, 135b	We are walking on the road.
61. water	18, 57b, 107, 112, 113, 134, 140, 159, 204, 218	Give him some water.
62. a) river		a) He throws a fishing trap into the river.
b) stream	88a	b) He throws a fishing trap into the stream.
c) lagoon, lake	59, 146b, 203ab	c) The lagoon (lake) is not deep.
63. hut	64, 68, 185b, 205b	There are five huts in your village.
64. village	63	There are five huts in your village.
65. a) fire	66, 163a	a) Snakes are afraid of fire.
b) firewood	147c	b) The women are tying up the firewood.
66. smoke		I can see the smoke of the fire.
67. ash		The ashes are still hot.
68. refuse, garbage	69, 171	There is refuse near the hut.
69. hole	98, 171	Throw the refuse into the hole.
70. calabash, gourd	107, 140, 204	Take the calabash (gourd).
71. knife	115, 150ab	Give me the knife.
72. rope	115, 174	Our rope is short.
73. a) spear	22, 172	a) The spear (assegai) pierced his right arm.
b) arrow		b) The arrow pierced his right arm.
74. war (combat)		The men are going off to war.
75. (article of) clothing	23, 96, 97, 146a, 199	We have a lot of clothes.

Linguistic Inventory Questionnaire

76. a) fishing trap	62ab	You (PL) have some fish in your fishing trap.
b) net		You (PL) have some fish in your nets.
77. a) animal	20, 21, 25, 30, 95a, 144, 170	a) The animals are running toward the hill.
b) meat	95b, 109, 114b, 147b, 187	b) It's good meat.
78. dog	5, 31, 118, 122, 125, 126, 143, 187, 187, 210	My father's three dogs are dead.
79. elephant	24, 154	He is afraid of elephants.
80. panther	12, 81	The panther killed the goat.
81. goat	80, 151, 169, 174, 200	The panther killed the goat.
82. bird	28, 120, 139	Birds eat (maize, millet, sorghum) seeds.
83. tortoise	158	The tortoise is sleeping.
84. snake	37, 65a, 103, 119, 125, 147a	There is a snake in the grass.
85. fish	76ab, 110a, 111a, 120, 124, 126, 139, 216	There are a lot of fish.
86. (head) louse		The children have lice in their hair head).
87. egg	124, 130, 131, 132, 149ab, 189	He ate some eggs.
88. a) tree	89, 92, 99b, 137	a) There is a big tree near the stream.
b) stick	104, 123, 210	b) I threw my stick a long way.
89. bark (tree)		He is sucking the bark of that tree.
90. leaf	53	I'm burning the dry leaves.
91. seed	82	The seeds are rotten.
92. root		Those trees have long roots.
93. grass	52, 84, 157	There is grass on the path.
94. salt		Give us a little salt.
95. a) fat		a) This animal has a lot of fat.
b) oil		b) He cooks the meat in oil.
96. old (worn)		Wash these old clothes.
97. new		I washed my new clothes.
98. deep	62c	The hole is deep.
99. a) big	25, 51, 88a	a) There is a big black stone over there.
b) tall	14	b) There is a tall tree over there.
100. small	1	I pick up a small stone.
101. wide		The road is wide.
102. narrow		The road is narrow.
103. long	3, 29, 92	He saw a long snake.
104. short	72	He picked up a short stick.
105. round		The lump of cassava (maize, millet ...) is round.
106. heavy		It's a heavy stone.

Questionnaire 2

107. full	18	The calabash (gourd) is full of water.
108. dry	56, 90	The ground is dry.
109. rotten, spoiled	91, 216	The meat is spoiled.
110. a) good (to the taste)	77b	a) This fish is good.
b) good (nice, kind)		b) That man is good.
111. a) bad (to the taste)		a) This fish is bad.
b) bad (wicked)		b) That man is bad.
112. cold		This water is cold.
113. hot	67	That water is hot.
114. a) hungry		a) The child is hungry.
b) hungry (for meat)		b) The man is hungry (for meat).
115. sharp		He cuts the rope with a sharp knife.
116. sad (different from weeping)		She is sad because her child is dead.
117. black	4, 99a	The ground on those hills over there is black.
118. white	13a	The white dog is sleeping.
119. red	28	Snake's blood is red.
120. one	30, 121	1 fish and 2 birds
121. two	48a, 120, 122	2 men and 1 woman
122. three	34, 78, 123	3 children and 2 dogs
123. four	38, 55, 124	4 sticks and 3 stones
124. five	63, 125	5 eggs and 4 fish
125. six	126	6 snakes and 5 dogs
126. seven		7 fish and 6 dogs
127. eight		8 men
128. nine		9 children
129. ten		10 women
130. twelve	149ab	12 eggs
131. twenty		20 eggs
132. hundred		100 eggs
133. to come	54b, 190–196b, 198, 203b, 213	You will come with him.
134. to send (dispatch)		I sent the child to fetch water.
135. to walk	60, 205a	a) He was singing as he walked.
		b) He is walking along the road.
136. to run	77a, 203a	The children were running, dancing, and laughing.
137. to fall	173, 212	The man fell out of the tree.
138. a) to leave	74, 154, 213	a) He left when you arrived.
b) to arrive		b) He left when you arrived.
139. to fly		Birds fly, but fish do not.
140. to pour		The woman is pouring water into the gourd.
141. to fight, struggle		They are not fighting, they are playing.
142. to hit	13b, 179, 210	She hit the child.

Linguistic Inventory Questionnaire

143. to bite (different from eat)	6	The dog bit the child.
144. a) to scratch b) to scratch oneself	7, 8, 13c, 26	The dog is scratching the ground.
145. to rub	2	He is rubbing his leg.
146. a) to wash b) to wash	15–17, 53, 96, 97 (15, 17)	a) She is washing her clothes. b) She is washing herself in the lagoon (lake).
147. a) to cut off b) to cut up c) to cut, to split	115	a) He cut off the snake's head. b) He cut up some meat. c) I cut some firewood.
148. to tie (up), attach	65b	He tied his feet (up).
149. a) to take b) to give	57b, 70, 61, 71, 94, 216	a) Take these twelve eggs. b) Give me those twelve eggs.
150. a) to look for b) to find	24	a) He is looking for his knife. b) He found his knife.
151. to steal		He stole our goats.
152. to squeeze		She is squeezing her breast.
153. to braid		She is braiding her sister's hair.
154. to hunt		They went to hunt elephants.
155. a) to cultivate b) to plant c) to bury, cover with earth		a) He is cultivating (cassava, taros, yams..., his field). b) He is planting (cassava,... a stake in the ground). c) He is burying (the cassava,...the corpse).
156. to prepare food (cook)	95b	My wife prepared the food.
157. to burn	90	I burned the grass.
158. to eat	20, 82, 87, 169, 197, 215	Those people do not eat tortoise.
159. to drink		We will drink water.
160. to vomit		He was vomiting everything he had eaten.
161. to suck	89	Don't suck on that bone.
162. to spit		They all spat on the ground.
163. to blow		a) He is blowing on the fire. b) He is blowing on the food (because it is too hot). c) He is breathing hard.
164. to swell	9	His arms and legs swell.
165. to give birth		My mother gave birth to me.
166. a) to sit down b) to be sitting/seated	202, 205b, 209 167b	a) Sit down over there. b) He is sitting on the ground.
167. a) to stand up b) to be standing		a) Stand up! b) Some are standing, others are sitting.
168. a) to lie down	57a	a) He is lying down but he is not sleeping.

b) to sleep	32, 48a, 83, 118, 201	b) He lay down but he is not sleeping.
169. to die	38, 55, 78, 116	The goat will die if it does not eat.
170. to kill	37, 80, 81	Man kills animals for food.
171. to throw (gen'l term)	62ab, 69, 88b	They throw the garbage into the hole.
172. to hurl		He hurled his spear a long way.
173. to push		When you push him (the child), he falls.
174. to pull	31	I am pulling (on) the goat's rope.
175. to sing	33, 135a, 186	The women sang all night.
176. to dance	33, 136, 183a	The men danced all night.
177. to play	141	The children are playing.
178. to laugh	136, 212	I can hear you (PL) laughing.
179. to cry, weep	39, 211	He is crying because his mother hit him.
180. to suffer, have a pain	183c	I have a pain on the arm.
181. to fear, be afraid	12, 45, 65a, 79	He is very afraid of his father.
182. a) to want		a) He wants some food.
b) to desire long for		b) He desires a woman.
c) to love		c) He loves his child very much.
183. to say	184	a) Your father said, "Don't dance!"
		b) I cannot hear what you say.
		c) I said that my feet hurt.
184. to think, reflect		He is not saying anything; he is thinking.
185. a) to see	19, 21, 40, 42, 46, 49, 66, 103	a) He was seen by his father.
b) to show		b) Show me your hut.
186. to hear	178, 183b	I hear the women singing.
187. to smell		The dogs smelled the meat.
188. to know, be acquainted		You (PL) know this person.
189. to count		I counted the eggs.
190. I		I came (and I am still here).
191. you (SG)		You came (and you are still here).
192. a) he		a) He came (and he is still here).
b) she		b) She came (and she is still here).
c) it		c) It came (and it is still here).
193. we		We came (and we are still here).
- dual		
- inclusive		
- exclusive		
194. you		You came (and you are still here).
- dual		
- masculine		
- feminine		

Linguistic Inventory Questionnaire

195. they - dual - masculine - feminine		They came (and they are still here).
196. who?		a) Who is it? b) Who came?
197. what?		What are you eating?
198. when?	138	When will you come?
199. how? (in what way?)		How do you wash your clothes?
200. where?		Where is my goat?
201. here	207	He sleeps here (close by).
202. there	99ab, 166a	He is sitting over there (at a distance).
203. a) toward (direction) b) from (place)	77a 137	a) She is running toward the lagoon (lake). b) She is coming from the lagoon (lake).
204. a) in b) into	44, 57b, 84 69, 140, 171	a) There is water in the lagoon (lake). b) He went into the hut.
205. behind (buttocks)	51, 59 (cf.17)	a) I am walking behind him. b) He is sitting behind the hut. c) The sun is behind a big cloud.
206. near	68, 88a	He is near the fire.
207. far, a long way	88b, 172	It is a long way from here.
208. right (direction)	73ab	It is on the right.
209. left		He is sitting to the left of his sister.
210. with	95b, 115, 133	Hit the dog with your stick.
211. not	36, 46, 139, 141, 161, 168, 169, 183ab 184, 215	Don't cry.
212. because	116, 179	I laughed because you fell.
213. if	169	If he comes, I (will) leave.
214. this		This is mine; that is yours.
215. that	214	I don't eat that.
216. other (different)	167	These fish are spoiled; give me some others.
217. all	21, 160, 162, 175, 176	I know them all (these men).
218. much, a lot	39, 44, 47, 54a, 75, 85 95a, 181, 182c	We drank a lot of water.
219. iron		
220. maize		
221. cowrie (shell money)		

Appendix 1: Verbal forms (modalities)

1. Infinitive	133–189, 134, 154, 170, 178, 183b, 186
2. Imperative	
- positive	61, 69, 70–71, 94, 96, 149, 166a, 210
- negative	161, 211
3. Present	
- habitual	12, 32, 45–46, 53, 65a, 79, 82, 139, 158, 170, 173, 181, 215
- continuous, progressive	7–8, 10, 13c, 15–17, 26, 50, 60, 65b, 83, 89, 90, 118, 135, 140, 141, 144–146, 150, 152–153, 163–164, 174, 177, 179, 180, 184, 201
- simple (aorist)	19, 36, 39, 43, 49, 57, 62, 67, 74, 77, 95, 100, 115–116, 155, 168, 169, 171, 178, 182, 183bc, 184, 186, 188, 197, 199, 203, 205, 213, 217
4. Future	54b, 133, 159, 169, 198
5. Past	
- preterite (completive)	6, 13b, 20, 24, 31, 33, 37, 40, 42, 48a, 54a, 73, 80, 87, 88b, 97, 103–104, 134, 137–138, 142–143, 147–148, 150b, 151, 154, 156, 162, 165, 172, 175–176, 179a, 183a, 185a, 187, 189–196, 212, 218
- imperfect (incompletive)	2, 21, 30, 135a, 136, 160, 209
6. Passive or participial to be + Adj.	cf. 96–119, 9, 13a, 38, 48b, 55–57, 78, 91, 107–109, 116, 137, 166b-167b-168, 185a, 202, 205b, 209, 216 4, 18, 28–29, 62c, 67, 72, 98, 101–102, 105–106, 110–113, 116–117, 119
7. Reflexive	2, 7–8, 10, 13c, 15–16, 26, 145–146b
8. Simultaneous	135a
9. to be	cf. to be + Adj. and to have = to be with; 35, 51, 59, 205–206, 214
10. it is, they are (indefinite)	41, 77b, 106, 196a, 207–208, 5, 139
11. to have	1, 3, 11, 14, 18, 27, 30, 34, 75, 76, 86
12. there is/are	22, 23, 44, 46, 47, 52, 57c, 58, 63, 64, 68, 84, 85, 88a, 93, 99, 204

Note: This table is merely a guide to help extract the verbal aspects in the languages studied. When necessary, use a different, better suited, table to present the particular verbal structures that you have discovered. If possible, mention the position of the different morphemes in the sentence, in particular with respect to the verb roots.

Linguistic Inventory Questionnaire

Appendix 2: Personal pronouns[7]

Subjects

		Singular	Plural
1st		12, 19, 24, 36, 42, 66, 88b, 90, 97, 100, 134, 147c, 157, 174, 178, 180, 183bc, 189, 190, 205a, 212–213, 215, 217	40, 45, 49, 60, 75, 159, 193, 218
2nd		18, 133, 138ab, 191, 187–189	76ab, 188, 194
3rd	M	3, 6–8, 11, 13–15, 20, 26, 27, ... 192a	2, 141, 154, 162, 171, 195a
	F	1, 10, 16–17, 116, 142, 146, 152–153, 192b, 203	195b

Objects

	Singular	Plural
1st	71, 149, 165, 185, 214, 216	94
		178
2nd		178
3rd	13b, 61, 133, 148, 173, 179, 205a	170, 217

---

[7] Ask whether there is a gender distinction in the 2nd and 3rd persons, and an inclusive/exclusive/dual distinction in the 1st person.

Appendix 3: Table of class agreements[8]

Meaning	No.	Classes[9]	my	your	his	our	your	...
...	...	...	...	...	...	...	...	...
...	...	...	...	...	...	...	...	...

Ask also:
- this, these, that, those, all, other(s)
- one, two, three, four, five, ...
- adjectives[10]
- subject referent, object referent, noun classifier

Appendix 3': Possessives

	Singular	Plural
my	34–35, 41–43, 78, 88b, 156, 200, 214	97
your	13, 18, 22, 37, 183, 185b, 210, 214	199
his / her	9, 17, 36, 73, 116, 150, 152, 153, 172, 179, 181, 185a, 209	4, 23, 146, 164
our	31, 72	151
your	63, 64	39, 76
their	38, 55	

The following distinctions must be indicated if they are made in the language:
- gender alternation:
    your (M) / *your* (F)
    his / *her*
- inclusive / exclusive in the 1st person plural
- differences in possessives according to the thing possessed:
    parts of the body / kinship terms / objects

---

[8]This table is only for languages that have noun class distinctions (cf. Appendix 3' for other languages); it may be expanded lengthwise, as follows:

Meaning	No.	Classes	Possessives	Demonstratives	Indefinites	etc.
...	...	...	...	...	...	...

[9]Enter the class marker in the second column, then, in the third column, a word from that class in the singular and, below it, the plural form. Enter as many words (in order) as there are classes in the language.

[10]Select as many adjectives as are needed to identify the distinctive characteristics of the language.

Linguistic Inventory Questionnaire

Demonstratives

this	25, 29, 30, 35, 47, 54a, 59, 89, 95a, 102, 110-112, 161, 188, cf.201, 214	these	96, 149
that	28, 40, 113 cf.202, 215	those	92, 117, 158

- plural
- connective *of*
- other morphological characteristics

Questionnaire 3
Questionnaire for an Extensive Survey

by Jacqueline M. C. Thomas

This questionnaire for an extensive survey or initial investigation was compiled on the basis of J. H. Greenberg's *List of Words for African Languages* (1–547) and A. E. Meeussen's *Supplement* (548–647)' designed for use with Bantu languages.

These basic questionnaires have been amplified and adapted for extensive investigation not limited to lexical data, but also various aspects of the morphology and syntax of the language concerned.*

Grammatical determiners of the Noun and Verb

A. I
    you (SG)
    he, she[11]
    we (we two, we all)   +   take
    you (you two, you all)   give (something)
    they (they two, they all)   eat PM_1
                                     come
                                     fall
                                     etc.

---

[11]For PM's of the 3rd person singular and plural in languages with noun classes, and for nPM's (e.g., in Bantu languages), all the different possible classes should be considered, e.g.,
'he (the man) falls' / 'they (the men) fall'
'it (the fruit) falls' / 'they (the fruits) fall'
'it (the animal) falls' / 'they (the animals) fall', etc.

B. me
    you (SG)
    him, her   he +   { takes }
    us   { gives } + B etc.
    you (PL)   { eats }
    them, etc.

C. to me
    to you (SG)
    to him, to her   he +   { takes }
    to us   { gives } + C etc.   PM$_2$
    to you (PL)   { eats }
    to them etc.

D. my
    your (SG)   ⎧ 30–47b, 51–55, 60–65,
    his, her   +   ⎨ 69, 86, 109–111, 122–132,   PM$_3$
    our   ⎪ 181–188, 192–195, 256–258,
    your (PL)   ⎩ 301–308, 329
    their

E. I (emphatic)
    you (SG)   { eat   }
    he, she   +   { come }   PMa
    we   { give }
    you (PL)
    they   etc.

F. the   +   ⎧ 30–47b, 51–55, 60–65,
    a, an   ⎨ 69, 86, 109–111, 122–132,   definite /
                        ⎪ 181–188, 192–195, 256–258, indefinite nPM$_1$*
                        ⎩ 301–308, 329

G. the, a   +   id.   singular /
    the, some   plural nPM$_2$*

H. this
    that   + id.   deictics, nPM$_3$*
    this / that ... in question

These different elements should be determined at the beginning of the survey and are to be combined with the words to which the above numbers correspond.

Tones

In the case of tone languages, look for a tone frame before starting on the word list. For languages with three tone levels, use a frame with mid tone; for those with four levels, use a frame with high and mid tone (avoid personal pronouns).

'here is X', 'it's X', 'it's not X', 'I see X', 'the big X', 'the small X', etc.

Extensive Survey

Do not use any frame until you have ascertained that it does not cause any tone perturbations in the words elicited (high, mid, or low).

Carrying out the survey

Begin the word list at No. 48, and leave Nos. 1–47c until the end. The latter cover terms of family relationship and numerals, which generally have special complexities, as well as phonological and morphological difficulties; furthermore, they are often difficult to investigate. It seems preferable, therefore, to tackle these problems when the survey is well under way, rather than at the outset.

Words that have been added to the original list are indented and bear a number followed by a letter, b, c, d, etc. (e.g., 53b nostril, 55b iris (of the eye)). Sentences illustrating the use of the words, which are also to be translated, bear the same number as the word in question and appear on the right-hand side of the page.

Lexical list

48.	face	
49.	skull	
50.	brain(s)	
51.	head	
52.	hair (of the head)	
53a.	nose	
53b.	nostril	+ 30–31, 113–114, 183, 192,
54.	ear	211, 233, 256, 296, 301
55a.	eye, eyes	
55b.	iris (of the eye)	
56.	cheek	
57.	beard	
58.	chin	
59.	jaw	
60.	mouth	
61.	lip	
62.	tongue	+ id.
63.	tooth	
64.	neck	
65.	nape of the neck	
66.	throat	
67.	chest	
68.	breast (of woman)	
69.	hand	
70.	fingernail / toenail	
71.	claw	
72a.	elbow	
72b.	wrist	
73.	shoulder	
74.	armpit	
75.	finger	

76a. back
76b. lower back, loins
77. heart
78. stomach, belly
79. liver
80. kidney
81. intestines
82a. leg
82b. calf
83. heel
84a. knee
84b. ankle
85. toes
86. foot   + id. + 297b
87. rib
88. lung
89. buttocks, bottom
90. anus
91. penis
92. vagina
93. testicles
94. thigh
95a. hip
95b. waist
96. navel
97. body
98. skin
99a. hair (body)
99b. pubic hair
100. blood
101. bladder
102a. bile, gall
102b. venom
103a. bone
103b. fishbone
104a. vein
104b. tendon
104c. nerve
105. urine
106. feces, excrement
107. sweat
108a. saliva
108b. nasal mucus
108c. sperm, semen
109. voice ⎫
110. name ⎬ + id.
111. ghost, spirit, soul ⎭
112. person, human being
113. man
114a. woman

Extensive Survey   203

114b. child
114c. adult
115.   boy
116.   girl
117.   baby
118a. young man
118b. bachelor
119a. young woman
119b. unmarried girl
120.   old man
121.   old woman
122a. chief, king
122b. master
123a. slave
123b. prisoner
124a. God
124b. earth spirit / water spirit / bush spirit / forest spirit
125.   doctor, witch-doctor
126.   medicine, remedy
127.   host, guest
128.   friend
129a. hunter
129b. fisherman
129c. crop farmer
129d. animal husbandman
130a. weaver
130b. blacksmith
131.   potter (M / F)
132.   thief
133.   water
134.   stream / river
135.   rain   135.   It's raining.
136.   cloud
137.   smoke
138.   dew
139.   fog
140.   thunder   140.   It's thundering.
141.   lightning
142.   sky
143.   wind
144.   sun   144.   The sun is shining.
145.   moon   145.   The moon is shining.
146a. star   146a. The stars are twinkling.
146b. Great Bear / Big Dipper
146c. Orion
147.   day   147.   Day is dawning.
148.   night   148.   Night is falling.
149a. morning   149a. He came this morning.
149b. noon   149b. He came at noon.
150.   afternoon   150.   He came this afternoon.

151.	evening	151.	He came this evening.
152.	dawn, daybreak	152.	Dawn is breaking.
153.	twilight, dusk	153.	Twilight is falling.
154a.	new moon		
154b.	first quarter		
155a.	full moon		
155b.	last quarter		
156.	month		
157.	year	157.	He died last year / ten years ago.
158.	rainy season		
159.	dry season		
160.	fire	160.	He is lighting the fire. He is reviving the fire. He is poking the fire.
161.	charcoal		
162.	ashes		
163a.	tree		
163b.	baobab tree - kapok tree		
163c.	mahogany tree		
163d.	umbrella tree		
164.	leaf		
165.	root		
166.	branch		
167.	bark		
168.	seed		
169.	trunk		
170.	fruit		
171.	flower		
172.	thorn		
173.	grass	173.	They are cutting the grasses.
174.	mountain		
175.	hill		
176.	earth, land	176.	He is raking the earth.
177.	soil, ground	177.	He puts the cooking-pot on the ground.
178a.	sand		
178b.	river sand		
179a.	mud		
179b.	clay		
179c.	white clay		
180.	dust		
181a.	forest		
181b.	bush, savannah, plains		
182.	village		
183a.	house, hut		
183b.	grand (of land) 'concession'		
184a.	room		
184b.	tomb		

Extensive Survey

185.	wall	
186.	door	+ 183
187.	roof	
188.	path, trail	+ 192
189.	road	
190a.	well	
190b.	waterhole	
191.	spring	
192a.	farm, agricultural estate	
192b.	field, land under cultivation	
193.	hoe	
194a.	sickle	
194b.	machete	
195a.	stone, pebble	
195b.	rock	
196a.	iron	
196b.	iron ore	
197.	copper	
198.	gold	
199.	silver	
200.	tin	
201.	animal	
202a.	hyena	
202b.	civet-cat	
202c.	genet	
203a.	bat	
203b.	flying-fox (lives in palmyras)	
204a.	scorpion	
204b.	galley-slug, centipede	
205a.	earthworm	
205b.	grub	
205c.	palm worm	
206.	chameleon(s)	
207.	termite(s)	
208.	ant(s)	
209.	termite's nest	
210.	lion	
211.	panther	
212.	elephant	
213.	buffalo	
214.	baboon, cynocephalus	
215a.	monkey(s)	
215b.	chimpanzee	
215c.	gorilla	
215d.	guenon	
215e.	mangabey, cercocebus monkey	
215f.	colobus monkey	
216a.	crocodile(s) (man-eating)	
216b.	crocodile (harmless)	
217a.	hippopotamus	

217b. hyrax
217c. wart-hog - koiropotamus
217d. rhinoceros
218a. lizard(s)
218b. gray lizard
219a. snake(s)
219b. python
219c. cobra
220. crab(s)
221a. tortoise(s) (land)
221b. turtle(s) (water)
222a. (house) spider(s)
222b. (bush) spider(s)
222c. mygale, trap-door spider
223a. (head) louse
223b. (body) louse
223c. crab-louse
224a. flea
224b. oyster
224c. mussel
225. mosquito
226a. fly (insect)
226b. tsetse fly
227. bee
228. honey
229a. frog(s)
229b. toad
230. squirrel
231. cow
232. bull
233. goat
234. he-goat
235. sheep (ewe)
236. ram
237. horse
238. mare
239. donkey
240. antelope(s)
241. horse antelope
242. blueduiker, yellow-backed duiker
243. bushbuck
244. sitatunga
245. waterbuck
246. rabbit, hare
247. chicken, hen
248. rooster
249a. (forest) guinea-fowl
249b. bush guinea-fowl
250. mouse
251a. striped field rat

Extensive Survey

251b. house-rat
251c. porcupine
251d. brush-tailed porcupine
251e. cane rat
252. turtle-dove
253. green pigeon
254a. domestic duck
254b. wild duck
255. hornbill
256. dog ⎫
257. cat ⎬ 30–31, 113–14, 129
258. bird ⎭
259. feather
260a. wing
260b. fin
261. egg
262a. vulture
262b. eagle
263. kite, falcon, sparrow-hawk
264. claws (of bird of prey)
265. horn
266a. tail
266b. proboscis, trunk (of animal, insect)
267. food
268. meat
269. fish
270a. soup
270b. gruel
271. milk
272. salt
273a. pepper
273b. pimento
273c. gelatin
274a. onion
274b. garlic
275. yam
276. guinea corn, great millet
277. (small) millet
278a. oil palm
278b. black rhun palm, African fan palm, Deleb palm
278c. coconut palm
279a. taro
279b. sweet potato
280. (haricot) bean
281. fonio *(Digitaria exilis)*
282. maize
283. manioc
284a. cooking banana
284b. sweet banana
285. earth pea, Bambara groundnut *(Voandzeia subterranea)*

286.	sesame
287.	oil
288.	grease, fat
289.	fat (of meat)
290.	groundnut, peanut
291.	cola, cola nut
292a.	stick
292b.	cane
293a.	spear, assegai
293b.	hunting spear
294.	sword - long knife - saber, machete
295a.	drum (made of skin)
295b.	wooden drum
296a.	basket
296b.	back-basket
296c.	sieve
296d.	bailer
297a.	mat (of straw)
297b.	bed
298a.	bow
298b.	crossbow
299.	arrow
300.	quiver ⎫
301a.	knife ⎬ + 30–31 / 113–14, 129
301b.	tattooing knife
301c.	circumcision knife
301d.	throwing knife
302.	(cold) chisel
303.	axe
304.	rope
305a.	calabash (for water)
305b.	calabash for wine
306a.	earthenware cooking-pot
306b.	iron cooking-pot
307.	thing
308a.	language, speech
308b.	word
309.	work
310a.	war, combat
310b.	ambush
310c.	hunting
310d.	fishing
311.	sleep
312.	dream
313a.	death
313b.	dead man
314.	corpse
315.	life	315. Life is short.
316a.	disease, sickness
316b.	leprosy

Extensive Survey

316c.	sleeping sickness		
317.	cough		
318.	fever	318.	He is shaking with fever.
			The fever has abated.
319a.	wound, scratch		
319b.	abscess	319b.	The abscess is swelling.
			He has an abscess on his arm.
319c.	scabies		
320a.	hole		
320b.	bump	320b.	The road is full of holes and bumps.
321.	truth		
322.	lie		
323.	place, spot	} general / personal	
324.	time, moment, turn		
325.	fatigue		
326a.	money		
326b.	dowry money		
327.	market		
328a.	load, burden		
328b.	package, bundle		
329.	boat, dugout canoe		
330a.	hunger		
330b.	hunger for meat		
331.	thirst		
332a.	shade, shadow		
332b.	darkness		
333.	light		
334a.	(dress), woman's clothing		
334b.	man's clothing		
335.	clothing, cloth		
336.	shoe		
337.	hat, head = gear		
338a.	ring		
338b.	bracelet		
339.	heavy	339.	The package is heavy.
			He is carrying a heavy package.
	+ 113–14,		It is heavy.
340.	light 201, 296,		
341.	white 301		
342.	black		
343.	red	(same)	
344.	green		
345.	yellow, ochre		
346.	blue, indigo		
347.	tall, high	347.	The tree is tall.
			He cut down a tall tree.
			It is tall.
348.	wide, big, immense	(same)	
349.	small, low		
350.	much, a lot, many	350.	He has a lot of goats.

			He ate a lot.
351.	little, few	351.	He has few goats.
			He ate little.
352.	all, everything	352.	He took all the kids.
			He ate everything.
353.	thick	353.	The book is thick.
			He took a thick book.
			It is thick.
354.	thin, slender	354.	(same)
355.	wide	355.	The door is wide.
			He made a wide door.
			It is wide.
356.	narrow	356.	(same)
357.	hard	357.	The fruit is hard.
			He took a hard fruit.
			It is hard.
358.	soft	358.	(same)
359.	sweet (sugar, fruit)	359.	The fruit is sweet.
			He took a sweet fruit.
			It is sweet.
360.	bitter (quinine)	360.	Quinine is bitter.
			He is eating some bitter quinine.
			It is bitter.
361.	sour, sharp (lemon)	361.	The lemon is sour.
			He is eating a sour lemon.
			It is sour.
362a.	sour (curdled milk)	362a.	Curdled milk is sour.
			He is eating curdled milk.
			It is sour.
362b.	sour (wine)	362b.	The wine is sour.
			He is drinking sour wine.
			It is sour.
363.	deep	363.	The hole is deep.
			He dug a deep hole.
			It is deep.
364.	shallow	364.	(same)
365.	long	365.	The stick is long.
			He is carrying a long stick.
			It is long.
366.	short	366.	(same)
367a.	good	367a.	The man is good.
			He is a good man.
			He is good.
367b.	well	367b.	He works well.
			It is well.
368a.	bad, wicked	368a.	(same as 367)
368b.	badly	368b.	(same as 367b)
369.	full	369.	The cooking-pot is full.
			She lifts the full cooking-pot.
			It is full.

367a–368b: + 30–31, 113–14, 211, 256

Extensive Survey

370a.	new	370a.	The garment is new.
			He put on a new garment.
			It is new.
370b.	young	370b.	The dog is young.
			He has a young dog.
			It is young.
370c.	old	370c.	The dog is old.
			He has an old dog.
			It is old.
370d.	worn, used	370d.	The clothing is worn.
			He put on worn clothing.
			It is worn.
371.	round - spherical	371.	The fruit is round.
			He takes a round fruit.
			It is round.
	round - circular		The hole is round.
			He is digging a round hole.
			It is round.
372.	dry, dried up	372.	The leaves are dry.
			He gathers up dry leaves.
			It is dry.
	dry, dried out		The garment is dry.
			He takes a dry garment.
			It is dry.
373.	dirty	373.	(same)
374.	clean	374.	(same)
375.	fat, big	375.	The man is fat.
			He is a fat man.
			He is fat.
376.	slim, thin	376.	(same)
377.	expensive	377.	The garment is expensive.
			He is buying an expensive garment.
			It is expensive.
378.	cheap, low-priced	378.	(same)
379.	close, nearby	379.	The village is nearby.
			He lives in a nearby village.
			It is nearby.
380.	distant, far(away)	380.	(same)
381a.	sharp (edge)	381a.	The knife is sharp.
			He has a sharp knife.
			It is sharp.
381b.	sharp	381b.	(same)
			(point)
382a.	blunt (edge)	382a. ⎫ (same)
382b.	blunt	382b. ⎭ (point)
383.	beautiful	383.	The woman is beautiful.
			He married a beautiful woman.
			She is beautiful.
384.	ugly	384.	The man is ugly.
			She married an ugly man.

			He is ugly.
385.	hot	385.	The water is hot.
			He washes with hot water.
			It is hot.
386.	cold	386.	The water is cold.
			He washes with cold water.
			It is cold.
387.	strong	387.	The man is strong.
			He is a strong man.
			He is strong.
388.	weak	388.	The man is weak.
			He is a weak man.
			He is weak.
389.	deaf	389.	The man is deaf.
			He is a deaf man.
			He is deaf.
390.	dumb	390.	(same)
391a.	blind	391a.	(same)
391b.	blind in one eye	391b.	(same)
391c.	hunchbacked	391c.	(same)
391d.	bow-legged	391d.	(same)
392.	today	392.	He came today.
			He is coming today.
393a.	yesterday	393a.	He came yesterday.
			Yesterday, he came.
393b.	day before yesterday	393b.	(same)
394a.	tomorrow	394a.	He will come tomorrow.
			Tomorrow, he will come.
394b.	day after tomorrow	394b.	(same)
395a.	where?	395a.	Where is the man?
			Where is the man going?
			Where is the man coming from?
395b.	if	395b.	If it rains, he will come.
			If the man comes, the woman will leave.
			He will come if he wants to.
396a.	when?	396a.	When will the man come?
			When are you leaving?
396b.	when	396b.	When it rains, he comes.
			When the man comes, the woman leaves.
			He comes when he wants to.
			He will come when he wants to.
			It was raining when he came.
397a.	how?	397a.	How did he come?
			How did he fall?
397b.	in order	397b.	The man came so that the that, so that woman may leave.
397c.	although	397c.	The man has come although the woman has left.

398a.	how much? how many?	398a.	How many hens does he have?
			How much did he pay for the cloth?
			How many men came?
398b.	as soon as	398b.	The man came as soon as the woman had left.
399a.	why?	399a.	Why did the man come?
			Why did he fall?
399b.	because	399b.	The man came because the woman left.
			He is crying because he is sad.
400a.	here (by me)	400a.	He is coming here.
400b.	here (by others)	400b.	He comes here.
401a.	there	401a.	He is there.
401b.	over there, down there	401b.	He is going over there.
402.	this one, this	402.	He gave me this (one).
403.	that one, that	403.	He gave me that (one).
404.	thus, like this	404.	It's like this.
			He did it thus.
405a.	who?	405a.	Who came?
			Who is it?
			Who said it?
405b.	because of whom?	405b.	Because of whom did he leave?
405c.	with whom?	405c.	With whom did he leave?
406a.	what?	406a.	What is it?
			What is he saying?
			What is he doing?
406b.	with what?	406b.	With what did he do that?
407a.	each (pron.)	407a.	They each take a hoe.
407b.	all	407b.	They all came.
			All (of them) came.
408a.	each (adj.)	408a.	Each hut has its owner.
408b.	all, every	408b.	All meat is good to eat.
409a.	not (at all)	409a.	He is not coming.
			He did not come.
			He will not come.
409b.	not (yet)	409b.	He has not come yet.
409c.	always	409c.	He is always crying.
			He always lies.
409d.	still	409d.	He is still living.
409e.	never	409e.	He never cries.
			He never lies.
			He never came.
410.	no one, nobody (anyone)	410.	No one came.
			He does not like anyone.
411.	nothing, anything	411.	Nothing fell down.
			He did not take anything.
412.	inside, in, into	412.	He put the cooking-pot into the hut.
			He put the cooking-pot inside.
413.	outside, out of	413.	He is bringing the cooking-pot out of the hut.

414.	on top, on, onto	414.	He brought the cooking-pot outside. He put the cooking-pot on (top of) the hut. He put the cooking-pot on top.
415.	underneath, under	415.	He put the cooking-pot under the table. He put the cooking-pot underneath.
416.	in front, in front of	416.	He put the cooking-pot in front of the hut. He put the cooking-pot in front. He walks in front of the women. He walks in front.
417.	behind, in back (of)	417.	He put the cooking-pot behind the hut. He put the cooking-pot in the back. He walks behind the women. He walks behind.
418.	to the left, left	418.	He turned left. His left hand is swollen.
419.	to the right, right	419.	He turned right. His right hand is swollen.
420.	between	420.	He put the cooking-pot between the table and the bed.
421.	in the north, north	421.	The north of the village burned down. He set off toward the north.
422.	in the south, south	422.	The south of the village burned down. He set off toward the south.
423.	in the east, east	423.	The east of the village burned down. He set off toward the east.
424.	in the west, west	424.	The west of the village burned down. He set off toward the west.
425.	to eat → food	425.	He is eating. He is eating meat. He is eating food.
426.	to drink → beverage	426.	He is drinking. He is drinking wine. He is drinking a hot beverage.
427.	to swallow	427.	He swallows the medicine. He swallows the seed.
428.	to urinate	428.	He is urinating.
429.	to defecate	429.	(same)
430.	to make, do	430.	He is making something. He is doing something.
431a.	to go	431a.	He is going away. He is going to the village.
431b.	to leave → departure	431b.	He is leaving. The moment of departure has come. He is leaving for the field.
432a.	to come → coming	432a.	He is coming. The coming of the chief made them run away.
432b.	to arrive → arrival	432b.	He has arrived.

			He arrived at the village. The arrival of the chief made them run away.
432c.	to abandon	432c.	He abandoned the village. He abandoned his child.
433a.	to return → return	433a.	He is returning to the village. The return of the chief made them run away.
433b.	to remake, redo (something)	433b.	He is remaking something. He is redoing the roof of his house.
434.	to enter, come/go into	434.	He is entering the hut. He went in.
435.	to come/go out	435.	He is coming out of the hut. He came out. He went out.
436.	to walk → pace	436.	He walks quickly. His pace is slow.
437.	to go/come up, climb	437.	He went up onto the roof. He went up. He is climbing the tree, the hill.
438.	to go down	438.	He is coming down from the roof. He is coming down the tree. He is going down the hill.
439.	to run → race	439.	He is running fast. They have run the race.
440.	to mount, ride (an animal)	440.	He rides a horse.
441.	to see → sight, view	441.	He sees the animal. The sight of the animal frightened him. He has a good view.
442a.	to hear → hearing	442a.	He hears the animal. He has sharp hearing.
442b.	noise	442b.	The noise of the animal frightened him. The people are making a lot of noise.
443a.	to smell → (sense of) smell	443a.	He smells the animal. He has a keen sense of smell.
443b.	smell, odor	443b.	The smell of the animal frightened him.
444a.	to touch → (sense of) touch	444a.	He is touching the animal. He has a gentle touch.
444b.	contact	444b.	Contact with the animal frightened him.
445a.	to taste → (sense of) taste	445a.	He tastes the meat. He has a keen sense of taste. The taste of the meat turns his stomach.
445b.	to try (on)	445b.	He tried on the garment. He tried to climb the tree.
446a.	to knock (against), bump	446a.	He knocked the cooking-pot. The canoe bumped into the rock.
446b.	to trip,	446b.	He stumbled on the tree stump. He tripped on the stone.
447a.	to hit, beat	447a.	He beats his wife.

		The wife is beaten every day.
		They hit each other.
447b.	to fight fight	447b. He is fighting his enemy.
		They are having a fight.
448.	to kill	448. He killed an animal.
		The animal was killed.
449.	to insult → insult	449. He insults the chief.
		It's a serious insult.
450.	to pull	450. He pulls the cord.
		He is pulling the package.
451.	to push	451. He is pushing the package.
452.	to carry, transport	452. He is carrying a package.
453.	to bring, take	453. He is bringing a package to the chief.
454.	to carry, lift	454. He lifts the parcel.
455.	to put down	455. He put down the parcel.
		He put the parcel (down) on the ground.
456.	to lie (down)	456. He lies down.
		He is lying down.
		He is lying (down) on the ground, on the bed.
457.	to sleep → sleep	457. He is sleeping.
		Sleep is good for a sick man.
458.	to dream → dream	458. He is dreaming.
		His dream woke him up.
		He had a bad dream.
459.	to rest → rest	459. He is resting.
		Rest cured him.
460.	to be tired → fatigue	460. He is tired.
		Fatigue killed him.
461.	to open → opening	461. He opened the door, his mouth.
		The opening is too big.
462.	to close → closing	462. He closed the door, his mouth.
		The closing is too small.
463a.	to bury	463a. He is burying the dead man.
		They buried the afterbirth.
463b.	to plant	463b. He is planting yams.
463c.	to sow	463c. He is sowing sesame.
463d.	to dig up, exhume	463d. He is digging up the dead man.
463e.	to pull up	463e. He is pulling up yams, taros.
463f.	to harvest	463f. He is harvesting sesame.
464.	to read	464. He is reading.
		He is learning to read.
465.	to write	465. He is writing.
		He is learning to write.
466a.	to gather, round up (inanimate, animate objects)	466a. He is gathering the drums together. He is rounding up the goats.
466b.	to assemble (people)	466b. He is assembling the villagers together.

467.	to accompany	467.	He accompanies the woman into the forest.
468.	to burn (down)	468.	He burned the grass. The hut burned down. The meat burned. He burned his hand.
469a.	to roast → roast	469a.	He is roasting the meat. He is eating roast meat. The meat is roasting.
469b.	to grill, roast → grilled, roasted	469b.	He is grilling the meat. He is roasting peanuts. He is eating grilled meat, roasted peanuts. The meat is grilling.
469c.	to fry → fried	469c.	He is frying the meat, the fish. He is eating fried fish. The fish is frying.
470a.	to boil → boiled	470a.	He is boiling the meat. He is eating boiled meat. The water is boiling. It is boiled water.
470b.	to braise (in leaves) → braised	470b.	He is braising the meat. He is eating braised meat. The meat is braising.
471.	to sing → song	471.	He is singing. It's a fine song. He is singing a dancing song. He is singing a mourning song.
472.	to say, tell	472.	He says he is eating. I say that he is eating. He is saying something to the chief. He tells proverbs. He tells riddles.
473.	to speak → word	473.	He is speaking to the chief. The chief's words are true.
474.	to tell, recount	474.	He is telling a story. He tells everything he hears.
475.	to ask (for)	475.	He is asking for a garment. He is asking him to come. He is asking the way. He is asking if he is coming.
476.	to reply, answer	476.	He is answering the chief. He replies that he is not coming.
477.	to want, desire, wish	477.	He wishes to leave. He wants a new garment.
478a.	to refuse	478a.	He refuses to come. He refused the garment. He refused to give him the garment he was asking for.
478b.	to accept, agree	478b.	He accepted the garment.

			He agreed to come.
			He agreed to give him the garment he was asking for.
479a.	to twist	479a.	He twists the strands of the string.
			He twisted the blade of the knife.
479b.	to wring out	479b.	He is wringing out the wash.
480.	to chop up	480.	He is chopping Gnetum (koko), tomatoes, meat.
481.	to cut → to cut away at	481.	He is cutting the meat.
			He is cutting away at the meat.
482.	to tear → to tear to shreds	482.	He is tearing the loincloth.
			He is tearing the loincloth to shreds.
483a.	to build	483a.	He is building the house.
483b.	to demolish	483b.	He is demolishing the house.
484.	to dress, put on	484.	He is getting dressed.
			He is putting on a garment.
			He is putting on a hat.
			He is putting on his shoes.
485.	to undress, take off	485.	He is getting undressed.
			He is taking off the garment.
			He is taking off his hat.
			He is taking off his shoes.
486.	to swim	486.	The man swims quickly.
			The fish swims quickly.
			The duck swims quickly.
487a.	to put/push aside, put in order	487a.	He pushed the people aside in order to pass.
			He is setting his things in order.
487b.	to sort	487b.	He is sorting nuts, shells, fruit.
488.	to hide → hiding-place	488.	He is hiding his money.
			He is hiding.
			His hiding-place is safe.
			He is eating in hiding.
489.	to steal → theft	489.	He stole some money.
			He steals.
			His theft was discovered.
490.	to help	490.	He helps his father cultivate the field.
			He helps his friends.
491a.	to fall	491a.	He fell.
			The calabash fell to the ground.
			He made the calabash fall.
491b.	to throw	491b.	He is throwing stones.
492.	to think → thought	492.	He thinks about his mother.
			He is thinking about his work.
			His thought was good.
			He has good thoughts.
			He thinks you are going to come.
493.	to know	493.	He knows how to count.
			He knows you are coming.
			He knows this song.

Extensive Survey 219

			He knows the chief.
			He knows the story.
494.	to remember	494.	He remembers the chief.
			He remembers the story.
495.	to forget	495.	He has forgotten the chief.
			He has forgotten the story.
			He forgot his knife.
			He forgot to come.
			He forgot that you were coming.
496.	to dig	496.	He is digging a hole.
497.	to weed, hoe	497.	He is weeding the field.
			The field is well weeded.
498.	to clear (of vegetation)	498.	He is clearing the plantation.
499.	to teach	499.	He is teaching the child to read.
500.	to learn	500.	The child is learning to read.
			He is learning to hunt.
501a.	to cry → tears	501a.	He is crying.
			Tears trickle from his eyes.
501b.	to shout → shout, cry	501b.	He is shouting.
			The cries of the animal frightened him.
502a.	to laugh → laughter	502a.	He is laughing.
			His laughter is loud.
502b.	to mock, make fun of → mockery	502b.	He makes fun of me.
			I was the target of his mockery.
503.	to set off (by car)	503.	He set off by car.
504.	to grab hold of, catch	504.	The panther caught the goat.
			He grabbed hold of the thief.
505.	to take	505.	He takes the meat.
			He took the meat from him.
			He takes some meat from the chief.
506.	to give	506.	He gives some meat.
			He gave him some meat.
			He gave some meat to the chief.
507.	to bite	507.	The dog bit his hand.
			He bites.
508.	to kick	508.	He kicked his buttocks.
			He kicks the dog.
509.	to sell	509.	He sells his goods to customers in the market.
			He has sold everything.
510.	to buy	510.	He buys.
			He bought his loincloth from the shopkeeper.
511.	to call → call	511.	He is calling the children.
			He heard his call.
512a.	to sit (down) be sitting	512a.	He is sitting on the ground. He sits down on the ground.
512b.	to get up, stand up	512b.	He gets up from his chair.
513.	to give birth to, father (M)	513.	He fathered a son.
514a.	to give birth to, deliver (F)	514a.	She gave birth to a son.

514b.	delivery	514b.	She had a difficult / long delivery.
515.	to throw (away) [cf. 491b]	515.	He threw his loincloth away.
			He threw his loincloth on the ground, into the rubbish.
516.	to follow	516.	He is following.
			He is following the chief.
517.	to die → death	517.	He is dying.
			Death is coming.
			He died a violent death.
518a.	to forge → forge, forging	518a.	He is forging.
			Forging is difficult.
			He is at the forge.
518b.	to paddle (a boat) → paddle	518b.	He is paddling.
			He is paddling back up the river.
			The paddle is broken.
518c.	to fashion, mold	518c.	He is molding the pottery.
519.	to increase, grow, rise	519.	The river is rising.
			The fever is increasing.
520.	to decrease, subside, lessen, abate	520.	The river is subsiding.
			The fever is abating.
521.	to dance → dance	521.	He is dancing.
			His dance, dancing is beautiful.
			He is performing a beautiful dance.
522.	to walk → walk, pace	522.	(same as 436)
523.	to fly → flight	523.	The bird is flying.
			The kite's flight is clumsy.
524.	to jump → jump, leap	524.	He is jumping.
			His jump was short.
525a.	to get up, rise	525a.	He gets up early in the morning.
525b.	to crouch (down)	525b.	He is crouching down.
525c.	to kneel (down)	525c.	He is kneeling down.
526.	to sneeze → sneeze	526.	He is sneezing.
			That was a loud sneeze!
527a.	to yawn → yawn	527a.	He is yawning.
			That was a loud yawn!
527b.	to belch → belch	527b.	He is belching.
			That was a loud belch!
527c.	to fart → fart	527c.	He is farting.
			That was a loud fart!
527d.	to cough → cough	527d.	He is coughing.
			That was a loud cough!
528.	to finish → end	528.	He has finished.
			He is finishing his work.
			The work is finished.
			It is the end.
			The end of the food is bad.
			The end of the road is difficult.
			The end of the dry season is coming.
529.	to begin → beginning	529.	He is beginning.
			He is beginning the work.

			The work has begun.
			It is the beginning.
			The beginning of the road is difficult.
			The beginning of the dry season is coming.
			He is beginning to eat.
530a.	to fill	530a.	He is filling the calabash.
			The calabash is getting filled (up).
530b.	to empty	530b.	He is emptying the calabash.
			The calabash is empty.
531.	to marry	531.	He married a pretty girl.
			She married a handsome boy.
			They got married.
532a.	to show	532a.	He is showing his fine clothes to his friends.
532b.	to point	532b.	He is pointing out the road out to the stranger.
533.	to dry	533.	He is drying the termites, the clothes in the sun.
			The termites / clothes are drying in the sun.
534a.	to be spoiled, damaged	534a.	The food is spoiled.
			The clothing is damaged.
534b.	to go bad → bad, rotten	534b.	The meat is bad.
			The fish is bad.
			It is bad.
			He is eating bad meat.
			He is eating bad fish.
535a.	to surpass, outdo overtake	535a.	He outdoes the chief.
			He overtook his friends in the race, on the way.
535b.	to equal	535b.	He equals the chief.
			He equals his friends in work.
535c.	to catch up with	535c.	He caught up with the chief.
			He will catch up with his friends on the way.
536.	to tie (up)	536.	He is tying up the goat.
			He is tying up the package.
537.	to untie	537.	He is untying the goat.
			He is untying the package.
538.	to pour, spill, overturn	538.	He is pouring some water on the ground.
			He spilled some water.
			He overturned the pot.
539.	to be damp, wet	539.	He is wet.
			The garment is damp.
			He is wetting his garment.
			It is a wet garment.
540a.	to sweep	540a.	He is sweeping the hut.
			The hut is well swept.

			It's a well-swept hut.
540b.	to clean	540b.	He is cleaning the cooking-pot.
			The cooking-pot is cleaned.
			It's a well-cleaned cooking-pot.
540c.	to coat, smear	540c.	He smears oil on his body.
			He coats his body with red wood powder.
			He coats his body with kaolin.
541.	to blow (wind)	541.	The wind is blowing.
542.	to blow (with the mouth)	542.	He is blowing on the fire.
543a.	to get, obtain	543a.	He gets what he wants.
			He obtained a good harvest.
543b.	to earn	543b.	He earns a lot of money.
543c.	to receive		He received a gift of goats and chickens.
			He received a beating.
544.	to weave	544.	He is weaving.
			He is weaving cotton.
545.	to plait, braid	545.	He is plaiting.
			He is braiding his hair.
			His hair is braided.
			It is braided hair.
			It's a braid.
546a.	to divide (up)	546a.	He divides the fruit in two.
			He divides the workers.
546b.	to share, apportion	546b.	He divided up the work.
			He divided the meat among the hunters.
547.	to break	547.	He breaks the stick.
			He broke his leg.
			His leg is broken.
			He broke the cooking-pot.
			The cooking-pot is broken.
			He took the broken cooking-pot.
			The cooking-pot was broken by the child.
548a.	other (person, kind)	548a.	He has another dog.
			It's another man.
			It's another one.
548b.	the one, the other	548b.	One came, the other stayed.
			Some ate, the others drank.
549.	shiny, glistening	549.	The mirror is shiny.
			His hands are glistening.
550.	ripe	550.	The fruit is ripe.
			He is eating a ripe fruit.
551.	green (unripe)	551.	(same)
552.	whole	552.	The fruit is whole.
			He is eating a whole fruit.
553a.	healthy	553a.	The animal is healthy.
			A healthy animal eats well.

553b.	ill, sick	553b.	The animal is ill.
			A sick animal does not eat.
554.	empty	554.	The cooking-pot is empty.
			She took an empty cooking-pot.
555a.	lazy	555a.	He is a lazy person.
			The lazy child is asleep.
			He is lazy.
555b.	industrious, hard-working	555b.	He is an industrious person.
			The industrious child is reading.
			He is industrious.
555c.	timid, fearful	555c.	He is a timid person.
			The timid child is running away.
			He is timid.
555d.	courageous	555d.	He is a courageous person.
			The courageous child is fighting.
			He is courageous.
556a.	rich	556a.	He is a rich man.
			The rich man is generous.
			He is rich.
556b.	poor	556b.	He is a poor man.
			The poor man is unfortunate.
			He is poor.
557.	oneself	557.	I do it myself.
			You (SG) do it yourself.
			He does it himself.
			We do it ourselves.
			You (PL) do it yourselves.
			They do it themselves.
			One does it oneself.
558.	alone, only, by oneself	558.	He did it alone.
			Only one man came.
			I took only one knife.
			I took only one of them.
			I go there by myself.
			You (SG) go there by yourself.
			He goes there by himself.
			We go there by ourselves.
			You (PL) go there by yourselves.
			They go there by themselves.
			One goes there by oneself.
559.	moment, time	559.	It's time to leave.
			He is coming in a moment.
560a.	bamboo (Chinese)		
560b.	bamboo (African)		
561a.	reed		
561b.	rattan		
562.	seed		
563.	bark, seed-case, chaff	563.	He separates the seeds from the chaff.
564.	flying ant		
565.	monitor lizard		

566.	wild cat (serval, tiger cat, bush-cat, etc.)		
567.	pig (domestic)		
568a.	shell (of snail)		
568b.	shell (of mussel, oyster, various shellfish)		
569a.	eyebrow		
569b.	eyelash		
569c.	moustache		
570.	arm	570.	He stretches out his arm.
571.	fist	571.	He clenched his fist.
572.	claws	572.	(same as 264)
573a.	bump (noun)	573a.	He got a bump on the head.
573b.	joint	573b.	He has painful joints.
574.	spark		
575.	arrow-head		
576.	grief, sorrow, trouble	576.	He has a lot of troubles. Grief is eating away at him.
577a.	poison (for testing)		
577b.	poison (ordinary)		
577c.	arrow poison		
577d.	fish poison		
578.	taboo	578.	He has a taboo for eating sheep.
579.	charm, spell	579.	A sorcerer cast a spell on him.
580.	to be equal, the same	580.	His field is equal to mine. That's all the same to him.
581.	to resemble	581.	He resembles his mother.
582.	to shine, light up	582.	The sun shines. The lamp lights up the hut. The fire is shining.
583.	to miss, lack	583.	He lacks manioc. Some people are missing. He missed the bus. He missed school yesterday. He missed the chief.
584.	to avoid	584.	He avoids the chief. He avoids the holes.
585.	to wait (for)	585.	He is waiting for the chief.
586a.	to be capable of	586a.	He is able to climb the palm tree.
586b.	to be incapable of	586b.	He is unable to climb the palm tree.
586c.	to succeed, do well	586c.	He succeeded. He succeeded in climbing the palm tree. He passed all his tests. He did his work well. He succeeded in selling it.
587a.	to get used to, accustomed to	587a.	He is getting accustomed to suffering. He is getting used to the cold.
587b.	to be used	587b.	He is used to eating a lot.
588.	to hurry	588.	He is hurrying. He is hurrying toward the village.

589.	to grow	589.	The corn (maize) is growing.
590a.	to swell → swelling	590a.	His hand is swelling.
			The swelling on his hand is going down.
590b.	to inflate, distend → inflation, distension	590b.	He is distending his bladder.
			The tire is well inflated.
			He has a distended belly.
			The distension of his belly is lessening.
591.	to stand up, be standing	591.	He is standing at the side of the road, in front of the door.
592.	to hang (up)	592.	He is hanging up his garment.
			He hangs the basket on the tree.
593a.	to slip	593a.	The calabash slipped from his hands.
593b.	to be slippery sticky,	593b.	The road is slippery after the rain.
			This fruit / this mushroom is sticky.
594a.	to breathe → breathing	594a.	He is breathing.
			He is breathing hard.
			His breathing stopped.
594b.	to snore → snore, snoring	594b.	He is snoring.
			He is snoring loudly.
			The snoring stopped.
595.	to lick, to suck	595.	The dog is licking the cooking-pot.
			The child is sucking the fruit.
596.	to nurse, feed at the breast	596.	The baby is nursing.
			The baby is feeding at its mother's breast.
597a.	to smoke	597a.	He is smoking.
			He smokes a pipe.
			He is smoking hemp.
597b.	to cure, smoke-dry	597b.	He is curing meat.
			He is eating cured meat.
598a.	to wake up	598a.	He is waking up.
			He wakes up early in the morning.
598b.	to revive, resuscitate	598b.	He is reviving.
			He has revived.
			He resuscitated the child.
599.	to live together, cohabit	599.	He lives with his brother.
			His two wives live together.
600a.	to vomit → vomiting	600a.	He is vomiting.
			He is vomiting bile, blood.
			The vomiting has stopped.
600b.	to have diarrhea → diarrhea	600b.	He has diarrhea.
			His diarrhea has stopped.
601a.	to tickle	601a.	He is tickling the baby.
601b.	itch	601b.	He has an itch on his foot.
601c.	to scratch, scrape	601c.	He is scratching his foot.
			He is scraping his skin.
602.	to put	602.	He put his loincloth in the sun.
			He put his foot into the water.
603a.	to cover	603a.	He covers the sleeping child.
			He covered the cooking-pot.

603b.	to kiss	603b.	He is kissing the child.
604a.	to hug, embrace	604a.	He is hugging the child.
			He is hugging the package in his arms.
604b.	to surround	604b.	They are surrounding the house.
605.	to wrap (up)	605.	He is wrapping up the package.
			He is wrapping the package with string.
606.	to add	606.	He adds salt to the soup.
607.	to gather together, pile up	607.	He is gathering the grasses together.
			He is piling the logs up.
608.	to join	608.	He joined the two ends of the rope.
609.	to separate	609.	He separated the two parts of the cola.
610.	to stir, turn	610.	He is stirring the gruel.
			He turned the meat over on the fire.
611.	to shake	611.	He is shaking the branch.
			He is shaking the basket.
			He is shaking the child.
612.	to pierce head	612.	He pierced the animal with the spear.
613.	to dig	613.	(same as 496)
614.	to bend, lower	614.	He bends his head.
			He lowers his eyes.
			He lowers his loincloth.
615.	to wipe (off), erase	615.	He is wiping the cooking-pot.
			He is erasing his tracks on the ground.
616.	to wash	616.	He is washing the cooking-pot.
			He is washing (himself).
			He is washing his hands.
617.	to look for → search	617.	He is looking for his knife.
			This search is futile.
618.	to find	618.	He found his knife.
			He found some game.
619.	to measure	619.	He is measuring the loincloth.
620.	to be silent	620.	He is silent.
621.	to agree, be in agreement	621.	He agrees.
			He agreed to leave.
			He agreed with me, you, him, etc.
622.	to allow	622.	He allows me to go there.
623.	to deny	623.	He denied the accusation.
			He denied stealing the chickens.
624a.	to announce	624a.	He announced the news of the death in the village.
624b.	to proclaim	624b.	He was proclaimed chief.
625a.	to threaten	625a.	He threatened to kill him.
			He threatened the chief.
625b.	to provoke	625b.	He provoked the chief.
			He provoked his friend to fight.
626.	to lie → lie	626.	He is lying.
			It's a lie.
			His lie astonished people.
627.	to cheat	627.	He cheats at the game.
628.	to whistle → whistling	628.	He whistles.

Extensive Survey

			He whistles loudly.
			The whistling frightened him.
629.	to send	629.	He sends a gift (a chicken) to the chief.
			He sends a child to tell the chief to come.
			He sends the child hunting.
630.	to leave (TRANS)	630.	He is leaving the village.
			He left his wife.
			He is leaving his friends in order to come back.
631a.	to strain, sift →	631a.	He is sifting the manioc.
			He took the sieve.
631b.	to filter → filter	631b.	He is filtering the wine, the oil.
			He made a filter for wine.
632.	to fight, war → war	632.	They are fighting.
			The war is over.
633a.	to cook	633a.	He is cooking the meat, the fish, the vegetables, the bananas.
633b.	to be cooked	633b.	The meat is cooked.
634.	to grind, crush	634.	He is crushing the nuts.
635.	to knead, to brew	635.	He is kneading the mucilage, the manioc.
			He is brewing the beer.
636.	to be angry → angry	636.	He is angry with his brother.
			He is angry with his son.
			He is angry.
			He was overcome with anger.
637.	to be ashamed → shame	637.	He is ashamed.
			He is ashamed of his son.
			He is ashamed of having stolen.
			He is overcome with shame.
638.	to be astonished, surprised → astonishment, surprise	638.	He is surprised to see him.
			He is surprised at his arrival.
			He is astonished at the chief's words.
			Astonishment keeps him from speaking.
639.	to fear, be afraid of → fear	639.	He is afraid of the chief.
			Fear causes him to run away.
640a.	malice	640a.	The malice of the chief haunts him.
640b.	vengeance	640b.	He wants to take vengeance for his brother's death.
641.	to lend	641.	He lent me some money to buy my house.
642.	to borrow	642.	He borrowed some money from me to buy his house.
643.	to pay (for)	643.	He has finishing paying for his house.
			He is paying his workers.
644a.	to bewitch, cast a spell on	644a.	The sorcerer cast a spell on the woman.
644b.	to poison	644b.	He poisoned the woman.
645a.	to need	645a.	He needs a new loincloth.

			He needs some water for washing.
645b.	to want, wish for	645b.	He wants a new loincloth.
			He wants some wine.
646a.	to love	646a.	He loves his son, his daughter.
			He loves his wife.
646b.	to like	646b.	He likes meat.
	have a liking for		He likes fine clothes.
647a.	to receive	647a.	He received a blow on the head.
			He received the money.
647b.	to accept	647b.	He accepted the money that I gave him.
648.	type, kind, breed, species	648.	There are two kinds of this thing.
			There are two types (species) of this tree.
			There are two breeds of this animal.
649.	more (comparative)	649.	He is taller than the chief.
	most (superlative)		He is more intelligent than the chief.
			He is the tallest.
			He is the most intelligent.
650.	less, not as (comparative),	650.	He is not as tall as the chief.
	least (superative)		He is less intelligent than the chief.
			He is the least tall.
			He is the least intelligent.
651.	as (comparative)	651.	He is as tall as the chief.
			They are equal.

* * *

1. one
2. two
3. three
4. four
5. five
6. six
7. seven
8. eight
9. nine
10. ten
11. eleven
12. twelve
13. thirteen
14. fourteen
15. fifteen
16. sixteen
17. seventeen
18. eighteen
19. nineteen
20. twenty

1. He gave me one (of them). One came.
2. He gave me two (of them). Two came.
etc.

+ 30–31, 50–55, 183, 195, 301, 329

21. twenty-one
22. thirty
23. forty
24. fifty
25. sixty
26. seventy
27. eighty
28. ninety
29. (one) hundred
30. father ⎫
31. mother ⎬ + 113, 122, 211, 256
32. paternal uncle (father's brother)
33. paternal aunt (father's sister)
34. maternal uncle (mother's brother)
35. maternal aunt (mother's sister)
36. brother ⎫
37a. sister ⎬ + 113, 122, 211, 256
37b. elder, eldest
37c. younger
37d. youngest
38. son
39. daughter
40. grandson (son's child; daughter's child)
41. granddaughter (son's child; daughter's child)
42. grandfather (father's father; mother's father)
43. grandmother (father's mother; mother's mother)
44. son-in-law (daughter's husband)
45. daughter-in-law (son's wife)
46a. father-in-law (husband's father; wife's father)
46b. husband
47a. mother-in-law (husband's mother; wife's mother)
47b. wife
47c. dowry

Grammatical Supplement

Some additional information about the verbal conjugation should be collected:

I
you
he

- come(s)
- came
- am/are/is coming
- is in the process of ...
- is setting out to come
- is beginning to come

- would come (if he could)
- was coming (this morning, yesterday, formerly)
- will come (this evening, tomorrow, later)
- let him come
- is coming (at this very moment)
- may (it is possible that he will) come

I you he	almost came is on the point of coming would like to come is (definitely) going to come is (possibly) going to come is still coming, still comes

I you he	eat(s) meat ate meat am/are/is eating meat is in the process of ... is setting out to ... is beginning to ...	would eat meat was eating meat will eat meat let him eat meat is (at this very moment) ... may (it is possible that he will) ...

I you he	almost ate meat is on the point of eating ... would like to eat ... is (definitely) going to eat ... is (possibly) going to eat ... is still eating ... , still eats ...

Eat! Drink! Come! etc.
To eat is good. To drink is good. To come is difficult. etc.
Eat the meat! Drink the wine! Come quickly! etc.

Similarly, information on sentence structure is needed:
He saw the man who came yesterday. He did not see the man who came yesterday. He saw the man who did not come yesterday. The man whom you saw yesterday is dead. The man whom you did not see yesterday is dead. The man whom you saw yesterday is not dead. It was he who came yesterday.

I eat. I eat meat. I eat meat in order to get fat. I am eating the meat so that you won't have any.

I take some water to drink. I take some water and I drink. I take some water, then I drink. I take some water in order to drink. I take some water but I do not drink. I do not take any water but I drink. I take some water without drinking. I do not take any water for fear of drinking. I take some water, which I drink. I took some water, which you are drinking. I am taking some water, for I am drinking. If I take some water, I drink. I take some water if I am drinking. When I take some water, I drink. I take some water when I drink.

> When this questionnaire is used in an extensive survey, it should be supplemented by the elicitation of a short text, preferably on a well-known topic, to facilitate comparison (for example, the topic of a race between two animals, one fast, the other slow: the latter wins through cunning).

Questionnaire 4
Phonological Guide

by Jacqueline M. C. Thomas

This guide is based on the structuralist method of phonological analysis. Its purpose is to show how the phonemes or distinctive sounds (minimal distinctive units, cf. Martinet 1956 and 1967) of the language being studied may be isolated. In the proposed analysis, various aspects of these sounds will be examined, such as their (articulatory) phonetic realization, their organization within the system, their distribution, frequency, combinations, etc.

Making a phonological analysis requires a minimum vocabulary. The amount will vary across languages, but on the average, the words and phrases of the Questionnaire for an Extensive Survey (Questionnaire No. 3, above and one or two texts of running discourse will provide a good basis.

A. Finding the Distinctive Sounds

In seeking to establish the phonological status of the sounds of a language, we will start with those most closed (stops) and work towards those most open (vowels), proceeding from the front (labials) to the back (glottals) and from segmentals (consonants - vowels) to suprasegmentals (e.g. stress). This order is useful, for the direct observation of forward articulations (action of the lips and the tip of the tongue, etc.) enables the investigator to become gradually more familiar with sounds that are foreign to him and makes it easier to perceive articulations that are more complex or more retracted.

On the basis of the Questionnaire 3, which will have been filed on slips and classified in phonetic order (cf. vol. 1, §5.2.1), a list should be made of words containing the different sounds in word-initial position. As far as possible, simple forms should be chosen (i.e., not compounds or obvious derivatives), comprising a minimum number of sounds, e.g., consonant + vowel, as in the following French words: [pɑ] *pas* 'step', [bɑ] *bas* 'low', [mɑ] *mât* 'mast', etc.; [yt] *hutte* 'hut', [oːt] *hôte* 'host', [ɔt] *hotte* 'back-basket', [ɑːt] *hâte* 'haste', etc.

From these words, we first select all those that are distinguished from one another by a single sound, (such as [yt] and [ɔt] above), or even by a single articulatory feature, as in [pɑ] and [bɑ] where the VOICELESS bilabial stop [p] is distinguished from the VOICED bilabial stop [b] only by the feature of voicing.

In this way, we make a list of nearly homophonous pairs of words, enabling the phonemes in initial position to be contrasted and isolated. If there are not enough pairs of words, an additional word that will form a pair with one already listed may be suggested to the speaker. A good speaker will quickly grasp the principle and will suggest words on his own, at least in simple cases.

Once a preliminary identification of the distinctive sounds found in initial position has been made, sounds in other positions will be considered in longer words: in word-final position, then in medial position (intervocalic in the case of consonants: VCV, interconsonantal in the case of vowels: CVC), and finally in clusters (consonant clusters and vowel clusters).

These sounds must be described phonetically and identified and defined phonologically, after being studied in all possible positions:

> initial, final, medial; in clusters;
> in initial, final, and medial phonetic syllables;
> in combinations.

This study starts within the WORD, i.e., the simplest unit elicited during the investigation. Such a unit, however, may turn out upon analysis to be a complex word (syntheme) or a phrase just as well as a simple moneme. In certain cases, e.g., in languages with noun classes, we must make a preliminary study within the framework of the moneme; then within the phrase level; and finally within the utterance level.

Simple segmental articulations *(p, b, m, t, d, n, s, z, ... i.e, ɛ, a ...)* and complex articulations *(ɓ, ɗ, kp, gb ... a^i, a^u ...)* should be studied separately, the former being correctly defined first, so that the latter may be compared with them. Similarly, a separate study should be made of pitch, which may have a different phonological status in different languages. The same applies to other phenomena, such as nasality, length, tenseness, and intensity.

All articulatory phenomena, of whatever kind, must be given a very careful and detailed phonetic description, whether they are distinctive or not. Since distinctive features, as well as distributions, conditioning, combinations, etc., are defined through substitution, it is essential to make lists of words showing the same phenomenon. By comparison and contrast, it will then be possible, in most cases, to establish the characteristics of the phonology of the language, or at least to identify the areas needing further investigation.

1 Consonants.

These are studied mainly by making substitutions and according to position:

within the word or moneme

	cv initial	cvc final	(c)vcv, etc. medial
French	[p⌊ɑ][12] *pas* 'step'	[p⌊a⌋p⌈] *pape* 'pope'	[p⌊a⌉ p⌊a] *papa* 'papa'
	[b⌊ɑ] *bas*		
	[m⌈ɑ] *mât*		

cc =	ccv ccv initial	(c)vcc (c)vcc final	(c)vccv (c)vccv, etc. medial

French	[p⌊ʁɛ] *prêt*	[ʁ⌉p⌊ɑ] *repas*	[kɑː⌋p⌈ʁ] *câpre*	[kaʁ⌋p⌈] *carpe*	[a⌋p⌊ʁɛ] *ápprêt*	[aʁ⌋p⌊i] *harpie*

phonetic = syllable	cv|cv initial	cv|cv final	cv|cv|cv internal	cv|cv|cv final	cv|cv|cv, etc. initial
French	[p⌊aʁe] *parer*	[ʁɑː⌋p⌊e] *râper*	[ʁe⌋p⌊aʁe] *réparer*	[deʁɑː⌋p⌊e] *déraper*	[p⌊aʁade] *parader*

within the phrase

c =	cv + cv [le ⌋p⌊ɛ̃] *les pains*	cvc + cv [lœʁ ⌉p⌊ɛ̃] *leur pain*	cvc + cv [na⌋p⌈ ʁɔ̃d] *nappe ronde* [na⌋p⌊ ʁɔ̃] *napperon*	cvc + cv, etc. [na⌋p⌊ ɔval] *nappe ovale*
cc =	cv + ccv [le ⌋p⌊ ʁɛ] *les prêts*	cv + ccv [le ʁ⌉p⌊ɑ] *les repas*	cvc + ccv [lœʁ ⌉p⌊ʁɛ] *leur prêt*	cvc + ccv , etc. [lœʁ ʁ⌉p⌊ɑ] *leur repas*

s = cv + cv|cv cv + cv|cv, cv|cv + cv cv|cv + cv,
cv + ccv|cv cv + cv|ccv, etc.

within the utterance

cv-cvcv-ccvc-v-ccv-cv-cvccv-cv-cvcvc, etc.
cv-cvcv-ccvc-v-ccv-cv-cvccv-cv-cvcvc, etc.

This study should bring to light:

a) neutralizations, e.g., neutralization of the voicing contrast in final position in Birom: *pá* 'remove' / *bá* 'knife' ≠ *mā* 'back', but only *gáp* 'strong' [gáp⌉ ~ gáb⌉] / *gám* 'he-goat', from which we see that, in final position, this language has oral archiphonemes contrasting with the nasals, whereas in initial position, there are contrasts between voiceless, voiced, and nasal sounds.

[12]The diacritics used represent: ⌋ (implosive), ⌊ (explosive), ⌉ (simple closure), ⌈ (simple release).

	initial	final
	p f t s k	P F T S K
	b v d z g	

These archiphonemes are realized as voiceless and unreleased in absolute final position (sentence-final), voiceless before a voiceless consonant, voiced before a voiced consonant, and fricative before a vowel: p [p⁷ ~ p ~ b ~ β].

b) variants, resulting, for example, from complementary distribution. Thus, in Ngbaka, there is only one phoneme /l/, but, according to position, it is realized as [l-] /lɔ́kɔ̀/ [lɔ́kɔ̀] 'hallucinogen sp.' and [-ɾ-] /kɔ́lɔ̀/ [kɔ́ɾɔ̀] 'to cut'. [l] never contrasts with [r], since the former occurs only in initial position and the latter only in intervocalic position;

c) conditioning, for example, the homorganic nature of the syllabic nasal in Birom: *Ǹ.mī* [m̀.mī] 'blood', *Ǹ.pēŋ* [m̀.pēŋ] 'whiteness', *Ǹ.bùs* [m̀.bùs] 'tin'; *Ǹ.fwīī* [m̀.fwīī ~ n̄.fwīī ~ m̞.fwīī] 'bark'; *Ǹ.dɔ́m* [n̄.dɔ́m] 'poison'; *Ǹ.jīk* [ɲ̄.jīk⁷] 'livers'; *Ǹ.kēn* [ŋ̄.kēn] 'life'; *Ǹ.kpēy* [ŋ̄m.kpēy] 'deafness'. In fact, in this language, the syllabic nasal is always actualized at the same point of articulation as the following consonant. Despite the numerous allophones (Ǹ = [m̀ ~ m̞ ~ n̄ ~ ɲ̄ ~ ŋ̄ ~ ŋm̀]), there is only one phoneme, whose articulation is conditioned by the environment—in this case, by the following consonant.

2 Vowels

Vowels are also studied primarily on the basis of substitutions and position:

within the word or moneme:

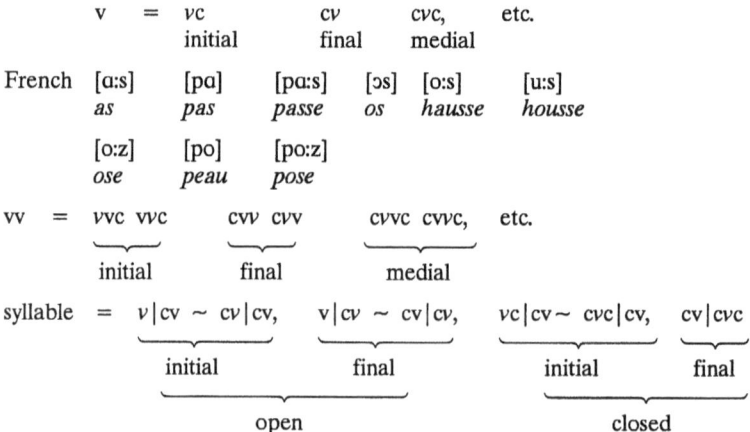

within the phrase:

v	=	cv + vc	cv + vc	cv + cv	cvc + vc, etc.
vv	=	cvv + vc	cvv + vc	cvv + cv	cvc + vvc,
		cvv + vc		cvv + cv	cvc + vvc, etc.
syllable	=	cv|cv + cv,	cv|cv|cv + cv,	cvc|cv + cv|cvc, cv|cvc cv, etc.
		cv|cv + cv,	cv|cv + vc, etc.		

within the utterance:

vc - cvcv - vvc - cvcvc - cvv - cvcvcc - vcv   etc.
vc - cvcv - vvc - cvcvc - cvv - cvcvcc - vcv   etc.

Oral and nasal vowels must be dealt with separately. The same applies to suprasegmental features that may affect vowels; from a phonological point of view, these should be considered differently according to the language concerned. Thus, length and tenseness (which may also affect consonants, or even whole syllables) should be examined separately, without prior assumptions and with the utmost phonetic precision, the usual procedures for phonological analysis being employed to define their distinctive characteristics.

Using the same conditions for position and distribution, first within the lexical unit and then in longer stretches, the investigation will thus cover those articulatory phenomena related to segmental articulation that may affect the various articulations from the most closed sounds (stop consonants) to the most open sounds (open vowels), namely, duration (long/short consonants or vowels), tenseness (tense/lax consonants or vowels), intensity (stressed/unstressed consonants and/or vowels) and pitch (the different registers and/or contours affecting consonants and/or vowels). A full and thorough analysis should result in a systematic treatment, not only of suprasegmental phenomena, but also of the manner and point of articulation for the segmental articulations, each covered separately in turn.

3 Tones (contour or level tones and glides).

Tone should also be studied through substitutions and by position, within the word or moneme, within the phrase, and within the utterance:

x x	x x	x	xx	xx	
(c)vcv	cvcv	cv	cvv	cvv	etc.

B. Phonological Description

The plan of a description must be flexible, varying according to the nature of the phonology of the language being described and the complexity of its problems. It is best to work from the simple to the more complex, beginning with either consonants or vowel phonemes, whichever are easier to handle and to define.

The consonant or vowel nature is not an absolute, transcendent fact in phonology, but has a functional phonological status. Any classification of phonemes into consonants and vowels must thus be treated as a definition whose validity must be demonstrated. The same applies to the definition of the phonological syllable.

1 Charting, description, and definition of phonemes

Each phoneme is presented and contrasted with all other phonemes with which it shares a relevant feature, in order to distinguish it from them. Thus, French /p/ would be contrasted with /b/, /m/, and /w/ and would thus be defined as voiceless (p/b), oral (p/m), and noncontinuant (p/w). It would also be contrasted with /f/ as bilabial (f being labiodental). It is pointless to contrast one phoneme with another unless they have at least one feature in common; e.g., in French, voiceless bilabial /p/ would not be contrasted with voiced central /ʒ/.

Depending on the language concerned, the phoneme may be shown in its various positions, or, to emphasize certain distributional phenomena, the different positions in which the phonemes occur may be examined in turn. In any case, it is recommended that the phoneme be presented and described so as to reveal all its characteristics, taking account of distribution, environment, etc. Finally, the characteristics pertaining to all the phonemes in a given position can be grouped together. In this way we present the phoneme: word pairs proving its distinctive status, the positions in which it occurs with the contrasts it manifests in these positions, its detailed phonetic description, and its phonological definition.

Example from French: the phoneme /p/

p/b: voiceless / voiced

pɑ	*pas*	bɑ	*low*	initial
po	*peau*	bo	*beau*	
pɛ̃	*pain*	bɛ̃	*bain*	
nap	*nappe*	nab	*nab*	final
apɔʁ	*apport*	abɔʁ	*abord*	medial
pʁize	*priser*	bʁize	*briser*	cluster: C_1C-
(p)œpl	*peuple*	(m)œbl	*meuble*	-C_1C
alp	*Alpes*	alb	*Albe*	-CC_2

p/m: oral / nasal

pɑ	*pas*	mɑ	*mât*

...

p/w: noncontinuant / continuant

p/f: bilabial / labiodental

Phonetic description. [p] is a voiceless bilabial oral stop, released in absolute initial and syllable-initial position, held and then released in absolute final position; in clusters, it is released in the position C_1C-, held and then released in the position -CC_2, etc.

Phonological definition. /p/ is a voiceless bilabial.

All the distinctive units of the language should be reviewed in this way. It would be logical to deal with these units either feature by feature or unit by unit, but it is customary to examine segmentals by units and suprasegmentals by their relevant features, insofar as the latter can or cannot combine individually with the former. Thus, depending on the language, pitch may be regarded as a relevant feature of the vowel, or as a suprasegmental feature affecting the entire syllable or meaningful unit or any other higher-level unit.

2 Identification problems

With the distinctive units catalogued, described, and defined, we now devote a few specific paragraphs to cases where the phonological choices made must be justified. We must prove the monophonemic character of complex articulations, in particular the labiovelars *(kp, gb, ŋm)*; prenasalized sounds *(mb, nd, nz, nj, ng)*; affricates *(pf, bv, ts, dz, ts, dz, tʃ, dʒ, tɬ, dɮ)*; palatalized, labialized, and glottalized sounds; and diphthongs *(aⁱ, aᵘ, ...)*. It must be shown that a double articulation is distinct from the sum of two simple articulations, when each exists elsewhere in the language, and that it constitutes a separate phoneme and not a cluster of consonants or vowels.

The consonant or vowel status of some particular phonemes is also difficult to determine, such as syllabic nasals, semi-vowels *(w, ɥ, y)*, and sometimes also the continuants *r, l*, etc. These, as well as problems of tone, stress, etc., where the phonological status is in question, must be dealt with whenever they arise. In addition, the phenomena of neutralization, variation, conditioning, etc., must be studied in their entirety.

3 Definition and classification of phonemes. Organization of the system

This requires a review of the phonemes established, their relevant features and the pattern these form when organized into orders and series in a system of two or more dimensions. Tables showing this organization should be drawn up, and the phonological choices made should be discussed and argued for.

4 Combinations, distribution, and frequency

Phonemes, themselves made up of a combination of articulatory features, combine turn with other phonemes to form a higher level unit, the syllable. Like the phoneme, the syllable is a two-sided entity, one side strictly phonetic, and the other phonological. The phonetic syllable is an articulatory unit which corresponds to all the sounds produced in a single emission of sound. It consists of one or more sounds combined in such a way that one peak combines with zero, one, or more margins, as in [o] 'oh', [no] 'no', and [nol] 'knoll'. The phonological syllable, which often coincides with the phonetic syllable, varies according to the language, and must be defined in accordance with the phonological system peculiar to the language concerned and not based on the articulatory unit of the phonetic syllable.

In a particular language, then, we must consider what combinations of phonemes make up the syllable and what types of syllables are thereby established, as well as the vocalic or consonantal function of certain phonemes with ambiguous, and sometimes ambivalent, status.

This will lead quite naturally to the systematic study of clusters of phonemes: consonant clusters and vowels clusters, and then mixed combinations. The different constituents must be considered, for the combination of the segments in itself may not be the most interesting feature; that of the significant features may be more enlightening, for example the combination of a voiceless consonant with a high-toned vowel. Combinations of noncontiguous phonemes should be examined, as well as contiguous combinations, at least within the moneme and within the syntheme. Studying combinations in this way may point up certain features of assimilation, dissimilation, harmony, etc. Thus, in French, we find regressive assimilation of nasalization, e.g., [mɛtnã] > [mɛ̃nnã] 'now', [lãdmɛ̃] > [lãnmɛ̃] 'the next day', etc.; in

Ngbaka-ma'bo, there is a series of gradual contrasts from voiceless to nasal sounds in the form C_1VC_2V in the simple word (e.g., words with the forms pVbV, bVmbV, mbVmV are rare, if not nonexistent).

Next we examine the distribution and frequency of each phoneme or each distinctive articulatory feature depending on the value of such a study in the type of language concerned, and of each type of phoneme combination, in increasingly complex situations from the moneme to the sentence. Thus, it might be a help in establishing the status of a phoneme to know its frequency of occurrence in the lexicon and in discourse, respectively. Frequency, combinations, and distribution, as well as phonetic realizations, are quite important for synchronic studies, and are basic to diachronic and comparative studies of phonology.

Lastly, the study of combinations should include the phenomena of saturation: saturation of the syllable, of clusters, of syllable combinations in the meaningful unit, etc., and any processes used to resolve saturation problems caused by contact, as in French consonant clusters.

Questionnaire 5
Morphology
Derivation and Compounding

by Luc Bouquiaux and Gladys Guarisma

A. Formation (Formal Processes)

There are many ways of forming derivatives and compounds, mostly related to affixation (the addition of prefixes, infixes, or suffixes). In a tone language, tone processes may be used in conjunction with affixation. Some languages have a rich morphology, especially those with noun classes, and others do not. On the level of morphology we will encounter a set of phenomena generally designated by the label fusion, which some include with the processes of morphophonemic analysis (cf. 4.2).

B. Parts of Speech Affected

The following parts of speech are most often affected:

Noun: adjectives, cardinal and ordinal numbers, a series of pronominal forms, including personal modifiers (usually subject and object or substitute pronouns), possessives, connectives, definite and indefinite articles, demonstratives, including connective demonstratives, determiners, interrogatives, and relative verbal forms. Thus, it is worthwhile to pay special attention to these categories when using the questionnaire on the noun phrase.

Verb: conjugated forms, reflexives, reciprocals, and pronominal infixes.

C. Lists of expressions that bring out these features

Questionnaires 6 (verb phrase) and 7 (noun phrase) are ideally designed to bring out these phenomena. It must be borne in mind that, in a language with noun classes, the class of a noun requires a specific set of agreements. Thus, the Birom adjective *réy* 'good, fine' occurs in the forms *rwéy, rèéy, bìrèéy, ērēy, bārēy, ǹrèéy, gòrwèéy, yèéy, yéy, kìrèéy*, depending on whether it qualifies a noun of class 1, 2, 3, 4, 5, 6^B, 6^N, 7, 8, 9, 10, or 11, respectively. Similar modifications are found in all categories found in the noun phrase.

D. Questionnaires on Specific Aspects

1 Roots

1.1 Derivation. Derived forms are formed by adding to a root moneme another moneme which is not a grammatical category, and does not exist as a free form in the language; it is not a syntagmatic expansion of the root.

For experimental purposes, we suggest the following list of words which, in many languages, may bring derivation relationships to light.

deverbal, verb-noun
    to eat / eating / food
    to run / running / race
    to sleep / sleeping / sleep
    to farm, cultivate / farming / field
    to see / the act of seeing / sight
    to drink / drinking / beverage

augmentative, diminutive
    thing/ big thing / small thing
    animal / big animal / small animal

frequentative, iterative
    to cut / to chop / to clip / to hack / to cut again
    to tear / to tear to pieces
    to chew / to munch / to chew again / to ruminate
    to tap / to pat / to tap again
    to hit / to bang (even harder) / to hit again

causative (implies the notion of causing to do something, helping to do, obliging to do, causing to become)
    to cut / to cause to cut
    to see / to make see / to show
    to eat / to make eat / to feed

passive
    to cut / to be cut

Morphology

applicative or prepositional, benefactive (the action is done in favor of or to the detriment of someone; or by means of, because of, next to, toward, onto someone or something)
    to give / to give to / to give for
    to lie / to lie to
    to work / to work for

reciprocal (indicates reciprocity, a mutual action; sometimes the action extends all around without discontinuity)
    to grab / to grab each other
    to love / to love one another
    to cultivate, farm / to farm all over, everywhere

reversive (expresses the opposite of the simple verb)
    to tie / to untie
    to go in / to go, come out
    to dress / to undress
    to cover / to uncover
    to open / to close

agent nouns
    dima 'to farm, cultivate' / *mu-dim-i* 'farmer, cultivator'

Of course, other types of derivatives may occur. The questionnaires dealing with formation will help to reveal these systematically.

1.2. Compounding

(a) Words often used as the basis of compounds

    mouth / head / eye / leg / arm / stomach / neck
    father / mother / chief / master / uncle
    male / female / child, little one
    hut / forest / brush / earth / water / tree / etc.

Birom	yīs.vwɔ́	'wrist bone'	/eye.arm/
	gɔ̀m.cūn	'acca owner'	/chief.acca/
	hwēy.cɔ̀kɔ̄t	'fruit, berry, seed'	/child.tree/
	dùk.cóŋōt	'henhouse'	/hut. chicken/
Ngbaka	lùkɔ́.ngó	'*Cola digitata*'	/cola.water/
	nzú.ngó	'straight-necked gourd'	/gourd.water/
	kú.ngó	'rapids'	/rope.water/
	báàmé.ngó	'giant kingfisher'	/kingfisher.water/
	bɔ́nɔ̄.ngó	'otter'	/dog.water/
	mbíà.tó	'*Thonningia sanguinea*'	/palm nut.earth/
	túlū.tó	'mushroom sp.'	/mushroom.earth/
	ngbɔ́lɔ́.tó	'peanut'	/kidney.earth/
	lù.tó	'*Cicindela* larva'	/weevil.earth/
	sómbò.tó	'white tailed mongoose'	/black-and-white colobus.earth/

(b) Agent nouns. These nouns are often formed in a specific way, e.g., 'the one (or the man) who does such and such a thing', or 'the one (or the man) of such and such a speciality'.

Ngbaka	wà.gbɔ̀.bɔ́lɔ́	'blacksmith'	/he (who).forges.forged objects/
	wà.tɔ̀kɔ̀.hő	'chef'	/he (who).makes.food/
	wà.bè.sībè	'singer'	/he (who).sings.songs/
	wà.bè.yàá	'porter'	/he (who).carries things/
	wà.mēnè.ndòkò	'adulterer'	/he (who).does.adultery/
	wà.pɔ	'debtor'	/he (of).debt/
	wà.mbáká	'mortal enemy'	/he (of).tenacious grudge/
	wà.ngàlà	'hunter'	/he (of).hunt/
Banda	èyī.ādɔ́	'disorderly person'	/he (of).disorder/
	èyī.āngbā	'thief'	/he (of).theft/
	èyī.ndàwò	'blacksmith'	/he (of).forging/
	èyī.kánɔ̀.ngáwò	'hunter'	/he (of).shooting.gun/
	èyī.kɔ́sò.lūsú	'potter'	/he (of).shaping.clay pots/
	àwō.nè	'beggar'	/he (who).begs/
	àwō.sù.lɔ́bà	'tailor'	/he (who).sews.garments/

(c) Neologisms. The introduction of techniques and articles of foreign origin entails a need for new terms. While a language sometimes resorts to borrowing, it also makes as much use as possible of its own creative processes, especially of compounding. Neologisms may be analogical, descriptive, or calques.

Birom	cǐi.rɔ̄.ǹvwá	'tsetsefly'	/fly.illness.sleep/	descriptive
Sango	bàtà.mè	'bra'	/protect.breast/	
Ngbaka	ngbɔ́lɔ́.tó	'peanut'	/kidney.earth/	
	6è.mbùnzú	'soursop'	/*Annonaceae*.european/	analogic
	bɔ́.bùnzū	'sweet banana'	/banana.european/	
	kètè.lāngɔ̄	'sleeping sickness'	/illness.sleep (pathologic) } calque	

The second part of the last compound is a loan from the trade language Sango, *lāngɔ̄* 'to sleep', which has become a noun in Ngbaka denoting sleep of a pathological nature (the Ngbaka word *lā,* a nominal derivative of *là* 'to sleep', is used for normal sleep).

2 Structures

(a) Inflectional derivation

Function. Inflection can make a change in grammatical category. A semantic shift may also be involved, e.g., the expression of the intensive, the opposition of definite and indefinite, etc.

Form. By inflection, we mean any modification in form apart from affixation, i.e., reduplication, changes in tones, consonants, or vowels, and possible combinations of these features.

Reduplication without tone change. Complete reduplication: the derivatives involves the reduplication of the whole of the root word. This reduplication may be simple (the

Morphology

root word is repeated once) or complex (the root word is repeated twice or more). The root form may still exist in the language or it may have disappeared.

$cv(c) \rightarrow cv(c).cv(c)$ $cv(c) \rightarrow cv(c).cv(c).cv(c) \ldots$
$cvcv \rightarrow cvcv.cvcv$ $cvcv \rightarrow cvcv.cvcv.cvcv \ldots$

Birom	yāŋ	'quiet'	yāŋ.yāŋ	'very quiet'
	tyɔ́ŋ	'little'	tyɔ́ŋ.tyɔ́ŋ	'very little'
Ngbaka	bī	'black'	bībībī	'very black'
*	ká		kákáká	'long time'
			kákákáká	'very long time'
			kákákákákáká	'indefinitely'
Banda *	dòló		dòló.dòló.dòló	'running continually'
	gùrù	'upset'	gùrù.gùrù	'upset'
	cūyó	'thin'	cūyó.cūyó	'gaunt'

Partial reduplication: the derivative involves the partial reduplication of the root word. For a monosyllabic word, only part is affected; for a dissyllabic or polysyllabic word, the reduplication affects either a part or the whole of one syllable.

$c_1vc_2 \rightarrow c_1vc_1vc_2 \sim c_1vc_2vc_2$
$c_1vc_2v \rightarrow c_1vc_1vc_2v \sim c_1vc_2vc_2v$ etc.

Bafia *	kpɔ́p		→	kpɔ́kpɔ́p	'plant'
	síā̃		→	sísíā̃	'fiber'
	púkà	'foam'	→	púpúkà	'subs (of soap)'

Reduplication with tone change. Complete reduplication of the segments of the root: the tone change may be total (in a dissyllabic word, both syllables change tone) or partial (in a dissyllabic word, only one syllable changes tone).

$cv́ \rightarrow cv̀.cv́ \sim cv́.cv̀ \qquad cv̀ \rightarrow cv̄.cv̀ \sim cv̀.cv̄$ etc.
$cv́cv́ \rightarrow cv́.cv́.cv̀cv̀ \sim cv̀cv̀.cv́cv́ \qquad cv̀ \rightarrow cv̀.cv̀.cv̀cv̄ \sim cv̄cv̄.cv̀cv̀$ etc.

Ngbaka	nō-	→	nònō	'foot (specific)'
Banda *	pītī	→	pītī.pìtì	'a large quantity'
Bafia *	kúdú	→	kúdú.kūdū	'hard to walk because of leprosy'
	dùn	'pound' →	dùmá.dùmá	'mortar'

Partial reduplication of the segments of the root word: the tone change affects the root word or the reduplicated part, or both.

$cv̀ \rightarrow cv̀cv́ \sim cv́cv̀ \qquad c_1vc_2v̀ \rightarrow c_1v̀c_1vc_2v̀ \sim c_1v́c_2v̀c_2v̀$ etc.
$c_1vc_2v̀ \rightarrow c_1v̀c_1v́c_2v̀$

Ngbaka	sì̄	'plant'	sìsíì	'the act of planting'
	hō̄	'eat'	hòhɔ́ɔ̀	'the act of eating'
	kpēlè	'deliver'	kpèkpélè	'the act of delivering'

Tonal inflection. Complete or partial tone change in the root word.

$cv̀ \rightarrow cv́ \sim cv̄$ etc.
$cv́ \rightarrow cv̀ \sim cv̄$ etc.
$cv́cv̀ \rightarrow cv̀cv́ \sim cv́cv́ \sim cv̀cv̀$ etc.

Ngabka	hō̄	'eat'	hő	'food'
	wɔ̀	'breathe'	wɔ́ɔ̀	'breath'
	zì	'steal'	zī	'theft'
	nɔ̄lɔ̀	'walk'	nɔ́lɔ̄	'a walk'
	yēngè	'sift'	yèngè	'sifter'
Banda	kāngà	'imprison'	kàngà	'slave'
	ngāʃà	'sneeze'	ngáʃā	'sneezing'

Vocalic inflection. Change in vowel quality (affecting one or more vowels) in the root word.

$$cv_1 \rightarrow cv_2 \qquad cv_1cv'_1 \rightarrow cv_1cv'_2 \sim c_2vc'_1v \text{ etc.}$$

Ngbaka	zókò	'good'	zúzúkò	'goodness'
	mólō		múmólō	'master'
	zākà	'design, paint'	zākā̀	'write'

Consonantal inflection. Consonant change in the derivative (as compared with the root word).

$$c_1v \rightarrow c_2v \qquad c_1vc'_1v \rightarrow c_1vc'_2v \sim c_2vc'_1v \text{ etc.}$$

Bafia	gáɓúú	'termite sp.'	kùù-kákáɓúú	'gáɓúú termite catching basket'
Fca	bāad	'applaud'	ngbāadɛ	'clapping'
	hāb	'kill'	pāb	'murder'
	hām	'harvest'	kām	'the harvest'
	gēg	'look for'	kēg	'research'

(Vocalic and consonantal inflection may occur with reduplication.)
  In all these cases, one should try to discover the function of the derivative in relation to its form. An attempt should be made, therefore, to show the tonal, vocalic, or consonantal patterns in the derivation. For example:
  The verb cv̄ corresponds to the noun cv́, expressing a result;
  The verb cv̀ corresponds to the noun cṽ, expressing a means of the action, etc.

(b) Affixal derivation

Function. Affixes can bring about changes in the meaning, and occasionally in the grammatical category, of the root. This process is the most common type of verbal derivation, but is also used for noun formation in many languages, especially those with noun classes.

Form. The affix may be a prefix, suffix, or infix, and may affect different segmental or tonal structures.

Form of the affix. segmental structure: v / cv(c) ~ (c)vc / c

Fca	ŋōs	'divide up'	ŋōs.ī	'pieces'
	yɔ̄s	'cut'	yɔ̄s.īrr	'chop'
	bɔ̄θ	'wring'	bɔ̄θ.īl	'twisted'

Morphology

Banda
nā	'walk'		á.ná	'a step'
mɔ̄	'ripen'		ɔ̄.mɔ̄	'ripe'
dū	'forge'		à.dú	'sledgehammer'
mèrɔ̀	'swell'		à.mérɔ́	'swelling'
wūtù	'leave'		kɔ́.wūtù	'act of leaving'

Birom
yērē	'cut'		yērē.s	'cut several times'
rāŋāl	'ask'		rāŋ.s.āl	'question'

The segmental structure of the affix is fixed (i.e., it remains unchanged regardless of the form of the root):

Banda prefix *kɔ́-*
ʔīmɔ̀	'stammer'	kɔ́.ʔīmɔ̀	'act of stammering'
ngāʃà	'sneeze'	kɔ́.ngāʃà	'act of sneezing'

prefix *à-*
gòrɔ̀	'pursue'	à.górɔ́	'pursuit'
ngbò	'reassemble'	à.ngbó	'meeting'

Ngbaka suffix *ngà-*
nzō	'drink, deny'	nzō.ngà	'swear'
yō	'call, name'	yō.ngà	'show, indicate'
zī	'turn'	zī.ngà	'divert'
hī	'know'	hī.ngà	'ask'

The segmental structure of the affix is variable (total or partial vowel or consonant harmony):

Banda prefix *v-* (the prefix vowel is the same as that of the root)
nā	'walk'	áná	'walk'
lō	'sleep'	ōlō	'sleep'
mī	'be thick'	ímí	'filled, trimmed'

Ngbaka suffix *-cv* (the suffix vowel is the same as that of the root)
dɔ̄	'trip'	dɔ̄tɔ̀	'stumble'	dɔ̄tɔ̀kɔ̀	'stamp foot'
mō	'tire'	mōlò	'kill'	mōlòkò	'massacre'
pì	'split'	pīkì	'fold up'		

Nzakara suffix *-kā ~ -kɔ̄* (the vowel quality of the suffix is conditioned by that of the root vowel)
ngbí	'lather'	kɔ̄.ngbí	'act of lathering'
ngbé	'cover with chaff'	kā.ngbé	'act of covering with chaff'

Tonal structure (considered separately from the segmental structure only in order to simplify the investigation/research). As for the segmental structure, two possibilities must be considered:

The tonal structure of the affix is fixed (remains unchanged regardless of the tones of the root; however, the tones of the root may be modified):

Ngbaka
tɔ̄	'germinate'	tɔ̄kɔ̀	'boil'
mōlò	'kill'	mōlòkò	'massacre'
tò	'bump against'	tōkò	'push in'

The tonal structure of the affix is variable (conditioned by the tone(s) of the root):

Bafia prefix *tì-*
    tí-én   'leaves'
    tī-ēē̆   'steps'
    tì-ɔ̀l   'smiles'

Position of the affix.
Prefixation (the affix is placed before the root):

Bafia   *tʌʔ*   'carry' → *ǹ.tʌʔ/mʌ̀.tʌʔ* 'luggage'

Banda   *dū*   'forge' → *à.dú*   'sledgehammer'

French *poser* → *reposer*   faire → *refaire*   dire → *redire*
             → *déposer*   → *défaire*   → *dédire*

Suffixation (the affix is placed after the root):

Ngbaka *kɔ̄* 'gather' → *kɔ̄.lɔ̀* 'cut' → *kɔ̄lɔ̄.kɔ̀* 'cut carelessly'
          ɓì 'get down' → *ɓī.tà* 'reverse, push'

French *chanson* → *chansonnette*   *maison* → *maisonnette*
        jupe → *jupette*   *fleur* → *fleurette*, etc.
        lav(er) → *lavage*   *mont(er)* → *montage*
        pli(er) → *pliage*   *sci(er)* → *sciage*

Infixation (the affix is placed inside the root):

Birom *rāŋāl* 'ask'   *rāŋ.s.āl* 'question'

(c) Derivations formed by both affixation and inflection.

We also find combinations of different modificational processes in a single derivation, or combinations of different affixation processes, or even combinations of modificational and affixation processes (which is rather common). We will consider the following possible combinations:
    affixation with reduplication
    affixation with tonal or vocalic or consonantal modification
    affixation with reduplication and tonal or vocalic or consonantal modifications

Bafia   *fép* 'blow' → *rù.fép/mʌ̀.fép*   'cold'   P
                              fèè.fèè/´bʌ̀.fèèfèè   'breeze'   P+R+Tm
                              bèp   'wind'   Tm+Cm
                              bèè.bèè   'air'   R+Tm+Cm
                              ǹ.féɓú/ɓʌ̀.féɓú   'bellows'   P+Cm+S
                              féèm.zèn   'breathe'   Tm+Cm+S
                              véèm.zén   'breath, sigh' Cm+Tm+S

N.B. P: prefix; R: reduplication; Tm: tonal modification; Cm: consonantal modification; S: suffix.

After some derivational processes (affixational or modificational) have been isolated, it is good to systematically explore all possibilities of their use with different root already known. For words whose form makes us suspect that they are derived, an attempt should be made to isolate their roots, and have speakers of the language identify them.

Morphology

Ngbaka roots	-kv̀	-lv̀	-tv̀	-nv̀	-ngv̀
pè 'make, jump, sift'	pēkè 'shake'	pēlè 'dust'	(pētè) x	pēnè 'turn and return'	(pēngè) x
bē 'hit'	(bēkè) x	(bēlè) x	bētè 'crouch'	bēnè 'plant nail'	bēngè 'sharpen'
zā 'touch'	zākà 'design'	zālà 'scrape'	(zātà) x	zānà 'dyed'	zāngà 'dye'

etc.

The forms *pētè, pēngè, bēkè, bēlè and zātà are not identified.
On the other hand, if we know these derivatives:

gāpà	'share, divide'
gāmà	'stammer, mumble, babble (divide the word)'
gānà	'pass, surpass, conquer, succeed, be difficult, reprimand'
gākà	'abandon, leave (separation, division)'

gāpàkà 'share (freq.)'

we may suppose that there is a root (or roots) gā or gà (the only two forms possible in the language). As a matter of fact, gā 'to be tall, big, immense, important, serious' exists and turns out to be the root of the derivative gānà.

There is no root *gà for gāpà, gāmà, and gākà, which are all derived from the same source. However, gã 'to cut, carve', which fits into the same set, may be the root, although it has been modified (perhaps through derivation) by nasalization of the vowel.

(d) Compounding

Function. Compounding is principally a noun-forming process, but it may also produce verbs, relators, clause-markers, interrogatives, or various types of markers. In some languages, there are special grammatical categories, such as the dependent noun (nominoid), which use compounding as a formation process. These dependent nouns cannot occur alone in discourse, but must be accompanied by a modifier, or else take on the form of a head or independent noun.

This formation of nouns and dependent nouns often yields a large number of plant and animal names, as well as names for the parts of the body, agents, persons, neologisms, etc.

Form. The form of compounds will be studied from three aspects:

1. the combination of their components
2. the recognizability of their components
3. the extent to which the compounds fit into the grammatical structures.

Combination of components. Compounds are classified by the number of their components, by the grammatical or lexical character of these components, and by the grammatical categories of the components.

Number of components. Compounds with two components:

Ngbaka   *nzò.nō-*   'toe'   /head.foot/
         wà.ngàlà   'hunter'   /he (of) hunt/

More than two components (consider 3, 4, etc. components in turn):

Ngbaka   *wà.gbɔ̀.bɔ́lɔ́*   'blacksmith'   /he.(who).forges.forged items/
         sōlōkō.mò.pa̋pa̋   'fork'   /tear.mouth.spoon/

Grammatical or lexical character of the components. Compounds with grammatical components:

Ngbaka   *wà.nè*   'this one'   /he.(of).here/   NM + P

N.B. A: adjective; D: derivative; DN: dependent noun or nominoid; N: nominal; NM: nominal modifier; P: possessive; Q: qualifier; R: relator; V: verbal; VN: verb = noun ~ noun modifier.

Compounds with lexical components:

Ngbaka   *sàlà.mò.dōkpē*   'crossroad'   /branch.mouth.route/   N + DN + N
         mɔ́kɔ́.tē   'canine tooth'   /male.tooth/   DN + DN
         pàpáà.bū   'miscarriage'   /passing.abdomen/   VN + DN

Mixed compounds (the order of the grammatical and lexical components varies according to the language and may be fixed or variable in the same language):

Ngbaka   *wà.mà*   'fetisher, healer'   /he (of) magic/   NM + N
         wà.mènè.ndòkò   'adulterous'   /he.does.adultery/   NM + V + N

Grammatical category of the components. Compounds may be classified on the basis of the word class of either the first or the last component.

The first component is:

noun
Ngbaka
    bɔ́.gő   'plantain sp.'   /banana.war/   N + N → N
    mbà.nzò   'tatooing knife'   /knife.head/   N + DN → N
    sàlà.mò.dōkpē   'crossroad'   /branch.mouth.route/   N + DN + N → N

dependent noun
Ngbaka
    sà.ɓākā   'armpit'   /beneath.wing/   DN + DN → DN
    nzò.tó.kò   'tomb'   /head.earth.cadaver/   DN + N + DN → DN
    sà.gúmà.kpā   'bend of the arm'   /beneath.middle.arm/   DN + DN + DN → DN

qualifier
Ngbaka
    sōlōkō.mò.pa̋pa̋   'fork'   /torn.mouth.spoon/   Q + DN + N → N
    ɲōkō.zè   'deafness'   /closed.ear/   Q + DN → N
    nūsū.pé.ngɔ̀lɔ̀   'hunchback'   /curved.above.neck/   Q + DN + DN → N

adjective
Ngbaka
    sítī.kpé   'forest spirit sp.'   /bad.day/   A + N → N
    ngénē.nō.mɔ̀ngɔ́   'pants'   /long.leg.clothes/   A + DN + N → N

Morphology

verb-noun
Ngbaka
    pìpû.túsù.ngō̄   'reconciliation'   /division.stomach.chicken/   VN + DN + N → N
    pàpáà.bū   'miscarriage'   /passing.abdomen/   VN + DN → N

verb
Ngbaka
    ɓàlà.dípā   'dung-beetle'   /roll.dung/   V + N → N
    dɔ̀-yò-kólí   'beetle (*Teflus megerlei*)'   /come.clothes.bereavement/   V + V + N → N
    dò.gbó.tē   'houserat'   /stay.inside.house/   V + DN + N → N
    dù.gítā.kémà   'grey hornbill'   /push in.buttocks.monkey/   V + DN + N → N
    dóò.pé.kénzé   'fish sp.'   /stay.upon.sand/   V + DN + N → N
    dúù.nō   'panties'   /push in.foot/   V + DN → N
    gbîè.hɔ́lɔ́   'running knot'   /pull.fast/   V + Adv → N
    hóò.gáā   'fish sp.'   /eat.canoe/   V + N → N

relator
Ngbaka
    ná.ɓō   'for'   /for.to/   R + R → R
    káà.ɓà   'as much as'   /again.as/   R + R → R
    káà.ɓú   'contrary'   /again.first/   R + R → P
    káà.bīā.ɓō   'nothing but'   /again.numerous.to/   R + V + R → R

noun modifier
Ngbaka
    wà.ngàlà   'hunter'   /he (of) the hunt/   NM + N → N

etc.

All grammatical categories that occur as the first component of a compound should be considered.

Word class of the compound. Finally, compounds are classified on the basis of the grammatical category of the compound as a whole.

noun
Banda
    èyī.āngbā   'thief'   /he.theft/   DN + N → N
    èyī.kánè   'beggar'   /he.begs it/   DN + VN → N
    àwō.nè   'beggar'   /he.begs/   Def + V → N
    èyī.wɔ́rɔ́gbɔ́   'well-being'   /he.strong/   DN + A → N
    bù.kɔ̀zɔ̀   'Brazza's monkey'   /black.monkey/   A + N → N
    cé.pá   'top'   /tie.above/   N + R → N
    àpà.ìʃì   'fork'   /spoon.thorn/   N + N → N

dependent noun
Ngbaka
    mɔ́kɔ́.tē   'canine tooth'   /male.tooth/   DN + DN → DN
    mò.dó.kèngé   'back of the head'   /mouth.stay.at neck/   DN + (V + R) + DN → DN

relator
Ngbaka
    ná.ɓō   'for'   /for.to/   R + R →
    káà.bīā.ɓō   'nothing but'   /again.numerous.to/   R + V + R → R

Identifiability of the components of compounds. Two types of compounds are distinguished: (1) all the components are still identifiable and occur as free forms in the language; (2) the components are only partly identifiable: at least one no longer occurs as a free form or cannot be identified (including forms which are probably compounds for phonological or morphological reasons).

Fully identifiable compounds. All the components occur as free forms in the language (apart from possible formal modifications), and can be identified by the speakers.

Banda	cé.là.gō	'village'	/place.surface.country/
	rà.kà	'sickness'	/thing.do bad/
Ngbaka	hṍ.bū.mbùlùyà	'balsam'	/food.stomach.sitatunga/
	ngénē.gálà	'fish sp.'	/long.side/
	dóò.pé.kénzέ	'fish sp.'	/stay.under.sand/
	mɔ̀.tē.έ.ngbò.béè	'glossy-backed Drongo'	/build.house.with.feather.his friend/

Partially identifiable compounds. Some compounds contain forms that have disappeared from everyday speech and are now found only in compounds. Some are still identifiable (by all or only some speakers), while some are not.

Component(s) no longer occurring except in compounds:

French	raz-de-marée	'tidal wave'	
	rez-de-chaussée	'ground floor'	
	potron-minet	'crack of dawn'	
	porte-faix, etc.	'porter'	
Ngbaka	pé.tɔ́kɔ́.kū.là	'upper eyelid'	/above.surface.cover eye/
Banda	tī.mà	'tongue'	/long, mobile appendage.mouth/
	tī.là.ngɔ̀rɔ̀	'uvula'	/appendage.in.mouth/
	yárádá.ōnū	'toes'	/ramification.foot/
	yárádá.ɔ̄ná	'fingers'	/ramification.hand/

One or more unidentified components:

Ngbaka	kpó.ngbó	'Calamus, sp.'	/large vine. —/
	ngbó.fiò	'Ancistrophyllum, sp.'	/—. —/
	(the second compound is only identifiable by comparison with the first)		
	mbóòó.ndí	'striped mongoose'	/—. savanah/
Birom	sīná.rɔ́kɔ́	'Acacia albida'	/—. thorn/
	dùk.kák	'cottage'	/house. —/
	sám.byá	'twins'	/—. two/
	gám.yòmō	'weak billy goat'	/billy goat. —/
	gbûŋ.bàyīs	'eyebrow'	/—. eyes/

Stems for compounding: certain stems are used productively in the formation of compounds; the discovery of such stems can help one to identify certain compounds in which one or more components are no longer identifiable.

Ngbaka -ngó   'water' (as the final element in compounds)
     lùkɔ́.ngó   'Cola digitata'   /cola.water/
     ʔí.bòló.ngó   'water serpent sp.'   /snake sp.(=mother.fish sp.). water/
     tèmé.ngó   'pebbles'   /stones.water/
     bɔ́nō.ngó   'otter'   /dog.water/

Compounds which yield to analysis:
     sí.mbò.ngó   'high water'   /full. — .water/
     sé.ngó   'grass of humid undergrowth' /—. water/
     kànzákà.ngó   'water spider'   /—. water/

Probable compounds: The form of some words suggests that they are compounds. For example, some languages have strict vowel harmony where certain vowel sequences never occur within the moneme. Similarly, restrictions on consonant or tone sequences may be clues of compounding.

Ngbaka mò.dɔ́kɔ́   'ceremonial staff'

This word is not recognized as a compound in present-day speech; however, knowing that mid vowels with different degrees of openness (o/ɔ and e/ɛ, or o/ɛ, or e/ɔ) are incompatible within the simple word, we are justified in assuming that mò.dɔ́kɔ́ is a compound. This hypothesis is strengthened by a study of the compounding stems/bases, which shows the importance of compounds with mò 'mouth, end, edge'.

Birom kwàándɔ̀ŋ   'ritual dance'

Although this word is not recognized as a compound in present-day speech, it may be interpreted as such because it has the following phonological characteristics that are not normally found in the simple word: the a/ɔ combination; the consonant cluster nd; and the rising tone, which normally occurs only at the end of words, but is on the first syllable here. We thus conclude that we have a compound kwàán.dɔ̀ŋ.

Integration into the grammatical structures of the language. Although derivation and compounds are discussed under different headings, they are not in fact completely separate. Similarly, it is often difficult to distinguish with certainty between characteristics/phenomena of compounding and relationships of modification. We thus consider compounds as to their syntactic or nonsyntactic character.

Syntactic (endocentric) compounds. This type of compound seems no different, at first glance, from phrases, or certain types of clauses (e.g., determinative noun phrases or relative noun phrases, or even a complete sentence).

French oeil-de-boeuf   'bull's eye window'   /eye.of.bovine/
        oeil-de-pie   'sail lacets'   /eye.of.magpie/
        pied-à-terre   'occasional lodging'   /foot.to.earth/
        pied-de-poule   'hound's tooth'   /foot.of.chicken/

English forget-me-not

Ngbaka nzē.té   'chance'   /blood.body/
        sítī.là.kpé   'fever'   /bad.eye.day/
        tɔ́.kpé   'morning'   /new.day/
        hɔ́.bū.mbùlùyà   'balsam'   /food.stomach.sitatunga/
        mā.hɔ̄.má.gɔ̄   'plantain sp.'   /(that) I.eat.(and) I.leave/

The above expressions may be classed as compounds for the following reasons:
(a) They belong in the substitution class of a grammatical category, seen by their possibilities of combination and use.
(b) The compound is indivisible, making a whole which cannot be analyzed as the sum of its parts.

Thus, in French, *oeil-de-boeuf* 'bull's-eye (window)' can substitute for *lucarne* 'skylight' in all contexts: 'a house with two skylights' ~ 'a house with two 'bull's eye windows'; 'the skylight is open' ~ 'the bull's eye window is open'.

Similarly, in Ngbaka, *tɔ́.kpé* 'morning' may be substituted for *wóndó* 'noon' and *mɔ̀kɔ̀lɔ̀* 'evening'.

These forms fit into the grammatical class of noun perfectly and behave as nouns in every way:

English
   a large skylight   ~ *a large bull's-eye window*
   my skylight   ~ *my bull's-eye window*
   the attic skylight is broken   ~ *the bull's-eye attic window is broken*

Although *bull's-eye window* can be expanded in the same ways as *skylight*, it is not possible, despite appearances, to separate its elements (by expansion, for example) without destroying its identity. *Skylight* is clearly indivisible, but *bull's-eye window* whose elements seem separable, loses its identity if they are separated: *an eye of a small bull* or *a bull's brown eye* no longer correspond in any way to the meaning *small round skylight*.

Similarly, in Ngbaka, *tɔ́.kpé* 'morning' and *mā.hō̄.má.gɔ́* 'plantain sp.' fit into the class of nouns just like *mɔ̀kɔ̀lɔ̀* 'evening' and *bɔ́* 'banana', and behave the same:

Ngbaka   ʔé dɔ́ té mɔ̀kɔ̀lɔ̀   'he came in the evening'
          ʔé dɔ́ té tɔ́.kpé   'he came in the morning'
          màá hō̄ bɔ́   'I ate a banana'
          màá hō̄ mā.hō̄.má.gɔ́   'I ate a plantain sp.'
          hà mā bɔ́-ɓīsì   'give me two bananas'
          hà mā mā.hō̄.má.gɔ́-ɓīsì   'give me two plantains sp.'
          ʔá bɔ́-ŋā   'it's my banana'
          ʔá mā.hō̄.má.gɔ́-ŋā   'it's my plantain sp.'

The indivisibility of the parts of the compound is also clear in these examples, which have different meanings:

Ngbaka   *zókò-tɔ́.kpé*   'a beautiful morning'
          tɔ́-zókò-kpé   'a beautiful new day'

Thus we try to define the extreme cases as much as possible, showing both that they are indivisible and belong to a grammatical category.

Nonsyntactic (exocentric) compounds. This type is immediately recognizable as a compound, since the combination of components is not like any phrase type found in the language. Furthermore, formal modifications characteristic of compounding may affect one or more of the components.

Morphology 253

nonsyntactic combinations

French	*pince-monseigneur*	'jemmy'	*ouest-allemand*	'West German'
	pause-café	'coffee break'	*oiseau-lyre*	'lyre bird'
	oiseau-mouche	'hummingbird'	*nord-africain*	'north African'
	non-lieu	'withdrawal of case'	*nord-ouest*	'northwest'
	fille-mére	'unmarried mother'		

None of these combinations could be considered some type of determinative phrase in French.

Birom	*mwāàt.rá.tɔ̀rɔ̀ŋ*	'baptiser'	/man + of.do.imposition of name/
	hwāà.lɔ́k.rōy	'potter'	/woman + of.make.pot/

The nonsyntactic character is evident here from the fact that the verb is nonfinite (unconjugated) and that the noun head precedes it. An attributive noun phrase in the language could never have this structure.

Ngbaka *ɓàlà.dípā* 'dung-beetle' /push.dung/

This is not a complete sentence (there is no subject) and cannot be regarded as an imperative utterance.

mɔ̀.té.ʔé.ngbò.béè 'glossy-backed Drongo' /build.house.with.feather.friend + his/

This is not a complete sentence (no subject) and cannot be regarded as an imperative (an imperative utterance would use a different possessive: *mɔ̀.té.ʔé.ngbò.bé.mɔ̀* /build. house. with. feathers. friend. 'your'/).

dɔ̀.yèlè.kólí 'lizard sp.' /come.exchange.bereavement/

This is not a complete sentence (no subject) and is not grammatically correct (no relator, as in *dɔ̀.ʔèé.yèlè.kólí ~ dɔ́ɔ́.yèlè.kólí* / comes + to.exchange.bereavement /).

dò.gbó.tē 'black rat, house rat' /stay.inside.house/

This is not a complete sentence (no subject) nor is it grammatically correct (no relator).
All these compounds have the form of incomplete agent nouns, without the noun determiner *wà* seen in *wà.gbɔ̀.bɔ́lɔ́* 'blacksmith' /the. strikes. forging/, which is itself a nonsyntactic form (cf. J. M. C. Thomas, *Parler ngbaka*, 154).

changes in form

Ngbaka	*dúù.nō*	'pants, underwear'	/push in.foot/
	dóò.pé.kénzé	'fish sp.'	/stay.upon.sand/
	záà.pé	'fixed part of the climbing belt'	/touch.palm tree/
	béè.tó	'swallow (bird)'	/hit.earth/
	zàzàlà.dèngbè	'*Streptogyna crinata*' herb sp.	/scrape.blue duiker/

All these compounds have components that are recognized as coming from verbs that still exist in the language, but in a form that hardly ever occurs by itself:

Ngbaka	*dúù.*	←	*dù*	'push in'
	dóò.	←	*dō*	'stay'
	záà.	←	*zā*	'touch'
	béè.	←	*bē*	'hit'
	zàzàlà.	←	*zālà*	'scrape'

In present-day speech, the forms *dúù, dóò, záà, béè, zàzàlà*, etc., are characteristic of compounds.

Similarly, in the following examples, the components are easily recognized as deriving from nouns, but they assume a special form in compounds:

Ngbaka

'place of chanting for the hunt' /place.word/
.*wò* comes from *wō* 'word'.
'counsel, proverb' /fruit.word/
.*wò* comes from *wō* 'word' (sometimes still, but rarely, found in the form *lé.wō*.
'well' /hole.water/
.*ngò* comes fron *ngó* 'water', here the compound form contrasts with the free form in the determiner *dú-ngó* 'water hole'. The compound form is found in *nò̀-ngò* 'spring', for which the first part is unknown.

Every type of nonsyntactic combination in the language concerned should thus be sought (along with the types of modifications of form) as a possible system of classifying compounds.

(e) The forms themselves in paradigms

Noun paradigms. In languages with agreement classes, one must examine systematically all parts of speech related to the nouns and try to discover the rules governing their formation. Of course, it is impossible to give general rules here, since these phenomena are specific to each language. As an example, consider Birom: the presence of the infix -y- characterizes classes 9 and 10, and the infix -w- characterizes classes 1 and 3. In some cases, these infixes fuse with the initial consonant or the vowel of the root, according to different rules. In order to discover these rules, one must examine all clusters of the types C + y + V and C + w + V, all nouns in classes 9/10 and 1/3, and all lexical modifiers (adjectives, qualifiers) and grammatical modifiers (possessives, demonstratives, etc) involved in the agreement system.

Study of C + w + V

Birom	*kwèn*	|k.w̄.èn|	/ *bìkèn*	|bì.k.`.èn|	'finger' SG/PL
	kwárá	|k.w̄.árá|	/ *kàrá*	|k.`.árá|	'enclosure'
	gwīk	|g.w̄.īk|	/ *bīgīk*	|bī.gīk|	'thief'
	pwēp	|p.w̄.ēp|	/ *pèp*	|p.`.ēp|	'bellows'

Study of classes 1/2 and 3/4

	vwɔ́	/ *vɔ̀*	(3/4)	'leg'	|v.w̄.ɔ́|	/ |v.`.ɔ́|
	hwītī	/ *hìtī*	(3/4)	'field'	|h.w̄.ītī|	/ |h.`.ītī|
	rókó	/ *ròkó*	(3/4)	'thorn'	|r.w̄.ókó|	/ |r.`.ókó|

In the last example, the infix -w- is not represented in the sequence r + w + o. the infix -w- of the sequence r + w + o is not represented.

	rwās	/ *bīrās*	(1/2)	'male'	|r.w̄.ās|	/ |bī.rās|
	kwēnèt	/ *bīkēnèt*	(1/2)	'host'	|k.w̄.ēnèt|	/ |bī.kēnèt|
	gwīk	/ *bīgīk*	(1/2)	'thief'	|g.w̄.īk|	/ |bī.gīk|
	sá	/ *bīsá*	(1/2)	'friend'	|s.w̄.á|	/ |bī.sá|

Morphology

In the last example, the -w- of the sequence s + w + a is not represented.
Study of the adjectives -rìm 'blue', -réy 'rich', and -sīt 'black' in classes 1/2 and 3/4.

rìm	/ bīrìm	(1/2)	|r.w̄.ìm|	/	|bī.rìm|
rìm	/ rìm	(3/4)	|r.w̄.ìm|	/	|r.`.ìm|
rwéy	/ bīréy	(1/2)	|r.w̄.éy|	/	|bī.réy|
rwéy	/ rèéy	(3/4)	|r.w̄.éy|	/	|r.`.éy|
swīt	/ bīsīt		|s.w̄.īt|	/	|bī.sīt|
swīt	/ sìt		|s.w̄.īt|	/	|s.`.īt|

Here, the infix -w- in the sequences s + w + i and r + w + e does show up, while in the sequence r + w + i it does not.

An exhaustive examination of classes 1/2 and 3/4 brings to light the following rules:

- -w- does not show up in the sequence C + w + V, where C = f; t, d; c, y; kp, gb, w.

- -w- may or may not show up in the sequence C + w + i/a (front V) but does not show up in the sequence C + w + a/u (back V), where C = n, r; s, z; k, g, ŋ.

- -w- shows up in the sequence C + w + i/a (front V), but does not show up in the sequence C + w + a/u (back V), where C = p; l; j; h.

- -w- shows up in the sequence C + w + a/u where C = b, m; v.

Verb paradigms. The verb conjugation is usually a special area, where fusion (often) occurs. Consider the case, common in Bantu languages, where the predicate phrase has the following form:

Subject pronoun + verbal marker + verb root

If the corresponding segmental pattern is, for example:

cv + v(c) + cv(cv)

one must find out exactly how the subject pronoun [cv-] and the verbal marker [-v(c)-] combine. The final vowel of the subject pronoun and the vowel of the marker generally fuse according to rules that must be determined; the tones and the fusion rules that govern them must similarly be examined.

Birom	má-cíŋ	'I dig'	|mé-ā-cíŋ|
	hò-cíŋ	'you dig'	|hò-ā-cíŋ|
	yè ā-cíŋ	'he digs'	|yè-ā-cíŋ|

In order to set up representations with the unfused forms (the structural or morphophonemic form, depending on the school), it is necessary to find out the root forms, i.e., canonical forms that are not represented in the language but deduced by analysis.

Thus, in a language with the predicate phrase form given above (subject pronoun + verbal marker + verb root), if the segmental pattern of the subject pronoun is sometimes cv and sometimes cvc, the verbal marker will be rather easily identifiable, since its initial vowel (in the above pattern - v(c)-) will not have fused with the vowel of the subject pronoun when the later has the structure cvc.

Birom

wōt ā-cíŋ	'we dig'	wōt à-cīŋ	'we dug'
yīn ā-cíŋ	'you dig'	yīn à-cīŋ	'you dug'
yèn ā-cíŋ	'they dig'	yèn à-cīŋ	'they dug'
wōt cíŋ	'that we dug'	wōt á-cíŋ	'we dug (yesterday)'
yīn cíŋ	'that you dug'	yīn á-cíŋ	'you dug (yesterday)'
yèn cíŋ	'that they dug'	yèn á-cíŋ	'they dug (yesterday)'

From this, we can analyze the following forms:

má-cíŋ	'I dig'	|mé-ā-cíŋ|
mà-cīŋ	'I dug'	|mé-à-cīŋ|
mé-cíŋ	'that I dug'	|mé-ø-cíŋ|
má-cíŋ	'I dug (yesterday)'	|mé-á-cíŋ|

Questionnaire 6
Verb Phrase

A. Thematic questionnaire
by Fr. Cloarec-Heiss

This questionnaire is based on the grammatical questionnaire drawn up by the SOAS. It has been revised, modified, and expanded in the light of its use with different languages studied by the members of ER 74.

Once the verb types in the language studied have been established (cf. Questionnaire on structures), conjugate one of each type in all persons.

1 Present

1.1. I
1.2. you (SG)
1.3. he / she / it
1.4. we (including you SG / you PL)
1.5. we (excluding you SG / you PL)
1.6. we two
1.7. you (PL)
1.8. you two
1.9. they (M) / they (F) / they (neuter)
1.10. they two (M) / they two (F) / they two (neuter)

} is walking / is not walking

} is making / is not making

1.11. What are you doing? I am crushing the grain.
1.12. He is coming to ask for a pestle.

2 Past

2.1. Did you see my son yesterday? Yes, I saw him. No, I did not see him.
2.2. What were you doing this morning? I was crushing grain.

2.3. What were you crushing this morning? I was crushing grain.
2.4. What did you kill yesterday? I did not kill anything. I killed a hare.
2.5. Whom, did you see in the village? I did not see anyone. I saw only an old man.
2.6. Who saw you going to the village? Nobody saw me. Only a little boy saw me.
2.7. He came just now.
2.8. He came this morning.
2.9. He came yesterday.
2.10. He came last year.
2.11. He came with his friend { yesterday. / just now. / last year.
2.12 He had come { yesterday. / last year. / just now. / ten years ago.

3 Immediate past

3.1. I (have) just finished skinning the antelope.
3.2. He (has) just left.
3.3. He (has) just arrived.
3.4. He left a second ago.

4 Future

4.1. I shall not do anything.
4.2. My cow is dead. What shall I do.?
4.3. Won't you go and see the shaman about that?
4.4. Will he arrive tomorrow? Yes, he will arrive tomorrow. No, he will not arrive tomorrow, but the day after.
4.5. Will you work for the chief today or tomorrow? I shall work for him tomorrow; today, I shall rest.
4.6. Who will go? I will go. So-and-so will go. Nobody will go.
4.7. He will come shortly.
4.8. He will come this evening.
4.9. He will come tomorrow.
4.10. He will come next year.

5 Immediate future

5.1. What are you going to sing?
5.2. He is going to come { shortly. / tomorrow. / this afternoon.
5.3. He is just about to leave.
5.4. He is going to leave any moment now.
5.5. He is leaving in a moment.
5.6. He will leave in a moment.

Verb Phrase

6 Indicative

6.1. He is going. He is coming. He is running.
6.2. He is eating.
6.3. He is eating gruel.
6.4. He is opening.
6.5. He is opening the door.

7 Reported speech

7.1.	He said that you were to come.	$S \neq S'$
7.2.	He(i) said that he(j) was to come.	$S \neq S'$
7.3.	He(i) said that he(i) will come.	$S = S'$
7.4.	He(i) said that he(i) was going to come.	$S = S'$
7.5.	He(i) said that he(j) was going to come.	$S \neq S'$
7.6.	He said that you were going to come.	$S \neq S'$
7.7.	He(i) said that he(i) would come.	$S = S'$
7.8.	He(i) said that he(j) would come.	$S \neq S'$

7.9. He said that you might come.
7.10. He said that he might come.
7.11. My brother says that he is ill.
7.12. My mother says that he is not ill, but just lazy, and that my father should beat him.
7.13. My sister says that she did not steal the meat, but that it was taken by the dog.
7.14. My father says that she is lying and that she stole it herself.
7.15. The chief says that his wife ran away and that he is coming to beat her.
7.16. The chief says, "Pay me ten goats!"
7.17. The chief says that I must pay him ten goats.
7.18. The chief said to me, "I am very angry with you, because you are a liar."
7.19. The chief told me that he was very angry with me because I was a liar.
7.20. The chief said that he was very angry with you because you are a liar.
7.21. I said that I was going to come.
7.22. You said that you were going to come.
7.23. We said that we were going to come.
7.24. You (PL) said that you were going to come.
7.25. They(i) said that they(i) were going to come. $\quad S = S'$
7.26. They(i) said that they(j) were going to come. $\quad S \neq S'$

8 Narrative

8.1. Yesterday I went to X ... , (I) bought some grain, (I) brought it home to my wife, (I) told her to cook it, she cooked it and we ate it.
8.2. Tomorrow I will go to X ... , (I) will buy some grain, (I) will bring it home to my wife, (I) will tell her to cook it, and we will eat it.

9 Infinitive

9.1. I want to beat you.
9.2. We do not want to die.

9.3. We hope to go to X ... tomorrow.
9.4. They are waiting to see you.
9.5. The chief does not want to come.
9.6. This child does not want to come.
9.7. The food is good to eat.
9.8. We are about to eat.
9.9. My friend helped me to build the house.
9.10. My friend prevented me from being bitten by a snake.
9.11. The children tried in vain to find the lost goat.
9.12. I do not know how to read.
9.13. My wife does not know how to cook.
9.14. My wife cannot do the cooking; she is ill.
9.15. My wife has never been able to do the cooking.
9.16. This child is dirty; he is not fit to go into the house.
9.17. We all want to come.
9.18. We want some water to drink.
9.19. We want a glass to drink out of.
9.20. To sleep is necessary. It is necessary to eat in order to live.
9.21. We want some water to wash ourselves.
9.22. Is this water fit to drink?
9.23. Beer is bad for children to drink.
9.24. Give me a calabash to put these eggs in.
9.25. Where is the hut for sleeping?
9.26. Where is your hut for sleeping?

10 Present and past participles

10.1. A singing child arrived.
10.2. The child arrived singing.
10.3. The past years have been warm.
10.4. The fallen child got up again.
10.5. His broken arm is hurting him.

11 Optative

11.1. Let us hope that he comes!
11.2. May I live long!
11.3. Let me live long!
11.4. Let the dance begin!
11.5. I hope he dies for all the evil he has done me.
11.6. May you die for all the evil you have done me.

12 Potential

12.1. He is able to come.
12.2. He is not able to come.
12.3. He is able to walk in spite of his illness.
12.4. He cannot read; he is blind.
12.5. He cannot speak; he is dumb.

Verb Phrase

13 Permissive

13.1. May I come tomorrow?
13.2. May I come and play with you?
13.3. You may go; the chief is allowing people to leave.

14 Obligative

14.1. You must eat in order to grow.
14.2. There is nothing to do but to go and look for him.
14.3. You must do it.
14.4. You will have to run to arrive in time.

15 Injunctive / Prohibitive

15.1. Sing! What should I sing? Don't sing!
15.2. Let him sing! Let him not sing!
15.3. Let's all sing together.
15.4. Let's not sing; he is sleeping.
15.5. Sing louder!
15.6. Don't sing, be quiet; people are sleeping.
15.7. Let them (F) sing if they want to.
15.8. Let them (F) not sing; I'm going to work.
15.9. Go right away; you are going to be late.
15.10. Don't go; it's going to rain.
15.11. Let him leave; I don't want to see him again.
15.12. Don't let him leave; I'm getting bored.
15.13. Let's leave; it's time.
15.14. Let's not go without him.
15.15. Leave quickly!
15.16. Don't leave!
15.17. Let them go; they weary me.
15.18. Don't let them leave without going to see the chief.

16 Volitional

16.1. If he wants to come, he will see him.
16.2. He wants to come.
16.3. He wanted to come but couldn't.
16.4. He tried to jump and fell.

17 Intentional

17.1. He came with the intention of seeing him.
17.2. He intends to come.
17.3. He intends to come and see.
17.4. He intended to come and see us.

18 Sequential (purposive or successive)

18.1. He went to have a drink of water. I came to see my sister.
18.2. He took your spear to kill some game.
18.3. I'll give you a knife to kill the chicken.
18.4. The old woman gave her son poison so that he would die.
18.5. The dog ate so much meat that he became ill.
18.6. He beat his son so hard that he died.
18.7. He put a curse on me so that I should die, but I am still very well.
18.8. She put poison in my food so that I would die, but it did not work.
18.9. He came and he saw him.
18.10. He came to see him.
18.11. He had come to see him.

19 Concessive

19.1. He came in spite of his illness.
19.2. Although his hut is far away, I visit him every day.
19.3. He hit me even though I had not done anything.

20 Negative

20.1.   + absolute

20.1.1. He does not come here (ever).
20.1.2. He will not come.
20.1.3. He does not eat catfish; it is taboo to him.
20.1.4. Muslims (Hausas / Arabs) do not eat pork.

20.2.   + completive

20.2.1. He did not come yesterday.
20.2.2. He did not eat this morning.
20.2.3. He did not eat the fish; he was not hungry.

20.3.   + incompletive

20.3.1. He has not come yet.
20.3.2. He has not eaten yet.
20.3.3. He has not eaten the fish yet.
20.3.4. He does not eat fish yet; he is still ill.

20.4.   + contrary-to-fact / hypothetical

20.4.1. He did not really see it.
20.4.2. It is not certain that it will rain today.

21 Positive

21.1.   + completive

Verb Phrase

21.1.1. He is really ill.
21.1.2. He certainly saw it.
21.1.3. He is bound to have gone down there, since he saw it.

21.2.   + incompletive

21.2.1. He has been cared for to no avail for two years; he is still ill.
21.2.2. He is looking for his knife in vain.
21.2.3. He came in vain; the chief had already left.

21.3.   + dubitative

21.3.1. Perhaps he is ill.
21.3.2. Perhaps he has lost his knife.
21.3.3. Perhaps he has seen the chief.

21.4.   + affirmative

21.4.1. He has certainly lost his dog in the forest.
21.4.2. It is certain that he saw him.

22 Interrogative

22.1.   + yes-no questions

22.1.1. Is he coming?
22.1.2. Has anyone seen him?

22.2.   + what

22.2.1. What are you doing?
22.2.2. What is he doing?
22.2.3. What is he eating?

22.3.   + who

22.3.1. Who gave you that garment?
22.3.2. Who is coming here?
22.3.3. Who told you that the chief had left?

22.4.   + circumstantial

22.4.1. How do you do it? (undifferentiated)
22.4.2. How did you catch it? (by what means?)
22.4.3. How do you say it? (with what word?)
22.4.4. Which one did you catch?
22.4.5. Which of the two do you want?

22.4.6. Where did you catch it?

22.4.7. Where did he go by?
22.4.8. Where is he going?
22.4.9. Where is he coming from?

22.4.10. How many of them did you catch?
22.4.11. How long did you stay?
22.4.12. Why did you go to the village? (for what purpose?)
22.4.13. Why are you crying? (for what reason?)
22.4.14. Why did you leave? (because of whom?)

22.4.15. When are you coming?
22.4.16. When did you catch it?
22.4.17. Until when are you staying?

23 Passive

23.1. Why is the child screaming? Because he is being beaten. By whom is he being beaten. He is being beaten by his father.
23.2. Why are you crying? I am crying because my brother was stung by a bee.
23.3. Where is the meat? It has been eaten. By whom was it eaten? It was eaten by the dog.
23.4. Where is the dog. It's dead. How did it die? It was killed by a blow from a spear. It was caught by a hyena / panther.
23.5. The cow has calved. The goat has dropped its young. The woman has given birth. I have given birth.
23.6. The calf was born. The child was born. I was born a long time ago. My wife was delivered of twins. Her twins were born yesterday.
23.7. The pot broke. The water spilled. The rope came untied. This pot was broken by the child. The water was spilled by me. The rope was untied by a boy.
23.8. Spears are used by the (Bandas) to fight with. The (Bandas) fight with spears.
23.9. Stones are used by the women of your village to grind grain.

24 Reciprocal

24.1. The two men killed each other.
24.2. We will kill each other.
24.3. The children are fighting against one another.

25 Reflexive

25.1. The man killed himself. The two men (each) killed themselves.
25.2. We shall kill ourselves.
25.3. The children are (each) beating themselves.
25.4. The child wounded himself with his knife.

26 Transitive - Intransitive / Obligatory transitive

26.1. What are you doing? I'm not doing anything.
26.2. What are you (PL) doing? We are not doing anything.

Verb Phrase   265

26.3.   I am sitting down. I am walking.
26.4.   I am cooking.
26.5.   We are ... (ethnic group).
26.6.   What are the people doing? The people are dancing, moving about, drinking beer, quarreling.
26.7.   What are you cooking? I am cooking meat.
26.8.   Is your wife cooking meat? No, she is cooking fish.
26.9.   Are you (PL) sleeping? No, we are just lying down.
26.10. He is drinking - He is eating - He is running.
26.11. He is drinking water - He is eating meat - He is running the race.
26.12. He drinks quickly - He eats quickly - He runs quickly.
26.13. He is drinking the water quickly.
26.14. He is singing.
26.15. He is singing a song.
26.16. He sings well.
26.17. He sings that song well.

27 Benefactive (action on behalf of others)

27.1.   For whom are you cooking? I'm cooking for my husband.
27.2.   Are you working for the chief? No, I am not working for the chief; I am working for my father. Don't work for your father; work for the chief.
27.3.   Did you cook something for your husband? Yes, I did. No, I didn't.
27.4.   What did you cook for him? I cooked some gruel for him.

28 Instrumental (≠ consecutive of purpose)

28.1.   What is this stone for? It's for grinding grain.
28.2.   What are you using this machete for? I am using it to chop wood.

29 Causative

29.1.   The man woke up. The child woke the man up.
29.2.   The baby is feeding at the breast. The mother is making the baby feed (at her breast).
29.3.   The boy is drinking some water. I made the boy drink some water. I let the boy drink some water.
29.4.   The cattle (goats) are running. Don't let your dog make the cattle run.
29.5.   Let's play. No, let's not play; it's too hot.
29.6.   Please, sir, let us play. No, I will not let you play; you are making too much noise.
29.7.   Let's all go to the chief together. Will the chief let us (make us) leave when the meeting is over?

30 Factitive

30.1.   He had his loincloth dyed.
30.2.   His arm turned black.
30.3.   He made his loincloth black.

31 Habitual

31.1. What do the ... (name of ethnic group) men do?
31.2. The ... men look after cattle (goats) / do the hunting, fishing.
31.3. What do the ... women do? The ... women prepare the food.
31.4. What do the children eat? The children eat gruel (boule, fufu).
31.5. Do the children drink beer, wine, etc ... ? No, the children do not drink beer; they drink milk / water.
31.6. Do the ... (name of ethnic group) eat python? No, they eat game.
31.7. The child has fallen asleep. The child is asleep now. The child sleeps every day.
31.8. Do the women do the same work as the men? No, they do not do the same things.
31.9. It is the women who make this pottery.
31.10. It is the men who weave mats.
31.11. It is the women who crush grain and fetch water.
31.12. It is the men who hunt.

32 Repeated action - Frequentative - Durative - Intensive

32.1. I folded the material (once, into two).
32.2. I folded (up) the material (several times, into many folds).
32.3. I tore the material (one tear). I tore the material into shreds.
32.4. Your shirt is torn. Your shirt is in tatters.
32.5. He is chopping the wood. He is sawing the wood. He is breaking the wood into pieces.
32.6. Blow on this flame (to extinguish it).
32.7. Blow on the fire (to revive it).
32.8. The mouse bit my finger.
32.9. The rat gnawed the wood.
32.10. Termites eat wood.
32.11. He chews for a long time before swallowing.
32.12. He pulled up a small tree.
32.13. He pulled the leaves off the tree.
32.14. He plucked (pulled the feathers out of) the chicken.
32.15. The dog bit me, then ran away.
32.16. The dog bit the child all over his body.
32.17. A bee stung me.
32.18. The mosquitos bit me all night.
32.19. It's raining.
32.20. It's pouring down (rain).
32.21. The sun is shining / the sun is blazing (is beating down).
32.22. He is eating / he is gorging himself.
32.23. It is still raining.
32.24. He is still eating.
32.25. He is getting up.
32.26. He gets up suddenly (with a leap).
32.27. He put the book on the table.
32.28. He put the book down on the table brusquely.

Verb Phrase

33 Iterative

33.1. He redid the work that was badly done.
33.2. He repainted his hut white.

34 Simultaneous

34.1. She sings while grinding the grain.
34.2. She laughs while preparing the food.
34.3. He sings at the same time he works the ground.
34.4. He weaves a mat while telling me a story.
34.5. While he was speaking to me, he was making faces.

35 Inchoative

35.1. He is coming (he is on his way).

36 Initiative

36.1. He is beginning to come / to walk.
36.2. He began to come / to walk.

37 Ingressive

37.1. He sets out to work.
37.2. He began to drink.
37.3. She started to cry.
37.4. He did not start work.

38 Inceptive

38.1. He is already working.
38.2. He is already eating.
38.3. He is already coming.

39 Progressive

39.1. He is (in the process of) weaving a mat.
39.2. She is (in the process of) preparing the meal.

40 Completive

40.1. Do you see a car over there? Yes, I see it. No, I don't see it.
40.2. Can you see something inside? Yes, I can. No, I can't.
40.3. I have finished the work.
40.4. She has finished grinding the grain.
40.5. He has arrived.

41 Incompletive

41.1. I am finishing the work.
41.2. I am not finishing the work.
41.3. I have not finished the work.

42 Hypothetical incompletive

42.1. He was going to come when his brother died.
42.2. He was getting ready to come when I arrived.
42.3. He was coming here when he was caught.

43 Contrary-to-fact completive

43.1. He almost came.
43.2. He was very ill and he almost died, but now he is well.
43.3. A little longer and she would have died.

44 Potential

44.1. He would do that for me.
44.2. He would kill his brother for money.

45 Dubitative

45.1. I think he came yesterday.
45.2. I wonder if he will come.
45.3. Perhaps he came yesterday.
45.4. I think he is going to come.
45.5. Perhaps it is going to rain.

46 Conditional

46.1. If he came, I would see him.
46.2. If he had come yesterday, he would have seen him.
46.3. He would come if he had the money for the trip.
46.4. He will not come if it rains.
46.5. He would have come if he had had some money.
46.6. If he comes tomorrow, he will see him.
46.7. If he wants to come, he will see him.
46.8. He would have come if you had asked him.
46.9. He would come if you asked him.
46.10. He could come if he wanted to.
46.11. If I go down there, I will be beaten.
46.12. If you stay here, you will be killed.
46.13. If the child loses the sheep, his father will beat him.
46.14. If you drink this medicine, you will die.
46.15. If the baby cries, you will give him some milk.
46.16. If the baby does not cry, you will not give him any milk.
46.17. If I had gone down there, I would have been beaten.

Verb Phrase

46.18. If you (PL) had stayed here, you would have been killed.
46.19. If the child had lost the sheep, his father would have beaten him.
46.20. If you had drunk this medicine, you would have died.
46.21. If the baby had cried, I would not have given him any milk.

47 Directional

47.1.   + movement away from speaker

47.1.1. Go (SG) away! Go (PL) away!
47.1.2. Run (SG)! Run (PL)! (away from me)
47.1.3. Drag the log away from me!
47.1.4. Drag it toward that man!
47.1.5. Go down into the well over there!
47.1.6. Climb up that tree over there!
47.1.7. The car left here yesterday and will arrive at x ... tomorrow.

47.2.   + movement toward speaker

47.2.1. Come (SG) here! Come (PL) here!
47.2.2. Run (SG)! Run (PL)! (toward me)
47.2.3. Drag the log toward me!
47.2.4. Come down from the tree and come here!
47.2.5. Come out of the well!
47.2.6. The car left x ... yesterday and will arrive here tomorrow.
47.2.7. Bring me some water! Take it back!
47.2.8. Come here! Go back!
47.2.9. Take this food away! Bring it back!
47.2.10. Go away! Come back!
47.2.11. Give me the money back!
47.2.12. Give him the money back!
(Give also the plural form of these last sentences.)

48 Motion

48.1. He went to dig a hole.
48.2. She went to fetch water.

49 Reference to source and goal

49.1. He will become a fisherman.
49.2. He will become a harvester.
49.3. His misfortunes have made him prudent.

50 Reversive

50.1. He is getting dressed.
50.2. He is getting undressed so that he can wash (himself).
50.3. She tied up the goat.
50.4. She untied the goat.

50.5. She opened the door.
50.6. She closed the door.

51 Augmentative

51.1. He is eating more and more.
51.2. My brother is getting fatter and fatter.
51.3. Every day, the river rises a little higher.
51.4. He gets more ill every day.

52 Diminutive

52.1. He works less and less.
52.2. He eats less and less.

53 Primordial

53.1. He was the first to leave.
53.2. It was he who told me first.

54 Pure verbal action

54.1. He does nothing but eat (= he is always, still eating / all he does is eat ...)
54.2. He is only passing through.
54.3. He simply passed by.

55 Generic - unactualized or actualized

55.1. He eats yam / he is eating a yam.
55.2. That demon catches people.
55.3. He is a man who talks loudly / today he is talking loudly.
55.4. During the rainy season, it rains / today, it is raining.

B. Questionnaire on Structures
by Jacqueline M. C. Thomas

First hypothesis:

The verb is monosyllabic: CV or CVC

Tone change
 $C\tilde{V}$ $C\acute{V}$ $C\grave{V}$ etc.

Vowel change
 $CV_1\, CV_2\, CV_3$ etc.

Consonant change
 $C_1V\, C_2V\, C_3V$ etc.

these three changes may be combined

$CV_1 + C\tilde{V} \rightarrow C\tilde{V}_1\, C\tilde{V}_2\, C\tilde{V}_3$ etc.

or

$CVC_1\, CVC_2\, CVC_3$ etc.

Verb Phrase

Each difference in form corresponds to a difference in meaning; if not, a morpho(phono)logical phenomenon is involved.

Tone change: the tone on the verb combines with a tone that precedes the verb (on the immediately preceding word or on the subject) or that follows the verb

⁻CV́ ⁻CV̌ ⁻CV̄ ⁻CV̂ ⁻CV   etc.
CV̄⁻ CV̄C⁻ / CV̂⁻ CV̂C⁻   etc.

Reduplication

C̲V̲CV - identical
C̲V̲CV - with a tone change   } [these] may be
C̲V̲₂CV₁ - with a vowel change   } combined
C̲₂V̲C₁V - with a consonant change }

An added tone
CV̀ + ´ → CV̌

An added vowel
CV + V → CVV / V + CV → VCV

An added consonant
CV + C → CVC / C + V → CV / C + CV → CCV
CVC + C → CVCC

An added syllable (CV or CVC)
CV + CV → C₁V₁C₂V₂ or C₁V₁C₂V₁
         → C₂V₂C₁V₁ or C₂V₁C₁V₁ etc.

Second hypothesis.

The verb has two, three, or more syllables:

CVCV or CVCVCV etc.
CVCVC or CVCVCVC etc.

the same possibilities as for monosyllabic verbs

changes in one syllable only

  CV̀(CV)   { CV́(CV) etc.
  CV₁(CV)   { CV₂(CV) CV₃(CV) etc.

or (CV)CV̌   { (CV)CV̀ (CV)CV́ etc.
   (CV)CV₁   { (CV)CV₂ (CV)CV₃ etc.

changes in two (or more) syllables:

$$C\bar{V}C\bar{V} \quad C\grave{V}C\grave{V} \quad C\acute{V}C\acute{V}$$
$$C\check{V}C\check{V} \quad C\grave{V}C\acute{V} \quad C\acute{V}C\grave{V}$$

possible change in stress CV'CV 'CVCV

with or without combination of these processes (tone + V + C +/- stress)

with or without combination with a preceding or following tone

with or without reduplication

Agreement

There may be agreement phenomena (gender, number, sex; noun classes, etc.)

xS   xV
Sx   Vx

Possible verb forms in the conjugation paradigm

inflected forms

simple $\bar{V} \; \acute{V} \; \grave{V}$ or $\hat{V} \; \check{V}$ etc.

with reduplication $\grave{V}\hat{V} \; \grave{V}\grave{V} \; \grave{V}\acute{V} \; \acute{V}\grave{V}$ etc. $\hat{V}\hat{V} \; \hat{V}\grave{V}$ etc.
(consider for both the 1st and 2nd hypotheses)

forms with affixes

suffixes: V-s (s may be V, CV, CVC, or C, etc.)
with or without fusion with the root

prefixes: p-V (p may be V, CV, CVC, or C, etc.)
with or without fusion with the root

infixes: V-i-V or V_1 = CV and V_2 = C-i-V, etc.
(i may be V, CV, or C, etc.)
with or without fusion with the root(s)

Affixes may be affected or combined with a preceding or following tone. The processes of modification and affixation may be combined.

auxiliary forms (V') or autonomous VM's

V' = affix (see forms with affixes, above)

V' ≠ affix

V' / ... / V
V / ... / V'

Consider V' in conjunction with both 1st and 2nd hypotheses

Verb Phrase

Consider agreement of V' (with S / with V)

Consider possible modified and affixed forms of V'

Consider forms of V (modified or affixed) possible with V'

Verbal forms of concord.

$P_1 = \bar{V} / P_2 = \acute{V} >$ concord in a following dependent clause (e.g., Ngbaka)

For the different modified and affixed forms of the V in P_1, consider the possible corresponding forms of the V in P_2, and the significance of this correspondence.

With the different clause-markers (if, when, as soon as, although, because, in order that, etc.), consider the modified and affixed forms of the V in P_1 for the possible corresponding forms of the V in P^2. (The order of P_1 and P_2 may be reversed.)

N.B.
C = consonant
V = vowel
C_1C_2 = different consonants
V_1V_2 = vowels of different qualities
´`` = tones
C<u>V</u>CV = reduplicated form
V = simple verbal form
VV = reduplicated verbal form
S = subject
x = agreement marker
s = suffix
p = prefix
i = infix
V^1 = root verb form
V^2 = modified verbal form (here infixed)
V' = auxiliary
P_1 = main clause
P_2 = dependent clause
VM = verbal marker

Questionnaire 7
The Noun and the Noun Phrase

by Nicole Tersis

This field work questionnaire focuses on the grammatical analysis of the noun and the noun phrase. Its systematic nature should help bring out the modifiers of the noun, and how they may or may not be combined. We distinguish two types of noun modifiers:

1. grammatical or monovalent or bound modifiers
2. lexical or polyvalent or free modifiers (cf. III)

The nouns in list B were chosen for languages with the most complex morphology, those with noun classes. Thus, this list includes terms of family relationship, terms relating to nature, parts of the body, liquids, foods, manufactured articles, animals, abstract terms and verb-nouns. For languages with a simpler morphology, it will not always be necessary to elicit the whole list.

A. Grammatical or Monovalent or Bound Modifiers

This type of modifier belongs to a closed class, whereas the head noun belongs to an open class. For each head noun in list B, e.g., chief (#1), all possible combinations with the modifiers in list A should be tried out: 01. a, an 02. the 03. some etc.; thus:

101. a chief / 102. the chief / 103. some chiefs 104. the chiefs / 105. both chiefs, the two chiefs 106. the three chiefs / 107. my chief / 108. my chiefs 109. my two chiefs, both my chiefs / 110. my three chiefs 111. this chief ...

This process should be repeated with the next word in list B:

201. a man / 202. the man / 203. some men / 204. the men 205. the two men, both men / 206. the three men 207. my man / 208. my man / etc.

1 One modifier

Types of modifiers	Column A Modifier	Column B Head noun
1. indefinite	1. a, an	1. chief
2. definite	2. the (SG)	2. man
- pluralizer		3. woman
indefinite	3. some	4. child
definite	4. the (PL)	5. father
dual	5. both, the two	6. mother
trial	6. the three	7. (uterine) uncle
3. possessive	7. my (SG)	8. brother
- pluralizer	8. my (PL)	9. river
- dual	9. both my, my two	10. field
- trial	10. my three	11. land
4. a) demon-		12. tree
strative	11. this (within view)	13. road
- near and	12. this	14. mouth
within view	13. that	15. nose
- close,	14. this particular	16. eye
unspecified	(this ... in question)	17. leg
- out of view	15. this ... from here	18. hand
b) anaphoric	16. these	19. neck
c) situational	17. both these, these two	20. head
- pluralizer	18. these three	21. water
- dual	19. the whole (of), a great	22. blood
- trial	number of, many	23. milk
5. quantifier	20. all (PL)	24. urine
- pluralizer	21. two, three, etc.	25. salt
6. numeral	22. no, not any, not one	26. fat
	23. (an)other	27. egg
	24. certain	28. meat
	25. each, every	29. cola
	26. same	30. sauce
	27. anywhere, no matter	31. honey
	where	32. knife
	28. any, no matter which	33. drum
	29. no, not one	34. hut
	30. nowhere	35. basket
	31. everywhere	36. canoe
	32. nobody, no one	37. mat
	33. several	38. loin-cloth
	34. which	39. calabash
	35. some, a few, any	40. dog
	36. any (whatever),	41. hare
	some (or other)	42. fish
	37. nothing	43. guinea-fowl
		44. cow

45. horse
46. thirst
47. fatigue
48. hunger
49. illness
50. time
51. eating
52. drinking
53. going to bed
54. getting up
55. sleeping

101. a chief
102. the chief
103. some chiefs
104. the chiefs
105. both chiefs, the two chiefs
106. the three chiefs
107. my chief
108. my chiefs
109. both my chiefs, my two chiefs
110. my three chiefs
111. this chief (within view)
112. this chief
113. that chief
114. this (particular) chief in question
115. this chief from here
116. these chiefs
117. both these chiefs, these two chiefs
118. these three chiefs
119. a great number of chiefs, many chiefs
120. all the chiefs
121. two chiefs, three chiefs ...

201. a man
202. the man
203. some men
204. the men
205. both men, the two men
206. the three men
207. my man
208. my men
209. both my men, my two men
210. my three men
211. this man (within view)
212. this man
213. that man
214. this (particular) man in question

215. this man from here
216. these men
217. both these men, these two men
218. these three men
219. a great number of men, many men
220. all the men
221. two men, three men, ...

301. a woman
302. the woman
303. some women
304. the women
305. both women, the two women
306. the three women
307. my woman
308. my women
309. both my women, my two women
310. my three women
311. this woman (within view)
312. this woman
313. that woman
314. this (particular) woman in question
315. this woman from here
316. these women
317. both these women, these two women
318. these three women
319. a great number of women, many women
320. all the women
321. two women, three women, ...

401. a child
402. the child
403. some children
404. the children
405. both children, the two children
406. the three children
407. my child
408. my children
409. both my children, my two children
410. my three children
411. this child (within view)
412. this child
413. that child
414. this (particular) child in question
415. this child from here
416. these children
417. both these children, these two children
418. these three children

Noun and Noun Phrase

419. a great number of children, many children
420. all the children
421. two children, three children, ...

501. a father
502. the father
503. some fathers
504. the fathers
505. both fathers, the two fathers
506. the three fathers
507. my father
508. my fathers
509. both my fathers, my two fathers
510. my three fathers
511. this father (within view)
512. this father
513. that father
514. this (particular) father in question
515. this father from here
516. these fathers
517. both these fathers, these two fathers
518. these three fathers
519. a great number of fathers, many fathers
520. all the fathers
521. two fathers, three fathers ...

601. a mother
602. the mother
603. some mothers
604. the mothers
605. both mothers, the two mothers
606. the three mothers
607. my mother
608. my mothers
609. both my mothers, my two mothers
610. my three mothers
611. this mother (within view)
612. this mother
613. that mother
614. this (particular) mother in question
615. this mother from here
616. these mothers
617. both these mothers, these two mothers
618. these three mothers
619. a great number of mothers, many mothers
620. all the mothers
621. two mothers, three mothers ...

Try to combine modifiers 22 to 37 with the head nouns listed in 1B and make a few sentences like these:

Not one man (No man) came.
I did not see any of them.
Not one tree (No tree) was burned.

I have another house.
It's another child.
It was not my dog that barked; it was another one.

Nests are found in certain trees.
He tells certain stories well.
He tells stories for certain people.

Each year, he comes to see us.
Every man needs to eat.
He gave some food to each one.

He is the same height.
They have the same voice.
They have the same shoes.

He left for no matter where (anywhere).
He chose no matter which (any) loincloth.
He did not find anywhere to eat.

He looked everywhere for something to eat.
He looked for his dog everywhere.
I did not see anybody.

No one will say so.

Several animals have died.
I saw several of them.
Which man came?

A few fruits fell from the tree.
He ate a few fruits.
He ate a few of them.

Give me any chicken (whatever).

There is nothing left.
He did not see anything.

Noun and Noun Phrase

2 Combination of two or more grammatical modifiers (monovalent or bound)

Try to combine two or more grammatical modifiers with a single head noun from list B. Repeat this process with all the words in list B.

A. Modifiers.

1. possessive + demonstrative	this chief of mine, this my chief
2. poss. + demons. + plural	these chiefs of mine, these my chiefs
3. possessive + anaphoric	the chief of mine in question, my chief in question
4. poss. + anaph. + plural	the chiefs of mine in question, my chiefs in question
5. possessive + quantifier	all (of) my chief, many a chief of mine
6. poss. + quant. + plural	all my chiefs
7. demonstrative + anaphoric	this chief in question
8. demons. + quant. + plural	these chiefs in question
9. demonstrative + quantifier	all (of) this chief, many (a) this chief
10. demons. + quant. + plural	all these chiefs
11. quantifier + anaphoric	all (of) the chief in question, many a chief in question
12. quant. + anaph. + plural	all the chiefs in question
13. possessive + indef. + demons.	this [, a] certain chief of mine
14. poss. + indef. + demons. + plural	these [,] certain chiefs of mine
15. poss. + demons. + quant.	all (of) this chief of mine, many (a) this chief of mine
16. poss. + demons. + quant.	all these chiefs of mine
17. quant. + poss. + anaph.	all (of) the chief of mine in question, many a chief of mine in question
18. quant. + poss. + anaph. + plural	all the chiefs of mine in question
19. poss. + demons. + anaph. + quant.	all (of) this chief of mine in question, many (a) this chief of mine in question
20. poss. + demons. + anaph. + quant. plural	all these chiefs of mine in question

B. Head noun.

1. chief	15. nose	29. cola	43. guinea-fowl
2. man	16. eye	30. sauce	44. cow
3. woman	17. leg	31. honey	45. horse
4. child	18. hand	32. knife	46. thirst
5. father	19. neck	33. drum	47. fatigue
6. mother	20. head	34. hut	48. hunger
7. (uterine) uncle	21. water	35. basket	49. illness
8. brother	22. blood	36. canoe	50. time
9. river	23. milk	37. mat	51. eating
10. field	24. urine	38. loin-cloth	52. drinking
11. land	25. salt	39. calabash	53. going to bed
12. tree	26. fat	40. dog	54. getting up
13. road	27. egg	41. hare	55. sleeping
14. mouth	28. meat	42. fish	

101. this chief of mine, this my chief
102. these chiefs of mine, these my chiefs
103. my chief in question, the chief of mine in question
104. my chiefs in question, the chiefs of mine in question
105. all (of) my chief, many a chief of mine
106. all my chiefs
107. this chief in question
108. these chiefs in question
109. all (of) this chief, many (a) this chief
110. all these chiefs
111. all (of) the chief in question, many a chief in question
112. all the chiefs in question
113. this certain chief of mine
114. these certain chiefs of mine
115. all (of) this chief of mine, many (a) this chief of mine
116. all these chiefs of mine
117. all (of) the chief of mine in question, many a chief of mine in question
118. all the chiefs of mine in question
119. all (of) this chief of mine in question, many (a) this chief of mine in question
120. all these chiefs of mine in question

201. this man of mine, this my man
202. these men of mine, these my men
203. my man in question, the man of mine in question
204. my men in question, the men of mine in question
205. all (of) my man, many a man of mine
206. all my men

Noun and Noun Phrase

207. this man in question
208. these men in question
209. all (of) this man, many (a) this man
210. all these men
211. all (of) the man in question, many a man in question
212. all the men in question
213. this certain man of mine
214. these certain men of mine
215. all (of) this man of mine, many (a) this man of mine
216. all these men of mine
217. all (of) the man of mine in question, many a man of mine in question
218. all the men of mine in question
219. all (of) this man of mine in question, many (a) this man of mine in question
220. all these men of mine in question

301. this woman of mine, this my woman
302. these women of mine, these my women
303. my woman in question, the woman of mine in question
304. my women in question, the women of mine in question
305. all (of) my woman, many a woman of mine
306. all my women
307. this woman in question
308. these women in question
309. all (of) this woman, many (a) this woman
310. all these women
311. all (of) the woman in question, many a woman in question
312. all the women in question
313. this certain woman of mine
314. these certain women of mine
315. all (of) this woman of mine, many (a) this woman of mine
316. all these women of mine
317. all (of) the woman of mine in question, many a woman of mine in question
318. all the women of mine in question
319. all (of) this woman of mine in question, many (a) this woman of mine in question
320. all these women of mine in question

401. this child of mine, this my child
402. these children of mine, these my children
403. my child in question, the child of mine in question
404. my children in question, the children of mine in question
405. all (of) my child, many a child of mine
406. all my children

407. this child in question
408. these children in question
409. all (of) this child, many (a) this child
410. all these children
411. all (of) the child in question, many a child in question
412. all the children in question
413. this certain child of mine
414. these certain children of mine
415. all (of) this child of mine, many (a) this child of mine
416. all these children of mine
417. all (of) the child of mine in question, many a child of mine in question
418. all the children of mine in question
419. all (of) this child of mine in question, many (a) this child of mine in question
420. all these children of mine in question

B. Lexical or Polyvalent or Free Modifiers

The lexical (polyvalent or free) modifier belongs to an open class, unlike the grammatical modifier.

1 Is there an adjective category?

A. One modifier. A language may have one or more categories of lexemes that correspond to what we call adjectives in English. These different categories may or may not combine with the noun in a relationship of secondary determinative. However, a verb or verboid or even an adverb may correspond to the English adjective in the questionnaire. In that case, they are involved in the primary clause-level relationship, and will not be considered on the phrase level. Certain languages favor this type of relation and do not even use an adjective category. In languages that do have an adjective category, there may be a derivation process involving the adjective, noun, and verb (without prejudging the direction of the derivation). It is important to discover how such a process works; the types of combinations given for each possible adjective in columns B, C, D, and E should help bring this out. In languages with noun classes, or genders, or which make use of other morphological processes, detecting such processes may require adding other forms that are better adapted for this purpose to the list given here. Similarly, one may be better able to discover certain phenomena by using each of the items suggested (and possibly others) in sentences of the following type:

I saw the white loincloth.
I saw the white one.
I did not buy the black loincloth, but this white one.
I saw some loincloths, (and) I bought a big one.
The small one (loincloth) is torn.
I saw some loincloths, (and) I bought those small ones.
The white one is clean, but the red one is dirty.
The loincloth that is white is long.
The loincloth that is black is short.
It is the white loincloth that is long.
It is the black loincloth that is short.
The black loincloth that is short is torn.
The black one that is short is torn.
I bought the white one that is long. etc.

Questionnaire 7

Column A	Column B	Column C
1. white	the white loincloth	It is white.
2. black	the black dog	It is black.
3. red	the red loincloth	It is red.
4. big	the big tree	It is big.
5. small	the small field	It is small.
6. wide	the wide river	It is wide.
7. narrow	the narrow path	It is narrow.
8. thick	the thick sauce	It is thick.
9. liquid	the liquid gruel	It is liquid.
10. fat	the fat woman	She is fat.
11. thin	the thin cow	It is thin.
12. hard	the hard stone	It is hard.
13. soft	the soft dough	It is soft.
14. sweet	the sweet honey	It is sweet.
15. bitter	the bitter cola	It is bitter.
16. deep	the deep well	It is deep.
17. shallow	the shallow furrow	It is shallow.
18. long	the long leg	It is long.
19. short	the short stick	It is short.
20. good	the good father	He is good.
21. naughty	the naughty child	He is naughty.
22. round	the round fruit	It is round.
23. dry	the dry ground	It is dry.
24. wet	the wet leaf	It is wet.
25. dirty	the dirty garment	It is dirty.
26. clean	the clean hut	It is clean.
27. beautiful	the beautiful woman	She is beautiful.
28. ugly	the ugly man	He is ugly.
29. hot	the hot meat	It is hot.
30. cold	the cold water	It is cold.
31. strong	the strong man	He is strong.
32. weak	the weak man	He is weak.
33. old	the old horse	It is old.
34. young	the young hare	It is young.
35. fresh	the fresh meat	It is fresh.
36. rotten, spoiled	the rotten fruit	It is rotten.
37. heavy	the heavy load	It is heavy.
38. light	the light sack	It is light.
39. skillful	the skillful child	He is skillful.
40. clumsy	the clumsy child	He is clumsy.

Noun and Noun Phrase

Column D	Column E
the whiteness of the loincloth	It's the white one.
the blackness of the dog	It's the black one.
the redness of the loincloth	It's the red one.
the bigness of the tree	It's the big one.
the smallness of the field.	It's the small one.
the width of the river	It's the wide one.
the narrowness of the path	It's the narrow one.
the thickness of the sauce	It's the thick one.
the liquidity of the gruel	It's the liquid one.
the fatness of the woman	It's the fat one.
the thinness of the cow	It's the thin one.
the hardness of the stone	It's the hard one.
the softness of the dough	It's the soft one.
the sweetness of the honey	It's the sweet one.
the bitterness of the cola	It's the bitter one.
the depth of the well	It's the deep one.
the shallowness of the furrow	It's the shallow one.
the length of the leg	It's the long one.
the shortness of the stick	It's the short one.
the goodness of the father	It's the good one.
the naughtiness of the child	It's the naughty one.
the roundness of the fruit	It's the round one.
the dryness of the ground	It's the dry one.
the wetness of the leaf	It's the wet one.
the dirtiness of the garment	It's the dirty one.
the cleanliness of the hut	It's the clean one.
the beauty of the woman	It/She's the beautiful one.
the ugliness of the man	It/He's the ugly one.
the heat of the meat	It's the hot one.
the coldness of the water	It's the cold one.
the strength of the man	It/He's the strong one.
the weakness of the man	It/He's the weak one.
the oldness of the horse	It's the old one.
the youth of the hare	It's the young one.
the freshness of the meat	It's the fresh one.
the rottenness of the fruit	It's the rotten one.
the heaviness of the load	It's the heavy one.
the lightness of the sack	It's the light one.
the skillfulness of the child	It/He's the skillful one.
the clumsiness of the child	It/He's the clumsy one.

2 The numeral modifier

one chief	the first chief	one man	the first man
two chiefs	the second chief	two men	the second man
three chiefs	the third chief	three men	the third man
four chiefs	etc.	four men	etc.
five chiefs		five men	
six chiefs		six men	
seven chiefs		seven men	
eight chiefs		eight men	
nine chiefs		nine men	
ten chiefs		ten men	

one woman	the first woman
two women	the second woman
three women	the third woman
four women	etc.
five women	
six women	
seven women	
eight women	
nine women	
ten women	

A. Combination of two or more lexical (polyvalent or free) modifiers

– two modifiers
201. the tall, old chief
202. the skillful young man
203. the tall, beautiful woman
204. the naughty, dirty child
205. the good old father
206. the beautiful young mother
207. the wicked old uncle
208. the thin, clumsy brother
209. the deep, wide river
210. the small, ruined field
211. the good, wet earth
212. the tall, black tree
213. the narrow, damp path
214. the cold, dirty water
215. the thick, hot sauce
216. the big old drum
217. the big black horse
218. the thin white cow
219. the bitter white cola
220. the swift, clever hare

– three modifiers
301. the tall, thin, old chief
302. the wicked, clever, young man
303. the tall, beautiful, young woman
304. the naughty, skillful, clever child
305. the short, fat young father

Noun and Noun Phrase

306. the beautiful, gentle young mother
307. the clumsy, wicked old uncle
308. the clumsy, dirty, wicked brother
309. the deep, wide, dirty river
310. the wet, ruined, little field
311. the beautiful, narrow little hand
312. the big, deep, light calabash
313. the beautiful, big, red loincloth
314. the big, round, old drum
315. the sweet, round, black fruit
316. the thick, hot, red sauce
317. the good, bitter, white cola
318. the beautiful, big black horse
319. the swift, clever young hare
320. the weak, old, white dog

– four modifiers
401. the good, tall, thin old chief
402. the clever, wicked, short young man
403. the beautiful, tall, gentle young woman
404. the dirty, naughty, clumsy, small child
405. the short, fat, good old father
406. the beautiful, gentle, short young mother
407. the cunning, clumsy, wicked old uncle
408. the long, wide, deep, dirty river
409. the big, black, beautiful old horse
410. the big, round, heavy old drum

– five modifiers
501. two good, tall, thin old chiefs
502. three clever, wicked, short young men
503. the second beautiful, tall, gentle young woman
504. the third big, black, beautiful old horse
505. five big, round, heavy old drums

B. Combination of lexical and grammatical modifiers

– One grammatical modifier (A) and one lexical modifier (B)
From the list of modifiers and the list of head nouns given in §1, we make the following combinations:

Type of modifier

1. indefinite   601. a (certain) tall chief
2. definite   602. the tall chief
3. pluralizer   indefinite   603. some tall chiefs
         definite   604. the tall chiefs
         dual   605. both the tall chiefs, the two tall chiefs
         trial   606. the three tall chiefs
4. possessive   607. my tall chief
         pluralizer   608. my tall chiefs
         dual   609. both my tall chiefs, my two tall chiefs
         trial   610. my three tall chiefs
5. demonstrative   611. this tall chief

          close and within view
          close, unspecified
          out of view
          anaphoric
          situational
          pluralizer
          dual
          trial
     6. quantifier
          pluralizer
     7. numeral

     612. this (here) tall chief
     613. this tall chief
     614. that (there) tall chief
     615. the tall chief in question
     616. the tall chief from here
     617. these tall chiefs
     618. both these tall chiefs, these two tall chiefs
     619. these three tall chiefs
     620. all (of) the tall chief, many a tall chief
     621. all the tall chiefs
     622. two tall chiefs, three tall chiefs
     623. the tall chief Paul

– two or more lexical modifiers

     701. a (certain) tall old chief
     702. the tall old chief
     703. some tall old chiefs
     704. the tall old chiefs
     705. the two tall old chiefs, both tall old chiefs
     706. the three tall old chiefs
     707. my tall old chief
     708. my tall old chiefs
     709. my two tall old chiefs, both my tall old chiefs
     710. my three tall old chiefs
     711. this (here) tall old chief
     712. this tall old chief
     713. that (there) tall old chief
     714. this tall old chief in question
     715. this tall old chief from here
     716. these tall old chiefs
     717. these two tall old chiefs, both these tall old chiefs
     718. these three tall old chiefs
     719. all (of) the tall old chief, many a tall old chief
     720. all the tall old chiefs
     721. two tall old chiefs, three tall old chiefs

– two or more grammatical modifiers
From the combinations of grammatical modifiers found in §II, we form the following sentences:

     801. this tall chief of mine
     802. these tall chiefs of mine
     803. my tall chief in question
     804. my tall chiefs in question
     805. all (of) my tall chief
     806. all my tall chiefs
     807. this tall chief in question
     808. these tall chiefs in question
     809. all (of) this tall chief
     810. all these tall chiefs
     811. all (of) the tall chief in question, many a tall chief in question

812. all the tall chiefs in question
813. this certain tall chief of mine
814. these certain tall chiefs of mine
815. all (of) this tall chief of mine
816. all these tall chiefs of mine
817. all (of) the tall chief of mine in question
818. all the tall chiefs of mine in question
819. all (of) this tall chief of mine in question
820. all these tall chiefs of mine in question

Other head nouns from list B may be used (cf. I).

– Combination of several grammatical (monovalent or bound) and lexical (polyvalent or free) modifiers

901. this tall old chief of mine
902. these tall old chiefs of mine
903. the tall old chief of mine in question
904. the tall old chiefs of mine in question
905. all (of) my tall old chief
906. all my tall old chiefs
907. this tall old chief in question
908. these tall old chiefs in question
909. all (of) this tall old chief
910. all these tall old chiefs
911. all (of) the tall old chief in question
912. all the tall old chiefs in question
913. this certain tall old chief of mine in question
914. these certain tall old chiefs of mine in question
915. all (of) this tall old chief of mine
916. all these tall old chiefs of mine
917. all (of) the tall old chief of mine in question
918. all the tall old chiefs of mine in question
919. all (of) this tall old chief of mine in question
920. all these tall old chiefs of mine in question

3 Noun modifiers

A. One modifier

Type:

1001. the chief's wife	a wife of the chief
1002. the chief's child	a child of the chief
1003. the chief's father	a chief's father
1004. the chief's mother	a chief's mother
1005. the chief's uncle	an uncle of the chief
1006. the chief's brother	a brother of the chief
1007. the chief's field	a field of the chief
1008. the chief's tree	a tree of the chief
1009. the chief's mouth	a chief's mouth
1010. the chief's head	a chief's head
1011. the chief's milk	a chief's milk

1012. the chief's meat   a chief's meat
1013. the chief's hut   a hut of the chief
1014. the chief's loincloth   a loincloth of the chief
1015. the chief's knife   a knife of the chief
1016. the chief's dog   a dog of the chief
1017. the chief's horse   a horse of the chief
1018. the chief's illness   an illness of the chief
1019. the chief's food   a chief's food
1020. the chief's getting up   a getting up of the chief
1021. a gold bracelet
1022. a water pot
1023. a meat pot
1024. a wood drum
1025. a clay hut
1026. a leather sack
1027. pottery clay
1028. Paul's dog (cf. 1016)
1029. Peter's illness (cf. 1018)
1030. the sack of bananas (cf. 1022)
1031. the banana sack
1032. an iron cooking-pot
1033. a pot of meat (cf. 1023)
1034. the handle of the basket
1035. the woman's arm
1036. the woman's basket

B. Sequence of modifiers

1101. the village chief's dog
1102. the chief's wife's head
1103. the chief's brother's field
1104. the child's mother's loincloth
1105. the tree of the child's village
1106. the woman's calabash of milk
1107. the child's uncle's knife
1108. the child's father's arm
1109. the lid of the woman's cooking-pot
1110. the door of the chief's hut

– Modification of the head noun

Lexical (polyvalent, free) modifier
1201. the chief's white loincloth
1202. the man's black dog
1203. the big calabash of milk
1204. the chief's fresh milk
1205. the child's sharp knife
1206. the cold river water / the cold water of the river
1207. the horse's heavy load
1208. the man's long leg
1209. the chief's four canoes

Noun and Noun Phrase

    1210. the woman's dirty garment

Grammatical (monovalent, bound) modifier
    1301. a (certain) calabash of milk
    1302. the calabash of milk
    1303. some calabashes of milk
    1304. the calabashes of milk
    1305. the two calabashes of milk / both calabashes of milk
    1306. the three calabashes of milk
    1307. my calabash of milk
    1308. my calabashes of milk
    1309. my two calabashes of milk
    1310. my three calabashes of milk
    1311. this (here) calabash of milk (within sight)
    1312. this calabash of milk
    1313. that (there) calabash of milk
    1314. this calabash of milk in question
    1315. this calabash of milk from here
    1316. these calabashes of milk
    1317. these two calabashes of milk, both these calabashes of milk
    1318. these three calabashes of milk
    1319. many calabashes of milk
    1320. all the calabashes of milk
    1321. two calabashes of milk, three calabashes of milk

C. *Combination of grammatical and lexical modifiers*

    1401. a (certain) big calabash of milk
    1402. the big calabash of milk
    1403. some big calabashes of milk
    1404. the big calabashes of milk
    1405. the two big calabashes of milk / both big calabashes of milk
    1406. the three big calabashes of milk
    1407. my big calabash of milk
    1408. my big calabashes of milk
    1409. my two big calabashes of milk / both my big calabashes of milk
    1410. my three big calabashes of milk
    1411. this big calabash of milk (within sight)
    1412. this big calabash of milk
    1413. that big calabash of milk
    1414. these big calabashes of milk
    1415. these two big calabashes of milk / both these big calabashes of milk
    1416. these three big calabashes of milk
    1417. many (a great number of) big calabashes of milk
    1418. all the big calabashes of milk
    1419. two big calabashes of milk, three big calabashes of milk ...

– Modification of the modifier

lexical (polyvalent, free) modifier

    1501. the calabash of fresh milk
    1502. the wife of the old chief
    1503. the bracelet of the beautiful woman
    1504. the young hare's paw
    1505. the water of the deep well
    1506. the trunk of the tall tree
    1507. the naughty child's knife
    1508. the tall chief's loincloth
    1509. the pot of hot meat
    1510. the door of the small hut

Grammatical (monovalent, bound) modifier

    1601. the calabash of a (certain) woman
    1602. the woman's calabash
    1603. the women's calabash
    1604. the two women's calabash
    1605. the three women's calabash
    1606. my woman's calabash
    1607. my women's calabash
    1608. my two women's calabash
    1609. my three women's calabash
    1610. the calabash of this woman (nearby)
    1611. the calabash of this woman
    1612. the calabash of that woman
    1613. the calabash of this woman in question
    1614. the calabash of this woman from here
    1615. these women's calabash
    1616. these two women's calabash / both these women's calabash
    1617. these three women's calabash
    1618. the calabash of many (a great number of) women
    1619. the calabash of all the women
    1620. two women's calabash, three women's calabash

Combination of lexical and grammatical modifiers

    1701. the calabash of a (certain) beautiful woman
    1702. the calabash of the beautiful woman
    1703. the calabash of the beautiful women
    1704. the calabash of the two beautiful women, the calabash of both beautiful women
    1705. the calabash of the three beautiful women
    1706. the calabash of my beautiful woman
    1707. the calabash of my beautiful women
    1708. the calabash of my two beautiful women, the calabash of both my beautiful women
    1709. the calabash of my three beautiful women
    1710. the calabash of this beautiful woman
    1711. the calabash of that beautiful woman

1712. the calabash of this beautiful woman in question
1713. the calabash of this beautiful woman from here
1714. the calabash of these beautiful women
1715. the calabash of these two beautiful women, the calabash of both these beautiful women
1716. the calabash of these three beautiful women
1717. the calabash of many (a great number of) beautiful women
1718. the calabash of all the beautiful women
1719. the calabash of two beautiful women, the calabash of three beautiful women

D. Modification of both the head noun and the modifier

1801. the big calabash of fresh milk
1802. the old chief's white loincloth
1803. the naughty child's sharp knife
1804. the round fruit of the big tree
1805. the tall woman's dirty garment
1806. the deep well of the neighboring village
1807. the cold water of the deep river
1808. the wicked man's black dog
1809. the old woman's long hand
1810. the hot meat of the small pot

C. Relator Noun Phrase

The words governed by the relator may belong to an open (lexical) or closed (grammatical) class. The relators may indicate:

1 Attribution
101. He gave the loincloth to the woman.
102. He gave the money to someone.
103. He gave money to some (of them).
104. He gave me some money; he gave you (SG) / him / her / us / you (PL) / them some money.
105. He gave some money to this one, to that one.
106. He gave some money to these, to those (people).
107. He gave money to everyone.

2 Restriction
108. He saw only the chief.
109. He came only with the child.
110. He ate only the meat. =/ He only ate.
111. He washed only his head. =/ He only washed (himself).
112. He bought only a loincloth.
113. He walked for only an hour. =/ He only walked.
114. He came with only some (people). =/ He only came.
115. He did not see your father; he saw only mine.
116. He did not see your children; he saw only mine.
117. She looked at the loincloths; she bought only this one.

118. She looked at the loincloths; she bought only these.
119. The child left only with me.

3. Comparison.
120. He ran like a hare.
121. He used to sing like a bird.
122. He swam like a fish.
123. The gruel is as clear as water.
124. He cried like a child.
125. Your loincloth is red like mine.
126. Your loincloths are red like mine.
127. He ran like me.
128. He bought a knife like this one, like that one.
129. He bought some knives like these, like those.
130. He began to dance like everyone.

4. Privation.
131. He came without the chief.
132. I saw the chief without his bow.
133. He sleeps without a mat.
134. He eats millet without sauce.
135. He went to the market without a calabash.
136. He came without anybody.
137. He left without anything.
138. He ate without me.
139. He took his bow; I followed him without mine.
140. He told me to come without this one.

5. Repetition.
141. He saw another bird.
142. He drank more water.
143. He caught another fish.
144. She bought herself another loincloth.
145. He made another drum.
146. He cured someone else (i.e., yet another person).
147. He came to fetch something else.
148. He lost his knife; he used mine again.
149. He lost his knives; he used mine again.
150. It was I again whom he struck.
151. The dog big this one, that one, those ones again.
152. The dog bit a lot more people.
153. He took three more of them.
154. He took three more papayas.

6. Destination.
153. He brought back a goat for the chief.
154. He went to fetch some milk for the child.
155. He bought a loincloth for the woman.
156. He brought some food for his cows.
157. He took some medicine for his leg.

158. Medicines are good for some people.
159. I brought back a goat for mine (my chief).
160. She prepared the meal for me.
161. She prepared the meal for this one, that one, these ones.
162. She prepared food for everyone.

7. Direction.
163. He set off toward the village.
164. He walked as far as the well.
165. He passed through the town.
166. He ran in the direction of the field.
167. He raised the liquid (up) to his lips.
168. He ran (in the direction of) someone, some (ones).
169. He ran toward something.
170. He ran toward me, you (SG), him, us, you (PL), them.
171. He ran toward everyone.
172. He saw the huts; he went toward mine (SG/PL).
173. He saw the children; he went toward mine.
174. He walked up to this one, that one, these (ones), those (ones).

8. Location.
175. He was sitting among (in the middle of) the children.
176. He put the meat in the middle of the plate.
177. There is a boundary line in the middle of the fields.
178. He kept the insect in the middle of his hand.
179. He made a stain in the middle of the loincloth.
180. He was sitting among some of them.
181. He was sitting among us.
182. He was sitting in the midst of them all.
183. He made a stain in the middle of this one.
184. He made a stain in the middle of mine.
184b. He sat down in the middle.

185. He came to the chief's home.
186. He stayed at the woman's home.
187. The guinea fowl ate at the hare's home.
188. He came to someone's home / some people's homes.
189. He did not stay at your father's home; he stayed at mine.
190. He came to my home (your home, his home, etc.).
191. He slept at this one's home, these ones' home.
192. He found hospitality in everyone's home.

193. He put some eggs into the calabash.
194. He dropped a stone into the well.
195. He went right inside the house.
196. He will come back in a moment.
197. He kept the fruit in his hand.
198. He put the sack into the canoe.
199. He put the sack into mine.
200. He put the sack into this one, these ones.
201. He put some eggs into something.

202. He put eggs into all of them (the calabashes).
202b. He put some eggs inside.

203. The bird is in the tree.
204. He put the fish onto the mat.
205. She put the cooking-pot on the fire.
206. The bird is flying over the river.
207. He has a wound on his leg.
208. He got onto the horse.
209. He got onto mine (SG).
210. He got onto mine (PL).
211. He got onto this one / these.
212. He got onto all (of them) (the horses).
213. She put the cooking-pot on something.
214. He put the garment on me.
214b. He put the garment on top.
215. The mat stayed under the bed.
216. The child fell asleep under the tree.
217. He crushed an insect under his foot.
218. He lit the fire under the cooking-pot.
219. He remained motionless in the rain.
219b. He put the garment underneath.
220. He lit the fire under something / under all (the cooking-pots).
221. His hut has been destroyed; he has come to find shelter under mine.
222. His hut has been destroyed; he has come to find shelter under this one.

223. The dog is sleeping near the hut.
224. She put her garment beside the tree.
224b. He put his garment aside.
225. She put her calabash beside the well.
226. He sat down near the fire.
227. The arrow passed close to his head.
228. The arrow passed close to mine (my head).
229. The arrow passed close to me.
230. The arrow passed close to this one / these ones / that one / those ones.
231. The arrow passed close to all (of them).
232. The arrow passed close to some (of them) / someone.

233. The men gathered around the chief.
234. The children are playing around the hut.
235. The cows are drinking around the well.
236. She put a necklace around her neck.
237. The sauce spread around the meat.
238. They gathered around someone / some (of them) / something.
239. They gathered around this one / these / that one / those.
240. The children are playing around mine (my hut).
241. The children are playing around (them) all (the huts).
242. The men danced around me.
242b. The chief came; the men gathered around.

243. The hare stopped in front of the hole.
244. The man is dancing in front of the musicians.

245. He came back before dark.
246. The child is walking in front of his mother.
247. The woman sat down in front of the cooking-pot.
248. The hare stopped in front of someone / some ones / something.
249. The child is not walking in front of his mother; he is walking in front of mine.
250. The child is walking in front of me.
251. The child is walking in front of this one / these (ones) / that one / those.
252. The child is walking in front of everyone.
252b. They left; the child was walking in front.

253. He disappeared behind the hut.
254. The woman hid behind a tree.
255. He came back after the night.
256. The dog stopped behind the cow.
257. He is walking behind someone / some (ones) / something.
258. He is walking behind me.
259. He is walking behind this one / these (ones) / that one / those (ones).
260. He is walking behind everybody (all).
261. He is not walking behind his father; he is walking behind mine.
261b. They are gone, the child walked behind.

262. He set off at the beginning of the day.
263. He met a monkey at the beginning of the road.
263b. They asked me to sing; I stopped at the beginning.

264. The donkey leaned over the edge of the water.
265. The fly fell on the edge of the vase.
265b. He ran to the river; he stopped just at the bank.

266. He hung a basket at the end of the stick.
267. He caught sight of a cow at the end of the field.
268. He hung a basket on the end of something.
269. He lost his stick; he hung his basket on the end of mine.
270. He hung his basket on the end of this one / these (ones) / that one / those (ones).
271. He took his fishing lines; he put some hooks on the end of (them) all.
271b. He took a stick; he hooked his basket over one end.

272. He has been working for three days.
273. I caught sight of him from the neighboring village.

274. The plants are broken because of the storm.
275. He did not sleep because of the noise.

276. He was cured thanks to the medicine.
277. He found his path again thanks to the chief.
278. He received the message thanks to the drum.
279. He received the message thanks to someone.
280. He received the message thanks to me.
281. He received the message thanks to this one / these (ones) / that one / those (ones).
282. He received the message thanks to everyone (all).
283. His canoe was in a bad condition; he was able to leave by means of mine.

284. The men held a meeting about a speech.
285. They talked about the harvest.
286. They held a meeting about someone / something.
287. They talked about us.
288. They talked about this one / these (ones) / that one / those (ones).
289. They talked about everyone.
290. They talked about women.
291. They talked about mine (my wife).

292. The lion and the hare set off.
293. They met the dog, the guinea-fowl, the hyena, and the monkey.

294. The woman spoke with gentleness.
295. The rain is falling violently.
296. The chief arrived with his wife and children.
297. He made the pot with clay and water.
298. The woman drew (out) the water with a calabash.
299. He arrived with someone / some (ones) / something.
300. My friend came with his wife; I came with mine.
301. My friend came with his children; I came with mine.
302. He chose several loincloths; he came with this one / these (ones).
303. He chose several loincloths; he came with that one / those (ones).
304. He chose several loincloths; he came with (them) all.
304b. He chose several loincloths; he came with (them)

305. The flies die at the time of the dry season.
306. He awakens at the time of prayer.
307. He puts on a white loincloth on festival days.

308. My hut is opposite (across from) the chief's hut.
309. The woman sat down opposite the tree.
310. The woman sat down opposite someone.
311. The woman sat down opposite this one / these (ones) / that one / those (ones).
312. The woman sat down opposite everybody (all).
313. The chief is sitting among his children; the woman is sitting opposite hers.
313b. The woman was standing up; I sat down opposite (her).

D. Relative Noun Phrase

1 The modifier is a verb.

head noun as agent

1. a singing bird   a bird that sings
2. a jumping animal   an animal that jumps
3. a drinking man   a man who drinks
4. a dancing woman   a woman who dances
5. a crying child   a child who cries
6. a thieving man   a man who steals
7. a lying man   a man who lies
8. a climbing animal   an animal that climbs

Noun and Noun Phrase

9. a begging man   a man who begs
10. bleeding meat   meat that bleeds

head noun as patient

11. a knife for cutting meat
12. a cup for drinking
13. a calabash for drawing water
14. a song for making the rain come
15. a mat for sleeping (on)
16. a bowl for preparing sauce
17. a spoon for stirring sauce
18. a needle for sewing nets
19. a hook for catching small fish
20. a basket for going to market

2 The modifier is a relative clause.

1. I saw the man who came yesterday.
2. I ate the meat that burned in the pot.
3. I cared for the cow that is sick.
4. I know the child who stole his brother's money.
5. He repaired the hut that was damaged during the storm.
6. He heard the rain that fell today.
7. The man who came yesterday is the chief's brother.
8. The meat that burned in the pot is mutton.
9. The cow that is sick lay down under a tree.
10. The child who stole his brother's money has been punished.
11. The hut that was damaged by the storm has been rebuilt.
12. The rain that fell today has ruined my father's field.
13. I saw the one who came yesterday.
14. I saw those who came yesterday.
15. The one who came yesterday asked me for some money.

E. Apposition

1. That man, he came.
2. The man, he is eating the yam.
3. The yam, the man is eating it.
4. The child, the tallest in the village, gave me some fruit.
5. I met the child, the tallest in the village.
6. He took the millet, that from last year.
7. I went to the well, { the one at the end of the village.
                        { which is at the end of the village.
8. The child, the chief's, is ill.

Questionnaire 8
Sentence Types

by Jacqueline M. C. Thomas

This questionnaire on structures is intended to supplement other parts of the study, such as the sentence questionnaire or the collection of texts, for a systematic exploration of the possible sentence types of the language. It can be used profitably only after a good deal of study of the language, since it takes account of what is already known.

1 Simple sentences

A. Types of functionemes (Sentence types functioning as dependent clauses). Grammatical categories and phrase types that may fill the different primary roles on the clause level (essential elements = S P / complement form S P + C).

1 Se = P
Does this constitute a complete, unmarked sentence or an incomplete and/or marked sentence?[13]
Does one or the other possibility (or both) occur in the language? Specify which ones(s).
P = verb and/or P = nonverb? e.g.: *Come!* is an incomplete, marked (imperative) sentence with P = V. *Dog* does not constitute a sentence in English, but in Turkish, a single noun such as this may constitute a complete, unmarked sentence, meaning 'It is a dog', with P = nonV. Which grammatical categories or phrase types may fill the P slot when Se = P?

2 Se = P C
Sentence type

---

[13]Se = Sentence; P = Predicate; S = Subject; C = Complement; Cm = Clause marker. Definitions of the sentence types are found in Chapter II, Elementary Grammatical Analysis, where the article on 'The Definition of Categories' by Luc Bouquiaux and Jacqueline Thomas appears.

- P = V and/or nonV e.g., *Come here!* is an incomplete, marked (imperative) sentence, with P = V.
- P = V : define C (which grammatical categories and/or types of noun or verb phrases it may be) e.g., 'Come here' or 'Come quickly' or 'Come running' or 'Come with the dog', etc.
- P = nonV : define C.

Which grammatical categories and phrase types may fill the P slot when Se = P C ? Possible combinations: if P = x (grammatical category / phrase), we have C = y' and y'' (grammatical category / phrase); if P = y (grammatical category / phrase (type)), we have C = y''', y'''', and z (grammatical category / phrase), etc. (for a certain P there are certain Cs, for a certain other P there are certain other Cs, etc.)

3. Se = P (C) Sp.[14]
   - sentence type e.g., *Do not come (here)* is an incomplete, marked sentence (negative imperative)
   - Sp : does the Sp affect the whole sentence or only the P?
   - Define Sp.
   - Define P and C (as in 1 and 2) when Se = P (C) Sp

4. Se = S P.
   - sentence type
   - definition of P
   - definition of S
   - possible combinations (cf. 2): e.g., in English, when Se = S P, we have for S 'He comes', 'Paul comes', 'The dog comes', 'Paul's dog comes', etc.

5. Se = S P C.
   - sentence type
   - definition of C^{15}
   - possible combinations for P, what may S be? For the various possible combinations of S P (cf. 4)
   - order of the C's free order or not e.g., 'He takes / his friend / and his suitcases / to the station / quickly / by car / in spite of the rain' or, 'In spite of the rain, / he takes / his friend / and his suitcases / to the station / by car / quickly', etc. Determine the syntactic possibilities and impossibilities (beware of semantic interference[16]). Ordering constraint = S P C_1 C_2 C_3 C_4 C_5 C_6 etc.

C_1 = personal pronoun direct object (M $P_{2.1}$) ⎫ without
C_2 = personal pronoun indirect object (M $P_{2.2}$) ⎬ relator
C_3 = nonlocative direct object (nonpers. pron.) ⎭
C_4 = nonlocative indirect object (nonpers. pron.) ⎱ with relator
C_5 = locative with or without relator
C_6 = adverb or adverbial phrase, etc.

---

[14]The sentential particle (Sp) is a sentence modifier, and may include one or more categories, e.g., negatives, affirmatives, positives, dubitatives, interrogatives, etc.

[15]Definition of S = which grammatical categories and phrase types may fill the S slot.

[16]The speaker may reject a sentence not because it is ungrammatical but because it seems semantically unacceptable, e.g., *The dog is meowing* (cf. Introduction).

Sentence Types   305

order fixed for some C's (free or partially free for other C's)
   C_t = temporal complement, the beginning or end of the sentence:
       S P C_1 C_2 C_t or S_t S P C_1 C_2
     - establish the order of the C's
     - define each type of C
     - Are some types mutually exclusive? Which ones?

6 Se = S P (C) Sp
     - sentence type
     - definition of Sp
     - possible combinations
     - with the different definitions and possible combinations of P
     - with the different definitions and possible combinations of S
     - with the different definitions and possible combinations of C (cf. 4 and 5)

7 Se = Cm P (C) Sp
Repeat the various questions found in 4, 5, and 6, replacing S with Cm e.g. 'It is he', 'It is Paul', 'It is the dog', 'It is Paul's dog', etc. In Ngbaka, *It is* = Cm 'he', 'Paul', 'the dog', etc. = P *ʔá yéè, ʔá Pólè, ʔá bɔ́nɔ̃, ʔá bɔ́nɔ́-kā Pólè*, ...

B. Possible order of the major constituents. Since the order S P (C) (Sp) is not common to all languages, the different possibilities must be considered. The major constituents of each sentence type should be analyzed as explained above (cf. 2 to 7).

1 Continuous constituents
   Se = S P Sp C
   Se = S C P Sp
   Se = P S C Sp or P Sp S C, etc.
   Se = P C S Sp or P Sp C S, etc. etc.

2 Discontinuous constituents. One or more of the major constituents may be discontinuous, i.e., may be broken up by other elements.
   Se = S sp P Sp ; e.g., French *Il ne vient pas.* 'He is not coming.'
   Se = S p Sp P ; e.g., English *He is not coming.*
   Se = S sp p Sp P C ; e.g., French *Il n'est pas venu ici.*
   Se = s C S P or S C s P etc.
   Se = S c P C (Sp) etc.
   Se = P s C S (Sp) etc.
   Se = S P C p etc.

2 Complex sentences

A. Secondary complex sentences: one of the major constituents of a simple sentence is expanded by a clause

1 Se = S_x P (C) (Sp)
           - S_x = S / relative (S) P (C) (Sp) /
                   e.g., 'the man whom/that you saw yesterday'

2. $Se = S\ P\ C_x\ (Sp)$.
   - $C_x = C$ $\overline{\diagup\ \text{relative (S) P (C) (Sp)}\ \diagup}$

3. $Se = x = $ relative Se' ($Se' = $ sentence governed by the relative).
   $Se' = S\ P\ C\ Sp$
   $Se' = S\ P\ C$ - possible sentence types
   $Se' = S\ P$ - possible verbal forms
   $Se' = P$ - dependent on the S or C of Se of which Se' is the expansion
   $Se' = \emptyset$ - not dependent on the S or C of Se of which Se' is the expansion.
   - definition of relative (category) - possible combinations (cf. 4–6) with Se' / of Se'
   - possible order of the constituents (B)
   - possible continuity or discontinuity of relative e.g., vō-ló ʔó hā ló nò 'the man whom they caught' //person|this one/catches this|ME-truly/... (Ngbaka)

4. $Se = S\ P\ C$
   $\underbrace{\underbrace{\overline{\diagup\ \text{relative S P C (Sp)}\ \diagup}}_{Se'}\ \text{(Sp)}}_{C_x}$
   - S of Se' = C of Se; or S of Se' ≠ C of Se
   - Sp exists for Se only, for Se' only, for Se' and Se

5. $Se = S$ $P\ (C)\ (Sp)$
   $\overline{\diagup\ \text{relative S P C (Sp)}\ \diagup}$
   - S of Se' = S of Se; or S of Se' ≠ S of Se
   - Sp exists for Se only, for Se' only, for Se' and Se

6. *Possible complexity of the complex sentence:*
   - $Se = S\ P\ C_x$ or $Se = S_x\ P\ C$
   - $Se = S\ P\ C$ (Sp)
   $\overline{\diagup\ \text{rel. S P C} \hspace{4em} \text{(Sp)}\ \diagup}$
   $\hspace{2em}\overline{\diagup\ \text{rel. S P (C)} \hspace{2em} \text{(Sp)}\ \diagup}$
   e.g., 'the man [who killed the woman [whom you saw yesterday]]'

B. Primary complex sentences: the whole of a simple sentence is expanded by a clause.

1 Without a clause marker governing the expansion clause (juxtaposed).
- $Se_x = S\ P\ (C)\ /\ S'\ P'\ (C')$
  $Se' = S'\ P'\ (C')$
  $P = V_1\ /\ P' = V_2$ (verbal forms in agreement)
  $S' = S$ or $S' \neq S$
  $S' = C$ or $S' \neq C$
- $Se_x = S\ P\ C\ /\ P'\ (C')$
  $C = (S')$
  Are the verbal forms in agreement?
- $Se_x = S\ P\ (C)\ /\ P'\ (C')$
  $S = (S')$
  Are the verbal forms in agreement?

Sp for Se only
Sp for Se' only
Sp for Se' and Se

2 With a clause marker[17] governing the expansion clause.
  $Se_x = S\ P\ (C)\ /\ cl\ S'\ P'\ (C')$
  definition of cl
    only one category of cl
    several categories of cl (in particular, distinction of the conditionals)
  composition of Se'
    possible sentence types (cf. 3)
    possible verbal forms
  possible combinations
    of Se
    of Se'
    of Se with Se' ($Se_x = Se\ /\ Se'$ or $Se'\ /\ Se$) For a given Se, this Se's may occur; for this other Se, we get this possible Se'; etc.
  If there are several categories of cl:
    definition of each category of cl
    composition of Se' according to the category of cl concerned
    sentence types
    verbal forms of Se and Se' in agreement, or dependent on the category of cl
    possible combinations of Se and Se'
- Examine the possible combinations with Sp for the whole of 2
  Sp for Se only
  Sp for Se' only   } possible effect on verbal forms
  Sp for Se' and Se

3 Examine the possible order of the major constituents (cf. IB) for the whole of IIB.

4 Possible continuity or discontinuity of cl (cf. IB1 and IB2).

---

[17] cl = clause marker; Se = sentence; Se_x = complex sentence; Se' = expansion clause of Se

Questionnaire 9
Sentence Questionnaire

by Jean-Pierre Caprile, France Cloarec-Heiss, Françoise Leduc and Jacqueline M. C. Thomas

A

1. The goat *abandoned* her kids.
2. They *abandoned* their village.
3. He is *about* to leave.
4. He asked me *abruptly* if I wanted to leave with him.
5. The *abscess* is coming to a head.
6. The head of the *abscess* is gone.
7. I have an *abscess* on my thigh.
8. He pierced the *abscess*.
9. He squeezed the *abscess*.
10. I have an *abscess*.
11. He was condemned in his *absence*.
12. Don't be *absent* tomorrow.
13. He is an *absent-minded* man.
14. The village chief is *absent*.
15. His remarks are *abusive*.
16. He *accepted* the clothing that I gave him.
17. He had an (automobile, hunting) *accident*.
18. She *accidentally* tipped over the pot.
19. He *accompanied* the child to the village.
20. Go *accompany* him to the village.
21. He is the *accomplice* of the thief.
22. That isn't in *accordance* with his tastes.
23. His *account* is accurate and detailed.
24. He aimed *accurately*.
25. He came to *accuse* him.
26. A man came to *accuse* your brother.
27. I *accused* him in court of stealing.
28. He *accused* him of stealing.
29. They *accused* me of stealing before the chief.
30. He is *aching* all over from a day of walking.
31. This lemon is *acidic*.
32. The accused man *acknowledged* his crime.
33. He is one of my *acquaintances*.
34. He has many *acquaintances*.
35. They quickly got *acquainted*.
36. He swam *across* the river.
37. Don't feel sorry for him—he's just putting on an *act*.
38. She is putting on an *act*.

39. This man is very *active;* he works a lot.
40. This child is not *adapted* to school life.
41. *Add* some salt to the soup.
42. He *added* a taro to the pile.
43. Forms of *address:* Hey you! (for a man) . . .
44. He was paid *adequately.*
45. The two huts are *adjacent* to each other.
46. The two huts are *adjacent.*
47. He *adjusted* the bedposts.
48. He never wanted to *admit* it.
49. He *admitted* that he had stolen it.
50. A monkey will not *adopt* his brother's child.
51. He *adopted* his brother's son.
52. He *adopted* the orphan child.
53. He has become an *adult.*
54. He committed *adultery* with the chief's wife.
55. He had to pay the chief five kids (young goats) for *adultery.*
56. I *advanced* him the money for the trip.
57. Take *advantage* of the lessons from your master.
58. He took *advantage* of the occasion to run away.
59. Events were to his *advantage.*
60. He is a wild *adventurer.*
61. He doesn't let *adversity* get him down.
62. He gives good *advice.*
63. I *advised* him to keep quiet.
64. I followed him from *afar.*
65. The *affair* is over (with).
66. The sight of blood doesn't *affect* him.
67. He is *affected* (in his manner).
68. Your sister has become *affected* (in manners) since she has been in the city.
69. She is *affectionate.*
70. The mother looks at her child *affectionately.*
71. The child is *afraid* of the storm.
72. Don't be *afraid.*
73. He ran *after* him.
74. He arrived three days *after* his father left.
75. He left *after* the tornado.
76. I will leave *after* you.
77. He will come this *afternoon.*
78. He arrived in the *afternoon.*
79. Everyone is *against* him.
80. That is *against* his interests.
81. He works in the fields *against* his will because his father makes him do it.
82. He left *against* his will.
83. Everyone comes up *against* that difficulty.
84. The men rowed *against* the current.
85. Go get the man leaning *against* the wall.
86. He never *ages;* he doesn't change.
87. Don't *aggravate* him.
88. He was *aggravated* by his chief.
89. He is *agile.*
90. He is very *agile.*
91. His face is *aging;* he has wrinkles.
92. The criminal's *agitation* gave him away.
93. They left three days *ago.*
94. That food doesn't *agree* with me.
95. His story doesn't *agree* with the facts.
96. Their stories didn't *agree.*
97. He arrived at the time *agreed upon.*
98. He *agreed* to let me go.
99. We *agreed* to meet after dinner.
100. He *agreed* with (approved of) the chief's decision.
101. The boat ran *aground* on the sand.
102. He got there five minutes *ahead* of him.
103. The preparations for the feast are moving *ahead.*
104. Go on *ahead.*
105. He *aimed* at the elephant.
106. The *air* is cold.
107. An *air* of hostility held sway over the men of the village.
108. He is looking into the *air.*
109. The bird flew away far into the *air.*

Sentence Questionnaire

110. The door of the hut fits poorly; it is *ajar*.
111. The woman gave birth to an *albino*.
112. They made a lot of *alcohol* for the feast.
113. He got drunk on corn *alcohol*.
114. The days follow one another, but no two are *alike*.
115. The two huts are exactly *alike*.
116. That custom is still very much *alive*.
117. He is still *alive*.
118. He left in *all* haste.
119. The child cried *all* night.
120. She is a woman who has *all* she could wish for.
121. He is an *all-around* fellow; he can do anything.
122. The chief *allowed* him to go.
123. *Almost* everyone went hunting.
124. He is a very generous man; he always gives *alms* to the poor.
125. He is *alone* with the chief in the hut.
126. He walked *along* the river.
127. The canoe drew *alongside* the shore.
128. It is *already* finished.
129. He raises manioc and millet *also*.
130. He is strong *although* short.
131. He is *always* there.
132. I *am* hungry.
133. He spoke in an *ambiguous* way.
134. He has no more *ammunition*.
135. The huts are scattered *among* the trees.
136. The chief gave him a certain *amount* of money.
137. He is an *amputee;* he has no arms.
138. He is an *amputee;* he has no hands.
139. He is an *amputee;* he has only one arm.
140. He is an *amputee;* he has only one hand.
141. She put an *amulet* around her baby's neck to make it grow quickly.
142. He put an *amulet* around his neck to protect him from the sickness.
143. The boat dropped *anchor* upstream from the village.
144. They weighed *anchor* yesterday.
145. He has *anemia*.
146. He is very *anemic*.
147. He has terrible fits of *anger*.
148. He is *angry*.
149. He became *angry*.
150. It is an *animal*.
151. There are many dangerous (wild) *animals*.
152. He twisted his *ankle* while running.
153. His foot rings hurt his *ankles*.
154. They *announced* the news of his death in the village.
155. He loves to *annoy* her.
156. She couldn't conceal her *annoyance*.
157. He *annoyed* me.
158. The chief is *annoyed* with him.
159. The *annual* harvest of sesame seed is increasing.
160. This knife is blunt; give me *another one*.
161. *Answer* my question.
162. The hunters killed five *antelopes* yesterday.
163. We must *anticipate* the worst.
164. They are making an *antidote* for him.
165. His *anus* hurts him.
166. Uncertainty about the future caused her *anxiety*.
167. He has an *anxious* nature.
168. You can't see *any* more; it is dark.
169. I didn't see *any* of them.
170. I couldn't do *anything else* but go there.
171. *Anything* will amuse him.
172. You can get used to *anything*.
173. His garment came *apart* at the seams.
174. Her husband is very ugly; he's a real *ape*.
175. That story is *appalling*.
176. It has the *appearance* of a man but it is a spirit.

177. The moon *appeared* on the horizon.
178. He *appeared* suddenly out of the shadows.
179. She *appears* older than her age.
180. It *appears* that the chief is sick.
181. He has a big *appetite* for meat.
182. He has a big *appetite*.
183. He *approached* him from behind.
184. He *approached* the bed.
185. That isn't *appropriate*.
186. She is *appropriately* dressed.
187. The branch must be well *arched* so that the trap is good and tight.
188. She *arched* her back.
189. They are always *arguing*.
190. His *arm* hurts.
191. He broke his *arm*.
192. He has an abscess on the *armpit*.
193. He cleaned up and cleared *around* his house.
194. The child ran *around* the hut.
195. The woman is sweeping *around* the hut.
196. There is nobody *around*.
197. He *arrived* at the village.
198. He *arrived* in town.
199. He *arrived* yesterday.
200. He is full of *arrogance*.
201. He shot an *arrow* with a bow.
202. He went *as far as* the river.
203. There are *as many* knives as forks.
204. He is not *as* big *as* he.
205. She is *as* pretty *as* can be.
206. Come *as* fast *as* you can.
207. He took her *as* his wife.
208. Do the work *as* it should be done.
209. Today I am *as* sad *as* I was happy yesterday.
210. He is *as* strong *as* an elephant.
211. I am *as* tall *as* you.
212. He arrived (just) *as* they were leaving.
213. He was quite *ashamed* to be caught red-handed.
214. The departure salt (in the Ngakola cult) is obtained from the *ashes* of that plant.
215. The chief put the food *aside*.
216. *Ask* him.
217. *Ask* permission.
218. He *asked* for his way.
219. The child is *asking* for his meal.
220. He fell *asleep*.
221. The people *assembled* at the burial place.
222. The people *assembled* in front of the chief's house.
223. *Assembling* this trap is difficult.
224. He is *asthmatic*.
225. He was quite *astonished*.
226. He is *at* Bangui.
227. I am *at* home.
228. He came *at* midnight.
229. Pay *attention* to what you are doing.
230. You must pay *attention* to what you are told.
231. The child wants to be the center of *attention*.
232. He is *attentive* to what he is told.
233. She put on her *finest attire* to go into town.
234. He *attracted* (enticed) the children to his home.
235. He is captivated by the *attraction* of novelty.
236. Those clothes make her (more) *attractive*.
237. He *attributed* the theft of the chickens to his brother.
238. He *avenged* one offense by another offense.
239. He is of *average* height.
240. On the *average*, ten cows die during the trip.
241. He *avoided* the blow.
242. He is not *aware* of his arrival.
243. He is *awkward* at courting girls.
244. His *awkwardness* in speaking is comical.
245. The cobbler pierced the leather with an *awl*.
246. The man is splitting wood with an *axe*.

B

247. The *baby* is crying.

248. She is cradling her *baby*.
249. The danger made him *back away*.
250. You can't talk with him; he'll *get his back up* right away.
251. He will soon be *back* in the village.
252. The *back* of the canoe is sinking down.
253. I am going to sit in the *back* of the car.
254. He is at the *back* of the line (queue).
255. He has a *backache*.
256. The children went to go fish in the *backwater* (water separated from a river).
257. He gave me *bad* advice.
258. Last night I had some *bad* dreams.
259. He's in a *bad* mood.
260. That's a *bad* omen.
261. He gave me a *bad* piece of meat.
262. The water from this well has a *bad* taste.
263. The weather is *bad*.
264. Your son is *bad-mannered;* he is not a good speaker.
265. You are *bad-tempered*.
266. These mats are *badly* made.
267. The *bag* is made of cloth.
268. He has *bags* under his eyes.
269. He put some *bait* in the trap to catch rats.
270. He put a piece of *bait* on the end of his line.
271. He walked *balancing* on the tree trunk.
272. *Balaphon insulator*.
273. The foot of the *balaphon* is broken.
274. He is playing the *balaphon*.
275. He is completely *bald*.
276. *Baldness* becomes him.
277. He made himself a mattress with the *bale* of rice.
278. They made a *bale* with the rice straw.
279. He carried the *bales* of cotton to market.
280. The thread is rolled up in a *ball*.
281. She made a manioc *ball*.
282. He *ballasted* his dugout canoe with rocks.
283. She spread a *balm* on her body.
284. He is carving a *bamboo* cane.
285. The *bananas* are full (green but not ripe).
286. The *bananas* are ripe.
287. I prefer *sweet bananas* to *cooking bananas*.
288. A *band* of buffaloes headed toward the hunters.
289. She put a *bandage* around his wounded head.
290. The doctor is changing the wounded man's *bandages*.
291. His head *banged* against the tree.
292. They are preparing a sheep *barbecue*.
293. The child goes around *barefoot*.
294. This tree is losing its *bark*.
295. The dog *barked* during the night.
296. The dog is *barking*.
297. The *barrel* of the rifle is still smoking.
298. The ewe is *barren* (sterile; has not yet carried young).
299. The soil is *barren;* nothing will grow in it.
300. The *basket* is made of wicker.
301. She carries the *basket* on her head.
302. She is weaving a *basket*.
303. She *bathed* her child.
304. All the young people *bathed* in the river.
305. *Bats* eat insects.
306. That woman *batters* her children.
307. The hunters use a *battue* (beating bushes to drive out the game).
308. Wait for him here; he won't *be* long.
309. She bought some red *beads*.
310. The necklace is made of blue *beads*.
311. The bird opened its *beak*.
312. The bird gives a *beakful* to its young.
313. His face *beams* with joy.
314. The *beans* are cooking.
315. She is shelling *beans*.

316. His *beard* grows quickly.
317. He has a sparse *beard;* it doesn't grow quickly.
318. Your son is still *beardless* (smooth-cheeked).
319. My suitcase was *beat up* during the trip.
320. He *beat* him black and blue.
321. He doesn't like to be *beaten* at games.
322. He deserves to be *beaten*.
323. He is *beating* his son.
324. The *beating* of his heart is rapid.
325. The blacksmith *beats* the iron on the anvil.
326. Look at the *beautiful* horse.
327. She is a very *beautiful* woman.
328. The *beauty* of her gestures touched us.
329. She is a woman of great *beauty*.
330. He *became* chief.
331. The man *became* old.
332. I excused him *because of* his age.
333. Close the door *because of* the little goats.
334. He isn't working *because* he is sick.
335. Why did he leave? *Because* his brother died.
336. He *goes to bed* late in the evening.
337. He made himself a *bed* of leaves.
338. The river left its *bed*.
339. He makes *beds*.
340. I'm going to the *bedside* of the sick man.
341. It is the *beer* festival.
342. The *beer* is fermenting.
343. The *beer* is just ready.
344. I'm thirsty; give me some *beer*.
345. The *bees* are swarming.
346. These *bees* make a lot of honey.
347. *Bees* sting a lot.
348. He is bothering the *bees*.
349. His father died two days *before* he returned to the village.
350. She got ready two days *beforehand*.
351. I *beg* you to leave me alone.
352. It *began* to rain again.
353. He *began* to work.
354. Yesterday I gave five francs (or other currency) to a *beggar*.
355. It reduced him to *begging*.
356. It's the *beginning* of the harvest.
357. He *begs*.
358. He *behaved* badly for me.
359. He *behaved* badly towards me.
360. He *behaves* like an adult.
361. He always *behaves* well.
362. His *behavior* is irreproachable.
363. Go *behind* him.
364. He got *behind* in his work.
365. He is *behind* the hut.
366. The child fell on his *behind*.
367. He is lagging *behind*.
368. Don't *believe* anything he tells you.
369. You can *believe* that man.
370. It is a *bell* for buying women (paying the bride-price).
371. He rang the *bell*.
372. His tone is *belligerent*.
373. He stuffed his *belly* full.
374. This hat *belongs* to me.
375. She fastened her *belt*.
376. He made a climbing *belt*.
377. He is carving a *bench* from the wood.
378. The river takes a *bend* here.
379. He is *bending* a branch.
380. He is *bending* his knees.
381. He is *bending* under the weight of his burden.
382. The wind *bent* the ears of grain over.
383. He *bent* the stem in an arc.
384. He *bent* the wood to make a bow.
385. The plank *bent* under the weight.
386. He *bequeathed* him all his property.
387. He did the *best* he could.
388. He is the *best* hunter in the village.
389. What he does *best* is play the harp.
390. That's the *best* piece of meat.
391. He *bet* ten francs on the first player.
392. You can *bet* on it.
393. His gestures *betrayed* his emotion.

394. He *betrayed* the chief's confidence.
395. They placed their *bets*.
396. He is singing *better* and *better*.
397. He is a *better* hunter than farmer.
398. He is in a *better* mood than yesterday.
399. This water is *better* than I thought.
400. The chief knows *better* than we do what needs to be done.
401. He sings *better* than you do.
402. My harvest was *better* than yours.
403. You will do *better* tomorrow.
404. For lack of anything *better* I had to accept his proposal.
405. You can find *better* but it will be more expensive.
406. It is difficult to do *better*.
407. I feel *better*.
408. There is nothing *better*.
409. I think more of him now that I know him *better*.
410. He cut a *bevelled edge* on the bamboo cane.
411. The witch doctor concocted a *beverage*.
412. That is *beyond* my control.
413. The plantation is *beyond* the village.
414. He has large *biceps*.
415. That is the *bier* for displaying the dead.
416. That is a *big* family.
417. He has some *big* problems.
418. He takes *big* steps.
419. This child is already *big*.
420. The legs of my trousers are too *big*.
421. He vomited *bile*.
422. The woodcock has a long *bill*.
423. They say he won more than a *billion*.
424. The *bird* was caught in the trap.
425. She gave *birth* to a boy.
426. The woman gave *birth* to two children.
427. That is my brother's *birthplace*.
428. Put the *bit* in my horse's mouth.
429. He *bit* into the meat.
430. Your dog *bit* me.
431. During the scuffle he *bit* my ear.
432. He is looking for the smallest *bit* of tobacco.
433. A snake *bite* can be fatal.
434. My dog *bite* has become infected.
435. The mosquito *bite* itches (hurts).
436. That is the scar from a horse *bite*.
437. It is *biting* cold at night.
438. The medicine is *bitter*.
439. The child cried *bitterly*.
440. It is pitch *black*.
441. The panther is speckled with *black*.
442. Smoke *blackened* the cooking pot.
443. The *blacksmith* shoed my horse.
444. He broke the *blade* of his knife.
445. The woman is picking up *blades* of grass.
446. He was *blamed* by the chief.
447. He has a *blank* look (on his face).
448. He sleeps under a *blanket*.
449. The fire is *blazing* (hot).
450. The lambs are *bleating*.
451. His wound is *bleeding* a lot.
452. He shot his arrow *blind* (by guesswork).
453. He was born *blind* in one eye.
454. His wound left him *blind* in one eye.
455. He became *blind* from his wound.
456. *Blind* with anger, he wanted to kill her.
457. He was born *blind*.
458. I was *blinded* by the sun.
459. Sunlight makes him *blink*.
460. He *blinked* his eyes because of the sun.
461. My shoe hurts me and I have a *blister* on my foot.
462. The burn gave him a *blister*.
463. There is a *block* of stone on the road.
464. The tree trunks *block* the river.
465. The path is *blocked up*.
466. The road is *blocked*.
467. Animals are *blocking* the road.
468. Family ties are *blood* ties.
469. The wounded man lost some *blood*.
470. That battle was a *bloody* one.
471. The tree is in *bloom*.

472. *Blow* on the fire.
473. He received a *blow* to the head.
474. *Blow* your nose!
475. She is gathering *blue* flowers.
476. The knife is *blunt*.
477. He told (it to) me *bluntly*.
478. The *boards* are nailed together.
479. There is nothing to *boast* about.
480. The *boat* went back up the river.
481. He gave himself *body* and soul to this undertaking.
482. They moved in a *body* toward the neighboring village.
483. His whole *body* was shaking.
484. She likes *boiled* caterpillars (grubs).
485. He *boiled* some water.
486. The water is *boiling*.
487. He is a *bold* warrior.
488. The fish *bone* got caught in his throat.
489. He is soaked to the *bone*.
490. He is so thin you can see his *bones* (skeleton).
491. His *bones* stick out.
492. This fish has a lot of *bones*.
493. His face is *bony*.
494. It is a *book*.
495. Their *booty* was impressive.
496. They collected *borassus* fruit.
497. That stream *borders* our territory.
498. He *bored* into the ground.
499. He *bores* me.
500. He was *born* prematurely, at seven months.
501. He *borrowed* some money from him.
502. The *boss* called his workers together.
503. His *boss* fired him.
504. He lets himself be *bossed* around by his wife.
505. He *botched* his work.
506. The news *bothered* me.
507. Leave me alone; you are *bothering* me.
508. He comes and *bothers* us every day.
509. He doesn't realize that he is *bothersome*.
510. He filled the *bottle* with wine.
511. She tore the *bottom* of his pagne (long garment).
512. He fell to the *bottom* of the tree.
513. He touched the *bottom* of the water.
514. I *bought* fish for the chief's wife.
515. The chief *bought* his old knife from him.
516. I *bought* sesame (seed) at the market.
517. I *bought* some fish from the chief's wife.
518. When she dances, her chest *bounces*.
519. They caught a thief and *bound* him hand and foot.
520. He *bound* the grasses together.
521. He went to the *boundaries* of the village.
522. That is the *boundary* of his field.
523. That is the *boundary* of the village.
524. He took his *bow* and arrows.
525. He shot three monkeys with his *bow*.
526. The child *bowed* his head.
527. He *bowed* his knees.
528. He has a large wooden *bowl*.
529. She put the sauce into a *bowl*.
530. He is drawing the *bowstring* tight.
531. He is going to buy a *box* of matches.
532. The witch doctor arranged the ritual objects in a *box*.
533. Her arm is covered with *bracelets*.
534. The woman is *braiding* her hair.
535. Her hair is plaited in small *braids*.
536. The man is eating sheep's *brain*.
537. The wound in the skull exposed the *brain*.
538. The roads *branch* off at that point.
539. The man cut the *branch*.
540. The *branches* hang over the path.
541. The herdsmen proceeded to *brand* their animals.
542. The herdsmen *branded* their livestock.
543. She is *brandishing* a knife.
544. He is *brave* in combat.
545. He *braved* the danger.
546. The donkey is *braying*.

547. For good *bread*, use good flour.
548. The traveler took a *break* at the village.
549. The chief decided to *break* the silence.
550. The sun is *breaking* through the clouds.
551. He is *breaking* up a block of stone.
552. The mother is feeding her child at the *breast*.
553. I am all out of *breath* from running.
554. We were looking for a *breath* of cool air.
555. He is holding his *breath*.
556. He ran until he was out of *breath*.
557. Leave me some time to *breathe* a little.
558. Man *breathes* through the nose.
559. I'm *breathing* in the fresh air.
560. The child is *breathing* regularly.
561. That animal is the result of crossing two *breeds*.
562. They began to *brew* the beer.
563. A storm is *brewing*.
564. He is crossing the *bridge*.
565. They built a wooden *bridge*.
566. He broke his *bridle*.
567. His speech was *brief*.
568. The house is *bright*.
569. I can't stand the *brightness* of the sky.
570. She filled her glass to the *brim*.
571. The hedgehog (porcupine, etc.) *bristled* its spines.
572. He is *broad* minded.
573. He has *broad* shoulders.
574. He is *broad-shouldered*.
575. He is *broadcasting* it to everyone.
576. The machine *broke* down.
577. The automobile *broke* down.
578. The man *broke* a horse in.
579. He *broke* a stick.
580. He *broke* his leg.
581. He *broke* his promise.
582. The glass *broke* into a thousand pieces.
583. The goat *broke* its tether (rope).
584. His story *broke* our heart.
585. He *broke* the stick.
586. The rope *broke*.
587. His moped is *broken down*.
588. The deal was *broken off*.
589. It was made of *bronze*.
590. He is making a *broom*.
591. He *brought* his brother with him.
592. He *brought* his chief with him.
593. They *brought* the drowned man back to life.
594. The doctor *brought* the patient out of danger.
595. He *brought* the pot to his father.
596. In this area the soil is *brown*.
597. He is suffering from light *bruises*.
598. There was a *brush* fire.
599. He is making a *brush*.
600. She *brushed* the clothes.
601. His gestures are *brusque*.
602. The shock was very *brutal*.
603. He is known for his *brutality*.
604. The child is making soap *bubbles*.
605. He filled the *bucket* with water.
606. He has many *buddies*.
607. He won't *budge* an inch.
608. The branches are covered with *buds*.
609. *Buffaloes* move in herds.
610. He plays the *bugle*.
611. He cleaned the mouthpiece of the *bugle*.
612. The *bugs* are biting.
613. Here is the *builder* of my hut.
614. I want my house to be built by a professional *builder*.
615. He is *building* a house.
616. He *built* the chief's hut.
617. He is well *built*.
618. He *bullies* his children.
619. He *bumped* his head.
620. It is a *bumpy* road.
621. The *bunches of bananas* are big this year.
622. The merchant arrived at the village with a *bundle* of fabric.
623. Her worries are quite a *burden* to her.
624. The corpse is *buried*.
625. He is dead and *buried*.

626. The witch doctor treated his *burn*.
627. He made a cigarette *burn*.
628. The meal *burned* (up).
629. The hut *burned* down.
630. The fire *burned* down the forest.
631. We *burned* the grasses.
632. The cooking pot is *burning* hot.
633. He is *burning* with fever.
634. There's a smell of *burning*.
635. This wood *burns* slowly.
636. The smoke *burns* the eyes.
637. Wood *burns*.
638. He *burst* in on me.
639. The river *burst* the dikes.
640. The abscess *burst*.
641. They are *burying* him today.
642. He took the *bus* to go to Bangui.
643. It is a small *bush* which grows after planting.
644. It is a large *bush* which grows after planting.
645. It is a *bush*.
646. He went into the *bush*.
647. He doesn't beat around the *bush*.
648. His eyebrows are *bushy*.
649. He is in *business*.
650. It is not my *business*; it is your business.
651. It's not a gourd I want, *but* a canary.
652. Not only is he dirty *but* insolent also.
653. It's not my fault *but* yours.
654. He is the *butt* of village jokes.
655. The buffalo *butted* him.
656. He doesn't *buy* that.
657. How much did you *buy* them for (what price)?
658. How many chickens did you *buy*?
659. There is no *buyer* for these goods.
660. Many *buyers* came.
661. I am *buying* peanuts.
662. You sell and he *buys*.
663. He is playing *by* (near) his mother.
664. You came *by* foot.
665. What do you mean *by* that?
666. He went along *by* the back (way).
667. He swears *by* the chief's head.
668. They are walking two *by* two.

C

669. He is building a *cabin*.
670. The hen *cackles*.
671. He planted a *cactus*.
672. The men went to the *cafe*.
673. He built a *cage*.
674. He poured wine into a small *calabash*.
675. He made a mistake in his *calculations*.
676. I hurt my *calf*.
677. We'll leave at the first *call* of the partridge.
678. *Call* the laborers to start the work!
679. The armed forces were *called* up.
680. He *called* his dogs.
681. He *called* his son Mark.
682. He *called* on God.
683. He was *called* to go see the chief.
684. He was *called* to order.
685. What is this tree *called*? this animal? this sickness?
686. His hands are *calloused*.
687. He has *callouses* on his feet.
688. He's the one who *calls* the shots.
689. The chief tried to *calm down* (pacify) the dissatisfied ones.
690. He listened to the news with the greatest *calm*.
691. The chief kept his *calm*.
692. The wind *calmed* down.
693. The shaman prepared him a *calming* drink.
694. He climbed up the tree and then *came back down* again.
695. After a month's absence, he *came back* to the village.
696. The sun *came into* the hut.
697. He entered his hut, then *came out* again.
698. A faint feeling *came over* him.
699. A change *came over* his character.
700. The chief *came* over to his opinion.
701. The village *came* together for the festival.
702. They *came* to an agreement.
703. The panther *came* up to the goat silently.

704. We saw a *camel* caravan passing by.
705. He prepared the *camping* equipment.
706. He *can* do anything.
707. That *can't* be! It's impossible!
708. Come tomorrow if you *can*.
709. The sugar *cane* must be cut.
710. He walks with a *cane*.
711. She's *caning* a chair.
712. He took the *cap* off the bottle.
713. He is *capable* of anything.
714. He's not *capable* of it.
715. That gourd has a greater *capacity* than this one.
716. He works in the *capital*.
717. She's a very *capricious* woman.
718. He *capsized* the canoe.
719. The canoe *capsized*.
720. They freed the *captive*.
721. The men *captured* the wild animal.
722. An animal *carcass* was found near the village.
723. They discovered an antelope *carcass*.
724. The mother takes *care* of her child.
725. She takes *care* of her children.
726. He always take good *care* of his little sister.
727. I don't *care* what happens to him.
728. She is cheerful and *carefree*.
729. He is *careful* in his work.
730. He is *careless*.
731. The air (breeze) *caressed* our faces.
732. The ship was emptied of its *cargo*.
733. That's a *carnivorous* animal.
734. That's a *carnivorous* insect.
735. The *carpenter* is absent.
736. The wind *carried* off the canoe.
737. The chief *carried on* with his story.
738. He *carried out* the orders.
739. His plans were *carried out*.
740. The wind *carried* him *off* to the north.
741. His voice *carries* a long way.
742. The mother *carries* her child on her back.
743. The vulture is a *carrion-feeding* bird.
744. He is *carrying* a piece of wood.
745. A train is made up of railroad *cars*.
746. He put a *cartridge* into the rifle.
747. He *carved* the meat.
748. He *carved* the wood with a chisel.
749. He nailed up the *case* for shipping.
750. I'll leave it there *in case* he comes.
751. In any *case* I won't leave.
752. In that *case* call me.
753. That's a completely different *case*.
754. The doctor's instruments are arranged in a *case*.
755. He went there just in *case*.
756. A spell was *cast* on him.
757. The blacksmith is *casting* a little bell.
758. It is a *castrated* sheep.
759. A ram was *castrated*. (They *castrated* a ram.)
760. It is a tiger *cat* (margay, jaguar).
761. The *cat* ate the food.
762. The *mother cat* nurses her *kitten*.
763. The epidemic was a *catastrophe* for the region.
764. You can leave first; I will *catch up* to you on the way.
765. He took every precaution against *catching* disease.
766. There is only one *category* of children.
767. Those are *caterpillar* droppings.
768. Edible *caterpillars* are gathered during the rainy season.
769. He climbed up the tree to get some *caterpillars*.
770. That's what is left of the leaves eaten by *caterpillars*.
771. He is *Catholic*.
772. He bought his cow at the *cattle* market.
773. The net got *caught* on a branch.
774. The hunter *caught* the animal in the trap.
775. The dog *caught* the bone that his master threw to him.
776. The panther *caught* the goat.
777. We *caught* the thief in the act.
778. He is pleading the *cause* of his friend.

779. The *cause* of his illness is unknown.
780. He is the *cause* of this discussion.
781. He is always very *cautious*; he never runs any risks.
782. Tell him the bad news *cautiously*.
783. The roof *caved* in.
784. He has a *cavity* in his tooth.
785. He is *cavorting* about.
786. *Cayman*—see *crocodile*.
787. A *ceiba* tree is growing near his hut.
788. The *ceiling* of the house is low.
789. They are *celebrating* the return from the hunt in the village.
790. Give me the *center of the bread* (inside the crust).
791. People meet in the *center* of the village.
792. I stepped on a *centipede*.
793. The chief put on his *ceremonial* clothes.
794. It is a *ceremonial* spear.
795. Everyone is preparing for the *ceremony*.
796. He is *certain* of having seen it.
797. He wears a *chain* around his neck.
798. The *chameleon* forewarned me.
799. The *chameleon* sheds its skin.
800. He never misses a *chance* to talk about it.
801. Give me *change* (for five dollars).
802. She *changed* her skirt.
803. The chameleon *changes* color.
804. He *changes* jobs often.
805. That boy's voice is *changing*.
806. That man does not lack *character*.
807. Her face has no *character*.
808. The buffalo *charged* at me.
809. He was *charged* with theft.
810. He is a *charitable* man.
811. That woman has great *charm*.
812. The woman *chased* the little goats out of the hut.
813. The hunter is *chasing* the elephant.
814. He fell into a *chasm*.
815. In initiation camps, *chastity* is the rule.
816. His wife *chats* away all day long.
817. The fever makes his teeth *chatter*.
818. We bought a lot of manioc because it is *cheap* in this village.
819. He has a pimple on his right *cheek*.
820. He has big *cheeks*.
821. He has hollow *cheeks*.
822. His *chest* is bare.
823. His *chest* is broad and muscular.
824. He filled his *chest* with air.
825. She is *chewing* a piece of tough meat laboriously.
826. He *chews* tobacco.
827. That *chicken* is still too young to be eaten.
828. The war *chief* is a Ngbaka.
829. Here is the village *chief*.
830. That man is our land *chief*.
831. A *chigger* got into my foot.
832. The *chigger* is a flea.
833. A *chigger* laid an egg in my foot.
834. Come take the *chigger* out for me.
835. That man acts *childishly*.
836. She had three *children*.
837. He climbs like a *chimpanzee*.
838. His *chin* is pointed.
839. He has a double *chin*.
840. His hat is held on by a *chinstrap*.
841. He has no *choice* but to leave.
842. He *choked* while eating.
843. He is *choking* with indignation.
844. The man is *chopping* (splitting) wood.
845. He is *chopping* the tobacco up.
846. He *chops* wood in the forest.
847. He *chose* the most beautiful woman in the village.
848. He *chose* to stay in the village.
849. That's a *chronic* illness.
850. He is *chubby-cheeked*.
851. He *chucked* the stick into the river.
852. *Cigarettes* are expensive.
853. He smokes *cigars*.
854. The roast is burned to *cinders*.
855. The villagers sat in a *circle* around the storyteller.
856. Blood *circulates* in the body.
857. *Circumcision* is an initiation rite.

Sentence Questionnaire

858. It is a *circumcision* knife.
859. The *circumcised* boys returned to the village.
860. There are extenuating *circumstances* in his case.
861. In some *circumstances* it is best to keep silent.
862. He returned under unfortunate *circumstances*.
863. To leave the city, you must ask for a permit at *city* hall.
864. His *claims* are excessive.
865. A great *clamor* arose from the crowd.
866. He *clapped* his hands.
867. The child *clapped* his hands.
868. The bell's *clapper* is heavy.
869. It is a large bell *clapper*.
870. He *clasped* her in his arms.
871. The panther showed his *claws*.
872. It is *clay* (used to close up holes in canoes).
873. There is white *clay* here.
874. He went to get some *clay*.
875. The dishes are *clean*.
876. That water is not *clean*.
877. The chicken has been *cleaned* out (gutted).
878. She is *cleaning* the cooking pot.
879. She is *cleaning* the salad.
880. The doctor is *cleaning* the wound.
881. The thread broke *cleanly*.
882. It's *clear*—there's nothing more to do but leave.
883. I want to be *clear* in my own mind about it.
884. He wanted to *clear* up the matter.
885. The water in the creek is *clear*.
886. The entrance to the village is *clear*.
887. The sky is *clear*.
888. He was not able to get himself *cleared* (of the accusation).
889. She *cleared* away the entrance to the house.
890. The man *cleared* himself a passage through the forest.
891. I *cleared* the entrance to the hut.
892. He *cleared* the ground for planting.
893. He *cleared* the ground of underbrush.
894. He *cleared* the path.
895. The men stopped in the *clearing*.
896. I am beginning to see *clearly* in this affair (matter).
897. The chief is *clearly* the strongest.
898. The outline of the mountain was *clearly* visible.
899. The water is of great *clearness*. The *clearness* of the water is lovely.
900. The chief showed *clemency* to the thief.
901. This man is *clever* at tricking people.
902. The *climate* is hot and humid here.
903. *Climb* up on the roof of my hut.
904. This is a steep *climb*.
905. He is out of breath from the *climb*.
906. He is *climbing* the hill.
907. The monkey is *climbing* the tree.
908. The old woman cut the *clitoris* of the initiates.
909. He threw a dirt *clod* at me.
910. They are very *close* (intimate).
911. *Close* the door again.
912. The chief's hut is located very *close* to mine.
913. Stay *close* to the house.
914. The day drew to a *close*.
915. She *closed* the cover of the pot again.
916. He is *closely* shaven.
917. Each day brings us *closer* to death.
918. He is my *closest* friend.
919. She put the clothes in the *closet*.
920. The shock caused him to have a blood *clot*.
921. This *cloth* doesn't wrinkle.
922. His *clothes* are all in tatters.
923. My *clothes* are worn out.
924. The blood *clotted* around the wound.
925. The blood has *clotted* around the wound.
926. The blood is *clotting* (coagulating).
927. His eyes are *clouded* with tears.
928. The sky is *clouding over*.
929. The sky is full of *clouds*.
930. The water is *cloudy*.

931. He hit him on the head with a *club*.
932. He got *clubbed*.
933. There is a *clump* of trees in the middle of the savannah.
934. This mat was woven *clumsily*.
935. His *clumsiness* keeps him from shooting a bow well.
936. I don't like the *clumsy* gait of the camel.
937. He is too *clumsy* to manage weaving a mat.
938. He is too *clumsy* to weave mats.
939. Pour water over the *coals*.
940. She is roasting the meat on the *coals*.
941. His manners are *coarse*.
942. The panther's *coat* is spotted.
943. He has a heavy *coat* to protect him from the cold.
944. She really likes to be *coaxed*.
945. The *cochineal* scales feed on cactus.
946. The *cockroach* is dead.
947. There is a big *cockroach* on the path.
948. The language of the drum is a *code*.
949. They are drying out the green *coffee* (beans).
950. She threw out the *coffee grounds*.
951. He has *coffee trees* on his plantation.
952. His child is *coffee-colored*.
953. I like strong *coffee*.
954. He is making a *coffin*.
955. There is no *coherence* to his ideas.
956. His story lacks *cohesion*.
957. The snake *coiled* up.
958. He is *coiling* the wire.
959. Your *coin* is counterfeit (fake).
960. His departure *coincided* with my arrival.
961. It is a *cola tree*.
962. He sells *cola* nuts.
963. It gets *cold* at nightfall.
964. It's *cold* today.
965. The child caught *cold*.
966. *Colic* is a serious disease among children.
967. The man *collapsed* from exhaustion.
968. The house *collapsed*.
969. The hut *collapsed*.
970. That house is *collapsing*.
971. His shirt *collar* is too tight.
972. He broke his *collarbone*.
973. The descendants of his ancestors are his *collateral relatives*. (cognates)
974. He is trying to *collect* his ideas.
975. There aren't any more *colonists*.
976. The *color* of that fabric has faded.
977. The rooster raised his (cocks) *comb*.
978. She *combed* out her hair.
979. She is *combing* her hair.
980. They are *combining* their effort to succeed.
981. Her hairdo is kept in place by *combs*.
982. He should *come back* tomorrow.
983. *Come out*, everybody!
984. The millet is starting to *come up*.
985. Where do you *come* from?
986. The chief will *come* here tonight.
987. All things *come* to those who wait.
988. *Come* up to the table.
989. *Come* with me; accompany me.
990. The road descends then *comes back up* again.
991. She came looking for me to *comfort* her.
992. She likes her *comfort*.
993. It is a *comfortable* seat.
994. He is *comfortably* settled underneath the tree.
995. The chief's words *comforted* him.
996. Water is *coming into* the canoe.
997. He is *coming out* from an interview with the chief.
998. It is *commendable* to work a great deal.
999. He *committed* adultery.
1000. That is *commonplace*.
1001. Some children are making a *commotion*.
1002. The rooms *communicate* with each other.

1003. He is a good *companion*.
1004. He left with his *companion*.
1005. That animal likes the *company* of people.
1006. He was in cheerful *company*.
1007. The shaman opened the small fetish *compartment*.
1008. The chief *compelled* us to work.
1009. He gave him a goat as *compensation*.
1010. The sick man is suffering without *complaining*.
1011. He addressed a *complaint* to the chief.
1012. The family was *complete*.
1013. The house is *completed*.
1014. He is *completely* mad.
1015. Don't *complicate* things. Don't make *complications*.
1016. It is too *complicated* for me.
1017. He *complied* with the chief's orders.
1018. She loves *compliments*.
1019. She is making fruit *compote*.
1020. The surface of the wood is *concave*.
1021. She *conceals* her feelings.
1022. It's hardly *conceivable*.
1023. You can't *conceive* of such a calamity.
1024. She *conceived* a baby.
1025. The chief *concentrated* before speaking.
1026. He *concentrated* his strength to jump. (gathered)
1027. This matter doesn't *concern* you.
1028. He isn't *concerned* about anything.
1029. He has a nice *concession* (piece of land).
1030. He granted him all kinds of *concessions*.
1031. They *concluded* a peace treaty.
1032. Its *conclusion* astonished everyone.
1033. I don't want to drink that awful *concoction*.
1034. They led the *condemned* man out.
1035. He was *condemned* to prison.
1036. He *condescended* to answer my letter.
1037. I'll lend it to you on *condition* that you give it back.
1038. He left in unfavorable *conditions*.
1039. I won't come under those *conditions*.
1040. He *conferred* with the chief.
1041. If you *confess* I won't do anything to you.
1042. He *confided* all his secrets to me.
1043. He is *confident* of his success.
1044. The news was *confirmed* to us.
1045. The chief's suspicions have been *confirmed*.
1046. The chief *confiscated* part of his goods.
1047. The two villages are in *conflict* with each other.
1048. His behavior is in *conflict* with his ideas.
1049. The liar was *confounded* (silenced).
1050. He fears a *confrontation*.
1051. They *confronted* the witnesses.
1052. His story is very *confused*.
1053. He *confuses* everything you tell him.
1054. It is a *congenital* disease.
1055. We *congratulated* him for his courage.
1056. We *congratulated* him on his success.
1057. They are *conniving* against me.
1058. That man has made many *conquests*.
1059. He gives presents when he has a guilty *conscience*.
1060. He is *conscientious* in his work.
1061. He lost *consciousness* before we arrived.
1062. He slept for six *consecutive* days.
1063. She bought a skirt without her husband's *consent*.
1064. You are the one who will suffer the *consequences* of it.
1065. His accident has not had any *consequences*.
1066. Let's *conserve* our strength because we still have a long way to go.
1067. That requires *considerable* work.

1068. He is *considering* leaving tomorrow.
1069. His work *consists* of supervising others.
1070. She came looking for *consolation* from me.
1071. They *conspired* against the chief.
1072. He shows a *constant* interest in his work.
1073. He is *constantly* sick.
1074. He can distinguish the different *constellations* in the sky.
1075. The news caused great *consternation* in the village.
1076. That food *constipates* him.
1077. He is always suffering from *constipation*.
1078. That action *constitutes* an offense.
1079. That child has a strong *constitution*.
1080. He suffers from a weak *constitution*.
1081. You can't make him work by *constraint*.
1082. The *construction* of the hut took several days.
1083. It is of excellent *construction*.
1084. He went to *consult* the spirit of the oracle.
1085. He never *consults* his father to decide what to do.
1086. They *consume* a great quantity of meat.
1087. The fire *consumed* the hut.
1088. The disease is *consuming* him.
1089. He came into *contact* with him.
1090. Laughter is *contagious*.
1091. That disease is very *contagious*.
1092. She couldn't *contain* her laughter.
1093. He doesn't know how to *contain* his anger.
1094. They *contained* the fire (brush fire, epidemic).
1095. The *container* is full to the brim.
1096. The plant *contains* poison.
1097. He *contaminated* the whole village.
1098. The creek water is *contaminated*.
1099. He is *contemplating* his work.
1100. When it is stormy he loses himself in the *contemplation* of the sky.
1101. That man is *contemptible*.
1102. He *contends* that he came yesterday.
1103. It doesn't take a lot to keep that child *content*.
1104. She poured the *contents* of the pot onto a plate.
1105. He *continued* working while I talked to him.
1106. The rain *continued*.
1107. He argues with me *continuously*.
1108. His face is *contorted* with pain.
1109. The dancer made *contortions*.
1110. He *contracted* a disease.
1111. The cold *contracted* his muscles.
1112. His acts *contradict* his words.
1113. The chief cannot bear to be *contradicted*.
1114. He enjoys *contradicting* me.
1115. The two stories are *contradictory*.
1116. I've never seen a *contraption* like that. What is it for?
1117. *Contrary* to his custom he kept quiet.
1118. He is *contrary*.
1119. I have nothing against him; on the *contrary*.
1120. The caution of the son *contrasts* with the audacity of the father.
1121. He *contravened* the law.
1122. She *contributed* to his success.
1123. His *contrite* expression disarmed me.
1124. He knows how to *control* his emotions.
1125. He is *in control* of himself; he never gets angry.
1126. He succeeded in bringing your horse under *control*.
1127. He *controlled* his anger.
1128. He can't stand *controversy*.
1129. He is just beginning his *convalescence*.
1130. He is always the one to open the *conversation*.
1131. The two friends *conversed* gladly.

Sentence Questionnaire

1132. They became *convinced* of his guilt.
1133. I am *convinced* of his sincerity.
1134. That argument is *convincing*.
1135. His face is *convulsed* with anger.
1136. Her child had *convulsions*.
1137. He broke out in a *convulsive* laugh.
1138. *Cook* the meat.
1139. She *cooked up* a good sauce for us.
1140. He is *cooking* the palm nut in the embers.
1141. She does the *cooking*.
1142. The wind is *cool*.
1143. His enthusiasm *cooled*.
1144. The shade of the trees gives some *coolness*.
1145. It *cools off* at night.
1146. His wives *cooperate* in working the same plantation.
1147. He isn't very *cooperative*.
1148. His efforts lack *coordination*.
1149. He built a *coping* around the well.
1150. She polished her *copper* bracelet.
1151. His welcome was most *cordial*.
1152. With *corn* you can make gruel (porridge) cakes and alcohol.
1153. We grow *corn*.
1154. I'm going to roast an ear of *corn*.
1155. He settled down at the *corner* of the table.
1156. Throw that into the *corner*.
1157. The *cornfield* is a little farther on.
1158. They buried the *corpse*.
1159. He is a walking *corpse*.
1160. He is trying to *correct* his mistakes.
1161. The hunter *corrected* his aim.
1162. It is easy to *corrupt* the young.
1163. That work *cost* him a lot of effort.
1164. How much does that *cost*?
1165. He is putting *cotton* on the wound.
1166. That blanket is made of *cotton*.
1167. He is *coughing*; his throat is irritated.
1168. That excitement *could* kill her.
1169. The men took *counsel* together before leaving.
1170. He can *count* well.
1171. He *counted* the goats.
1172. The chief has a vigorous *countenance*.
1173. He succeeded in *countering* his adversary.
1174. He is *counting* on leaving tomorrow.
1175. He speaks the language of the *country*.
1176. He left his *country*.
1177. He left *courageously* without turning back.
1178. The combatants fought *courageously*.
1179. Are you coming with us? *Of course* I am.
1180. I will go in the *course* of the month (some time this month).
1181. He followed the *course* of the river.
1182. The affair followed its *course*.
1183. The *court* condemned the criminal.
1184. He is in the *courtyard* of the house.
1185. *Cover* yourself *up* with your pagne.
1186. A straw roof *covers* the house.
1187. He is looking *covetously* at the food.
1188. He *covets* the chief's position.
1189. His *cowardice* is terrible.
1190. He ran away in a *cowardly* way. (like a)
1191. That man is *cowardly*.
1192. *Cowards* are not good warriors.
1193. He gave some *cowrie shells* to his wife's parents.
1194. That boy is full of *crabs* (lice).
1195. He catches *crabs* in the river.
1196. He filled in the *crack* in the wall.
1197. She *cracked* her knuckles.
1198. The wall is *cracked*.
1199. The ground is *cracking*.
1200. The dead branches *crackled* under his feet.

1201. The fire is *crackling*.
1202. She is very *crafty*.
1203. He has been swimming for a long time; he has a *cramp* in his leg.
1204. They are *cramped* for space.
1205. They put the vegetables in *crates*.
1206. He *craves* the honor of being invited by the chief.
1207. A snake *crawls*.
1208. My neighbor is *crazy*.
1209. He is *crazy*.
1210. His face is full of *creases* and wrinkles.
1211. The artist *created* a work of art.
1212. The merchant gave him *credit*.
1213. It is a corn *crib* (storage compartment).
1214. The guilty one is accused of a *crime*.
1215. He is *crippled*.
1216. They *criticized* his attitude heavily.
1217. The toads are *croaking*.
1218. The *crocodile* came out of the water.
1219. The *crocodile* caught a fish.
1220. That *crocodile* doesn't eat humans.
1221. The *crocodile* is warming himself in the sun.
1222. It's a man-eating *crocodile*.
1223. That man is a *crook*.
1224. His legs are *crooked*.
1225. There were some seeds in the chicken's *crop*.
1226. He had his hair *cropped*.
1227. We are going to put the *crops* in a safe place.
1228. *Cross* your legs.
1229. These two roads *cross*.
1230. The chief *crossed* the doorway of the house.
1231. They *crouch* around the fire.
1232. The men are gathering in a *crowd*.
1233. There was a terrible *crowding* to get in.
1234. We'll leave at the first *crowing* of the rooster.
1235. Their mother is nasty to them; she is a *cruel* mother.
1236. The chief treated them *cruelly*.
1237. The ants are coming to get the *crumbs*.
1238. The man is *crushing* the tobacco leaves.
1239. The mother *cuddled* her child.
1240. He is a *cuddly* child.
1241. The *culprit* was found out.
1242. He is as *cunning* as a fox.
1243. He *curbed* the resistance of his horse.
1244. He likes *curdled* milk.
1245. I am *cured*.
1246. That child is very *curious*.
1247. She *curled up* in his arms.
1248. She has *curly* hair.
1249. The *current* of this river is swift.
1250. The drought is a *curse* on the village.
1251. The sorcerer's *curse* was effective.
1252. He *cursed* his son.
1253. The river makes a wide *curve*.
1254. That road is full of *curves*.
1255. That is an old *custom* of the country.
1256. He must *cut down* his expenses.
1257. The knife *cut into* the skin.
1258. They *cut up* the animal.
1259. He *cut* down a tree.
1260. I *cut* him short.
1261. The player *cut* the cards.
1262. He *cut* the rope.
1263. This knife *cuts* well.
1264. He is *cutting off* the branches.
1265. He has a *cyst* on his head.

D

1266. The duck is *dabbling* in the pond.
1267. The hail has done *damage* to the crops.
1268. The storm caused much *damage*.
1269. The storm *damaged* the houses.
1270. He *damaged* the machine.
1271. The ground is *damp* from the rain.

1272. We *danced* a lot.
1273. She is *dancing* the belly dance.
1274. His life is in *danger*.
1275. He is in *danger;* he is shouting "Help!"
1276. The child doesn't *dare* speak.
1277. He is a *daring* warrior.
1278. The sky is getting *dark* (clouding over); it is going to rain.
1279. He is very *dark-skinned*.
1280. It is *dark;* night is falling.
1281. Clouds *darkened* the sky.
1282. Your daughter is *darling*.
1283. He is *dauntless;* he doesn't fear danger.
1284. Do not *dawdle* on the way.
1285. The sky is getting light; *dawn* will be here soon.
1286. They traveled all night and arrived at *dawn*.
1287. We will see each other the *day after tomorrow*.
1288. He got weaker *from day to day*.
1289. He will come the *day* after tomorrow.
1290. He lives one *day* at a time.
1291. One *day* he met an ant who said this to him.
1292. He will arrive any *day* now.
1293. He does more work in one *day* than you do in three!
1294. After a *day's* work he can only think of sleeping.
1295. It isn't night any more; it is *day(time)*.
1296. It's the news of the *day*.
1297. It is a *feast day*.
1298. He left again the *next day*.
1299. We all fear the arrival of our last *day*.
1300. It is *daylight*.
1301. The *days* are getting shorter.
1302. For several *days* he couldn't walk.
1303. He spends his *days* sleeping.
1304. The sun *dazzles* the eyes.
1305. Lightning *dazzles* the eyes.
1306. I found a *dead* bird.
1307. The path is a *dead* end (has no outlet).
1308. We bury the *dead* here.
1309. He was found *dead*.
1310. This poison is *deadly*.
1311. He is *deaf;* he can't hear.
1312. She didn't make a big *deal* of her present.
1313. I made a *deal* with him.
1314. That view is *dear* to me.
1315. He will pay me *dearly* for that.
1316. He loves his children *dearly*.
1317. *Death* came to take him.
1318. He was already *at the point of death* when we arrived.
1319. He had a gentle *death*. (peaceful)
1320. He is *deathly* pale.
1321. He has many *debts*.
1322. He *deceived* the chief.
1323. This piece of clothing is still quite *decent*.
1324. The chief is the one to *decide*.
1325. It is a *deciduous* tree.
1326. The village is all *decked out* for the festival.
1327. He was *declared* guilty.
1328. They *declared* war.
1329. He *declined* all responsibility.
1330. The sick man is *declining* (in strength).
1331. The house is *decorated* with flowers.
1332. He *deducted* a sum from his savings.
1333. Stealing is a bad *deed*.
1334. You have done a good *deed*.
1335. He took a *deep* breath.
1336. He is digging the hole *deep*.
1337. The well is very *deep*.
1338. He *defeated* his adversary.
1339. They were *defeated* in the vote.
1340. He *defends* the weak.
1341. Don't *delay;* make up your mind.
1342. The chief *delayed* his departure for two days.
1343. The sick man is *delirious*.
1344. If he thinks I'm going to give him money, he's *deluding* himself.
1345. The chief *demands* obedience.
1346. They *demolished* the village.
1347. How can I *demonstrate* my gratitude to you?

1348. They *demonstrated* his innocence.
1349. On that occasion they *demonstrated* in the streets.
1350. He *demonstrates* his anger by shouting.
1351. *Demonstrations* were forbidden.
1352. A number of *demonstrators* were shouting in the streets.
1353. He *denies* that he came yesterday.
1354. He *denigrates* all men.
1355. The fog is *dense*.
1356. The *density* of the population is high.
1357. He is preparing for his *departure*.
1358. He is not *dependent* on anyone.
1359. That *depends* on the circumstances.
1360. Epidemics have *depopulated* the country.
1361. He paid a *deposit* on his wife's dowry.
1362. The currency *depreciated*.
1363. He is always *depressed*.
1364. Fear *deprived* him of his means.
1365. They *deprived* him of his property.
1366. He was *deprived* of food.
1367. He is quick-witted but without *depth*.
1368. This village was *deserted* by its inhabitants.
1369. He *deserves* a reward.
1370. He *deserves* to be punished.
1371. She always draws the same *design* on her pots.
1372. He *despises* the poor.
1373. He refuses to work in the fields *despite* his father's orders.
1374. He became completely *destitute*.
1375. They are *destitute*.
1376. The hut was *destroyed*.
1377. He *detests* lying.
1378. The man made a *detour* through the field.
1379. The storm *devastated* the farming land.
1380. The fire caused great *devastation*.
1381. His ideas have *developed* a great deal.
1382. You must not meet up with the *devil* at night.
1383. He is a *devious* character.
1384. He *devoted* himself to his work.
1385. He *devotes* all his time to fishing.
1386. The caterpillars *devoured* the leaves.
1387. She wrapped the baby in its *diapers*.
1388. He got *diarrhea* from eating green corn.
1389. He got up and I *did the same* (did so too).
1390. He is going to *die* any day now.
1391. They will *die* of hunger.
1392. The chief's anger has *died down*.
1393. His horse *died* of glanders.
1394. The sick man was put on a starvation *diet*.
1395. Those children are *different*.
1396. Since he came back to the village he is completely *different*.
1397. It is *difficult* to tell someone the truth. (uncomfortable)
1398. This work is *difficult*.
1399. I have *difficulty* believing you.
1400. The sun *diffuses* light.
1401. He can't *digest* meat well.
1402. He is *digging* a hole in the ground.
1403. The animal is *digging* in the ground.
1404. The current carried the *dike* away.
1405. Water *dilutes* the salt.
1406. The heat has *diminished* today.
1407. The bow of the boat *dipped* (down).
1408. This way is *direct*.
1409. The man went in the *direction* of the river.
1410. He has a good sense of *direction*.
1411. He followed the chief's *directions*.
1412. The child is running in all *directions*.
1413. The child has *dirty* hands.
1414. The hut is *dirty*.
1415. Deafness is a *disability*.
1416. He *disabled* his opponent.

1417. Everything has its *disadvantages*.
1418. They are in *disagreement*.
1419. He has *disappeared* from the village.
1420. The sun *disappeared*.
1421. He *disappointed* his hopes.
1422. He *disapproves* of his project.
1423. The epidemic was *disaster* for the population.
1424. That defeat was a *disaster*.
1425. He remained *disconcerted* by it.
1426. You have *discouraged* me from working.
1427. No difficulty *discourages* him.
1428. He *discovered* what he was looking for.
1429. The scandal *discredited* him.
1430. We *discussed* the question.
1431. He had a *discussion* with the chief.
1432. He gets lost in useless interminable *discussions*.
1433. Nobody likes him because he is *disdainful*.
1434. We don't know what *disease* he has.
1435. It is a contagious *disease*.
1436. We don't know how to care for the *diseases* of millet (manioc . . .).
1437. The passengers *disembarked* on the far shore.
1438. She *disentangled* the string.
1439. That's a *disgrace*—such a disgrace!
1440. It's a *disgrace*.
1441. He comes home at *disgraceful* hours.
1442. He had *disguised* his voice and I didn't recognize him.
1443. That action *disgusted* him.
1444. That food *disgusts* him.
1445. She is preparing a meat *dish*.
1446. His conduct is *dishonest*.
1447. That merchant is *dishonest;* his prices are too high.
1448. His *dishonesty* is well known; nobody trusts him any more.
1449. I have a *dislike* for this man.
1450. I *dislike* that man.
1451. He *dislikes* it in his hut.
1452. He *dislocated* his kneecap.
1453. He has a *dislocated* shoulder.
1454. His knee is *dislocated*.
1455. That song is *dismal*.
1456. That news really filled me with *dismay*.
1457. She *dismissed* him.
1458. He *dismissed* his servant boy.
1459. He *disobeyed* the chief.
1460. The sun *dispelled* the clouds.
1461. The chief *displayed* an interest in me.
1462. He *displayed* his merchandise.
1463. I *displeased* him by telling him the truth.
1464. He has a nervous *disposition*.
1465. He has an ugly *disposition*.
1466. They submitted their *dispute* to the village judge.
1467. He *disregarded* the insults.
1468. He spoke *disrespectfully* to the chief.
1469. He has no reason to be *dissatisfied*. (discontented)
1470. He *dissolved* some sugar in the water.
1471. Salt *dissolves* in water.
1472. Over there *in the distance* I see a flock.
1473. He left for *distant parts*.
1474. I feel a *distaste* for food.
1475. Her child has a *distended* stomach.
1476. His skin is *distending* with age.
1477. He *distills* alcohol.
1478. He can't *distinguish* the true from the false.
1479. That child has trouble *distinguishing* colors.
1480. He *distracted* him from his work.
1481. The mother *distributed* the food to her children.
1482. The chief *distributes* the fields.
1483. Leave all *distrust* behind.
1484. The village people *distrust* strangers.
1485. That child is very *distrustful*.
1486. His sleep was *disturbed* by the noise.
1487. Excuse me for *disturbing* you.

1488. The situation is *disturbing*.
1489. The vulture *dived* onto its prey.
1490. Their opinions *diverge*.
1491. He *diverted* the stream.
1492. The seasons *divide up* the year.
1493. The invaders *divided up* the land between them.
1494. The river *divides* the field into two parts.
1495. I am *dizzy*; my head is spinning.
1496. *Do* what you want.
1497. He doesn't know what to *do*; he's bored.
1498. The boat is at *dock*.
1499. The *doctor* came to treat him.
1500. A *doe* has no antlers.
1501. His face had a *doleful* expression.
1502. During colonization the Whites *dominated* the Blacks.
1503. He is *donefor*; he'll never get better.
1504. They bought a *donkey*, a *she-donkey* and a *donkey's* foal.
1505. The sick man was *doomed* to die (there was no hope for him).
1506. The *door* of the hut is closed.
1507. He went in through the *door*.
1508. He stepped over the *doorstep*.
1509. The bird came in by a *dormer window*.
1510. There is no *doubt* about it.
1511. The woman is kneading the *dough*.
1512. The path is *down below*.
1513. *Get down!* (duck!)
1514. He put his head *down*.
1515. He is going *downhill*.
1516. There is no longer a bridge *downriver* from Bangui.
1517. The visitors stopped *downstream* from the village.
1518. He has not finished paying the *dowry* money.
1519. I detest *drafts* (of air).
1520. He is *dragging* his feet.
1521. Your pagne is *dragging* on the ground.
1522. It is a *dragonfly*.
1523. He *drags* himself around; he can hardly walk.
1524. They *drained off* the dirty water.
1525. The fever *drained* me.
1526. He *drank* too much; he is drunk.
1527. Our life was *drastically changed* by the arrival of the white man.
1528. He is *drawing* water from the spring.
1529. He *dreamed* last night.
1530. He's *dreaming* of the future.
1531. He has a *dreamy* look.
1532. He threw out the *dregs* of the millet beer.
1533. It was a *drenching* rain.
1534. Her *dress* is made of printed cotton.
1535. *Dress* lightly.
1536. He put his horse through *dressage* movements to train him.
1537. Help her get *dressed*.
1538. The child is hardly *dressed*.
1539. She is *dressing* the child.
1540. He *drew* (unsheathed) his knife.
1541. He *drew* the bowstring tight.
1542. The heat *dried out* the plants.
1543. The well *dried* up.
1544. A whaling boat *drifted* by.
1545. I'm going to *drink* the water.
1546. As soon as he gets money he begins to *drink*.
1547. He only likes cold *drinks*.
1548. It hasn't rained a *drop* in months.
1549. You *dropped* something.
1550. He *drowned* in the river.
1551. He plays the *drum*.
1552. He is striking with the balaphon *drumstick*.
1553. He *gets drunk* every day.
1554. He is *drunk*.
1555. The air is *dry*.
1556. My throat is *dry*; I'm thirsty.
1557. The meat is *drying out*.
1558. The laundry is *drying* in the sun.
1559. The *(female) duck* led her brood toward the creek.
1560. He walks like a *duck*.
1561. The wild *ducks* took flight.
1562. He ran after the *ducks*.
1563. He *dug up* a tree.
1564. He paddled the *dugout canoe* forward.

1565. He heard a *dull* thud.
1566. That object isn't shiny; it is *dull*.
1567. This cloth is *durable*.
1568. He left the village *during* the night.
1569. *During* the rainy season he stays in the village.
1570. The wind makes the *dust* fly.
1571. He *dyed* his pagne.
1572. The traditions are *dying* out.
1573. He was *dying* to leave.
1574. He is *dying*.
1575. The sick man lay *dying*.
1576. He is in danger of *dying*.

E

1577. The father brought a present for *each* of his children.
1578. *Each* person brought his own food.
1579. The chief gave something to *each* person.
1580. That child is *eager* to learn.
1581. The *eagle* flew away.
1582. The *eagle* is gliding.
1583. The *eagle* swooped down onto its prey.
1584. He ate the *ear* of corn.
1585. He is only listening with one *ear*.
1586. He has a sharp *ear*.
1587. He gets up *early* in the morning.
1588. He is an *early* riser.
1589. He was so afraid of being late that he arrived *early*.
1590. He got up *early*.
1591. This operation *earned* him some money.
1592. She wants some *earrings*.
1593. It is an (old-fashioned) *earthenware* plate.
1594. That is *easily* worth twice as much.
1595. He went away toward the *east*.
1596. It's *easy*.
1597. Antelopes don't *eat* meat.
1598. We *eat* three times a day.
1599. Today I didn't have time to *eat*.
1600. Your brother is a big *eater*.
1601. The . . . people are snake-*eaters* (termite-*eaters*).
1602. Rats are *eating away* at the clothing.
1603. He is *eccentric;* he never does anything like anyone else.
1604. The *echo* answered.
1605. The *edge* of his pagne is frayed.
1606. He planted some trees along the *edge* of his property.
1607. He stopped at the *edge* of my field.
1608. They stopped at the *edge* of the village.
1609. I saw a horse antelope at the *edge* of the woods.
1610. It's the season for *edible* caterpillars.
1611. This manioc is not good; it is just barely *edible*.
1612. That mushroom isn't *edible*.
1613. He caught two *eels*.
1614. The disease has had long term *effects*.
1615. This work demands a great deal of *effort*.
1616. The chicken laid an *egg*.
1617. She grows *eggplant* in her house garden.
1618. It is a white *egret* (a long-legged white bird which lives along the river).
1619. He is resting his *elbows* on the table.
1620. The *elders* of the village met for a discussion.
1621. The drugs *eliminated* the pain.
1622. Go and do your foolishness *elsewhere*.
1623. This illness has left him *emaciated*.
1624. They *embarked* yesterday (for . . .).
1625. She blushed with *embarrassment*.
1626. The *embers* are almost finished burning.
1627. Meat is roasted in the *embers*.
1628. The crocodile *emerged* from the water.
1629. The doctor came for an *emergency*.

1630. That man has an *empty* stomach.
1631. *Empty* the water from the bottle.
1632. He came back *empty-handed*.
1633. He is *empty-headed;* he has no ideas.
1634. My stomach is *empty;* I'm hungry.
1635. The hut is *empty;* there is no furniture in it.
1636. He *enclosed* his field.
1637. He is at the *end* of his strength.
1638. Go to the *end* of the road.
1639. He cut the *end* of the stick.
1640. She lives at the far *end* of the village.
1641. The chief put an *end* to the dissension.
1642. He got his way in the *end*.
1643. The matter *ended* badly.
1644. He achieved his *ends*.
1645. That man *endured* great suffering.
1646. They gave him an *enema*.
1647. They are *enemies*.
1648. The chief has a lot of *energy*.
1649. The locomotive is driven by the *engineer*.
1650. The man is *engraving* the stones.
1651. You must *enjoy* the present moment.
1652. He *enjoys* good health.
1653. He *enlarged* his plantation.
1654. He *enlarged* the hole.
1655. The woman is *enlarging* the mat.
1656. There is not *enough* salt in the soup.
1657. There are not *enough* workers to move this log.
1658. That's *enough!*
1659. There are *enough*. There are not *enough* for me.
1660. The animal got *entangled* in the net.
1661. *Enter* the house.
1662. He *entered* the house in secret.
1663. He will stay an *entire* day.
1664. He did it *entirely* by himself.
1665. He ate the *entrails* of the animal.
1666. She *entrusted* her children to him for the whole day.
1667. He *envies* him his knife.
1668. The climate of the region is *equable* (unchanging).
1669. He was *equal* to his task.
1670. These two amounts are *equal*.
1671. The two amounts are *equivalent*.
1672. He *erased* the tracks.
1673. The prisoner *escaped*.
1674. I bought this *especially* for you.
1675. Water is *essential* to man.
1676. This custom is well *established*.
1677. The water *evaporated* in the sun.
1678. He isn't *even* capable of lifting a hoe.
1679. He drank so much that he forgot *even* his own name.
1680. They killed *even* the women and children.
1681. He never acts like *everyone* else.
1682. The chief can't be *everywhere* at once.
1683. The *evidence* was overwhelming against the accused man.
1684. He wishes *evil* on his youngest brother.
1685. In the cities there are *evildoers* who live just by stealing.
1686. You must choose the lesser of two *evils*.
1687. The *ewe* gave birth to a baby lamb.
1688. That's *exactly* right.
1689. He *examined* the place.
1690. He comes every day *except* Sunday.
1691. It's *excessively* hot.
1692. This work does not tire him *excessively*.
1693. They *exchanged* gifts.
1694. He walked in the *excrement*.
1695. Please *excuse* me.
1696. He *executed* the orders.
1697. The work *exhausted* him.
1698. He *exhausted* the animal.
1699. Farming *exhausted* the soil.
1700. He *exorcised* the demons.
1701. He *expanded* his farming land.
1702. He was *expelled* from the village.
1703. That cloth is very *expensive*.
1704. *Explain* it to me carefully.
1705. The land ought to be *exploited*.
1706. He has *explored* the whole region.
1707. He *expressed* his feelings.

1708. This gift is an *expression* of my friendship.
1709. He gave free *expression* to his joy.
1710. He had a worried *expression*.
1711. The forest *extends* from the river to the village.
1712. The road *extends* through the forest.
1713. His remarks were *extreme*.
1714. He cannot *extricate* himself from the mud.
1715. He keeps an *eye* on everything.
1716. She has long *eyelashes*.
1717. They plucked out his *eyelashes*.
1718. His *eyelids* are closed; he is asleep.
1719. The chief followed him with his *eyes*.

F

1720. His *face* is bony.
1721. The *face* is the expression of character.
1722. His *face* is thin.
1723. The hut *faces* east.
1724. The colors *fade* in the sun.
1725. The flowers are *faded*.
1726. The cloth has *faded*.
1727. He is *failing* (in health) from day to day.
1728. The chief's memory is *failing*.
1729. The light is *failing*.
1730. His project is doomed to *failure*.
1731. He *fainted*.
1732. He is *fainting* with hunger.
1733. That is not *fair*.
1734. They fought *fairly*.
1735. He always acts in *fairness*.
1736. That is only a *fairy* tale.
1737. He took a *fall* from the top of the tree.
1738. The waters have begun to *fall*.
1739. It's the time when the leaves *fall*.
1740. They had a *falling* out.
1741. Rain has been *falling* for several days.
1742. You can't do anything to prevent hair from *falling* out.
1743. Night is *falling*.
1744. This field is always *fallow*.
1745. That area is lying *fallow*.
1746. What he says is *false*.
1747. He *faltered* in his speech.
1748. That voice is *familiar* to me.
1749. They are from the same *family*.
1750. They started a *family*.
1751. The village is dying of *famine*.
1752. He is *famous* for his courage.
1753. The animal is showing his *fangs*.
1754. The lion is still *far* away from us.
1755. My village is *far* away.
1756. He was *far* from expecting to see you.
1757. It is not *far* from noon.
1758. It is *far* from the village to the river.
1759. We are *far* from the village.
1760. *How far* is it from here to Bangui?
1761. The dry season is not very *far* off.
1762. He left for a *faraway* country.
1763. The *farmer* works the fields.
1764. Who *farted*?
1765. Go a little *farther* and you will find the village.
1766. She is dressed *fashionably*.
1767. His *fast* lasted three days.
1768. He runs very *fast*.
1769. He *fasted* for three days.
1770. He *fastened* a piece onto the calabash.
1771. She is *fat* (big) woman.
1772. He has a *fat* face.
1773. The aulacode is *fat(ty)*.
1774. This animal has lots of *fat*.
1775. He is frying the meat in *fat*.
1776. It is a *fatal* illness.
1777. He wounded him *fatally*.
1778. He is trusting his *fate*. He has confidence in his *fate*.
1779. It's the *fateful* moment.
1780. My *father* is coming tomorrow.
1781. His *father* is dead.
1782. He is the *father* of two children.
1783. I'm suffering from *fatigue*.
1784. He is *fattening* (up) the hens.
1785. It's his *fault*.

1786. The chief granted him *favor*.
1787. The climate was *favorable* for such a request.
1788. The circumstances were *favorable*.
1789. His request was *favorably* received.
1790. Events *favored* him.
1791. He *favors* the children of his first wife.
1792. I *fear* death.
1793. He is trembling with *fear*.
1794. That chicken's *feathers* are white.
1795. The *features* of his face are regular.
1796. I'm *fed up* with seeing you.
1797. That child is well *fed*.
1798. The mother *feeds* her children.
1799. He has walked so much that he can't *feel* his legs any more. (has no more *feeling* in . . .)
1800. I *feel* ill.
1801. I am *feeling* fine.
1802. He has a *feeling* of admiration for the chief.
1803. I had a *feeling* that he wouldn't come.
1804. His shoes hurt his *feet*.
1805. He is *feigning* illness.
1806. He *fell over* backwards.
1807. The responsibilities *fell* on the chief.
1808. The child *fell* to the ground.
1809. The doctor *felt* the sick man's stomach.
1810. The wine is *fermenting*.
1811. This animal is *ferocious*.
1812. This land is *fertile*.
1813. The snake is his *fetish*.
1814. The child is hot; he has a *fever*.
1815. That man is *fickle* in his friendships.
1816. He has a *fickle* temperament.
1817. There were at least *fifty* people at the place.
1818. We are going to share *fifty-fifty*.
1819. Men must *fight* to live.
1820. He likes to *fight;* he is very aggressive.
1821. The *fighting* was terrible.
1822. He is *figuring out* his chances of success.
1823. The blacksmith has a *file*.
1824. He is in the middle of *filing down* a spearhead.
1825. They *filled in* the pothole in the road.
1826. The wind *filled out* the sail.
1827. Success *filled* him with pride.
1828. He *filled* me with horror.
1829. He *filled* up the basin with water.
1830. He is *filling in* the hole.
1831. She is *filtering* the water.
1832. The wind *filters* in through the cracks.
1833. He was unspeakably *filthy*.
1834. He stammers; he can't *find* his words.
1835. *Find* out if he has arrived.
1836. He took a *fine* goat to his parents-in-law (wife's parents).
1837. He is a *fine* man.
1838. This sand is *fine*.
1839. The woman put on her holiday *finery*.
1840. He pointed it out with his *finger*.
1841. His *fingernails* are very long.
1842. The woman kneaded the dough with her *fingers*.
1843. My wife is *finicky;* she is very set in her ways.
1844. *Finish* your work first, then we will go for a walk.
1845. He *finished* his meal.
1846. We have *finished* the work.
1847. Have you *finished* your work?
1848. My work is *finished*.
1849. His work is *finished;* he can leave.
1850. When will you have your work *finished*?
1851. He *finishes* his meal.
1852. The *fire* went out.
1853. He is making a *fire*.
1854. The fire is burning in the *fireplace*.
1855. He speaks with a *firm* tone.
1856. The meat of this fish is *firm*.
1857. I am *firmly* convinced of it.
1858. At *first* he was nice.

Sentence Questionnaire   335

1859. The child took his *first* steps.
1860. He gets up *first* thing in the morning.
1861. Go *first*.
1862. Eat *first;* you can go afterwards.
1863. The fisherman caught a lot of *fish*.
1864. The river is *full of fish*.
1865. The *fisherman* brought back a lot of fish.
1866. He *fishes* with a hook.
1867. He is going *fishing*.
1868. He clenched his *fists*.
1869. He bought *five* goats.
1870. That child is *five* years old.
1871. He has a *fixed* stare.
1872. He *fixed* the broken machine.
1873. The flag is at the top of the *flagpole*.
1874. The fire doesn't make *flames*.
1875. Suddenly he felt a *hot flash*.
1876. There are *flashes of lightning* in the sky.
1877. The merchant laid out some *flashy* objects.
1878. The terrain is *flat*.
1879. That *flatters* his vanity.
1880. This pottery is *flawed*.
1881. The dog is covered with *fleas*.
1882. Fear made him *flee*.
1883. That is a *fleshy* fruit (its pulp is thick).
1884. The bird *flew away*.
1885. The flame is *flickering*.
1886. That man *flies* (runs fast) like a zebra.
1887. There are a lot of *flies* here.
1888. He shot the bird in full *flight*.
1889. The bird took *flight*.
1890. She is a *flirt* with her friends.
1891. The stick is *floating* on the water.
1892. The river *flooded* the land.
1893. The rain caused *flooding*.
1894. The *floor* of the house is wood.
1895. The woman is making dough with the *flour*.
1896. His health is *flourishing*.
1897. The water is *flowing* in torrents.
1898. The Ouaka River *flows into* the Ubangi at Kwango.

1899. His face was completely *flushed*.
1900. A *fly* bit me.
1901. This water is full of *foam*.
1902. All eyes *focused* on the defendant.
1903. There is a lot of *fog* (haze) today.
1904. The *fog* came in after the rain.
1905. The *fold* of the hem has been marked.
1906. He *folded* his arms on his chest.
1907. He *folded* his hands. (clasped)
1908. He sleeps with his legs *folded*.
1909. *Follow* me; come behind me.
1910. You must *follow* your first impulse.
1911. I don't *follow* your speech.
1912. He *followed* orders.
1913. He came back the *following* day.
1914. *Folly* took a hold of him.
1915. He is very *fond* of his children.
1916. He loves to *fool* people.
1917. Don't *fool* yourself!
1918. He lets himself be *fooled* by everyone. (he lets everyone *fool* him)
1919. He *fooled* the chief.
1920. It is a *foolhardy* venture.
1921. He is *fooling* himself.
1922. How *foolish* he is!
1923. He did something *foolish*.
1924. He was scolded because he did something *foolish*.
1925. That's what *fools* you.
1926. He left *for* a long time.
1927. That woman is remarkable *for* her beauty.
1928. She left *for* her parents' house.
1929. All the better *for* him.
1930. Go get me some sugar cane *for* me to suck.
1931. *For* pity's sake! Let me go.
1932. I have been sick *for* six days.
1933. Don't worry yourself *for* so little.
1934. Pray *for* them.
1935. Thanks *for* your gift.
1936. I *forbid* you to enter.
1937. The chief has *forbidden* him to enter.
1938. He gave in to *force*.
1939. He had a *forced* smile.

1940. He *forded* the creek.
1941. His *forehead* is high and wide.
1942. He lacks *foresight*.
1943. All their troubles have not cured them of their lack of *foresight*.
1944. The *forest* is impenetrable.
1945. These clouds *foretell* rain.
1946. The prophets *foretold* the coming of the Messiah.
1947. He is working at the *forge*.
1948. He *forged* on ahead.
1949. He *forges* iron (is forging iron).
1950. I *forget* which it is.
1951. *Forgetting* comes with the passage of time.
1952. A sin confessed is a sin half *forgiven*.
1953. He *forgives* easily; he is lenient.
1954. He *forgot* his friends.
1955. He *forgot* his worries.
1956. I have not *forgotten* that he is supposed to come tomorrow.
1957. Go to the next *fork* and go to the left.
1958. They *formed* a close friendship.
1959. He saw his *former* wife again.
1960. *Formerly* he was rich.
1961. He is a *formidable* adversary.
1962. It was very *fortunate* for him.
1963. I *found* a hat.
1964. He lost his wife and *found* himself alone again.
1965. The chief can be *found* in his hut.
1966. He *found* refuge with the chief.
1967. A compass indicates the *four* cardinal points.
1968. This child has *fragile* health.
1969. Gather up the *fragments* of glass.
1970. He is leaning against the door *frame*.
1971. The men are putting up the *framework* of the hut.
1972. The baby goat was born with two heads; it's a *freak*.
1973. This man is *free* (at large).
1974. He is *free* to do as he pleases.
1975. We are not *free*.
1976. He *freed* the prisoner.
1977. *Freedom* is a precious thing.
1978. He acted *freely*.
1979. He has some *frenzied* ideas.
1980. He eats *fresh* fish.
1981. His *friend* gave him some clothing.
1982. He left for the bush with his *friends*.
1983. They showed each other much *friendship*.
1984. I *frightened* you.
1985. He lives on the *fringe* of the village (life).
1986. The *frog* is croaking.
1987. She was divorced *from* him.
1988. I heard the news *from* my brother.
1989. He went away *from* the forest.
1990. He came back *from* the forest.
1991. She took refuge *from* the rain.
1992. Since he was in a hurry, he went *in front of* me.
1993. He wounded the antelope on its *front* legs.
1994. The man got in *front* of him.
1995. Go in *front* of me.
1996. He left in *front*.
1997. He *frowned*.
1998. This tree produces *fruit*.
1999. His attempts remain *fruitless*.
2000. He feels a great *frustration*.
2001. She is *frying* the dough.
2002. It's a *full moon*.
2003. He has a *full* face.
2004. It's a *full* moon.
2005. That boy is *full* of health. (bursting with health)
2006. The glass is *full* to the brim.
2007. He has repaid his debts in *full*.
2008. He has not *fully* recovered from his illness.
2009. The children are having *fun* (a good time).
2010. He did it for *fun*.
2011. The *funeral* ceremony will take place tomorrow.
2012. He told a *funny* story.
2013. He is very *funny*.
2014. The panther's *fur* is spotted.
2015. It makes *furniture*.
2016. The face of the old man is *furrowed* with wrinkles.

Sentence Questionnaire

2017. The plow digs *furrows* in the ground.
2018. She really likes people to make a *fuss* over her.
2019. A great *fuss* was made about the event.

G

2020. The horse set off at a *gallop*.
2021. I don't like that *game*.
2022. I don't know the rules of this *game*.
2023. All this *gang* (horde) is noisy.
2024. They all *ganged up* on him.
2025. The boy *gapes* in admiration for his father.
2026. His story is full of *gaps*.
2027. There are flowers in the *garden* around his house.
2028. He grows vegetables in his *garden*.
2029. The *gardener* sold me some vegetables.
2030. He is in the middle of *gardening*.
2031. He is opening the *gate*.
2032. Bees *gather* pollen.
2033. He *gathered* branches and made a fire.
2034. He *gathered* the workers together.
2035. When I arrived there was already a big *gathering* at the burial place.
2036. He thought he would eat it all but he *gave up* before finishing.
2037. He *gave up* his place to the chief.
2038. The branch *gave way* under his weight.
2039. The man *gave way* under the weight.
2040. The rope *gave way*.
2041. The woman *gave* birth to a son.
2042. The woman *gave* birth to twins.
2043. The woman *gave* birth yesterday.
2044. The guilty man *gave* himself *up*.
2045. He *gave* in to my stubbornness.
2046. Here's the fishing *gear*. (equipment)
2047. He showered us with *generosity*.
2048. He's very *generous*.
2049. Go *gently*.
2050. He *gestured* with his hand.
2051. *Get up* on your horse.
2052. He will not *get* there before the rain.
2053. I'm going to *get* to work.
2054. He *gets up* early in the morning.
2055. That *gets* me *down*.
2056. He is *getting* old.
2057. The sickness is *getting* worse.
2058. The wine made him *giddy*.
2059. He made him a *gift* of the money.
2060. He brought his wife a *gift*.
2061. Thank you for your *gift*.
2062. She *girded* a pretty skirt around her waist.
2063. The rain made him *give up* his trip.
2064. *Give* me some salt.
2065. We will *give* them battle here.
2066. She always *gives in* to her children.
2067. It *gives off* a bad smell.
2068. The necklace is made of *glass* beads.
2069. *Glass* breaks easily.
2070. He wears *glasses*.
2071. Her eyes are *gleaming* with malice.
2072. The knife blade is *gleaming*.
2073. The bird is *gliding* in the sky.
2074. He gets up at the first *glimmer* of dawn.
2075. The mirror *glistened*.
2076. She loves the *glitter*.
2077. They are *glorifying* (giving glory) to the chief.
2078. He makes *glue*.
2079. He *glued* the two pieces together.
2080. I'm in a *glum* mood this morning.
2081. In the evening there are a lot of *gnats* near the river.
2082. The dog *gnaws* at the bone.
2083. *Go* in front; I'll follow you.
2084. Let *go!*
2085. His *goal* is to have a lovely plantation.
2086. The *goat* gave birth to a kid.

2087. He tied the *goat* to a tree.
2088. The men are going to hunt the (*billy*) *goat*.
2089. His parents raise *goats* (caprines).
2090. *God* loves decent people.
2091. He fears the wrath of *God*.
2092. The sun is *going down*.
2093. I am *going* to the village.
2094. Get *going!* Leave quickly.
2095. Where are you *going?*
2096. The swelling in my foot has *gone down*.
2097. We have not yet *gone* into town.
2098. That man is a *good* blacksmith.
2099. This is a *good* cure for stomach aches.
2100. He is *good* for nothing.
2101. She's a *good* girl but not very bright.
2102. The men had a *good* hunt.
2103. He is a *good* husband.
2104. That's a *good* knife.
2105. We had a *good* laugh.
2106. The bananas are *good*.
2107. That did him *good*.
2108. He is lazy; that is not *good*.
2109. Your daughter has *gorgeous* eyes.
2110. She really loves *gossip*.
2111. He is a *gossiper*.
2112. The story teller *got* (gained) the attention of his audience.
2113. He *got off* on shore.
2114. The affair *got off* to a bad start.
2115. He *got over* his surprise.
2116. The child fell and then *got up* again.
2117. The hole in his clothing *got* bigger.
2118. He *got* down on his knees.
2119. The chief *got* him some money.
2120. He *got* nothing from the chief.
2121. Since the arrival of the new chief the work has *gotten* better.
2122. The *gourd* is cracked.
2123. The *balaphon gourd* is cracked.
2124. The man sewed up the tear (break) in the *gourd*.
2125. He *grabbed* a branch and clung onto it.
2126. He was about to fall when he *grabbed* hold of a branch.
2127. He *grabbed* the knife from his hand.
2128. She dances with *grace*.
2129. The people eat mostly *grain* here.
2130. He sowed the *grain*.
2131. The carpenter cuts the wood along the *grain*.
2132. This soil is *grainy*.
2133. He is his paternal great *grandfather*.
2134. He is his maternal great *grandfather*.
2135. The chief *granted* him the right to leave.
2136. *Grasses* grow in the fields.
2137. He is *grateful* to the chief for his help.
2138. He thanked him with *gratitude*.
2139. He is suffering from a *grave* illness.
2140. The dead man was buried in the *grave*.
2141. The goat will have to *graze* where it is tied up.
2142. He *grazed* his hand.
2143. The sheep are *grazing*.
2144. His face is black with *grease*.
2145. He is *greedy* for meat.
2146. That man is *greedy* for riches.
2147. That man loves money; he is *greedy*.
2148. He's very *greedy*.
2149. Trees' leaves are *green*.
2150. He came to *greet* me at the entry of the village.
2151. When he returned, his brother *greeted* him poorly.
2152. I *greeted* the chief.
2153. He has much *grief*.
2154. His *grievances* are justified.
2155. She made a *grimace*.
2156. He *grimaced* in disgust.
2157. His skin is covered with *grime*.
2158. He is *grimy* (filthy); he doesn't like to bathe.
2159. I am going to *grind* these seeds.
2160. The woman is *grinding* flour.

Sentence Questionnaire

2161. He is *grinding* his teeth.
2162. She is *grinding* the corn in the mortar.
2163. She is *grinding* the peppercorns.
2164. Go sharpen this knife on the *grindstone*.
2165. He has ganglions in the *groin*.
2166. The *groom* has not arrived yet.
2167. He *groped* around to find his knife.
2168. It's a *gross* error.
2169. He has a *grouchy* nature.
2170. It rained and the *ground* is soaked.
2171. He is eating *ground* meat.
2172. The enemy is gaining *ground*.
2173. The child fell to the *ground*.
2174. He stood his *ground*.
2175. His anger is *groundless*.
2176. Coffee *grounds* are not good for anything.
2177. What are the *grounds* for their argument?
2178. Hunting is a *group* activity.
2179. The elephants moved in a *group*.
2180. They are in the same age *group*.
2181. They *grow* millet here.
2182. The child is *growing* fast.
2183. Corn *grows* slowly.
2184. Those people's hut is *grubby*.
2185. He holds a *grudge* against him for his lie.
2186. He left me *grudgingly*.
2187. The woman is preparing the *gruel*.
2188. He found some *gruesome* remains when digging behind his hut.
2189. The pig is *grunting*.
2190. I can *guarantee* it to you.
2191. He *guessed* his secret.
2192. The walker used the sun as a *guide*.
2193. He is *guiding* the traveler.
2194. The *guilty one* confessed his crime.
2195. I hear the cry of the *gulls*.
2196. The sick person *gulped* down the potion.
2197. She is cleaning out the *guts*.
2198. He's a good *guy*.

H

2199. He has picked up a bad *habit*.
2200. He eats out of *habit*.
2201. The *habits* of bees are strange.
2202. *Haggle*.
2203. You must always *haggle* before paying.
2204. After *haggling* I paid 60 (francs) for the knife instead of 100 (francs).
2205. It is *hailing*.
2206. He is going to get his *hair* cut.
2207. They cut his *hair* in a circle.
2208. She washes her *hair* often.
2209. The cat is losing its *hair(s)*.
2210. She is in the middle of *doing* (arranging) *her hair*.
2211. He already has white *hair*.
2212. He's got a good crop (full head) of *hair*.
2213. She has lovely *hair*.
2214. He is *half* drunk.
2215. Two is *half* of four.
2216. The village team won the first *half* of the soccer game.
2217. Give me *half* of your tobacco.
2218. He sold him the cloth at *half* price.
2219. He is a *half-breed*.
2220. They use a *half-gourd* to drink out of.
2221. He works *half-heartedly*.
2222. The hut is in a *half-light*.
2223. Cut the ball of millet in *half*.
2224. He stopped *halfway* down the road.
2225. *Halfway* from the village you will see a small hut.
2226. He stopped *halfway*.
2227. He tied up his horse with a *halter*.
2228. He hurt his *ham(string)*.
2229. The blacksmith uses a *hammer*.
2230. The blacksmith is *hammering* a piece of iron.
2231. He was wounded in the *hand* and in the arm.
2232. A monkey caught his *hand* in the trap.

2233. My right *hand* is more skillful than my left *hand*.
2234. They *handed over* the fugitive to the soldiers.
2235. He took a *handful* of salt.
2236. I don't have any *handkerchiefs*.
2237. It is dangerous to let a child *handle* an axe.
2238. He broke the *handle* of the axe.
2239. He took the *handle* off the pickaxe.
2240. He put a *handle* on the knife.
2241. He took the lid by the *handle*.
2242. This knife has an iron *handle*.
2243. The potter *handles* clay all day long.
2244. He *handles* his canoe well.
2245. My *hands* are dirty.
2246. They shook *hands*.
2247. Monkeys *hang* from trees.
2248. The dog's tongue is *hanging out*.
2249. Her skirt *hangs down* in the back.
2250. Her dress *hangs down* to her feet.
2251. A great misfortune *happened* to him.
2252. Her *happiness* was to have all her children about her.
2253. I would be *happy* to (do it).
2254. She is *happy* to leave.
2255. He is very *happy*.
2256. He *harassed* his prey until it was worn out.
2257. He has a *hard* heart.
2258. The trip was a *hard* one.
2259. This wood is *hard*.
2260. The heat *hardened* the earth.
2261. The child has *hardly* begun to walk.
2262. He caught a *hare*.
2263. He has a *harelip*.
2264. The two are in perfect *harmony*.
2265. Alcohol *harms* his health.
2266. He plays the *harp*.
2267. He is fishing with a *harpoon*.
2268. He spoke *harshly*.
2269. The manioc *harvest* was good.
2270. He began to *harvest*.
2271. The *harvesters* are at work.
2272. Now he *has* a job.
2273. She *has* a lovely plantation.
2274. She *has* a new pagne.
2275. He *has* good memories of his trip.
2276. Come in all *haste*.
2277. The weather made him *hasten* his departure.
2278. His *hat* fell off.
2279. He bought a *hat* in town.
2280. The hen *hatched* the eggs.
2281. He *hates* me.
2282. She *hates* waiting.
2283. He has a *hatred* for him.
2284. He *hauled* the dugout in.
2285. I *have* a headache.
2286. His children *have* courage.
2287. I *have* nothing against you.
2288. I *have* nothing to do.
2289. It is *hazy* this morning.
2290. Has *he* come?
2291. *He* is eating.
2292. That is a *he-mule*.
2293. My *head* is reeling; I'm dizzy.
2294. The chief is the *head* of the village.
2295. He's a *head* taller than his brother.
2296. He bumped his *head*.
2297. The chief is at the *headquarters*.
2298. That wine is very *heady*.
2299. The wound *healed* quickly.
2300. The wound is not *healing* (scabbing up) well.
2301. They put *healing* herbs on him.
2302. The chief is in poor *health*.
2303. He is not *healthy*; he is sick.
2304. There is a *heap* of rubbish in front of his hut.
2305. He doesn't want to *hear* it.
2306. I have *heard* a lot about the chief of this village.
2307. He *heard* a noise.
2308. He is hard of *hearing*.
2309. He has a *heart* condition (bad heart).
2310. He died of *heart* disease.
2311. His *heart* is beating quickly.
2312. They offered him the *heart* of the animal they killed.
2313. They got lost in the *heart* of the forest.

2314. I don't have the *heart* to abandon my children.
2315. She didn't have the *heart* to punish her child.
2316. That accusation still weighs on his *heart*.
2317. His father's death broke his *heart*.
2318. He is kind *hearted*.
2319. He ate *heartily*.
2320. He is *heartless*.
2321. He had a *hearty* meal.
2322. The *heat wave* makes me tired.
2323. The *heat* of the sun is intense at that time.
2324. The fire gave off an intense *heat*.
2325. They had a *heated* discussion.
2326. She *heated* the water over the fire.
2327. The chief *heaved* a sigh.
2328. He will go to *heaven* (paradise).
2329. He is *heavily* loaded down.
2330. He has a *heavy* gait.
2331. He walks with a *heavy* tread.
2332. Your basket is *heavy*.
2333. Her dress falls around her *heels*.
2334. He drew himself up to his full *height*.
2335. The man *held out* his hand to tell me good-day.
2336. He *held* his hat in his hand.
2337. He *held* out his arm to catch his clothing.
2338. His *helmet* has a metal *chin piece*.
2339. I couldn't *help* but go there.
2340. Come *help* me carry the basket.
2341. He *helped* me build my hut.
2342. The chief gave me some *helpful* advice.
2343. He grows *hemp*.
2344. The *hen* is sitting on its eggs.
2345. I shall go to see *her* tomorrow.
2346. A buffalo broke away from the *herd*.
2347. He threw the garbage *here and there*.
2348. *Here* he comes.
2349. *Here* is where he fell.
2350. From *here* you can see the river.
2351. Come *here!*
2352. Come by *here*.
2353. They passed by *here*.
2354. He lives near *here*.
2355. He's not from *here*.
2356. Did he come all the way *here?*
2357. His disease is *hereditary*.
2358. This bottle is *hermetically* sealed.
2359. He fought like a *hero*.
2360. We *hesitated* between the two roads.
2361. After *hesitating* for a long time he made a decision.
2362. I've got the *hiccups*.
2363. He *hid* the thing from everyone.
2364. He *went away and hid* to eat.
2365. *Hide* it well; someone might steal it.
2366. The child discovered the *hideout*.
2367. She *hides* it well.
2368. She is *hiding* from me.
2369. The hut is very *high*.
2370. Let *him* eat.
2371. I gave *him* some millet.
2372. It's from *him* that I learned that you were coming.
2373. He looked in front of *him*.
2374. Who broke the pot? *Him*.
2375. He looked around *him*.
2376. He came *himself*.
2377. He knows nothing about it *himself*.
2378. He has a good opinion of *himself*.
2379. The woman sways her *hips* when she walks.
2380. His loincloth wraps around his *hips*.
2381. The child lost *his* balance and fell.
2382. He has *his* glasses on *his* nose.
2383. That is *his*.
2384. That knife is *his*.
2385. He *hit* (shot) the animal with the rifle.
2386. A *hitch* (unforeseen difficulty) kept me from coming.
2387. Bees make honey in the *hive*.
2388. He got *hoarse* from shouting.
2389. I am *hoarse*.
2390. He put something in *hock*.
2391. He was *hoeing* in his plantation.
2392. He *hoisted* the flag.

2393. *Hold out* your hand to me.
2394. The pillars *hold up* the house.
2395. *Hold up* your head.
2396. He is *holding* his breath.
2397. He killed him by *holding* his head under water.
2398. The chief *holds* the same opinions.
2399. His pagne has a *hole* in it.
2400. He dug a *hole* in the ground.
2401. That tree is *hollow*.
2402. The spoon was *hollowed* out of wood.
2403. They paid *homage* to the chief.
2404. He doesn't feel at *home* here.
2405. He is quite *at home* there.
2406. He likes to stay *home* with his family.
2407. The Central African Republic is his *homeland*.
2408. He is *homesick;* he wants to return to his village.
2409. He's an *honest* man.
2410. The *honey* has hardened.
2411. He is going to collect *honey*.
2412. The goose is *honking*.
2413. That would *honor* him too much.
2414. It's a debt of *honor*.
2415. The man raised the *hood* of the car.
2416. The fish bit the *hook*.
2417. He has a *hooked* nose.
2418. The hunter *hooted* (hallooed) after the animal.
2419. The owl *hoots*.
2420. There's no longer any *hope*.
2421. He is *hoping for* a good crop.
2422. He *hopped* forward.
2423. The children are playing *hopscotch*.
2424. The sun sank behind the *horizon*.
2425. The *horse dealer* sold me this horse.
2426. He is *hostile* to this project.
2427. His welcome was *hostile*.
2428. The sauce is *hot* (spicy).
2429. Be careful—it's *hot*.
2430. The water is *hot*.
2431. He has a fever; his head is *hot*.
2432. Today it is very *hot*.
2433. It's a *wood house (brick house stone house)*.
2434. Your sister is doing the *housework*.
2435. *How* are you (doing)?
2436. *How* did you do that?
2437. *How* expensive it is!
2438. Look *how* he runs.
2439. I don't know *how* she'll take that.
2440. The sky is covered with *huge* clouds.
2441. The boat's *hull* is full of water.
2442. The prisoner is being treated *humanely*.
2443. He has a *humble* way about him.
2444. This setback is *humiliating*.
2445. You can hear the bees *humming* around the hive.
2446. He is *hunchbacked*.
2447. The herd consisted of about a *hundred* elephants.
2448. More than a *hundred* men went hunting.
2449. He does it a *hundred* times better.
2450. He *hung up* his clothes.
2451. He *hung* his hat on the end of the stake.
2452. He *hung* the bunch of bananas under the roof of the hut.
2453. He didn't eat enough to satisfy his *hunger*.
2454. I am *hungry*.
2455. They *hunt* buffalo.
2456. *Hunting* is done in the rainy season.
2457. The men went *hunting*.
2458. He *hurled* abuse at us.
2459. The *hurricane* uprooted the trees.
2460. He left *hurriedly*.
2461. He's in a *hurry* to leave.
2462. *Hurry* up!
2463. *Hurry* up.
2464. Where does it *hurt*?
2465. Where do you *hurt*? My head *hurts*.
2466. Her *husband* beats her.
2467. That man is her *husband*.
2468. The coconut is surrounded by a *husk*.

Sentence Questionnaire

2469. The *hut* fell over.
2470. He covered the *hut*.
2471. It is a round *hut*.
2472. He built an earthen *hut*.
2473. It is a *hybrid*.
2474. He is a *hypochondriac*.

I

2475. *I* (intensive) like mangoes a lot.
2476. *I* alone can resist him.
2477. *I* will come tomorrow.
2478. The *ibis* has a long beak.
2479. An *idea* occurred to me.
2480. He was very happy at the *idea* of going back to the village.
2481. Their *idea(l)* of beauty is different from ours.
2482. He had this *idea*.
2483. He's an *ideal* husband.
2484. The world you're talking about would be an *ideal* world.
2485. He is an *idealist*.
2486. He *idealizes* the memory of his father.
2487. He only has good *ideas*.
2488. He just can't express his *ideas*.
2489. The twins are completely *identical*.
2490. The two knives are *identical*.
2491. My brother could *identify* this bird.
2492. You *idiot!*
2493. He is the village *idiot*.
2494. He is an *idiot*.
2495. That is completely *idiotic*.
2496. He remained *idle* all day long.
2497. He leads an *idle* life.
2498. He cannot stay *idle*.
2499. Come tomorrow *if* (it is) possible.
2500. Too bad *if* I arrive late.
2501. *If* only I could sleep!
2502. This wood *ignites* (catches fire) easily.
2503. He is an *ignoramus*.
2504. His *ignorance* is amazing.
2505. He is *ignorant*.
2506. He fell *ill* a week ago.
2507. He felt *ill* because he hadn't eaten for two days.
2508. She spoke *ill* of your sister.
2509. The people of the village are *ill-disposed* towards you; they won't help you.
2510. That is *illegal*.
2511. This page is *illegible*.
2512. He writes *illegibly*.
2513. He is an *illegitimate* child.
2514. He is *illiterate*.
2515. Your reasoning is *illogical*.
2516. Your *illogicality* irritates me.
2517. A number of fires *illuminate* the village square.
2518. It was only an *illusion*.
2519. I don't have any more *illusions* about him.
2520. He prefers his *illusions* to reality.
2521. This book is *illustrated*.
2522. He is *illustrious*.
2523. He is the *image* of his father.
2524. He invents *imaginary* exploits.
2525. He prefers the *imaginary* to reality.
2526. He has a lot of *imagination*.
2527. Your son is *imaginative*.
2528. He can't *imagine* that anyone would oppose him.
2529. He *imagined* the whole thing.
2530. He *imagines* that we are going to help him.
2531. He is *imagining* things.
2532. He is an *imbecile*.
2533. He can *imitate* the call of all the animals.
2534. He *imitated* the chief's voice.
2535. That cry can't be *imitated*.
2536. He *imitates* all his father's gestures.
2537. He is *imitating* the walk of a lame man.
2538. He is a good *imitator*.
2539. This material is *immaculately* white.
2540. The spirit is *immaterial* (intangible).
2541. That young man is *immature*.
2542. His *immediate* reaction was to refuse.
2543. This medicine gave me *immediate* relief.

2544. He arrived *immediately* after you left.
2545. The man left and *immediately* the woman turned into a kite.
2546. He is *immensely* rich.
2547. Many *immigrants* have settled in this area.
2548. He is *immobilized* by the wound in his leg.
2549. He drinks *immoderately* (excessively).
2550. Your behavior is *immodest*.
2551. His behavior is *immoral*.
2552. His *immorality* is reprehensible.
2553. The gods are *immortal*.
2554. He won *immortality* (eternal fame) by his exploits.
2555. He is *immune* to pity.
2556. No one has *immunity* for a crime like that.
2557. Our laws are *immutable* (unchanging).
2558. He *impaled* an animal.
2559. This judge is *impartial*.
2560. He judged *impartially*.
2561. In the rainy season this road is *impassable*.
2562. We are at an *impasse*.
2563. He remained *impassive*.
2564. He is full of *impatience*.
2565. He is *impatient*.
2566. These woods are *impenetrable*.
2567. With an *imperative* gesture I told him to leave.
2568. His pulse is *imperceptible*.
2569. The change is *imperceptible*.
2570. He has an *imperious* nature.
2571. His *impersonation* of the chief was very well done.
2572. I don't like his *impertinence*.
2573. Your brother is *impertinent*.
2574. He is *impervious* to pity.
2575. He does everything *impetuously*.
2576. Our enemies are *implacable*.
2577. He didn't say it; it was *implicit*.
2578. He *implored* our help.
2579. He *implored* the chief.
2580. He did an *impolite* thing.
2581. You are *impolite*.
2582. What he said is of great *importance*.
2583. He is an *important* person.
2584. It is an *important* question.
2585. He knows how to *impose* (himself).
2586. In the past the Muslims *imposed* a heavy tax of millet on us.
2587. A chief that we don't like was *imposed* on us.
2588. Our chief has an *imposing* air (about him).
2589. It is *impossible* to cross the river here.
2590. It is not *impossible* to do but it will be difficult.
2591. The solution that you propose is *impossible*.
2592. He attempted the *impossible*.
2593. He is an *imposter*.
2594. His *imposture* was discovered.
2595. Her husband is *impotent*.
2596. This project is *impracticable*.
2597. The information he gave me is *imprecise*.
2598. The Arabs' fortress was *impregnable*.
2599. The male *impregnates* the female.
2600. He *impressed* them.
2601. He made a good *impression* on me.
2602. What is your *impression*?
2603. My wife is *impressionable*.
2604. He is *impressive* when he puts on his weapons.
2605. The accused man was *imprisoned*.
2606. It is *improbable* that he will come.
2607. It is *improper* to be unfriendly with a guest.
2608. His remarks are *improper*.
2609. He was forced to *improvise* an answer.
2610. He has no shame; he is *impudent*.
2611. He is young and *impulsive*.
2612. The water is *impure*.
2613. He was speaking *in* Ngbaka.
2614. *In* animals the sense of instinct is highly developed.

2615. I would like to see him *in* order to discuss the matter with him.
2616. Take some quinine; *in* that way you will be healed.
2617. There are fish *in* the water.
2618. In the rainy season the village is *inaccessible* without a canoe.
2619. His version of the story is *inaccurate*.
2620. His attitude is *inadmissible*. (intolerable)
2621. He *inadvertently* came in without knocking. (by mistake)
2622. This event had *incalculable* consequences.
2623. He is *incapable* of lying.
2624. He is *incapable* of running a business.
2625. He can talk *incessantly* on this subject.
2626. The trip went (off) without *incident*.
2627. He made an *incision* in the bark of the tree.
2628. He is *inclined* to be lazy.
2629. His words are *incoherent*.
2630. She is *incomparably* beautiful.
2631. These two components are *incompatible*.
2632. This man is *incompetent* in his work.
2633. The listing is *incomplete*.
2634. He speaks an *incomprehensible* language.
2635. It is an *incomprehensible* riddle.
2636. The defense of the accused man is full of *inconsistencies*.
2637. He showed *inconsistent* behavior.
2638. His grief is *inconsolable*.
2639. His success is *incontestable*.
2640. That child is *incorrigible*.
2641. The judge proved *incorruptible*.
2642. He has made *incredible* progress.
2643. He struck him with *incredible* violence.
2644. His disease is *incurable*.
2645. His dress is *indecent*.
2646. He has an *indecisive* nature.
2647. That viewpoint is absolutely *indefensible*.
2648. The color of his clothes is *indefinable*.
2649. The stain is *indelible*.
2650. The defeated people had to pay war *indemnities*.
2651. The country is fighting for its *independence*.
2652. The room is in an *indescribable* mess.
2653. The material is *indestructible*.
2654. There are only vague *indications* of his guilt.
2655. He is *indifferent* to the world.
2656. He has *indigestion* because he ate too much.
2657. His conduct made everyone *indignant*.
2658. He is *indiscreet;* he asks too many questions.
2659. His superiority is *indisputable*.
2660. The bonds of marriage are *indissoluble*.
2661. *Indistinct* noises were heard.
2662. His voice is *indistinct*.
2663. Man is an *individual* being and a social being.
2664. Society is composed of *individuals*.
2665. He has an *indolent* air about him.
2666. His will is *indomitable*.
2667. He *induced* me to do it.
2668. The *industry* of this country is thriving.
2669. This meat is *inedible*.
2670. He left an *ineffaceable* remembrance of him.
2671. This remedy is *ineffective*.
2672. The *ineffectiveness* of their efforts discourages them.
2673. The catastrophe was *inevitable*.
2674. His negligence is *inexcusable*.
2675. The spring is *inexhaustible*.
2676. His curiosity is *inexhaustible*.
2677. That young man is still *inexperienced*.
2678. His behavior is *inexplicable*.
2679. The hut is in an *inextricable* mess.
2680. It is an *inextricable* problem.
2681. The medicine is *infallible* against a cough.

2682. Nobody is *infallible;* anyone can make a mistake.
2683. The wound became *infected.*
2684. The *infection* became widespread.
2685. This is an *infectious* disease.
2686. He is very *inferior* to him.
2687. It is an *infernal* heat.
2688. The horse is galloping at an *infernal* speed.
2689. The ground is *infertile;* nothing grows.
2690. His will is *inflexible.*
2691. They *inflicted* a penalty on him.
2692. He acted under the *influence* of his anger.
2693. He changed a lot under the *influence* of the chief.
2694. I don't want to *influence* your decision.
2695. He lets himself be *influenced* easily.
2696. That man is easily *influenced.*
2697. They *informed* him of the event.
2698. He is an *informer.*
2699. This man has committed an *infraction* of discipline (the rules).
2700. That *infuriates* me.
2701. Let the plants *infuse.*
2702. It is an *ingenious* invention.
2703. The child answered *ingenuously.*
2704. The *inhabitants* have left their village.
2705. The act of breathing consists of *inhaling* and exhaling.
2706. It is *inherent* in its nature.
2707. The (joint) heirs will divide the *inheritance.*
2708. He came into a big *inheritance.*
2709. I *inherited* a house from my father.
2710. The chief treats him *inhumanely.*
2711. We must find the *initial* cause.
2712. The priest is responsible to *initiate* the faithful.
2713. He *initiated* him into the profession of a carpenter.
2714. The initiates left for the *initiation camp.*
2715. That ceremony is an *initiation* rite.
2716. He took the *initiative* for the movement.
2717. He did that on his own *initiative.*
2718. He is the victim of a terrible *injustice.*
2719. He has *innate* knowledge.
2720. His gifts are *innate.*
2721. We recognized his *innocence.*
2722. He is as *innocent* as a newborn baby.
2723. It is an *inopportune* moment.
2724. He is *inordinately* angry.
2725. He is an *insane* man.
2726. His thirst is *insatiable.*
2727. He lives in *insecurity* (in the fear of the future).
2728. He is *insensible* to pain.
2729. The chief remained *insensitive* to their pleadings.
2730. The two brothers are *inseparable.*
2731. It is cooler *inside* the hut.
2732. There is nothing *inside.*
2733. Put your millet *inside.*
2734. Put it *inside.*
2735. Shall I wait for you outside or *inside*?
2736. His behavior is *insidious.*
2737. She has an *insignificant* face.
2738. What are you *insinuating* by that?
2739. Be *insistent* with her; perhaps she will accept.
2740. He implores the chief *insistently.*
2741. I understood; there's no use *insisting.*
2742. He was *insolent* with the chief.
2743. This problem is *insoluble.*
2744. Worry keeps him from sleeping; he has *insomnia.*
2745. The chief *inspected* each one's work.
2746. There he had a flash of *inspiration.*
2747. He has no *inspiration.*
2748. The chief was truly *inspired.*
2749. *Instead of* going by canoe we will go on foot.
2750. You are sleeping *instead of* working.
2751. Come tomorrow *instead.*

2752. The *instigator* of the plot was discovered.
2753. He did that *instinctively*, without thinking.
2754. The chief gave him some *instructions*.
2755. He plays a wind *instrument*.
2756. His resources are *insufficient* to live on.
2757. It is an *insult* to his honor.
2758. That's an *insult* to reason.
2759. The chief *insulted* him.
2760. His remarks are *insulting*.
2761. The chief directed *insults* at him.
2762. The obstacle is *insurmountable*.
2763. The barrier is *insurmountable*.
2764. His reputation is *intact* (spotless).
2765. The inheritance remained *intact*.
2766. He is becoming *integrated* into the community.
2767. The people are defending the *integrity* of their territory.
2768. The brain is the seat of the *intellect*.
2769. He is of superior *intelligence*.
2770. His speech is *intelligible*.
2771. The child's speech is barely *intelligible*.
2772. I *intend* to leave tomorrow.
2773. He *intends* to leave.
2774. The light is *intense*.
2775. He works *intensely*.
2776. He did that *intentionally*.
2777. The chief *interceded* on his behalf.
2778. He borrowed at *interest*.
2779. I listened to her with *interest*.
2780. That story *interested* me greatly.
2781. He has an *interesting* face.
2782. She always acts in her own *interests*.
2783. They were *interfering* in the village's affairs.
2784. I don't know how to *interpret* his behavior.
2785. *Interrogate* him.
2786. Don't *interrupt* me all the time.
2787. He *interrupted* his trip.
2788. They *interrupted* their conversation.
2789. He stopped at the major *intersection*.
2790. This road *intersects* another.
2791. The rains return at regular *intervals*.
2792. She is ready to *intervene* (to act).
2793. He *intervened* on my behalf.
2794. I am counting on your *intervention*.
2795. He has parasites in his *intestine*.
2796. His authority *intimidates* me.
2797. He went *into* the bush.
2798. They were walking *into* the wind.
2799. The heat is *intolerable*.
2800. The situation became *intolerable*.
2801. His attitude is *intolerant*.
2802. Alcohol *intoxicates*.
2803. He is *intransigent*; he never gives in.
2804. I am *intrigued* by this matter.
2805. He is *introducing* a visitor.
2806. I have an *intuition* as to what will happen.
2807. They *invaded* the village.
2808. He has done me an *invaluable* service.
2809. He is *invariably* late.
2810. God is *invisible*.
2811. The chief *invited* him to the ceremonial meal.
2812. He *invited* me to come to the village.
2813. The whole family is *invited* to the meal.
2814. The chief *invoked* the law against the guilty man.
2815. The blade of the knife is made of *iron*.
2816. His words are *ironical*.
2817. His fear is *irrational*.
2818. Their interests are *irreconcilable*.
2819. This proof is *irrefutable*.
2820. The defeat was *irremediable*.
2821. It is an *irreparable* disaster.
2822. The situation was *irreparably* compromised.
2823. His behavior is *irreproachable*.
2824. His illness made him *irritable*.
2825. The child *irritates* his older brother.
2826. Smoke *irritates* the eyes.
2827. The man *is to* leave tomorrow.

2828. There *is* a snake under that rock.
2829. It *is* daylight.
2830. How *is* he? He is fine.
2831. He *is* worried.
2832. There's an *island* in the middle of the lake.
2833. There's an *island* in the middle of the river.
2834. That is an *isolated* case.
2835. He is *isolated* from the rest of the world.
2836. Give *it* (for various objects) to me.
2837. *It* is going well.
2838. *It* is raining.
2839. *It* is true that he is tall.
2840. His buttons make him *itch*.
2841. That *itches* (me) a lot.
2842. Elephant's teeth are made of *ivory*.

J

2843. The *jackal* feeds on what the wildcats leave.
2844. His *jacket* fastens at the waist.
2845. He won the *jackpot*.
2846. He *jammed* his finger in the door.
2847. *January* is the first month of the year.
2848. The *jar* contains water.
2849. There is water in the *jar*.
2850. That is *jasmine*.
2851. He has a big *javelin*.
2852. He broke his rival's *jaw* with a punch.
2853. One of the hyena's paws had been caught in the *jaws* of the trap.
2854. He is *jealous* of your brother.
2855. He is *jealous* of your good luck.
2856. He is *jealous*.
2857. *Jealousy* is gnawing away at him.
2858. He was stung by a *jellyfish*.
2859. He is *jeopardizing* his health.
2860. He is fishing from the *jetty*.
2861. She likes *jewels* very much.
2862. He is very attached to his *jewels*.

2863. His ideas don't *jibe* with his actions.
2864. Clearing land is too difficult a *job* for women.
2865. It's the *job* of the doctor to care for the sick.
2866. He has a good *job*.
2867. He *joined* the discussion.
2868. They *joined* together to do the work.
2869. The *joke* was in poor taste.
2870. That was only a *practical joke*.
2871. We can't talk seriously; he is always *joking*.
2872. I'm not in the mood for *joking*.
2873. I am not *joking;* this is serious.
2874. The car *jolted* down the trail.
2875. The *journey* from the village to Bangui is long.
2876. They sang to while away the time of the *journey*.
2877. He is *jovial*. (jolly)
2878. His *joviality* is well known.
2879. His *joy* was great.
2880. He felt great *joy*.
2881. Why do you look so *joyful* today?
2882. He greeted me *joyfully*.
2883. He is the *judge* of the village.
2884. It is more difficult to *judge* oneself than to *judge* others.
2885. Your grandfather will *judge* this matter.
2886. He gave an equitable *judgment*.
2887. He gave me some *judicious* advice.
2888. He can *juggle* well.
2889. He crushed the fruit and some *juice* came out.
2890. This fruit is *juicy*.
2891. In *July* it rains a lot.
2892. The antelope will *jump up* when someone approaches.
2893. The animal *jumped* over the obstacle.
2894. The squirrel *jumps* from branch to branch.
2895. It is *June*.
2896. He got lost in the *jungle*.
2897. He is two years my *junior*.
2898. He *just barely* escaped the lion.

2899. He is a *just* man.
2900. It is my grandfather who dispenses *justice*.
2901. There is no *justification* for such a horrible act.
2902. His fears are not *justified*.
2903. His refusal is not *justified*.
2904. The end *justifies* the means.
2905. His efforts were *justly* rewarded.
2906. The house on piles *juts out* over the river.

K

2907. She took off the *kapok* (fibers) which cover the ceiba tree's seeds.
2908. He has *keen* sight.
2909. That child is *keen* to learn.
2910. *Keep* this secret to yourself.
2911. You're *keeping* things from me.
2912. She *keeps* the food in a gourd.
2913. Policemen wear *kepis*.
2914. The chief *kept* his promise.
2915. He *kept* the fire going.
2916. He is breaking the palm nut stones to get the *kernels*.
2917. He is eating some corn *kernels*.
2918. That *key* doesn't work.
2919. He provided the *key* to the mystery.
2920. That garment is *khaki*.
2921. The horse *kicked*.
2922. You won't get your *kicks* here!
2923. The child tugged on the *kid's* beard.
2924. A *kid's* hair is bristly.
2925. He gave several goat *kids* to his wife's family.
2926. The poison *killed* him.
2927. The epidemic *killed* many people.
2928. I have two *kilograms* (unit of mass . . .) of manioc.
2929. We are five *kilometers* (unit of distance . . .) from the village.
2930. He is a very *kind* man.
2931. That man is very *kind* to others.
2932. That's the same *kind*.
2933. He is too *kind*.
2934. This woman is *kind*.
2935. His father is a *kindly* man.
2936. He was treated with *kindness*.
2937. He eats all *kinds* of vegetables.
2938. *Kiss* her.
2939. She gave her mother a *kiss*.
2940. She works in the *kitchen*.
2941. She is *kneading* the dough.
2942. She is *kneading* the dough.
2943. The potter *kneads* the clay with her hands.
2944. He is *kneeling* on the mat.
2945. He went into the water up to his *knees*.
2946. She got down on her *knees*.
2947. He is sharpening his *knife*.
2948. He threw his *throwing-knife*.
2949. The child *knit* his brow.
2950. He *knit* his brows.
2951. The bones *knit* together with age.
2952. She is *knock-kneed*.
2953. The boats *knocked* against each other on the river.
2954. Someone *knocked* at the door.
2955. He *knocked* everything *over* as he went by.
2956. Somebody's *knocking* at the door.
2957. The village is built on a *knoll*.
2958. The *knot* is too loose; it will come undone.
2959. He is *knotting* the two pieces of rope together.
2960. I don't *know* if he will come back.
2961. He doesn't *know* me.
2962. *Let* him *know* that I am back.
2963. I *know* the way.
2964. He doesn't *know* what to do.
2965. He doesn't *know* who I am.
2966. I *know* why he is angry.
2967. They exchanged a *knowing* look.
2968. He did it without my *knowledge*.
2969. He is gone, along with all his *knowledge*.
2970. He is *known* for his courage.
2971. The news was already *known*.
2972. I might have *known;* I suspected it.
2973. He cracked his *knuckles*.

L

2974. He works as a *laborer* in the cotton mill (factory).
2975. It is a *laborious* enterprise.
2976. The (shoe) *lace* broke.
2977. He couldn't go out for *lack* of money.
2978. He *lacked* the strength to finish the work.
2979. He speaks *laconically*.
2980. The *ladybug* flew away.
2981. It is a *lagoon*.
2982. He *laid down* his burden on the ground.
2983. He was *laid low* by the disease.
2984. The chicken *laid* an egg.
2985. She *laid* the mat on the ground.
2986. The chief *laid* the responsibility at his feet.
2987. There are many fish in that *lake*.
2988. They live in a *lakeside* village.
2989. The people of the village make fun of the *lame man*.
2990. He bought a kerosene (oil) *lamp*.
2991. He *lanced* the abscess.
2992. The *land* has been overly cultivated and is becoming exhausted.
2993. This *land* is fertile.
2994. It is a rich *land*.
2995. He *landed* the canoe.
2996. The canoe *landed*.
2997. He planted coffee trees along the *lane* leading to his house.
2998. Animals have no *language*.
2999. I don't understand their *language*.
3000. The chief moderated his *language*.
3001. He speaks several *languages*.
3002. She is *languid*.
3003. I am *languishing* without you. (in your absence)
3004. The waves *lapped* at the hull of the boat.
3005. I hear the cat *lapping up* water.
3006. He made up for his *lapse* of memory.
3007. That is a *larva*.
3008. The rain *lashed* at our faces.
3009. He *lashed* her legs with a whip.
3010. That is not the *last* time.
3011. He arrived *last*.
3012. The rainy season *lasts* a long time.
3013. It's better to wait as *late* as possible.
3014. The sick man feel asleep *late* in the night.
3015. It is too *late*.
3016. He arrived a bit *late*.
3017. There was *latent* conflict between the parties.
3018. He arrived a few minutes *later*.
3019. The soap makes a *lather*.
3020. Soapy water *lathers*.
3021. Show me the way to the *latrines* (outhouse).
3022. There is nothing to *laugh* about.
3023. His was a mocking *laugh*.
3024. He broke out *laughing*.
3025. He respects the *law*.
3026. My grandfather knows our *laws* well.
3027. It is a *laxative*.
3028. The flooring is made up of superimposed *layers*.
3029. He gave way to *laziness*.
3030. He is too *lazy* to get up.
3031. We *lead* a hard life.
3032. Your brother will take the *lead* and you will take up the rear.
3033. Rifle bullets are made of *lead*.
3034. He is a (born) *leader* of men.
3035. He is the *leader* of the herd.
3036. They left under the *leadership* of the chief.
3037. He's the one who *leads* the dance.
3038. This road *leads* to the river.
3039. The container is *leaking*.
3040. *Lean* against the wall of the hut.
3041. *Lean* back against this tree.
3042. The wind made the trees *lean* over.
3043. This meat is *lean*; it doesn't have any fat.
3044. He *leaned* his elbows on the table.
3045. Go get the man who is *leaning* against the tree.

3046. He is *leaning* against the wall of the house.
3047. He jumped over the obstacle (hurdle) in one *leap*.
3048. They *leaped* to the attack.
3049. He *leapt up* indignantly.
3050. He *learned* the news yesterday.
3051. The chief is very *learned;* he knows many things.
3052. He is *learning* to read.
3053. He tied up his dog with a *leash*.
3054. It is at *least* a day's walk to return to the village.
3055. He is the *least* courageous of us all.
3056. That's the *least* of my worries.
3057. Those shoes are made of *leather*.
3058. *Leave* me alone.
3059. *Leave* some millet for your brother.
3060. *Leave* the door open.
3061. He gave him *leave* to go.
3062. If you *leave*, I will *leave* too.
3063. New *leaves* are coming out.
3064. That thought never *leaves* him; it's an obsession.
3065. Your husband is *lecherous*.
3066. His stubbornness *led* to calamity.
3067. He *left* for Bangui yesterday.
3068. He *left* his luggage in the car.
3069. He *left* his wife and went away on a trip.
3070. He *left* on foot.
3071. There is a lot *left* to eat.
3072. Walk on the *left*.
3073. The *leftover* meat is in the pot.
3074. He tore the *leg* of his pants.
3075. He broke his *leg*.
3076. He left me a *legacy*.
3077. That is *legal*.
3078. He is a *legendary* hero.
3079. He knows many *legends*.
3080. He has the power to *legislate*. (make the laws)
3081. He has the right of *legislation*.
3082. He is a *legislator*. (lawmaker)
3083. He is a *legist*. (law specialist)
3084. His complaint is *legitimate*.
3085. A panther has four *legs*.
3086. In his *leisure time* he plays the harp.
3087. *Lemon oil* repels mosquitoes.
3088. He sells *lemonade*.
3089. There are a lot of *lemons* this year.
3090. The *length* of his nose is ridiculous.
3091. The *length* of my stick is not enough to reach the mango.
3092. He explained his problem to me at *length*.
3093. He *lengthened* the legs of his trousers.
3094. He shows great *leniency* with his children.
3095. He isn't *lenient;* he is strict.
3096. Honey is a good *lenitive* for the throat. Honey is soothing for the throat.
3097. The *leopard* caught a goat.
3098. That is a *leopard's* skin.
3099. *Leprosy* is a disease.
3100. He has *leprosy*.
3101. She is a *lesbian*.
3102. He works *less and less*.
3103. I will not sell you this knife for *less* than 100 francs.
3104. He is *less* than fifteen years old.
3105. He worked *less* than he did yesterday.
3106. He works *less* than this brother.
3107. He works even *less* than you do.
3108. He works much *less* than you do.
3109. He doesn't work any *less* than you do.
3110. Be fear *less*.
3111. He works *less*.
3112. He *let go of* his knife.
3113. I *let* him leave.
3114. He *let* himself be swept along by the current.
3115. He *let* me *down*.
3116. *Let* me *go;* you are hurting me.
3117. *Let* me through.
3118. A state of *lethargy* came over him.
3119. I received a *letter*.
3120. He can't form his *letters*.
3121. The *level* of the water varies according to the season.
3122. The water came up to waist *level*.

3123. He used a *lever* to tip the rock over.
3124. He is the biggest *liar* in the village.
3125. He offered *libations* to the gods.
3126. His head is full of *lice*.
3127. Only some *lichens* were growing on those rocks.
3128. The dog *licked up* what was left in the bottom of the pot.
3129. The dog is busy *licking* himself.
3130. He is *licking* the honey from his fingers.
3131. She covered the pot with a *lid*.
3132. He *lied* to his sister.
3133. He *lies* compulsively.
3134. You only tell *lies*.
3135. I owe my *life* to him; he saved me.
3136. They are friends for *life*.
3137. She *lifted* the lid of the pot.
3138. A gentle *light* bathed the countryside.
3139. You showed it to me in its true *light*.
3140. Your suitcase is *light*.
3141. The fire doesn't give much *light*.
3142. The truth will come to *light*.
3143. The bird *lighted* (landed) on the branch.
3144. He is *lighting* the fire in his new house.
3145. The fire is not *lighting* things *up*.
3146. The *lightness* of this bag surprises me.
3147. *Lightning* caused the house to burn down. (Lightning struck the house.)
3148. They make fire with *lignite*.
3149. Do *like* (as) he does.
3150. I *like* bananas a lot.
3151. People do not *like* being beaten.
3152. You must not do it *like* that.
3153. He does not *like* this man.
3154. What would you *like*?
3155. That supposition is *likely*.
3156. He *likes* being in the village.
3157. He *likes* to sing and dance but he doesn't like working.
3158. He acquired a *liking* for his work.
3159. He finally found work to his *liking*.
3160. He broke all four *limbs*.
3161. The hut was whitewashed with *lime*.
3162. His imagination is *limitless*.
3163. His ambition is *limitless*. There is no *limit* to his ambition.
3164. The water is *limpid* (clear).
3165. Ever since he was wounded he *limps*.
3166. His field ends at the *line* between that tree and the rock.
3167. He drew a *line* in the sand with a stick.
3168. They planted a *line* of trees the length of the road.
3169. Trees *line* the trail.
3170. *Line* up the children in front of the house.
3171. He fishes with a (fishing-) *line*.
3172. The soldiers got in *line*.
3173. They are from the same *lineage*.
3174. He *lined* up the boxes in his canoe.
3175. Her dress is made of *linen*.
3176. The *links* of the chain are solid.
3177. That road *links* the village and Bangui.
3178. He captured two *lion* cubs.
3179. The *lion* killed a goat.
3180. It is a *lioness*.
3181. His *upper lip* is cracked.
3182. His *lower lip* is cracked.
3183. She has thick *lips*.
3184. *Liquids* flow.
3185. Blood and water are *liquids*.
3186. *Listen* to me.
3187. He *lit* his cigarette-lighter (torch to set fire to the bush).
3188. I *lit* my pipe.
3189. The fire is *lit*.
3190. He is *literate*.
3191. That gourd contains two *liters* (unit of liquid measure . . .) of water.
3192. The Tuaregs cover the lower part of their face with a *litsam*.

3193. He is traveling in a *litter*.
3194. We need to change the horse's *litter*. (bedding)
3195. He left just a *little while* ago.
3196. It's a *little* cool.
3197. That has *little* importance.
3198. He is a *little* older than I.
3199. A *little* patience, please.
3200. It matters *little*.
3201. The wives of the same man don't *live together*.
3202. They *live* in a hut.
3203. You must work in order to *live*.
3204. The eyes of that child are full of *liveliness*.
3205. He *lives on* vegetables.
3206. He *lives* down there at Bangui.
3207. The *livestock* is quite good-looking in this area.
3208. You can't make a *living* from that job.
3209. He is *living* with me.
3210. He is still *living*.
3211. In that region there are a lot of *lizards*.
3212. Take your *load* and leave.
3213. She's carrying a *load* on her head.
3214. He came back from town *loaded down* heavily.
3215. Help me get *loaded*.
3216. They are *loading* the goods onto the canoe.
3217. It bit his ear *lobe*.
3218. It is a *local* custom.
3219. He has no *lodging*. (housing)
3220. What he says is not *logical*.
3221. He went to get *logs* for the fire.
3222. We shall remember him a *long time* after his death.
3223. He died a *long time* ago.
3224. Your son hasn't come to the village for a *long time*.
3225. He is here for a *long time*.
3226. Will he stay here a *long time*?
3227. You can stay here as *long* as you want.
3228. He has a *long* neck.
3229. We spent a *long* time.
3230. The day seemed interminably *long* to me.
3231. The day seemed *long* to me.
3232. I waited a *long* while.
3233. This is a *long-standing* custom.
3234. Her hair is *long*.
3235. His spear is very *long*.
3236. His field is . . . (unit of measure) *long*.
3237. His field is three times *longer* than it is wide.
3238. Don't delay any *longer*.
3239. The days are becoming *longer*.
3240. The *longevity* of your grandfather surprises the whole village.
3241. *Look* around here.
3242. Things *look* bad.
3243. He has a malicious *look* in his eyes.
3244. The man *looked away*.
3245. The chief *looked* him straight in the face.
3246. He is *looking for* excuses not to work.
3247. He is always *looking for* his things.
3248. He was *looking for* his wife in the crowd.
3249. The law is *looking for* the thief.
3250. He is *looking for* work.
3251. She is *looking* after her children.
3252. He is on the *lookout* for the dugout to pass by.
3253. He *looks upon* him as a slave.
3254. He *looks* sick.
3255. She made a *loop* with the rope.
3256. *Loose* soil is easy to work.
3257. The war caused many *losses*.
3258. He *lost a lot of weight* during his illness.
3259. She *lost* consciousness.
3260. The child *lost* his appetite.
3261. He *lost* his knife in the bush.
3262. He *lost* his left arm.
3263. The traveler *lost* his way.
3264. I *got lost* in the forest.
3265. His cries got *lost* in the tumult.
3266. The fisherman brought back a *lot of* fish.

3267. He is very tired; he is working *a lot*.
3268. He organized a *lottery*.
3269. He protested *loudly*, crying his innocence.
(cried . . . protesting . . .)
3270. He speaks *loudly*.
3271. His mother has more *love* for him than for his brother.
3272. He has a lot of *love* for his mother.
3273. It is his daughter's *lover* that he beat yesterday.
3274. You are talking too *low* (softly); I can't hear you.
3275. The water is *low* in the river.
3276. The cows *lowed* all night long.
3277. He *lowered* his head.
3278. He *lowered* his loin cloth.
3279. We can trust him; he is *loyal*.
3280. His *loyalty* is well known.
3281. It's a *lozenge* (shape).
3282. Oil is a *lubricant*.
3283. He has a *lucid* mind.
3284. He has no *luck* with women.
3285. Good-bye and good *luck!*
3286. Bad *luck!*
3287. It was a stroke of good *luck*.
3288. He has no *luck*.
3289. He is *lucky* at gambling.
3290. He doesn't have a wife yet; he doesn't know how *lucky* he is!
3291. It's a *lucrative* work.
3292. The *luggage* was heavy.
3293. He has a *lump* in his throat.
3294. He filled his *lungs* with air.
3295. He fishes with a *lure*.
3296. He *lures* the animals to the trap with a bait.
3297. He is *lustful*.
3298. He looked at me *lustfully*.
3299. *Lustfulness* is his greatest fault.
3300. The vegetation is *luxurious*.
3301. He lives *luxuriously*.
3302. He loves *luxury*.
3303. He killed a *lycaon* (African hunting dog).
3304. The *lynx* (caracal) fled.
3305. I saw a *lynx*.

M

3306. I have *macabre* dreams every night.
3307. He cut the branches with his *machete*.
3308. There are some big *machines* at the cotton mill.
3309. The *mackerel* is a bony fish with a green and blue back.
3310. He went *mad*.
3311. The child *made out* the voice of his mother.
3312. That *made up for* his trouble.
3313. He *made* a bow.
3314. He *made* a mistake.
3315. I *made* an opening in the fence.
3316. The explosion *made* noise.
3317. This bedroom wasn't *made* to eat in.
3318. His handkerchief is made of *madras* (silk and cotton).
3319. He put several bullets into the *magazine* of his rifle.
3320. The people of the village don't know anything about *magic*.
3321. Only sorcerers practice *magic*.
3322. A magnet attracts anything made of iron because it is *magnetic*.
3323. He gave me a *magnificent* gift.
3324. Imagination *magnified* the dangers.
3325. The package arrived in the *mail*.
3326. After he was *maimed*, he doesn't talk to anyone any more.
3327. The *main* thing has been done.
3328. Her *main* virtue is perseverance.
3329. The police *maintain* order in the region.
3330. This great river is *majestic*.
3331. Our chief has an air of *majesty*.
3332. The *major* part of the harvest was lost.
3333. Together the huts *make up* a beautiful village.
3334. *Make* him obey.
3335. I did not *make* it up; it is the truth.
3336. The child *makes* up stories.

3337. He is *making fun* of us.
3338. She is *making up* her face.
3339. The mosquitoes gave him *malaria*.
3340. Quinine is the remedy for *malaria*.
3341. He is an eternal *malcontent*.
3342. With most animals, the *male* is stronger than the female.
3343. The child is of the *male* sex.
3344. That child had a *malformation* of the foot at birth.
3345. She said some *malicious* things about her neighbor.
3346. Watch out for him—he's *malicious*.
3347. He is more stupid than *malicious*.
3348. He used a *mallet* to drive the stakes in.
3349. *Malnutrition* is severe in that village.
3350. This *man* is in the prime of life.
3351. He is becoming a *man*.
3352. It's not a *man*; it's an animal.
3353. You can *manage* on your own.
3354. He cannot *manage* to catch the goat.
3355. A bird's beak consists of two *mandibles*.
3356. The praying mantis has large *mandibles*.
3357. The *mandrill* is a big monkey with an elongated muzzle like a dog's.
3358. Your little dugout canoe is *maneuverable*.
3359. It is the horses' *manger*.
3360. Our ancestors were not acquainted with the *mango tree*.
3361. The *mango* is a fruit with yellow flesh.
3362. The fruit of the mangosteen tree is the *mangosteen*.
3363. That tree is a *mangosteen*.
3364. He has the *mania* of thinking that everyone is out to get him. (obsession)
3365. The *manioc* harvest was poor.
3366. This morning I ate some *manioc*.
3367. There are several types of *manioc*: . . . .

3368. They need *manpower* at the motorscooter factory.
3369. The *mantis* is an insect with two large legs and a small head.
3370. Weaving requires great *manual* dexterity.
3371. *How many* eggs are there in that basket?
3372. *Many* men have left to work in town.
3373. *How many* men stayed in the village?
3374. I don't know *how many* there are.
3375. The people wore *many-colored* clothing.
3376. The *marabou* is large bird with white and gray plumage.
3377. Muslims make pilgrimages to the tomb of the *marabout*.
3378. We are going to get some marble from a *marble quarry* near the hill.
3379. *Marble* is a stone of varied colors.
3380. The *mare* gave birth.
3381. He reads the Koran on sheets with wide *margins*.
3382. It's a *marine* plant.
3383. The death of his father left its *mark* on him.
3384. He made a *mark* on the tree with his knife.
3385. The runners will start from the *mark* that I drew on the ground.
3386. The soldiers *marked* time.
3387. This tree was *marked* with a notch.
3388. I am going to the *market* to buy some soap.
3389. The *market-gardener* raises lettuce and tomatoes.
3390. The *marketplace* is at the end of the village.
3391. She has *marks* all over her body from having been hit.
3392. That stone *marks* the boundary of his field.
3393. He is related by *marriage*.
3394. His *marriage* is near.
3395. Your daughter is *marriageable*.

3396. He *married beneath his station*.
3397. Your son and my daughter are to be *married*.
3398. He is *married*.
3399. I don't want to get *married*.
3400. He broke the bones to suck out the *marrow*.
3401. It's time to *marry* your daughter.
3402. You can see *Mars* in the sky.
3403. It is not wise to put a village in the middle of a *marsh*.
3404. The horse's *martingale* is made of leather.
3405. That work is a *marvel*.
3406. The sunset was *marvelous*.
3407. That animal is our good luck *mascot*.
3408. That woman is too *masculine*.
3409. A *mask* is worn for this dance.
3410. He carved a wooden *mask*.
3411. The sorcerer *masked* his face.
3412. The *mason* is making bricks now.
3413. The potter began to knead a *mass* of clay.
3414. The *mass* of the people was shouting.
3415. He *massaged* her legs.
3416. The *mast* of the boat is broken.
3417. He's a *master* of mat weaving.
3418. The dog threw himself in front of his *master*.
3419. He has complete *mastery* of his emotions.
3420. The little boy is *masturbating*.
3421. He spread out the *mat* on the ground and lay down on it.
3422. The man made me a *mat* to sleep on.
3423. He has never found an adversary that was a real *match* for him.
3424. Don't *match* yourself against him; he is stronger than you.
3425. The chief's testimony *matches up* with mine.
3426. Go fetch some *matches*.
3427. His humor is *matchless*.
3428. She is a *matchmaker*.
3429. The *material* is made of cotton.
3430. That grass is the *material* used for building huts.
3431. The body of man is *material* but not his soul.
3432. Clay is a pliable *material*.
3433. Oil is a fatty *material*.
3434. It was a *matricide*.
3435. They met to discuss the *matter*.
3436. He sleeps on a straw *mattress*.
3437. Bananas must be picked before they reach complete *maturity*.
3438. The mangoes have not yet come to *maturity*.
3439. That flower is *mauve*.
3440. The basket is full to *maximum*.
3441. In *May* it's already the rainy season (adapt to the area).
3442. Is it going to rain? *Maybe*.
3443. The *mayor* of the capital is from the . . . X . . . people.
3444. It is a *maze*.
3445. Give *me* some tobacco.
3446. The chief? That's *me*.
3447. The river *meanders*.
3448. He crossed the river by *means* of a dugout canoe.
3449. The chief *means* to be obeyed.
3450. This money is *meant* for him.
3451. *Measure* the length of that piece of cloth.
3452. That piece of cloth *measures* . . . .
3453. Give me two *measures* of cloth. (lengths)
3454. The *meat* has been boned.
3455. The *meat* is cooked; you can eat it now.
3456. The *meat* of that animal is very good.
3457. He has an inflammation of the urinary *meatus*. (tract)
3458. The *mechanic* will come to repair the truck.
3459. She was *mechanically* stirring the pot with the stick while thinking about something else.
3460. He *meddles* in other people's business.
3461. He served as a *mediator*.

3462. This *medication* has a bad taste. (medicine)
3463. That is a *medicinal* herb.
3464. He took some *medicine* for the fever.
3465. He has *mediocre* intelligence.
3466. He is *meditating*.
3467. He went out to *meet* the strangers.
3468. The village chief called a *meeting* of the elders.
3469. From their first *meeting* she has liked that man.
3470. They had a family *meeting*.
3471. He is a dreamer and *melancholic*.
3472. He has bouts of *melancholy*.
3473. In the *melee* he got hit with a spear.
3474. I like the *melody* of this song.
3475. Buy a *melon*.
3476. It was a *memorable* event.
3477. I have a bad *memory*.
3478. She is *mending* the linen.
3479. After *menopause*, a woman can no longer have children.
3480. Her *menstrual bleeding* (menses) comes every 25 days.
3481. Her *menstruation* only lasts a short time.
3482. The Banda don't have the same *mentality* as the Sara.
3483. He made *mention* of a shortcut to the next village.
3484. She didn't *mention* the name of her village.
3485. The cat goes *"meow."*
3486. I heard a *meowing* (from a cat).
3487. Your cat is *meowing*. What does she want?
3488. That night someone robbed a Hausa of his *merchandise*.
3489. The *merchants* are Hausas.
3490. He is *merciful* towards others in calamity.
3491. He is *merciless*.
3492. *Mercury* is a liquid metal.
3493. He showed him *mercy* for his debts.
3494. The crops are at the *mercy* of the drought.
3495. The stick is drifting at the *mercy* of the waves.
3496. The *merino* is a type of sheep.
3497. There is no *merit* in telling the truth when there's no way to lie.
3498. Fish get caught in the *mesh* of the nets.
3499. The cat made a *mess* inside the hut.
3500. This situation is a bloody *mess*. 'un vrai merdier'
3501. Nobody understands any of this *mess*. (imbroglio)
3502. Your wife gave me a *message* to pass on to you.
3503. I sent him a *messenger* to tell him the news.
3504. That child is a *messy* eater.
3505. I *met* the chief by the river.
3506. We have already *met*.
3507. Iron and copper are *metals*.
3508. The caterpillar was *metamorphosed* into a butterfly. (transformed)
3509. He knows the *method* for making charcoal.
3510. He works *methodically*.
3511. He is very *meticulous*.
3512. He works *meticulously*.
3513. In that rock there are small shiny pieces of *mica*.
3514. He caught the arrow in *mid-air*.
3515. The *middle finger* is the longest finger of the hand.
3516. He broke his *middle finger*.
3517. The *middle* finger is the longest.
3518. The hyena hid in the *middle* of a thicket.
3519. He threw himself into the *middle* of the fight.
3520. The child woke up the *middle* of the night.
3521. He walked in the *middle* of the road.
3522. Cut this stick in the *middle*.
3523. His hair is separated by a part in the *middle*.
3524. You will come at *midnight*.
3525. It is *midnight*.

3526. We must clean the path *midway* between our two huts.
3527. The *midwife* helps women give birth.
3528. It *might* well rain tomorrow.
3529. I have a *migraine* (headache).
3530. The *migration* of the (storks, eels, . . .) is about to begin.
3531. It is a *migratory* bird.
3532. That is a *mild* sickness.
3533. The wind is *mild*.
3534. The millet will *mildew* if you leave it damp.
3535. There is *mildew* on the manioc.
3536. That goat gives *milk*.
3537. Babies drink *milk*.
3538. He *milks* the goats.
3539. I saw the *Milky* Way.
3540. It is a *mill*.
3541. We have been established in this village for a *millennium* (thousand years).
3542. Give me some (white, red, . . .) *millet*.
3543. That car costs a *million* francs.
3544. The *millstone* for crushing grain is activated by a donkey.
3545. He can *mime* anything he wants.
3546. He is a good *mime*.
3547. She changed her *mind* and went back to her husband.
3548. His *mind* is elsewhere.
3549. That idea went through my *mind*.
3550. He has a quick *mind*.
3551. He changed his *mind*.
3552. Take your hoe and give me *mine* back.
3553. There is an iron *mine* near here.
3554. Your crop was poor, but *mine* was good.
3555. That spear is *mine*.
3556. *Miners'* work is hard.
3557. The damage was *minimal*.
3558. You *minimize* the role of your father.
3559. We need a *minimum* amount of money.
3560. He did a *minimum* of work.
3561. That child is still a *minor*.
3562. They are in the *minority*.
3563. That child is not responsible; he's still in his *minority*.
3564. Fix us some *mint* tea.
3565. 10 *minus* 3 is 7.
3566. Wait for me a *minute*.
3567. Only a *miracle* could save him.
3568. He only escaped from the lion by a *miracle*.
3569. In the desert you see *mirages*.
3570. She broke her *mirror*.
3571. The trail is *miry*.
3572. That marriage would be a *misalliance*.
3573. He doesn't like anybody; he is a *misanthrope*.
3574. His *mischief* drives him to make fun of people.
3575. He is *mischievous;* he likes to have fun at others' expense.
3576. He is guilty of many *misdeeds*.
3577. He is *miserable* because his wife died.
3578. His clothes are *miserable*.
3579. The *misery* of the people in this village is great.
3580. The death of the chief was a great *misfortune* for the village.
3581. He had the *misfortune* to get sick just at harvest time.
3582. He encountered a *mishap*.
3583. He *misled* me.
3584. He is a *misogynist*.
3585. His *misogyny* is great.
3586. He doesn't *miss* a chance.
3587. His arrow *missed* the bird.
3588. The rifle shot *missed*.
3589. He *misses* his youth.
3590. The string to that bow is *missing*.
3591. He accomplished his *mission* well.
3592. They gave him a difficult *mission*.
3593. He is a monk from the *mission*.
3594. He is a Catholic *missionary*.
3595. There is a blanket of *mist* on the river.
3596. That man has made a *mistake*.
3597. He made a *mistake*.
3598. Anyone can make a *mistake*.
3599. She *mistreats* her children.
3600. He who *mistreats* his houseboy is a bad boss.

3601. There is a slight *misunderstanding* between your brother and me.
3602. Their argument arose from a *misunderstanding*.
3603. They got *mixed up* in the fight.
3604. There are both men and women—it's a *mixed* gathering.
3605. It is a *mixed* marriage.
3606. In this region several peoples have *mixed* together.
3607. She is *mixing* water with the clay.
3608. I don't like the *mixture* of water and wine.
3609. She *moaned* all night long.
3610. The child is *moaning* with pain.
3611. That animal is very *mobile*.
3612. He can't stand *mockery*.
3613. He has a *mocking* nature.
3614. Draw your inspiration from that *model*.
3615. He *models* his behavior on that of the chief.
3616. He is *moderate* in his words and actions.
3617. He spoke with *moderation*.
3618. He is *modern*.
3619. Agriculture must be *modernized*.
3620. You are *modest*.
3621. *Modesty* is sometimes a fault.
3622. He has a sense of *modesty;* he is timid.
3623. That is not *modifiable*. (can't be modified)
3624. My experience made me *modify* my viewpoint.
3625. That is made of *mohair*.
3626. His eyes are *moist* with tears.
3627. After *moistening*, the clay becomes workable again.
3628. He has an aching *molar*.
3629. The potter is *molding* a pot.
3630. The blacksmith is making some *molds*.
3631. He caught some *mollusks* in the river.
3632. My *mom* left for the market.
3633. Where is your *mom*?
3634. He arrived at the very *moment* I was going to leave.
3635. He thought for a *moment* that you were angry with him.
3636. At this *moment* he is in the bush country.
3637. Wait; hold on for a *moment*.
3638. This situation is *momentary*.
3639. There are difficult *moments* in life.
3640. *Mommy*, give me some water.
3641. Our *monetary* unit is the franc.
3642. He earned a lot of *money*.
3643. They don't use *money;* they have a barter system.
3644. That child suffers from *mongolism*.
3645. The *mongoose* is an animal that kills reptiles.
3646. Among the (Mbay Kaba Gbaya ...) the men are *monogamous*.
3647. Your brother is *monogamous*.
3648. He gave a *monologue*.
3649. That is a *monologue*.
3650. He responds in *monosyllables*.
3651. He sings in a *monotone*.
3652. I don't like the *monotony* of his voice.
3653. He killed a child; he's a *monster*.
3654. He does not believe the storyteller's tales of *monsters*.
3655. That one-eyed hunchback is *monstrous*.
3656. There are 12 *months* in a year.
3657. It's a lovely *monument*.
3658. The child is in a good *mood*.
3659. He is *moody*.
3660. I don't like the *mooing* of the cows.
3661. The cow is *mooing*.
3662. I see the *moon*.
3663. I don't go out on *moonless* nights.
3664. There's a lovely *moonlight*.
3665. There is such lovely *moonlight*.
3666. The dugout broke free from its *moorings* and is drifting away.
3667. He married a *Moorish* woman.
3668. The *Moors* are Muslims.
3669. Their *moral standards* are not ours.
3670. I don't like the *moral* of that story.

3671. He has no *moral* sense; he sees no difference between good and evil.
3672. That isn't *moral*.
3673. He is a *moralist*.
3674. He is always *moralizing*.
3675. He has no *morals*.
3676. He has dissolute *morals*.
3677. His sister is *far more* courageous than his wife.
3678. What *more* do you need?
3679. The story is becoming *more* interesting.
3680. He could work *more*.
3681. I want some *more*.
3682. The *mores* (customs) of the Sara are different from those of the Gbaya.
3683. The *morgue* is next to the hospital.
3684. Every *morning* he goes to work the land.
3685. He worked all *morning* long.
3686. Venus is the *morning* star.
3687. The *morning* sun is not very hot.
3688. He has a *morose* character.
3689. All men are *mortal*.
3690. The *mortality rate* is high in this village.
3691. His *mortar* (bowl) got smashed.
3692. The mason bound the brick together with *mortar*.
3693. I'm going to get a *mosquito net*.
3694. The *mosquitoes* bit me.
3695. Some *moss* is growing on that tree.
3696. These stones are *mossy*.
3697. That's the *most* I can pay.
3698. He spends *most* of his time drinking.
3699. He sleeps *most* of the time.
3700. My clothes are *moth-eaten*.
3701. His *mother* has big feet.
3702. *Motherhood* did not bring her joy.
3703. She is *motherly* towards her husband.
3704. *Moths* are attracted by light.
3705. *Moths* have made holes in your clothes.
3706. An antelope is standing *motionless* next to the tree.
3707. He remained *motionless*.
3708. His *motorcycle* is broken down.
3709. He climbed onto the *mound* to see better.
3710. He doesn't know how to *mount* a horse.
3711. There is a *mound* of stones at the entrance to the village.
3712. There is a *mountain* to the north.
3713. It is a *mountainous* region.
3714. They live near the *mountains*.
3715. He is *mourning* the death of his father.
3716. The woman is in *mourning*.
3717. The *mouse* ate his clothes.
3718. He has a *moustache*.
3719. She is talking with her *mouth* full.
3720. He lives *from hand to mouth*.
3721. The crocodile opened its *mouth*.
3722. He opened his *mouth*.
3723. I won't *move* from here.
3724. *Move* the children *away* from the fire!
3725. If you don't *move*, I won't hurt you.
3726. Don't *move*.
3727. He *moved off* abruptly.
3728. He *moved* the table.
3729. He said he had seen a *movement* in the bushes.
3730. He made a sudden *movement*.
3731. He *moves* around a lot.
3732. You know how *much* I love her.
3733. He works half as *much* as you do.
3734. It is *much* later than I thought.
3735. The rice didn't yield *much* this year.
3736. He is not worth *much*.
3737. He always has *mucus* in his nose.
3738. After the rain, the path was a pool of *mud*.
3739. It was an unbelievable *muddle*.
3740. Despair had *muddled* his mind.
3741. The road is *muddy*.
3742. The cow came and rested its *muffle* on my arm.
3743. The noise is *muffled* and far away.

Sentence Questionnaire 361

3744. He is a *mule-driver*.
3745. That bird is *multicolored*.
3746. 28 is a *multiple* of 7.
3747. The *multiplication* of 8 by 2 gives 16.
3748. There was a *multitude* of people around the chief.
3749. Don't *mumble*; speak up.
3750. I can't understand what you are saying; you're *mumbling*.
3751. We will *mummify* his body.
3752. That is a *mummy*.
3753. You can hear him *munching* corn.
3754. There was a *murder* in the village last year.
3755. Someone *murdered* the village chief.
3756. The *murderer* has not been found.
3757. He is the *murderer*.
3758. I heard a *murmur*.
3759. What are they *murmuring*?
3760. Nobody dares move a *muscle* in front of him.
3761. He has big *muscles*.
3762. His legs are *muscular*.
3763. The so-called guinea fowl *mushroom*.
3764. Birdlime from *mushrooms*.
3765. My father doesn't want me to eat *mushrooms*.
3766. In that region there are a lot of *mushrooms*.
3767. That *music* is pretty.
3768. He is a *musician*.
3769. He is a *Muslim*.
3770. He found some big *mussels*.
3771. He is *mustached*.
3772. He is *mute*.
3773. I didn't understand what he *muttered*.
3774. I don't like your *muttering*.
3775. They made *mutual* concessions to each other.
3776. They have *mutual* trust (in each other).
3777. I sold *my* cow.
3778. That is *my* father.
3779. I broke *my* hoe.
3780. That is *my* knife.
3781. That is *my* mother.

3782. Come to *my* place.
3783. *My* wife died.
3784. *My* words are sound.
3785. Only the initiated know those *mysteries*.
3786. This business is quite *mysterious*.
3787. It is a *mystery*.
3788. He is *mystical*.
3789. That is only a *myth*.
3790. Sou (T, . . .) is a *mythical* hero.
3791. Their *mythology* speaks of many gods.
3792. I don't know their *mythology*.
3793. You can never believe what he says; he's a *mythomaniac*. (habitual exaggerator)
3794. He can tell us many *myths*.

N

3795. He is driving a *nail* into the plank with a hammer.
3796. Pull the skin tight so I can *nail* it down.
3797. I am not so *naive* as to believe that lie.
3798. He has a *naive* expression.
3799. She is completely *naive*.
3800. He seems *naive*.
3801. He is *naked* from the waist up.
3802. The accused man refused to *name* his accomplices.
3803. My *name* is Thomas.
3804. What is your *name*?
3805. You can't talk (reason) with him; he is *narrow-minded*.
3806. It was a *nasty* injury.
3807. He is *nasty*.
3808. It is my *native* country.
3809. He is a *native* of the village.
3810. He has a *natural* liking for music.
3811. His gestures are simple and *natural*.
3812. It's in the *nature* of things.
3813. That is against his *nature*.
3814. He has a violent *nature*.
3815. The child did some *naughty* things.
3816. Be quiet; you are *naughty*.

3817. He is *nauseated*. *(wants to vomit)*
3818. The sight of food makes him *nauseous*.
3819. He is *nearsighted*.
3820. The inside of the hut is *neat* and clean.
3821. It is *necessary* that we talk about it.
3822. We will do what is *necessary*.
3823. I accepted by *necessity* more than by choice.
3824. The *neck* of the gourd is chipped.
3825. He has a long *neck*.
3826. He threw his arms around her *neck*.
3827. He is in trouble up to his *neck*.
3828. She put on a *necklace* for dancing.
3829. The bees came to gather *nectar* in the area.
3830. There is no *need* to tell him.
3831. Take something to use if it's *needed*.
3832. Now he earns his living without *needing* anyone.
3833. Give me a *needle* to sew up my loin-cloth.
3834. His father *needs* him to go hunting.
3835. He *needs* money for the trip.
3836. His response was *negative*.
3837. The result of the investigations was *negative*.
3838. That woman *neglects* her children.
3839. He *neglects* his health.
3840. You must love your *neighbor* as yourself.
3841. The horse is *neighing*.
3842. He said *neither* yes *nor* no.
3843. His *nerves* are tense.
3844. The noise gets on his *nerves*.
3845. That gets on my *nerves*.
3846. Waiting makes him *nervous*.
3847. The bird fell from its *nest*.
3848. He catches birds in the *net*.
3849. The chief remained *neutral* in the quarrel.
3850. I will *never* be rich.
3851. I *never* saw him.
3852. I will *never* see you again.
3853. Better late than *never*.
3854. He is nice; *nevertheless* I don't get along with him.
3855. It's quite simple *nevertheless*.
3856. He put on some *new* clothes.
3857. He bought a *new* knife.
3858. The hut was done up like *new*.
3859. What's *new*?
3860. The chief has had *news* of him.
3861. The *news* spread throughout the whole village.
3862. Have you heard the *news*?
3863. He bought a *newspaper*.
3864. His hut is *right next to* ours (adjoining).
3865. I'm going to his place *next* week.
3866. The dog *nibbled* at my hand.
3867. He has no appetite; he just *nibbles*.
3868. The child is *nibbling* at his bread.
3869. This food is *nice*.
3870. It is *nice* to rest in the shade.
3871. The chief came the *night before*.
3872. *Night* is falling.
3873. It is *night*.
3874. I didn't sleep all *night*.
3875. He works at *night*.
3876. They came back at *nightfall*.
3877. The results were *nil*.
3878. The *nipple* of the mother's breast is sore because her child has been nursing a lot.
3879. That woman is *no longer* very young.
3880. *No* man came yesterday.
3881. I have *no* need of it.
3882. Do you want some? *no* thanks.
3883. I didn't say *no*.
3884. He is weak; he can't say *no*.
3885. Have you decided—yes or *no*?
3886. That woman's features are *noble* and regular.
3887. There was *nobody* in the hut.
3888. The chief made an affirmative *nod* of the head.
3889. In town the *noise* is unbearable.
3890. She walks *nonchalantly*.
3891. You are talking *nonsense*.

3892. He eats in the morning, at *noon,* and in the evening.
3893. I will come to see you at *noon.*
3894. It is *noon.*
3895. The situation has become *normal* again.
3896. He isn't his *normal* self.
3897. He went up the stream to the *north.*
3898. His *nose* is bleeding.
3899. He breathes through the *nose.*
3900. *Not* a chance! (*no* chance!)
3901. He can stay; he is *not* bothering me *at all.*
3902. That's *not* new.
3903. He has made *notable* progress.
3904. The child is proud of his new *notebook.*
3905. She likes rice; she'll eat *nothing* else.
3906. That has *nothing* to do with it.
3907. There is *nothing* to understand.
3908. Thank you very much.—It was *nothing.*
3909. The chief didn't *notice* his absence.
3910. I *notice* that you are not working.
3911. His infirmity is *noticeable.*
3912. The whole village was *notified* (knew about) of my arrival.
3913. Just a minute ago he was laughing but *now* he is crying.
3914. She *nudged* him with her elbow.
3915. Fatigue *numbed* her.
3916. I don't know their exact *number.*
3917. The enemy is superior in *numbers.*
3918. The woman *nurses* her child.
3919. The goat is *nursing* her kid.
3920. That food is *nutritious.*

O

3921. He uttered an *oath* (swear word).
3922. The chief has authority; he knows how to make people *obey.*
3923. If you see no *objection,* I will leave tomorrow.
3924. He makes *objects* from wood.
3925. You are under no *obligation* to leave.
3926. The chief sees that the customs are *observed.*
3927. She is *observing* her facial features.
3928. That is his *obsession.*
3929. The accused man *obstinately* persists in keeping silent.
3930. The foliage is *obstructing* the path.
3931. It is *obvious* that he is angry.
3932. The village people put on their finery for the *occasion.*
3933. She appears cheerful on all *occasions.*
3934. He asked the question on three *occasions.*
3935. He would need an *occupation* a trade.
3936. He is an *odd* man rather strange.
3937. It's an *odd* number.
3938. He is *odd.*
3939. They are at *odds.*
3940. His crime is *odious.*
3941. The spoon is made *of* wood.
3942. That music *offends* my ears.
3943. He took *offense* at the chief's words.
3944. The *offense* is punished by the law.
3945. He is *offensive* but doesn't realize it.
3946. The enemy has taken the *offensive.*
3947. He accepted the chief's *offer.*
3948. We *offered* him money in exchange for his services.
3949. He *offered* his congratulations to the chief.
3950. He *offered* me money.
3951. I (He) made *offerings* so that the sick man might recover.
3952. He *often* comes here.
3953. Stop *ogling* my wife.
3954. He extracted the *oil.*
3955. It is an *old* abandoned plantation.
3956. How *old* are you?
3957. It's an *old* custom.
3958. He rebuilt his *old* hut.

3959. He is an *old* man.
3960. They found the *old* village.
3961. She's an *old* woman.
3962. He is ten years *old*.
3963. My clothes are *old;* they are worn.
3964. My *older* brother went to Damara.
3965. That is my *older* brother.
3966. That is my *older* sister.
3967. It is my *oldest* daughter.
3968. The *oldest* of the children came.
3969. The *oldest* of the girls led them into the forest.
3970. It is my *oldest* son.
3971. It's a bad *omen*.
3972. Sit down *on it*.
3973. His hat is *on* his head.
3974. He kept *on* the defensive.
3975. She set the cooking pot *on* the fire.
3976. He stretched out *on* the mat.
3977. He comes here *once* a month.
3978. Don't all speak at *once*.
3979. That isn't the *one* I lent you.
3980. Come forward *one* by *one*.
3981. He is the *one* who broke the pot.
3982. That's the chief's *only* concern.
3983. It's the *only* solution.
3984. Water is *oozing* down the wall.
3985. The wound is *oozing*.
3986. He received his friend with *open* arms.
3987. The chief spoke with an *open* heart.
3988. He cut *open* his skull in falling. (when he fell)
3989. He sailed on the *open* sea.
3990. The door is wide *open*.
3991. The plant *opened out* its flowers.
3992. We *opened up* a path through the bush.
3993. The bird *opened* its beak.
3994. The chief *opened* the discussion.
3995. This year a new school *opened*.
3996. He made an *opening* in the forest.
3997. The *opening* of the hut is too small.
3998. He is *opening* the box.
3999. This key *opens* the door to the hut.
4000. The chief has a bad *opinion* of him.
4001. Our *opinions* are divergent.
4002. The chief is categorically *opposed* to it.
4003. He passed by on the *opposite* bank.
4004. The two men had *opposite* opinions.
4005. Just the *opposite!*
4006. He is gathering *opposition*.
4007. He lives in luxury and *opulence*.
4008. Give it to me right away *or* else you will be punished.
4009. It's all *or* nothing.
4010. The chief is a persuasive *orator*.
4011. You must work *in order to* live.
4012. I *order* you to be quiet.
4013. The hut is in *order*.
4014. Let's proceed in *order*.
4015. He doesn't like to be *ordered* around.
4016. She *ordered* him to leave.
4017. He didn't do what the chief *ordered*.
4018. He obeyed the chief's *orders*.
4019. That is iron *ore*.
4020. He has a mind for *organization*.
4021. He loses a lot of time; he doesn't know how to *organize* himself.
4022. He is of French *origin*.
4023. The cloth has lost its *original* color.
4024. His ideas are *original*.
4025. He is *orphaned* of both his mother and father.
4026. He's not the one who hit me; the *other* one did.
4027. He has no *other* clothing.
4028. Some went fishing, *others* went to the village.
4029. You must not steal from *others*.
4030. He doesn't know how to do *otherwise* (any other way).
4031. Your ideas are not always the same as *ours*.
4032. The patient is *out* of danger.

4033. That is *out* of the ordinary.
4034. The fish jumped *out* of the water.
4035. He threw it *out*.
4036. Each tried to *outdo* the other in shouting.
4037. He *outlived* all his children.
4038. He has avenged the *outrage*.
4039. The *outside* of the house is dirty.
4040. You can go put it *outside*.
4041. He arrived at the *outskirts* of the village.
4042. That assassination was an *outstanding* event.
4043. He *overcame* his adversary.
4044. He *overcame* his fear.
4045. The sky is *overcast* (covered) with clouds.
4046. He is *overcome* with jealousy.
4047. The river *overflowed* its banks.
4048. The water has *overflowed* the vase.
4049. The hill *overlooks* the river. (towers over)
4050. He has an *overnight* case for traveling.
4051. He changed his mind *overnight*.
4052. The cloud *overshadowed* the sun.
4053. She was *overwhelmed* when she heard the news.
4054. He is *overwhelmed* with work.
4055. He is *overworked*.
4056. He *owes* me some money.
4057. The *owl* hoots.
4058. The *owl* is a nocturnal bird.
4059. I heard him with my *own* ears.
4060. He sold everything he *owned*.
4061. The *owner* decided to close the factory.
4062. I saw a flock of wild *oxen*.
4063. He suffocated from lack of *oxygen*.
4064. He is gathering *oysters*.

P

4065. Justice should make *peace* reign.
4066. He works at an amazing *pace*.
4067. He *paced back and forth* in front of the building.
4068. He has a *pack* of dogs.
4069. The *package* arrived by mail.
4070. The ground is *packed down* in that spot.
4071. He *packed* down the tobacco in the pipe.
4072. He *paddles* forcefully.
4073. I lost the key to the *padlock*.
4074. This book has a hundred *pages*.
4075. The chief *paid* me.
4076. *Pain* made him yell out.
4077. It is *painful* for me to see him sick.
4078. She put some *paint* on her face.
4079. He is *painting* the cloth blue.
4080. That child has some *paints*.
4081. Those two birds form a *pair*.
4082. He clicked his tongue against his *palate*.
4083. It is dawn and the light is *pale*.
4084. The *palm* of his hand is round.
4085. She *pampers* her children.
4086. One *pane* of the window is broken.
4087. He was *panic-stricken* when he saw the buffaloes.
4088. The army was overcome with *panic*.
4089. The buffaloes *panicked*.
4090. Running makes him *pant*.
4091. His *pants* are too big for him.
4092. The *paper* is all crumpled.
4093. He had an attack of *paralysis*.
4094. Fear *paralyzes* him.
4095. This *parcel* is badly tied up.
4096. He gave him *pardon* for his debts.
4097. The condemned man was *pardoned*.
4098. He lost his *parents;* he is an orphan.
4099. The whole village takes *part* in the festival.
4100. The handle is a *part* of a basket.
4101. He is *part* of the family.
4102. His hair is divided by a *part*.
4103. He *parted* with his money.
4104. The village invited him to *participate* in the festival.

4105. The man is making a *partition* in the house.
4106. He doesn't have a *pass*.
4107. During the rainy season the roads are not *passable*.
4108. The traditions are *passed down* from father to son.
4109. The chief *passed on* his power to him.
4110. He *passed* me.
4111. The traveler only *passed* through the village.
4112. Time *passes* quickly.
4113. The storm is *passing*.
4114. He has a *passion* for travel.
4115. What is the *password*?
4116. Let's forget the *past* and make peace.
4117. *In the past* everyone stayed in the village.
4118. There's a lot of water on the *path*.
4119. *Patience!* This is a bad time to go on.
4120. She cannot be *patient*.
4121. He is very *patriotic;* he loves his country.
4122. She drew *patterns* on her daughter's head.
4123. The animal wounded its *paw*.
4124. He is a *pawnbroker*.
4125. Leave me in *peace*.
4126. He is *peaceful* by nature.
4127. He is sleeping *peacefully*.
4128. The child is sleeping *peacefully*.
4129. He liked the *peacefulness* of the area.
4130. He likes eating *peanuts*, peanut cake and peanut sauce.
4131. They are pulling up *peanuts*.
4132. She is crushing the *peanuts*.
4133. You can see round *pebbles* at the bottom of the stream.
4134. The hens *pecked* at each other (with the beak).
4135. The chickens *pecked* at the grain.
4136. The birds are *pecking* in the courtyard of the village.
4137. He is a *peculiar* fellow.
4138. He let go of the *pedals* of the bicycle.
4139. The *pedlar* arrived in the village. (colporteur)
4140. She *peeled* the beans.
4141. She threw out the fruit *peels*.
4142. The *penalty* imposed by the chief is just.
4143. The chief has *penetrated* his secret.
4144. The *people's* traditions are disappearing.
4145. The ministers are elected by the *people*.
4146. *Pepper* is ground into powder.
4147. She is *perceptive*.
4148. A bird is *perched* on the branch of the tree.
4149. The bird is *perching* on the branch.
4150. *Perhaps* he will come tomorrow.
4151. The excursion was *perilous*.
4152. The festival *period* has begun.
4153. His fever returns *periodically*.
4154. Meat is a *perishable* food.
4155. The chief *perished* in the war.
4156. That rock is *permeable;* it absorbs water.
4157. That is not *permitted;* it's forbidden.
4158. He works with *perseverance*.
4159. The odor is *persistent*.
4160. The pain is *persisting* despite the treatment.
4161. He is an old *person*.
4162. That man has a strong *personality*.
4163. He *persuaded* me to leave with him.
4164. That man is *perverse;* he loves to do harm.
4165. Religion is *perverted* by superstition.
4166. He bothers everyone with his *pet fad*.
4167. It is a *pet*.
4168. They are collecting signatures for a *petition*.
4169. The children *petted* the animal.
4170. She has a pretty *petticoat* (slip).

4171. His *pettiness* shows itself in continual reproaches. (meanness)
4172. His attitude is very *petty*. (He has a *mean* attitude.)
4173. His strength is *phenomenal*.
4174. His *physical* strength is very great.
4175. He has declined a great deal *physically*.
4176. The child is *picking up* pebbles.
4177. She is *picking* fruit.
4178. She is *picking* her teeth.
4179. She made a pagne from a *piece* of material.
4180. Give me a *piece* of meat.
4181. It is a *piece* of pottery.
4182. The chief gave him a five franc *piece*.
4183. The plank is *pierced* by several holes.
4184. He *pierced* his ears to put rings in.
4185. The child let out a *piercing* cry.
4186. They killed a *pig*.
4187. There are some black *pigs*.
4188. We *pile* the wood in front of the house.
4189. *Pile* up the grasses in a heap behind the hut.
4190. There was a traffic *pile-up* on the highway.
4191. He put the sweepings in a *pile*.
4192. Thieves came to *pilfer* in the fields of the village.
4193. We don't leave the chickens outside at night to avoid *pilfering*.
4194. The soldiers *pillaged* the town.
4195. He is *piloting* the boat as far as the port.
4196. She has a *pimple* on her nose.
4197. *Pin* down the skin.
4198. He *pinched* himself in closing the door.
4199. The crab *pinched* his finger.
4200. I found some *pineapples* in the bush.
4201. He planted a field of *pineapples*.
4202. He lost a *pipe* cleaner.
4203. The chief shot the *pistol*.
4204. The engine's *piston* is broken.
4205. This fruit has a big *pit*.
4206. They buried the corpse in a *pit*.
4207. The poor man is *pitiable*.
4208. She let out some *pitiful* cries.
4209. The hut is in a *pitiful* state.
4210. The chief had *pity* on him.
4211. For *pity's* sake! Let me sleep.
4212. He *pivoted*, making a half-turn.
4213. The feast took *place* in the neighboring village.
4214. What *place* is he going to?
4215. A basket took the *place* of a hat for him.
4216. He stayed in the same *place*.
4217. It's a large *place*. They found a large *place* to hold the meeting.
4218. She *placed* the pot on the hearth.
4219. His worries *plague* him.
4220. The village was hit by the *plague*.
4221. The explanation was *plain* and clear.
4222. The *plain* is grassy.
4223. That's the *plain* truth.
4224. He is drawing the *plan* of the house.
4225. His *plan* was carried out.
4226. The sun is one of the seven *planets*.
4227. The chief's *plans* were carried out.
4228. He is a rich *plantation* owner.
4229. Beside the village there is a large *banana plantation*.
4230. The storm ruined the *plantations*.
4231. He is *planting* vegetables.
4232. Trees are *plants*.
4233. He is uprooting the *plants*.
4234. He broke his *plate*.
4235. The village is situated on a *plateau*.
4236. Go clean the *plates*.
4237. His explanation is *plausible*.
4238. There is some *play* in the head of that spear.
4239. You made a *play* on words.
4240. He can *play* the harp.
4241. The children are at *play*.
4242. He *played* (the part of) the victim.
4243. He *played* a dirty trick on me.
4244. Which *player* won?

4245. He is an unlucky *player*.
4246. He is a harp *player*.
4247. He is *playing* dead.
4248. The children are *playing* war.
4249. He is *playing* with his dog.
4250. The chief is *pleading* the accused man's cause.
4251. This village is *pleasant*.
4252. He did that to *please* me.
4253. He tries to *please* the chief.
4254. She only seeks to *please*.
4255. He is *pleased* with him.
4256. He only does as he *pleases*.
4257. That gives me great *pleasure*.
4258. That child has a *pliable* nature.
4259. Clay is *pliable*.
4260. The men *plodded on* slowly through the forest.
4261. The *plot* of this story is complicated.
4262. I have nothing to do with the *plot*.
4263. They *plotted* to kill me.
4264. He has an old *plow*.
4265. He *plowed* his field.
4266. It is *plowing* time.
4267. We *pluck* poultry before cooking it.
4268. He *plunged* his head into the water.
4269. The dugout canoe *plunged* into the water.
4270. He caught cold and got *pneumonia*.
4271. His *pockets* are full of holes.
4272. She is taking the vegetables out of their *pod*.
4273. He is a great *poet*.
4274. They have this *point* in common.
4275. He is still at the same *point* in it.
4276. The chief shares my *point* of view.
4277. He stared at a *point* on the horizon.
4278. He is attaching a *point* to the spear.
4279. He has a *pointed* nose.
4280. He *pointed* out the way to him.
4281. The spear is *pointed*.
4282. The *poison* killed him.
4283. He put *poison* on the arrows.
4284. The child is suffering from food *poisoning*.
4285. The *police* keep order.
4286. The criminal is being sought by the *police*.
4287. The stone is *polished* and it shines.
4288. He is *polishing* his shoes.
4289. You must be *polite* to older people.
4290. He is a *political* prisoner.
4291. The *political* situation is critical.
4292. Tolerance is necessary in *politics*.
4293. In that direction there is a *pond* in the middle of the brush.
4294. He speaks *poor* French.
4295. The millet harvest was *poor* this year.
4296. The village is *poor*.
4297. His health is very *poor*.
4298. The soil here is *poor;* nothing grows in it.
4299. The millet is growing *poorly* this year.
4300. The cork *popped* out.
4301. The chief is very *popular*.
4302. The area has a small *population*.
4303. The boat is leaving *port*.
4304. The *porter* took the bags.
4305. He ate his *portion* of meat.
4306. He received his *portion* of the inheritance.
4307. The painter did a *portrait* of the chief.
4308. This matter *poses* some grave problems.
4309. The chief is in a bad *position*.
4310. He is in a sitting *position*.
4311. His response was *positive*.
4312. He *is* not *in full possession* of his faculties.
4313. Keep it in your *possession*.
4314. There are only two *possibilities*.
4315. It is *possible* that it will rain.
4316. That's not *possible!*
4317. Come as soon as *possible*.
4318. Come tomorrow if *possible*.
4319. He left his *post* (job).
4320. The *post* office is open.

4321. The roof is held up by *posts*.
4322. She's boiling water in the *cooking pot*.
4323. He makes *pottery* in the kiln.
4324. *Pour* me some wine.
4325. She *poured out* the water from the basin.
4326. He had a scornful *pout* on his face.
4327. He is *pouting*.
4328. We are *poverty-stricken*.
4329. He is putting *powder* into the cannon.
4330. The sugar is in *powder*.
4331. The chief's *power* is limitless.
4332. The *power* of God is infinite.
4333. That isn't within my *power*.
4334. He is a *powerful* person.
4335. The army is *powerful*; it will defeat the enemy.
4336. We are *powerless* in the face of death.
4337. The chief has a long *practical experience* in sailing.
4338. He has a *practical* understanding of it.
4339. That tool is *practical*.
4340. The cobbler *practices* his trade well.
4341. Customs are made up of a set of *practices*.
4342. The faithful observe the religious *practices*.
4343. He has a *pragmatic* mind.
4344. He *praised* him for his work.
4345. He sang the *praises* of the chief.
4346. The faithful say their *prayers*.
4347. He *prays* for the dead.
4348. The priest *preaches* the gospel.
4349. He is in a *precarious* situation.
4350. We took all possible *precautions* against an accident.
4351. Time is *precious*; it must not be wasted.
4352. These jewels are *precious*; they are worth a lot.
4353. The chief gave him *precise* directions.
4354. He is a *precocious* child for his age.
4355. Do as you *prefer* however you like best.
4356. I have no *preference*; it doesn't matter to me.
4357. Her numerous *pregnancies* wore her out.
4358. That woman is *pregnant*.
4359. He got her *pregnant*.
4360. That idea *preoccupies* and torments him.
4361. She *prepared* a delicious dish.
4362. The chief is *preparing* a military operation.
4363. The village is *preparing* for the festival.
4364. The woman is *preparing* the meal.
4365. The doctor *prescribed* a remedy for the sick man.
4366. He did that in my *presence*.
4367. The *present* chief is very good.
4368. Heaven *preserve* me!
4369. It is difficult to *preserve* meat here.
4370. He *pressed* his finger into the manioc paste.
4371. The atmospheric *pressure* is high.
4372. The chief decided under the *pressure* of events.
4373. The title of chief gives *prestige*.
4374. He is *pretending* to be sad.
4375. That girl is *pretty*.
4376. That cloth is *pretty*.
4377. The law makes peace and order *prevail*.
4378. He *prevented* him from fleeing.
4379. *Previously* they grew sorghum here; now they only grow manioc.
4380. He is *prey* to jealousy.
4381. The vulture is a bird of *prey*.
4382. He paid a high *price* for his success.
4383. What is the *price* of this cloth?
4384. The dog *pricked up* its ears.
4385. His attitude is full of *pride*.
4386. The *priest* celebrates mass.
4387. The millet (manioc) crop is of *primary* importance to us.
4388. He died in the *prime* of life.
4389. He is a person without *principles*.
4390. The thief was put into *prison*.

4391. May I speak to you in *private?*
4392. The chief abuses his *privileges.*
4393. It is hardly *probable* that he'll come.
4394. The *problem* has several solutions.
4395. There is a *problem* in this matter.
4396. The *problem* was badly stated.
4397. The prisoner *proclaimed* his innocence.
4398. The accused man *proclaims* his innocence.
4399. He is a child *prodigy;* he's very precocious.
4400. This land does not *produce.*
4401. This palm tree *produces* beautiful fruit.
4402. That tree *produces* fruit.
4403. The *production* of manioc has slowed down.
4404. He chose the military *profession.*
4405. He is *making good progress* in his work; he can rest a bit.
4406. The student is not making any *progress.*
4407. The work has begun and is in *progress.*
4408. The *projectile* hit him on the head.
4409. This breed is *prolific.*
4410. The chief kept his *promise.*
4411. The chief *promised* to help him.
4412. You are forgetting your *promises.*
4413. His answer *prompted* me to think that he is innocent.
4414. He *pronounces* certain words badly.
4415. That *proof* is not convincing.
4416. That plant has medicinal *properties.*
4417. This hut is my *property.*
4418. That family is rich; they have *property.*
4419. The hut is of generous *proportions.*
4420. The chief's *proposal* was rejected.
4421. He *propped up* the foot of his seat.
4422. The industry is in full *prosperity.* (is prospering greatly)
4423. He *prostrates* himself before God.
4424. My God *protect* you.
4425. The chief took him under his *protection.*
4426. He took on a *protective* tone.
4427. The roof *protects* us from the rain.
4428. Don't *protest!*
4429. He *protested* indignantly against that accusation.
4430. This man is *proud* of his strength.
4431. That doesn't *prove* anything.
4432. They *proved* his innocence.
4433. They *proved* that he was lying.
4434. That remains to be *proven.*
4435. Divine *providence* is unfathomable.
4436. That event was *providential.*
4437. The chief *provides* them with food.
4438. It's a *provisional* agreement.
4439. Don't *provoke* me.
4440. He *provoked* the chief's anger.
4441. The animal is *prowling* near the village.
4442. He is *pruning* the palm trees.
4443. It is a *public* meeting; anyone can come.
4444. Her hair *puffed out* around her head.
4445. He *puffed out* his chest for the photographer.
4446. He *puffed* out his chest.
4447. The man calmly took several *puffs* on his pipe.
4448. He has a *pug* nose.
4449. They are going to *pull* up the manioc.
4450. He *pulled out* a jigger (boring insect).
4451. She *pulled the leaves off* the branches.
4452. He *pulled* out the vines surrounding the tree.
4453. He *pulled* the door *to* behind him.
4454. He *pulled* up the stumps.
4455. He is *pulling* on the rope.
4456. The *pulp* (flesh) of the fruit is tender.
4457. His *pulse* is rapid and he has a fever.

Sentence Questionnaire

4458. He is stopping at the gasoline *pump*.
4459. *Pumpkin seed 1328.* He cut the *pumpkin* in the middle.
4460. They gather *pumpkin* leaves.
4461. He cut the stalk of the *pumpkin*.
4462. God *punished* him.
4463. The child was *punished*.
4464. The chief *punishes* the lazy ones.
4465. He laughed at his *puns*.
4466. It is a *puny* tree.
4467. He makes *puppets*.
4468. The water is *pure* and clear.
4469. His intentions are *pure*.
4470. He *purified* the water for drinking.
4471. What is the *purpose* of your visit?
4472. He did it *on purpose*.
4473. He is being *pursued* by his creditors.
4474. *Pus* has formed in the wound.
4475. *Push* that plate up to me.
4476. He *pushed* the door with his foot.
4477. He *put on* a hat which suits him well.
4478. He *put out* the fire.
4479. Evidence was *put together* against the accused man.
4480. He *put up* (erected) a house.
4481. He *put* a stamp on the envelope.
4482. I'm going to *put* him *up*.
4483. They *put* his eyes *out*.
4484. He *put* his hat on his head.
4485. *Put* my advice into practice.
4486. *Put* that on the ground.
4487. *Put* that thing *back* in its place.
4488. *Put* the mangoes into your basket.
4489. I *put* the net into the dugout.
4490. She *put* the pestle (pounding stick) next to the pot.
4491. They *put* their money together.
4492. *Put* this trap *up* on the tree.
4493. He *put* together some branches to make a stretcher.
4494. Don't *put* yourself out.
4495. He *puts* hunting before everything else.
4496. She is *putting* the spoon into her mouth.
4497. He ran away from the *python*.

Q

4498. The men spread out a net to catch *quail*.
4499. The chief has many good *qualities*.
4500. The merchandise is of good *quality*.
4501. There is a little *quarrel* (spat) between them.
4502. Don't pick a *quarrel* with me.
4503. The chief calmed the *quarrel*.
4504. Come back in a *quarter* of an hour.
4505. The moon is in its first *quarter*.
4506. He *quenched* his thirst.
4507. The *question* is complex and it's difficult to respond to.
4508. It's a *question* of life and death.
4509. The chief *questioned* him about his intentions.
4510. He will *quibble* over anything; he is a *quibbler*.
4511. Get away *quick*!
4512. He is a *quick-tempered* child.
4513. His mind is *quick*; he understands quickly.
4514. The chief spoke *quickly*.
4515. Watch out for *quicksand*.
4516. He is *quiet* by nature.
4517. It was a *quiet* evening.
4518. He has a *quiet* spirit.
4519. He walks with a *quiet* step.
4520. *Be quiet!*
4521. She made the children be *quiet*.
4522. The chief is *quiet*; he doesn't talk much.
4523. The blacksmith has *quite a bit* of money.
4524. I think he's *quite* young for that.
4525. She is weaving a *quiver*.
4526. The water is *quivering*; it's going to boil.

R

4527. It is a *rabbit*.
4528. The children are making a lot of *racket*.

4529. His smile is *radiant*.
4530. Her skirt is worn out; it's nothing but a *rag*.
4531. These clothes are in *rags*.
4532. He is dressed in *rags*.
4533. The *rain* is falling in torrents.
4534. Before the end of the tornado the *rainbow* appeared.
4535. A *rainbow* surrounding the sun is rare.
4536. It's *raining* in torrents.
4537. The *rainy* season is beginning.
4538. The weather is *rainy*.
4539. He *raised* his arm.
4540. He *raised* his head.
4541. The antelope *raised* its head.
4542. He *raised* the horn to his lips.
4543. They *raised* the workers' pay.
4544. They are *rallying* around the chief.
4545. The *ram* led the flock toward the river.
4546. He *ran away* yesterday.
4547. He *ran off*.
4548. He *ran up* and jumped.
4549. The children *ran* up (here).
4550. The village people *ran* up in a crowd to see him.
4551. The oil is *rancid*.
4552. He walks with a *rapid* pace.
4553. The *rapids* are dangerous.
4554. This plant is *rare*.
4555. The brush *rat* ran off.
4556. It is *rather* hot.
4557. The chief distributes the *rations*.
4558. The dying man gave the death *rattle*.
4559. Rain *ravaged* the harvest.
4560. A torrent runs at the bottom of the *ravine*.
4561. The meat is *raw*.
4562. The sun's *rays* are warming.
4563. The *razor* cuts very well.
4564. I could not *reach* him. (get in contact with him)
4565. He keeps his gun within *reach*.
4566. He *reached* old age without ever being sick.
4567. They *reached* the river.
4568. The dugout (canoe) *reached* the shore.
4569. The chief had an angry *reaction*.
4570. He cannot *read*.
4571. At school children learn how to *read*.
4572. He is *reading* a book.
4573. The meal is *ready*.
4574. That's a *real* and incontestable fact.
4575. His story doesn't square with *reality*.
4576. He has *really* changed a lot.
4577. He is *really* dead.
4578. You *really* want me to leave.
4579. The horse *reared up* when he approached.
4580. He has good *reason* to complain.
4581. That is not a *reason*.
4582. They fought without any *reason*.
4583. Be *reasonable;* don't demand the impossible.
4584. His *reasoning* is unassailable.
4585. He *rebelled* against the chief's authority.
4586. I don't *recall* any more.
4587. She *recalled* the memory of him.
4588. He *received* a package in the mail.
4589. The chief *received* him in his hut.
4590. By my *reckoning* he will arrive tomorrow.
4591. I *recognized* him by his voice.
4592. The chief *recommended* that he be moderate.
4593. The chief could not *reconcile* the adversaries.
4594. The two enemies were *reconciled*.
4595. Time lost cannot be *recovered*.
4596. The ashes are still *red*.
4597. His sickness *reduced* him to doing nothing.
4598. He *reduced* the length of the arrow.
4599. The wood burned and was *reduced* to ashes.
4600. He is playing the *reed pipe*.
4601. His face is *reflected* in the water of the river.

4602. He saw his *reflection* in the water of the river.
4603. On *reflection* I won't leave today.
4604. The chief *reformed* the laws.
4605. The chief took *refuge* in silence.
4606. He *refuses* to acknowledge his wrongs.
4607. There's no *refuting* that argument.
4608. He *regained* his health.
4609. The sick man is *regaining* his strength.
4610. He *regards* others with scorn.
4611. This *region* is particularly dry.
4612. He has traveled over the whole *region*.
4613. He left the village with *regret*.
4614. He *regrets* having come.
4615. His breathing is *regular*.
4616. He visits the chief *regularly*.
4617. The *regulations* make provision for obedience to the chief.
4618. This dish is cold; we will have to *reheat* it.
4619. The man *reinforced* the wall of his hut.
4620. He has a good *relationship* with the chief.
4621. Those two events have no *relationship*.
4622. The chief ordered the *release* of the prisoners.
4623. He *released* the animal caught in the trap.
4624. The prisoner was *released*.
4625. He went well out of sight to *relieve* himself.
4626. The medicines *relieved* his pain.
4627. He *relieved* the porter of his burden.
4628. He *relives* the past with his memories.
4629. The *remedy* cured the sick man.
4630. I *remember* him.
4631. *Remember* and don't forget.
4632. He *remembers* everything you tell him.
4633. He *removed* the leaves from the tree.
4634. He *removed* the stool.
4635. He *renewed* his request to the chief.
4636. He *rented* a motor-scooter.
4637. The doctor *reopened* the wound.
4638. The cobbler *repairs* shoes.
4639. They always *repeat* the same mistakes.
4640. He *repeated* his story several times.
4641. The chief gave a negative *reply*.
4642. He made a *representation* of his plan by drawing it on the sand.
4643. He is *repressing* his anger.
4644. I don't *reproach* him for anything.
4645. His look is full of *reproach*.
4646. The chief *reproached* him for his conduct.
4647. This account *reproduces* the facts. (is *faithful* to the facts)
4648. The army *repulsed* the invaders.
4649. The enemy was *repulsed*.
4650. He lost his *reputation* of being wise.
4651. He has a bad *reputation*.
4652. This work *requires* a lot of attention.
4653. That child *resembles* his father.
4654. The chief has *reservations* about his plan.
4655. The chief stayed on the *reserve*.
4656. The chief is *reserved* in his remarks.
4657. He has great *reserves* of energy.
4658. He *resigned* himself to staying in the village.
4659. He has a very great *resistance* to fatigue.
4660. He is putting up an obstinate *resistance* to the chief's proposals.
4661. These colors are water- *resistant*.
4662. He *resisted* the disease well.
4663. I've made my *resolution*.
4664. The tom-tom is very *resonant*.
4665. I *respect* that man.
4666. He works without *respite*.
4667. He spent the *rest* of his money.
4668. The animal is at *rest*.
4669. The chief doesn't have time to *rest*.

4670. The sick man is *restless* with fever.
4671. The doctor's treatment *restored* the chief to health.
4672. The medicine *restored* the strength to the patient.
4673. He is trying to *restrain* his anger.
4674. *Restrain* your anger.
4675. He is *restraining* his anger.
4676. The chief got some excellent *results*.
4677. The chief *retired* to his hut.
4678. Peace and quiet have *returned* after the festival.
4679. The chief *returned* his money to him.
4680. He *returned* to the village.
4681. We *revived* the wounded man.
4682. The tribe *revolted* against the chief.
4683. The meal was *revolting*.
4684. The earth *revolves* around the sun.
4685. The chief promised a *reward*.
4686. His efforts were *rewarded*.
4687. The music has a quick *rhythm*.
4688. The women are dancing in *rhythm*.
4689. He was so thin that you could count his *ribs*.
4690. Only the *rich* can borrow.
4691. The subsoil is *rich* in ore.
4692. He got *rid* of his clothes.
4693. He is making himself an object of *ridicule*.
4694. His hat makes him look *ridiculous*.
4695. He took his *rifle* to go hunting.
4696. He is loading the *rifle* with powder.
4697. He *put right* his wrongs.
4698. He is at the village *right* now.
4699. You're not putting it on the *right* side.
4700. You are *right*.
4701. She took the *ring* and put it on her finger.
4702. His ears are *ringing*.
4703. She put on her arm and leg *rings* to go dancing.
4704. She has *rings* under her eyes.
4705. This fruit is not *ripe*.
4706. Let that fruit *ripen*.
4707. The child *ripped* his clothing.
4708. The temperature is on the *rise*.
4709. The smoke is *rising* straight into the sky.
4710. It rained a lot and the river is *rising*.
4711. The temperature is *rising*.
4712. He isn't *risking* anything.
4713. This undertaking is full of *risks*.
4714. He performed the funeral *rites*.
4715. The two *rivals* are in conflict.
4716. He went down the *river* by boat.
4717. The *river* is swollen.
4718. A *river* waters this region.
4719. The *riverbank* is very high at this point.
4720. The *riverbed* is dry.
4721. The *road* is narrow.
4722. The traveler took to the *road*.
4723. The beast *roared*.
4724. He *roasted* the antelope.
4725. She's *roasting* some corn.
4726. I was *robbed* of all my money.
4727. He is between a *rock* and a *hard place*.
4728. This *rock* is hard.
4729. The wave *rocked* the boat.
4730. She *rocks* her child in her arms.
4731. It is a *rocky* path.
4732. He *rolled* the fish in the flour.
4733. The ball is *rolling*.
4734. The *roof* of the hut is made of wood.
4735. The table takes up a lot of *room*.
4736. The house consists of several *rooms*.
4737. The crowing of the *rooster* announces dawn.
4738. He was *rooted to the spot* by it.
4739. The tree's *roots* are deep.
4740. He put the *rope* around his neck.
4741. The animal *rose up* on its hind legs.
4742. The weather today is *rotten*.
4743. His teeth are *rotten*.
4744. The egg is *rotten;* you shouldn't eat it.

4745. The water of the river is *rough* (choppy).
4746. He is very *rough* with his family.
4747. It's *rough* work.
4748. The thief was *roughed up* by the crowd.
4749. Your son has a *round* face (with big cheeks).
4750. He has gone *round* the world.
4751. Straighten up; you're getting *round-shouldered* (hunchbacked).
4752. The people gathered *round*.
4753. The sun is *round*.
4754. He took the longest *route* there.
4755. He took a *roundabout route* to get here.
4756. He is taking a strange *route*.
4757. There's going to be quite a *row*.
4758. These three huts form a *row*.
4759. He is *rowing* toward the shore.
4760. The *rubber* is made to solidify. They make the rubber coagulate.
4761. He has a *rubber* plantation.
4762. He tapped the *rubber* vine.
4763. She is *rubbing* her child to warm him up.
4764. There is a pile of *rubbish* behind his hut.
4765. You are talking *rubbish*.
4766. His wife is *rude;* she receives (welcomes) his friends badly.
4767. He shook out the *rug*.
4768. The rain *ruined* my shoes.
4769. The rain *ruined* the crops.
4770. The chief is *ruining* his health working.
4771. The hut is in *ruins*.
4772. Ten years ago Europeans were the *rulers* of this country.
4773. The *rules* of courtesy should be respected.
4774. He observes the *rules* scrupulously.
4775. The thunder is *rumbling*.
4776. The cow is *ruminating* (chewing the cud).
4777. The *rumor* of his death spread quickly.
4778. He had *rumors* of the affair.
4779. He is eating the chicken's *rump*.
4780. Her skirt is *rumpled*.
4781. *Run* after him *run* quickly; he's going to get away.
4782. He is *running* a great danger.
4783. His nose is *running*.
4784. Blow your nose; it's *runny*.
4785. The airplane landed on the *runway*.
4786. We mustn't *rush* it.
4787. The army *rushed* at the enemy.
4788. *Rust* attacks iron.

S

4789. They *sacrificed* some animals to the gods.
4790. His thoughts are *sad*.
4791. He rides horseback without a *saddle*.
4792. He put his money in a *safe* place.
4793. All danger is gone; he is in *safety*.
4794. The boat has a large *sail*.
4795. The boat *sailed* away.
4796. He is a good *sailor*.
4797. He got his *salary*.
4798. She sprinkled the meat with *salt*.
4799. This food is too *salty*.
4800. It amounts to the *same thing*.
4801. They have the *same* character.
4802. They are of the *same* opinion.
4803. It is always the *same* people who do the work.
4804. He says the *same* stupid things every day.
4805. We are from the *same* village.
4806. The doctor took a blood *sample* from him.
4807. The boat ran aground on a *sand* bank.
4808. The boat *sank*.
4809. The tree is full of *sap*.
4810. He ate to *satiation*.
4811. The chief gave him *satisfaction*.
4812. It *satisfied* his curiosity.
4813. He *satisfied* his hunger.
4814. I am *satisfied* with my lot.
4815. The sponge is *saturated* with water.
4816. This cloth is *saturated* with water.

4817. Tomorrow is *Saturday*.
4818. The meat *sauce* is liquid.
4819. She put a *saucepan* on the fire.
4820. He looks *savage* and brutal.
4821. The *savannah* is full of animals.
4822. The sick man has been *saved*.
4823. He is *saving* himself for the end.
4824. I *saw* myself in the mirror.
4825. I *saw* right through you.
4826. The carpenter *sawed* wood.
4827. The *sea* breeze is cool.
4828. They left to go fish in the *sea*.
4829. The man affixed a *seal* (stamp) to the paper.
4830. The men *sealed up* the hold in the canoe.
4831. He *sealed* the envelope.
4832. We abandoned the *search* for the culprit.
4833. It's a *seaside* town.
4834. The rainy *season* is here.
4835. That plant makes a good *seasoning*.
4836. The *seat* is low.
4837. That is the *seat* of the disease.
4838. They found out the *secret* of the matter.
4839. The chief let me in on the *secret*.
4840. The matter is *secret*; no one knows about it.
4841. Bees *secrete* honey.
4842. He is *secretive*.
4843. That man is *secretive*; he says little.
4844. He *seduced* a woman.
4845. The chief came to *see* me yesterday.
4846. Go *see* what happened.
4847. I don't *see* what it is all about.
4848. The child can't *see*; he's blind.
4849. The plant went to *seed*.
4850. The lemon is a fruit with *seeds*. (pips)
4851. It *seems* pointless to me to tell that to the chief.
4852. The meal *seems* to be sufficient.
4853. Water is *seeping* out.
4854. He is *seething* with impatience.
4855. He lacks *self-confidence*.
4856. He is a *self-seeking* man.
4857. The merchant *sells* fruit at a high price.
4858. He feels a burning *sensation*.
4859. What he says makes no *sense*.
4860. His hope is *senseless*.
4861. The chief brought him back to his *senses*.
4862. His decision is *sensible*.
4863. The chief's hearing is *sensitive*.
4864. He *sent* the child home.
4865. The *sentence* (punishment) was severe.
4866. He passed an equitable *sentence*.
4867. He is *sentimental*.
4868. The river *separates* the two countries.
4869. A *series* of catastrophes happened.
4870. It is a *serious* moment.
4871. He is *serious*; he doesn't joke around.
4872. He takes everything *seriously*.
4873. The *servant boy* is making the meal.
4874. The knife *serves* to cut up the meat.
4875. He did the chief a *service*.
4876. He is a *serviceman* (in the military).
4877. He *set up* a fishing camp.
4878. You should have *set* about it beforehand.
4879. Someone *set* fire to his hut.
4880. He *set* his dog to chase after me.
4881. He *set* the date of his departure.
4882. They *set* the prisoner free.
4883. A conflict has *set* the two villages *against* each other.
4884. He suffered a *setback*.
4885. It's a lovely *setting* (for jewelry etc.).
4886. That's a magnificent *setting* (for the jewel).
4887. The question was *settled* after a long discussion.
4888. He *settled* down comfortably to eat.
4889. We got him *settled* in his new quarters.
4890. He *settled* in the region.

4891. Dust *settled* on the furniture.
4892. The chief has *settled* the quarrel.
4893. I *settled* up with him.
4894. A week has *seven* days.
4895. That happened *several* times.
4896. The judge proved *severe*.
4897. The punishment is *severe*.
4898. She is *sewing* two pieces of cloth together.
4899. He is *shabbily* dressed.
4900. The boys built themselves a *shack*.
4901. The trees give *shade*.
4902. He cast a *shadow* on the wall.
4903. The *shaft* of the pipe is clogged.
4904. Hoe *shafts* (handles) are made of wood.
4905. She is *shaking* the blanket.
4906. The child is *shaking* with fever.
4907. That's a *shame!*
4908. She felt *shame*.
4909. They lowered their eyes in *shame*.
4910. These two dugouts have the same *shape*.
4911. My *share* is not big enough.
4912. The hunters *shared* the game.
4913. He has a *sharp* eye.
4914. The knife is well *sharpened*.
4915. He is *sharpening* his knife.
4916. I am *sharpening* the knife.
4917. I was completely *shattered* by it.
4918. The cooking pot *shattered*.
4919. His chin is *shaven*.
4920. He bought a *she-mule*.
4921. It is *shea nut* oil.
4922. She ground the *shea nuts*.
4923. He is near the *shea* tree.
4924. A lot of blood was *shed* during the war.
4925. The widow *shed* many tears.
4926. He is building a *shed*.
4927. During the *shedding season* that animal has a lot of fur.
4928. The snake *sheds* its skin.
4929. A flock of *sheep* is arriving.
4930. The man goes into the *sheepfold*.
4931. He suspended a *shelf* from the hut.
4932. He broke the *shell* to eat the egg.
4933. The tortoise went back (withdrew) into its *shell*.
4934. He withdrew into his *shell*.
4935. The chick came out of its *shell*.
4936. She *shelled* the beans.
4937. The man *shelled* the millet.
4938. He gathers *shellfish* in the river.
4939. He found *shelter* from the sun.
4940. He is building a *shelter* in the bush for the wine harvest.
4941. He built a *shelter* in the forest.
4942. Let's make a *shelter* quickly.
4943. They are weaving *shields*.
4944. The sun *shines* brightly.
4945. The cat *shines* its fur by licking it.
4946. I see the first ray of sunlight *shining*.
4947. Her hair is *shiny*.
4948. The boat was *shipwrecked*.
4949. The man's *shirt* suits him well.
4950. She is washing her *shirt*.
4951. He bought a *short-sleeved shirt*.
4952. He cried *"shit!"*
4953. The cold makes you *shiver*.
4954. The child is *shivering* with cold.
4955. The news gave him a *shock*.
4956. His ways *shocked* the whole village.
4957. The *shoemender* resoles shoes.
4958. Wait for me; I'm *putting* my *shoes on*.
4959. He bought some (leather) *shoes* in town.
4960. The animal *shook* its tail.
4961. He *shook* the bottle.
4962. The storm *shook* the houses.
4963. It is a *shooting* (throbbing) pain.
4964. He practiced *shooting* the bow.
4965. There are many *shopkeepers* in town.
4966. He is *short* in stature.
4967. He has *short* legs.
4968. She has a *short* memory.
4969. May I have a *short* moment with you?
4970. This village is *short* of meat.
4971. She is *short-tempered;* she gets annoyed easily.
4972. His hair is cut *short*.

4973. We are one chicken *short*. *Where is it?*
4974. *Shorten* your speech.
4975. He *shortened* his hair.
4976. He should arrive very *shortly*.
4977. The hunters *shot* down five buffaloes.
4978. He *shot* the rifle.
4979. A *shot* went off.
4980. The man *should* leave tomorrow.
4981. He has broad *shoulders*.
4982. He *shouted* for joy.
4983. He can't talk without *shouting*.
4984. He *shoved* me.
4985. *Show* him how to use a rifle.
4986. *Show* him the path to the village.
4987. *Show* me your rifle.
4988. He is a *show-off*.
4989. It is a throwing knife for *show*.
4990. He *showed himself* a good student at school.
4991. When he laughs he *shows* his beautiful teeth.
4992. His wife is a *shrew*.
4993. She is a real *shrew*.
4994. He is too *shrewd* to be easily fooled.
4995. The boy is very *shrewd*.
4996. He won't *shrink back* for anything.
4997. They wrapped him in a *shroud*.
4998. He *shut* him *up* in the hut.
4999. He *shut* the door.
5000. *Shut* your eyes.
5001. Since she became pregnant she has *sick feelings*.
5002. There are a lot of *sick people* in that village.
5003. I'm as *sick* as a dog.
5004. My father is *sick*.
5005. He is a *sickly* child.
5006. That child is thin and *sickly*.
5007. My son has a weak constitution; he is *sickly*.
5008. The two companions walked *side by side*.
5009. He walked by the *side* of the river.
5010. He lives on the other *side* of the village.
5011. He slept on his *side*.
5012. He lay down on his *side*.
5013. The chief *sided* for peace.
5014. He drew designs on the *sides* of his canoe.
5015. She is shaking the *sieve*.
5016. The flour passed through the *sieve*.
5017. The flour is *sifted*.
5018. He let out a *sigh* of relief.
5019. My *sight* is failing; I see worse and worse.
5020. The *sight* of blood upsets me.
5021. I hear the panther but it is staying out of *sight*.
5022. He indicated in *sign language* (by gesticulations) that he didn't want to come.
5023. That's a bad *sign*.
5024. *Signal* them with your hand.
5025. He shows *signs* of fatigue.
5026. Be *silent!* Keep quiet!
5027. The *silhouette* of the tree is reflected in the river.
5028. How *silly* he is!
5029. The *silt* near the river is fertile.
5030. The river water is *silt-laden*.
5031. Let the meat *simmer* in the pot a while longer.
5032. He made a *simple* knot.
5033. She has a *simple* smile.
5034. Every *sin* can be forgiven.
5035. It has been five years *since* he left.
5036. *Since* when have you been there?
5037. The repentance of the guilty man is *sincere*.
5038. The birds *sing* very early.
5039. He doesn't have a *singleness* of purpose.
5040. He *sings* well.
5041. That man has a *sinister* look.
5042. He confessed his *sins*.
5043. His *sister* is younger than he.
5044. *Sit* on my right and you sit on my left.
5045. The bird *sits on* its eggs to make them hatch.
5046. He is *sitting* on the chair.
5047. My financial *situation* is prosperous.

5048. The chief is examining the *situation*.
5049. This field is of a large *size*.
5050. She *skewered* the fish.
5051. He works with great *skill*.
5052. He is *skillful* with his hands.
5053. He *skimps* on everything he buys.
5054. She is taking the *skin* off the animal.
5055. He is working the buffalo *skin*.
5056. She *skinned* the animal.
5057. He *skinned* the buffalo.
5058. His *skinniness* is frightful.
5059. Your horse is *skinny*; he doesn't have enough to eat.
5060. She has a red *skirt*.
5061. She *skirted around* the hut.
5062. A stone broke his *skull*.
5063. The *sky* is overcast.
5064. The stars are twinkling in the *sky*.
5065. The rope is *slack*.
5066. She left *slamming* the door.
5067. You have *slandered* me.
5068. Your wife is a *slanderer*. (scandalmonger)
5069. He is *slandering* us.
5070. He gave a *slanderous* speech.
5071. The roof is on a *slant*.
5072. The chief gave him a friendly *slap*.
5073. She gave him a *slap*.
5074. The warriors *slaughtered* their enemies.
5075. He is a *slave* to his passions.
5076. He treats him like a *slave*.
5077. He drove in a stake with a *sledgehammer*.
5078. Let's *sleep* on it.
5079. Elephants *sleep* standing up.
5080. The mother *put* the child *to sleep*.
5081. He slept a deep *sleep*.
5082. He has *sleeping sickness*.
5083. He *sleeps* poorly.
5084. The *sleeves* of his shirt are too short.
5085. She cut the meat into *slices*.
5086. There is a *slight* difference between those two colors.
5087. At the *slightest* movement I'll kill you.
5088. That young woman is *slim*.
5089. He is repairing the *sling* of the rifle.
5090. He has a *slingshot*.
5091. That was a *slip* of the tongue.
5092. The knife *slipped out* of his hands.
5093. That *slipped* my mind.
5094. His foot *slipped*.
5095. The child is *slobbering*.
5096. He went halfway up the *slope*.
5097. The path descends in a gentle *slope*.
5098. The road *slopes* at a gentle angle.
5099. His dress is *slovenly*. (sloppy)
5100. He is *slow-witted*.
5101. He is *slow*.
5102. His watch is five minutes *slow*.
5103. He approached the lion *slowly*.
5104. His *slowness* exasperates me.
5105. I stepped on a *slug*.
5106. The man left with his rifle *slung over his shoulder*.
5107. He left his wife *on the sly*.
5108. He only brought back *small game*.
5109. He has *small* feet.
5110. Smoke makes the eyes *smart*.
5111. He *smashed up* the inside of the hut.
5112. The bowl fell and *smashed* to pieces.
5113. The children are all *smeared*.
5114. The *smell* is bad.
5115. These flowers *smell* strong.
5116. That *smells* like meat.
5117. The closets are *smelly* (foul-smelling).
5118. He always has a *smile* on his face.
5119. The child is *smiling*.
5120. The fire is giving off *smoke* (making smoke).
5121. The fire filled the hut with *smoke*.
5122. The woman is preparing *smoked* meat.
5123. He is *smoking* the meat.
5124. The man is *smoking* tobacco.
5125. That pottery is quite *smooth*.

5126. The surface of the lake was calm and *smooth*.
5127. He *smoothed* out the floor of the hut.
5128. The potter *smoothed* out the inside of the pot.
5129. It is the potter's *smoothing-tool*.
5130. That *snake* is poisonous.
5131. He knows how to *snap* his fingers.
5132. The dog *snapped* up the meat.
5133. He set up a *snare* for the hares. (noose to catch hares)
5134. The child *sneezed*.
5135. The animal *sniffed* at its food.
5136. He *snores* every night.
5137. The horse *snorted*.
5138. You can't eat *so* much without getting sick.
5139. The forest is *so* big that you can get lost.
5140. Go get me a stick *so* that I can beat the rug.
5141. It is *so*.
5142. The healer let the leaves *soak* in the water.
5143. My clothes got *soaked* in the rain.
5144. She *soaked* the laundry in water.
5145. The wood *soaked* up the water.
5146. He is *sober*.
5147. The child broke into *sobs*. (burst into tears)
5148. He has a very *sociable* nature.
5149. He is very *sociable*.
5150. Clay is *soft*.
5151. Her skin is *soft*.
5152. Wax is *soft*.
5153. He kneaded the skin to *soften* it.
5154. The skin is well *softened* now.
5155. He is *softening*; he will give in soon.
5156. He walked *softly* so as not to make any noise.
5157. The *soil* is fertile at that place.
5158. The *soil* is poor.
5159. He *soiled* his clothes.
5160. He has a *solemn* face.
5161. The cobbler is repairing the *soles* of the shoes.
5162. He *solicited* a favor from the chief.
5163. That jewelry is *solid* gold.
5164. He isn't fat but he's *solidly* built.
5165. He leads a *solitary* life.
5166. The chief needs *solitude*.
5167. The problem has no *solution*.
5168. *Some* stayed in the village but others left.
5169. I waited for him for *some* time.
5170. I'm looking for *something* else just as beautiful.
5171. He had *something* to do with this affair.
5172. I'm afraid *something* will happen to him.
5173. He comes here *sometimes*.
5174. You're making too much noise; go play *somewhere else*.
5175. If I do not want to stay here I shall go *somewhere* else.
5176. He ran away *somewhere* but I don't know where.
5177. She has a *son* and a daughter.
5178. That *song* is very lovely.
5179. He knows many *songs*.
5180. The chief's laugh is *sonorous*.
5181. *As soon as* the one moved forward the other moved back.
5182. They will come back *soon*.
5183. He arrived *sooner* than I thought.
5184. The *sorcerer* was killed.
5185. The fetishist caught the *sorcerer*.
5186. One man's joy is another man's *sorrow*.
5187. I am very *sorry* about his misfortune.
5188. I don't feel *sorry* for him; he deserved his punishment.
5189. We heard the *sound* of a rifle shot.
5190. I heard the *sound* of an elephant.
5191. You can barely hear the *sound* of his voice.
5192. He said some *sound* things.
5193. Don't make a *sound*.
5194. The chief's health is *sound*.
5195. The child is sleeping *soundly*.
5196. We all appreciate the *soundness* of his advice.
5197. The pot *sounds* hollow.
5198. The wine is *sour*.

5199. God is the *source* of the universe.
5200. He traveled up the river to its *source*.
5201. The ground has been plowed and *sown*.
5202. We are short of *space*.
5203. He calls a *spade* a spade.
5204. He cut into the earth with a *spade*.
5205. He doesn't have much *spare time* during the millet harvest.
5206. They *spared* the prisoner's life.
5207. A *spark* started the fire.
5208. Joy *sparkled* in her eyes.
5209. I like the *sparkling* of the water.
5210. The water is *sparkling*.
5211. The sun is *sparkling*.
5212. The corn is *sparse*.
5213. *Speak* clearly; I can't understand you.
5214. They have not been on *speaking terms* for a long time.
5215. He *speaks* French fluently.
5216. The *spear's* point has been sharpened.
5217. He lost his *spear*.
5218. This animal is from a different *species*.
5219. He *sped* up his running pace.
5220. The car is losing *speed*.
5221. He left at full *speed*.
5222. The sorcerer cast a *spell*.
5223. It is a fetish designed to ward off evil *spells*.
5224. He *spends* his time sleeping.
5225. I *spent* all my money.
5226. The chief *spent* the day at the river.
5227. They *spent* the night in the forest since they could not get back to the village before dusk.
5228. The fly is caught in a *spider* web.
5229. He caught a big *spider*; it might be a mygale.
5230. *Trap door spiders* are spiders that live in holes.
5231. The hunter *spied on* the animal.
5232. He *spilled* some water on the ground.
5233. Wine makes his head *spin*.
5234. That man has a curved *spine*.
5235. He is *spineless;* anyone can order him around.
5236. The *spinelessness* of that man is insufferable.
5237. She is *spinning* cotton.
5238. He is dead; his *spirit* has gone.
5239. Men have a *spirit*.
5240. The horse is *spirited*.
5241. Here's where he leaves offerings to the *spirits* of his ancestors.
5242. He calls up the *spirits* of the ancestors.
5243. He stuck the *spit* (pin) into the animal's body to cook it.
5244. He *spit* in his face.
5245. In *spite* of the drought the harvest will be good.
5246. He acted out of *spite* for the pleasure of harming us.
5247. He spoke *spitefully* to him.
5248. She is coughing and *spitting* blood.
5249. The fruit was *spoiled* by the moisture.
5250. The meat is *spoiled*.
5251. Fallen fruit *spoils*.
5252. She is making a *spool* of cotton.
5253. He eats with a *spoon*.
5254. He works *sporadically*.
5255. The thief was caught on the *spot*.
5256. The panther has black *spots*.
5257. The wood of the bow *sprang back*.
5258. He *spread* (open) his legs.
5259. The news *spread around* the village.
5260. The bird *spread out* its wings to fly.
5261. He *spread out* the manioc in the sun.
5262. She *spread out* the mat on the ground.
5263. The smell of smoke *spread* through the hut.
5264. The news *spread* throughout the village.
5265. The news *spread*.
5266. He is going to draw water from the *spring*.

5267. She *sprinkled* water on me.
5268. The corn is *sprouting*.
5269. The blood was *spurting* out from his wound.
5270. He works in *spurts*.
5271. I am all *square* (with him); I don't owe him anything more.
5272. He has *square* shoulders.
5273. His account doesn't *square* with the facts.
5274. The hut is *square*.
5275. Don't *squat* near the door.
5276. The birds are *squawking*.
5277. She is *squeezing* the fruit to extract the juice.
5278. He is *squinting*.
5279. He *stabbed* with his spear.
5280. This metal is *stable*.
5281. She *stacked* (up) some wood.
5282. Water *stagnates* in the pond.
5283. He *stained* his clothes.
5284. Her dress is *stained* with mud.
5285. His pagne is covered with *stains*.
5286. He was still *stammering* from anger.
5287. He *stamped* his foot on the ground.
5288. *Stand up* straight.
5289. The cold makes the animal's hair *stand* on end.
5290. *Stand* the bottle up(right).
5291. He is so sleepy that he can hardly *stand* up any more.
5292. *Stand* up!
5293. The *standard* of living has risen.
5294. He *stands* by what he said yesterday.
5295. The sky is sprinkled with *stars*.
5296. We have to *start* all *over*.
5297. They *started* a brush fire.
5298. I *started* here.
5299. It's *starting* to rain.
5300. They are not of the same *station* (social condition).
5301. He stood straight as a *statue*.
5302. The chief is tall of *stature*.
5303. He made a brief *stay* at the village.
5304. He is *staying* in front of the hut without moving.
5305. The water is boiling; *steam* is rising from the (sauce) pan.
5306. The river flows between *steep* banks.
5307. The banks of the river are *steep*.
5308. He *steered* the dugout toward the south.
5309. The *stem* is growing high.
5310. He *stemmed* (stopped up) the flow of blood.
5311. *Step forward;* don't be afraid.
5312. The child won't *step* away from his mother for a moment.
5313. The chief took a *step* forward.
5314. He *stepped* on my foot.
5315. You (have to) climb three *steps* to enter his hut.
5316. He retraced his *steps* when he came upon the wild beast.
5317. She took little *steps*.
5318. She is *sterile*.
5319. The *stick* broke.
5320. He cut a reed walking *stick*.
5321. She hit him with a *stick*.
5322. The *stickiness* in the air is unpleasant.
5323. His skin is *sticky* with sweat.
5324. He seems *stiff* (starchy).
5325. The corpse is *stiff*.
5326. He is *still* alive.
5327. The child can't keep *still*.
5328. She had a *stillborn* child.
5329. He is weak and needs to be *stimulated*.
5330. Wine *stimulates* him.
5331. Pull the bee's *stinger* out of my arm.
5332. He is not liked because of his *stinginess*.
5333. This wound *stings* a lot.
5334. Smoke *stings* the eyes.
5335. He has always been *stingy*.
5336. The meat has spoiled and it *stinks*.
5337. We'll have to *stir up* the fire that went out.
5338. She *stirred* the batter.
5339. The leaves *stirred*.
5340. She took the *stitches* out of the material.

5341. Put his feet in the *stocks*.
5342. She felt a pain in the *stomach* (*guts*).
5343. He is going on an *empty stomach*.
5344. She has an empty *stomach*.
5345. He sleeps on his *stomach*.
5346. The child has a *stomachache*.
5347. His heart is as hard as *stone*.
5348. He is rubbing a flint *stone*.
5349. They *stoned* the guilty man.
5350. He can throw *stones* a long way.
5351. He *stood up* to see better.
5352. He *stood up*.
5353. His hair *stood* up on his head.
5354. He *stooped down* to enter the forest.
5355. The traveler made a *stop* at the village.
5356. *Stop* here.
5357. He *stopped* (arrested) the thief.
5358. His nose is *stopped up*.
5359. The work *stopped* at noon. (They stopped work at noon.)
5360. He *stopped* at the village to sleep.
5361. He *stopped* working when I arrived.
5362. The boat *stopped*.
5363. We can go out now; the rain has *stopped*.
5364. The man put a *stopper* on the bottle.
5365. The chief never *stops* praising him.
5366. I bought this plastic bowl at the sub-prefecture *store*.
5367. Nobody knows what the future holds in *store*.
5368. *Stork*
5369. A *storm* is menacing.
5370. A *storm* is taking shape; the sky is growing dark.
5371. His speech created a *storm*.
5372. The sky is *stormy*.
5373. He is the best *storyteller* in the village.
5374. He sat *straddling* the log.
5375. He is *straddling* the tree trunk.
5376. *Straighten* up the things in the hut.
5377. The financial situation was *straightened out*.
5378. The chief *straightened* out the situation.
5379. He is twisting the *strands* of the rope.
5380. He looks *strange*.
5381. He is a *stranger;* he's not from the village.
5382. He *strangled* him with a rope.
5383. The carrying *strap* is made of leather.
5384. He threatened his child with a *strap*.
5385. He made a whip from a leather *strap*.
5386. He is covering his roof with *straw*.
5387. She is weaving a basket out of *straw*.
5388. He *strayed* from the path.
5389. The *stream* is almost dry.
5390. The *street* is busy.
5391. He is walking in the *streets*.
5392. He has a lot of *strength*.
5393. *Stretch* out on the bed.
5394. He *stretched* (out) his legs.
5395. He *stretched out* the net to catch the prey.
5396. He *stretched* out his legs under the table.
5397. The ground was *strewn* with pottery fragments. (shards)
5398. The regulation is *strict*.
5399. She took long *strides*.
5400. He tightened (braced) the *string* of his bow.
5401. He made a lovely plantation on this *strip* of land.
5402. The animal's skin is *striped*.
5403. He *stripped* me of everything.
5404. He *stripped* the scales off the fish.
5405. He had a *stroke* of genius.
5406. He died of a *stroke*.
5407. He is a *strong* supporter of the revolt.
5408. There is a *strong* wind blowing.
5409. This man is big and *strong*.
5410. He *struck up* a friendship with my brother. He *made* friends with my brother.
5411. Lightning *struck*.

5412. The *struggle* with our neighbors has lasted for ten years now.
5413. He *struggled* like a madman.
5414. They burned the *stubble*.
5415. You can't convince him; he's *stubborn*.
5416. He is really *stubborn*.
5417. He is *stubborn;* he always answers no.
5418. The fever is *stubborn;* we can't get rid of it.
5419. I *stuck to* my opinion.
5420. He *stuck* a piece of wood into the ground.
5421. He got *stuck* in the mud.
5422. He *stuck* the spear (assegai) into the ground.
5423. In spite of our protests he *stuck* to his order.
5424. That *stuck* to my hand.
5425. My foot is *stuck*.
5426. He *stuffed* his hands in his pockets.
5427. He *stumbled* against a stone.
5428. The *stump* of his amputated arm hurts.
5429. He is burning the *stump* of the tree.
5430. She was *stung* by a scorpion.
5431. The chief told him some *stupid things*.
5432. Stop acting *stupid!*
5433. He is *stupid*.
5434. His *stupidity* is unmatched.
5435. He is *sturdily* built.
5436. He *stutters;* I have trouble understanding him.
5437. That dress is *stylish*.
5438. One must *submit* to the laws.
5439. His anger *subsided*.
5440. Oil is a fatty *substance*.
5441. The son *succeeded* his father as blacksmith.
5442. He *succeeded* in climbing to the top of the palm tree.
5443. The prisoner *succeeded* in escaping.
5444. His plan *succeeded*.
5445. He *succumbed* to his injuries and died.
5446. I have never had *such* a fright.
5447. I am *sucking* a lemon.
5448. He felt a *sudden* pain.
5449. The *sudden* return of the rain surprised us.
5450. She learned the news *suddenly*.
5451. He died *suddenly*.
5452. His injury causes him great *suffering*.
5453. That's a necessary and *sufficient* condition.
5454. The smoke is *suffocating* me.
5455. The heat is *suffocating* me.
5456. The chief *suggested* that he go fishing.
5457. That is the *suggested* way to do it.
5458. These clothes do not *suit* you very well.
5459. This road is *suitable* for cars.
5460. He chose the *suitable* moment to ask him for money.
5461. He can't keep from *sulking*.
5462. He is in a *sullen* mood.
5463. He was *summoned* before the court.
5464. The *sun* faded this cloth.
5465. The *sun* is rising.
5466. The *sunlight* is blinding.
5467. The *sunlight* is dazzling me.
5468. He starts work at *sunrise*.
5469. The wound is *superficial*.
5470. It is *superfluous* to insist.
5471. The animal's body is *supple*.
5472. He *supplied* himself with provisions for three days.
5473. He laid up a *supply* of water.
5474. The beams *support* the roof.
5475. The chief is *suppressing* his anger.
5476. It is *sure* and certain.
5477. He made *sure* that no one was there before going in.
5478. That is *surely* the nicest boy in the village.
5479. He is a *surly* man but *nice*.
5480. The enemy attacked by *surprise*.
5481. That news *surprised* him.
5482. He *surprised* me from behind.
5483. The forest *surrounds* the village.
5484. We *suspect* him of being the thief.

Sentence Questionnaire 385

5485. Our *suspicions* were confirmed; he is the guilty one.
5486. Those are *swaddling clothes* (bands).
5487. He *swallowed* a raw egg whole.
5488. He was so hungry that he *swallowed* everything at once.
5489. He was quiet and *swallowed* his anger.
5490. The man *swallowed* it down the wrong way.
5491. He *swam* across the river.
5492. There are crocodiles in the *swamps*.
5493. It is better to avoid going that way because the land is *swampy*.
5494. The bees are *swarming*.
5495. The heat makes him *sweat*.
5496. The woman is *sweeping* the inside of the hut.
5497. There is a pile of *sweepings* (trash) near the village.
5498. The *sweepings* are thrown behind the hut.
5499. Honey is *sweet*.
5500. The river is *swelling*.
5501. She *swept* under the bed.
5502. He *swims* like a fish.
5503. He has an irritating face. He has the sort of face that just asks to be *swiped*.
5504. The wind is raising *swirls* of dust.
5505. His face is *swollen up* from being punched.
5506. His eyes are *swollen* from lack of sleep.
5507. Her eyes were *swollen* with tears.
5508. His lips are *swollen*.
5509. He *swore* all day long!
5510. He *swore* he would never start over.
5511. He *swore* that he told the truth.
5512. The monkey *swung* across the path.
5513. The doctor injected the liquid with a *syringe*.

T

5514. The *table* is made of wood.
5515. She put the cooking pot on the *table*.
5516. The elephant's *tail* is long.
5517. He fell on his *tailbone*.
5518. The heat *taints* meat.
5519. I *take back* what I said.
5520. The doctor made him *take* a remedy.
5521. *Take* it away!
5522. *Take* the knife *out* of his hands.
5523. The fire went out; it won't *take*.
5524. The table *takes up* a lot of room in the hut.
5525. This work *takes* all my time.
5526. She *takes* her wishes for reality. (She indulges in wishful thinking.)
5527. It *takes* him all his strength to speak.
5528. He is *taking* the bones *out* of the fish.
5529. His *talk* is offensive.
5530. He is very *talkative*.
5531. He is *talkative*.
5532. They *talked* a lot about the village chief.
5533. He *tamed* the animal.
5534. She *tangled up* the string.
5535. The hide is *tanned*.
5536. The child is throwing a *tantrum*.
5537. He aimed poorly and missed the *target*.
5538. The fruit has an acid *taste*.
5539. He only *tasted* (sampled) his vegetables.
5540. This food is *tasteless*.
5541. They have the same *tastes*.
5542. He swallowed without *tasting*.
5543. His clothes are in *tatters*.
5544. He had his stomach *tattooed*.
5545. His chest is covered with *tattoos*.
5546. The rope is *taut*.
5547. We pay *taxes*.
5548. He *teaches* the children to read.
5549. He is *teaching* him to trap animals.

5550. *Tears* ran down his cheeks.
5551. The child was all in *tears*.
5552. The baby antelopes suck at their mother's *teats*.
5553. A sow has twelve *teats*.
5554. The *teeth* are growing.
5555. You bite with your *teeth*.
5556. *Tell* it to me.
5557. Go *tell* the doctor quickly.
5558. The chief is (re) *telling* a story.
5559. Don't leave without *telling* me.
5560. In the evening my father *tells* stories.
5561. That man always *tells* the truth.
5562. He has a sullen *temperament*.
5563. He has a *temperamental* nature.
5564. He is *temperate*; he drinks little.
5565. The *temperature* has fallen and it is colder.
5566. The doctor took the patient's *temperature*.
5567. He is bad*tempered*.
5568. That trip *tempts* me a great deal. (is very tempting)
5569. He has a *tendency* to be lazy.
5570. He has a *tendency* to exaggerate.
5571. He has a *tender* heart.
5572. The meat is *tender*.
5573. *Tense* up your muscles.
5574. The features of his face are *tense*.
5575. He *tensed* up the features of his face.
5576. His muscles are *tensed*.
5577. He is on good *terms* with the chief.
5578. They are on good *terms*.
5579. He speaks of the chief in respectful *terms*.
5580. The heat is *terrible* today.
5581. The drought is *terrible*.
5582. He has a *terrific* appetite.
5583. The army is defending the *territory* of . . . .
5584. He is dumb with *terror*.
5585. He *tested* his courage.
5586. He told him "*thank* you."
5587. The chief *thanked* him for his gift.
5588. It is a *thankless* job.
5589. Take *that one; this one* isn't any good.
5590. *That* isn't important.
5591. *That* makes him bad-tempered.
5592. Are you coming with me? Where is *that* to?
5593. I don't like *that* woman.
5594. Look at *that!* Isn't *that* what you were looking for?
5595. *That's* the man who told me.
5596. Take *that*.
5597. I'm tired of all *that*.
5598. What's *that?* It's a dugout canoe.
5599. *The* blacksmith is my friend.
5600. *The* mother died this morning.
5601. He was convicted of *theft*.
5602. All *their* children died.
5603. *Their* dugouts are in bad shape.
5604. Our son is tall, but *theirs* is short.
5605. Give *them* (for various objects) to me.
5606. I told *them* not to come any more.
5607. Come to see me again tomorrow; between now and *then* I'll think about your problem.
5608. He arrived, and *then* he left again.
5609. Go up on the hill; from *there* you will see the river.
5610. From *up there* you will see what they are doing.
5611. Do not stay here; go *there*.
5612. Don't stay here; go *over there*.
5613. Let's go *there*.
5614. Is your brother *there?*
5615. It is *therefore* a mongoose.
5616. The *thermometer* measures temperature.
5617. *These* children are unbearable.
5618. *They* are eating.
5619. She has *thick* lips.
5620. He is *thick-lipped*.
5621. The batter is *thick*.
5622. Her hair is *thick*.
5623. The clouds *thickened*.
5624. The darkness is *thickening*.
5625. The liquid *thickens* when heated.
5626. The *thief* was captured.
5627. It is as big as my *thigh*.
5628. The old man has *thin* hair.
5629. The mat is very *thin*.

Sentence Questionnaire

5630. The chief gave some*thing* to each one.
5631. It's not a *thing* to talk about.
5632. The chief laughs at the slightest *thing*.
5633. Tidy your *things*.
5634. Those are my *things*.
5635. I can't *think of* his name.
5636. Leave me some time to *think* about it.
5637. That question makes you *think*.
5638. I am *thirsty*.
5639. Give me *this*.
5640. We laughed *thoroughly*.
5641. He lost his train of *thought*.
5642. His face had a *thoughtful* expression.
5643. That tree is more than a *thousand years* old.
5644. It is a herd of a *thousand* cows.
5645. That costs a *thousand* francs.
5646. The stars shone by the *thousand* in the sky.
5647. This village has five *thousand* inhabitants.
5648. The one *thousandth* inhabitant of the village was just born.
5649. The cloth is *threadbare*.
5650. She is weaving the *threads*.
5651. He *threatened* to beat them.
5652. They *threatened* us.
5653. He spoke to me in a *threatening* tone.
5654. I'm not afraid of his *threats*.
5655. He *threw* a bone to his dog.
5656. His horse *threw* him to the ground.
5657. He *threw* himself at my knees.
5658. I *threw* out my old pants.
5659. He *threw* rocks at me.
5660. He *threw* stones at my dog.
5661. Plants *thrive* in this climate.
5662. I've got a sore *throat*.
5663. The dog leapt at his *throat*.
5664. The pain *went through* his stomach.
5665. She looked out *through* the window.
5666. It is a *throwing* weapon.
5667. The child is sucking his *thumb*.
5668. He gave him a friendly *thump*.
5669. A peal of *thunder* rang out.
5670. It's *thundering*.
5671. Let it remain *thus*.
5672. The weather *thwarted* our plans.
5673. Don't *tickle* me.
5674. That *tickles*.
5675. The *flood tide* arrives very quickly here.
5676. The water will not rise very high because the *tide* is weak right now. (neap tide)
5677. You must be careful not to be carried away by the *ebb tide*.
5678. She is *tidying up* the inside of the hut.
5679. You must *tie* the baggage down well in the car.
5680. *Tie* your shoelaces.
5681. I *tied up* his hands with a rope.
5682. The goat is *tied* to the post.
5683. He broke his *ties*. *(with them)*
5684. These pants are too *tight* for me.
5685. His clothes are *tight*.
5686. These clothes are *tight*.
5687. He *tilted* his head.
5688. The *timbre* of his voice is pleasant.
5689. We have all the *time* in the world.
5690. He came at the *time* of my marriage.
5691. He found that *time* passed slowly.
5692. It's *time* to go to bed.
5693. This work can be finished *in no time*.
5694. It happened just at the wrong *time*.
5695. They arrived at the same *time*.
5696. I don't have *time*.
5697. He took a *timely* step.
5698. He is *timid;* he can't make a decision.
5699. They set fire to the *tinder*.
5700. He threatened me with a *tiny* knife.
5701. He cut the meat into *tiny* pieces.
5702. He broke the *tip* of the wood.
5703. The child stood up on *tiptoe*.
5704. The bicycle *tire* is punctured.

5705. That walk *tired* him *out*.
5706. He *tired* himself out working.
5707. He *tired* his horse out.
5708. He never *gets tired* of singing.
5709. I'm dead *tired*.
5710. He feels *tired*.
5711. The chief is a *tireless* walker. (untiring)
5712. The heat makes the work *tiresome*.
5713. It is ten minutes *to* (before) seven.
5714. I really want *to* (do it).
5715. I am going *to* Damara.
5716. He gave medicine *to* him.
5717. He gave meat *to* the dog.
5718. They went *to* the hunt.
5719. He went *to* the market.
5720. He told the men *to* come.
5721. The *tobacco* he smokes smells good.
5722. He is rolling *tobacco*.
5723. The children of *today* no longer respect their parents.
5724. He will arrive *today*.
5725. They went in *together* for the pay.
5726. Let's go into the forest *together*.
5727. I have to go to the *toilet*.
5728. He is going to the *toilets*.
5729. He *told* the news to the village people.
5730. The chief shows *tolerance*.
5731. He is *tolerant*, respecting the freedom of others.
5732. The chief does not *tolerate* abuse.
5733. The sick man *tolerates* the medicine well.
5734. The *tomatoes* are ripening.
5735. That cat is a big *tomcat*.
5736. I am leaving *tomorrow*.
5737. It will rain *tomorrow*.
5738. The chief raised the *tone* of his voice.
5739. The blacksmith picked up the metal with his *tongs*.
5740. My *tongue* is completely dry.
5741. He bit his *tongue*.
5742. The snake stuck out its *tongue*.
5743. The doctor gave him some *tonic* medicine.
5744. He lied *too much* for anyone to believe him.
5745. *Too* bad for you—it's your fault!
5746. It is *too* good to be true.
5747. He *took along* his bow and arrows.
5748. The chief *took back* the money he had lent me.
5749. He *took off* his clothes.
5750. He *took off* his shoes.
5751. He *took to* (escaped into) the country.
5752. The people *took up* arms.
5753. He *took* a long trip.
5754. He *took* a pinch of salt.
5755. The matter *took* a turn for the worse.
5756. The thief *took* flight.
5757. He *took* four days to make that dugout canoe.
5758. She *took* her child to see the shaman.
5759. The woman *took* her child's clothes *off*.
5760. The father *took* him to the river.
5761. The disease *took* its course.
5762. He *took* the trouble to do it.
5763. Bring your working *tools*.
5764. I have a *toothache* (a stomachache, . . .).
5765. I have a *toothache*.
5766. He fell from the *top* of the tree.
5767. He climbed to the *top* of the tree.
5768. It is filled to the *top*.
5769. Sit *on top*.
5770. See if you see it *on top*.
5771. He made a *torch* to light the way.
5772. He *tore* his clothes *to shreds*.
5773. The wind *tore* off the straw from the roof.
5774. The animal *tore* the meat to pieces.
5775. He is *tormented* by his conscience.
5776. Hunger is *tormenting* me.
5777. The *torrent* is swift.
5778. It's raining in *torrents*.
5779. The heat is *torrid* (scorching).
5780. The condemned man was *tortured*.

5781. The waves *tossed* the canoe about.
5782. There was *total* silence.
5783. He is *totally* healed.
5784. The *touch* of the animal made him shudder.
5785. Don't *touch* the rifle; it's dangerous.
5786. He is *touchy* and jealous by nature.
5787. His skin became *tough* in the sun.
5788. He turned his head *toward* me.
5789. The dugout is heading *towards* the north.
5790. She wiped the plates with a *towel*.
5791. It is a *toy* for your son.
5792. He broke his *toy*.
5793. He has been *toying* with that idea for a long time.
5794. He *tracked down* a boar.
5795. That dog is a good *tracker*.
5796. The hunter is *tracking* the animal.
5797. The hunter followed the animal's *tracks*.
5798. It is a good *trade*.
5799. It is a *tradition* of the people.
5800. The traveler took the wrong *trail*.
5801. He made the trip by *train*.
5802. The cloth of his pagne is practically *transparent*.
5803. The dugout canoe is used for water *transportation*.
5804. The panther was caught in the *trap*.
5805. He *traveled* over the whole region on foot.
5806. That woman is *treacherous;* she is unfaithful.
5807. While digging in the ground we found a *treasure*.
5808. The doctor prescribed a *treatment* for the sick man.
5809. The chief *treats* him as an equal.
5810. The doctor *treats* the sick.
5811. They cut down all the *trees*.
5812. Emotion made his voice *tremble*.
5813. He is *trembling* with fever.
5814. He went through a hard *trial*.
5815. That *tribe* lives in the mountains.
5816. The Mpoko River is a *tributary* of the Ubangi.
5817. He found a *trick* to get his brother to do the work.
5818. He got that information by *trickery*.
5819. He *tried out* his strength. (tested)
5820. He *tried* my patience.
5821. Our case will be *tried* today.
5822. He is *trimming* his pagne.
5823. He just came back from a *trip*.
5824. I am leaving on a *trip*.
5825. The army *triumphed over* the enemy.
5826. They exchanged *trivial* words.
5827. Her *trouble* is that she always meddles in other people's business.
5828. He went to a lot of *trouble* to buy a sewing machine.
5829. Speak more slowly—I have *trouble* understanding you.
5830. He is *troubled* and sad.
5831. The chief's words *troubled* me.
5832. His expression is *troubled*.
5833. It is the goats' eating *trough*.
5834. He put on his *trousers*.
5835. He got the *truck* on its way.
5836. He is a *true* native.
5837. That isn't *true*.
5838. The sorcerer's stories are *true*.
5839. The elephant is *trumpeting*.
5840. He attacked him with a *truncheon*.
5841. Put your basket into the *trunk* in the back of the car.
5842. That *trunk* is full of clothes.
5843. He doesn't deserve our *trust*.
5844. He *trusted* me with a secret.
5845. He is too *trusting* by nature.
5846. That's the plain *truth*.
5847. Tell the whole *truth*.
5848. You are telling the *truth;* you're right.
5849. *Try* to wake up early.
5850. You've always got to *try* your luck.
5851. The child is *trying* to sleep.
5852. *Tuberculosis* is a contagious disease.
5853. He sings *in tune*.
5854. He *tunes* his harp.

5855. He *turned over* the soil with the hoe.
5856. They *turned* him *against* his family.
5857. He *turned* his back on the chief.
5858. The situation has *turned* out badly.
5859. He is now *turning over* his field.
5860. The canoe is *turning* (and) changing direction.
5861. He moves like a *turtle*.
5862. I've told you *twenty* times!
5863. He is starting the fire with *twigs*.
5864. She had *twins* (boys).
5865. They are *twins* (girls). Those girls are *twins*.
5866. He *twisted* his ankle (while) jumping.
5867. His mouth was *twisted* with annoyance.
5868. His eyelids are *twitching*.
5869. The father and mother have *two* sons.
5870. He is *tying* the goat to the tree.
5871. The father is *tyrannical* towards his children.
5872. The chief is not a *tyrant*.

U

5873. The cow's *udder* is full of milk.
5874. That female goat has a full *udder*.
5875. Your cow has injured its *udder*.
5876. His *ugliness* frightened the children.
5877. She is an *ugly girl*.
5878. He is *ugly*.
5879. Your offer is *unacceptable*.
5880. He is *unaware* of his actions.
5881. I was *unaware* of that news.
5882. He has an *unbearable* nature.
5883. The heat is *unbearable* today.
5884. The glare of the light is *unbearable*.
5885. That noise is *unbearable*.
5886. His story is *unbelievable*.
5887. Justice proved *unbending* with the accused man.
5888. The air is *unbreathable*.
5889. He *unbuttoned* his shirt.
5890. The result of his undertaking is *uncertain*.
5891. The weather is *uncertain*. (unsettled)
5892. He is in a state of *uncertainty* about his future.
5893. That woman is *unchaste*.
5894. This position is very *uncomfortable*.
5895. The heat makes me *uncomfortable*.
5896. The chief remains *uncompromising*.
5897. He is *unconcerned* about the danger.
5898. His courage is *unconquerable*.
5899. He fell *unconscious*.
5900. She *uncorked* (uncapped) the bottle.
5901. The river is *uncrossable* here.
5902. He is still *undecided* between the two solutions.
5903. This proof is *undeniable*.
5904. He took shelter *under* the umbrella.
5905. He is swimming *under* the water.
5906. You *underestimate* your adversary.
5907. He is *underhanded* in business.
5908. He arranged them *underneath*.
5909. Put it *underneath*.
5910. The snake is hidden *underneath*.
5911. Your brother's *undershirt* is dirty.
5912. I don't *understand* what you are saying.
5913. He didn't *understand* why I was crying.
5914. They live in perfect *understanding* (of each other).
5915. They were speaking in an *undertone*.
5916. At this time of year the island is *under water*.
5917. The accused man *underwent* interrogation.
5918. His presence is *undesirable*.
5919. He *undid* the braid.
5920. The troops are *undisciplined*.
5921. The laws are *undisputed*.
5922. *Undoubtedly*.

5923. She *undressed* her child and put him to bed.
5924. This millet beer is *undrinkable*.
5925. His condition makes me *uneasy*.
5926. He is an *uneducated* man.
5927. There is a lot of *unemployment*.
5928. These men are of *unequal* height.
5929. He has an *uneven* temper.
5930. That *unexpected* event surprised us.
5931. His *unexpected* visit surprised me.
5932. The result was *unexpected*.
5933. He arrived *unexpectedly*.
5934. His departure is *unexplainable*.
5935. This region is still *unexplored*.
5936. That punishment is *unfair*.
5937. He was *unfaithful* to his word.
5938. That woman is *unfaithful*.
5939. The depths of the sea are *unfathomable*.
5940. This work is *unfinished*.
5941. This land is *unfit* for farming.
5942. She is an *unfit* mother.
5943. He *unfolded* the pagne.
5944. His arrival was *unforeseeable*.
5945. He was an *unforgettable* character.
5946. Your mistake is *unforgivable*.
5947. He made an *unfortunate* move and the pot fell and broke.
5948. *Unfortunately*, I lost the machete you lent me.
5949. He is generous to *unfortunates*.
5950. He is *ungrateful* to his benefactor.
5951. It is *unhealthy* to live in marshy areas.
5952. He is in poor health; he is *unhealthy*.
5953. The climate of the area is *unhealthy*.
5954. The region is *unhealthy*; you'll catch malaria there.
5955. He had *unhoped-for* success.
5956. He came out of the accident *unhurt*.
5957. This story concerns a *unicorn*.
5958. The soldier is wearing a *uniform*.
5959. That is *unimaginable*.
5960. The hut is *uninhabitable*.
5961. He spoke *unintelligibly*.
5962. He broke the plate *unintentionally*.
5963. That story is *uninteresting*.
5964. The husband and wife live in conjugal *union*.
5965. The inhabitants of the village form a *unit*.
5966. They all *united* against him.
5967. The family is *united* by blood ties.
5968. The punishment is *unjustified*.
5969. The child has an *unknown* father. (The father of the child is unknown.)
5970. These problems are *unknown* to him.
5971. He *unleashed* his dog.
5972. This story is *unlikely*.
5973. His riches are *unlimited*.
5974. They *unloaded* a shipload of wood.
5975. He is too *unlucky* to become rich.
5976. Your son is *unmanageable*.
5977. He is still *unmarried*.
5978. This reward is *unmerited*.
5979. He is *unmoved* by entreaties.
5980. In that costume he won't go *unnoticed*.
5981. That hut is *unoccupied*.
5982. The house is *unoccupied*.
5983. The chief is *unpopular*.
5984. This land is *unproductive*.
5985. He is often *unpunctual* for appointments.
5986. The crime went *unpunished*.
5987. That mask makes him *unrecognizable*.
5988. He went *unrecognized*.
5989. This food is *unrefined*.
5990. He is an *unrepentant* drunkard.
5991. She *unrolled* the mat on the ground.
5992. Despite the insults he remained *unruffled*.
5993. My hunger remained *unsatisfied*.
5994. The weather is *unsettled*.
5995. His resolve is *unshakeable*.
5996. He will leave on an *unspecified* date.
5997. Her pagne became *unstitched*.

5998. He has discovered *unsuspected* prospects.
5999. That animal is *untamable*.
6000. He *untangled* a complicated case.
6001. His view is *untenable*.
6002. That story is *unthinkable*.
6003. He is very *untidy* (muddle-headed).
6004. He *untied* the rope.
6005. You will wait for me *until* I return.
6006. He stayed *until* the end of the discussion.
6007. *Until* when will you stay in the village?
6008. I'll stay *until* your return.
6009. His gaiety is *untimely*.
6010. He started repeating the same gesture *untiringly*.
6011. These trousers are *unwearable*.
6012. You look *unwell*.
6013. The heat makes him *unwell*.
6014. He is *unworthy* of the chief's confidence.
6015. The man *unwound* the string.
6016. The water came *up to* his neck.
6017. Look *up* in the air!
6018. He has been *up* since dawn.
6019. *Up* to today he had never gotten drunk.
6020. Hold your hand *up*.
6021. One of the *uprights* (posts) of the ladder is broken.
6022. The storm *uprooted* the trees.
6023. He stopped *upstream*.
6024. Nothing is *urgent;* the matter can wait.
6025. He doesn't see *us*.
6026. The sick man lost the *use* of his voice.
6027. What is that tool *used* for?
6028. The children aren't *used* to being alone.
6029. I'm *used* to doing that.
6030. My eyes are getting *used* to the darkness.
6031. The chief gave me some *useful* advice.
6032. It is *useless* to insist.
6033. That individual is *useless* to society.
6034. She only *uses* fresh meat.
6035. He came late, as *usual*.
6036. He *usually* comes in the evening.
6037. That's what he *usually* does.
6038. The spoon is a kitchen *utensil*.
6039. My *uvula* tickles me.

V

6040. She left on *vacation*.
6041. He leads a *vagabond* life; he travels constantly.
6042. The chief gave *vague* instructions.
6043. The reasons he gives are *vague*.
6044. He is making *vain* efforts; it's a waste of time.
6045. That man is *vain;* he is quite pleased with himself.
6046. The chief's arguments are not *valid*.
6047. This object has great *value*.
6048. The weather changes often; it is *variable*.
6049. There are several *varieties* of vegetables.
6050. Customs *vary* from place to place.
6051. The bush (country) is *vast*.
6052. The village square is *vast*.
6053. The wind made the dugout *veer* off course.
6054. Fruit is a *vegetable* food (comes from plants).
6055. I don't like *vegetables*.
6056. He raises *vegetables*.
6057. Her *veil* is torn.
6058. The heat makes the *veins* swell.
6059. The dress is made of *velvet*.
6060. The *venom* of certain snakes is fatal to man.
6061. He has a *venomous* tongue; he is a malicious man.
6062. They didn't want to *venture* into the bush.
6063. The *verdict* was negative; the guilty man was condemned.
6064. She was on the *verge* of tears.
6065. This meat is *very* good.
6066. It is *very* hot.
6067. What I said were the *very* words of the chief. (I repeated the *very* ...)

6068. The blood flows through the blood *vessels*.
6069. The harp string is *vibrating*.
6070. There are panthers in the *vicinity*.
6071. He was the *victim* of an accident.
6072. He is the *victim* of an illusion.
6073. Our points of *view* are divergent.
6074. The trees block the *view*.
6075. The crime is a *vile* deed.
6076. He is a *vile* fellow.
6077. The whole *village* participates in the festival.
6078. *Violations* (breaches) of custom are punished in several ways.
6079. His character is *violent* and quick-tempered.
6080. The storm was *violent*.
6081. The chief spoke *violently*.
6082. Patience is a great *virtue*.
6083. His sleep is haunted by *visions*.
6084. The chief paid me a *visit*.
6085. The doctor *visited* the sick man.
6086. That memory remains very *vivid*.
6087. The colors of his pagne are *vivid*.
6088. He spoke in a low *voice*.
6089. The chief spoke with a loud *voice*.
6090. The *volume* of water in the river is increasing.
6091. The child *vomited* his meal.

W

6092. He gave me a *wad* of tickets.
6093. He *waddled* from one foot to the other.
6094. That *wailing* kept me from sleeping. (awake)
6095. He went into the water up to his *waist*.
6096. He seized his adversary *around the waist*.
6097. He went into the water up to his *waist*.
6098. He went into the water up to his *waist*.
6099. If you *wait* a little longer he will come.
6100. *Wait* for me; I'm coming.
6101. The panther is lying in *wait* for the game.
6102. He *waited* for her a long time.
6103. *Wake up*. It is late.
6104. Don't make any noise or you'll *wake* him *up*.
6105. I'm going to go *walk* by the river.
6106. My feet hurt too much to *walk*.
6107. He *walked backwards*.
6108. He is a good *walker*.
6109. That's a *walking* song.
6110. Long *walks* through the bush tired her out.
6111. We built a *wall* of earth.
6112. He *walled* up the door with bricks.
6113. He is *wandering* in the forest.
6114. I *want* some more (meat, . . .).
6115. What do you *want*?
6116. The child *wants* to eat.
6117. *War* broke out.
6118. They entered the *war*.
6119. The shaman *warded off* the wrath of the ancestors' spirits.
6120. The president made a *warlike* speech.
6121. That warrior looks *warlike*.
6122. The lizard *warmed* himself in the sun.
6123. The wood is *warped*.
6124. He went to *wash* himself in the river.
6125. The *wash* is not yet done.
6126. He did not *wash* my clothes.
6127. She put the *wash* out to dry in the sun.
6128. She went to do the *wash*. (wash the linen)
6129. He *washes* himself every day.
6130. He went to the *washing place*.
6131. She left to do the *washing*.
6132. That garment needs a good *washing*.
6133. That's a *waste* of time.
6134. He *wastes* his money.
6135. You will *watch* (take care of) the meat on the fire.
6136. *Watch out;* you are going to fall!
6137. I bought a beautiful *watch*.
6138. He *watched* his language.

6139. The woman *watches over* her sick husband every night.
6140. She is *watching* over the children.
6141. The *water* is cold.
6142. He plunged into the *water*.
6143. There is a *waterfall* in that place.
6144. His eyes are *watering*.
6145. This cloth is *waterproof*.
6146. The gardener *waters* the vegetables to make them grow faster.
6147. His eyes are *watery*.
6148. *Wave* to them with your hand.
6149. The *waves* are swelling.
6150. The boat is making *waves*.
6151. He has *wax* in his ears.
6152. His ears are full of *wax*.
6153. Bees make *wax*.
6154. That palm tree produces *wax*.
6155. I don't like the *way* he smiles.
6156. Her *way* of life is different from ours.
6157. I don't see any other *way* out of the situation.
6158. The *way* seemed long to us.
6159. The hunter cleared a *way* through the brush.
6160. He knows a *way* to earn a lot of money.
6161. He doesn't know the *way* to use a rifle.
6162. He has lost his *way*.
6163. Stay; you won't be in the *way*.
6164. There are several *ways* to prepare a sauce.
6165. He has a *weak* personality.
6166. His condition is very *weak*.
6167. He was greatly *weakened* by the sickness.
6168. Hunger has *weakened* him considerably.
6169. The *wealth* of the country is great.
6170. The mother *weaned* the child.
6171. His wife complained of having nothing to *wear*.
6172. My *weariness* was great.
6173. He *wears* a ring on his finger.
6174. I am *weary* of your lies.
6175. The *weather* is hot and dry.
6176. The village was exposed to bad *weather*.
6177. She is *weaving* a basket.
6178. She is *weaving* cotton.
6179. There will be a *wedding* tomorrow.
6180. He put a *wedge* under the foot of the table.
6181. He *wedged* the door of the hut.
6182. The man is *weeding* the fields.
6183. The festival will take place this *week*.
6184. Smoke makes you *weep*.
6185. The *weevil* bores into the corn.
6186. The merchant *weighed* the merchandise on a balance.
6187. She *weighs* a lot.
6188. The threat of a storm *weighs* heavy on the region.
6189. The food makes him put on *weight*.
6190. Gold is sold by *weight*.
6191. *Welcome!*
6192. The chief *welcomed* me warmly.
6193. That must be *well* cooked.
6194. The work was *well* done.
6195. He will *do well* to keep quiet.
6196. The child is very *well behaved*.
6197. You look *well*.
6198. The chief *went beyond* his rights.
6199. A dugout *went down* the river.
6200. They *went in together* to buy him a present.
6201. He *went up* the hill.
6202. He *went up* the river by canoe.
6203. The price of manioc *went up* this year.
6204. He *went* away.
6205. He *went* to the creek.
6206. He *went* to the window.
6207. That *went* well.
6208. *What* are you thinking about?
6209. *What* day is it today?
6210. *What* did you say?
6211. *Whatever* happens, I'll be there for the festival.
6212. Don't listen—he's a *wheedler*.
6213. A bicycle has two *wheels*.
6214. At the time *when* he arrived it was raining.

6215. You will offer him something to eat *when* he comes.
6216. *When* he has finished studying he will work.
6217. *Where* are you going?
6218. *Where* do you come from?
6219. I know *where* he lives.
6220. The child follows his mother *wherever* she goes.
6221. Your friend came.—*Which* one?
6222. *Which* one of you took my knife?
6223. I saw him a little *while* ago.
6224. In a little *while* there won't be any more millet.
6225. He stayed there a long *while* without moving.
6226. He came *while* you were sick.
6227. The corn will not ripen for a *while*.
6228. His *whining* gets on my nerves.
6229. The child is *whining*.
6230. She *whispered* something in his ear.
6231. The girls *whispered* something while laughing.
6232. The bird is *whistling*.
6233. The wind is *whistling*.
6234. He wears *white* clothing.
6235. *White* men don't like to live in the bush.
6236. This fabric is very *white*.
6237. His hair is all *white*.
6238. His hair is *turning white*.
6239. She was dressed in *white*.
6240. They *whitewashed* the house.
6241. *Who* is that man?
6242. He is eating *wholemeal* bread.
6243. This food is *wholesome*; it won't make you sick.
6244. The boy to *whom* you are speaking is my son.
6245. He is coughing because he has *whooping cough*.
6246. Tell me *why* you came.
6247. The *wick* of the lamp is too short.
6248. He stared *wide-eyed*.
6249. She opened the window *wide*.
6250. That river is *wide*.
6251. The road is *wide*.
6252. That blanket is *wide*. (broad)
6253. The river *widens* out.
6254. He is *widowed*; his wife is dead.
6255. The *width* of this fabric is . . . .
6256. He took her as his *wife*.
6257. That is a *wild* animal.
6258. It is a *wild* animal.
6259. That man has *will power*; he is vigorous.
6260. He is a *willful* man; he's determined.
6261. The child obeys *willingly*.
6262. The *wind* drove away the clouds.
6263. The *wind* is blowing strongly.
6264. The flag is flying in the *wind*.
6265. The *wine* is not yet made.
6266. He is drinking palm *wine*.
6267. He broke the bird's *wing* with his sling.
6268. The bird's *wings* are black.
6269. The dragonfly's *wings* are transparent.
6270. He *winked* at the girl.
6271. The woman is *winnowing* the corn.
6272. He *wiped off* his feet.
6273. The chief gave him some *wise* advice.
6274. You couldn't *wish* for anything more.
6275. My *wishes* came true.
6276. Those were the last *wishes* of the deceased.
6277. He tied the bag *with* a string.
6278. *With* all his spirit (hard work) he remains poor.
6279. He came to an agreement *with* him.
6280. He fought *with* his best friend.
6281. He is angry *with* me.
6282. The chief responded *with* silence.
6283. *With* the rain that had fallen we couldn't go on.
6284. Here people get up *with* the sun.
6285. If he doesn't come *within* three days we will go back to the village.
6286. He is a man *without* scruples.
6287. It is raining *without* stopping.
6288. The army *withstood* the attacks of the enemy.

6289. I *witnessed* their dispute.
6290. The *witnesses* were brought face to face in court.
6291. The noise *woke* him up.
6292. This *woman* is old.
6293. She has an inflammation of the *womb*.
6294. He *won* a lot by gambling.
6295. He *won* her *over* to his ideas.
6296. He *won* the chief's good will.
6297. The men cut *wood* in the forest.
6298. She anointed the fetish with red *wood* powder and oil.
6299. I'm going to fetch some *wood* to make a fire.
6300. He put a sachet of *"wood"* into the wine.
6301. He carved a paddle from the *wood*.
6302. The woodcutter sent the *woodchips* flying.
6303. He is learning *woodworking*.
6304. *Wool* is made from sheep's hair.
6305. That blanket is *woollen*.
6306. What does this *word* mean?
6307. He didn't say a *word* to me.
6308. I am not familiar with that *word*.
6309. You have not kept your *word*.
6310. He broke his *word*.
6311. That is not a common *word*. (*everyday*)
6312. The chief weighed his *words* carefully.
6313. They exchanged a few *words*.
6314. He makes plays on *words*.
6315. His sick feeling *wore off*.
6316. You must *work* in order to earn money.
6317. After *work* he rests.
6318. This basket is nice *work*.
6319. Building a hut requires *work*.
6320. That's a long-term *work*.
6321. Don't be afraid; I've *worked* it all *out*.
6322. The *workers* work as a team.
6323. The blacksmith has been *working* since the age of twenty.
6324. He is in the carpenter's *workshop*.
6325. The *world* is big.
6326. She *wormed* the information out of him.
6327. *Worms* have eaten into the wood.
6328. He is a schemer; he *worms* his way into everything.
6329. He has intestinal *worms*.
6330. The sick man is *worn out*.
6331. The soles of my shoes are *worn*.
6332. I am *worried* about what will happen to him.
6333. He is getting *worried*.
6334. The chief looks *worried*.
6335. That child *worries* his parents.
6336. Her health *worries* me.
6337. *Worries* overwhelmed him.
6338. Don't *worry* about my business.
6339. He is *worse* than his brother.
6340. Everything that people said *worsened* his grief.
6341. I expect the *worst*.
6342. Manioc is not *worth* much.
6343. That is not *worth* talking about.
6344. That man is *worthy* to be chief.
6345. The *wound* has closed up.
6346. His *wound* hasn't healed.
6347. The *wound* is deep.
6348. The *wound* is open.
6349. She dressed his *wound*.
6350. He was *wounded* in the leg.
6351. He *wounded* me.
6352. The elephant is *wounded*.
6353. She *wrapped up* the child in the mat.
6354. He brought down the *wrath* of the ancestors.
6355. They *wrestled* together.
6356. He is *wretched* (pitiful).
6357. That *wrings* your heart.
6358. His face is furrowed with *wrinkles*.
6359. He raised himself up by (the strength of) his *wrists*.
6360. The man is *writing* on paper.
6361. The child is stroking the dog the *wrong way*.
6362. It is *wrong* not to submit to the decisions of the traditional judge.
6363. He took the *wrong* road.
6364. He took your joke the *wrong* way and got angry.

6365. The chief is not *wrong*.
6366. He was condemned *wrongly*.

Y

6367. It's a bush *yam*.
6368. She's cooking some *yams*.
6369. He grows *yams*.
6370. I heard a *yap(ping)*.
6371. Your dog *yapped*.
6372. He began to *yawn*.
6373. He is suffering from *yaws*.
6374. He only has a *year* to live.
6375. I will go to see him next *year*.
6376. He came last *year*.
6377. I saw him last *year*.
6378. His uncle has been dead for two *years*.
6379. The chief is *yelling* his head off.
6380. Lemons are *yellow*.
6381. In this spot the soil is *yellowish*.
6382. Answer *yes* or no.
6383. Are you satisfied—*yes* or no?
6384. He came *yesterday* afternoon.
6385. The child has been sick since the day before *yesterday*.
6386. He arrived *yesterday*.
6387. He has not come *yet*.
6388. The *yield* of this land is diminishing.
6389. That *yoke* is heavy.
6390. That food will make *you* sick.
6391. Hey *you!* What's your name?
6392. He is nicer than *you*.
6393. All the *young people* are leaving the village for the city.
6394. He is my *younger* brother.
6395. That man is *younger* than you.
6396. Close *your* door.
6397. Put on *your* pagne.
6398. That isn't *yours*—it's mine (hat).
6399. You are to love your neighbor as *yourself*.
6400. *Youth* is carefree (happy-go-lucky).
6401. In my *youth* the village had many inhabitants.
6402. He has a *youthful* enthusiasm.

Z

6403. The *zebra* runs fast.
6404. He runs like a *zebra*.
6405. The drunk man walked *zigzagging*.
6406. Lightning *zigzags* across the sky.

3
Thematic Approach Questionnaires

Questionnaire 10

Traditional Technologies

Outline

1. Basic ways of acting on matter
    - 1.1 General
        - 1.1.1 Acting upon matter
        - 1.1.2 Transmission of force to an active part
        - 1.1.3 Impulsion
    - 1.2 Action of fire on matter
        - 1.2.1 General
        - 1.2.2 Lighting a fire
        - 1.2.3 Maintaining a fire
    - 1.3 Action of water on matter
        - 1.3.1 Use of the physical properties of water
        - 1.3.2 Use of the dynamic properties of water
        - 1.3.3 Use of the chemical properties of water
    - 1.4 Action of air on matter
2. Transportation
    - 2.1 General
        - 2.1.1 Carrying by man, by animal
        - 2.1.2 Riding
    - 2.2 Navigation
    - 2.3 Routes of communication
3. Techniques
    - 3.1 General
        - 3.1.1 Techniques for making and producing things

       3.1.2 Techniques for consuming

  3.2 Techniques for manufacturing things
       3.2.1 Stable solids
       3.2.2 Semi-plastic solids
       3.2.3 Plastic solids
       3.2.4 Supple solids
       3.2.5 Fluids

  3.3 Techniques for acquisition
       3.3.1 Fishing
       3.3.2 Hunting, warfare
       3.3.3 Animal husbandry
       3.3.4 Food gathering
       3.3.5 Agriculture
       3.3.6 Extraction of minerals

  3.4 Techniques for consumption
       3.4.1 Food
       3.4.2 Clothing
       3.4.3 Dwellings

Appendix

Index

Traditional Technologies 403

This questionnaire is designed to help linguists collect a significant list of words concerning traditional techniques, most particularly those of central Africa. It was revised and expanded for the second edition, but does not claim to be exhaustive.

The classification of techniques is based on *L'Homme et la Matière (Man and Matter)*, by André Leroi-Gourhan. In addition, we have drawn from materials in various regional ethnological monographs.

Only those words in roman characters are to be translated. Other instructions are indicated in italics.

Figures 6, 12, 13, 15, 17, 20, 24, 25, 30, 41, 43, 44, 48, 50–59, 61, 64, 89a, 90, 116, 122, 123, 137, 138, and 139 are borrowed from Leroi-Gourhan's *L'Homme et la Matière*. Figures 11, 32, 93–96, 144, 146, 155, 159, and 160 are taken from *Moeurs et coutumes des Manjas (Customs and ways of the Manja)*, by Vergiat. Figures 106, 107, and 108 come from *Tâches quotidiennes et travaux saisonniers en pays bwa (Daily tasks and seasonal work in Bwa country)*, by G. Manessy. Figures 69, 70, and 71 were taken from *La Préhistoire (Prehistory)*, by Leroi-Gourhan, from the chapter on the classification of pottery by Hélène Balfet.

It is recommended that the investigation begin at §3.2 and that §§1, 2, and 3.1 be left for the end. The basic means of action are actually the trickiest for linguistic examination, but they are placed at the beginning of the classification of the techniques since they underlie all of them.

1. Bent finger
(hook)

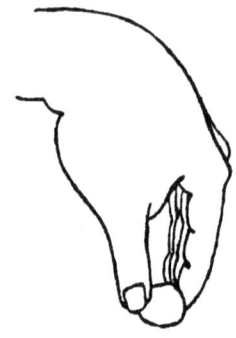

2. Thumb and index finger
(tongs)

3a. Axe: cutting edge of the blade is parallel to the axis of the handle.

3b. Adze: the cutting edge of the blade is perpendicular to the axis of the handle

Basic Actions

1 Basic Ways of Acting Upon Matter

1.1 General

The different ways of acting upon matter may be presented as the set of gestures, movements and tools that exist in the culture under study. With this approach, we must make inventory of all the names of tools in the language, and all the verbs which correspond partially or exactly to one or several of the basic actions.

Such a list can be presented with the following classification:

Action   by prehension
          by percussion
          by conveyance
Transmission   (of force to the active part)
                   (source of the force)

1.1.1. Acting upon matter.
to act (upon matter)
the blade of the knife *acts* on the wood (cuts it)
the blade of the knife *doesn't act* on the wood (because it is dull)

There is a good chance that 'to act on' = 'to cut' in this case, and that in general each specific tool has its own verb (a point pierces, a file files, a millstone crushes or grinds, a club clubs, etc.). Still, it is interesting to know if there is a more general verb, indicating action apart from the tool used. Try to use this term in as many different contexts as possible (such as those indicated above).

Also, find out the term(s) which designate the active part of a tool, which carries out the action:

e.g.,   cutting edge (of an iron head, blade)
       point (of an iron head, blade)
       flat part (of a millstone)
       active part, head (of a hammer)
       the (space described) inside of the noose of a snare
       harness of a weaving loom
       inside of baskets (of various types)
       incisor tooth (human)
       molar tooth (human)

1.1.1.1. Acting on matter by grasping (prehension).
hand: thumb / index finger / middle finger / ring finger / little finger
      (5 terms) thumb / other fingers (2 terms)
palm; hollow of the hand
to take, to grab hold of, to act by grasping (try to see if the following or other distinctions exist)
to take with a hooked finger; (a vine); to hook, hang (cf. fig. 1)
      the hook caught (hooked) a fish
      I hang up the basket on the nail (the nail holds the basket)

to take between the fingers, to pinch (cf. fig. 2): between the thumb and index finger, between index and middle fingers
> I pick up a stone with tongs
> I take one strand over two to braid (between the thumb and index finger)

to take up in the open hands, in the fists; to catch (in the hollow of the hand)
> the basket contains holds the seeds
> I take up a fish with a hoop net
> I hold a butterfly (with the hollow of the hand, the hand hollowed)
> I take a pile of seeds in the hand

to hold, hold tightly
examples of tools that act by grasping:

curved finger:	hook, fish hook
thumb and index finger:	tongs,
	harness of weaving loom
hollow of the hand:	hoop net
	basket
	spoon
	hunting net
	cage trap

1.1.1.2. Acting on matter by striking. Find out if there is a general term for the notion of: acting by blows, striking

> to split (wood)
> to hammer (iron)
> to prune (trees)
> to polish (stone)
> to divide (matter)

These words all express the action of hitting, banging, or beating, and should be researched according to the material and tools being used, and according to the results of these actions.

tools: axe, hammer, etc.

1.1.1.2.1. Acting on matter by percussion without striking.
to cut, to gash, to notch, to peel, to cut to a point
> I cut the meat with a knife (= cut up into chunks)
> I cut up a thread with the knife
> The knife cuts well; it is sharp
> The knife cuts poorly; it is blunt
> I stick the shovel into the ground (its cutting sharp edge cuts into the earth)

tools: knife (hunting knife, woman's knife, ceremonial knife)
scissors (sewing)
shears (iron)
spade, shovel

to scratch, scrape, plane, saw, file, polish:
> I scrape the skin with the scraper
> I sawed the board with the saw
> I file the wood with the file

tools: scraper, plane, saw, file, polisher, claw

to pierce:
> the needle bores into the cloth
> the awl pierces the leather

tools: needle, awl, stiletto

Traditional Technologies

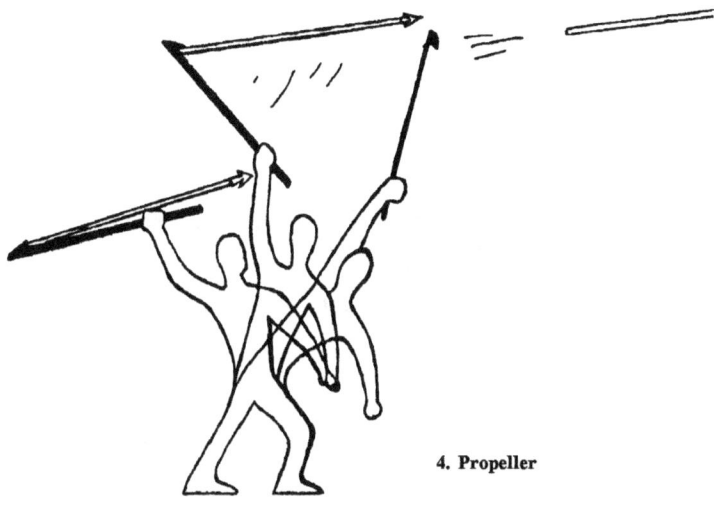

4. Propeller

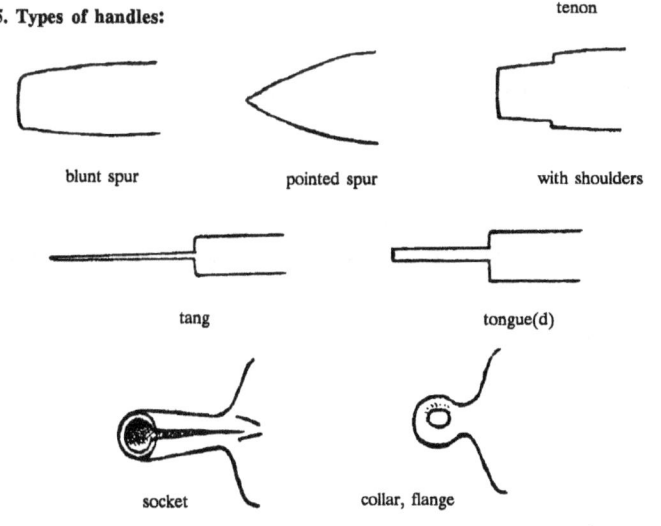

5. Types of handles: tenon

blunt spur   pointed spur   with shoulders

tang   tongue(d)

socket   collar, flange

Basic Actions

to crush, grind, mold, squeeze
>   I crush the grain with the mill
>   I press the palm nut with the oil press
>   I mold a pot (with the fist)
>   tools: mill, press, mold, ...

1.1.1.2.2. Acting on matter by percussion by throwing.

to hurl, hew, strike, beat, give a blow, give several blows
>   I strike the tree with the axe, I cut down the tree, I hew the stone
>   I strike the iron with the hammer
>   I beat the bark with a beater
>   I hit my enemy / the antelope with my fist / the spear / the club
>   I shoot the gun
>   I thrust the dagger in
>   I throw the throwing knife
>   I shoot the arrow with the bow
>   The bow casts the arrow far off
>   I shoot an arrow with the blowgun
>   The air that I produce in the blowgun propels the dart far off
>   I crush the seeds by pounding / flinging the pestle against the bottom of the mortar

>   tools: axe, machete, billhook, pick(axe), hoe
>   adze / axe (fig. 3)
>   mallet, hammer, club, beater
>   dagger, pike, spear, throwing knife, (pronged) harpoon
>   bow, crossbow, spring-loaded and spiked traps
>   blowgun
>   pestle, mortar
>   gun

1.1.1.2.3. Action by percussion applied with an instrument.

Find out if there is a general word that corresponds to this action: striking with an instrument, and an intermediary
>   I cut away at the wood with a hammer and chisel
>   tools: wood chisel, gouge (fig. 21–22)
>   burin (= iron chisel, cold chisel)
>   striking instrument (iron hammer, sledgehammer, etc.)

1.1.1.3. Acting on matter by conveying.

to carry, transport
>   I carry a basket
>   I carry water in the calabash from the well to the hut

to lift up, move, roll
>   I lift up the load
>   Move that mat; roll it up!

to pull, push
>   I pull on the rope to bring the bucket out of the well
>   I pull the child by the hand
>   The men push the tree trunk to clear the trail

Traditional Technologies

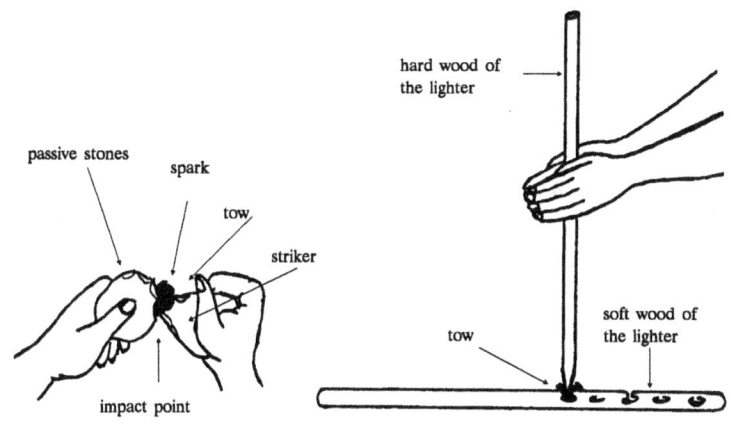

6. Flintstone

7. Friction lighter

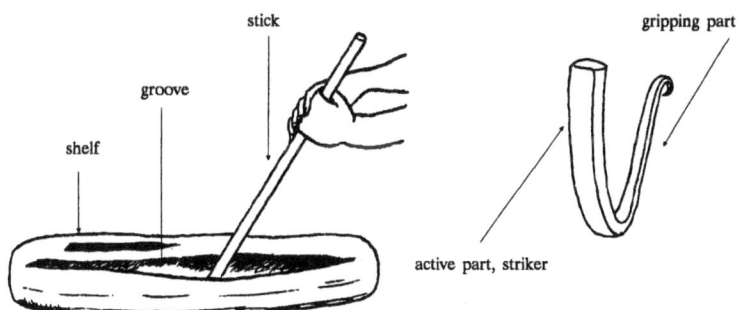

8. Friction lighter

9. Flint lighter

Fire

tools: pack (container), bag, sack, basket (general name)
           packsaddle, saddle
           bucket
to turn, make turn
    The potter makes his wheel turn with the stick
    I make the spindle go round
to swim, sail
to fly (bird, airplane)
to walk, run
    tools: paddle, oar
               dugout, canoe

1.1.2. Transmission of force to the active part.

Is the notion of transmitting movement consciously expressed?
    the axe handle transmits force from my arms to the blade
    I throw the spear with the propeller (fig. 4)
    tools: handle
               propeller
               press
               pulley
               spindle
               wheel, gearwheel
               crank
    types of handles (fig. 5):
            tang
            tongue
            spur (stub, heel)
            tenon
            groove (of a pulley)
            socket
            collar, flange

1.1.3. Impulsion.

to give impulse, to propel
    the bowstring gives impulse to the arrow
    the blacksmith gives impulse to the hammer in striking the iron
        human force, animal force
        a strong, weak man
        with force, without force
        muscle, motor

1.2 Action of Fire on Matter

1.2.1. General.

fire { hearth fire
       brush fire
to make a fire { by friction (wood)
                      by striking (stones, matches)

1.2.2. Lighting a fire.
to carry fire (embers, faggots, straw)
to light the fire
to be lit, to be blazing, flaming
lighter (general term)
    different types of lighter:
        a) flintstone (scientific names of the stone(s) used: e.g., flint cf. fig. 6
            striker (iron, stone)
            passive stone
            spark
            tow, oakum (what material is it made of: touchwood, . . . leaves, fruit fibers, etc.)
        b) friction lighter (cf. 7 and 8)
            hard wood of the lighter ⎫
            soft wood of the lighter ⎬ what kinds of wood are used?
            tow (made of what material?)
        c) flint lighter (for the different parts, see part a, and fig. 9)
            European lighter (are the different parts specified?
                e.g., wick, stone, reservoir, wheel, etc.)
            matchbox
            match, friction strip (to strike a match)

1.2.3. Care of the fire.
to look after (a fire)
    to burn: the fire is burning well
                  this wood burns well
    to stir up (the fire): by blowing, fanning
                          by stirring the coals, fuel
    to break up wood (for the fire)
    to feed (the fire)
    Fuel
        twigs   ⎫
        branches ⎬ what types of wood and grasses are preferred?
        logs   ⎬ are these woods used in a particular order?
        charcoal ⎭
    hearth
        (European) cooking oven
        woodpile
        ember pot (for carrying the coals)
        ember
        live coals, ashes, smoke
    to put out the fire

Effects of fire.
to burn: the fire burned the grass; I burned the grass; the house burned
to heat
to carbonize
to roast / grill
to soften by heating (metals)

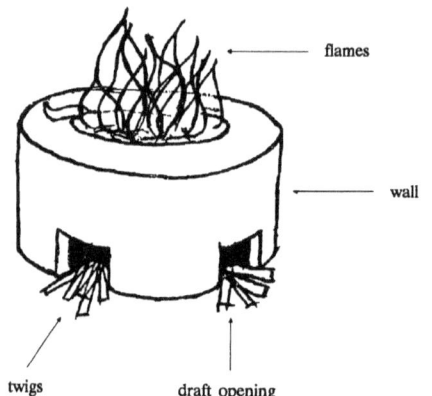

10. Air draft

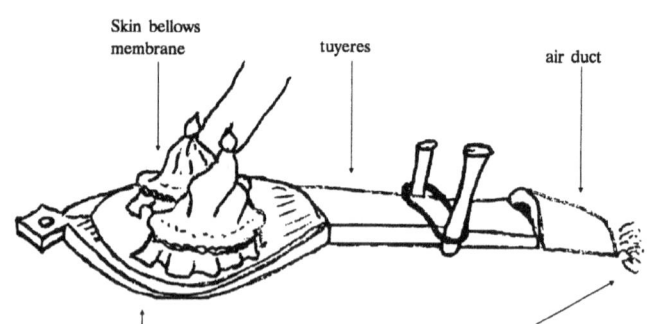

11. Bellows of a forge

Air

Traditional Technologies

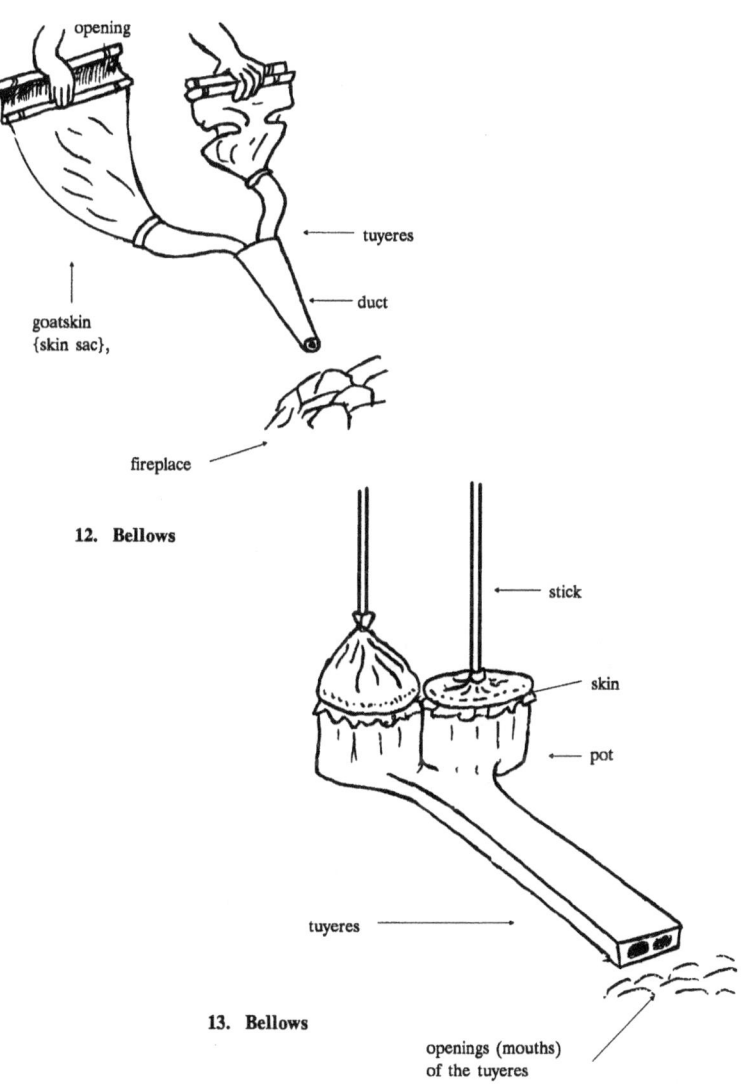

12. Bellows

13. Bellows

to splinter (wood, grass)
to iron (clothes)

1.3 Action of Water on Matter

water

1.3.1. Use of the physical effects of water.
to impregnate (with water, dye) to swell up or to make flexible
    he soaks the hide to permeate it well with dye
    a well-saturated hide is more flexible
to dissolve adhesive substances (dyes, waterproofing substances, glues), certain foods (sauces, etc.) to make them liquid
    I dissolve the sugar
to cool off (metals)
to heat up (in cooking food)

1.3.2. Use of the dynamic effects of water.
current of water
    stream, spray   { if they are used as a force:
    spout, flood   e.g., for washing food
to wash, washing (the soil—to separate ore; the body; clothes)
to decant (intentionally) into a liquid (to separate the grit from the clay when preparing it for molding
    coffee grounds, dregs, deposit, sediment
    the clay settles
    I decant the water to make it clear
to boil, beat up, whip, soak, dry out by hanging (clothes)

1.3.3. Use of the chemical effects of water.
solution, mixture (general term)
    tanning, coloring baths; dyes
    fermented drinks
    sauces
    poisons
    etc.
to mix, prepare a solution

1.4 Action of Air on Matter

air, wind
Make note of all technological uses of air (air = means of acting)
to blow with the mouth (man)
to blow (wind)
    whistle (different types)
    musical wind instruments (used to attract game)
    scarecrow (if based on the principle of wind)
    blow-gun
    fan
    (European) air conditioner, ventilator

Traditional Technologies

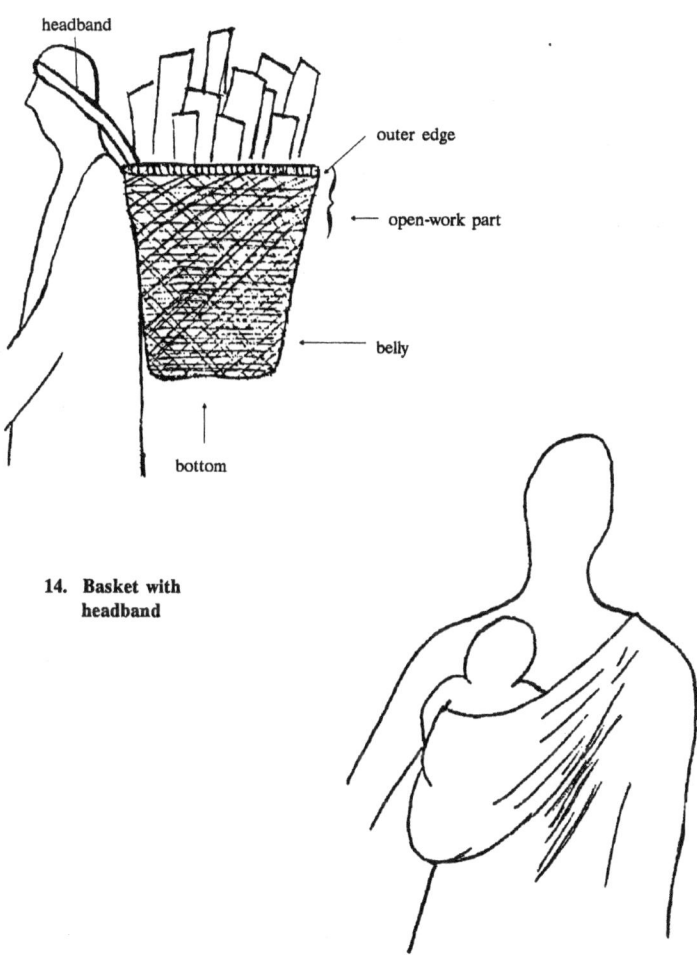

14. Basket with headband

15. Hood for carrying babies

Transportation

to dry (by hot air current, in open air, etc.)
to revive the fire (with air)
    drawing (open fire oriented in the direction of the wind)
        (by a device with sides and openings) fig. 10
    blowtorch (what is it made of?)
    bellows of a forge (cf. fig. 11, 12, 13) or foundry
        nozzle ⎧ from what trees does the
        body (of wood, skin, clay) ⎨ wood used come from?
        skin membranes, goatskins ⎩ what skins are used?
to activate the bellows

Traditional Technologies

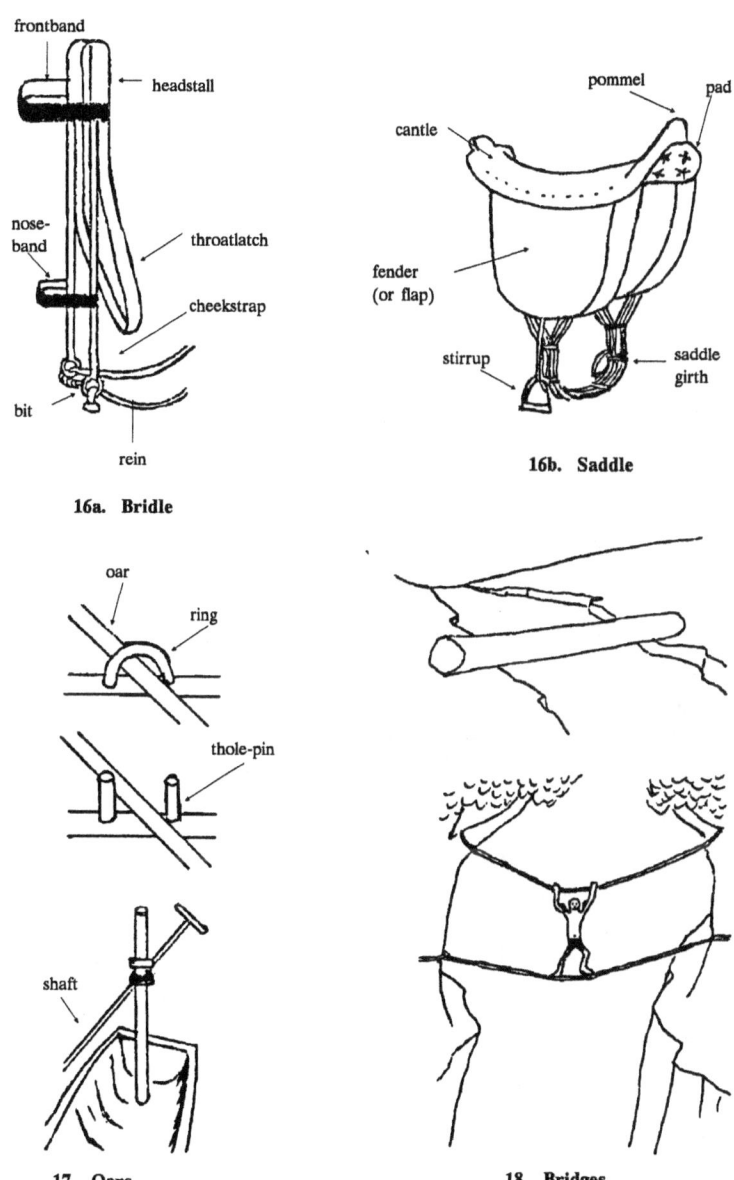

16a. Bridle

16b. Saddle

17. Oars

18. Bridges

Transportation

2 Transportation

2.1 General

    nomadic
    settled
to carry (find different verbs depending on:
        the place of carrying   -head, arm, etc.
        the object carried   -child, water, fruits, etc.
        the container   -basket, bottle, etc.
to transport
to lift
to load, unload
to pull, drag; pulling (whom or what does one pull? on what?)
    portage, porter
to run, travel (vehicle)

2.1.1. Carrying by man, animal.

baggage
package, pack, bundle
load
    handle (for carrying a load)
    pad (for carrying on the head), made of what (cloth rolled up, circle of straw)
    cord, tie, strap (to fasten the load on the back or shoulders)
    strap over the shoulders or back
    headband (fig. 14)
    belt for carrying babies (made of what?)
    hood in the clothes for carrying a baby (cf. fig. 15)
for nomadic peoples:
    horse, donkey; bovine animals (which?)
    camel
    dromedary
        bridle   { cheekstrap
        (fig.   headstall
        16a)   noseband
                      bit
                  reins
        saddle   { padding
        (fig.   saddle-girth
        16b)   stirrup
                  arch
                  packsaddle
containers for carrying:
    basket with headband (cf. fig. 14)
    baskets (various, depending on use)
    Indicate the use of each basket, the different parts, the material used
        for making it, the user (man or woman), the maker
    basket carried on the back
    satchel, bag

calabash
leaf for wrapping (from which plants?)

2.1.2. Vehicles.
to ride (a car, a bicycle)
    bicycle, motorcycle
    car, auto
    truck, van
different parts distinguished on these vehicles: handlebar, steering wheel, cab (cabin), engine, pedal, brake, axle, tire, wheel, chassis, ... (deflate), to blow out (tire)

2.2 Navigation

to navigate
    raft (logs tied together)—made of what? wood, reeds, etc.
    dugout canoe (different types: large, small, etc.)
    parts of the canoe—determine the materials used for each:
        stern, prow
        port, starboard
        bottom, seams (skin), seats
        carved trunk, or carcass, skin, or bark for covering the frame of the canoe
        pole ⎫
        paddle ⎬ type of wood used?
        oar (requires a fulcrum) ⎭ (cf. fig. 17)
        bailer, bailing scoop
        anchor ⎫
        cable, rigging (gear) ⎬ European boat
        mast, sail ⎭
    to paddle, paddler
    to steer, guide
    to embark, to land, to draw alongside
        pier, port
    to float (on the water)
    to drift (from shore), to capsize, to sink
        river, stream, tributary, upstream, downstream

2.3 Communication routes

path, way, lane, trail
European road, street
intersection, direction
to get one's bearings (are the stars used?)
to make (reference) marks (by banding trees, setting up objects, etc.)
landmark: broken branch, etc.
to get lost
ford for passing over, crossing water
bridge: trunk, vines tied fast (cf. fig. 18)
European bridge
airplane, airport

3 Techniques (Traditional Technologies)

3.1 General

3.1.1. Techniques of manufacture and production.
Elicit the following terms in sentences.
to construct, make
> He is making a basket.
> He is constructing a house.
> He is making a hoop net.
> I am putting together a trap.
> He is fashioning a pot.
> He is making a hoe.

to produce (=cultivate, raise, grow, gather, hunt, fish, etc.)-general term
> The village produces a lot of coffee.
> We produce food for the village by hunting and fishing.

to transform (raw material into a finished product)
> The artisan transforms the raw wood into a mortar.

3.1.2. Techniques of consumption.
to consume (=eat, drink, wear a garment, inhabit, etc.)-general term
> We consume food by eating and drinking

to use, use up, wear out; worn, worn out:
> This garment is worn out; I'm throwing it out.
> When you use a hoe, the blade wears down and becomes dull.

to care for, repair
> You must care for the blade of the hoe by sharpening it.
> Repair this calabash!

product, to produce / reproduce
> This crop is the product of my work (fruit of my labor).
> This field produces sesame; sesame reproduces itself every year.

3.2 Manufacturing Techniques

3.2.1. Stable (Unchangeable) solids.

3.2.1.1. Stone working.
> stone (hard or soft): granite, sandstone, graphite, chalk, etc .... uses
> bone, ivory
> shell—what is made with it? (earrings, necklaces, stone sculptures, etc.)
> tools: chisel, hammer, drill

to polish, drill, sculpt(ure)

3.2.1.2. Fibrous solids: wood.
> wood / tree / trunk / branch / root / base of the trunk

Traditional Technologies   421

to cut wood
    woodcutter, wood artisan (makers of seats, mortars, drums)
    carpenter, joiner ⎫
    sawmill   ⎬ European
to cut down a tree
to split wood; to split (v.i.)
to saw, to break wood
to carve, notch
to file, to rasp, to drill
to tap a tree
to sculpture wood
    board, plank
    wooden chest
    wood shavings, off-cuts
    worm-eaten, dry, brittle
    tools: wood knife (cutting edge in the same axis as the handle) ⎫ cf. fig. 19
               graver (cutting edge perpendicular to the axis of the handle) ⎭
               awl
               saw, sawtooth
               file, rasp (made of what?)
               polisher, sandpaper (made of what?—plants, etc.)
               piercer, drill (cf. fig. 20a)   hand drill
                                                  rolled in the palms
                                                  string drill
                                                  bow drill
               bit (cf. fig. 20b)
               axe, hatchet (cf. fig. 23)
               adze (cf. fig. 3b)
               chisel (cf. fig. 21)   narrow blade
                                             one-bevelled
                                             two-bevelled
               gouge (cf. fig. 22)
               wooden mallet
               plane

Make note of all trees, bushes, etc. used as wood. Note what the wood of each tree is used for, and if certain tools are only used for certain trees.

3.2.2. Semi-plastic solids.

metal
    iron, silver, gold, copper, bronze, lead, brass
to (s)melt metal
    foundry work
    ore
    blast furnace (cf. fig. 24)   Is there one or several shafts?
                                             chimney
                                             furnace mouth
                                             shaft

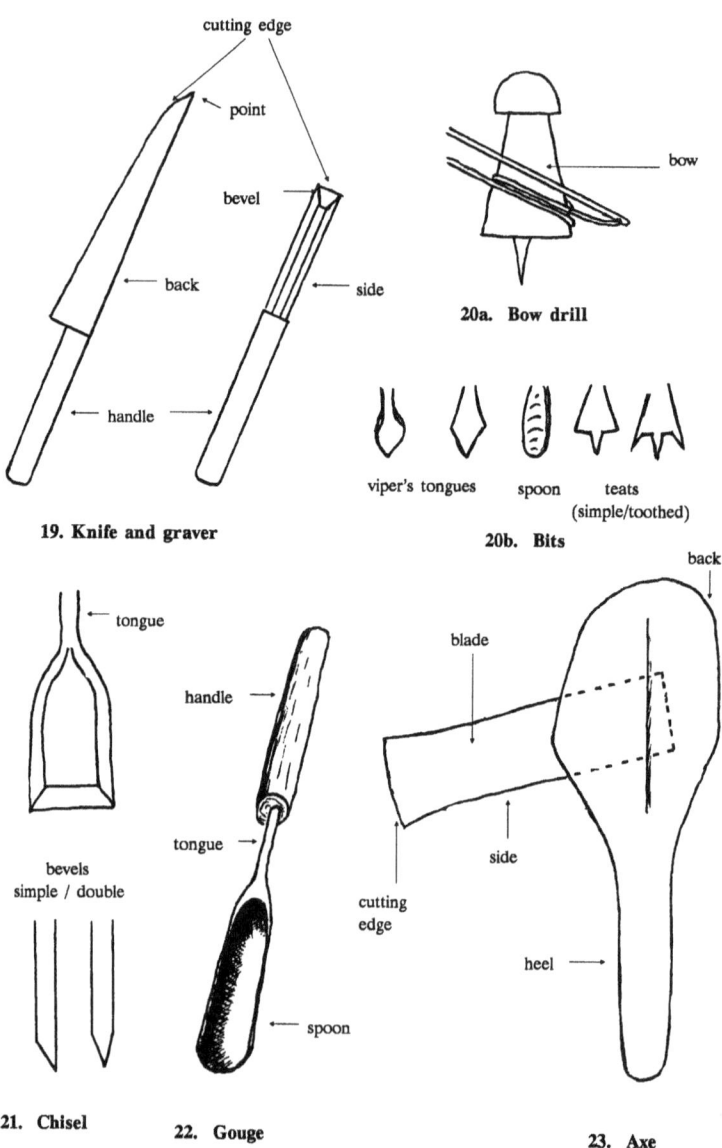

Tools for Stable Solids

Traditional Technologies

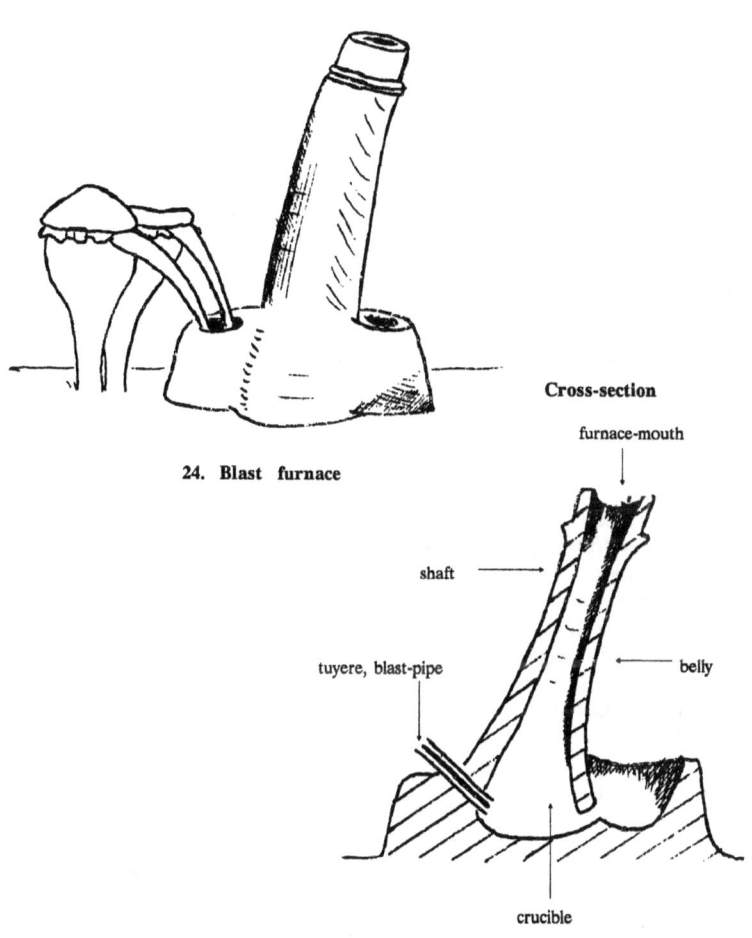

24. Blast furnace

Tools for Semi-Plastic Solids

        belly (widest part of the blast furnace)
        crucible
        blast pipes
        fire-rake (rod of iron or vine filled with water for recovering the cast iron)
mixture of ore and combustible material (for example, charcoal)
    cast iron (= alloy of iron and carbon); gangue containing the *loop;*
        loop of cast iron
to shingle cast iron, to purify it (possibly)
to cut up the *loop*
place where the blast furnace is set up
different materials for the construction of the furnace:
    blocks from a termite's nest
    earthen mortar, etc.
founder, smelter (only if distinct from the blacksmith: is it always the same person who smelts and forges?)
lost wax casting; molding the iron (cf. fig. 25)
    mold (stone, soft material, etc.)
    crucible (of clay)
    wax object (that is melted after being enveloped in the mold)
    to heat the mold (in order to melt the wax)
    to break the mold (to recover the iron)
blacksmith, to forge, forge (cf. fig. 26)
    forge work, forging
    mass of stone
    tools: hammer, anvil (the latter may be a stone of the type illustrated in fig. 26)
        burin graver, pliers (forceps), tongs, awl, drill, file
        fireplace, firebox
        bellows
    to hammer / to shingle / to beat
    to purify iron
    to shape while hot
    to become red in the fire
    to be incandescent

3.2.3. Plastic solids.

3.2.3.1. Weakly cohesive plastic solids (earth).
earth, soil, space for drying manioc (top of termite's nest, flat stone)
    sand, mud. Types of soils.
to break up the earth
    hoe, stick for digging loose soil-agriculture
    pickaxe, mattock (hard soil)-mines, earthworks
to move earth
    shovel, container (made of what?), basket, spade
to pack down the earth (the floor of a house, walls)
    rammer, plank, and hoe

Traditional Technologies

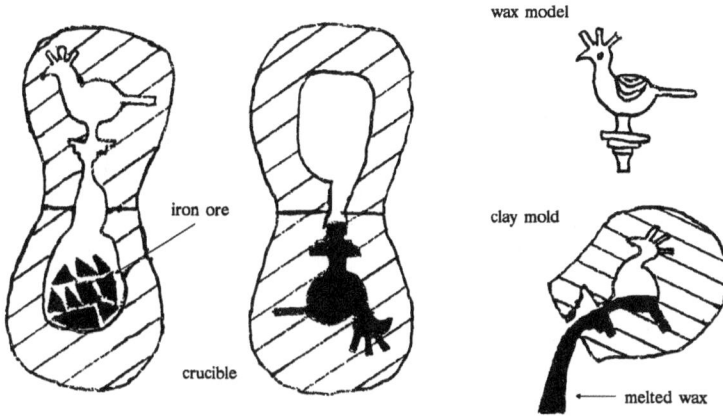

25. Lost wax casting

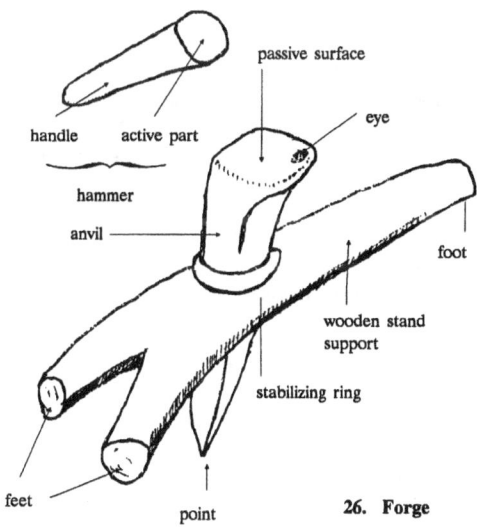

26. Forge

Tools for Semi-Plastic Solids

3.2.3.2. Truly plastic solids (pottery).

3.2.3.2.1. Preparation.
clay earth, place where clay is gathered
    lump of rough clay
clay, kaolin—other materials used for firing
        to purify the raw clay
        to pound, sift the clay—clay powder
        to form the wet clay.
        to degrease (= to mix materials with the wet clay to decrease plasticity)
degreasing agent (straw, grass, sawdust, ashes, hair, feathers, sand, latex, ground glass, etc.)
to knead, beat clay
clay beater (to make the clay of the desired consistency)

3.2.3.2.2. Shaping.
to model, mold, turn
    potter (m. or f.), potter's workshop

3.2.3.2.2.1.a. Normal modelling.
lump of raw shaped clay (cf. fig. 27)
    to dig out the lump; to build up the sides; to lengthen the clay
    to smooth the exterior—smoother (pottery shard)
    to polish the exterior—polisher (roller)
    to scrape out the interior (to remove irregularities)—scraper (of shards, of iron)
    to shape the lips of the neck (by turning them out)
    to turn the neck progressively out on itself (if there is no wheel)
    shaping stand: broken pottery on the bottom, basin, shelf
    receptacle full of water in which the tools soak (scraper, smoother, toothed wheel, ...) while in use

3.2.3.2.2.1b. Coil modelling.
coil pottery-making (process), cf. fig. 28
    to wind around in a spiral (the clay coils)
    clay coil
    to polish, to bind the joints

3.2.3.2.2.2. Molding.
mold
lost frame (straw framework), cf. fig. 30

3.2.3.2.2.3. Turning.
wheel (cf. fig. 29)

3.2.3.2.3. Treatment before firing.
to dry the pottery in the sun (after shaping)
to coat the pottery with oil (to facilitate the application of the decorations)
to imprint the decoration
    Toothed wheel, cf. fig. 32: cylinder, braided or of fluted wood
    iron ring, twisted (fig. 32) or toothed

Traditional Technologies

27. Lumps of clay

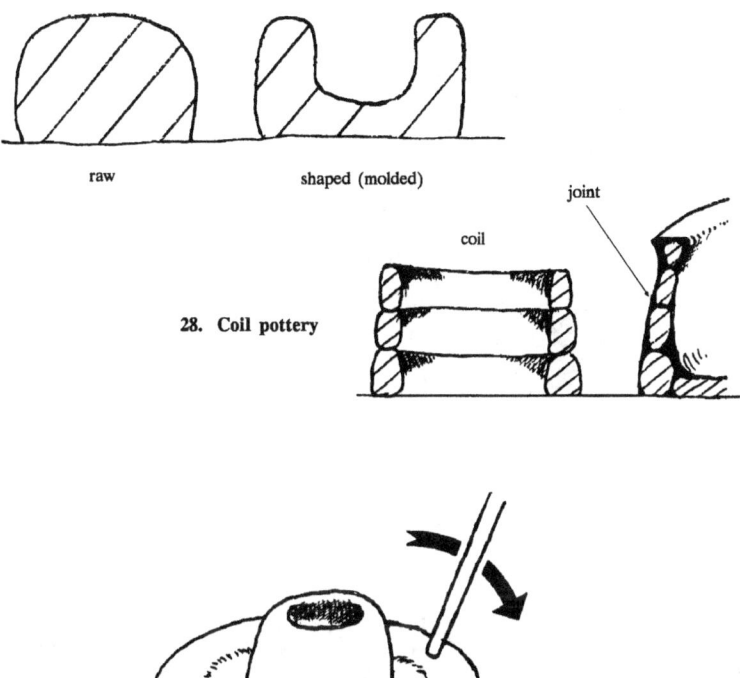

raw   shaped (molded)

28. Coil pottery

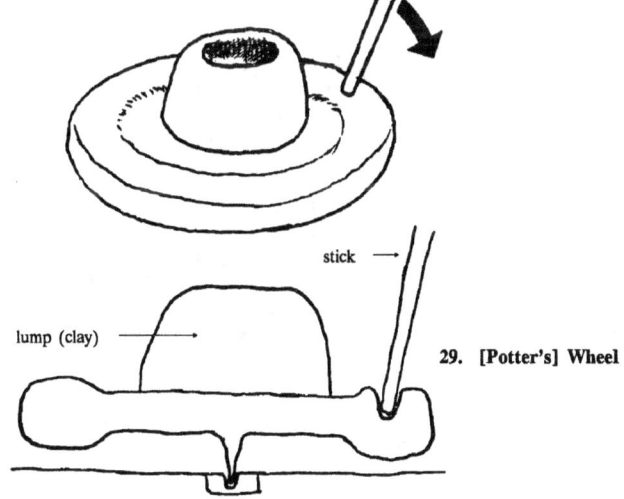

29. [Potter's] Wheel

Tools for Plastic Solids

428   Questionnaire 10

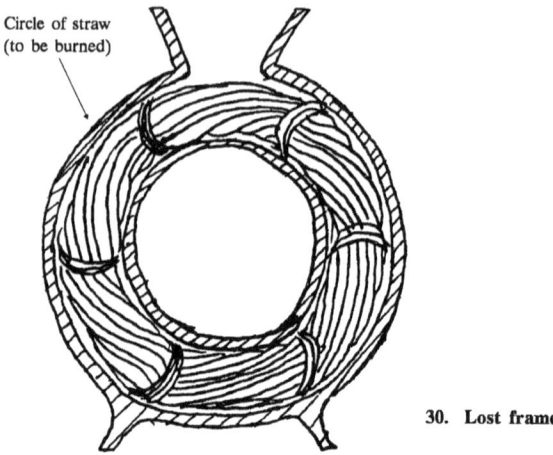

30. Lost frame pottery

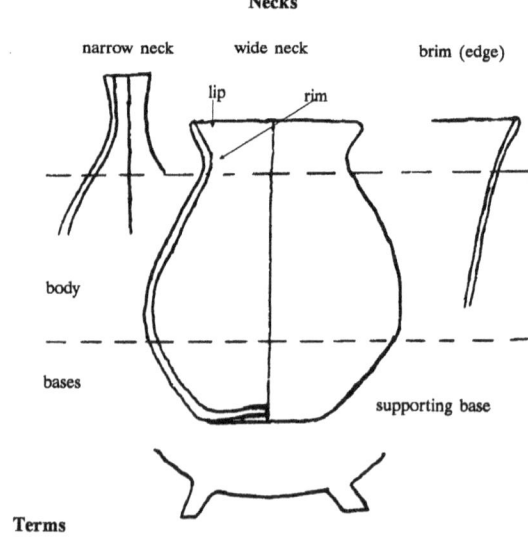

31. Terms

Pottery Terms

Traditional Technologies

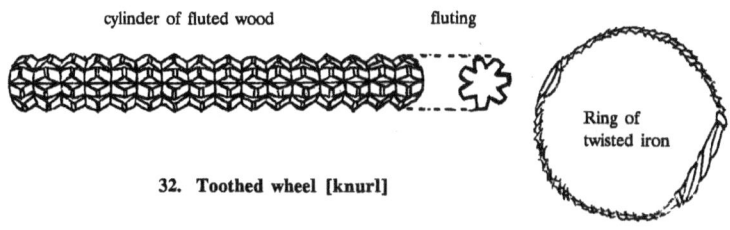

32. Toothed wheel [knurl]

33. Non-masonry potter's kiln: combustible material

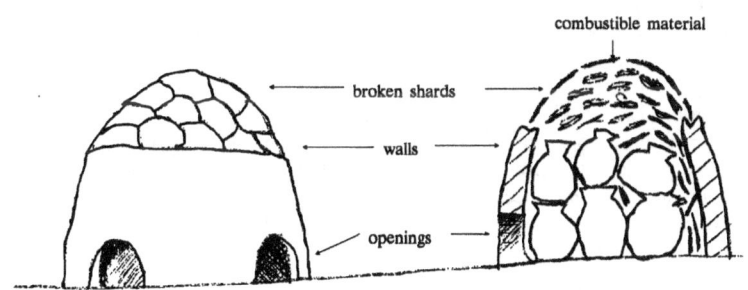

34. Masonry work kiln

Pottery Firing

to incise the decoration
  tip of an iron bracelet, smooth bracelet
to apply slip
  slip (=clay coating on the pottery surface, before firing)
  glaze (=substance which vitrifies on firing: what is it obtained from?
      resin, minerals, etc ...)
    solutions of mineral colors;
      (black) graphite base
      chalk base (reds, whites, yellows). Application before or after firing etc ....

3.2.3.2.4. Firing.
to fire, firing of pottery
nonmasonry kiln (cf. fig. 33): is there a word for this notion?
  combustible material used (wood, carbon, peat, grass, etc.)
masonry work kiln (cf. fig. 34)
  upper shell of old shards
  openings (for the draft)
breakage (=% of vessels broken in firing)

3.2.3.3. Plastic adhering solids.

3.2.3.3.1. Colors and dyes.
color
  to color (something): general term + different verbs depending on the color
  coloring agent: charcoal, soils (which?), fruit juices (which?), tree sap,
wood (e.g., mahogany gives red wood which is ground into powder)
  to grind (mineral or plant powders)
  to thin out with water, with oil
  painting: of the body, on a wall, or of an object (weapons)
  to paint, to coat
  to dye, dye (n.) (different types according to color, preparation, etc.)
    material from which the dye is taken (bark, etc.)
    (=material containing or giving off metallic oxides which fix a dye in cloth:
    it is put into the dyeing vat along with the dye before adding the cloth)
    (=chemical substance for fixing dye)
    to thrust, immerse items to be dyed into the vat

3.2.3.3.2. Glues and gums.
glue (different types according to the components: blood for sticking light objects,
    feathers; flour and plant juice; tree resin, beeswax: make note of the preparation,
    use, etc.)
to glue two pieces together, to join by gluing
to stick a piece onto an object to repair it (calabash, etc.)
birdlime (for trapping small animals, birds)
    (make note of the different components, mixtures, and where each one comes
        from)

Traditional Technologies 431

> to daub a spot with birdlime
> rubber tree
> rubber
> latex
> to collect latex, sap

since colonization
(grown commercially)

3.2.3.3.3 Roughcast
to roughcast
    roughcast: soils, mortars,
                   cob (= soil + agglutinant)
                   animal (dung)
                   plant (straw, etc.)
                   mineral (lime, plaster)
    plaster, cement (European)

3.2.4 Flexible solids

3.2.4.1 Bark
bark (what trees? specify the use of different types)
    to strip, remove the bark from a tree
    tools for the removal, if specific to this activity
    what is made with this bark? doors, receptacles, clothing, basketwork
    to cut up the bark (to get pieces of the desired size)
        sewn bark
        to stitch, join bark
           awl (cf. fig. 35)
           to soften bark (how?)
           tapa (= cloth made by pounding strips of wet bark, with parallel fibers), cf. fig. 37
           strip of bark for making tapa
               to soak the strips
               to scrape the strips   } to get rid of their outer layer
               scraper
           to superpose the layers of the strips
           to beat, hammer, pound the strips
               beater (cf. fig. 36) (made of what?)
           to moisten, dampen the strips
               bark cloth, clothing

3.2.4.2 Skin hide
untreated, raw skin (uses of the skin of each animal?)
    to skin, take off the skin
    to dry the skin, drying (cf. fig. 38)
    to nail down the skin (to stretch it out and dry it on the ground)
    to scrape the skin (to pare it, to remove the hair)
        scraper (for scraping)
    to tan the hide
        tanning solution (what is it made of?)
    to soften the hide
        by crumpling

432 Questionnaire 10

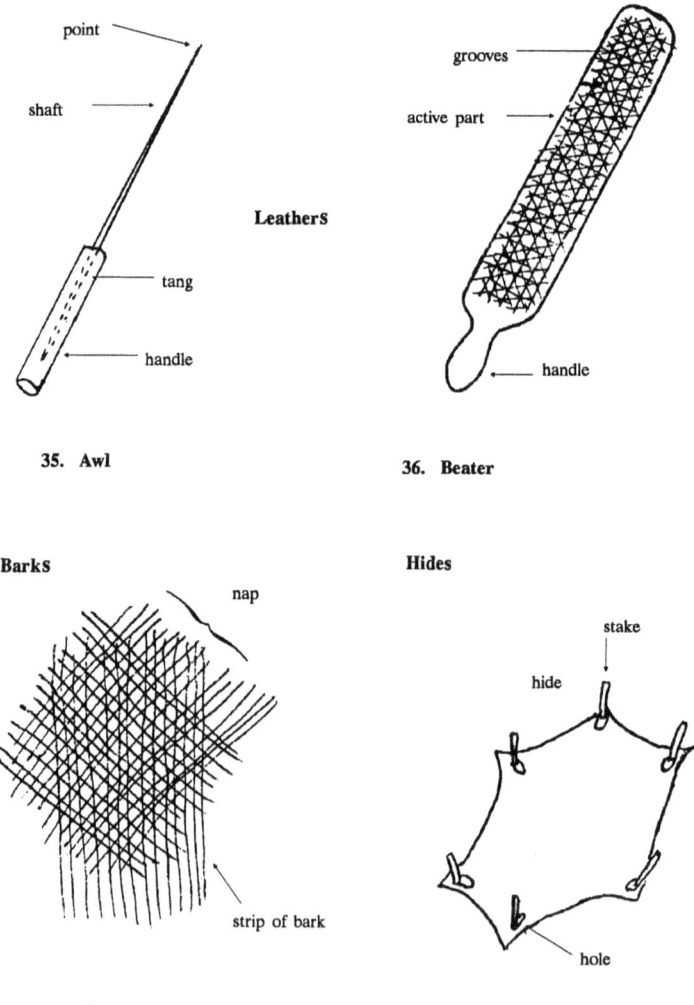

Leathers

35. Awl

36. Beater

Barks

Hides

37. Tapa

38. Drying

Leatherworking

Traditional Technologies

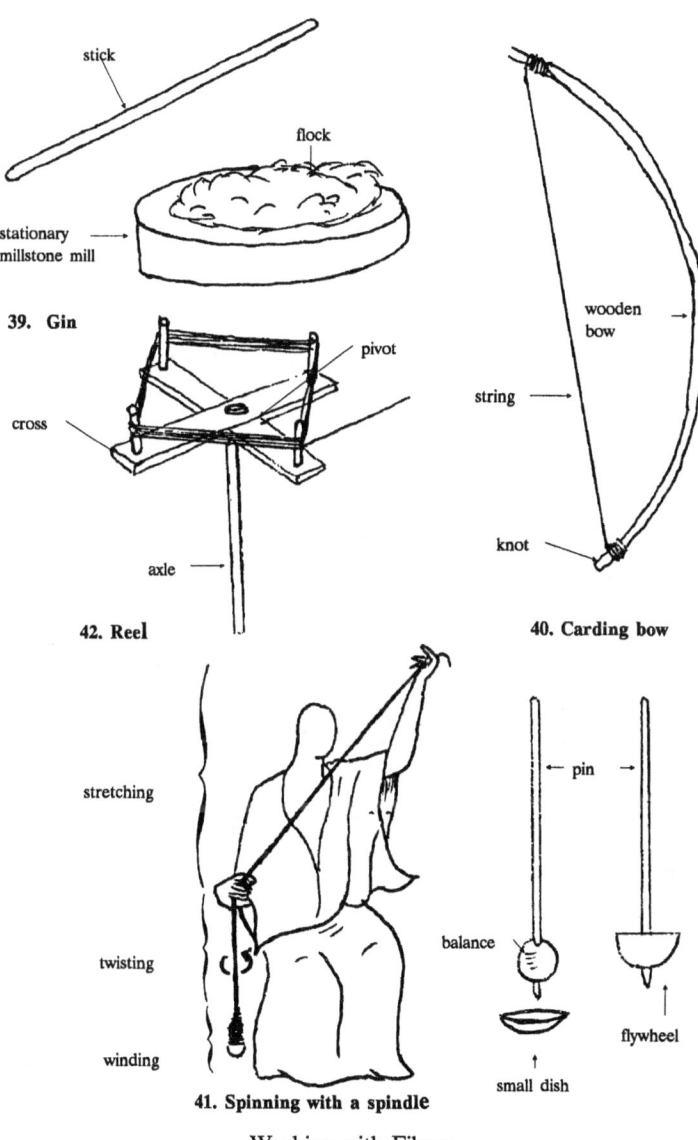

39. Gin
40. Carding bow
42. Reel
41. Spinning with a spindle

Working with Fibers

by beating (alone or with leaves) (which ones?)
to get a shine, sheen,
to crumple, to beat
to cut the hide into strips
tanned hide, leather

3.2.4.3. Spinning.
to spin (twist fibers to make thread), spinner, spinning
tools: thread, string, rope

3.2.4.3.1. Preparation.
raw, unprepared fiber (plants used?)
       flax   if used to make thread
       hemp
- retting, to ret (= soaking in water to separate the thready (fibrous) bark from the stem)
    - retting-pond (= place to put things to ret)
    - to crumple (to divide the fibers contained in the stem)
    - to beat (to soften it)
    - to comb (the fibers to disentangle them)
        cotton (two senses: textile fiber; finished thread)
    - to stretch out the thread in the sun
    - to unravel (by hand)
    - ginning, to gin (= to separate the flock from the seeds)
        gin (cf. fig. 39)
    - to card (to separate the fibers and set them in the same direction)
        carding bow
    - to join, gather the strands together
        distaff (from a stalk, a grass, or other)

3.2.4.3.2. Twisting, spinning.
to stretch / pull (the thread), drawing / stretching cf. fig. 41a
to twist, twisting
to wind, winding
to roll the fibers
    between the fingers
    between the palm and the thigh
to spin onto the spindle
spindle (cf. fig. 41b)   pin
                             flywheel, balance
                             small dish
                             spinning powder (to make the thread slide better)
to wind up the thread
    reel (= instrument allowing the winding); cf. fig. 42   axle
                                                                 cross
                                                                 pivot
                                                                 skein
                                                                 bobbin of thread

3.2.4.3.3. Putting together.

a) by weaving
    to assemble threads by braiding
    to braid
        (to make a thicker thread than the fibers: thin thread, string, rope)
        braid with 2, 3, 4, or more strands (cf. fig. 43)

b) by knotting
    to tie a bond, to knot
    to tie a knot (different terms depending on type of knot)
    to tighten a knot
    to be well knotted, well tied
    to be loose, poorly tied
    to undo quickly, with a snap (for a slip knot)
    to knot a net, to weave a net (cf. fig. 45)
    to intertwine (by tying)
    to entangle, tangle up the thread
    to knit (recent)

bond, tie, knot (cf. fig. 44):
    simple knot (roofing, house frame)
    reef knot (net)
    slip knot (trap)
    strap knot
    whipping (when putting two parts together, when putting a handle on a tool)

tools: marlinespike, awl for untying knots
    clip, buckle (to join two parts)
    knitting needles (European, stems of bushes, bicycle spokes)

3.2.4.4. Sewing.

to stitch, unstitch
to hem
to mend, darn
to double (the thread)
to cut (a piece of cloth)
    leather knife (= knife to cut leather, cloth); cf. fig. 48
    scissors

tools: awl   } for piercing (cf. fig. 46)
    awl with handle
    needle (cf. fig. 47): eye, point, shaft
        to thread a needle
        sewing thread
    thimble or protective device (e.g., skin in the hollow of the hand)
    sewing machine

3.2.4.5. Cloth.

3.2.4.5.1. General.

to braid / to weave (general term covering both)
    I braid, weave a basket, a hoop net
    I weave material
    naps of parallel components

436

Questionnaire 10

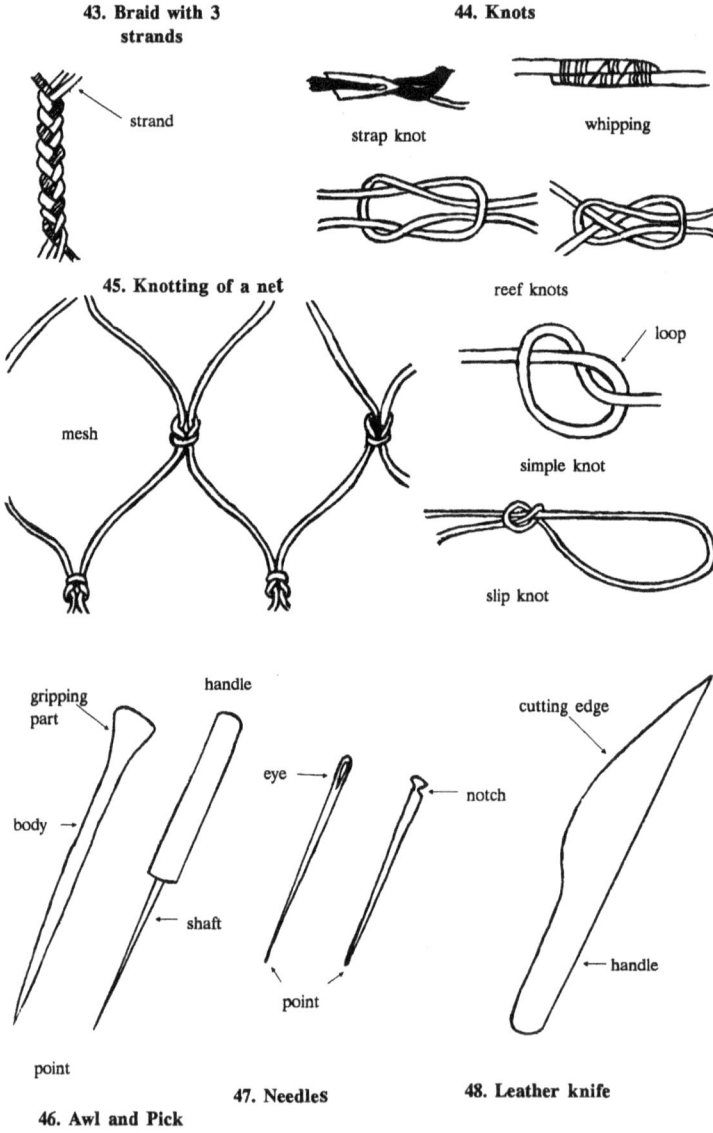

43. Braid with 3 strands
44. Knots
strap knot
whipping
reef knots
45. Knotting of a net
mesh
loop
simple knot
slip knot
gripping part
handle
body
eye
notch
cutting edge
shaft
point
handle
point
46. Awl and Pick
47. Needles
48. Leather knife

Knots and Tools

Traditional Technologies

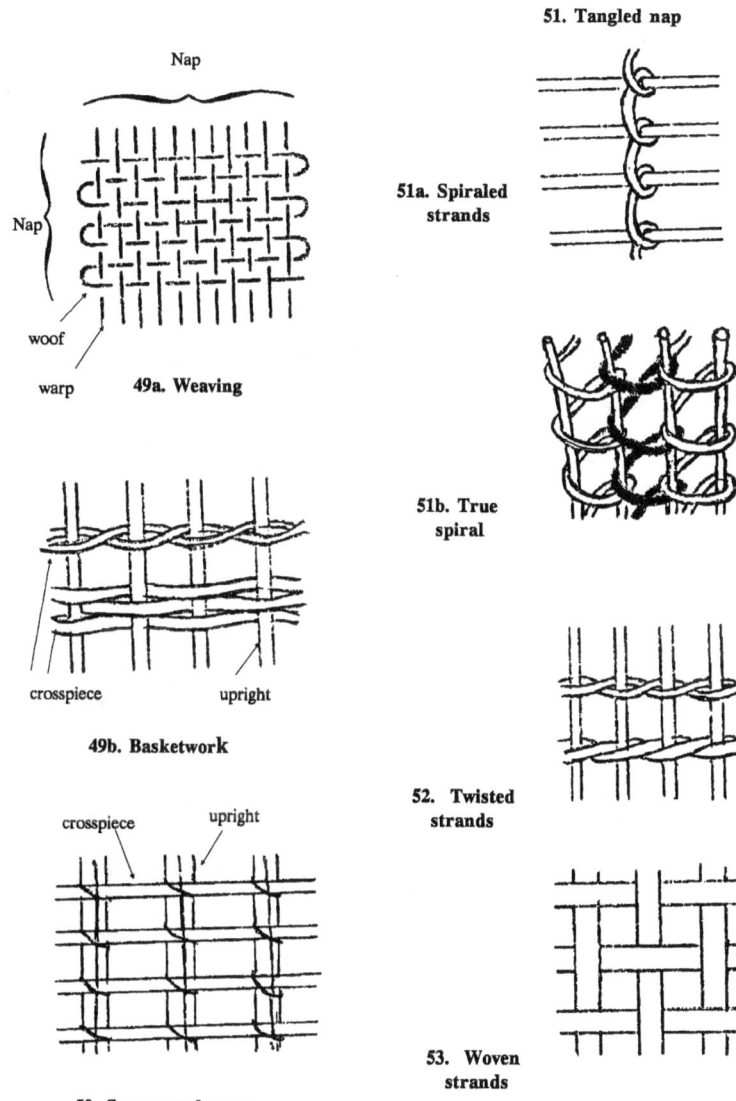

Weaves

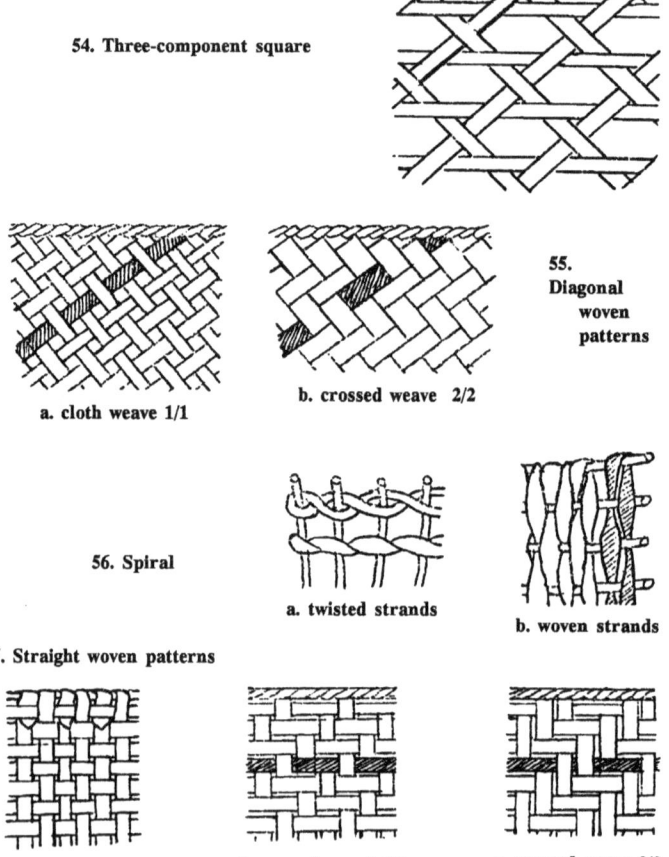

54. Three-component square

55. Diagonal woven patterns

a. cloth weave 1/1

b. crossed weave 2/2

56. Spiral

a. twisted strands

b. woven strands

57. Straight woven patterns

a. cloth weave 1/1

b. serge [weave] 2/1

c. crossed weave 2/2

Basketry

Traditional Technologies

weaving = warp—woof (cf. fig. 49a)
basketwork = upright—crosspiece (cf. fig. 49b)
superposed naps (in construction, fig. 50)
tangled naps (basketry, weaving):
- spiral strand basketry (the moveable piece goes around each fixed element (fig. 51a, b)
- corded basketry (the moveable elements are twisted in pairs around the fixed pieces: fig. 52); example: hoop net
- woven basketry (the moveable elements go around the fixed pieces without twisting

tools:
awl (to separate the rows of the warp so that the woof thread can more easily be inserted)

3.2.4.5.2. *Basketry.*

basketry (note for each technique the basketwork that illustrate(s) it)
   a) diagonal
      3-component square (cf. fig. 54)
      cloth weave (under one, over one), cf. fig. 55a
      crossed weave (under two, over two; advanced one element in each row), cf. fig. 55b: mats, baskets
      serge weave (2/1, 3/1, 4/1)—edges of mats
   b) straight
      spiralled: superposed naps
      true spiral (cf. fig. 51b)
      twisted strands (cf. fig. 56a)
      woven strands (cf. fig. 56b)
      twisted (cf. fig. 52)
      woven: cloth weave 1/1 (cf. fig. 57a)
      cross 2/2 (cf. fig. 57c)
      serge 1/2 (cf. fig. 57b)
      3/3, etc.
   starting from the bottom of the basket (beginning of the weaving)
      to begin weaving a basket
      to start into the weaving
      fastening of the edge of basket, basketwork: the finishing
      to finish   the weaving of a basket
                weaving
to weave, do basketwork / to braid (hair, braids)
basket-maker

3.2.4.5.3. *Weaving.*

weaving, to weave, weaver
   warp (situated in front on a frame)
   woof (active part)
   to (set up the) warp
tools: reel (for preparing the threads during the warping)
      loom   with 2 rows of rails (cf. fig. 58)
                 with 1 row of rails (cf. fig. 59)
      frame

warp/beam
cloth/beam
blocking device   of the cylinder   (pawl, bar, brake)
                        of the rod
harness equipment (for the two-rail loom)
spreading bar
heddle
heddle rod
mesh
pulley
treadle
step (=space created by the alternating movement of the beams
    into which the woof thread is put)
lease rods
reed
comb or knife
spool
shuttle
fabric, cloth:
    weaves (cf. fig. 62)   cloth 1/1
                                      crossed 2/2
                                      serge 1/2, 1/3, 1/4, etc.
pit (under the loom, where the pedals are); cf. fig. 61
name of a cloth pattern

Make note of the different names of the different manufactured and European cloths: plaid, blend, wool, etc.

What are the warp thread, woof thread, the wood of the posts, vine strands made of? (rattans, grasses, etc.)

3.2.5. Fluids.

fluids = liquids, flour, grains, etc.
treatment by means of objects used to contain, transport, or release fluids

3.2.5.1. Collecting fluids.

to collect, to gather, to gather up a pile / to gather objects one by one, etc.
tools: dam (for fishing)—different types
well: winch
           rope
           coping
           hole
           bottom
tank, cistern (to collect water)
waterjar, flour jar, grain jar
granary (cf. fig. 63, 64), made of what?
              wood
              earth
              basketry (for grains, agricultural products)
              how?   on piles
                           on the ground

Traditional Technologies

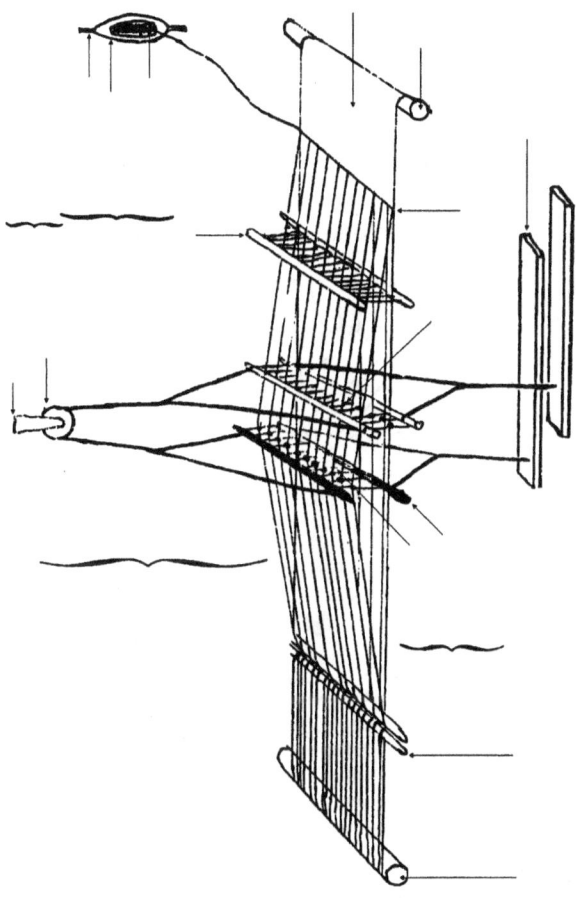

58. Two-Rail Weaving Loom

Weaving

442

Questionnaire 10

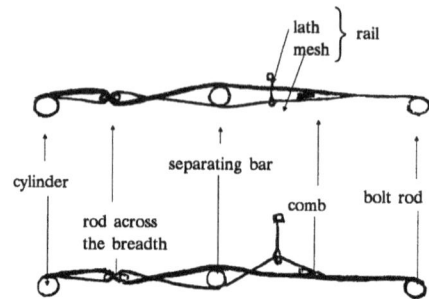

59. Weaving loom with one row of rails

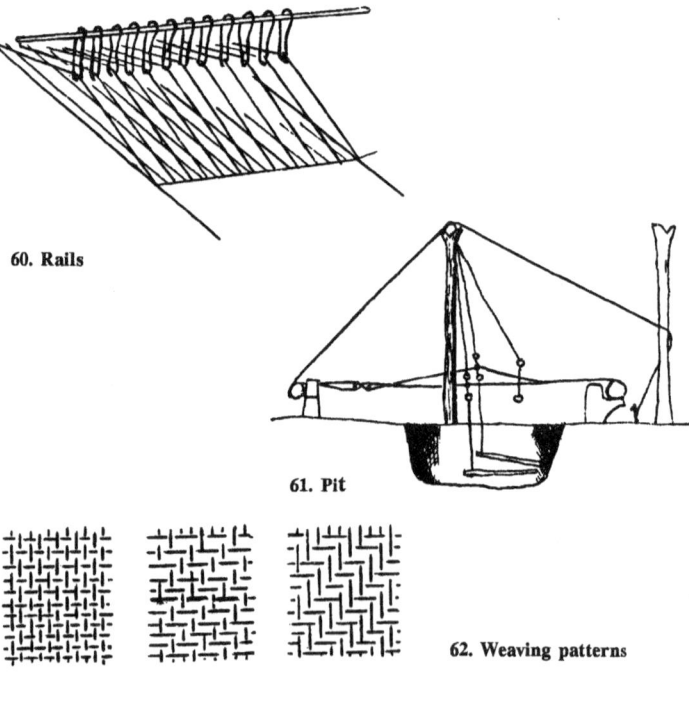

60. Rails

61. Pit

62. Weaving patterns

cloth weave 1/1   serge weave 2/1   crossed weave 2/2

Weaving

Traditional Technologies

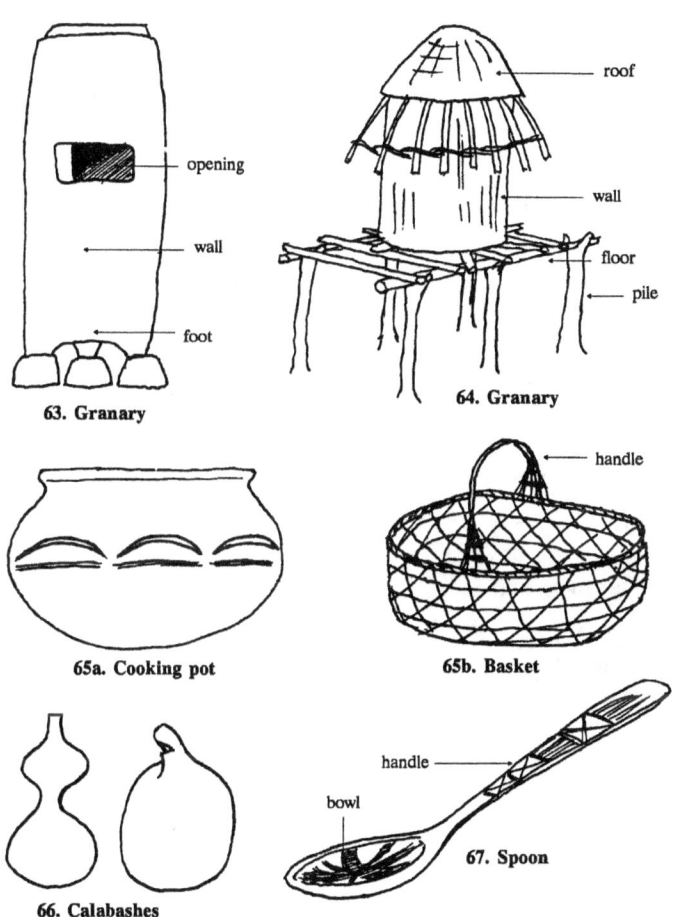

63. Granary
64. Granary
65a. Cooking pot
65b. Basket
66. Calabashes
67. Spoon

Containers

(grain) silo
>> large-sized portable containers
>>> jar, baskets (cf. fig. 65b)
>>> barrel, vat,
>> small-sized portable containers
>>> keg, jar, pitcher, bottle
>>> tub, basin, cooking pot (cf. fig. 65a)
>>> bowl, beaker, calabash (cf. fig. 66)
>>> flat basket, basin, shallow bowl, dish, goblet, spoon (cf. fig. 67)

3.2.5.2. Transporting fluids.

to draw (water)
- by hand, with a bucket or a waterskin, goatskin, rubber pouch, leaf
- by rope, with a bucket, etc.
- pulley well
- sump (= hole dug in the ground where the water shows on the surface)
- pipes (dug in the soil) for irrigation for example (of what material can they be made?)
- channel
- gutter
- hand-carrying:
  - bridle (= stationary or fixed strap)
  - straight or curved handle (cf. fig. 68)
  - lip (cf. fig. 69)
  - nipple (cf. fig. 70)
  - handle (cf. fig. 71)
  - spoon handle

3.2.5.3. Transferring fluids.

to transfer, decant, seep
to fill a receptacle
to be full
to water
- stopper (measuring cap)
- faucet
- lip (cf. fig. 72)
- neck (cf. fig. 73)
- spout, neck on side (cf. fig. 74)
- funnel: different types depending on size, use, form, etc. (cf. fig. 75)
  - upper and lower openings
    - pin to keep the leaf rolled up—what is it made of?
      - what tree does the leaf come from?
- filter (inside the funnel), made of what?
- funnel for oil, for salt, for wine
  - small, large
  - wooden, iron, leaf, etc.
- sieve
- pipe for the flow of sap into a calabash (cf. fig. 76)

Traditional Technologies

68. Handle   69. Lip   70. Nipple   71. Handle

72. Lip   73. Neck

74. Spout (on the side)

Containers

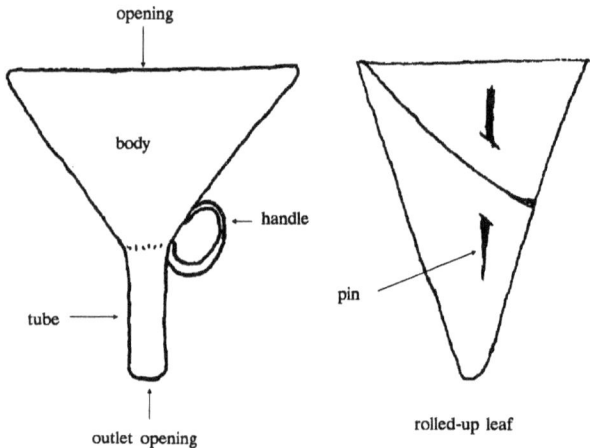

75. Funnels

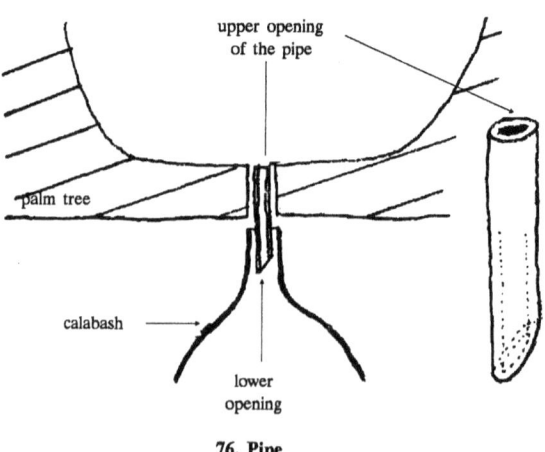

76. Pipe

Transferring Liquids

Traditional Technologies

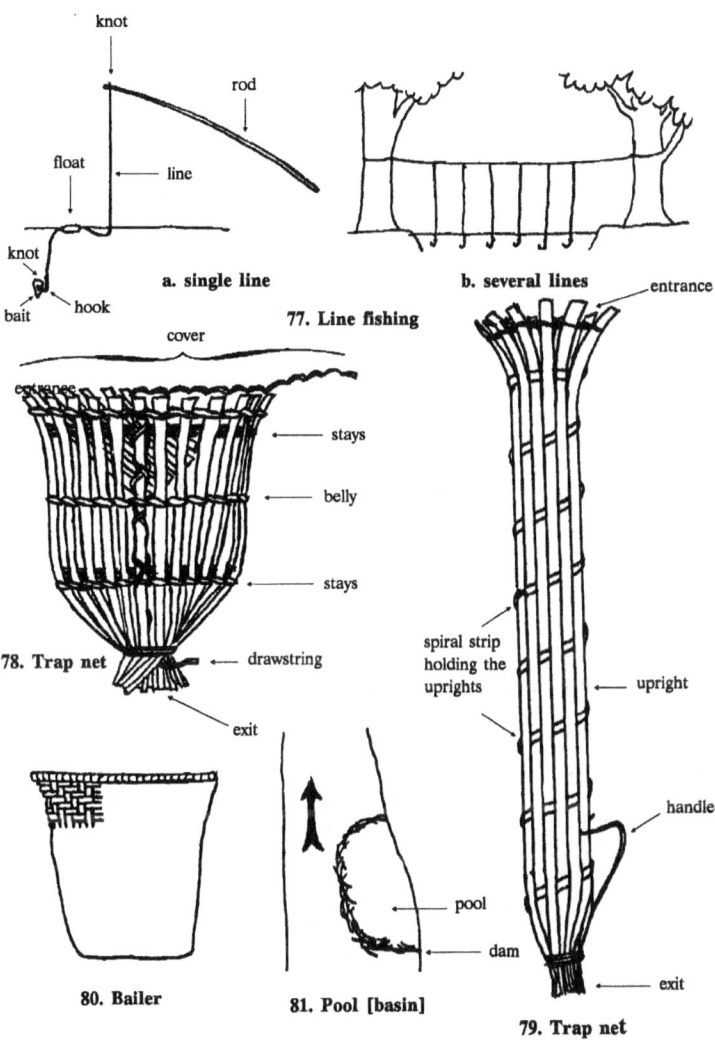

a. single line
b. several lines
77. Line fishing
78. Trap net
79. Trap net
80. Bailer
81. Pool [basin]

Fishing

3.3 Techniques for Acquiring Things

3.3.1. Fishing.

fishing, fisherman, fisherwoman
 collective fishing ⎫
 individual fishing ⎪
 spear fishing ⎪
 fishing by hook with or without a rod, net fishing, ⎬ specify for each
  hoop net fishing ⎪ whether it is men's
 harpoon fishing ⎪ or women's activity
 fishing with poison ⎪
 fishing with weir dam or blocked-off river that is emptied ⎭
to fish, to scoop up water to gather fish
to fish (different terms depending on the procedure used)
fishing shelter (made of what kind of wood and leaves?)
holes in the river where fish live (which kinds?)
river full of fish
tools: harpoon: head
      shaft
  float (made of what material: shards, bark, ... ?)
  fishing spear: barbed point
       hook
       tie
  fishing rod (cf. fig. 77a)
  fishing net (of vine, bark, etc.)
  hook (what materials?)
  float
  bait (worms, insects, leaves, fish plants, etc.)
  lines cast (3, 4 hooks) (cf. fig. 77b)
    several lines
  landing net, simple or double
     ⎧ with one entrance (different types
   trap ⎨ depending on shape, use, and size
     ⎪ cf. fig. 78–79
     ⎩ with 2 or 3 successive entrances
   entrance to the trap ⎫
   bottom ⎬ what
   stays reinforcing the bottom, middle, top ⎬ different
   body ⎭ materials
             are used?
 weir dam (enclosure)
  dam to empty (side pool, cf. fig. 81)
  basket bailer (or pottery bailer) (cf. fig. 80)
   woven tightly for emptying water from the pool; what is it made of?
to dam up the river to make a pool
to erect, construct a dam
to drain
fishing net (different types: casting net (thrown), net (set), ...)
 net bottom
 mesh
  ballast (stones, copper rings, etc., hung on the bottom of the net)

Traditional Technologies

3.3.2. Hunting, war.

hunting
hunter
to proclaim, announce the hunt
to hunt
    collective hunting (by net, by fire, without fire) ⎫ different
    individual hunting, to hunt for one's personal use ⎭ types
hunting meeting (to set the methods and date of the hunt)
hunting master / hunter, beater / net-setter ... (in collective hunting)
hunting rites
place where hunters meet before beginning net hunting
hunting meeting (just before the hunt)
place of the great hunt (forest, savannah, etc.)
share of the hunt; division (specify the methods)
              empty-handed, to be emptyhanded
animal, game, meat; first animal killed by a man in his life, or each year
war, different types: latent war between villages, codified (feud) war, conflict, raid
    combat ⎰ between 2 people
            ⎱ between 2 villages
    warrior, soldier
    ambush
    hostage, prisoner of war
        slave (captured in war)
            fetters, shackles (put where? made of what?)
to wage war, to fight
    tracks, footprints ⎰ animal
                      ⎱ human
trail (different according to the animal)
    space trampled down by large animals (which ones?)
burrow
entrenched camp or village
siege
pack of dogs
to smell, to sniff (out)
to watch (out), to lie in wait ⎰ for someone
                            ⎱ for an animal
to crawl
    look-out (n.)
to pursue a man/game by his/its tracks
to pursue, chase (by running)
to flush out (a man, game)
to surround, encircle (a man, an animal)
to attack
to pounce on
to overpower
to catch, to seize (a prey)
to give a blow, hit someone/an animal with a weapon

450   Questionnaire 10

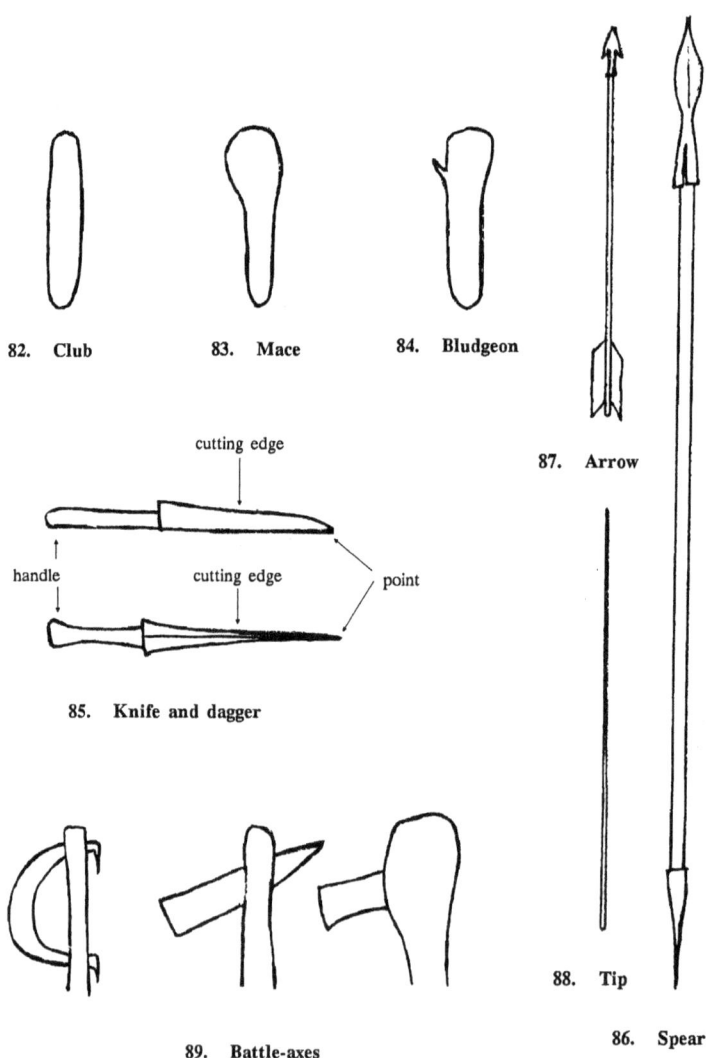

82. Club   83. Mace   84. Bludgeon

85. Knife and dagger

87. Arrow

88. Tip

89. Battle-axes

86. Spear

Arms

Traditional Technologies

to stab, pierce through (with a spear)
to wound (a man, an animal)
to kill: different terms depending on the weapon, the victim, etc.
to finish off, to give the death blow

3.3.2.1. Weapons.
club (cf. fig. 82)
mace (cf. fig. 83)
bludgeon (cf. fig. 84)
knife, different types: hunting knife, man's knife, etc. (cf. fig. 85a)
dagger (2 blade edges)
(battle-)axe, hatchet (if used as a weapon) cf. fig. 89
pike (does not leave the hand, is not thrown)
spear (projectile, distant and nearby combat)
assegai (projectile, distant combat only)
assegai   (general term) cf. fig. 86
spear   numerous types, according to size, shape, ethnic group, etc.
        point, tip ⎫
        rib, head ⎬   iron
        socket   ⎭
                shaft
                lower end (iron), decorations (copper spirals, etc.)
throwing crook (type of boomerang)
throwing knife   (general term) cf. fig. 93
              different according to shape, use, etc.
throwing hatchet, axe
throwing club
to throw, to hit
arrow (cf. fig. 87): tip
              shaft
              feathering ⎧ if feathers, from which animal? or
                           ⎩ if from a plant, which one?
    arrow poison (what is it made up of?)
        wooden tip (cf. fig. 88)
        bow (cf. fig. 90) different types
        quiver (different types)
to shoot a bow, a crossbow
to bend a bow
crossbow (cf. fig 91): body
                      bow-head
                      tail
                      top side, bottom side
                      thrust, spring
                      catch—device which keeps the string taut
                      groove—shaft for the arrow
For all these weapons, make note of the type of wood and other materials used to make them.
gun, rifle (general term), cf. fig. 92: different types:
    flintlock rifle
    cap gun

452   Questionnaire 10

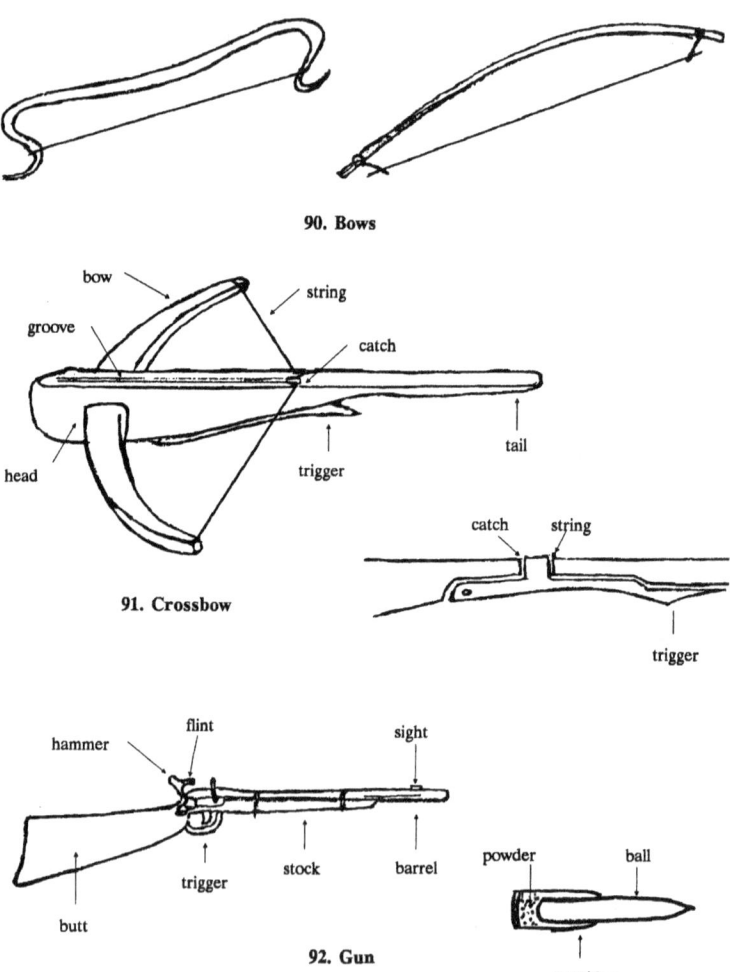

90. Bows

91. Crossbow

92. Gun

Arms

Traditional Technologies

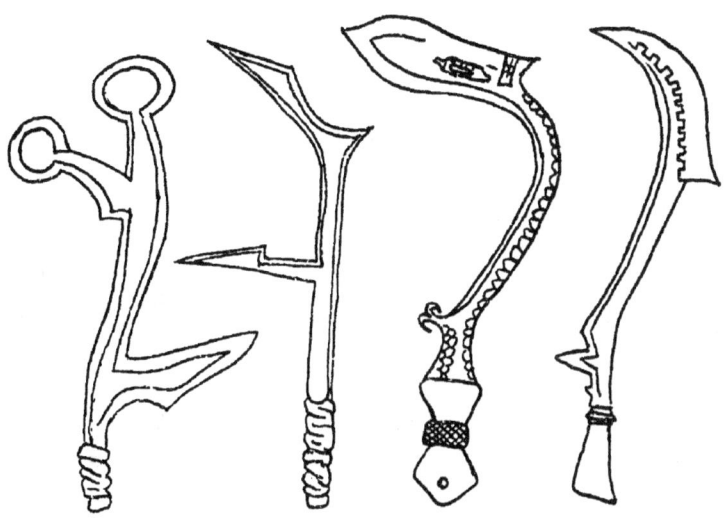

93. Throwing Knives

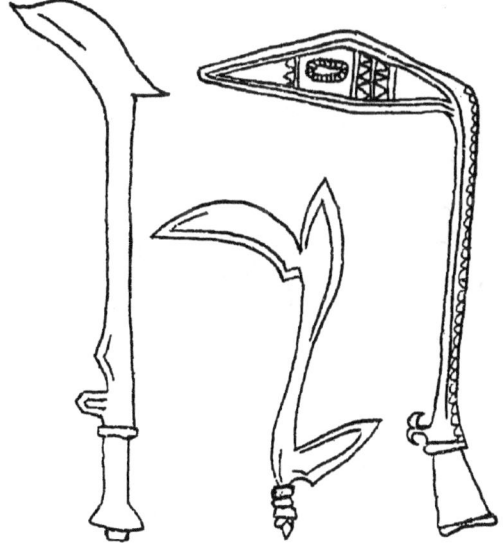

Arms

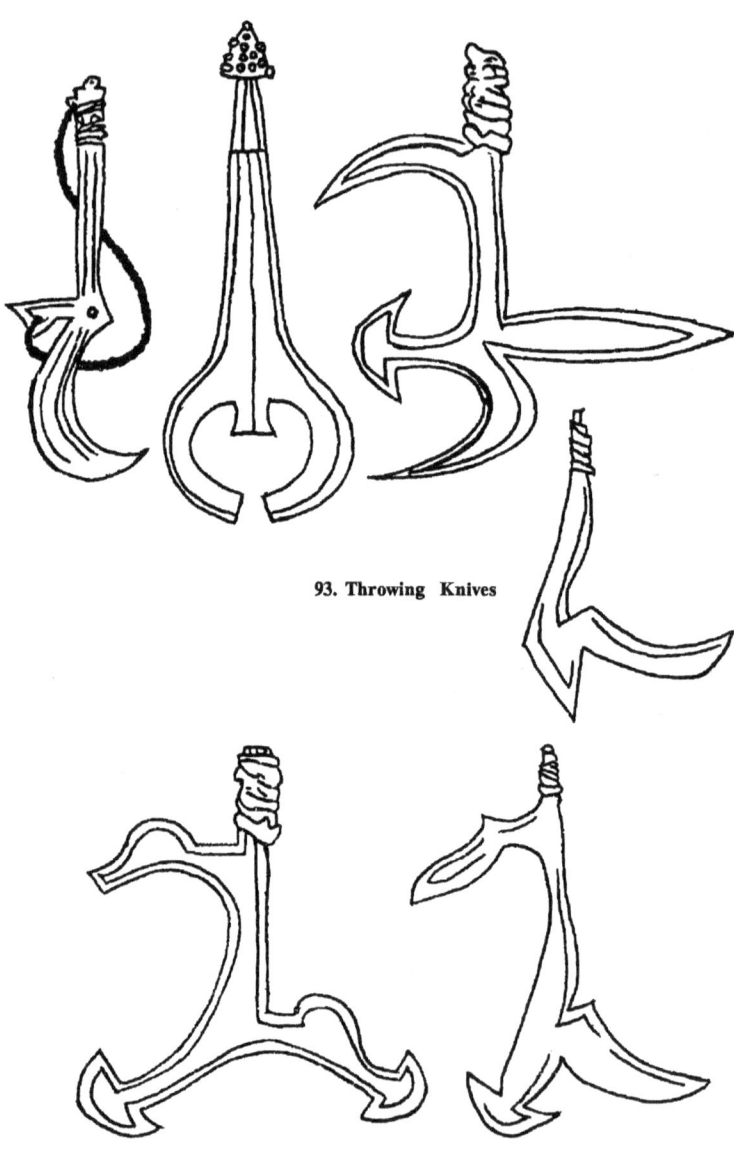

93. Throwing Knives

Arms

Traditional Technologies

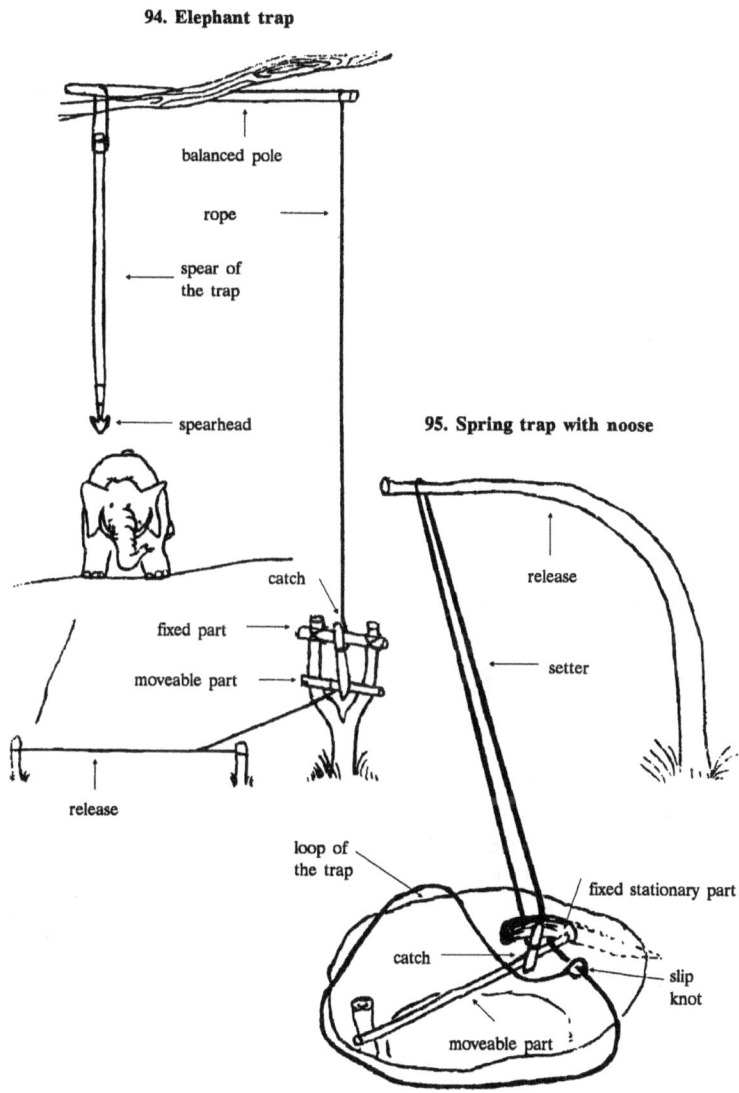

94. Elephant trap

95. Spring trap with noose

Traps

percussion rifle
machine gun
> barrel
> muzzle
> hammer
> butt
> stock, trigger-guard
> sling
> trigger
> sight(-finder)

cartridge (cf. fig. 92b): powder, cartridge case, bullet
to lift the hammer
to cock, to load
to aim, take aim
to fire, shoot
to jam
bang, click, sound of the submachine gun
shield—different types and different parts: front, back, strap

3.3.2.2. Traps.
to trap
to make traps
to set a trap
to catch in a trap, a pit, or a hole
to slide (open)
the trap slides (open and shut).
to get caught, be caught in a trap
> fall-trap (cf. fig. 94 and 96), different types:
> > for elephant
> > for buffalo
> > for rat
> > elephant trap: spear
> > (spear)head
> > rope
> > balance
> > release mechanism
> > fork and mechanism
> spring traps (cf. fig. 95)
> > snare trap
> > noose trap

different types depending on the animal (rabbit, bird, rat, squirrel), the bait (termite white ant, banana, manioc, peppers, various plants), or the means of activation (hole, net, bait)
> release (= bent branch)
> setter (attaches the release to the catch)
> fixed part that the catch rests on
> catch
> movable crosspiece (causes activation of the trap)
> loop, noose
> slip knot of the noose

Traditional Technologies 457

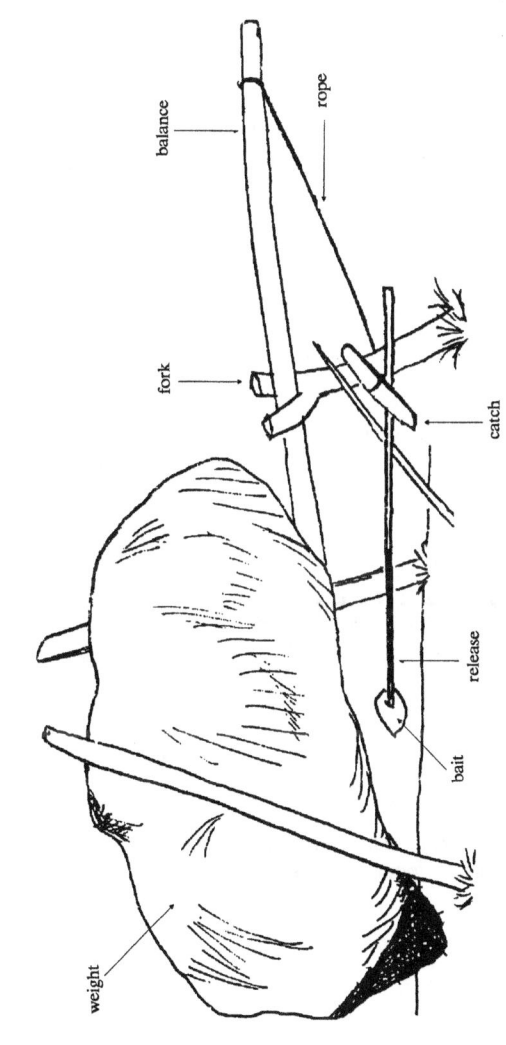

96. Rat trap

Traps

bait, lure (general term), different types: fruit, grain, etc.
    which ones?
    for which animals?
pit, trap (branch-covered)
cage-trap: spring-loaded
    guillotine
    guillotine door
    basket-cage (closed with the foot when the animal is caught)
to set a net (in order to make a barricade in the brush)
personal hunting net (different types depending on the animal: pigeon,
    mongoose, ...)

3.3.3. Animal husbandry.
to raise, rear, breed; breeder
to ruminate, chew the cud
to milk
    cat, dog
    horse
    camel
    ox, cow, zebu (determine the varieties)
    pig, sow
    sheep, ewe lamb, ram
    kid, goat
    elephant (if domesticated—rare)
    rabbit
    henhouse, hen, rooster, chicken, chick
        to sit on (incubate), to lay (eggs)
    domestic pigeon, guinea-fowl
        pigeon house
to domesticate, to train
to brand, mark (the ears)
to castrate an animal
    castrated animal, castrato
    castration, spaying
Do specialized constructions for animals exist? Which ones?
    (sheep fold, cowshed, stable, open-air pen, ...)

3.3.4. Food gathering.
to gather fruit, mushrooms
to cut off, pick ⎫ vegetable fruits
to fall   ⎭
to fall (caterpillars)
to pick up, to look for (caterpillars, crickets, tubers, firewood, straws, etc.)
to feel a fruit
ripe, just ripe
to be ripe, to be green
to gather, collect honey
    basket for gathering honey, for keeping gathered items
        (termites, berries, etc.)
    beehive

fruit pole (cf. fig. 97) to make fruit fall from the tree
collecting palm wine
    climbing belt (for a tree), cf. fig. 98
    permanent part in rattan
    flexible part in palm rib
    attachment points for the two parts
    ladder cut into the tree   { natural
                                     { dug by man (cf. fig. 98b)
    step
to go up a tree
to move the belt along in jerks
palm tree being worked (which ones?)
    to tap, lance the palm tree
    cold chisel (for lancing the palm tree) cf. fig. 99   other
    mallet (to drive in the cold chisel) cf. fig. 100   possible uses?
        what is it made of? (base of the palm stalk?)   what are they?
    bill-hook (to lance the palm tree finely), cf. fig. 101
other uses, possibly?
    long chisel (to bore a hole in the palm tree for the flow of the sap),
        cf. fig. 102; other uses?
    pipe (for the flow of the palm sap into a calabash), cf. fig. 76
    wine calabash (for collecting palm sap), cf. fig. 103
    funnel (cf. fig. 75)

3.3.5. Agriculture.

3.3.5.1. General.
dry season (= clearing, harvesting)
rainy season (= planting)
months of the traditional year, of the Christian year
year
agricultural cycle (general term)
cultivation zones: deep forest
                  forest near the village
                  heavily wooded savannah
                  savannah near the village
                  savannah
    What is grown in each zone?
    field (different names according to the place
        -savannah, gallery, forest
        -what is grown.)
    field boundaries (how is it marked?)
    cultivation, garden, little field
    planting (of coffee, for example)
    earth (material)
    mud, dust, hardened road
    cultivable place, without stones
    unproductive, rocky place
    barren land
    lands near the village (permanently cultivated?)

460 Questionnaire 10

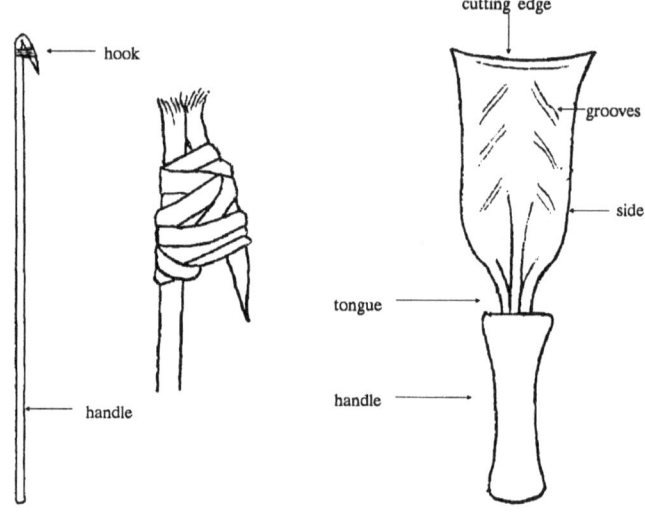

97. Fruit pole

99. Cold chisel

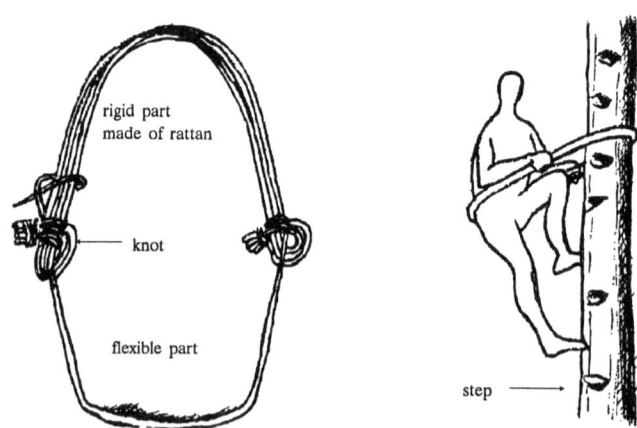

98. Climbing belt

Food Gathering

Traditional Technologies

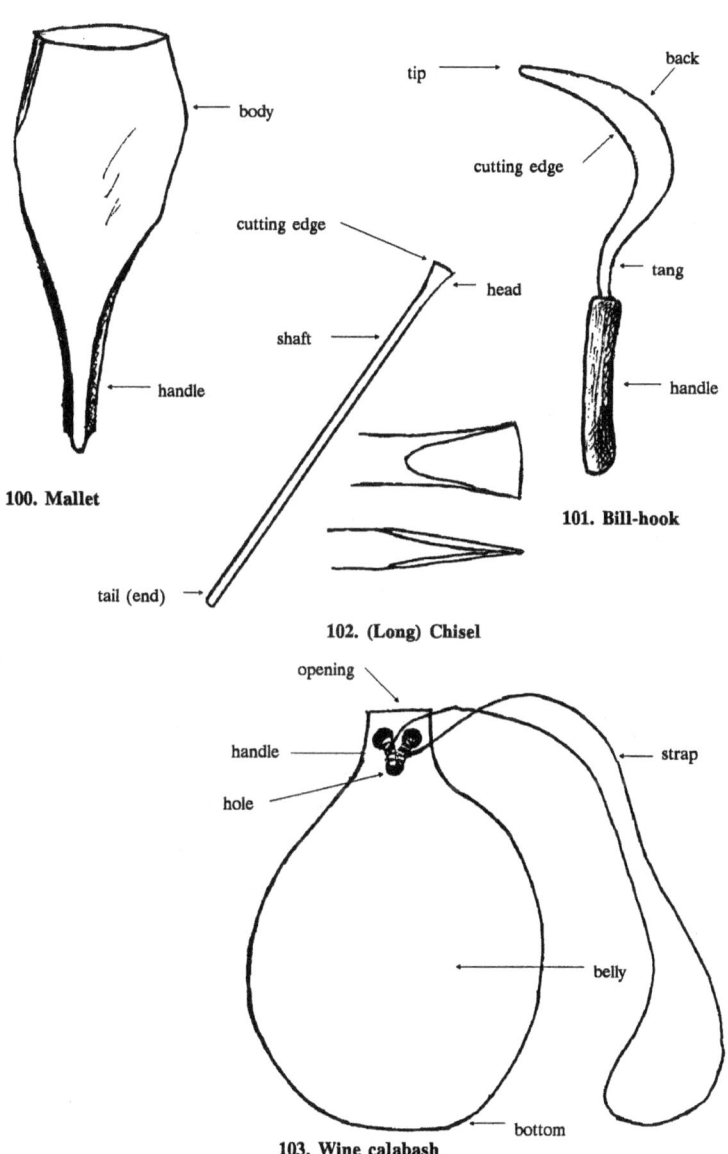

100. Mallet
101. Bill-hook
102. (Long) Chisel
103. Wine calabash

Food Gathering

Questionnaire 10

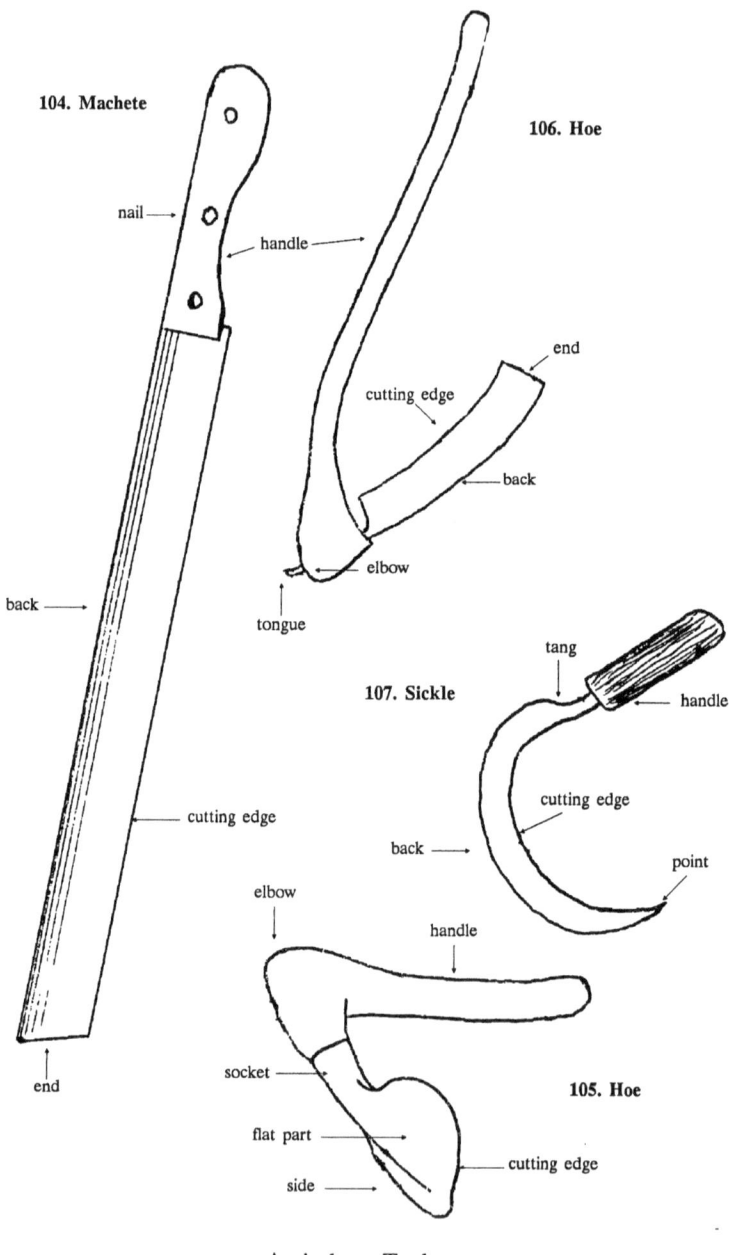

Agriculture Tools

Traditional Technologies

    land under cultivation + fallow land = the whole of cultivated lands
    plants (which ones? give their name) with information on the quality of the soil
        (= if they grow well, the soil is usable)
cultivator, farmer

3.3.5.2. Preparation of the field.
new plantation, piece of land reclaimed from the bush or forest
fallow land (old abandoned plantation)
to clear a fallow field (= to clear an old cultivated plantation)
to clear the brush (for the first time for a new plantation)
    tools: adze (for cutting down shrubs)   ⎫   for fallow
                mattock (for pulling up the undergrowth) ⎭   ground
                axe (for cutting down trees), cf. fig. 23
                European machete (cf. fig. 104)
                light machete (made with indigenous materials on the model
                          of the European machete)
I cut down a tree
I pull up ⎫
I dig out ⎭ a stump
I pull out the weeds
I cut the vines, the grasses, the stalks
I clean up, I clear the area around a tree that is not to be burned
What trees are saved? e.g., nere tree, shea tree, baobab, etc.
I pile up the brushwood at the foot of the stumps and trees to be destroyed
I spread out the vines on the field before the fire to help it
I set the brushwood on fire; it is a plantation fire
The field is burning
firebrush (to contain the fire to the burning field)
stirring up of the plantation fire by the wind
brushwood ashes   ⎫   which remain
blackened stubble (after the plantation fire) ⎭   after the fire
to break up the soil, to plow deeply
to turn over the earth superficially
    tools: hoe (to lift and turn aside the earth), cf. fig. 105–106
                mattock (for deep plowing), cf. fig. 108
                European hoe, cf. fig. 109
      I smooth out
      I mound up the earth, I make mounds   for which plants
      I made ridges, a ridge   ⎫ does one do one
                                        ⎭ or the other?
      I pile up the earth onto the ridge
          (to keep tubers from being exposed by the rains)

3.3.5.3. Sowing and plant care.
seeds (objects to be planted or sown)
    seedling   ⎫
    cutting, slip ⎭ planted
    graft
    (grain) seeds   sown

to plant, to put into the earth, to bury, to bed out
   I plant a cutting of yam, manioc, taro
   I bed out a tobacco plant, a millet shoot
   hole in the earth (for planting)
   I dig a hole with { the hand; I put the tuber in and fill in the hole
                     { the finger
to sow (general term): sow by (broad)casting (small seeds / large seeds?)
   sow in hills (for example for sesame)
   I sow millet seeds in hills, at the top of a ridge
   I broadcast the seed
to weed
   with a mattock
   with a hoe
   by hand
to thin out (= to take out a certain number of plants to give the seedlings more
      room)
to prune (close) (= to cut a seedling near the ground or near the graft; e.g., to cut
      back coffee plants)
to thin out the leaves
to break off the extra branches
tools for caring for the plants:
   hoe, pruning shears, machete, etc.
   fence around the field (to keep out animals; which ones?)
   watchtower (to watch over the field: how constructed? with what?)
   hut for spending the night in the field   -to watch over it
                                             -to avoid long trips to and
                                              from the village
   scarecrow (how is it made?)
   different means for keeping animals away;
      for example, a catapult (how are they constructed?); bows, etc.
to germinate, to grow and get larger
maturity (of a plant)
   The manioc is ripe, ready to be harvested
   The fruit is ripe
Look for verbs indicating the effects of maturity for each plant; for example: swelling and changing color for fruits, drying of the covering of the ear of corn, falling of the leaves of the peanut (groundnut), etc.

3.3.5.4. Harvesting.
to harvest
to gather
different verbs   -depending on whether you pull out, break off, cut, take
                     off one by one, take off several, remove the plant
                  -depending on the nature of the plant harvested
to bear fruit, to produce, to yield (harvest)
What tools are used for harvesting?
      knife } rice, acca, sesame, etc.
      sickle } (cf. fig. 107)
      mattock   to dig up tubers
stubble (left on the field)—possible use?

Traditional Technologies 465

ear (of corn) -cut
             -uncut

3.3.6. Minerals (extraction).
to extract metal
    extraction, mining, miner
to treat, prepare metal
to wash metal
    gold
    nugget
    gold-bearing sand
to look for specks in the bed of a watercourse
    who does it? men, women, the old, etc.
to pan for gold
    panning (= swirling sand in a calabash / bamboo tube / conical trough
                      -which method is used?
                      -to separate the powder or specks from the soil
    who pans?
    calabash for washing the gravel
impure metal
purified metal
    copper
    copper ore
iron
iron ore
mine   -open air
          -underground (cf. fig. 110)
shaft
gallery
supporting works (possibly; rare)
colored soils (for body painting)
which ones? (clay, ...)
edible soils (exceptional)
which ones?
salt (if exploited with mines in the swamps and saltwater lakes)
other mineral products taken from the ground
what are their uses?

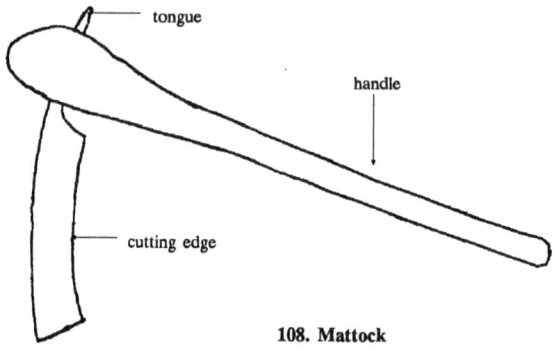

108. Mattock

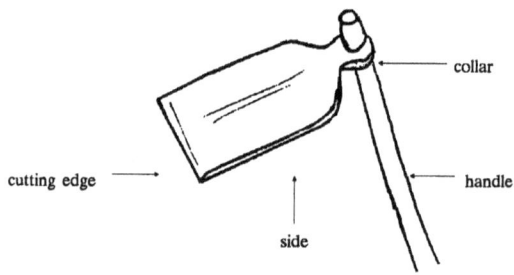

109. (European) hoe

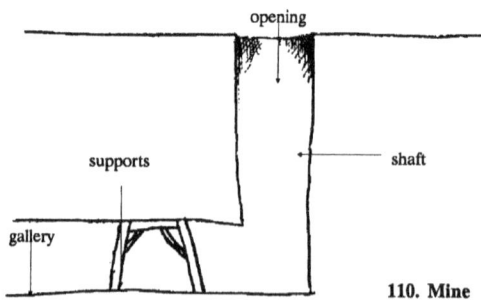

110. Mine

Agriculture and Mining

Traditional Technologies 467

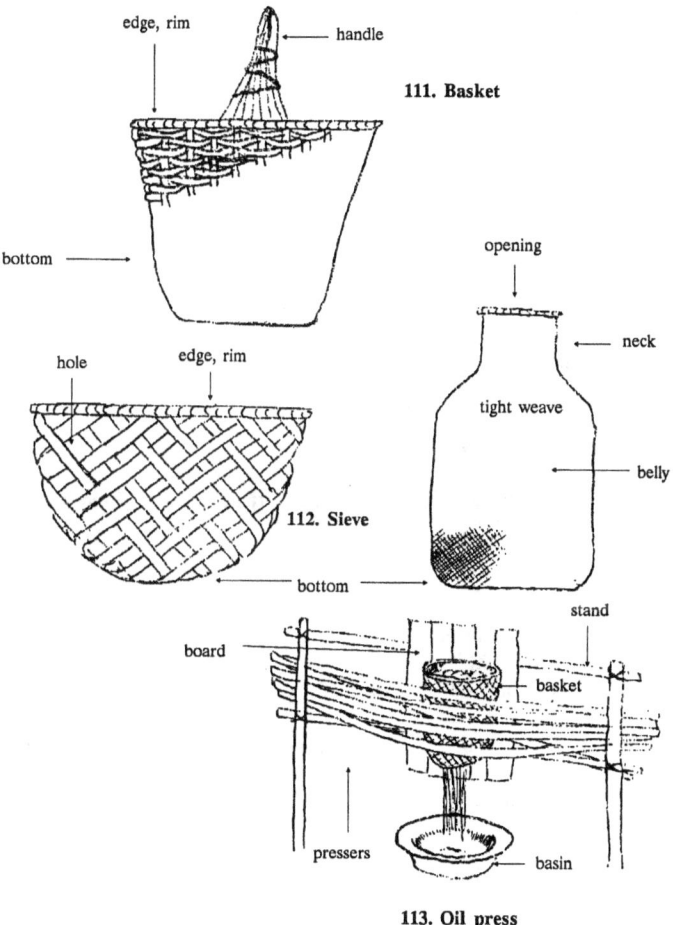

111. Basket
112. Sieve
113. Oil press

Food Preparation

3.4 Consumption techniques

3.4.1. Food.

3.4.1.1. Food preparation.

3.4.1.1.1. General.
cooking, cookery
to do the cooking, to make a meal
to cook

3.4.1.1.2. Sorting, operation of separating out.
to shell (= to extract the grain from its husk)
(= to pull off the grain from the stalk)
treading out the grain (if practiced)
beater, thresher
threshing by hand (on a screen or board)
scraper (for scratching off the ears)
comb (for separating the grain from the sheaf)
to clean the grain, the food
to wash food in water
calabash for cleaning grain (it is poured out from above into the wind: the chaff and debris blow away, and the grain falls)
winnowing basket (for tossing the grain)
basket for tossing up caterpillars (cf. fig. 111)
to sort (seeds, etc.) to separate the good from the bad seeds
to winnow, toss grain (to remove dirt, to singe off caterpillars' hairs in the fire, etc. Specify)
to shake food in a basket
to filter
to drain, strain
basket, sieve, strainer (in basketwork) ⎱ for straining
skimmer (in baked clay, with holes) ⎰
sieve (in basketwork), for what product? cf. fig. 112
to sift
filter (in a funnel, etc.)—what is it made of? male palm flower, cloth, etc.

3.4.1.1.3. Cutting up the food.
to cut up (animal and plant products)
to skin, dismember, carve up
to shell, to remove (the flesh from the bones)
to debone
to peel
to pluck; to remove the hair (pig, cane rat)
to remove the bark
to crumble (manioc)
to cut, chop, mince
to scale a fish, a pangolin
to husk, pare

Traditional Technologies

tools: vegetable board ⎫   for chopping
          chopping board ⎭
          knife for cutting up meat
          knife for mincing herbs
          woman's knife, other kinds of knife
          cleaver (for cutting bones—very rare)
to scratch, scrape
to grate
grater, grinder (for what? what is it like?)

3.4.1.1.4. *Mixing, crushing, grinding, etc.*
to mix, stir (a liquid, foods, similar or different ingredients . . .)
to stir and blend in (a liquid, sauce)
to mix up, knead (batter, dough)
to squeeze, wring (in the hand: leaves, dough, lemon, . . .)
to press, squeeze (using a press)
    oil press (cf. fig. 113):
    basket
    board
    wooden branch (press)
    frame, (support stand)
to empty by squeezing (caterpillars)
to milk
to grind, crush, break up (by striking; what?)
    crusher (millstone; flat beater; bulbous or bent pestle; . . .)
to break, smash, crack
    nutcracker, stone with hollows (indentations) (cf. fig. 114)
to flatten out (by pressing down, by rolling a bottle)
to mill
to pound finely, reduce to a pulp
to crush in a mortar
mortar (cf. fig. 115)—what tree's wood is it made of?
what is crushed in it?
pestle

3.4.1.2. *Cooking.*
to cook (trans., intrans.)
to be cooked, cooked just right
    cooking
    raw, uncooked
to heat, reheat, heat up (trans., intrans.)
to boil (trans., intrans.)
to burn
to roast, grill (trans., intrans.)
to fry (in oil) (trans., intrans.)
to braise (in the embers)
Make note of the foods prepared by each of these processes (large categories)
to stir in the saucepan
to put on a spit, skewer (whole animals)
    spit, skewer (what is it made of?)

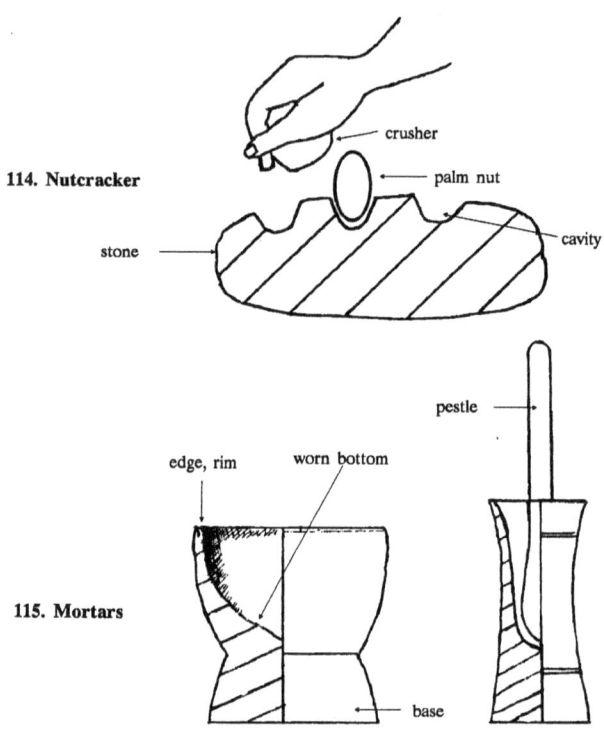

114. Nutcracker — crusher, palm nut, stone, cavity

115. Mortars — edge, rim; worn bottom; pestle; base

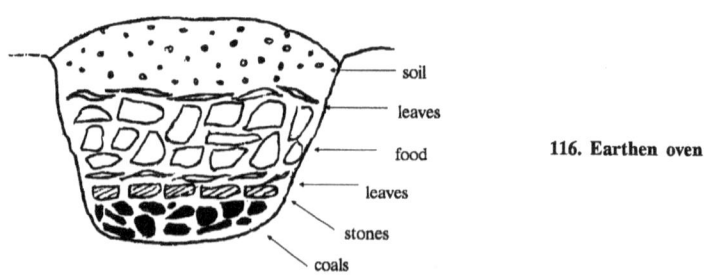

116. Earthen oven — soil, leaves, food, leaves, stones, coals

Food Preparation

earthen oven (cf. fig. 116)
steaming, braising
hearth: -block of earth or stone (forming the triangle of the hearth)
    -iron trivet
    earthen cooking pots (different types: determine the criteria for
        distinguishing them, for example by shape, usage, contents, etc.)
    cooking pot lid
    leaves for wrapping foods (to cook them in the coals) (leaves of which plants?)

3.4.1.3. Food preservation.
to dry, dry out in the sun (food) (trans., intrans.)
    drying
    drying area
    drying shed (for sesame, etc.)
    drying screen (for sesame, manioc, etc.)
    drying mat (different types if appropriate)
to smoke (for preservation)
to smoke, cure meat / fish
    granary, loft ⎫
    silo   ⎬ different types, of wood, clay, etc.
    baskets   ⎫ numerous types; discover the criteria
    boxes, chests ⎭ for distinguishing them
    different grasses used in packing for preservation: which ones?
    demijohn, carboy (European)
    pot, jar, calabash
    iron *touque* (European)
    bottle, stopper, cap
to cork, cap, stop up; to unstop, uncap
to keep, preserve
to put away, store, arrange tightly packed
    supplies, reserves, stocks
    old stock
    spoiled, rotten, tainted
    leftovers, fragments, crumbs
to be hungry, thirsty
    famine, food shortage
to be plentiful, abundant, overabundant
to be lacking, short

3.4.1.4. Foods consumed.
food

3.4.1.4.1. Animal products.
antelopes, hares, monkeys, wildcats, cattle, sheep, goats, elephants, birds, rats, squirrels, poultry, etc.
leg, haunch
quarters, large chunks of meat
viscera, tripe, entrails, intestines, livers, hearts, lungs, heads, brains, tails, feet: who gets these parts, and what social value do they have?

eggs
reptiles, snakes
amphibians (frogs)
crocodiles, turtles
fish
mollusks
insects (grasshoppers, worms, larvae, caterpillars, etc.)

Make note of the different varieties of each animal, and the name of each animal category as related to food consumption

3.4.1.4.2. Plant foods.
tuber, root, stem or stalk (bark + pith, core)
leaf, flower, fruit, seed
a) farinaceous plants (general term)

Indicate the names of the different kinds of each: for example, depending on whether the food is wild, cultivated, prepared, etc.

    manioc
    large white millet = sorgo   *Sorghum sp.*
    small millet   *Pennisetum sp.*
    white rice   *Oryza sativa*
    red rice   *Oryza glaberrima*
    corn   *Zea sp.*
    acca   *Digitaria exilis*
    yam   *Dioscorea sp.*
    sweet potato   *Ipomaea batatas*
    pea   *Voandzeia subterranea*
    bean   *Vigna unguiculata*
    groundnut, peanut   *Arachis hypogaea*
    roselle   *Hibiscus sabdariffa*
    kenaf, okra   *Hibiscus esculentus*
    potato
    coco-yam
    wheat, barley
    bean
    millet
    squash
    seeds of certain trees (which ones?)
    pumpkin
    various legumes
    trees with tubers, etc.
    preparations of farinaceous plants:
        mush, puree
        pancake
        flour
        dough, batter (of groundnuts, sesame)
        leaven
        dough ball
        bread (of millet, manioc; European bread)
        doughnut (of manioc, millet, wheat, groundnut)
b) fleshy plants

Traditional Technologies

    edible mushrooms (many kinds)
    fruits: bananas (different varieties)
    papaya, papaya tree
    orange, orange tree
    mandarin orange, tangerine, mandarin orange tree
    Cithere apple
    groundnut
    mango, mango tree
    custard-apple
    avocado, avocado tree
    palmyra tree *(Landolphia)* fruit
    shea tree fruit *(Butyrospermum parkii)*
    nere fruit *(Parkia biglobosa)*
    cola nuts
    etc.

c) green plants
    various grasses: yielding vegetables for stew, spinach greens
    Gnetum africanum Welw.
    leaves of different trees and especially of plants
    occasionally, flowers of some trees (the flower of the banana tree yields spinach greens)

All these grasses may be cultivated, but are most often used in the wild state.

3.4.1.4.3. Mineral foods.
earth, earth cake, clay

3.4.1.4.4. Seasonings.
native salt, ash salt
vegetable ashes
block of potash salt (obtained after evaporation)
salt cake (pieces obtained by breaking up the above block)
salt plants (make note of the different species)
European salt
pepper
pepper plants   *Piper guineense* (Piperaceae)
hot pepper   *Capsicum frutescens* L. (Solanaceae)
garlic (plants)   *Hua gabonii* (Sterculiaceae)
other condiment plants; for example *Ocimum americanum* (Labiateae)
lemon (juice)   *Citrus medica* (Rutaceae)
                            acida
sweet-smelling insects serving as condiments: which ones?
sugar
sugar cane   *Saccharum officinarum* L. (Gramineae)
                       other varieties?
bees' honey
bee, honeybee
honeycomb
natural beehive
to make honey
to melt, to dissolve sugar / salt

juice, sauce
sticky substances (obtained from which plants? sesame, kenaf, various herbs)
oil, fat (are these two ideas distinguished?)
    palm oil, palmetto oil
    peanut oil
    honey oil
    sesame oil, squash oil (various kinds)
    palm nut
    cluster of palm nuts
    spine of the cluster
    pulp of the nut
    stone of the nut
    kernel of the stone
    animal, vegetable fats: karite butter
    etc.

3.4.1.4.5. Beverages.

drink, beverage (general term)
liquid (general term)
    water (is it drunk or used? and for what?)
    milk
    citronella
    coffee
    coffee tree (cultivated)
    palm wine
    banana wine
    corn wine
    corn beer
    mead beer
    millet beer
    sprouted corn for making alcohol
    alcohol
    foam, froth (of wine)
    dregs, sediment (of wine)
    deposit in the bottom of a liquid
    condiments for drinks, e.g., bitter bark for palm wine
to ferment

3.4.1.4.6. Stimulants, narcotics.

tobacco (plant): different varieties
smoking tobacco (prepared), cigarette
nicotine
marijuana *(Cannabis sativa)*
cola nut
other narcotics—which ones?

3.4.1.5. Means of consuming.

3.4.1.5.1. Consuming foods.

wooden (copper, clay, etc.) dish

soup bowl, shallow bowl, hemispheric container
plate (cf. fig. 117) ⎫
basin ⎬ European
shallow bowl, pouring receptacle with or without spout
hand(ful) (= container)
(wooden) spoon: of gourd, calabash (which one?)
              of wood (from what?), etc.
ladle
cup (cf. fig. 119) ⎫ of what? gourd, wood,
goblet, mug (cf. fig. 118 and 120) ⎬ fruit skin . . .
goblet: different European types
European glass
table knife (very rare)
European fork
to eat
to drink
to swallow
to taste
to be good / to be bad (to the taste)
to appreciate, like
to cut (with the incisors)
to chew (with the molars)
to masticate, grind, crush
to lick
to suck (while breathing in)
to suck (in the mouth)
to salivate (upon seeing something good)
to choke (on food)
to take in handfuls,
    a spoonful
    a full, heaping spoonful
to pour out (a liquid)
bland, without taste
strong-flavored, full of taste (gamy meat)
sweet, sugary
acrid, bitter
sour, tart; sour (milk)

3.4.1.5.2. Consuming stimulants.
to chew (cola)
to take (snuff)
    snuffbox
    tobacco mortar
    pestle
to smoke
    roll of tobacco, bag of tobacco
    cigarette, pack of cigarettes
    pipe components; made of what?
        pipe bowl
        stem

476 Questionnaire 10

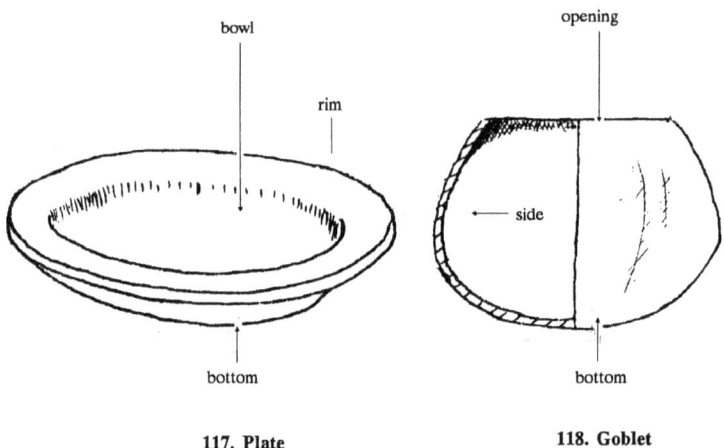

117. Plate **118. Goblet**

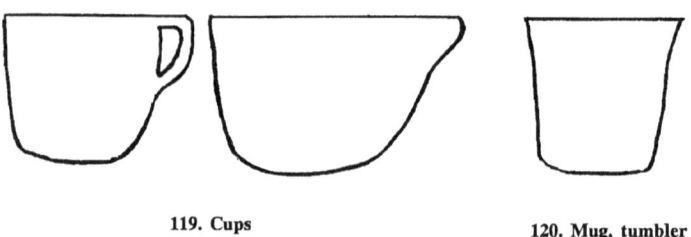

119. Cups **120. Mug, tumbler**

Eating Utensils

Traditional Technologies 477

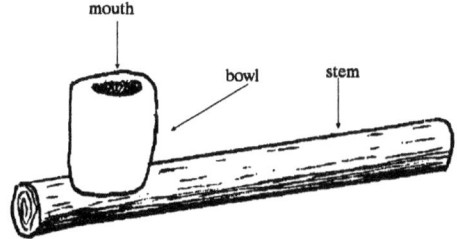

121. Pipe

122. Straight pipe

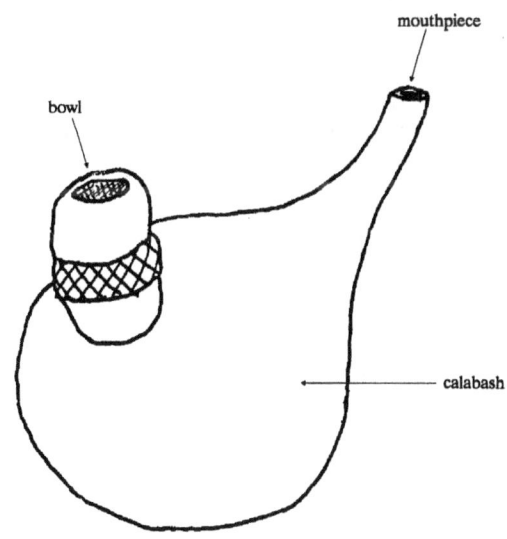

123. Water pipe

Smoking

mouthpiece
filter (with the leaves of which plant?)
different types of pipes (cf. fig. 121, 122): ordinary pipe, chief's pipe, European pipe, etc.
pipe cleaner, water pipe (cf. fig. 123)

3.4.2. Clothing.

3.4.2.1. General.
clothing, dress
piece of clothing, costume
    linen (cloth, clothing, rags, etc.)
    I am clothed.
    I am not clothed; I am naked.
to clothe, to clothe oneself
to get dressed
to wear a garment (different terms according to type of clothing, the place and means of attaching it, ...)
to cover, wrap oneself
to undress, get undressed
to take off (hat)
to button, fasten
to unbutton, undo (one's clothes) / to button up
to take off (one's shoes) / to put on one's shoes
to be tight, skimpy (garment) / to be roomy, large
to pull up one's sleeves
to turn a garment up
to change (clothes)
to crumple, crease; to be worn, threadbare, torn, tattered (in rags)
to turn inside out (back to front / inside to outside)

3.4.2.2. Head, neck.
headgear, headdress (general term)
veil
head kerchief
(head)scarf
military forage cap
hat (different types / plaited leaves, ...)
turban, Muslim skullcap, etc.
scarf, neck scarf
neck sash ⎫
           ⎬ what are they made of?
(neck)tie ⎭

3.4.2.3. Shoulders, waist, extremities.
cape of fur or skin
outer loincloth (draped), boubou (African shirt)
blouse, dress (European)
upper garment, top

Traditional Technologies

shirt
long-sleeved pullover
short-sleeved pullover } European
undershirt
brassiere
belt
bark loincloth } specify the materials used
leaf loincloth
man's, woman's loincloth, etc.
Make note of the different sorts of loincloths that can be found and that have different names.
G-string
briefs, panties
shorts, skirt
pants
pocket
button, zipper
buttonhole
sleeve
collar (of a shirt, pullover)
fly (of trousers)
socks
thongs
sandals } different traditional types
shoes
boots
parasol, sunshade
umbrella
raincoat
flyswatter

3.4.2.4. Everyday care, upkeep.
gathered together, up
    This dress is gathered at the waist.
fringe
    This shawl has fringes.
to dirty (a garment)
to wash (the linen)
to scrub, rub, lather
to wring out, soap
to wring out (the water), to press, to wring
to iron
    (flat)iron
to mend: patch a tear

3.4.2.5. Adornment.
finery, adornment, jewelry—earrings
coronet, head band for keeping hair in place
Make note of the different types of decorative hair styles, the occasions on which they are worn, the materials used (feathers, skins, leaves, etc.)

necklace (different types: made of beads, animal teeth, etc.)
   chain, neck chain
ring (general term—different types: bracelet for arm, ankle; ring for finger, nose; ankle bell)
bead (made of what? seeds, etc.); cowrie shells (different types)
to string (beads)
to pierce the ears, the nose, the lips (for inserting rings)
pendant—braid, medal, military uniform, forage cap, epaulettes
convict's dress

3.4.2.6. Tattooing.
tattooing (general term), cf. fig. 152–154
different types: of face, chest, arms, back, etc.
to tattoo, prick
tattooing knife (cf. fig. 155)
other instruments used for tattooing: hook, bundle of needles
   Make note of the ingredients of the materials used in tattooing: kaolin, oils, various juices and decoctions placed onto the bleeding tattoo (e.g., powdered charcoal, red wood, charred fruit, manioc flour, sawdust, etc.)

3.4.2.7. Care of the body.
to remove hairs, eyelashes, eyebrows
to style, to plait, to comb the hair
to trim, shave, cut (the hair)—to shave (the face)
razor-comb (cf. fig. 157); different types: European comb, etc.
needle for untangling hair
hair styles: different types (cf. fig. 158)
beard, moustache, sideburns
to shape the teeth—scrapers for shaping the teeth (cf. fig. 159)
different types of shapes for the teeth (cf. fig. 160)
   Make note of the different names: tooth brush (generally the stem of a plant: which one?)
tooth pick

3.4.2.8. Body decoration.
body painting (note the materials used: sap of trees (which ones?) red powder from the mahogany tree, black dye (from which trees?), kaolin, etc.)
to paint, to draw (patterns) on the body
to rub, soap, massage, smear, anoint (the body)
soap (how is it made? with what?)

3.4.2.9. Perfume.
pleasant odor / perfumes
plants with various scents: are they smeared on or is it worn (at the neck, waist, etc.)?
to give out a fragrance, to perfume, scent

Traditional Technologies 481

152. Nose tattoos

153. Forehead and chin tattoos

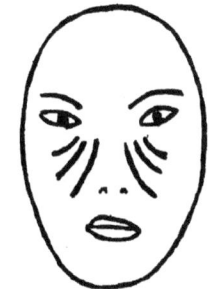
154. Cheek tattoos

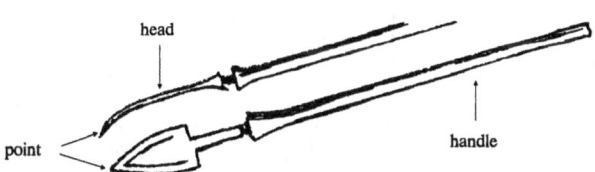
155. Knife

Ornamentation

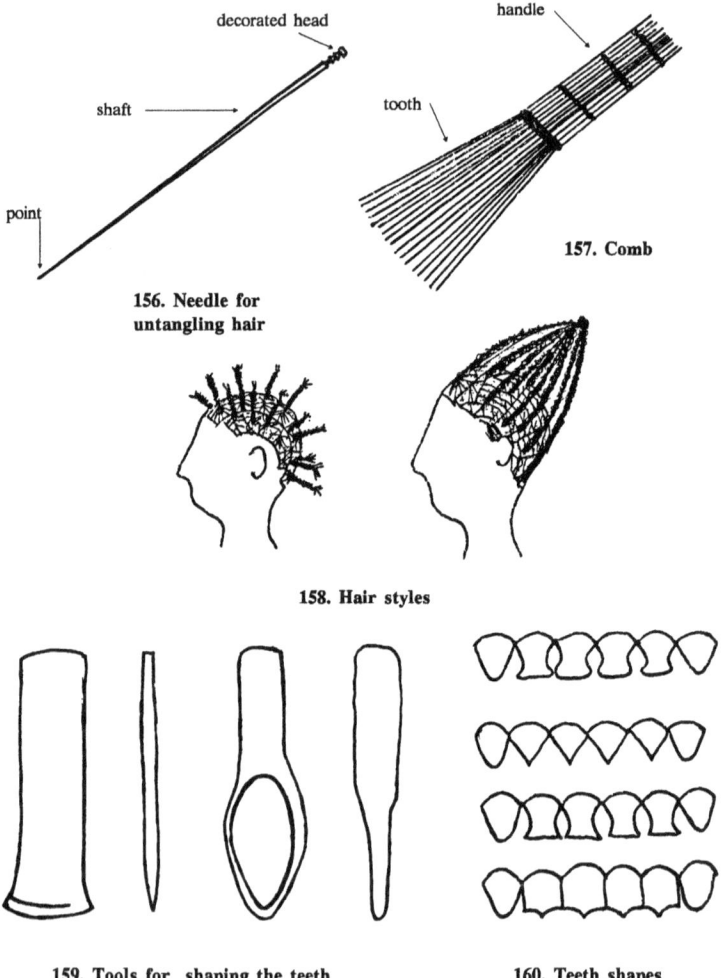

156. Needle for untangling hair

157. Comb

158. Hair styles

159. Tools for shaping the teeth

160. Teeth shapes

Ornamentation

Traditional Technologies 483

3.4.3. Dwellings.

3.4.3.1. General: types of dwellings.
city
covered market, market hall
building
street, square
church, mosque
school, town hall, administrative buildings; prison, shop, etc.
village
    site of the village
    site of a house
    place, home
    clearing of the village—natural
    obtained by clearing the brush
    center of the village   (geographic)
                                (social)
cabin, house (general term: communal, family, unmarried persons')
shelter, encampment (far from the village, for fishing, hunting, etc.; forest camp, bush camp, war camp, etc.)
    (Make note of the different types of encampment distinguished)
        leaf hut, Pygmy hut
Make note of the most common shape of houses in the village (round, rectangular, etc.), the materials used; indicate what the houses are like which are different from this (permanent modern house, chief's house, sanctuary place of worship, house shape borrowed from other groups, etc.)

3.4.3.2. Construction.
to construct, built, erect, put up
    I build the house (of bricks, leaves, cob, ...
        and the general term)
    I make the foundations
    I construct the frame
    I put up the main beam
to drive in a post, to stick into the ground (for the frame)
to straighten up a post (if it is not straight)

3.4.3.2.1. Foundation (possibly).
posts that the dwelling is erected on
    pile (marshy ground), cf. fig. 124a
    piling, support ⎫
    posts   ⎭ (dry ground), cf. fig. 124b
Make note of the trees used to make these posts.

3.4.3.2.2. Framework.
frame(work), the whole of the frame set up (cf. fig. 125, 126, and 127)
    forked post (general term)
    post supporting the main beam
    post supporting the ridgepole

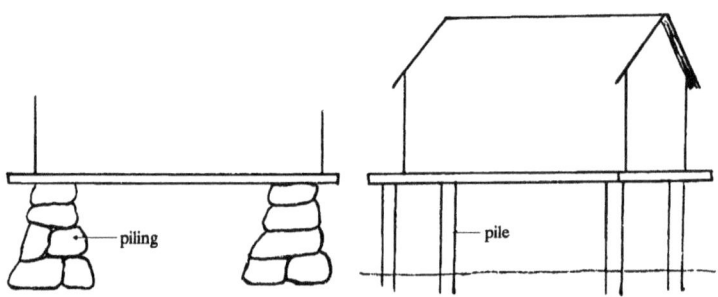

124. Foundations

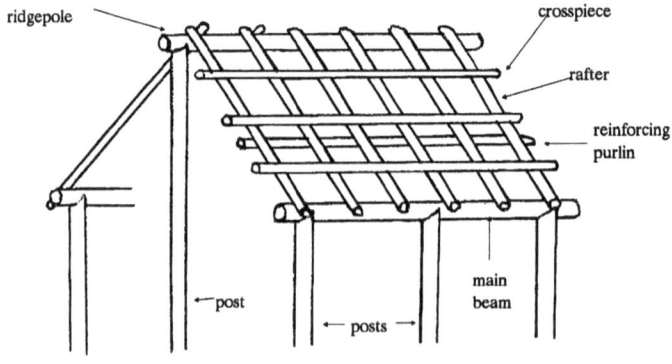

125. Frame

Building

Traditional Technologies 485

  main beam purlins ⎫
  ridgepole   ⎬ purlins
  principal rafter (only if the purlins rest on it), cf. fig. 126
  rafter
  crosspiece, wattle fastened perpendicular to the
  rafters and parallel to the purlins
 reinforcing purlin (fastened under the rafters and parallel to the purlins; only found when the rafters bear a great weight) the structure of fanned-out rods forming the framework of a conical roof (cf. fig. 127)
  rod
  horizontal ring holding the rods, hoop
  trees whose wood is used for the different parts of the frame
  vines used for fastening the different parts of the frame
  other possible means of fastening—be specific: nails, etc.
to put the frame onto the house (in the case of a conical roof)

3.4.3.2.3. Roofing.
roof
  slope of the roof; ridge of the roof (general terms)
  roof covering (cf. fig. 128)
  bamboo tiles
  rigid riser upright post, crosspiece of the tile
  foliole forming the fabric of the tile
    needle for attaching the folioles
    small bundle of folioles   ⎫ for transporting
    large bundle comprising several small ones ⎭ the folioles
  plants used for the different parts of the tile
    bamboo tile is the local name for this type of roof covering; most often it is not made of bamboo and is not really a tile
  straw; truss of straw
  various grasses, thatch
    determine the names of these plants
  sheet metal, European type tiles
to roof
  vines used in making the covering
  top (crest) of the roof (cf. fig. 129 and 130)
  inverted pot or pottery crest cone (conical houses)
  straw cap (conical house)
  ridge tiles (rectangular house)

3.4.3.2.4. Walls, flooring.
outer wall, interior wall or partition
  framework of wall: laths, horizontal crosspieces attached to vertical
    posts (cf. fig. 131)
  determine the types of wood used
body of the wall
  made of branches, leaves (from which trees?)
  made of thin vertical stalks (from which grasses, plants?)
  made of wickerwork (what framework is used?)
  made of bark (planks)

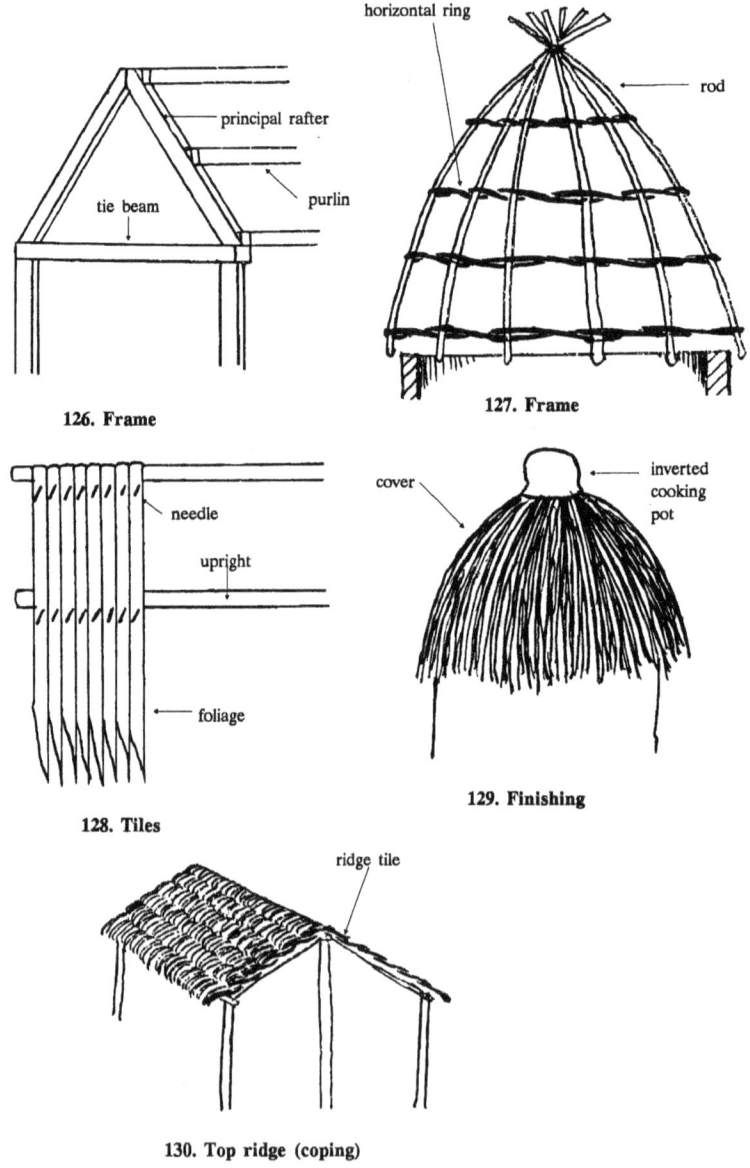

126. Frame

127. Frame

128. Tiles

129. Finishing

130. Top ridge (coping)

Building

Traditional Technologies

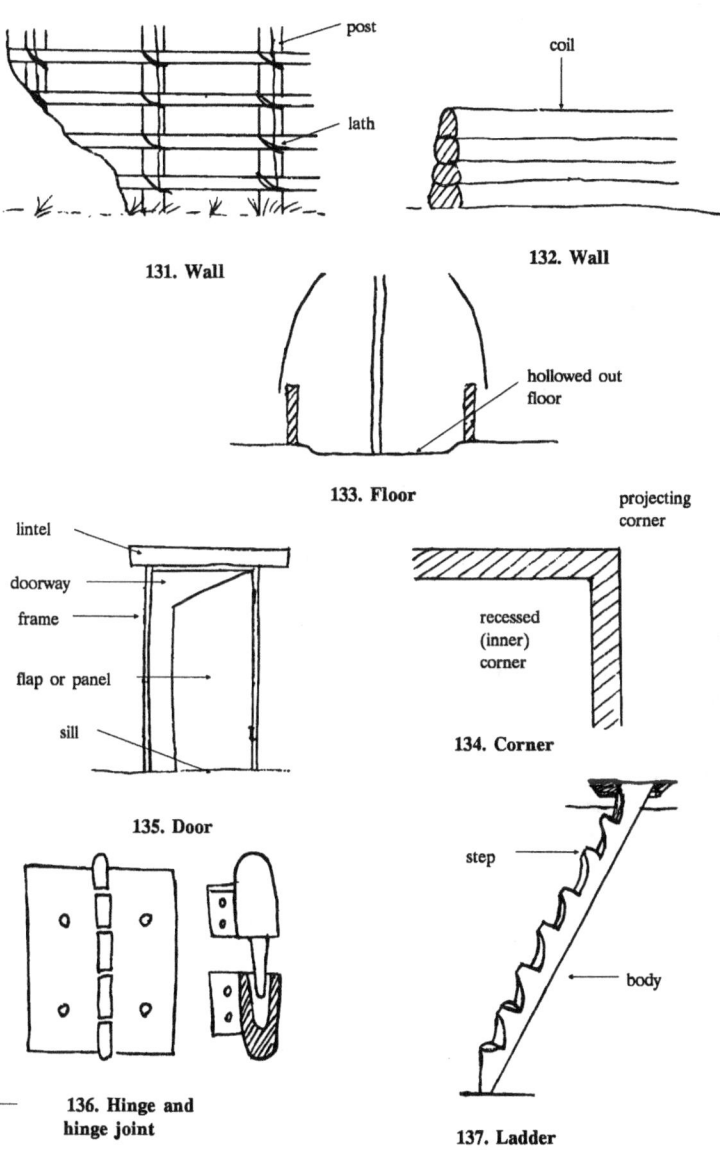

131. Wall
132. Wall
133. Floor
134. Corner
135. Door
136. Hinge and hinge joint
137. Ladder

Building

    clay mortar
        mud and clay kneaded together and thrown onto the framework
    clay coil (cf. fig. 132—name of each coil)
    bricks of unbaked clay
    brick mold
to build, construct
    I am throwing handfuls of mud onto the framework
    I am building the walls with coils; I am putting up bricks
to paint a wall
to whitewash a wall with lime, kaolin
    lime, kaolin
to flake off (wall)
    a crack, chink
    small crack (in paint)
    hole in a wall
    floor of a hut
    hollow (if hollowed out like a basin—cf. fig. 133)

3.4.3.3. Different parts of the dwelling.
bedroom or private area / public area
kitchen
granary, loft, attic
chicken coop   if they are inside the house
stable
lavatory, toilet
courtyard
storeroom, lumber room, shed
hall, vestibule
storage shelter
women's hut
back (inside) of the hut
corner of the house   recessed (cf. fig. 134)
                  projection
veranda
canopy for resting under (near the hut)
pleasure garden, flowered area
enclosure
    fence
    enclosing wall, ditch, stockade, fortifications (in the past, in wartime)
    live hedge (of plants)
    Take inventory of the plants used for enclosing
to enclose, fence in

3.4.3.4. Doors and windows.
door (cf. fig. 135)
    door sill; threshold, doorway
    lintel
    door frame
    flap or panel (of a single or double door)
    entrance door / back door

Traditional Technologies 489

    window
    lintel
    frame
    flap or panel
    window sill
    shutter
    hinge ⎫
    hinge joint ⎭   (cf. fig. 136) (of leather, iron, ...)
ladder (cf. fig. 137)
    step, upright post, rung
    notched post
lock (cf. fig. 138 and 139): cord bolt (fig. 138),
    pin bolt (fig. 139)
    bolt
    bolt cord
    bolt cavity
    key
system of locking from the inside (cf. fig. 140)
to open, unlock a door
to close, lock a door

3.4.3.5. Furnishings.

3.4.3.5.1. Furniture.
couch, place to lie down
bed (different types—fig. 141–144)
earthen bed
wooden bed
raised bed
bed of leaves (which kind?) in an encampment (temporary bed)
top of the bed
head of the bed
    foot of the bed
    side of the bed
    edge of the bed
    frame, crosspiece, lath or slat (cf. fig. 143)
    mat (for sleeping)—different types
    top, bottom, edge
Make note of the pertinent features by which the different types are distinguished: differences in weaving, shape, pattern, color, etc.; make note also of the plants from which the mats are made.
    blanket
    sheet
seat (general term) (cf. fig. 145–147)
wooden head-rest (cf. fig. 147)
    foot ⎫
    body ⎭ which wood is used?
stool, low seat
    top
    foot

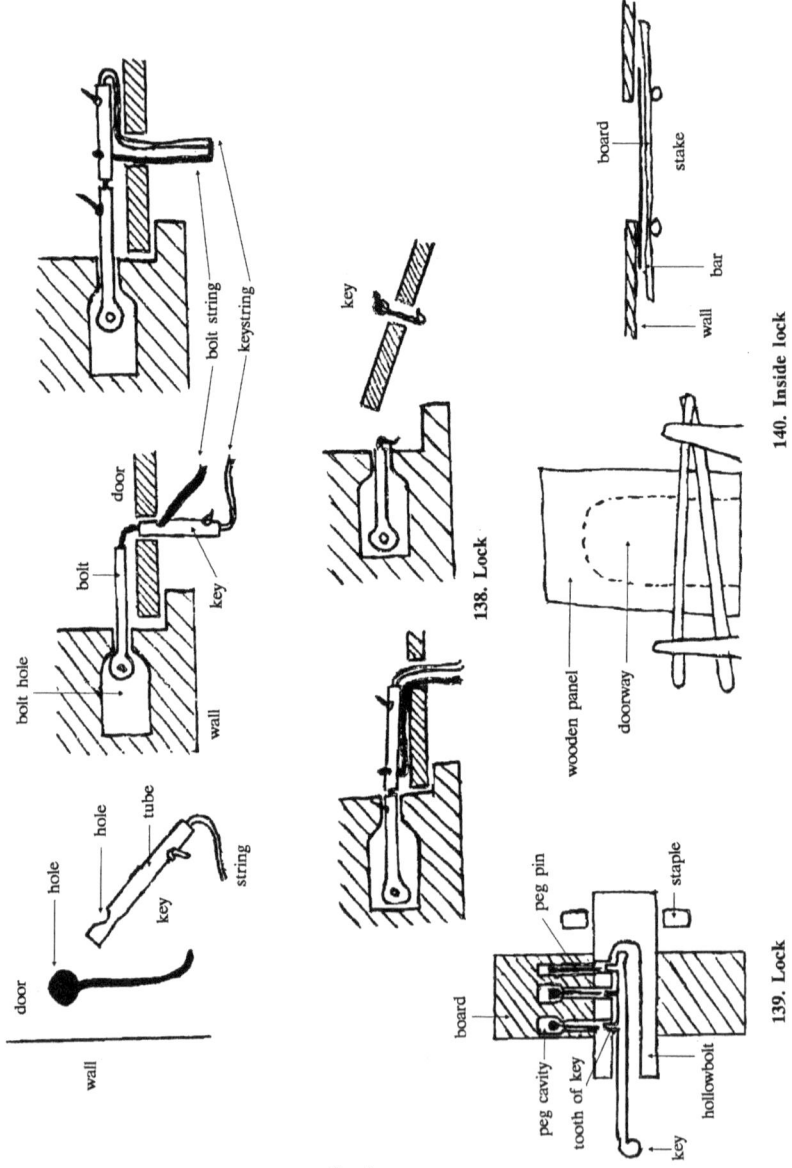

Locks

Traditional Technologies

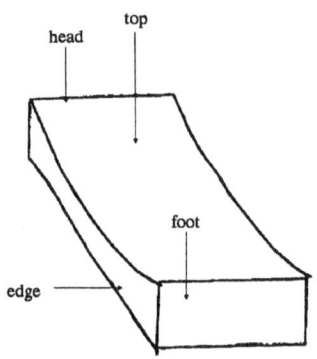

141. Earthen bed

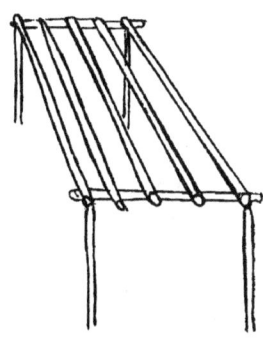

142. Pole Bed

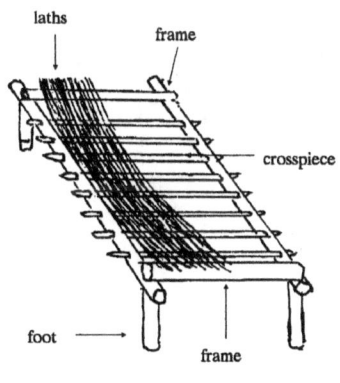

143. Bed

144. Bed

Furniture

chaise lounge ⎫
chair   ⎬ recent; which woods and leathers are used?
bench   ⎭
mirror
cupboard, wardrobe, chest, shelves, stand (cf. fig. 148)
different types of stands *(claie):* small, large, etc.
specify the function of each item of furniture

3.4.3.5.2. Lighting.
traditional lamp (cf. fig. 149) (iron, hollowed-out tuber, . . .)
    fuel:
    oil
    shea butter
    paraffin, kerosene, etc.
    resinous woods (which ones?)
    animal fats
European lamps   pressure lamp (cf. fig. 151)
                       kerosene lamp

This vocabulary will undoubtedly be borrowed from a European language.

3.4.3.5.3. Heating.
open hearth, fireplace:
    hearth bordered by stones or ashes
    brazier (cf. fig. 150) made of iron, clay, . . .
    fireplace with a draught:
cavity for the fuel
    opening at base for the draught
    chimney ⎫
                 ⎬ rare
    hood   ⎭

3.4.3.5.4. Housekeeping.
to prepare the bed, the bedroom
to sweep
    broom: handle, body, active part (different types: for outside, for
        inside, etc.)
    what is it made of?: what kind of wood? which stalks?
shovel for picking up rubbish (made of bark)
clean, swept out
dirty, unswept
dust
rubbish, dirt
rubbish dump (hole or heap)
path leading to the dump
to clean, wipe off
Make note of the names of leaves used for cleaning or polishing
plant sponge (which plant?)
to wash (someone, the dishes)
to tidy up, arrange, set in order
to put things away, to pack together

I am putting away the calabash on the shelf
The woman is arranging her valuables in a basket
I am tidying up the bedroom

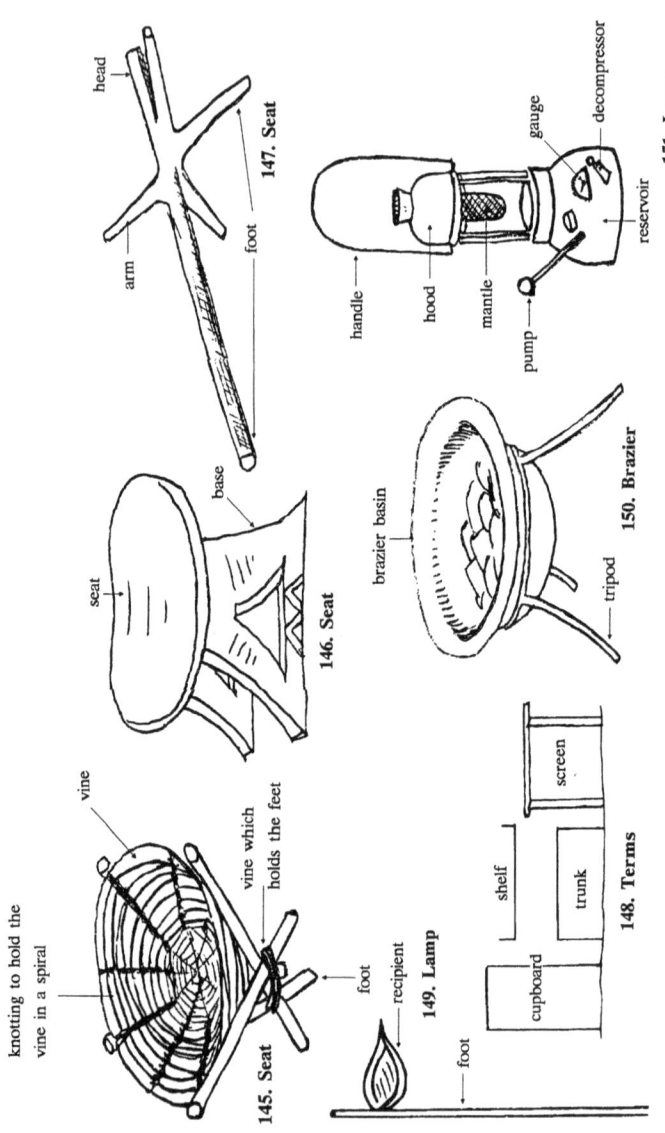

Furnishings

Alphabetical Index of Terms

acca: 3.3.5.4, 3.4.1.4.2
acrid, bitter: 3.4.1.5.1
adornment: 3.4.2.5
adze/axe: 1.1.1.2.2, 3.2.1.2, 3.3.5.2
agricultural cycle: 3.3.5.1
air, wind: 1.4
air conditioner: 1.4
airplane: 2.3
airport: 2.3
alcohol: 3.4.1.4.5
ambush: 3.3.2
amphibians, frogs: 3.4.1.4.1
anchor: 2.2
animal: 3.3.2
animal fat: 3.4.3.5.2
animal force: 1.1.3
ankle bell: 3.4.2.5
antelopes: 3.4.1.4.1
apple: 3.4.1.4.2
arch (of the saddle): 2.1.1
arrow: 3.3.2.1
arrow poison: 3.3.2.1
ashes: 1.2.3, 3.2.3.2
avocado: 3.4.1.4.2
avocado tree: 3.4.1.4.2

awl: 1.1.1.2.1, 3.2.1.2, 3.2.2, 3.2.4.1,
  3.2.4.3.3, 3.2.4.4,
axe (for cutting down trees): 3.3.5.2
axe, hatchet: 1.1.1.2, 1.1.1.2.2, 3.2.1.2
axle: 2.1.2, 3.2.4.3.2
back (inside) of the hut: 3.4.3.3
bag: 1.1.1.3, 2.1.1
bag of tobacco: 3.4.1.5.2
baggage: 2.1.1
bait: 3.3.1, 3.3.2.1
balance: 3.2.4.3.2
bamboo tiles: 3.4.3.2.3
banana: 3.4.1.4.2
banana wine: 3.4.1.4.5
bar: 3.2.4.5.3
bark: 3.2.3.3.1, 3.4.1.4.2
bark cloth: 3.2.4.1
bark loincloth: 3.4.2.3
barley: 3.4.1.4.2
barrel: 3.2.5.1, 3.4.1.3
barren land: 3.3.5.1
basin: 3.2.5.1
basket: 1.1.1.1, 1.1.1.3, 3.2.3.1, 3.2.5.1,
  3.3.1, 3.4.1.1.2, 3.4.1.3
basket carried on the back: 2.1.1
basket for gathering honey: 3.3.4

basket with headband: 2.1.1
basket-maker: 3.2.4.5.2
basketry (for grains): 3.2.5.1
basketry: 3.2.4.5.1, 3.2.4.5.2
beak, lip: 3.2.5.3
beaker: 3.2.5.1
bean: 3.4.1.4.2
beard: 3.4.2.7
beating, flap: 3.2.4.5.3
bed: 3.4.3.5.1
bedframe: 3.4.3.5.1
bedroom: 3.4.3.3
bee: 3.4.1.4.4
beehive: 3.3.4, 3.4.1.4.4
bees' honey: 3.4.1.4.4
bellows: 3.2.2
bellows of a forge: 1.4
belly (wide part of blast furnace): 3.2.2
belt: 3.4.2.3
belt for carrying babies: 2.1.1
bench: 3.4.3.5.1
beverages: 3.4.1.4.5
bicycle: 2.1.2
billhook: 1.1.1.2.2, 3.3.4
birdlime: 3.2.3.3.2
birds: 3.4.1.4.1
bitter: 3.4.1.5.1
blackened stubble (after plantation fire): 3.3.5.2
blacksmith: 3.2.2
bland, without taste: 3.4.1.5.1
blanket: 3.4.3.5.1
blast furnace: 3.2.2
block of earth: 3.4.1.2
block of potash salt: 3.4.1.4.4
blocks from a termite's nest: 3.2.2
blouse: 3.4.2.3
blowgun: 1.1.1.2.2, 1.4
blowtorch: 1.4
bludgeon: 3.3.2.1
board, plank: 3.2.1.2, 3.4.1.1.4
bobbin of thread: 3.2.4.3.2
body: 1.4
body of the wall: 3.4.3.2.4

body painting: 3.4.2.8
boiler, boiling scoop: 2.2, 3.3.1
bolt: 3.4.3.4
bolt cavity: 3.4.3.4
bolt cord: 3.4.5.1
bond, tie: 3.2.4.3.3
bone: 3.2.1.1
boot: 2.1.1, 3.4.1.3
bottle: 3.2.5.1, 3.4.1.3
bottom: 3.2.5.1
bottom of the dugout canoe: 2.2
bovine animals: 2.1.1, 3.4.1.4.1
bow: 1.1.1.2.2, 3.3.2.1
bow drill: 3.2.1.2
bowl: 3.2.5.1, 3.4.1.5.1
boxes, chests: 3.4.1.3
bracelet for arm: 3.4.2.5
braid: 3.4.2.5
braids: 3.2.4.3.3
brains: 3.4.1.4.1
braising: 3.4.1.2
brake: 2.1.2, 3.2.4.5.3
branches: 1.2.3
brand (ember): 1.2.3
brassiere: 3.4.2.3
brazier: 3.4.3.5.3
bread: 3.4.1.4.2
breakage: 3.2.3.2.4
brick mold: 3.4.3.2.4
bricks of baked clay: 3.4.3.2.4
bridge: 2.3
bridle: 2.1.1, 3.2.5.2
bridle cheek strap: 2.1.1
bridle noseband: 2.1.1
briefs: 3.4.2.3
brittle: 3.2.1.2
bronze: 3.2.2
broom: 3.4.3.5.4
brush fire: 1.2.1
brushwood ashes: 3.3.5.2
bucket: 1.1.1.3
buckle: 3.2.4.3.3
building: 3.4.3.1
bunch (cluster) of palm nuts: 3.4.1.4.4

Traditional Technologies 497

bundle: 2.1.1
burn: 1.2.3, 3.4.1.2
burn the field: 3.3.5.2
burrow: 3.3.2
button hole: 3.4.2.3
button: 3.4.2.3
cab, cabin: 2.1.2
cable, rigging gear: 2.2
cage trap: 3.3.2.2
calabash: 2.1.1, 3.2.5.1, 3.4.1.1.2, 3.4.1.1.3, 3.4.1.5.1
camel: 2.1.1, 3.3.3
cane rat: 3.4.1.1.3
canopy: 3.4.3.3
cap gun: 3.3.2.1
cape of fur: 3.4.2.3
cape of skin: 3.4.2.3
capsule: 3.4.1.3
car: 2.1.2
carbon: 1.2.3, 3.2.3.2.4
carboy: 3.4.1.3
carding bow: 3.2.4.3.1
carpenter: 3.2.1.2
cartridge: 3.3.2.1
carved trunk (canoe): 2.2
cask/keg: 3.2.5.1
casonet: 3.4.2.5
cast iron: 3.2.2
castrated animal: 3.3.3
castration: 3.3.3
cat: 3.3.3
caterpillars: 3.4.1.4.1
cavity for the fuel: 3.4.3.5.3
cement: 3.2.3.3.3
chain: 3.2.4.5.1, 3.2.4.5.3, 3.4.2.5
chain link of mail: 3.2.4.5.3
chair: 3.4.3.5.2
chaise lounge: 3.4.3.5.2
channel: 3.2.5.2
charcoal: 1.2.3, 3.2.3.3.1
chemical substance for fixing dye: 3.2.3.3.1
chest of wood: 3.2.1.2
chests: 3.4.1.3, 3.4.3.5.2

chick: 3.3.3
chicken: 3.3.3
chicken coop: 3.4.3.3
chimney: 3.4.3.5.3
chisel: 3.2.1.1, 3.2.1.2
chopping board: 3.4.1.1.3
church: 3.4.3.1
cigarette: 3.4.1.5.2
cistern, tank (to collect water): 3.2.5.1
citronella: 3.4.1.4.5
city: 3.4.3.1
claw: 1.1.1.2.1
clay: 3.2.3.2.1, 3.4.3.2.4
clay coils: 3.2.3.2.2.1b, 3.4.3.2.4
clean: 3.4.3.5.4
clearing of the village: 3.4.3.1
cleaver (for cutting bones): 3.4.1.1.3
climbing belt (for a tree): 3.3.4
cloth: 3.2.4.5.3
cloth weave: 3.2.4.5.2, 3.2.4.5.3
clothing: 3.4.2.1
club: 3.3.2
club (tool): 1.1.1.2.2
club (weapon): 3.3.2.1
cob: 3.2.3.3.3
coco-yam: 3.4.1.4.2
coffee: 3.4.1.4.5
coffee tree (cultivated): 3.4.1.4.5
coil pottery making process: 3.2.3.2.2.1b
cola nuts: 3.4.1.4.2, 3.4.1.4.5
cold chisel: 3.3.4
collar: 3.4.2.3
collar, flange: 1.1.2
collecting palm wine: 3.3.4
color: 3.2.3.3.1
colored soils: 3.3.6
coloring agent: 3.2.3.3.1
coloring baths: 1.3.3
comb: 3.2.4.5.3, 3.4.1.1.2, 3.4.2.7
combat (between 2 people): 3.3.2
combustible material: 3.2.3.2.4
container: 3.2.3.1
convict's uniform: 3.4.2.5

cooking, cookery: 3.2.3.2.4, 3.4.1.1.1, 3.4.1.2, 3.4.3.3
cooking oven: 1.2.3
cooking pot: 3.2.5.1, 3.4.1.2
cooking spit: 3.2.4.3.2
coping: 3.2.5.1
copper: 3.2.2, 3.3.6
copper dish: 3.4.1.5.1
cord, tie: 2.1.1
cord (string) bolt: 3.4.3.4
cord for lashing tool: 3.2.4.3.3
corn beer, wine: 3.4.1.4.5
corn, maize: 3.4.1.4.2
corner of the house: 3.4.3.3
cotton: 3.2.4.3.1
couch: 3.4.3.5.1
courtyard: 3.4.3.3
covered market: 3.4.3.1
cow: 3.3.3
cowrie shell: 3.4.2.5
crack, chink: 3.4.3.2.4
crank: 1.1.2
crocodiles: 3.4.1.4.1
cross: 3.2.4.3.2
crossbow: 1.1.1.2.2, 3.3.2.1
crossed weave: 3.2.4.5.2
crossed: 3.2.4.5.2, 3.2.4.5.3
crosspiece (basketwork): 3.2.4.5.1
crosspiece: 3.2.4.5.1, 3.4.3.2.2, 3.4.3.5.1
crucible: 3.2.2
crumbs: 3.4.1.3
crusher: 3.4.1.1.4
cultivated land: 3.3.5.1
cultivated plot: 3.3.5.1
cultivation zones: 3.3.5.1
cup: 3.4.1.5.1
cupboard: 3.4.3.5.1
current of water: 1.3.2
custard-apple: 3.4.1.4.2
cut down a tree: 3.2.1.2
cut down: 3.3.5.2
cutting edge of a blade: 1.1.1
cutting edge of iron head: 1.1.1
cutting, slip (of plant): 3.3.5.3

cutting, slip, graft: 3.3.5.3
cylinder: 3.2.4.5.3
dagger: 1.1.1.2.2
dagger (2 blade edges): 3.3.2.1
dam (for fishing): 3.2.5.1
dam to empty (side pool): 3.3.1
dancing shoes: 3.4.2.3
decoration: 3.2.3.2.3
degreasing agent: 3.2.3.2.1
demijohn, carboy: 3.4.1.3
detonation: 3.3.2.1
diagonal: 3.2.4.5.2
dig out: 3.3.5.2
direction: 2.3
dirt: 3.4.3.5.4
dirty: 3.4.3.5.4
dish: 3.2.5.1
distaff: 3.2.4.3.1
ditch: 3.4.3.3
dog: 3.3.3
domestic pigeon: 3.3.3
donkey: 2.1.1
door: 3.4.3.4
door frame: 3.4.3.4
door sill, threshold: 3.4.3.4
dough ball: 3.4.1.4.2
dough, batter: 3.4.1.4.2
doughnut: 3.4.1.4.2
drawing (open fire oriented in the direction of the wind):
dregs in a liquid: 3.4.1.4.5
dress: 3.4.2.1
drill: 3.2.1.1, 3.2.2
drill rolled in the palms: 3.2.1.2
drill/bit: 3.2.1.2
dromedary: 2.1.1
dry: 3.2.1.2
dry season: 3.3.5.1
drying: 3.2.4.2
drying (dessication): 3.4.1.3
drying mat: 3.4.1.3
drying screen: 3.4.1.3
drying shed: 3.4.1.3
dugout canoe: 1.1.1.3, 2.2

Traditional Technologies

dust: 3.3.5.1, 3.4.3.5.4
dye: 1.3.3, 3.2.3.3.1
ear: 3.2.5.2
ear of corn: 3.3.5.4
earrings: 3.4.2.5
earth: 3.2.3.1, 3.4.1.4.3
earth cake: 3.4.1.4.3
earth granary: 3.2.5.1
earthen bed: 3.4.3.5.1
earthen mortar: 3.2.2
earthen oven: 3.4.1.2
edible mushrooms: 3.4.1.4.2
edible soils: 3.3.6
eggs: 3.4.1.4.1
elephant: 3.3.3, 3.4.1.4.1
ember pot (for carrying coals): 1.2.3
encampment: 3.4.3.1
encircle: 3.3.2
enclosing wall, enclosure: 3.4.3.3
engine: 2.1.2
entrails: 3.4.1.4.1
entrenched camp, village: 3.3.2
epaulettes: 3.4.2.5
European bridge: 2.3
European machete: 1.1.1.2.2, 3.3.5.2, 3.3.5.3
European road: 2.3
European type tiles: 3.4.3.2.3
European ventilator: 1.4
ewe lamb: 3.3.3
extinguish the fire: 1.2.3
extraction: 3.3.6
eye of needle: 3.2.4.4
fabric: 3.2.4.5.3
fall trap: 3.3.2.2
fallow land: 3.3.5.2
famine: 3.4.1.3
fan: 1.4
farinaceous plant: 3.4.1.4.2
farthingale: 3.2.4.5.3
fat (seasoning): 3.4.1.4.4
faucet: 3.2.5.3
feathering: 3.3.2.1
feathers: 3.2.3.2

fence: 3.3.5.3, 3.4.3.3
fermented drinks: 1.3.3
fetters, shackles: 3.3.2
fiber: 3.2.4.3.1
field, field boundaries: 3.3.5.1
file: 1.1.1.2.1, 3.2.1.2, 3.2.2
filter: 3.2.5.3, 3.4.1.1.2
finery: 3.4.2.5
fingers: 1.1.1.1
fire: 1.2.1
fire brush: 3.3.5.2
fire rake/poker: 3.2.2
fireplace with a draught: 3.4.3.5.3
fireplace, firebox: 3.2.2
fish: 3.4.1.4.1
fishing: 3.3.1
fishing by hook, with or without a rod: 3.3.1
fishing net, rod: 3.3.1
fishing shelter: 3.3.1
fishing with poison: 3.3.1
fishing with weir dam or blocked off river that is emptied: 3.3.1
fist: 1.1.1.2.1
flat basket: 3.2.5.1
flat part of a millstone: 1.1.1
flax: 3.2.4.3.1
flintlock rifle: 3.3.2.1
flintstone: 1.2.2
float: 3.3.1
floor of a hut: 3.4.3.2.4
flour: 3.4.1.4.2
flower: 3.4.1.4.2
fly (of trousers): 3.4.2.3
fly wheel: 3.2.4.3.2
flyswatter: 3.4.2.3
foam, froth (of wine): 3.4.1.4.5
food: 3.4.1.4
food shortage: 3.4.1.3
footprint: 3.3.2
forage cap: 3.4.2.5
ford: 2.3
forest: 3.3.5.1
forge, forge work: 3.2.2

fork: 3.4.1.4.5
forked post: 3.4.3.2.2
fortifications: 3.4.3.3
founder, smelter: 3.2.2
fragments (remnants): 3.4.1.3
frame: 3.2.4.5.3, 3.4.3.4
frame (of the canoe): 2.2
framework: 3.4.3.2.1, 3.4.3.2.4
friction lighter: 1.1.1.2.1, 1.2.2
friction strip (to light a match): 1.2.2
fringe: 3.4.2.4
fruit: 3.4.1.4.2
fruit gathering pole: 3.3.4
fruit hairs: 1.2.2
fruit juice: 3.2.3.3.1
fuel: 1.2.3, 3.4.3.5.2
full: 3.2.5.3
full of taste: 3.4.1.5.1
funnel: 3.2.5.3, 3.3.4
furnace mouth: 3.2.2
g-string: 3.4.2.3
gallery: 3.3.6
garden: 3.3.5.1, 3.4.3.3
garlic: 3.4.1.4.4
gather: 3.2.4.3.1
gathered together: 3.4.2.4
get larger (plants): 3.3.5.3
gin: 3.2.4.3.1
ginning (to separate the flock from the seeds): 3.2.4.3.1
glass: 3.4.1.5.1
glaze: 3.2.3.2.3
glue: 3.2.3.3.2
goat: 3.3.3, 3.4.1.4.1
goblet, mug: 3.2.5.1, 3.4.1.5.1
gold: 3.2.2, 3.3.6
gold-bearing sand: 3.3.6
gouge: 1.1.1.2.3, 3.2.1.2
granary: 3.2.5.1
granary loft: 3.4.1.3, 3.4.3.3
grass: 3.2.3.2, 3.2.3.2.4
grasshoppers: 3.4.1.4.1
grater: 3.4.1.1.3
graver: 3.2.1.2

groove (of a pulley): 1.1.2
ground glass: 3.2.3.2.1
ground nut, peanut: 3.4.1.4.2
grounds (coffee) dregs: 1.3.2
group fishing: 3.3.1
guinea fowl: 3.3.3
gun: 1.1.1.2.2
gutter: 3.2.5.2
hair pin: 3.4.2.7
hair styles: 3.4.2.7
hair: 3.2.3.2
hall, vestibule: 3.4.3.3
hammer: 1.1.1.2, 1.1.1.2.2, 3.2.1.1, 3.2.2
hammer of a gun: 1.1.1.2.3
hand: 1.1.1.1
hand drill: 3.2.1.2
handful: 3.4.1.5.1
handle (for carrying a load): 2.1.1
handle: 1.1.2, 3.2.5.2
handlebar: 2.1.2
hard wood of the lighter: 1.2.2
hardened road: 3.3.5.1
hares: 3.4.1.4.1
harness equipment: 3.2.4.5.3
harness of a weaving loom: 1.1.1
harpoon: 1.1.1.2.2
harpoon fishing: 3.3.1
hat: 3.4.2.2
head (of hammer): 1.1.1
head band: 2.1.1, 3.4.2.5
head kerchief: 3.4.2.2
headgear: 3.4.2.2
heads: 3.4.1.4.1
headstall of the bridle: 2.1.1
hearth: 1.2.3, 3.4.1.2
hearth fire: 1.2.1
hearts: 3.4.1.4.1
hemispheric container: 3.4.1.5.1
hemp: 3.2.4.3.1, 3.4.1.4.5
hen: 3.3.3
henhouse: 3.3.3
hinge: 3.4.3.4
hit someone with a weapon: 3.3.2
hoe: 1.1.1.2.2, 3.2.3.1, 3.3.5.2, 3.3.5.3

Traditional Technologies

hole: 3.2.5.1
hole in a wall: 3.4.3.2.4
hollow: 3.4.3.2.4
hollow of the hand: 1.1.1.1
home: 3.4.3.1
honey bee: 3.4.1.4.4
honeycomb: 3.4.1.4.4
hood: 3.4.3.5.3
hook: 1.1.1.1, 3.3.1
hoop net: 1.1.1.1
horse: 2.1.1, 3.3.3
hostage: 3.3.2
hot pepper: 3.4.1.4.4
house: 3.4.3.1
human force: 1.1.3
hunger: 3.4.1.3
hunter, hunting: 3.3.2
hunting game: 3.3.2
hunting knife: 1.1.1.2.1, 3.3.2.1
hunting master: 3.3.2
hunting net: 1.1.1.1
hunting rites: 3.3.2
hut: 3.3.5.3, 3.4.3.1
immerse: 3.2.3.3.1
impulse: 1.1.3
incandescent: 3.2.2
incisor tooth (human): 1.1.1
index (finger): 1.1.1.1
individual fishing: 3.3.1
insects: 3.4.1.4.1
inside of baskets: 1.1.1
instruments: 1.4
interior wall or partition: 3.4.3.2.4
intersection, direction: 2.3
intestines: 3.4.1.4.1
inverted pot: 3.4.3.2.3
iron: 3.2.2, 3.3.6
iron (flat): 3.4.2.4
iron chisel: 1.1.1.2.3, 3.2.2
iron hammer: 1.1.1.2.3
ivory: 3.2.1.1
jar: 3.4.1.3
jewelry: 3.4.2.5
joiner: 3.2.1.2

juice: 3.4.1.4.4
kaolin: 3.2.3.2.1
kenaf, gombo: 3.4.1.4.2
kernel of the stone: 3.4.1.4.4
kerosene, paraffin: 3.4.3.5.2
key: 3.4.3.4
kid (goat): 3.3.3
knife: 3.2.4.5.3, 3.3.5.4, 3.4.1.1.3, 3.4.1.5.1
knot: 3.2.4.3.3
ladder: 3.4.3.4
ladder cut into tree: 3.3.4
ladle: 3.4.1.5.1
lady: 3.2.3.1
lamp: 3.4.3.5.2
landing net: 3.3.1
landmarks: 2.3
landolphia fruit: 3.4.1.4.2
lane: 2.3
large white millet, sorghum: 3.4.1.4.2
larvae: 3.4.1.4.1
latex: 3.2.3.2, 3.2.3.3.2
lath, slat (rail): 3.4.3.5.1, 3.2.4.5.3
lavatory, toilet: 3.4.3.3
lead: 3.2.2
leaf, leaflet: 3.4.1.4.2, 3.4.3.2.3
leaf for wrapping: 2.1.1
leaf for wrapping foods: 3.4.1.2
leaf hut: 3.4.3.1
leaf loincloth: 3.4.2.3
leather: 3.2.4.2
leather knife: 3.2.4.4
leaven: 3.4.1.4.2
leftovers: 3.4.1.3
leg, haunch: 3.4.1.4.1
lemon juice: 3.4.1.4.4
lever: 1.1.2
lime: 3.4.3.2.4
linen: 3.4.1.5.1
lines: 3.3.1
lintel: 3.4.3.4
liquid: 3.4.1.4.5
little finger: 1.1.1.1
live coals: 1.2.3
livers: 3.4.1.4.1

load: 2.1.1
lock: 3.4.3.4
log: 1.2.3
long-sleeved pullover: 3.4.2.3
look-out (person): 3.3.2
loom: 3.2.4.5.3
loose: 3.2.4.3.3
lost wax casting: 3.2.2
lumber room: 3.4.3.3
lump of clay: 3.2.3.2.2.1a
lungs: 3.4.1.4.1
machine gun: 3.3.2.1
main beam: 3.4.3.2.2
mallet: 1.1.1.2.2, 3.3.4
man's knife: 3.3.2.1
man's loincloth: 3.4.2.3
mandarin orange (tangerine) tree: 3.4.1.4.2
mango, mango tree: 3.4.1.4.2
manioc: 3.4.1.4.2
market hall: 3.4.3.1
marks: 2.3
marlinspike: 3.2.4.3.3
masonry work kiln: 3.2.3.2.4
mast: 2.2
mat: 3.4.3.5.1
match: 1.2.2
matchbox: 1.2.2
mattock: 3.2.3.1, 3.3.5.2, 3.3.5.4
maturity of a plant: 3.3.5.3
meat: 3.3.2
medal: 3.4.2.5
mesh: 3.3.1
metal: 3.2.2, 3.3.6
middle finger: 1.1.1.1
military forage cap: 3.4.2.2
military uniform: 3.4.2.5
milk: 3.4.1.4.5
mill: 1.1.1.2.1
millet: 3.4.1.4.2
mine: 3.3.6
minerals: 3.2.2, 3.3.6
mirror: 3.4.3.5.2
miss the target: 3.3.2

mixture (general term): 1.3.3
molar tooth (human): 1.1.1
mold: 3.2.2, 3.2.3.2.2.2
molding the iron: 3.2.2
molding: 3.2.3.2.2.2
mollusks: 3.4.1.4.1
monkeys: 3.4.1.4.1
months of the year: 3.3.5.1
mortar: 3.2.3.3.3, 3.4.1.1.4
motor: 1.1.3
moustaches: 3.4.2.7
mud: 3.3.5.1, 3.4.3.2.4
muscle: 1.1.2, 1.1.3
mush: 3.4.1.4.2
naked: 3.4.2.1
nap: 3.2.4.5.1
native saw: 3.2.1.2
neck chain: 3.4.2.5
neck of a bottle: 3.2.5.3
neck sash: 3.4.2.2
neck scarf: 3.4.2.2
necklace: 3.4.2.5
necktie: 3.4.2.2
needle: 1.1.1.2.1, 3.2.4.4
nere fruit: 3.4.1.4.2
nicotine: 3.4.1.4.5
nipple: 3.2.5.2
nomad: 2.1
non-masonry kiln: 3.2.3.2.4
noose trap: 3.3.2.2
notched post: 3.4.3.4
nugget: 3.3.6
nutcracker: 3.4.1.1.4
oar: 1.1.1.3, 2.2
oil: 3.4.1.4.4, 3.4.3.5.2
okra: 3.4.1.4.2
open hearth, fireplace: 3.4.3.5.3
openings: 3.2.3.2.4, 3.2.5.3
orange, orange tree: 3.4.1.4.2
outer loincloth: 3.4.2.3
outer wall: 3.4.3.2.4
outfit (set of clothes): 3.4.1.5.1
overabundant: 3.4.1.3
ovines (sheep): 3.4.1.4.1

Traditional Technologies

ox, bull: 3.3.3
pack bundle (container): 1.1.1.3, 2.1.1
pack of dogs: 3.3.2
pack saddle: 1.1.1.3
package: 2.1.1
pad (for carrying on the head): 2.1.1
padding (saddle): 2.1.1
paddle: 1.1.1.3, 2.2
painting: 3.2.3.3.1
palm: 1.1.1.1
palm nut: 3.4.1.4.4
palm tree (domesticated): 3.3.4
palm wine: 3.4.1.4.5
palmyra tree fruit: 3.4.1.4.2
pancake: 3.4.1.4.2
panning: 3.3.6
panties: 3.4.2.3
pants: 3.4.2.3
papaya (pawpaw), papaya tree: 3.4.1.4.2
paraffin, kerosene lamp: 3.4.3.5.2
parasol: 3.4.2.3
passive stone: 1.2.2
path: 2.3, 3.4.3.5.4
pawl: 3.2.4.5.3
paws: 3.4.1.4.1
pea: 3.4.1.4.2
peat: 3.2.3.2.4
pedal: 2.1.2, 3.2.4.5.6
pendant: 3.4.2.5
pepper: 3.4.1.4.4
percussion rifle: 3.3.2.1
perfume: 3.4.2.9
personal hunting net: 3.3.2.2
pestle: 1.1.1.2.2, 3.4.1.1.4, 3.4.1.5.2
pick axe: 1.1.1.2.2, 3.2.3.1
pier: 2.2
pig: 3.3.3
pigeon house: 3.3.3
pike: 1.1.1.2.2, 3.3.2.1
pile up: 3.3.5.2
piling, support: 3.4.3.2.1
pin: 3.2.5.3
pin bolt: 3.4.3.4
pipe: 3.2.5.3, 3.3.4, 3.4.1.5.2

pipe cleaner: 3.4.1.5.2
pit: 3.2.4.5.3, 3.3.2.2
pitcher: 3.2.5.1
pith, core, marrow: 3.4.1.4.2
pivot: 3.2.4.3.2
place: 3.4.2.4
plane: 1.1.1.2.1
plank: 3.2.3.1
plant ashes: 3.4.1.4.4
plant juice: 3.2.3.2.3
plant sponge: 3.4.3.5.4
plantation: 3.3.5.2
planting: 3.3.5.1
plants: 3.3.5.1, 3.4.1.4.2
plaster: 3.2.3.3.3
plate: 3.4.1.5.1
pleasant odor: 3.4.2.9
pliers (forceps): 3.2.2
pocket: 3.3.5.3, 3.4.2.3
point, tip: 1.1.1, 3.2.4.4
poisons: 1.3.3
pole: 2.2
polisher: 3.2.1.2
port: 2.2
porter, portage: 2.1
posts: 3.4.3.2.1
pot: 3.4.1.3
potato: 3.4.1.4.2
poultry: 3.4.1.4.1
preserve: 3.4.1.3
press: 1.1.1.2.1, 1.1.2, 3.4.1.1.4
pressure lamp: 3.4.3.5.2
principal rafter: 3.4.3.2.2
prisoner of war: 3.3.2
product: 3.1.2
pronged: 1.1.1.2.2
propeller: 1.1.2
prow (bow): 2.2
pruning shears: 3.3.5.3
pull up: 3.3.5.2
pulley well: 3.2.5.2
pulley: 1.1.2, 3.2.4.5.3
pulling: 2.1
pulp of the nut: 3.4.1.4.4

pumpkin: 3.4.1.4.2
pygmy hut: 3.4.3.1
quarters, large chunks of meat: 3.4.1.4.1
quiver: 3.3.2.1
rabbit: 3.3.3
raft: 2.2
rafter: 3.4.3.2.2
rail: 3.2.4.5.3
raincoat: 3.4.2.3
rainy season: 3.3.5.1
raised bed: 3.4.3.5.1
ram: 3.3.3
rasp: 3.2.1.2
rats: 2.4.1.4.1
raw: 3.4.1.2
razor: 3.4.2.7
red rice: 3.4.1.4.2
reel: 3.2.4.3.1, 3.2.4.5.3
reinforcing purlin: 3.4.3.2.2
reptiles: 3.4.1.4.1
reserves, stocks: 3.4.1.3
reservoir: 1.2.2
resinous wood: 3.4.3.5.2
retting: 3.2.4.3.1
retting pond/pit: 3.2.4.3.1
ridge: 3.3.5.2
ridge tiles: 3.4.3.2.3
ridgepole: 3.4.3.2.2
rifle stock: 3.3.2.1
rigging (gear): 2.2
ring: 3.4.2.5
ring (for finger): 3.4.2.5
ring (framing): 3.4.3.2.2
ring finger: 1.1.1.1
ripe: 3.3.4
river, stream: 2.2
river full of fish: 3.3.1
rocky place: 3.3.5.1
rod: 3.4.3.2.2
roll of tobacco: 3.4.1.5.2
roof: 3.4.3.2.3
rooster: 3.3.3
root: 3.4.1.4.2
rope: 3.2.4.2

rotten: 3.4.1.3
rough cast: 3.2.3.3.3
rubber, rubber tree: 3.2.3.3.2
rubbish dump (hole or heap): 3.4.3.5.4
rung ladder: 3.4.3.4
sack: 1.1.1.3
saddle: 1.1.1.3, 2.1.1
saddle-girth: 2.1.1
sail: 2.2
salt: 3.3.6, 3.4.1.4.4
salt plants: 3.4.1.4.4
sand: 3.2.3.1
sandals: 3.4.2.3
sandpaper: 3.2.1.2
satchel: 2.1.1
sauce: 1.3.3, 3.4.1.4.4
saw: 1.1.1.2.1
sawdust: 3.2.1.2
sawmill: 3.2.1.2
sawtooth: 3.2.1.2
scarecrow: 1.4, 3.3.5.3
scarf (head): 3.4.2.2
school: 3.4.3.1
scissors: 3.2.4.4
scraper: 1.1.1.2.1, 3.2.4.1, 3.2.4.2, 3.4.1.1.2
scrapers (files): 3.4.2.7
seams (canoe skin): 2.2
seat: 3.4.3.5.2
seats of the canoe: 2.2
seed: 3.4.1.4.2
seed for sowing: 3.3.5.3
seedling: 3.3.5.3
seeds (grain): 3.3.5.3
separating (spreading) bar: 3.2.4.5.3
serge: 3.2.4.5.2, 3.2.4.5.3
settled: 2.1
sewing machine: 3.2.4.4
sewing scissors: 1.1.1.2.1
sewing thread: 3.2.4.4
sewn bark: 3.2.4.1
shaft: 3.3.6
shallow bowl: 3.2.5.1, 3.4.1.5.1
shard: 3.2.3.2.2.1a
shea nut butter: 3.4.1.4.4, 3.4.3.5.2

Traditional Technologies

shea tree fruit: 3.4.1.4.2
shears (iron): 1.1.1.2.1
shed: 3.4.3.3
sheep: 3.3.3
sheet: 3.4.3.5
sheet metal: 3.4.3.2.3
shelf: 3.2.3.2.2.1a
shell: 3.2.1.1
shelter, encampment: 3.4.3.1
shield: 3.3.2.1
shirt: 3.4.2.3
shoes: 3.4.2.3
short-sleeved pullover: 3.4.2.3
shorts: 3.4.2.3
shoulder strap: 2.1.1
shovel: 1.1.1.2.1, 3.2.3.1, 3.4.3.5.4
shutter: 3.4.3.4
shuttle: 3.2.4.5.3
sickle: 3.3.5.4
siege: 3.3.2
sieve, strainer: 3.2.5.3, 3.4.1.1.2
silo (grain): 3.2.5.1, 3.4.1.3
silver: 3.2.2
site of the house, village: 3.4.2.4
skein: 3.2.4.3.2
skewer: 3.4.1.2
skimmer (in baked clay): 3.4.1.1.2
skin hide: 3.2.4.2
skin membranes: 1.4
slave: 3.3.2
sledge hammer: 1.1.1.2.3
sleeve: 3.4.2.3
sling on clothing to carry baby: 2.1.1
slip (as in pottery): 3.2.3.2.3
slope of the roof: 3.4.3.2.3
small crack (in paint): 3.4.3.2.4
small dish: 3.2.4.3.2
small, thin blade: 3.2.3.2.2.1a
smoke: 1.2.3
snake: 3.4.1.4.1
snare trap: 3.3.2.2
snuffbox: 3.4.1.5.2
soap: 3.4.2.8
socket: 1.1.2

socks: 3.4.2.3
soft wood of the lighter: 1.2.2
soils: 3.2.3.1, 3.2.3.3.1, 3.2.3.3.3
soldier: 3.3.2
solution: 1.3.3
sorrel: 3.4.1.4.2
soup bowl: 3.4.1.5.1
sour: 3.4.1.5.1
spade: 1.1.1.2.1, 3.2.3.1
spark: 1.2.2
spear: 1.1.1.2.2, 3.3.2.1
spear fishing: 3.3.1
spiked trap: 1.1.1.2.2
spindle, shuttle: 1.1.2, 3.2.4.3.2
spinner: 3.2.4.3
spinning powder: 3.2.4.3.2
spiralled: 3.2.4.5.2
spoiled: 3.4.1.3
spool: 3.2.4.5.3
spoon: 1.1.1.1, 3.2.5.1, 3.4.1.5.1
spout: 3.2.5.3
spout, flood: 1.3.2
spring trap: 3.3.2.2
spring-loaded trap: 1.1.1.2.2
sprouted corn, maize: 3.4.1.4.5
spur (stub, heel): 1.1.2
square: 3.4.3.1
square, of 3 component: 3.2.4.5.2
squash: 3.4.1.4.2
squirrels: 3.4.1.4.1
stable: 3.4.3.3
stage: 3.4.3.5.2
stand: 3.2.3.2.2.1a, 3.4.3.5.2
starboard: 2.2
steering wheel: 2.1.2
stem or stalk: 3.4.1.4.2
step: 3.2.4.5.3, 3.4.3.4
stick: 3.2.3.1, 3.2.4.5.3
stick across the breadth: 3.2.4.5.3
sticky: 3.4.1.4.4
stirring up: 3.3.5.2
stirrup: 2.1.1
stock: 3.4.1.3
stockade: 3.4.3.3

stone: 1.1.1.2.2, 1.2.2, 3.2.1.1
stone of the nut: 3.4.1.4.4
stone with hollow cavities: 3.4.1.1.4
stool: 3.4.3.5.1
stopper, measuring cap: 3.2.5.3, 3.4.1.3
storage shelter: 3.4.3.3
storeroom: 3.4.3.3
strap: 2.1.1
straw: 3.2.3.2, 3.4.3.2.3
stream (of water): 1.3.2
street: 2.3, 3.4.3.1
stretch out the vines: 3.3.5.2
stretching: 3.2.4.3.2
striker: 1.2.2
striking: 1.1.1.2.3
string: 3.2.4.3
string drill: 3.2.1.2
strip of bark: 3.2.4.1
strong man: 1.1.3
stubble: 3.3.5.4
sugar: 3.4.1.4.4
sugar cane: 3.4.1.4.4
sump: 3.2.5.2
sunshade: 3.4.2.3
supplies: 3.4.1.3
supporting works: 3.3.6
sweet potato: 3.4.1.4.2
sweet, sugary: 3.4.1.5.1
table: 3.4.3.5.2
tails: 3.4.1.4.1
tainted: 3.4.1.3
tang: 1.1.2
tank: 3.2.5.1
tanned hide: 3.2.4.2
tanning solution: 1.3.3, 3.2.4.2
taro: 3.4.1.4.2
tart: 3.4.1.5.1
tattooing: 3.4.2.6
tenon: 1.1.2
thatch: 3.4.3.2.3
thimble: 3.2.4.4
thirst: 3.4.1.3
thread: 3.2.4.3, 3.2.4.4

thresher, beater: 1.1.1.2.2, 3.2.3.2.2.1a,
  3.2.4.1, 3.4.1.1.2
threshing by hand: 3.4.1.1.2
throwing club: 3.3.2.1
throwing crook (type of boomerang):
  3.3.2.1
throwing hatchet, axe: 3.3.2.1
throwing knife: 1.1.1.2.2
thumb: 1.1.1.1
tie: 2.1.1
tip: 3.3.2.1
tire: 2.1.2
to (set up the) warp: 3.2.4.5.3
to act by blows: 1.1.1.2
to act upon matter: 1.1.1
to activate the bellows: 1.4
to aim: 3.3.2.1
to anoint: 3.4.2.8
to apply: 3.2.3.2.3
to appreciate, like: 3.4.1.5.1
to arrange, set in order: 3.4.3.5.4
to assemble threads: 3.2.4.3.3
to attack: 3.3.2
to be abundant, plentiful: 3.4.1.3
to be bad to the taste: 3.4.1.5.1
to be blazing, flaming: 1.2.2
to be good to the taste: 3.4.1.5.1
to be green: 3.3.4
to be in wait: 3.3.2
to be lacking, short: 3.4.1.3
to be tight (garment): 3.4.2.1
to bear fruit: 3.3.5.4
to beat, hammer, the strips: 3.2.4.1
to beat: 1.1.1.2.2, 1.3.2, 3.2.3.2.1, 3.2.4.2,
  3.2.4.3.1
to become red in the fire: 3.2.2
to bed out: 3.3.5.3
to bend a bow: 3.3.2.1
to block off a river: 3.3.1
to blow: 1.4
to boil: 1.3.2, 3.4.1.2
to bore, pierce: 1.1.1.2.1
to braid the hair: 3.4.2.7
to braid: 3.2.4.3.3, 3.2.4.5.1, 3.2.4.5.2

Traditional Technologies

to braise: 3.4.1.2
to break the mold: 3.2.2
to break up the soil: 3.3.5.2
to break wood: 1.2.3, 3.2.1.2
to break: 3.4.1.1.4
to build, erect: 3.4.3.2, 3.4.3.2.4
to burn: 1.2.3
to burst, blow out a tire: 2.1.2
to bury: 3.3.5.2
to button: 3.4.2.1
to capsize: 2.2
to carbonize: 1.2.3
to card: 3.2.4.3.1
to care for: 3.1.2
to care for the fire: 1.2.3
to carry fire: 1.2.2
to carry: 1.1.1.3, 2.1
to carve up: 3.4.1.1.3
to carve: 3.2.1.2
to cast: 1.1.1.2.2
to castrate an animal: 3.3.3
to catch: 3.3.2
to catch: (in hollow of hand): 1.1.1.1
to change clothes: 3.4.2.1
to chew: 3.4.1.5.1
to choke: 3.4.1.5.1
to clean: 3.4.3.5.4
to clean food: 3.4.1.1.2
to clean grain: 3.4.1.1.2
to clean up: 3.3.5.2
to clear brush, a field: 3.3.5.2
to clear the area: 3.3.5.2
to climb a tree: 3.3.4
to clip: 3.2.4.3.3
to close, lock a door: 3.4.3.4
to clothe: 3.4.2.1
to cock, load: 3.3.2.1
to collect: 3.2.5.1
to collect honey: 3.3.4
to collect latex: 3.2.3.3.2
to color (something): 3.2.3.3.1
to comb: 3.2.4.3.1
to comb one's hair: 3.4.2.7
to construct: 2.3, 3.4.3.2, 3.4.3.2.4

to consume: 3.1.2
to contain: 1.1.1.1
to cook: 3.2.3.2.4, 3.4.1.1.1, 3.4.1.2
to cool off (metals): 1.3.1
to cover: 3.4.2.1
to crawl: 3.3.2
to crease: 3.4.2.1
to crumble: 3.4.1.1.3, 3.2.2
to crumple: 3.2.4.2, 3.2.4.3.1, 3.4.2.1
to crush: 3.4.1.1.4
to crush by pounding: 1.1.1.2.2
to cut: 1.1.1.2.1, 3.2.4.4, 3.3.4, 3.4.1.5.2, 3.4.1.5.1
to cut away: 1.1.1.2.3
to cut down/back: 3.3.5.3
to cut hair: 3.4.2.7
to cut into the earth: 1.1.1.2.1
to cut the hide: 3.2.4.2
to cut up into chunks: 1.1.1.2.1
to cut up the bark: 3.2.4.1
to cut up: 3.4.1.1.3, 3.2.2
to cut wood: 3.2.1.2
to dampen: 3.2.4.1
to debone: 3.4.1.1.3
to decant the water (make clear): 1.3.2
to decant: 3.2.5.3
to deflate: 2.1.2
to degrease: 3.2.3.2.1
to dig out: 3.2.3.2.2.1a, 3.3.5.3, 3.2.2
to dirty: 3.4.2.4
to dissolve: 1.3.1
to divide matter: 1.1.1.2
to domesticate: 3.3.3
to double: 3.2.4.4
to drain, strain: 3.3.1, 3.4.1.1.2
to draw (water): 3.2.5.2
to draw alongside: 2.2
to draw patterns on the body: 3.4.2.8
to drift (from shore): 2.2
to drill: 3.2.1.1, 3.2.1.2
to drink: 3.4.1.5.1
to drive in a post: 3.4.3.2
to dry: 3.2.3.2.3, 3.4.1.3
to dry (in open air etc.): 1.4

to dry a skin: 3.2.4.2
to dry out by hanging clothes: 1.3.2
to dry out: 3.4.1.3
to dye: 3.2.3.3.1
to eat: 3.4.1.4.5
to embark: 2.2
to empty: 3.4.1.1.4
to enclose, fence in: 3.4.3.3
to entangle: 3.2.4.3.3
to extract: 3.3.6
to fall: 3.3.4
to feed (the fire): 1.2.3
to feel a fruit: 3.3.4
to ferment: 3.4.1.4.5
to fight: 3.3.2
to file: 1.1.1.2.1, 3.2.1.2
to fill: 3.2.5.3
to filter: 3.4.1.1.2
to finish off, (give death blow): 3.3.2
to fish: 3.3.1
to flatten out, crush: 1.1.1.2.1, 3.4.1.1.4
to float on water: 2.2
to flush out (in hunting): 3.3.2
to fly (bird, airplane): 1.1.1.3
to forge: 3.2.2
to fry: 3.4.1.2
to gather: 3.2.5.1, 3.3.4, 3.3.5.4
to germinate: 3.3.5.3
to get dressed: 3.4.2.1
to get lost: 2.3
to get one's bearings: 2.3
to get undressed: 3.4.2.1
to give a blow: 1.1.1.2.2, 3.3.2
to give impulse, propel: 1.1.3
to give out a fragrance: 3.4.2.9
to glue two pieces together: 3.2.3.3.2
to grab hold of: 1.1.1.1
to grate: 3.4.1.1.3
to grind: 1.1.1.2.1, 3.2.3.3.1, 3.4.1.1.4
to grow: 3.3.5.3
to guide: 2.2
to hammer (iron): 1.1.1.2
to hammer: 3.2.2, 3.2.4.1
to hang: 1.1.1.1

to harvest: 3.3.5.4
to heat: 1.2.3, 3.2.2, 3.4.1.2
to heat the mold: 3.2.2
to heat up (food): 1.3.1
to hem: 3.2.4.4
to hew: 1.1.1.2.2
to hit: 1.1.1.2
to hold: 1.1.1.1
to hook: 1.1.1.1
to hunt: 3.3.2
to hurl: 1.1.1.2.2
to impregnate (with water, dye): 1.3.1
to imprint: 3.2.3.2.3
to intertwine by tying: 3.2.4.3.3
to iron: 3.4.2.2
to jam: 3.3.2.1
to join: 3.2.4.3.1
to keep: 3.4.1.3
to kill: 3.3.2
to knead: 3.2.3.2.1
to knot: 3.2.4.3.3
to land (a boat): 2.2
to lather, soap: 3.4.2.4
to lay (eggs): 3.3.3
to lengthen (draw out) the clay: 3.2.3.2.2.1a
to lick: 3.4.1.5.1
to lift: 2.1
to lift the hammer: 3.3.2.1
to lift up: 1.1.1.3
to light (the fire): 1.2.2
to load: 2.1, 3.3.2.1
to look for: 3.3.4
to lure: 3.3.2.1
to make: 2.3
to make a fire: 1.2.1
to massage: 3.4.2.8
to masticate, grind, crush: 3.4.1.5.1
to melt, to dissolve: 3.4.1.4.4
to mend, darn: 3.2.4.4
to milk: 3.3.3, 3.4.1.1.4
to mill: 3.4.1.1.4
to mix a solution: 1.3.3
to mix up, to knead: 3.4.1.1.4

to model: 3.2.3.2.2
to moisten: 3.2.4.1
to mold: 1.1.1.2.1, 3.2.3.2.2
to move: 1.1.1.3
to move the earth: 3.2.3.1
to nail down the skin: 3.2.4.2
to navigate: 2.2
to notch: 1.1.1.2.1, 3.2.1.2
to open a door: 3.4.3.4
to overpower: 3.3.2
to pack down the earth: 3.2.3.1
to pack together: 3.4.3.5.4
to paddle: 2.2
to paint: 3.2.3.3.1
to paint a wall: 3.4.3.2.4
to paint the body: 3.4.2.8
to pan for gold: 3.3.6
to perfume: 3.4.2.9
to pick up: 3.3.4
to pierce: 1.1.1.2.1, 3.4.2.5
to pile up earth onto the ridge: 3.3.5.2
to pinch: 1.1.1.1
to plane: 1.1.1.2.1
to plant: 3.3.5.3
to plow: 3.3.5.2
to pluck: 3.4.1.1.3
to polish: 3.2.1.1, 3.2.3.2.2.1b
to polish (stone): 1.1.1.2
to pounce on: 3.3.2
to pound: 3.4.1.1.4
to pour out: 3.4.1.5.1
to prepare: 3.3.6
to prepare a solution: 1.3.3
to prepare the bed: 3.4.3.5.4
to press: 3.4.2.4
to prick: 3.4.2.6
to produce: 3.1.1, 3.1.2, 3.3.5.4
to propel: 1.1.1.2.2
to prune trees: 1.1.1.2
to pull: 1.1.1.3
to pull up, to turn up: 3.4.2.1
to pull, drag: 2.1
to purify: 3.2.3.2.1
to purify iron: 3.2.2

to pursue: 3.3.2
to push: 1.1.1.3
to put away: 3.4.1.3
to put into the earth: 3.3.5.3
to put on a spit: 3.4.1.2
to put on one's shoes: 3.4.2.1
to put things away: 3.4.3.5.4
to put up: 3.4.3.2
to rasp: 3.2.1.2
to reduce to a pulp: 3.4.1.1.4
to reheat: 3.4.1.2
to remove: 3.3.4, 3.4.1.1.3
to remove hairs: 3.4.2.7
to remove the bark from a tree: 3.2.4.1
to repair: 3.1.2
to reproduce: 3.1.2
to ret: 3.2.4.3.1
to revive the fire: 1.4
to ride a vehicle: 2.1.2
to roast, grill: 1.2.3, 3.4.1.2
to roll: 1.1.1.3
to roll fibers: 3.2.4.3.2
to roughcast: 3.2.3.3.3
to rub: 3.4.2.8
to ruminate, chew the cud: 3.3.3
to run: 1.1.1.3
to run, travel: 2.1
to sail: 1.1.1.3
to salivate: 3.4.1.5.1
to saw: 1.1.1.2.1
to saw wood: 3.2.1.2
to scale: 3.4.1.1.3, 3.4.3.2.4
to scrape, scratch: 1.1.1.2.1, 3.4.1.1.3
to scrape the skin: 3.2.4.2
to scrape the strips: 3.2.4.1
to scrub: 3.4.2.4
to sculpt: 3.2.1.1
to sculpt wood: 3.2.1.2
to seize: 3.3.2
to set a net: 3.3.2.2
to set in order: 3.4.3.5.4
to shake: 3.4.1.1.2
to shape the teeth: 3.4.2.7
to shape while hot: 3.2.2

to shave: 3.4.2.7
to shell, to remove flesh from bones: 3.4.1.1.3
to shell: 3.2.4.3.1, 3.4.1.1.2
to shingle, coat (purify) iron: 3.2.2
to shoot a bow: 3.3.2.1
to shoot the gun: 1.1.1.2.2, 3.3.2.1
to sift: 3.4.1.1.2
to sink: 2.2
to sit on (eggs): 3.3.3
to skewer: 3.4.1.2
to skin: 3.2.4.2, 3.4.1.1.3
to slide (open): 3.3.2.1
to smash, crack: 3.4.1.1.4
to smear, to daub: 3.2.3.3.2, 3.4.2.8
to smell: 3.3.2
to smelt metal: 3.2.2
to smoke (for preservation): 3.4.1.3
to smoke: 3.4.1.5.2
to smooth: 3.2.3.2.2.1a
to smooth (the exterior): 3.2.3.2.2.1a
to smooth out, level: 3.3.5.2
to sniff (out): 3.3.2
to soak: 1.3.1, 1.3.2
to soak the strips: 3.2.4.1
to soap: 3.4.2.8
to soften: 3.4.3.3.4
to soften bark: 3.2.4.1
to soften by heating (metals): 1.2.3
to soften skin: 3.2.4.2
to solder: 3.2.3.2.2.1b
to sort: 3.4.1.1.2
to sow: 3.3.5.3
to spin: 3.2.4.3
to spin onto a spindle: 3.2.4.3.2
to split wood: 1.1.1.2, 3.2.1.2
to sprout: 3.3.5.3
to squeeze, press: 1.1.1.2.1, 3.4.1.1.4
to stab, pierce through: 3.3.2
to steer: 2.2
to stick into the ground: 3.4.3.2
to stir: 3.4.1.1.4, 3.4.1.2
to stir up (the fire): 1.2.3
to stitch: 3.2.4.1

to store tightly packed: 3.4.1.3
to straighten up a post: 3.4.3.2
to stretch: 3.2.4.3.2
to stretch out the thread: 3.2.4.3.1
to strike: 1.1.1.2.2
to strike a match: 1.2.2
to strip (bark from tree): 3.2.4.1
to style the hair: 3.4.2.7
to suck: 3.4.1.5.1
to surround: 3.3.2
to swallow: 3.4.1.5.1
to sweep: 3.4.3.5.4
to swim: 1.1.1.3
to take (snuff): 3.4.1.5.2
to take a spoonful, a heaping spoonful: 3.4.1.5.1
to take aim: 3.3.2.1
to take in handfuls: 3.4.1.5.1
to take in the hands: 1.1.1.1
to take off (one's shoes): 3.4.2.1
to take off: 3.4.2
to take up: 1.1.1.1
to take with a hooked finger: 1.1.1.1
to tan: 3.2.4.2
to tangle: 3.2.4.3.3
to tap a tree: 3.2.1.2, 3.3.4
to taste: 3.4.1.5.1
to tattoo: 3.4.2.6
to thin out: 3.2.3.3.1, 3.3.5.3
to thread: 3.2.4.4, 3.4.2.5
to throw: 1.1.2
to thrust: 3.2.3.3.1
to tidy up: 3.4.3.5.4
to tie a band: 3.2.4.3.3
to train: 3.3.3
to transfer: 3.2.5.3
to transform: 3.1.1
to transmit a movement: 1.1.2
to transport: 1.1.1.3, 2.1
to trap: 3.3.2.1, 3.3.2.2
to treat: 3.3.6
to trim the hair: 3.4.2.7
to turn: 3.2.3.2.2, 3.2.3.2.2.1a
to turn a garment up: 3.4.2.1

Traditional Technologies 511

to turn over the earth: 3.3.5.2
to turn, make turn: 1.1.1.3
to twist: 3.2.4.3.2
to unbutton: 3.4.2.1
to uncork, uncap: 3.4.1.3
to unload: 2.1
to unravel: 3.2.4.3.1
to unstitch: 3.2.4.4
to use: 3.1.2
to walk: 1.1.1.3
to wash: 1.3.2, 3.4.2.4, 3.4.3.5.4
to wash metal: 3.3.6
to watch (out): 3.3.2
to water: 3.2.5.3
to wear a garment: 3.4.2.1
to wear out: 3.1.2
to weave: 3.2.4.5.1, 3.2.4.5.3
to weed: 3.3.5.3
to wind: 3.2.4.3.2
to wind around in a spiral: 3.2.3.2.2.1b
to winnow: 3.4.1.1.2
to wring: 3.4.1.1.4, 3.4.2.4
to yield harvest: 3.3.5.4
tobacco: 3.4.1.4.6
tobacco mortar: 3.4.1.5.2
tongs: 1.1.1.1, 3.2.2
tongue: 3.4.1.3
tongue (type of handle): 1.1.2
toothbrush: 3.4.2.7
toothed wheel: 3.2.3.2.3
top (crest): 3.4.3.2.3
top of the bed: 3.4.3.5.1
touchwood: 1.2.2
tow, oakum: 1.2.2
tower: 3.2.2
tracks: 3.3.2
traditional lamp: 3.4.3.5.2
trail: 2.3, 3.3.2
trap: 1.1.1.1, 3.3.1, 3.3.2.1
treading out the grain: 3.4.1.1.2
treadle: 3.2.4.5.3
tree: 3.2.1.2
tree sap: 3.2.3.3.1
tributary: 2.2

trigger mechanism, click: 3.3.2.1
tripes: 3.4.1.4.1
trivot (tripod): 3.4.1.2
truck: 2.1.2
trunk: 2.3, 3.2.1.2
tub: 3.2.5.1
tuber: 3.4.1.4.2
turtles: 3.4.1.4.1
tuyeres (blast pipes): 1.4, 3.2.2
twigs: 1.2.3
twisted: 3.2.4.5.2
twisting: 3.2.4.3.2
umbrella: 3.4.2.3
undershirt: 3.4.2.3
upper garment: 3.4.2.3
upright post: 3.4.3.4
upright: 3.2.4.5.1
van: 2.1.2
vat: 3.2.5.1
vegetable board: 3.4.1.1.3
vegetable fat: 3.4.3.5.2
veil: 3.4.2.2
ventilators: 1.4
veranda: 3.4.3.3
village: 3.4.3.1
vines tied fast: 2.3
viscera: 3.4.1.4.1
war: 3.3.2
wardrobe: 3.4.3.5.1
warrior: 3.3.2
washing: 1.3.2
washing soil to extract ore: 1.3.2
watchtower: 3.3.5.3
water: 1.3, 3.4.1.4.5
waterjar: 3.2.5.1
wattle: 3.4.3.2.2
wax object: 3.2.2
way: 2.3
weak (man): 1.1.3
weaving: 3.2.4.5.3
weir dam: 3.3.1
well: 3.2.4.5.3
wheat: 3.4.1.4.2
wheel, gearwheel: 1.1.2, 3.2.3.2.2.3

whistle: 1.4
white rice: 3.4.1.4.2
wick: 1.2.2
wildcats (wild animals): 3.4.1.4.1
winch: 3.2.5.1
wind: 1.4
wind instruments: 1.4
winding: 3.2.4.3.2
window sill: 3.4.3.4
window: 3.4.3.4
wine calabash: 3.3.4
winnowing basket: 3.4.1.1.2
wipe off: 3.4.3.5.4
woman's knife: 1.1.1.2.1
woman's loincloth: 3.4.2.3
women's hut: 3.4.3.3
wood: 3.2.1.2, 3.2.3.2.4, 3.2.3.3.1
wood chisel: 1.1.1.2.3
wood for burning: 1.2.2

wood granary: 3.2.5.1
wood knife: 3.2.1.2
wood shavings: 3.2.1.2
woodcutter: 3.2.1.2
wooden bed: 3.4.3.5.1
wooden dish: 3.4.1.5.1
wooden head rest: 3.4.3.5.2
wooden mallet: 3.2.1.2
woodpile, stockpile: 1.2.3
woof: 3.2.4.5.1, 3.2.4.5.3
worm: 3.4.1.4.1
worm-eaten: 3.2.1.2
worn, worn out: 3.1.2
wound: 3.3.2
woven: 3.2.4.5.2
yam: 3.4.1.4.2
year: 3.3.5.1
zebu: 3.3.3

Questionnaire 11
Ethnobotany

by Jacqueline M. C. Thomas

1 Plant names

This questionnaire was inspired in part by the series of ethnobotanical questionnaires devised by Claudine Friedberg-Berthe of the Laboratoire d'Ethnobotanique of the Museum of Paris, but it concentrates on the linguistic and ethnolinguistic aspects. Thus it does not make the later questionnaires on ethnobotany superfluous.

No.:   Ethnic group: Language:
Collector: Informant:

1.1 Name of the plant

vernacular name   synonyms
meaning
why was it given this name?
name in English, French, and/or trade language or local widely-spoken language

1.2 Geographic locality

place where it was growing   place where it is used
how did it get there? (market, crop from olden times, etc.)

1.3 Description

tree / bush / grass / vine / succulent / epiphyte[13] / parasite

---

[13] An epiphyte uses another plant as a support but does not live at its expense, as opposed to a

- size (height - diameter)
- colors (leaves - flowers - ripe fruit)
- shape (leaves - flowers - ripe fruit)
- habitat (large wet/dry forest - forest gallery - wooded savannah - grassy savannah - prairie - steppe) (marsh - flood zone - mangrove swamp - shoreline)

1.4 Production

Is the plant wild / domestic[14] / cultivated?

1.5 Localization with respect to the village

(in the last two cases, for domestic or cultivated plants)
- distance from the village
- outside the village (roadside / fallow ground / weed in the field / hedge / border of the field / place of worship / watering places / brush shelters / etc.)
- around the village (where? field / garden / enclosure / outside the fence / inside the fence / etc.)
- in the village (where? street / square / around the houses / place of worship / hut's garden / etc.)
- in the concession area (where? hut's garden / place of worship / protective plants / etc.)

1.6 Exploitation

- Is the plant planted? / not planted?
- If planted: when? by whom? for how long has it been planted? why?
- Is it protected / exploited // exterminated?

1.7 Cultivation methods

- complete field
- grown dry / irrigated / watered / on burnbeat field-permanent field with / without being left fallow (how long?)
- do you plant: seeds / tubers / cuttings
- how? bedding out / manuring / terraces or low walls etc.
- method of harvesting: pulling up / cutting down / etc.
- method of storing (granaries / silos / etc. - where?) / immediate consumption / etc.

1.8 Planting

Who does the planting? the upkeep? the harvesting? etc.
Where? when? how? Is there an accompanying ritual?

---

parasite which draws its sustenance from another plant.

[14]A domestic plant is found in the human environment; it may be exploited, protected, and cared for, but is not cultivated.

Ethnobotany 515

1.9 Uses

- How produced: gathering / domestication / cultivation (for food / for making things)
- How exploited: for subsistence (occasional / seasonal / daily) / commercial purposes / ritual purposes

1.10 Technological

- General:
    * wood (for the sawmill, for working)
    * fibrous plants and tying
    * dyes
    * perfume plants
    * poisons
    * for burning and lighting
    * pastes, resins, latex, glues
    * wrapping, receptacles
    * narcotics and tonics
    * making tools, weapons, and parts of tools and weapons
- In preservation
- In production:
    * gathering
    * fishing
    * artisanal: forge, pottery, basketry, ...
    * hunting and trapping
    * clearing land and cultivation, animal husbandry
- In consumption:
    * construction and habitat, furniture
    * clothing, toilet (hairdressing, tattooing, ornaments)
    * household articles
    * ornamental plants
    * musical instruments and toys

1.11 Alimentary

- Basic foods
    * starchy (farinaceous) foods
    * oil-producing (oleaginous) foods
    * stew and green vegetables
- Supplemental foods
    * fruits, seeds, various foods
    * soups, salads
    * sauce plants and thickening agent
- Condiments
    * salt plants
    * various condiments (pepper, hot pepper, garlic, ...)
- Drinks and stimulants
    * water plants
    * wine plants
    * (herbal) tea
    * alcohol plants
- Foods in time of famine

1.12 Medicinal

- Symptoms (headaches, fainting, dizziness, fever, swelling, etc.)
- Skin (dermatological ailments) (wounds, infections, ulcers, sores, boils, abscesses, tattooings, etc.)
- Skin parasites (scabies, facial swelling or lump, jiggers, threadworm, mycosis, etc.)
- Endemic diseases (leprosy, yaws, elephantiasis, sleeping sickness, malaria, etc.)

- Ear, nose, throat, and lung ailments (earache, nose and throat infections, lung ailments: bronchitis, bronchial pneumonia, pneumonia, lung congestion, tuberculosis, ...)
- Eye ailments
- Ailments of the digestive system (teeth problems, gastroenterological ailments, pain in the spleen, liver troubles, intestinal parasites)
- Cardiovascular ailments
- Gynecological and urinary ailments and venereal diseases (menstrual pains, sterility, abortion-inducing and -preventing agents, aphrodisiacs, etc. - care at delivery, milk-producing and -promoting agents, etc. - gonorrhea, syphilis)
- Mental illnesses
- Childhood diseases
- Bone problems (fractures, curvatures, problems with the joints, etc.)

1.13 Magical and ritual

- Protective (evil spirits, sorcerers, enemies, wild animals, rivals, etc.)
- Propitiatory (trapping and hunting, fishing, growing crops, harvesting, marketing; for the home, children, love, weather, etc.)
- Malefic (hindering others from trapping, hunting, fishing, growing crops, etc.)
- Relationships with the supernatural (contacts with spirits, genies, demons, etc. - clairvoyance, mediums, etc. - ordeals, oaths, etc. - ancestor worship, cults of twins, etc.

1.14 Social role

- Familial organization: rituals or behaviors and incidentals (making and breaking alliances, etc.)
- Political and social organization: rituals or behaviors and incidentals (assembly places-different attributes, messages, explanations, marks of passage, boundaries, etc.)
- Juridical organization: rituals or behaviors and incidentals (finding the guilty, tests of truth, punishments, reconciliations, etc.)
- Religious organization: rituals or behaviors and incidentals

1.15 Beliefs

- Biological characteristics (anatomy, physiology, etc.)
- Relationship to the environment (soil, other plants, animals: attracts some animal, some animal eats it or lives on it, etc.)
- Taxonomy (considered in the same category as such and such another plant: what is the type of relationship? For what reasons (criteria) are they considered to be related?)
- Taboos or veneration (is the plant the object of it? which taboos, etc.?)

1.16 Literature

Is the plant mentioned (in different contexts) in myths, legends, epics, stories, poetry, songs, liturgy, proverbs, riddles, etc.?
- Main character (hero / principal subject / agent)

Ethnobotany

- Other character (favorable / unfavorable): object / patient
- Incidental (positive / negative)

1.17 Proper names

- Can the name of the plant by itself be a proper name?
- Or is it used in making up proper names?
    * of persons (patronymics, personal names, surnames, given names, etc.)
    * of lineages, clans, etc.
    * of domestic animals
    * of villages, localities, etc.

1.18 Symbolism

Does the plant have symbolic value (sex / life / death / war / feelings, etc.)
For each use indicated, specify:
- the part of the plant used (leaf, flower, root, stem, bark, sap, etc.)
- how it is used (ground, crushed, cut, heated, burned to ashes, boiled, unraveled, etc.)
- whether it is used alone or in conjunction: with other plants (which ones?) and/or animal matter (which ones?) and/or inorganic matter (which ones?)
- if it is eaten, or how it is used (for §§1.12, 1.13, and 1.14)
- the terms designating different stages of its use: parts, products, transformations, uses
- the persons entitled to use it (where? when? how? why these people and not others?)

2 Ethnobotanical Questionnaires
by Claudine Friedberg-Berthe

2.1 Wild Plants

Country: Collector: No.:

Scientific Name*

              Family: Genus:
              Species: Variety:

* This part of the questionnaire is designed to be completed by a local botanist, if there is one.

Vernacular Name

Detailed Geographic Location
1. of the place where the collector obtained the plant
2. of the place where it was growing
3. of the place where its role was observed (people, village)

(If these last two places are different, specify how the plant is obtained from the outside by the people being studied: bought in the market, or from a peddler; harvested at a great distance by members of the community.)

Description
- Tree, bush, grass, vine, crassula (succulents and cactus), epiphyte
- Height: maximum height that the species attains:
- Leaves (color):   flowers (color):
- Fruits (color at maturity, shape when fresh):

Habitat
- Forest: deciduous, evergreen, semi-deciduous (half of the trees are deciduous, gallery forest (alongside rivers in savannah country)
- Bush form: deciduous, evergreen (characteristic of high-altitude tropical vegetation, in particular), xerophytes (with thorns; cactus or crassula plants)
- Grassy vegetation: savannah (tall grasses), savannah with trees, steppe (spread-out grasses), prairie (low grasses forming a continuous cover)

Specify the proportion of annual and perennial plants.
Indicate if trees are scattered among the grasses.

Vegetation With Respect To Water
- Marsh (with trees, bushes, or grasses-fresh water, brackish water-mangrove swamp), peat bog, plant living beside the water. (Indicate if the ground is periodically flooded.)

Collection
- Who harvests the plant? How? When? Is there a harvesting ritual?

Use

Indigenous Taxonomy. For plants considered by the _____ as a variety of this one, see No. _____.

2.2 Domestic Plants

Country: Collector: No.:

Scientific Name*
                            Family: Genus:
                            Species: Variety:

* This part of the questionnaire is designed to be completed by a local botanist, if there is one.

Vernacular Name

Detailed Geographic Location
1. of the place where the collector obtained the plant
2. of the place where it was growing
3. of the place where its role was observed (people, village)

(If these last two places are different, specify how the plant is obtained from the outside by the people being studied: bought in the market, or from a peddler; harvested at a great distance by members of the community.)

Description
- Tree, bush, grass, vine, crassula (succulents and cactus), epiphyte
- Height: maximum height that the species attains:
- Leaves (color): flowers (color):
- Fruits (color at maturity, shape when fresh):

Habitat
- Outside the village: roadside, fallow field, weed in the field, hedge, field borders, around the field houses, near places of worship, watering places, ...
- In the village: street, square, around houses, places of worship, community-type buildings, inside the enclosures of houses, near places of family worship, on walls, etc.
- In the zone surrounding the village
- In the cemetery, etc.

If the people live spread out, pin down the locality of the plant.
Specify if the plant is: not planted, protected, planted (on what occasion? by whom? how long ago?)
Is there a planting ritual? a harvesting ritual?

Use

Indigenous Taxonomy. For plants considered by the _____ as a variety of this one, see No. _____.

2.3 Cultivated Plants (involved in the agricultural cycle)

Country: Collector: No.:

Scientific Name*

                  Family: Genus:
                  Species: Variety:
                       Determinavit:

* This part of the questionnaire is designed to be completed by a local botanist, if there is one.

Vernacular Name

Detailed Geographic Location
1. of the place where the collector obtained the plant
2. of the place where it was growing
3. of the place where its role was observed (people, village)

(If these last two places are different, specify how the plant is obtained from the outside by the people being studied: bought in the market, or from a peddler; harvested at a great distance by members of the community.)

Description:
- Tree, bush, grass, vine, crassula (succulents and cactus), epiphyte
- Height: maximum height that the species attains:

- Leaves (color):   flowers (color):
- Fruits (color at maturity, shape when fresh):

Localization With Respect To Human Settlements
- Concentrated settlements: cultivated far from the village (at what distance?); around the village; within the village proper; within the yard of the house
- Scattered settlements: consider the case where people live spread out

Growing Methods
- Connected area where the same plant is cultivated; approximate number of plants
- Grown dry, irrigated, watered; with burnbeating (How long is the same land used?); permanent field (What is the sequence of crops? Is the field left to lie fallow? How long?)
- How is the ground prepared?
- Methods of manuring
- What is planted? seed (in furrows, by broadcasting, each separately in holes); tubers (in furrows, in separate holes; Do you make mounds?); cuttings (How are they prepared?) Are they bedded out?
- Precautions taken against erosion (controlling the direction of the furrows, presence of low walls, terraces)

Planting And Harvesting
- Who does these jobs? Does a ritual accompany them?

Use

Indigenous Taxonomy. For plants considered by the _____ as a variety of this one, see No. _____.

Questionnaire 12
Ethnozoology

by Jacqueline M. C. Thomas

1 Animal Names

This questionnaire is based in part on the series of ethnozoological questionnaires that Jacqueline M. C. Thomas devised for the Société d'Ethnozoologie et d'Ethnobotanique. Those questionnaires, however, were concerned only with African artiodactyls, and thus contained a detailed description of the animal, which does not appear here. Here we are seeking to emphasize the ethnolinguistic aspect of the investigation.

No.: Ethnic group: Language:
Collector: Informant:

1 Name of the animal

vernacular name synonyms
meaning
why does it have this name?
name in English, French, and/or other trade language or widespread local language

2 Geographic location

place where it was living
place where it is used
how did it get there? (from market, far-off expedition, etc.)

3 Description

+ *Category*
mammal / bird / turtle / crocodile / lizard / snake / amphibian / fish / mollusk / spider / insect / myriapod / crustacean / segmented worms (earthworm / leech) / nematodes (filaria / threadworm / roundworm, etc.) / flatworms (tapeworm / fluke, etc.) / echinoderm (sea urchin, starfish, etc.) / coelenterate (hydra, sea anemone, coral, etc.) / sponge

+ *Morphology*
- size
- colors (quality and distribution: spots, stripes, etc.)
- sex-determined features (horns, mane, tuft, crest, etc.) Give their vernacular names.
- outstanding characteristics (other than sexual): tusks, outgrowths of flesh, shape of the paws, areas of bare (and colored) skin, etc. Give their vernacular names.

+ *Habits (noted by the collector)*
- activity (diurnal, nocturnal, sedentary, etc.)
- habitat (burrow: built by itself / usurped // shelter: thickets / grasses / reeds / etc.)
- food (grass, seeds, fruits ...) meat, carrion, etc.)
- cry (onomatopoeic), excrements, etc.

+ *Social characteristics*
- solitary / pairs / herd / etc.
- timid / friendly
- rare / somewhat common / common / etc.

+ *Distribution*
- plains / mountains
- desert / sahel / steppe / grassy savannah / wooded savannah / fringing forest / forest border / sparse forest / dense forest / stand forest of tall trees / copse / etc.
- barren ground / dry / irrigated / marshy / stream or river bank / stagnant water / running water / shallow water / deep water / etc.

4 Relations With Man

Is the animal: wild / domestic / friendly?

5 How Exploited

Is the animal: ignored? / systematically exterminated? / hunted ~ fished ~ gathered? / exploited? regularly ~ periodically ~ occasionally / tamed? usually ~ occasionally / domesticated? with ~ without being cared for / raised?

6 Domestic Animals

For a domestic animal, specify the vernacular names for:
- male / female / baby / castrate / breeders (male / female) / the young (one year old / two years old)
- racing animal / combat animal / portage animal / draft animal / etc.

Ethnozoology

- female which has never borne / pregnant female / female which has young
Is the animal considered to be the representative of a variety, a breed, or a blood-line?
What are criteria for selecting it? (size, color, distinctive physical characteristic, etc.)
Indicate the terms used.

7 Methods of raising them

- far from / near / within human dwellings
- with / without their own dwellings (what are they called?)
- with / without feeding or special care, etc.
- reproduction uncontrolled / controlled (how?)
- Does one ethnic group / social group / individual specialize in the care / guarding of the animals?

8 How Obtained

- Who does the hunting / fishing / gathering / exploiting / supplying / raising? Characteristics and number of participants
- Where? (geographic and social locale)
- When? (time of year, season, etc.)
- How? (method: hunting with fire, net, trap, ... ; fishing by line, ... ; etc. / means: net, spear, canoe, poison, bait, etc.)

Rituals accompanying the various phases
Terms, cries, or exclamations used to call, round up, disperse, lead, etc. the animals / the participants.

9 Uses

- Type of production: hunting ~ fishing ~ gathering / exploiting / raising (for food / for industrial uses)
- Type of exploitation: for subsistence (occasional / seasonal / daily) / for commercial purposes

10 Techniques

+ *General techniques*
- hides and skins (to work)
- fats, oils
- straps, threads, felts
- receptacles, packing materials
- coloring agents
- perfumes
- poisons, narcotics, stimulants
- making of tools, weapons and parts of tools and weapons

+ *Preservation techniques*

+ *Production techniques*
- gathering

- hunting and trapping
- fishing
- clearing and farming, animal husbandry
- artisanal: forging, pottery, basketry

+ *Consumption techniques*
- construction, dwellings, furnishings
- household articles
- clothing, toilet (+ hairstyles, tattooing, adornment)
- art and games

11 Food

+ *Basic foods*
- flesh (meat, fish, etc.)
- fat (butter, fats, etc.)
- milk

+ *Supplemental foods*
- eggs
- by-products (cheeses, etc.)

+ *Foods for time of scarcity*

12 Medicines

13 Magic and rituals

14 Social role

For details on these headings, see the corresponding headings in Questionnaire 11.1, Plant names

15 Beliefs

+ *Distinctive biological characteristics.* (anatomy, physiology, behavior: walk, postures, manner of lying down, digging, flying, etc.); terms that designate them (e.g., trot, gallop, soar, glide, etc.); possibly, terms of technical usage derived from them. (Terms that designate the cry of the animal (e.g., to bleat, bleating / to trumpet, trumpeting / etc.)

+ *Relationship with the environment.* (ground / other animals: kills, is parasitic of, tolerates, attracts, hunts, feeds, lodges such-and-such animal, etc. / plants: eats, is attracted by, avoids, lives in such-and-such plant, etc.)

+ *Taxonomy.* (considered to be in the same category as what other animal(s)): what is the type of similarity for what reasons are they considered related (criteria)?

+ *Taboos or worship.* (is the animal the object of either? of what sort?)

Ethnozoology

16 Literature

Is the animal mentioned (in various connections) in myths, stories, legends, epics, poetry, songs, liturgy, proverbs, riddles, etc.)?

+ *Main character:* hero / principle subject / agent (positive or negative)

+ *Secondary character* (favorable ~ unfavorable): object / patient

+ *Accessories* (positive ~ negative)

In each case, is the animal strictly animal / personified / animal in name only?

17 Proper names

+ Can the name of the animal in itself constitute a proper name?
+ Or does it enter into the composition of proper names?—of persons (patronyms, individual's names, surnames, given names, etc.)—of lineages, clans, etc.—of domestic animals—of villages, localities, etc.

18 Symbolism

+ Does the animal have a symbolic value (sex / life / death / war / feelings / etc.)?
In all cases of the uses mentioned, specify:
- if the whole animal is involved, or only a part (which parts: skin, hair or fur, horn, teeth, venom, etc.)
- how it is used (tanned, dried, boiled, fried, grilled, roasted, (burned to ashes), etc.)
- if it is used alone, or in conjunction with other animals or animal products (which?) and/or plant products (which?) and/or mineral products (which?)
- if it is consumed, or in what particular manner it is used (for §§12, 13, and 14)
- the terms to designate the different stages in its use: the parts, the products, the transformations, and the usages
- the persons entitled to use it, for what purpose(s) and how:
* Who can use / consume this animal or this part of the animal? Where? When? How?
* May the one who catches the animal use it or not? why? If not, what must he do?

1

Field Methods in Ethno-Zoology
with special reference to the New Guinea Highlands

by R. N. H. Bulmer

1 Introduction and acknowledgments

This document is intended primarily for the guidance of ethnographers and lexicographers. Biologists using indigenous field assistants from preliterate societies may also find some sections of it useful. It will be circulated to ethnographers and also to a score or so of biologists who have cordially assisted the author and other ethnographers working in New Guinea. Criticisms and suggestions will be welcomed and will be taken into account in a revised version, if and when one appears to be justified.

The author hopes that readers will not take offense at the didactic quality of these notes. They are very much based on his own experience: he has himself encountered nearly all the difficulties he describes, and has made almost every mistake he warns against. He also hopes that intending fieldworkers will not be discouraged by the length and complexity of the instructions. Some sections may be relevant even to the anthropologist who has no intention of collecting a single zoological specimen, if only to help him understand the status of his own data and of the data of colleagues.

For help in the drafting of this paper the author is greatly indebted to J. I. Menzies, Senior Lecturer in Biology at the University of Papua and New Guinea.

Throughout his field-work in the New Guinea Highlands (totalling approximately three years between December 1954 and the present date 1976)) the author has been engaged at least in part in ethno-biological enquiries. For periods since 1963, in which he has specifically concentrated on this field, he gratefully acknowledges support from the U. S. National Institutes of Health (N. H. 07957–01), the New Zealand University Research Grants Committee, the Golden Kiwi Lotteries Fund Scientific Research Grants Committee of New Zealand, the University of Papua and New Guinea, and the Wenner-Gren Foundation for Anthropological Research.

2 Identifying animals:
preliminary considerations and elementary pitfalls

Ethnographers and linguists need to identify animals, so that they can report accurately which species are ecologically, economically or technologically significant to the peoples among whom they work, or so that they can adequately gloss folk taxonomies which may be relevant in lexical studies and also in studies of ritual, art, folklore and cosmology. A few, like the present author, may be concerned to make detailed studies in ethno-zoology a main theme of their field enquiries.

The task of identification has two aspects. One is to ascertain how folk taxonomies relate to certain material phenomena–individual birds, mammals, reptiles, insects, etc. The other is to ascertain how species and other categories of the zoological taxonomist apply to the same phenomena. In part the task thus consists of eliciting, comparing and cross-relating two lists of names for one set of phenomena. However it is hardly ever as simple as that. The eliciting of names should always be ancillary to or supplemented by observation in natural contexts of the use of these, and of the use of, or behavior towards, the phenomena to which they refer; and should also be supplemented by questioning. Even if names are recorded accurately, in large numbers, and with due consciousness of the contexts in which they are being applied, the ethnographer cannot know, from these records alone, to what other objects or in what other contexts the same names might also be applied; nor can he know what other names might also be applied to the objects under examination in different contexts. Nor can he necessarily ascertain the criteria by which a particular name is being applied rather than any other, without asking questions.

No enquiry can be completely exhaustive. There is bound to be some degree of ambiguity or indeterminacy in the glosses applied to any vocabulary list, however much care has been taken in its compilation. Nevertheless, regardless of the scope of an enquiry, even if for example the investigator requires only a rather small number of folk taxonomies glossed and kinds of animals scientifically identified, he needs to guard against the five following elementary pitfalls.

(1) Premature assumption of equivalence between folk-taxonomies and scientific taxa, and particularly of equivalence between lower-order folk taxonomies and biological species. This error, which characterizes the work of traditional lexicographers, all too many ethnographers and even many biological fieldworkers, is discussed in §3.

(2) Failure to appreciate the elasticity of a natural language that words, including those applied to animals, can mean different things in different contexts (see §3).

(3) Misinterpretation of atypical or inaccurate information from speakers (inaccurate, that is, according to the canons of the culture concerned) or responses by speakers to specimens, pictures, or inadequately observed living animals. Creatures removed from their natural context frequently elicit atypical responses from speakers, and this hazard is increased if they are dead and if the form of their preservation changes their natural shape or color (see §6.4). Preliterate naturalists are also, in the author's experience, just as prone as their Western equivalents to make family identifications or hazard insupportable guesses as to the identity of inadequately observed living creatures. Cultural variables are also involved here. In the two New Guinea Highlands societies best known to the author, members of one took pride in providing some kind of answer to any question, and providing some kind of name for any creature or object presented to them, and showed little or no embarrassment if their information was subsequently contradicted. In contrast, members of the other society were almost pedantic in their concern with accuracy, were quite prepared to admit when they did not know what some creature was, and if contradicted on some identification would debate the matter seriously.

(4) Inadequate note-taking and labelling of specimens. Inconsistencies in orthography in fieldnotes and on labels, inaccurate transcriptions of speakers' statements and inadequate notes on the context of an observation

or a speaker's statement, can easily lead to inaccurate and anomalous results.

(5) Inaccurate or inadequate scientific identifications of phenomena observed or collected. Either the fieldworker himself may arrive at incorrect identifications of material he observes or handles; or supposed better-informed European sources may mislead him; or zoological taxonomists to whom he refers specimens may incorrectly identify these, providing only incomplete identifications, or provide no identification at all. Where the zoologist appears to have let the fieldworker down, this may be because the fieldworker has not himself taken the trouble to preserve or label specimens adequately or it may mean that the fieldworker is making demands which are for other reasons impossible to fulfill.

It is difficult, if not impossible, to eliminate these hazards entirely. Pitfalls (1), (2), and (3) can be avoided to the extent that the fieldworker has the time, skill and language-control to question speakers adequately, opportunity to observe creatures in natural contexts on multiple occasions, opportunity and preparedness to make extensive collections when they are necessary, and knowledge of the total potential faunal list for the area, so that he can gauge the possibility that species he has not observed or collected may be subsumed in folk-taxa also applied to creatures which he has observed. Nevertheless in any study, however painstaking, there is bound to be a residue of folk-taxa for creatures which the investigator has never seen and cannot identify with certainty from circumstantial evidence, and a further number of taxa for which field identifications and specimens are too few and verbal information too limited for more than provisional identifications to be provided. In these cases it is important that the investigator should not delude himself or mislead others as to the status of his data, and should indicate the provisional nature of his glosses.

Little need be said about pitfall (4) except that the occasional lapse in orthography or reporting may be difficult to detect in a small body of data, but will often stick out like a sore thumb in a long enough series of identifications or notes, and therefore stand a much better chance of being rechecked or relegated to the doubtful class. Pitfall (5) will be discussed further in §§7 and 8.

3 Folk taxonomies and scientific taxonomies

This is not the place for a general treatise on semantics and primitive or prescientific modes of thought. Nevertheless it is necessary to consider certain basic similarities and differences between scientific taxonomy and nomenclature on the one hand and folk taxonomies and nomenclature on the other, in order both to justify the use of the categories of scientific biology in glossing folk-taxa and to indicate the limits of such use.

Folk-taxonomies applied to animals are like modern scientific zoological taxonomy to the extent that many of the taxa in the former and all in the latter case are natural units in the logical sense, that is units discriminated from others of like order by multiple criteria of morphology and behavior. The units of scientific zoological taxonomy are also natural units in the genetic or phylogenetic sense, actually or putatively sharing a common ancestry which is different from that of other units of like order. This is necessarily the case in terms of the theory of evolution which provides the rationale for modern biological taxonomy. The units, and especially lower-order units, of a folk-taxonomy may also correspond to natural units in a genetic or phylogenetic sense, but if they do this is only because creatures which share many attributes are likely to share some measure of common ancestry not because common ancestry in itself is likely to be a taxonomically significant principle.

The approximation of many lower-order units in folk-taxonomies to the species and genera of scientific zoology both justify the use of technical zoological terms in glossing terms for folk-taxa and create the hazard of premature assumption of equivalence between the two which was mentioned above. If folk-taxonomy bore no relation to scientific taxonomy, but was entirely based on biologically arbitrary but culturally relevant discriminations, there would be no point in obtaining zoological identifications for the creatures concerned, no way of relating biological information about them to ethnographical information about the uses to which they were put or the manner in which men conceptualized them.

Further, it is because folk-taxa applied to animals are in so many cases natural units, defined by multiple and in some cases infinitely extendable series of criteria, that there is no economical way of glossing these except by the use of scientific zoological identifications. If folk-taxonomies could be satisfactorily analyzed in terms of a straight-forward series of binary oppositions applied to single characters, the most economical way of glossing terms applied to these would simply be to codify these binary oppositions, and to that extent zoological identifications of the creatures classified would be redundant.

At the same time, the fact that, at least in the author's experience (see Bulmer n.d. (1); but for a contrasting view of the nature of folk-taxonomies see Berlin, Breedlove and Rave 1966), a large proportion of lower-order taxa in a zoological folk-taxonomy are natural units in a logical sense, and a fair proportion coincidentally correspond to species, does not mean that in any individual case a correspondence can be assumed.

Thus in the case of the Karam of the New Guinea Highlands roughly sixty percent of minimal taxa applied to vertebrate animals appear to correspond to species: the proportion is probably considerably lower for invertebrates. The following deviations were recorded:

(1) Two or more zoological species lumped in the same minimal folk-taxon, in some cases closely related species within the same genus or family (e.g., cuckoos of genus *Cacomantis*; kingfishers, all of certain genera of family Alcedinidae), in other cases very distantly related (e.g., the oriole, *Oriolus szlayi*, grouped with the friar-bird, *Philemon novaeguineae*).

(2) A single zoological species represented by two or more folk taxa, dimorphic sexes and/or morphologically contrasting immature and mature individuals being discriminated (e.g., certain birds of paradise, parrots, small honey-eaters, frogs, small lizards); or contrasting forms of highly variable or polymorphic species being placed in separate taxa (e.g., certain lorikeets, frogs).

(3) Combinations of (1) and (2), morphologically similar sexes or life-stages of different species being placed in the same folk-taxon, while contrasting sexes or life stages are placed in different taxa (e.g., certain birds of paradise, flower-peckers, frogs); or the immature examples of one species being lumped with members, both mature and immature, of another species, while mature examples of the first species are placed in a separate taxon (e.g., certain rodents, marsupials, frogs).

It should be noted that the fact that folk-taxa do not correspond to zoological species does not necessarily mean that speakers are unaware of biological realities. For example, in respect of some of the taxa they apply to birds of paradise, Karam knew perfectly well that certain taxa apply to mature male birds only, while others include both mature females and immature birds of both sexes. Many speakers were also aware that minimal taxa applied to certain birds included two or more forms contrasting both in their morphology and in aspects of their behavior, even though they had no standardized names for these. In other cases, however, biologically inadequate taxonomy was linked to a failure to observe or interpret biological relationships correctly, as when speakers did not appreciate the existence of consistently linked morphological and behavioral differences between different species of birds (e.g., swiftlets, *Collocalia* spp.) or invertebrates; or asserted, incorrectly, that certain of their taxa applied to rodents and small marsupials included individuals who would in time grow and change into members of other taxa which they applied to different, larger marsupial species (cf. Bulmer n.d. (2)).

Higher order folk-taxa, at least in the New Guinea Highlands, rather seldom correspond to zoologically valid taxa such as bird, marsupial, rodent, reptile, insect, etc. For examples see Glick 1964, Diamond 1966, Bulmer 1967.

Scientific zoological taxonomy not only contrasts with folk-taxonomies in that it is based on the theory of evolution, and that its units are at least putatively genetic or phylogenetic groupings, but in the rigor of the prescriptive codification which determines nomenclatural usage. In this respect it is unlike all folk-taxonomies, including contemporary Western European ones which in many respects have been influenced by the development of biological science and scientific taxonomies.

It is not only that the units of a folk-taxonomy which receive standardized names are those which it may be important to label for a range of quite miscellaneous reasons, whereas the units of a scientific taxonomy are, at least in theory, labelled in accordance with an ordered set of rules derived from a single guiding principle. The terms used to denote the units of a folk-taxonomy are part of natural language, and as such can be used intuitively and imaginatively, with different referents in different contexts and with new referents in new contexts; in contrast to terms used in biological taxonomy, usage of which is explicitly restricted with the object of minimizing ambiguity.

Thus in folk-taxonomies it is quite in order that the same term should be applied to two or more related taxa of different order (as e.g., in U. K. English 'thrush' = 'song-thrush' *(Turdus philomelos)* in contrast to 'blackbird' *(Turdus merula)* or = 'song-thrush' plus 'mistle-thrush' *(Turdus viscivorus* in contrast to 'blackbird,' 'fieldfare' *(T. pilaris)* and 'redwing' *(T. musicus),* depending on immediate contexts; or may be used as a generic category which includes all these species. Many exactly parallel cases can be found in New Guinea Highlands folk-taxonomies.

In some instances the investigator may have good general grounds for assuming or suspecting the existence of a folk-taxon and yet find that there is no single exclusive standard term for this. An example is provided by the intermediate taxa within the Karam primary taxon *as* which includes all frogs and certain small marsupials and rodents. The investigator failed for many months to elicit any standard terms for distinguishing frogs collectively from small marsupials and rodents collectively. Either or both could in certain contexts be referred to as *as yb* ('real' *as*). Eventually the information was volunteered to him that if necessary frogs could be referred to as *as ng-ket* ('water-haunting' *as*), the small mammals as *as lwm-ket* ('ground-haunting' *as*), though he has still never heard this discrimination used in a natural context. However he was eventually able to strike a spontaneous situation where it was necessary for people to make the distinction in his hearing. A group of girls had captured a number of both frogs and rats, and were discussing with each other which of them to sell to the ethnographer. They referred to the rats as *kmn,* the term properly, so all speakers both previously and subsequently insisted, applied only to game mammals (larger furred mammals hunted by males), a taxon contrasting with *as.* The use of a familiar term in unusual or novel contexts creates difficulties for the investigator. Take the case where taxon x is normally applied exclusively to zoological species y, which is locally common and familiar. Eventually an individual example of a different but somewhat similar and very much rarer species, z, is observed or collected, and speakers also place this in folk-taxon x. Does this indicate that they do not perceive any significant differences between this individual and individuals of species y? Or does it indicate that they do indeed note differences, but are consciously and legitimately extending the referents of the term they use for x and in so doing are creating a new, more inclusive taxon with the same name? This process is inevitable if speakers are removed from familiar territory and asked to identify species new to them in a new environment. An example from English may illustrate this point. To the English bird-watcher on his home territory 'blackbird' can only mean *Turdus merula* and 'robin' can only mean *Erithacus rubecula.* However on being first confronted with an American robin *(Turdus migratorius)* the Englishman is more than likely to react, 'That's not a robin, it's a blackbird,' an entirely legitimate response, since the American robin is indeed closely related to the English Blackbird, and the two species are equally distantly related to the English Robin. The criteria speakers use in extending their categories under novel circumstances themselves merit attention. Karam speakers brought to New Zealand applied the taxon *koqds,* applied at home as a generic category to certain species of Whistler *(Pachycephala* spp.), to birds as diverse as Mynas *(Acridotheres tristis)* and House Sparrows *(Passer domesticus),* in the first case on account of voice and context of observation in trees, in the second case on account of size and plumage.

Finally, as Conklin (1962:121) and other authors have pointed out, although there is likely to be some general consistency between naming practices and taxonomic discriminations, nomenclature and taxonomy must each be examined in its own right, and names considered in isolation can be wholly or partially misleading. Thus not all blackbirds are black, not all house-sparrows live around houses, and silverfish are not fish at all, though goldfish are. Parallel cases must be expected in any language.

4 Levels of scientific identification required

If the arguments in §§2 and 3 are accepted, it will be seen that the ethnographer has no option but to get zoologically adequate identifications of fauna. Section 5 discusses problems involved in identifying different groups of animals, before advice on particular techniques of obtaining information from speakers is offered in §6. However it is worth first making the general point that the level of scientific identification and detail of supporting information required is not the same for all groups of animals in any one folk-taxonomy, nor even, necessarily, for all genera or species within a single wider group.

In most cases the ethnographer or linguist will need identifications at the species level. But in some cases, where folk-taxa are splitting or cross-cutting species, he will need to know whether sexual dimorphism, life-stages, polymorphism or other forms of biological variation underlie these discriminations, and the identifications of individual specimens will need to include diagnoses of sex, maturity, polymorphism, etc.

In other instances, scientific identifications need not be taken as far as the species or even the generic level. Some years ago the author proudly presented a small freshwater crab to an elderly museum taxonomist for identification, and was somewhat taken aback by the response, 'It's a yabbie (Australian folk-taxon applied to fresh-water crabs and/or fresh-water crayfish). Surely you can see that for yourself. What more do you need to know?' The point was well taken. The New Guinea Highlanders from whom the author had collected the specimen had only one taxon applied to crabs, and applied this to no other kind of creature, and indeed there was apparently no other creature locally present which either the ethnographer or the Highlanders could possibly confuse with a crab. Why should the Museum man have been put to the trouble of giving it a species identification which would probably have been highly tentative in any case? It would have been a different matter if the Highland community had distinguished *two* kinds of crabs; or if the author had collected crabs in the territories of two different communities one of which ate them while the other didn't. Though even in this case identifications at the generic or even family level might have been quite adequate for the ethnographer's purpose, provided that they distinguished the same groups that the folk-taxa did, and that the zoological could give him some estimate of the probability that all specimens ascribed to a particular folk-taxon, or obtained from a particular area, belonged to the same species, even if he did not have the reference material to name this.

5 Problems in obtaining identifications of particular groups of animals

Problems of identification are of different magnitude in different geographical regions and with different groups of animals. In parts of the world where most groups of animals of ethno-biological significance are well-known to zoologists and where local faunal lists, good modern handbooks and identification keys are available, the ethnographer's task is very much easier than in regions like New Guinea where general faunal lists are still far from complete, local faunal lists virtually nonexistent, the zoological taxonomy of many groups is under or awaiting revision, and handbooks and keys, accessible and intelligible to the amateur naturalist, are lacking for nearly all groups. Nevertheless, although the following notes apply particularly to New Guinea conditions, some parts may have wider applicability.

5.1 Mammals

Folk-taxa applied to New Guinea mammals are in many cases extraordinarily difficult for the ethnographer to investigate adequately, both because the creatures themselves are difficult to observe and relatively difficult to collect, and because the zoological literature is so incomplete, particularly on details of ecology and behavior which are often of considerable importance to folk-classifications. Although it is unlikely that there are many mammal species in New Guinea as yet scientifically undescribed, there is no handbook or field-guide to New Guinea mammals, there are no adequate local faunal lists, and the best identification key (Ziegler and Lidicker 1968) does not go beyond the generic level. An older key with some useful illustrations which does take marsupials to the species level, is Husson (1955), but this is not in

Ethnozoology

English and is in any case difficult to use in the field. Laurie and Hill (1954) provide a general list of mammals of New Guinea and the Celebes: to the extent that New Guinea shares certain species with Australia, these can be looked up in Marlow (1962), Troughton (1966) and other Australian publications while a few endemic New Guinea species are illustrated and described in Walker (1964).

New Guinea mammals are mainly nocturnal, and for this reason are difficult to observe. Many New Guinea species of marsupials, rodents and bats are superficially very similar to their congeners, and even, in some cases, to members of related genera. Zoological taxonomists rely to a great extent on examination of dentition to determine species identifications. Apart from a few very striking and distinctive creatures, there is at present no satisfactory means for identifying most New Guinea mammals except by collecting them. Collecting and preserving larger mammals is a costly and time-consuming business. Photographs, measurements (as prescribed in Marlow 1962:6) and, especially, preservation of crania and mandibles, is a fairly adequate substitute for preserving an entire large marsupial or rodent, but Museum taxonomists to whom such remnants are referred may understandably express irritation at not receiving the whole specimen if it is in any way unusual. If the investigator lacks taxidermic expertise, small mammals can be preserved in seventy percent alcohol (see also §7.3).

Problems involved in the use of skeletal material and pelts obtained from native hunters, for eliciting folk-taxa, are discussed in §6.4.4. Legal restrictions on collecting and exporting mammals and other fauna are discussed in §7.0.

5.2 Birds

Compared with mammals, many kinds of birds are relatively easy to observe and identify. In general New Guinea Highlanders are interested in them and knowledgeable about them. The main problem the investigator faces in most parts of New Guinea is that there is such a very rich local bird fauna. It is not at all unusual for upwards of 150 species to be present in the area with which members of one particular local community are familiar. Some of these will be uncommon, others shy and difficult to observe, and many may be quite difficult to distinguish from their congeners in natural contexts and possibly even in the hand. Fortunately New Guinea's birds are better known to science than any other group of her fauna (it is unlikely that there are more than a handful of species yet to be described), and there is a good modern handbook (Rand and Gilliard 1967) which is indispensable to the fieldworker. The colored illustrations in Iredale 1950 and 1956 are also helpful, though these works should be treated as supplementary to Rand and Gilliard and not as substitutes for it. Collectors' reports providing regional bird lists of varying degrees of completeness are listed in Rand and Gilliard (pp. 608–609); see also Schoddo and Hitchcock 1968, Gilliard and Leeroy 1968).

5.3 Reptiles

There are no good handbooks or good local faunal lists of New Guinea reptiles, and the taxonomy of most groups is awaiting or currently under revision. A few of the more conspicuous snake species, which are common to Australia and New Guinea, are described in such Australian guides as Worrell 1963a or McPhee 1959, which are also helpful in suggesting to the fieldworker which family or genus a particular species may belong to. Loveridge 1946 is also useful. Slater's (1956) booklet listing venomous snakes is useful: Worrell's (1963b) book on the same subject is incomplete for New

Guinea species. In the Highlands above 5,000 ft. there are few reptiles other than small skinks but at lower altitudes New Guinea is rich in both snakes and lizards, certain of which tend to have considerable economic or ritual importance.

5.4 Frogs

The only amphibia known in the Melanesian region are frogs. These are very numerous in some parts of New Guinea and are of importance as a subsidiary food resource in some areas. The three main groups present are the Hylidae ('tree-frogs'), Ranidae (to the North-West European, 'typical' frogs) and Microphylidae (a group embracing an astonishing range of mainly rather small frogs, some of very curious appearance). Although there is a useful modern taxonomic review, with identification keys, of the genus *Hyla* (Tyler 1968), one of the two genera of the Hylidae present in New Guinea, it is likely that even in this genus there are species yet to be discovered described. It is thus quite necessary for the ethnographer requiring identifications to make collections.

A study of the classification of frogs by the Karam of the New Guinea Highlands (Bulmer and Tyler n.d.) notes that ecological information, call-notes, smell and sliminess, as well as morphological criteria, are relevant in folk-classification and identification.

In some areas tadpoles are also a food resource. It is worth collecting these, even though at the present stage the authorities can only relate these to particularly species in a few cases.

5.5 Fish

The author has no experience of the study of the folk-classifications of sea fish and other marine fauna, or of fish in lowland rivers where these are common. In many Highland rivers eels (*Anguila* sp. or spp.) appear to be the only fish present, though generally below 4,500 ft., and in some places at higher altitudes, other species occur. A well-illustrated modern handbook of New Guinea fish (Munro 1967) is available, but it is unlikely that this is in any sense complete as regards smaller freshwater fishes. Cochrane (1968) is a useful booklet for any ethnographer in a coastal community.

5.6 Invertebrates

Comprehensive study of folk-classifications of invertebrate animals presents the most appalling difficulties of all. In contrast to the situation with vertebrate animals, where, at least in the New Guinea Highlands there appears to be generally a rough equivalence in numbers of folk-taxa and numbers of species present, numbers of invertebrate species run into thousands while folk-taxa are likely to number one or two hundred at the most. With some groups of local economic importance (e.g., grasshoppers and other Orthoptera) folk-classification may approach the complexity of scientific taxonomy. In other cases minimal folk-taxa may lump any number of species and span not only genera and families but even orders and classes. Further useful handbooks and keys are not available for any of the invertebrate groups. Novices in entomology, and particularly those lacking even lay familiarity with Australasian insects, will find a popular illustrated introduction to Australian insects, such as Child (1960), a most useful field aid. Curran's (1946) guide to insects of the Pacific basin is equally helpful. Invertebrate animals, such as Buchsbaum (1966), can be helpful, suggesting more obvious possibilities for, e.g., the identity of worm or worm-like creatures, and of various kinds of internal parasites of which the people make take note.

A special problem with insects, though it can occur to some extent with vertebrate groups, is that different life-stages of the same creature may look entirely different and be placed in different folk-taxa, and the people may or may not correctly relate these. Where the immature form is of much greater interest to the people than the adult (as is the case with many kinds of caterpillars versus adult butterflies and moths, and wood-boring beetle larvae versus adult beetles) it may be particularly hard to get precise identifications, for even where the mature insect may be well known to science, its larval form may not have been described, or, if it has, be very difficult to distinguish from those of related species.

Fortunately anthropologists and linguists do not often need many invertebrate identifications at the species level, identification at the generic or even family level being quite adequate for their purposes. Use of elementary guide books of the kind specified above, and a little help from a biologist with some general interest in invertebrates, can achieve this. But even for these purposes a fair amount of collecting may be necessary. To get collections adequately identified to species, or even, in some cases, generic level, will require patient assistance from a host of specialists. Some impression of the logistics of such an enquiry may be gained from Wyman and Bailey's (1964) painstaking study of Navaho Indian ethno-entomology; for a critique of method employed in this see Bulmer 1965.

Molluscs require special mention. In the interior of New Guinea the imported marine shells which are important in personal adornment and in exchange are fortunately nearly all of a rather small number of well-known species. Any Museum conchologist in the Pacific region can identify most of these in a moment, but unfortunately there is no convenient handbook which will enable the ethnographer to do this for himself. Cernohorsky (1967) is misleadingly titled and only covers certain groups. What is important for the ethnographer to enquire into is which of these species were well-known before direct and indirect European contact influenced trade patterns, the directions from which they were obtained, and so forth. Land-snails and fresh water mollusks generally raise the same problems of zoological identification that do most other invertebrate groups.

6 Obtaining identifications and information

As in so many other fields of ethnography, an appreciation of the context in which information is obtained, and to which it relates, is crucial in ethno-biology. When eliciting names for animals one must consider first how the interview or test situation relates to normal, natural contexts; and second, even in quite spontaneous natural contexts of recording identifications one must consider what range of information the identifier is permitted to use or is restricted from using, e.g., by locality, conditions of visibility, audibility, etc. There is of course nothing wrong with the investigator creating artificial test situations for experimental purposes, provided that he does this consciously and makes clear in his reports the status of data so obtained.

6.1 Obtaining lists of names

The two most obvious methods of starting to elicit information are to ask the names of creatures observed, and, once terms for generic taxa have been obtained, asking for lists of subsidiary taxa. Three cautions are necessary here. First, when one initially obtains a name for some particular individual creature, one has no way of knowing, without further inquiry, if this applies to a generic, intermediate or minimal taxon. Thus, in English a particular creature may equally accurately be described as a bird, a duck or a teal. Without asking whether or not there are other kinds of birds/ducks/teals or without taking detailed notes on the use of their taxa in other contexts, one can have no idea of the status of the taxa to which they apply. Second, speakers, even if not being deliberately unhelpful or overhelpful (consciously trying to provide the investigator with the answers they think he seeks), tend initially to gear their responses to what they estimate to be the level of the fieldworker's sophistication in the subject matter under discussion. If, for example, they realize that the fieldworker is knowledgeable about birds they are unlikely to deliberately hold back information about finer points of ornithological classification. But if they realise that he is an ignoramus they can hardly be expected to volunteer information that in their view he would not understand or appreciate. Thus the author has been assured by more than one fieldworker that Highlanders among whom they have worked lump certain bird species in a single taxon (e.g., the two common local species of cuckoo-doves, *Macropygia*), and do not have minimal taxa applied to these separately. In every case he has inquired into personally, the two cuckoo-doves are in fact terminologically distinguished. In contrast the author knows nothing about geology or rocks. The Karam evidently appreciated this fact and never provided him with more than the most simple-minded information on rock sources and stone technology. When, however, he was visited in the field by a petrologist, they very quickly grasped that the newcomer was expert in this field, and enthusiastically regaled him with technical information. Thirdly, when speakers provide lists of taxa in the abstract, these are, with the best... will in the world, hardly ever anywhere near exhaustive. After twelve months of fieldwork among the Karam, spread over nine years, the author still learns of additional bird taxa on each successive trip.

6.2 Obtaining descriptions of taxa

Abstract descriptions of taxa, both as provided spontaneously by speakers and in response to questions as to how these contrast with other taxa of like order, are very valuable and indeed essential data to the student of folk-taxonomies. At the same time they are seldom an adequate basis for establishing the scientific identity of the creatures referred to. The method is only reliable to the extent that the fieldworker is himself familiar with the wider group of fauna concerned, so that he is satisfied that he can match up unambiguously discriminatory features mentioned by speakers with characters which he knows objectively to be restricted to a particular species, group of species, etc. This can be surprisingly difficult.

6.3 Use of bilingual speakers

In some cases a fieldworker has a vocabulary list in another language with which his speakers have at least partial familiarity, so that he can ask what the term for creature x (in the original study) is in the language he is studying, or what the equivalent in the

Ethnozoology

other language is for taxon *y* in his own study-language. Even assuming that the glosses in the original study are adequate (see appendix B) this is a method which must be employed with great caution. Any two New Guinea linguistic groups even close to each other are likely to be living in territories of somewhat different ecology, and certain creatures familiar to one group are likely to be less familiar to the other. Further, there is no reason to assume that in detail their taxonomies will correspond precisely, even though there is a tendency on the part of bilinguals to insist that, in most instances, they do. The same difficulties apply when a field worker has adequately explored the categories of one language and attempts to elicit equivalent terms in a neighboring language.

Some special hazards are involved in using trade languages as a medium for investigation. Some widely used trade language terms for animals have no precise equivalents in most vernacular languages. Examples are *mumut* (= bandicoot) and *trelanggau* (= hawk); Highlands languages with which the author is familiar have terms for different kinds of bandicoot and for different kinds of hawk, but no generic terms for these groups. In contrast, but even more confusingly, other vernacular terms such as *kapul* or *sinek* are generally used by native speakers of Highland languages to equate primarily with terms in their own language, but the taxa to which these refer differ from language to language and seldom if ever correspond precisely to what Europeans assume the terms to mean (i.e., 'marsupial' and 'snake' or 'reptile' respectively).

6.4 Identification of specimens, pictures, tape recordings

6.4.1. The animal in its natural state. The ideal identification-datum is provided when the investigator and his speakers together observe a living creature in its natural state and discuss its identity and the criteria by which it is identified, then capture it and examine it in the hand, giving the speaker the opportunity to change his mind if need be, and justify any such change: and finally the creature is either conclusively identified zoologically by the use of reference works or the investigator's personal knowledge before being released, eaten or otherwise disposed of; or it is preserved for later identification by a professional zoologist. This situation gives both the speaker and the investigator opportunity to take the maximum number of possibly relevant variables into account–location, call-note, posture and movement, feeding, display, nesting or other behaviors, size color, shape and other morphological characters, odor, tactile qualities, etc. Comparison of the consistency of identifications obtained under these ideal circumstances with those offered by speakers when circumstances restrict the range of information available to them can offer valuable information on the ranking of criteria they may in fact apply, for comparison with their verbal rationalizations about processes of identification.

Field observation of creatures which are not subsequently captured and examined in the hand, will, in any extended study, provide a very large part of the total data reported. Reliance that can be placed on such observations depends essentially on the investigator's skill as a field naturalist and on his skill in estimating the probability that either he or his speakers may be wrong in any particular instance.

6.4.2. The animal out of context. Identifications of animals, either alive or newly dead, examined out of context are, at least in some groups, less consistent than identifications where contextual information is available. For Karam women, who specialize in collecting small rodents, certain taxa are morphologically indistinguishable, but may be separated out by the shape and location of the burrows in which they are found and the size of the colony inhabiting these. Call notes are likely to be significant in identification of birds, frogs and certain insects. Odor can be a key character in identifying frogs and earthworms, but it is apparently only on initial capture that some species emit a scent which is distinct, and different species of frogs jumbled together in the same bundle of leaves or plastic bag may, even if still alive, all smell much the same a few hours later.

6.4.3. Use of preserved specimens. Because dead creatures cannot move or assume their characteristic postures they are less satisfactory objects for identification than living ones. Preserved creatures, e.g., stuffed birds or pickled frogs, more than likely have lost their characteristic shape, while fleshy parts, and in the case of pickled specimens, the whole animal, may have lost their characteristic color. These difficulties are not significant in the case of birds or mammals with really striking and distinctive plumage or furs, but in the case of birds with more nondescript markings, identifications from dried pelts / skins may be very unsure. Insofar as color drawings are useful in identifying frogs and many invertebrates, pigmentation changes in preservative make use of pickled specimens an almost complete waste of time, particularly if the shape of the creatures has also changed.

6.4.4. Use of animal parts. Native peoples may have in their possession collections of plumes and fur made for ornamental purposes, skeletal material kept as hunters' trophies or for ritual or technological reasons, and occasionally reptile skins and other animal parts. Some of this material can be used to advantage in obtaining identifications.

Plumes. On the whole people who use plumes regularly in trade and display are very consistent in their identifications. But three cautions are necessary here. One is that plumes and skins may be traded for considerable distances–even, from remote parts of New Guinea. Thus people may be in the possession of feathers of species with which they are totally unfamiliar in life. In some cases they may be lumping these, quite consistently, with species with which they are familiar. In others they may be guessing. A second consideration is that many of the birds whose plumes are used in ornaments are sexually dimorphic, and also show marked contrast between the adult and immature plumage. Because mature male plumes used in decoration are consistently identified by a certain term does not mean that this term is equivalent to a zoological species designation: it is not at all unlikely that female and immature male birds will be placed in different taxa. A third problem is that the fieldworker himself may find it difficult to identify small quantities of feathers or parts of dismembered skins, even with the aid of a Handbook. While it is not necessarily desirable or even legal for anthropologists to collect whole skins, unless they are doing this with official sanction and for the benefit of a scientific institution, it may prove necessary for them to make small collections of certain native prepared plumes of species which they only see in dismembered forms.

Mammal fur. Use of ornamental pieces of mammal fur present the same problems as use of native prepared plume ornaments, except that here problems of zoological identification are likely to be more difficult, both because of the absence of accessible literature and because a piece of fur may, by itself, be difficult even for the museum worker with a good reference collection to assign to a particular species.

Skeletal material. The people may keep skeletal material of larger mammals, and to a lesser extent of birds, reptiles and fish, as trophies, for technological or ornamental purposes, and for magical or other ritual reasons. This material is often inexpensive and easy to acquire. Mammal crania and mandibles can in almost all cases be confidently identified to the species level by a professional mammologist. Unfortunately this material is not, as useful for eliciting folk-taxa as one might expect. Some peoples are astonishingly inconsistent in the naming of mammal crania and mandibles, in spite of the fact that until recently the incisors and mandibles of certain species were of some technological importance to them as graving tools. Without further checking however, one must accept with confidence native identifications of skeletal material.

Skeletal material other than crania and mandibles is at present unlikely to offer possibilities of identifications beyond the generic level.

Students wishing to rough-sort crania and mandibles into generic categories for themselves, and thus obtain some check on the reliability of their speakers while they are still in the field, will find Ziegler and Lidicker (1968) useful. For marsupials Brazenor (1950) is also helpful.

6.4.5. Use of pictures. Showing book and magazine illustrations to speakers is a great way of eliciting vocabulary, but can produce some astonishing results. Many speakers find differences in scale difficult to cope with, particularly in composite plates in which a number of different bird or mammal species are figured. Book illustrations done from museum skins, which do not accurately capture the natural shape of a bird, are not as helpful as they might be. Good quality and large scale color photographs, are the most consistently identified. A final warning to the unwary is that some speakers insist on putting a name to any creature whose picture is presented to them. Once one is aware of what they are doing, analysis of the diagnostic features they are using is a revealing though complicated routine. But at all costs such identifications should not be taken at face value and appear in vocabulary lists.

6.4.6. Tape recordings. Many peoples rely on the call notes of birds, frogs, and other creatures extensively, in order to locate and identify and sometimes to hunt them. Recordings both of the natural noises that the creatures make, and of imitations that people provide, can be a very useful check on their skill and consistency of identifications. Tape recordings of calls of birds common over wide areas can be useful in eliciting vocabulary rapidly, but the same list of cautions apply as in the use of pictures, or of names in another language with which bilinguals may be familiar.

7 Collecting

7.0 General

It will be apparent from the above that any field worker is likely to need to do at least some collecting of specimens if he is to obtain adequate identifications of most groups of fauna relevant to his study. Some general principles may be laid down here:

1. The field worker should conform scrupulously to the laws on collecting fauna of the country within which he is working. If the hunting, possession, or export of animals is government-related, it is necessary to obtain the required authorization

before making any collection. Such permits are generally granted only to bona fide collectors for museums or other research institutions.

2   The fieldworker should behave ethically in regard to the customary rights and prohibitions of the indigenous communities among which he works, ensuring that he is neither infringing local hunting rights himself without freely-given consent, nor encouraging his assistants to do so.

3   The fieldworker should behave ethically with regard to the conservation of wildlife. He should not collect or kill creatures unless he has some good reason for doing so, ensuring that the information thus obtained will be of positive scientific value either in his own studies or to professional zoologists or both; nor should he encourage local hunters to kill more than they normally would on his behalf without good reason. This is particularly true regarding rare creatures especially if they have been well described, and if a good handbook is available, the need for collecting is greatly reduced.

4   Before he starts collecting the fieldworker should ensure that some institution or individual research worker will be prepared to receive and examine his collections. He should also make sure what the requirements of the recipients are as to the condition, method of preservation and documentation of specimens.

5   The fieldworker should ensure that the specimens he collects are as well preserved and documented as possible, not only for his own record, but in the interests of the institutions and research workers who will receive these specimens (see §§7.4 and 7.5).

6   The fieldworker should collect intelligently and as economically as possible, in the interests of his own time and budget, using common sense and the advice of his zoological collaborators in deciding when a single specimen of a particular species is an adequate sample, or when long runs of specimens are desirable.

7.1 Obtaining specimens

7.1.1. Gift or purchase. Any ethnographer is likely to obtain most of his specimens from members of the communities among whom he works, and to reward captors or others from whom he receives them. Disadvantages, or features to be taken into account in the use of this method, are:

1   Depending on mode of capture, specimens may not be received in ideal condition for identification or preservation–birds shot with multiple-prong barbed arrows can be very mangled, and a marsupial bludgeoned to death by its captors makes a sorry specimen.

2   Statements by vendors as to the taxa to which a specimen is assigned, and precise location and circumstances in which it was obtained, may require careful checking, particularly when an animal passes through several hands before it reaches the investigator. Also, if people grasp that the investigator is keen to get as comprehensive a range of specimens as possible, there will almost inevitably be some tendency to assert that specimens fall in new, hitherto uncollected taxa, whereas they would admit in other circumstances that they are of the same kind as those previously obtained. To the extent that the investigator becomes personally familiar with the fauna he is collecting this risk is minimized, but it is

necessary to cross-check any doubtful identifications with other speakers who lack pecuniary interest in the specimens concerned.

3 Specimens brought to the investigator for sale will neither constitute a representative sample of the total fauna in the groups concerned, nor necessarily correspond closely in range and proportion to the selection usually obtained by hunters for their own purposes. To take the second point first, hunters may withhold certain species from the investigator for ritual or economical reasons, may collect creatures for him they would not normally bother to obtain, may take special efforts to get rewards by producing a highly diversified bag, or may simply go flat out to get the largest numbers of the commonest taxa they can, even though if they were hunting for themselves they would not give these the highest priority. It is desirable for the fieldworker to check the lists and the numbers of specimens of different taxa offered against lists of creatures obtained by hunters for their own purposes. As regards the representativeness in relation to the total fauna of collections made by hunters, whether for themselves or for the investigator, it will certainly be found that modes of hunting and collecting, as well as differential economic and ritual values attributed to different animals, will affect the sample. For example, in a study of Karam classification of small rodents and marsupials, researchers found that Karam women obtained these creatures mainly by digging up burrows or pulling out nests. Their catch was quite a different range of species from those caught by the investigators themselves who used break-back and box traps, though none of these specimens were entirely unfamiliar to speakers. Interestingly, the investigator found from examination of owl *(Tyto tenebricosa)* pellets that the predatory bird was obtaining a different sample of rodents from either group of human hunters.

Thus there is often a case for the ethnographer to extend his collections by obtaining specimens for himself, or by employing specialist staff.

7.2 Employment of professional hunters

In an intensive ethnozoological study, as in zoological collecting expeditions, there may be a case for employing full-time professional hunters, who have had special briefing and who show particular skill in obtaining material which would not otherwise be discovered. Few anthropologists are likely to find this necessary or desirable. The employment of a professional hunter who is not a local man can cause social problems for the fieldworker.

7.3 Personal collecting by the fieldworker

There are considerable advantages in the fieldworker's collecting at least some specimens of certain groups of animals for himself. Even if he is not obtaining anything different from the species brought in by local people, the contexts in which he himself obtains, for example, particular frogs or insects will give him some check on the accuracy and detail of the local collectors' reports on the circumstances in which they obtain their specimens. Beyond this, his use of techniques not available to local people (fire-arms, metal traps, mist nets, fishing lines) may be expected to obtain specimens of species he would not otherwise be able to examine.

7.3.1. Fire-arms. No one totally inexperienced in the use of fire-arms should be advised to take up shooting as a hobby in the field. The returns are likely to be meager and the risks of doing injury to someone, though slight, are sufficient to act as a deterrent. Many anthropologists find a .22 rifle an economical and convenient way of improving their living conditions by shooting pigeons for the pot. Unfortunately a .22 makes too much of a mess of any but the largest New Guinea birds or mammals to be recommended as a collector's weapon. A 12-bore or .410 shotgun are useful collecting weapons, though the 12-bore tends to blow small birds or mammals to pieces, while the .410 lacks the range or power to make it double up economically as a weapon for shooting for the pot. In either case if a shotgun is to be used for collecting, cartridges with lighter-weight shot than the No. 4 or No. 6 will be required. The author has found it simpler to repack cartridges himself with No. 8 shot rather than go through the rigmarole of importing or specially ordering No. 8 cartridges.

7.3.2. Traps. For obtaining small terrestrial mammals, simple break-back rat and mouse traps are very effective. These are cheap, readily available and good for gift and trade. They do, however, tend to damage specimens rather badly. Also, if set in exposed locations, they kill and mangle birds as well as rodents. In our limited use of them, humane traps are not nearly as productive as the break-book traps, but they allowed us to catch species never taken in the latter. They have the great advantage that they do not damage specimens, and unless a captive dies of shock or exposure, do not kill them, so that they can be released again.

7.3.3. Mist-nets. Ornithologists with experience find mist-nets useful for obtaining bird species which may not easily be examined in the hand by use of any other method. Bats can also be caught in these devices. However the novice should not attempt to use them without help and guidance: setting them involves a certain measure of skill and extracting birds from them alive and undamaged requires a considerable knack.

7.3.4. Fishing tackle. In many areas local people are now using fishing lines with steel hooks as well as traditional technologies. It is worth any anthropologist's while to take hooks, line and steel trace with him, in the hope of catching eels. These are an excellent addition to his diet, provided that he can catch and eat them without infringement of local riparian property rights or ritual prohibitions. At the same time he may be able to do some scientifically useful collecting.

In special circumstances an ethnographer may find it desirable to use chemicals to stun or poison fish, but he should only do this after full consultation with experts and with the explicit consent of the authorities.

7.4 Preparation and preservation of specimens

The most important advice here is that the fieldworker follow the instructions and suggestions of the institutions or research-workers destined to receive his collections. Many museums have printed sheets of instructions for the preservation of different kinds of animals.

7.4.1. Killing. Many specimens to be preserved are, fortunately, dead before they come into the hands of the fieldworker-collector. Humane and efficient methods of killing animals, which do not damage them as specimens, are not always described in the literature on collecting methods. For invertebrates a killing-jar containing cyanide is the most efficient device, though this is a poison and can only be obtained on prescription or from a research laboratory, and has to be handled with care. For small vertebrates a large jar containing a piece of cotton-wool moistened with chloroform can be used. For frogs and small reptiles an injection in the gut of thirty-seven percent formalin will both kill rapidly and preserve the internal organs. Birds may be killed by pressing firmly on either side of the thorax with thumb and first finger, which constricts movement of the heart and lungs. Mammals may be choked or injected with nembutal. I know of no satisfactory means of killing a large snake or eel which does not involve considerable physical damage to the cadaver. A brutal but often inescapable method of disposing of larger reptiles is to push them straight into the drum of preserving fluid so that they are both drowned and preserved in this. However, if this method is used, the specimens must be extracted again from the preserving fluid soon after death and suitable incisions then be made to allow the fluid to enter the body cavity.

7.4.2. Taxidermy. The most useful method to prepare bird or mammal specimens is by accompanying dried skins with the skull and mandible, which have been separately dried and preserved. Although it is possible to learn taxidermy with the aid of a do-it-yourself manual and a certain amount of practice, skill in this technique is more easily acquired by direct instruction by a museum preparator or other skilled craftsman. However, skinning is a time-consuming activity even for a skilled worker, and few anthropologists can afford to devote themselves to this. In a specialist study, it may be desirable to employ a trained indigenous preparator, if one is available, or to seek field assistance from a zoologist prepared to do some preparation of skins himself, or to arrange for a preparator to accompany him. The alternatives to taxidermy are, in the rare cases where local facilities are available for this, to put bird or mammal specimens on ice; or to treat them as most other vertebrates will be treated and preserve them in alcohol. A compromise in the case of larger mammals is to rough-skin them, removing trunk and main sections of limbs but leaving skull and lower section of limbs in the skin for immersion in preserving fluid.

7.4.3. Use of preservative fluids. The simplest method of preserving any kind of small vertebrate and many kinds of invertebrates is by submerging these in solutions of 70% alcohol. An incision of appropriate size in the abdomen should be made to permit the fluid to preserve the internal organs: alternatively, the gut should be injected with 40% formalin, in quantities ranging from one cc. for an animal weight 25 gms.

Care should be taken to ensure that the alcohol solution is neither too weak nor too strong. If too weak, as tends to be the case if large quantities of body-fluids dilute what was originally 70% spirit, creatures begin to decompose, as they also do if they are too tightly packed in the jar or drum so that the fluid cannot circulate around them. If the solution is too strong, the specimens become extremely rigid and distorted in shape. One way of preventing this undesirable rigidity and distortion in frogs and small reptile specimens is by adding glycerine to the 70% alcohol in proportion of approximately 1 part in 50.

Some collectors use 8% formalin (3.7% formaldehyde solution) rather than alcohol. This has the advantage of being both cheaper than alcohol and transportable in highly concentrate form (normally, as purchased, 37% formaldehyde solution), thus saving space and special negotiation with airlines which will not permit the transport of alcohol and other inflammable fluids on flights also carrying passengers. Laboratory workers dislike formalin because it is unpleasant to work with. Also, its use tends to produce rigid brittle specimens. However, it can be washed out and replaced with 70% alcohol when the specimens are brought to a laboratory.

It is important that specimens are fixed in an extended position and not simply dropped, curled up, into a container of fluid. It is recommended that small animals (rats, frogs, lizards) be laid out straight, limbs and digits extended, in a shallow dish, covered with the preserving liquid, and allowed to harden before being transferred to the main storage vessel.

7.4.4. Special treatment of certain invertebrate groups. Most kinds of insects, spiders and other invertebrates can simply and safely be preserved in either alcohol or formalin, though in some groups, e.g., grasshoppers, this may result in the loss of natural pigmentation. For some kinds of insects, e.g., butterflies and moths, preservation in alcohol is obviously even less satisfactory. For butterflies, preparation in papillates is the preferred method; and nonfleshy insects should be placed on layers of carded cotton treated with paradichlorobenzene and arranged in wooden boxes. Some other invertebrates, e.g., earthworms, also require a measure of special treatment. Advice on preferred techniques should be sought from specialists who are to receive these collections.

7.5 Documentation of collections

Specimens collected by an ethnozoologist require more extensive documentation than those acquired by most straightforward zoological collectors. The fieldworker must provide not only the data required by the zoologist who will examine the specimens, but as much information as is necessary for his own objectives, i.e., evaluating the folk-taxon or folk-taxa applied to them.

7.5.1. Labeling and field registers. Each specimen requires its own label, firmly attached to it or attached to its individual container, and minimally inscribed with a unique reference number which cross-checks with a field register entry. The only exception to this rule of individual labeling and numbering is the case of a group of specimens obtained in precisely the same place and at the same time and unambiguously designated to the same folk-taxon by speakers: these may be given a group number, or a series of numbers placed in their collective container.

In the case of bird or mammal skins or other large dry specimens it may be a convenience for later study to write comprehensive labels, giving name of fieldworker-collector, date and location (including altitude) of acquisition, notes on sex, breeding condition, crop and stomach contents, and folk-taxon or taxa applied. Regardless of whether or not such information goes on the label, it should also go in the field register, together with other biologically or ethnographically relevant information, such as notes on the creature's activities at the time of capture, vegetation in which it was taken, name and relevant personal details of indigenous collector, and comment or explanation offered by the collector or other speakers regarding the specimen. It is a useful practice to use duplicate books with carbon sheets for field registers, so that sheets can be torn out and mailed off to accompany collections. Leave either a broad margin column blank for addition of later notes or identifications of the specimens, or a blank opposite page for the same purpose.

All labels should be sturdy and written with materials that do not fade in the sun when specimens are put out to dry (as many kinds of ball-point ink do), or dissolve in water. Labels attached to specimens in liquid preservatives require particular attention.

Ethnozoology

It is depressing to find how frequently paper or card labels disintegrate in preserving fluid, particularly when the laboratory worker comes to remove, an intricately entwined mass of rigid and distorted frogs, labels and string attachments from a jar. It is also disconcerting to find how often labels work loose from the specimens to which they were originally tied. For these reasons small labels on rather short cords are better than large ones, because they are less likely to get tangled up, even if there is only space on them to inscribe an index number and no other details. Bold marking with a soft lead pencil is less likely to be obliterated in preservative than other substances. There is much to be said for the use of cloth labels or pre-stamped numbered metal tags, as provided by some museums, though even these are not fool-proof.

Finally, labels should always be attached at the first possible moment to minimize the risk that these get wrongly attached. Inevitably there will be some cases where delay or confusion occurs. If the fieldworker has the least suspicion that labels have become wrongly attached, he must make a note to this effect in his field register.

7.5.2. Ancillary documentation. Where specimens change shape, size or color in the process of preservation, photographs (preferably in color) and measurements can be vital supporting information. If it is possible to take photographs of creatures in life, assuming characteristic postures, these are preferred over photographs of dead specimens.

7.6 Packing and transportation

A beautifully preserved and documented collection might as well never have been made if it is damaged, destroyed or lost in transit to its eventual home. Packing materials are as vital to the collection as preserving materials.

For transportation of spirit specimens most of the liquid can be emptied out of containers, and specimens will not deteriorate much as long as the containers are air-tight and contents remain moist. However, packing materials must be inserted to prevent damage by specimens banging about in drums or jars. Alternatively, specimens can be sealed in polyethylene bags or roll tubular polythene for transport. Specimens require careful handling at each re-sorting and re-packing, if some are not to lose their labels.

Removing preserving fluid greatly reduces weight and thus lowers costs of transport. However it increases the necessity for relatively rapid shipment to base, if material is not to deteriorate. In most areas air freight, in spite of higher cost, is amply justified: sea freight is slow, and long periods of waiting at the exit port or at transit ports waiting for transshipment can mean disaster both to incompletely sealed spirit specimens and to skins and other dried specimens which risk becoming moldy or infested with vermin. If the fieldworker is unable to consign his material himself, he should seek out a reliable agent and give him full and explicit instructions. Above all he should be certain that his export permits (see §7.0) are in order and in the hands of his agent. He should be careful that the addressees are aware of the impending arrival of the collection and that there are no formalities regarding the import of animal materials to the country of reception which he has not looked into.

7.7 Basic collecting equipment and supplies

The following list is not exhaustive. It assumes that the fieldworker will not be doing taxidermy, but will be preserving specimens in alcohol and/or formalin. Quantities will obviously depend on the scale of collecting which is envisaged.

Alcohol. High grade Industrial Methylated Spirit (=98% EtOH) is best, but can only be obtained through research or medical institutions. Colored methylated spirit (also 98% EtOH) sold commercially is not as good for obvious reasons, though the coloring matter precipitates when water is added and does not make much difference to most specimens.

Remember, too that in many regions the commercial sale of methylated spirits is prohibited. 98% alcohol is hygroscopic, i.e., absorbs water from the atmosphere. Thus alcohol left in a part empty drum will draw moisture from the air in it, and will not remain 98% for long. When diluting to 70% etc. for preservation of specimens, this must be borne in mind.

Formalin. Formalin as purchased is an approximately 37% solution of formaldehyde. For use it should be diluted with water 12 times, giving an approximate 8% solution of formalin (or 3% formaldehyde solution).

Glycerine. Glycerol is the technical term for this.

Syringes and needles. Expendable syringes are cheap and perfectly satisfactory. No. 14 is an appropriate size for needles. Finer needles tend to get blocked; larger ones may be difficult to insert.

Forceps. For handling specimens in preservative.

Shallow dishes. Specimen trays, or baking or roasting pans, are necessary for initial preservation of specimens in extended position, and for later sorting.

Killing-jars. With tight-fitting lids.

Poisons and anaesthetics. Nembutal for injections. Chloroform or cyanide for killing jars, but note warning concerning latter in §7.4.1.

Containers. For large specimens, plastic containers such as plastic milk sacks are best. The disadvantage of metal drums is that in time they rust and stain specimens particularly if they are not fully air-tight. Formalin corrodes metal, so drums and tins are not suitable for materials preserved in this. For medium sized specimens (smaller rats, frogs, etc.) plastic containers or screw top glass jars (old pickle-jars, etc.) can be used. For most insects and other creatures too small for labels to be attached to them, small glass vials and jars are indispensable. These enable the fieldworker to check his data by showing specimens to speakers. For convenience of packing, and to ensure an ample supply, it pays to buy a selection of sizes by the gross or half-gross. Screw tops or inserted plug-type plastic tops are preferable to clip-on plastic tops. Do not pack glass vials or jars containing liquids in cotton wool or other absorbent materials. If one jar breaks it will dampen the cotton wool

Ethnozoology

and cause this to contract. This will allow other jars to shake about and smash, and damage will be compounded.

Labels. Large numbers of pre-tested labels of varying sizes are a necessity.

Cotton-wool, kapok or similar packing material. (Dry moss is useful as a temporary packing material.)

Polyethylene bags of selected sizes, or rolls of tubular polyethylene which can be cut and sealed into bags.

Cloth bags, of assorted sizes, for carrying live animals.

Insecticides and repellants. Napthaline or paradichlorobenzene flakes or some equivalent are necessary for packing with feathers, bones and other dried animal parts to discourage cockroaches and other insects from devouring either these or their labels.

Cartons, crates, metal trunks or patrol boxes, for packing specimens.

Sisalcraft or similar water-proof packing paper, for wrapping cartons and other parcels.

Copra sacks or hessian, together with yarn and sail needles, for outer covering of packages.

Scotch-tape, for sealing packages; and waterproof plastic tape, for sealing glass jars, etc.

Marking crayons or marking pens, for clear labeling of crates, trunks or packages.

8 Collaboration with zoologists

Unless the fieldworker is in the unusual situation of requiring very few identifications and being able to make these for himself on the basis of available literature, he is going to need some assistance and advice from professional zoologist or other specialists. The extent of this assistance may range from extended collaboration in fieldwork itself to limited consultation on a few particular points or identification of a handful of specimens.

Whatever the scale of this dependence, two essential principles apply. The first is one that should be well known to anthropologists, the principle of reciprocity. Professional zoologists, and especially museum taxonomists, are generally over-worked and much put-upon people. If the anthropologist is asking them for help he should do his best to lighten their task by providing material in a good condition, as well documented as possible, and to provide them with specimens and data of interest and value from the point of view of their own studies. In the case of the most valuable kind of assistance of all, collaboration in observation and collecting in the field, the zoologist is only likely to welcome this arrangement if this enables him to obtain data and materials he could not otherwise acquire. For his part, the anthropologist should go out of his way to try to grasp what the zoologist's professional interests and objectives are, and to ensure that his own knowledge of the region and communication with the local population are at the service of his collaborator.

For want of a better term, the second principle may be dubbed the principle of ethnographic relativity. Anthropologists who lack academic training in the natural sciences tend to be astonishingly naive in their dealings with and expectations of real scientists. They regard them, as oracles of absolute truth, and display shock and dismay when these authorities contradict themselves or each other, produce what appear to be inadequate identifications or answers to questions, or even supply no answers or identifications at all. In fact although the degree of inconsistency and indeterminacy in a professional biologist's identifications of fauna is likely to be lower than those of indigenous persons, it will nevertheless be present and the scientist's responses must be anticipated and evaluated by the ethnographer in fundamentally the same way that he evaluates the indigenous person's responses. He must firstly do his best to understand the principles, both ideal and empirical, by which the scientist reaches his conclusions. In general ethnographers must learn to treat their scientist collaborators with the same courtesy, humility and caution that they adopt in dealings with their most knowledgeable and reliable indigenous speakers.

8.1 Choosing your zoologist

8.1.1. For reception and identification of specimens. The most fortunate ethnographer is the one who works in an institution which also employs biologists who are regional specialists in his own area of study. Where this is the case he obviously goes to them for advice. Otherwise, the fieldworker has two initial choices. The first is to find an institution or individual who will receive his total collection, make such identifications as are possible on the basis of knowledge and reference collections, and farm out the rest to research workers elsewhere. The second option is for the fieldworker himself to negotiate with zoologists who are specialists in the groups of fauna he has collected.

The first solution may be the most economical in terms of the fieldworker's own time, limiting the number of consignments he needs to write. It can work well if his total collections are small, or when he is dealing with an institution which is specifically concerned with all or most kinds of fauna from the region in which he is working, if it employs taxonomists in most relevant fields, and holds good reference collections.

The disadvantages of this solution are that not all the specialists expert in faunal groups in the collecting area, or enthusiastic about finding time to work on the required identifications; that if they in turn send material on to specialists in other institutions, the fieldworker is likely not to establish direct personal contact, and may miss out on valuable advice and information supplementary to the identification list. He may experience considerable frustration if they are tardy or inefficient in their work. Authorities in an under-staffed museum, may be slow in sending collections on.

If the fieldworker prefers the second choice, and negotiates directly with individual specialists he should choose individuals who are professionally competent and enthusiastic. Finally, the best kind of specialist to consult is usually one who has had personal field experience in the region of study.

Having first chosen your institution or individual specialists and ascertained that they are prepared to receive your specimens, it is important to find out what their requirements are regarding condition of specimens and documentation. Some museums have printed instructions for collectors. Some institutions have prepared data-sheets which they like to have completed for each specimen.

8.1.2. For collaboration in the field. The increasing scale of biological as well as ethnographical field research means that some ethnographers can enjoy collaboration with biologists in their field enquiries. In negotiating such an arrangement, the following points should be borne in mind.

Ethnozoology

1 Any experienced ethnographer will realize that teamwork or collaboration in field enquiries includes risks of personal dissension, though these are normally reduced if the co-workers have separate and well-defined professional interests to avoid quarrels over interpretation of data and publication of results. It is obviously desirable that two people who are to live together in the bush should know one another reasonably well before they embark on this venture, and have some estimate of each other's personal tastes, prejudices, and styles of living.

2 It is unwise for an ethnographer to have visitors in the field at early stages of his enquiry before he feels that he understands the local situation well. He needs to reach the point where he knows everybody has established some means of communication, has some impression of who the knowledgeable and reliable speakers, skilled hunters and bushmen are, and has good local geographical knowledge, so he can identify places rapidly and knows their approximate altitude, vegetational cover, etc. He should also prepare in advance basic vocabulary lists relevant to the phenomena in which his visitor will be interested. Without this degree of preparation he can neither take full advantage of his visitor's expertise nor give his visitor as much help as would be desirable. It is also not a good idea to receive a visitor at the very end of one's field period. Any fruitful visit will result in new perspectives for the fieldworker and a host of new questions, and it can be very frustrating not to have time to go into these further.

3 The local people should be prepared for the visitor's arrival, so that they understand what his work and interests are, and are in a position to give him the maximum assistance.

4 The ethnographer should have a clear understanding of the professional interests, objectives and methods of fieldwork of his visitor, so that he can be of maximum assistance in the period of time available.

5 Conversely, the ethnographer must do all he can to ensure that his visitor has a clear idea of his own objectives, at least as they relate to their joint enquiries. Natural scientists tend to view the theoretical propositions of anthropologists with suspicion, while anthropologically untrained biologists often find it surprisingly hard to grasp the subtleties of folk-taxonomy and the degree of noncoincidence of folk-taxa with what seem to them to be obvious biological taxa. There is an almost inevitable tendency for a biologist, particularly on a short collection trip when he hopes to amass a lot of material to cut corners and not get the maximum ethnological data on each individual specimen. The biologist may be tempted to place all specimens of some particular group (such as frogs or rats) which have been obtained in one place on the same date, in the same plastic bag, to be individually labeled and numbered later, and merely to rough-sort them out into apparent species or genus categories at this stage of his enquiry. This can be maddening to the ethnographer, whose speakers are providing a host of identifications for the unsorted or rough-sorted specimens. Since shortage of time and the shortage of volume of material obtained are key features in this situation, the ethnographer may be able to alleviate it himself if he is permitted to assist with the sorting, labeling and preservation of specimens. Above all, the ethnographer must make sure that his own notes are individually cross-indexed to the zoologist's field registration numbers.

6 The ethnographer cannot expect any one zoologist to be a specialist in all groups of fauna of ethnobiological relevance, or to be equally interested in all groups. It

is unreasonable to expect a herpetologist to help him out with birds or longicorn beetles, though he may be able to suggest authorities to be consulted and elementary methods of collecting and preserving specimens.

7 If the visiting zoologist is only to be in the field for a short period, the ethnographer should do all he can to organize his own routine to render the zoologist maximum aid. If an important ceremony, a death or unanticipated political crisis occurs, the visitor will understand that the ethnographer may simply have to abandon him and pay attention to this. But normally it is discourteous and professionally foolish, to turn a visiting zoologist loose to make out as best he can while the ethnographer goes about his everyday business. As he observes the procedures a biologist adopts in the field, the ethnographer can learn to evaluate in evaluating the differences and similarities between folk-biology and biological science.

Appendix B

Analysis of a list of vernacular bird-names collected by a professional zoologist.

A professional ornithologist with an extensive record of fieldwork in Oceania laudably made the practice of providing local vernacular names for birds in the reports of his expeditions. In one such report, based on a period of two weeks' collecting in a particular area, he gave local names for 45 of the species he collected. Understandably, since he was not trained in phonetics and no phonemic or otherwise standardized orthography for the language was available to him, he wrote the names down as they might be spelled if they were English words.

In this case, the author evaluated the list of local names in the light of an ethnographic enquiry in the same area, which included a fairly comprehensive study of knowledge and classification of birds. The status of the 45 terms appears to be as follows:

(1) Terms orthographically recognizable and accurately applied to single species 16

(2) Terms probably unrecognizable, for orthographic reasons, but accurately applied to single species * 7

(3) Terms correctly applied to species designated, but also to other species for which vernacular names were either not recorded or inaccurately recorded. (All these terms properly relate to generic, and not specific or minimal taxa.) 7

(4) Terms accurately applied to species, but not accurately restricted to dimorphic sexes and/or stages of maturity 3

(5) Terms totally inaccurately applied 10

(6) Terms, or species to which applied, unknown to ethnographer, so status uncertain 2

It will be seen that, at the most charitable estimate, only two thirds of this list of names could be deemed accurate.

The point of this analysis is not to demonstrate that professional biologists are wasting their time to collect and record vernacular vocabulary. On the contrary, this list, which is in no way atypical of the majority of lists provided by biologists which the author has himself utilized, would certainly be useful to other biologists and ethnographers, provided they treated it with caution. But it should certainly not be accepted uncritically: while to use it with bilingual speakers as a basis for eliciting bird identifications in yet another language, would only compound the errors and ambiguities it contains.

Bibliography

Berlin, B., D. E. Breedlove and P. H. Raven. 1966. Folk-taxonomies and biological classification. Science 154:273–75.
Conklin, H. C. 1962. Lexicographical treatment of folk-taxonomies. International Journal of American Linguistics 28(2):119–41.
Diamond, J. M. 1966. Zoological classification system of a primitive people. Science 151: 1102–04.

Austronesia

Brazenor, C. W. 1950. The mammals of Victoria. Melbourne: Brown-Prior and Anderson.
Buchsbaum, R. 1966. Animals without backbones, 1 and 2. Harmondsworth: Pelican.
Cernohrsky, W. O. 1967. Marine shells of the Pacific. Sydney: Pacific Publications.
Child, J. 1960. Australian insects. Sydney: Periwinkle. 1968 revised edition. Melbourne: Cheshire-Lansdowne.
———. 1965. Australian spiders. Sidney: Periwinkle.
Curran, C. H. 1946. Insects of the Pacific world. New York: Macmillan.
Iredale, T. 1956. Birds of New Guinea, 1 and 2. Melbourne: Georgian House.
Laurie, E. M. O. and J. E. Hill. 1954. List of land mammals of New Guinea, Celebes and adjacents islands. London: British Museum.
Loveridge, A. 1946. Reptiles of the Pacific world. New York: Macmillan.
Main, B. Y. 1964. Spiders in Australia. Brisbane: Jacaranda.
Marlow, B. 1962. Marsupials of Australia. Brisbane: Jacaranda.
Munro, I. S. R. 1967. The fishes of New Guinea. Port Moresby: Department of Agriculture, Stock and Fisheries.
McPhee, D. R. 1959. Snakes and lizards of Australia. Brisbane: Jacaranda.
Rand, A. L. and E. T. Gilliard. 1967. Handbook of New Guinea birds. London: Weidenfeld and Nicolson.
Schodde, R. and W. B. Hitchcock. 1968. Contribution to Papuasian ornithology, I: Report on the birds of the Lake Kutuba area, Territory of Papua and New Guinea. Melbourne: C.S.I.R.O.
Slater, K. R. 1956. A guide to the dangerous snakes of Papua. Port Moresby: Government Printer.
Troughton, E. 1968. Furred animals of Australia. Sydney: Angus and Robertson.
Tyler, M. J. 1968. Papuan hylid frogs of the genus Hyla. Leiden: Zoologische Verhandelingen 96.
Worrell, E. 1963a. Reptiles of Australia. Sydney: Angus and Robertson.
———. 1963b. Dangerous snakes of Australia and New Guinea. Sydney: Angus and Robertson.

Africa

Chopard and A. Villiers 1950. Contribution à l'étude de l'Aïr. Paris: Larose, IFAN (Mémoires).

Malbrant, R. 1952. Faune du Centre africain français: mammifères et oiseaux. Paris: Paul Lechevalier.
—— and A. Maclatchy. 1949. Faune de l'Equateur africain français: I. Oiseaux, II. Mammifères, 1 et 2. Paris: Paul Lechevalier.
Williams, J. G. 1967. A field guide to the national parks of east Africa. London: Collins.

MAMMALS

Bigourdan, J. and R. Prunier. 1943. Les mammifères sauvages de l'Ouest africain et leur milieu. Paris: Paul Lechevalier.
Dekeyser, P. L. 1955. Les mammifères de l'Afrique Noire française. Dakar: IFAN.
Dorst, J. and P. Dandelot. 1970. A field guide to the larger mammals of Africa. London: Collins.
Haltenorth, T. and H. Diller. 1985. Mammifères d'Afrique et de Madagascar. Paris: Delachaux et Niestlé.
Jeannin, A. 1936. Les mammifères sauvages du Cameroun. Paris: Paul Lechevalier.
Schouteden, H. 1944–46. Les mammifères du Congo belge et du Ruanda Urundi. Tervuren: M.R.C.B.

BIRDS

Bannerman, D. A. 1953. The birds of west and equatorial Africa, 1 and 2. London: Edinburgh, Oliver and Boyd.
Bates, L. G. 1930. Handbook of the birds of west Africa. London: John Bale and Daniellson.
Bouet, G. 1955. Oiseaux de l'Afrique tropicale. Paris: Larose, 2 vol.
Dekeyser, P. L., and J. H. Derivot. 1967. Les oiseaux de l'Ouest africain. Dakar: IFAN, 2 vol.
Heim de Balsac, H. 1924. Contribution à l'ornithologie dans le Sahara septentrional, en Algérie et en Tunisie. Paris: Paul Lechevalier.
Schouteden, H. 1948. Les oiseaux du Congo Belge et du Ruanda Urundi. Tervuren: M.R.C.B.
Williams, J. G. 19xx. A field guide to the birds of east and central Africa. London: Collins.

REPTILES

Angel, F. 1933. Les serpents de l'Afrique occidentale française. Paris: Larose.
Cansdale, G. 1955. Reptiles of west Africa. London: Penguin Books.
FitzSimons, V. F. M. 1970. A field guide to the snakes of southern Africa. London: Collins.
Villiers, A. 1963. Les serpents de l'Ouest africain. Dakar: IFAN.

FISH

Blache, J. 1964. Les poissons du bassin du Tchad et du bassin adjacent du Mayo Kebbi. Fort-Lamy: Ministry of Agriculture.
Irvine, F. R. 1947. The fishes and fisheries of the Gold Coast. London: Crown Agent for Col.

Micha, J-C. 1973. Etude des populations piscicoles de l'Oubangui et tentatives de sélection et d'adaptation de quelques espèces à l'étang de pisciculture. Paris: Ed. C.T.F.T.
Pellegrin, J. 1923. Poissons d'eau douce de l'Afrique occidentale. Paris.
Poll, M. n.d. Familles et genres de poissons africains. Tervuren: M.R.C.B.
Reed, W. 1967. Fish and fisheries of northern Nigeria.

INVERTEBRATES

Villiers, A. and H. Stempffer. 1957. Les lépidoptères de l'Afrique noire française, 1–3. Dakar: IFAN.
Williams, J. G. 19xx. A field guide to the butterflies of Africa. London: Collins.

Asia

Pfeffer, P. 1970. L'Asie. Paris: Hachette.

MAMMALS

Prater, S. H. 1965. Book of Indian animals, revised edition. Bombay: Bombay Natural History Society.
Tate, G. H., J. E. Hill, and T. D. Carter. 1946. Mammals of the Pacific world. New York: Macmillan.

BIRDS

Ali, S. and S. Dillon. 1970. Handbook of the birds of India and Pakistan. Together with those of Nepal, Sikkim, Bhutan and Ceylan. New York: Oxford University Press.
Etchecopar, R. D. in preparation. Les oiseaux de la Chine.
Hue, F. and R. D. Etchecopar. 1970. Les oiseaux du proche et du moyen Orient de la Méditerranée aux contreforts de l'Himalaya. Paris: Boubée.
King, B., M. Woodcock, and E. C. Dickinson. 1975. A field guide to the birds of Burma, Malaya, Thailand, Cambodia, Vietnam, Laos, Hainan and Hong Kong. London: Collins.
Lekagul, B. in revision. Bird guide of Thailand. Bangkok: The Association for the Conservation of Wild Life.
Yamashina, Y. 1967. Birds in Japan: A field guide. Tokyo: Tokyo News Service.

REPTILES

Bourret, R. 1936. Les serpents de l'Indochine: études sur la faune. Toulouse: Imprimerie Henri Basuyau.
———. 1941. Les tortues de l'Indochine. Institut Océanographique de l'Indochine.
Deuve, J. 1970. Les serpents du Laos. Paris: ORSTOM.
Lanza, B. 1972. I vertebrati inferiori dell'Eurasia. Florence: Loi tipi dell'Istituto Geografico Militare.

FISH

Bleeker. 1972. Papers on fishes in particular of the Indonesian Archipelago. Amsterdam: Asher.

INVERTEBRATES

Baltazar, C. R. and N. P. Salazar. 1979. Philippine insects: An introduction. Quezon City: U.P. Press.

South America and Central America

Dorst, J. 1969. L'Amérique du sud et l'Amérique centrale. Paris: Hachette.
Rohl, E. 1949. Fauna descriptiva de Venezuela. Caracas: Tipografia americana (Boletin de la Academia de ciencias fisicas, matematicas y naturales).

MAMMALS

Cabrera, A. 1957. Catálogo de los Mamíferos de America del Sur. Buenos-Aires: Museo Argentino de Ciencias Naturales (out of print).
Wawrin, Marquis de. 1951. Les bêtes sauvages de l'Amazonie. Paris: Payot.

BIRDS

Peterson, R. T. and E. L. Chalif. 1973. A field guide to the Mexican birds and adjacent Central America. Boston: Houghton Mifflin Company.
Meyer de Schauensee, R. 1970. A guide to the birds of South America. Edinburgh: Oliver and Boyd.

General Works

REPTILES

Angel F. 1949. Petit atlas des amphibiens et des reptiles, 1 et 2. Paris: Boubée.
Pritchard, P. C. H. 1967. Living turtles of the world. Jersey City: T.F.H. Publ.
Schmidt, K. P. and R. F. Inger. 1960. Les reptiles vivants du monde. Paris: Hachette.
———. 1968. Poisonous snakes of the world: A manual for use by U.S. Amphibious Forces (U.S. Department of the Navy Bureau of Medicine and Surgery). Washington: United States Government Printing Office.

FISH

Axelrod, H. R. and C. W. Emmens. 1975. Poissons exotiques d'eau de mer. Hong Kong: T.F.H.
Goldstein, R. J. 1973. Cichlids of the world. Hong Kong: T.F.H.
Pujol, R., ed. 1975. L'homme et l'animal, premier colloque d'ethnozoologie. Paris: Institut International d'Ethnosciences.
Randall, J. E. 1968. Caribbean reef fishes. Hong Kong: T.F.H.
Sterba, G. 1959. Süsswasser aus aller Welt. Berlin: Urania Verlag.

Questionnaire 13
Anatomy and Physiology
Animals and Plants

by Corinne Venot

1 Anatomy: plates and vocabulary

The numbers on these drawings indicate various parts of the body, or expressions, positions, and postures of man, animals, and plants. The English terms given may not have equivalents in the language, and conversely, the language may have a specific term which is lacking in English. For this reason, using pictures is better than a nonillustrated list, and the terms included here do not constitute a closed list.

External Anatomy

Fig. 1, 2
The Body: Female and Male
  A. The Head
  B. The Trunk
  C. The Limbs

1. arm } limbs
2. leg   }
3. hair
4. neck
5. nape
6. dowager's hump
7. hollow behind the collarbone
8. shoulder
9. clavicle (collarbone)
10. chest
    a. breast (ask whether men have breasts)
       1. areola
       2. nipple
    b. chest hair
11. sternum (breastbone)
12. back
13. shoulder blades
14. rib, side, flank
15. waist
16. hip
17. stomach
    a. navel
18. groin
19. pelvis
20. spine, backbone, vertebral column
21. lumbar region
22. buttocks
    a. crack, part in the buttocks
23. pubis
24. female genitals
    a. female pubic hair
25. male genitals
    a. male pubic hair
26. biceps (is there a special word or no word at all for this muscle in women?)
27. elbow
28. bend of the arm
29. forearm
30. armpit (underarm)
    a. underarm hair
31. wrist
32. hand
33. thigh
34. knee
    a. kneecap
    b. bend of the knee
    c. back of the knee (ham)
35. inner thigh
36. leg
37. tibia (shinbone)
38. calf
39. ankle
40. Achilles' tendon
41. foot
42. heel

Anatomy and Physiology/Animals and Plants 559

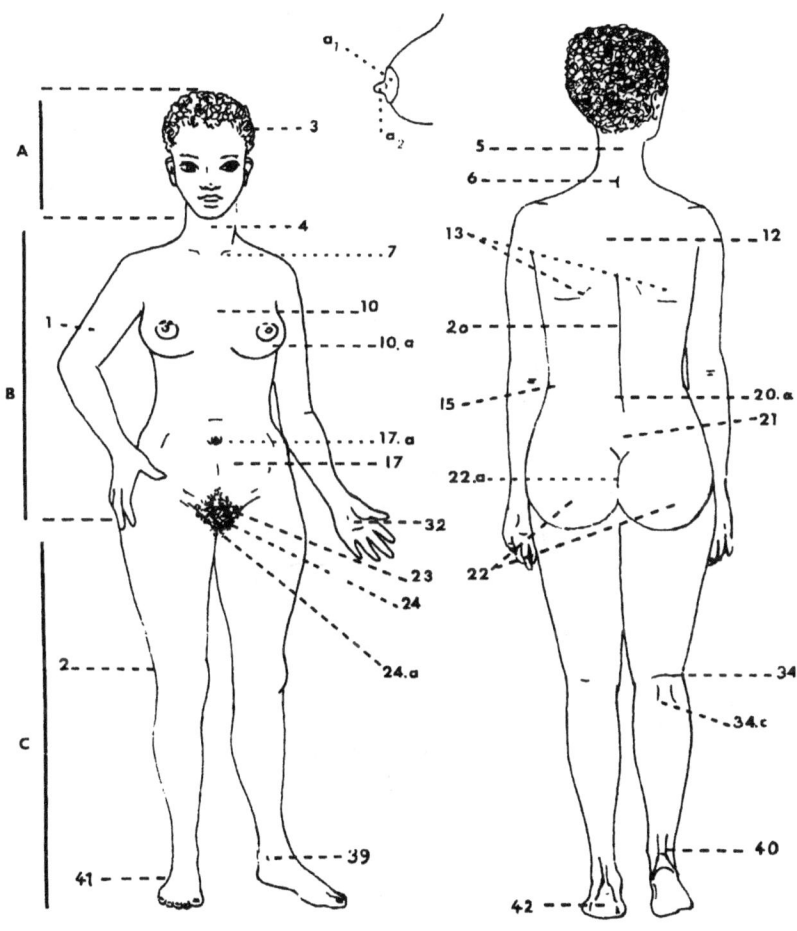

Fig. 1 The Female Body

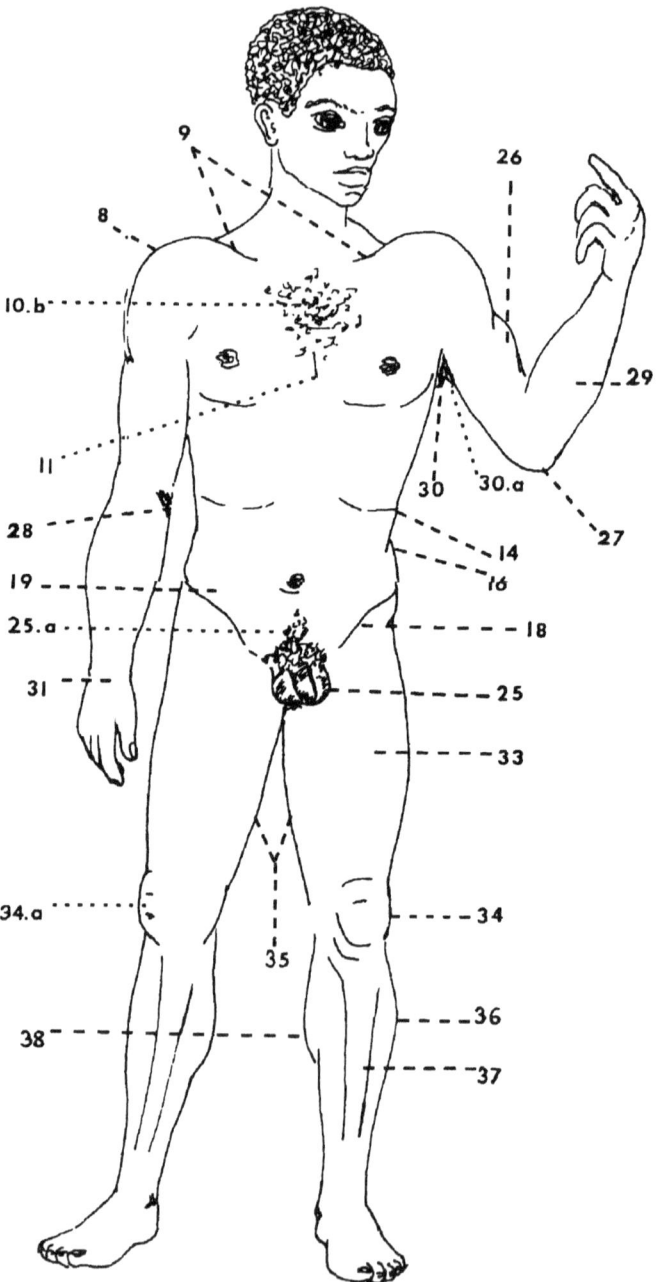

Fig. 2 The Male Body

External Anatomy

Fig. 3, 4
The Head

A. & B. front views
C. profile
D. three-quarters view

1. hair
2. hairstyle (ask the names of different hairstyles)
   a. part
3. hairline
4. skull, bald skull, bald
5. suture line
6. fontanel
   a. anterior
   b. posterior
7. occiput (back of the head)
8. temple
9. bump (hump) of the forehead
10. forehead
    a. wrinkle in the forehead
11. eyebrow
12. space between the eyebrows (lacking = jealous eyebrows)
13. eye
14. upper eyelid
    a. eyelashes
15. white of the eye
16. iris
17. pupil
18. (inner) corner of the eye
19. lower eyelid
20. 'crow's feet'
21. bags under the eyes
22. rings, shadows under the eyes
23. nose
24. bridge of the nose
25. nostril
26. nasal openings, nares
27. tip of the nose
28. cheek
29. cheekbone
30. space from the condyle to the lower jaw
31. expression lines
32. mouth (ask for the corners of the mouth)
33. lips
    a. upper lip
    b. lower lip
34. space between nose and lips
35. groove under the nose
36. chin
37. fold of the chin
38. Adam's apple
39. wen
40. mole, beauty mark (flat or raised)
41. wart
42. ear
    a. pinna, auricle
    b. lobe
    c. earhole, ear canal
43. dimple
44. baldness on top
45. widow's peak
46. bald spot
47. cleft chin
48. harelip

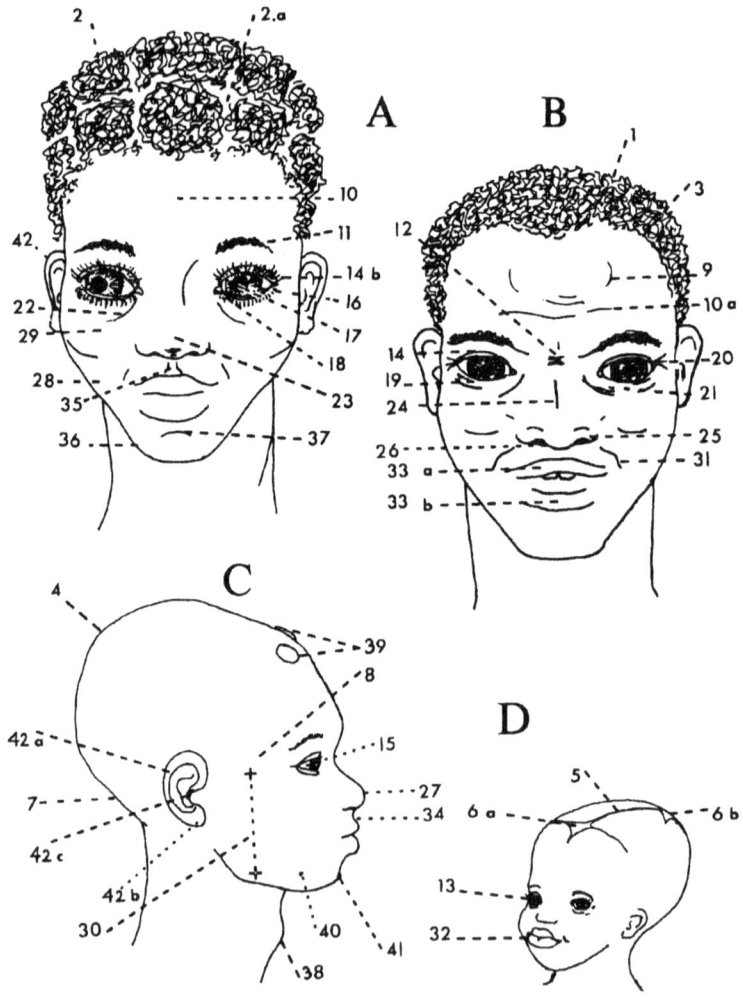

Fig. 3 The Head

Anatomy and Physiology/Animals and Plants 563

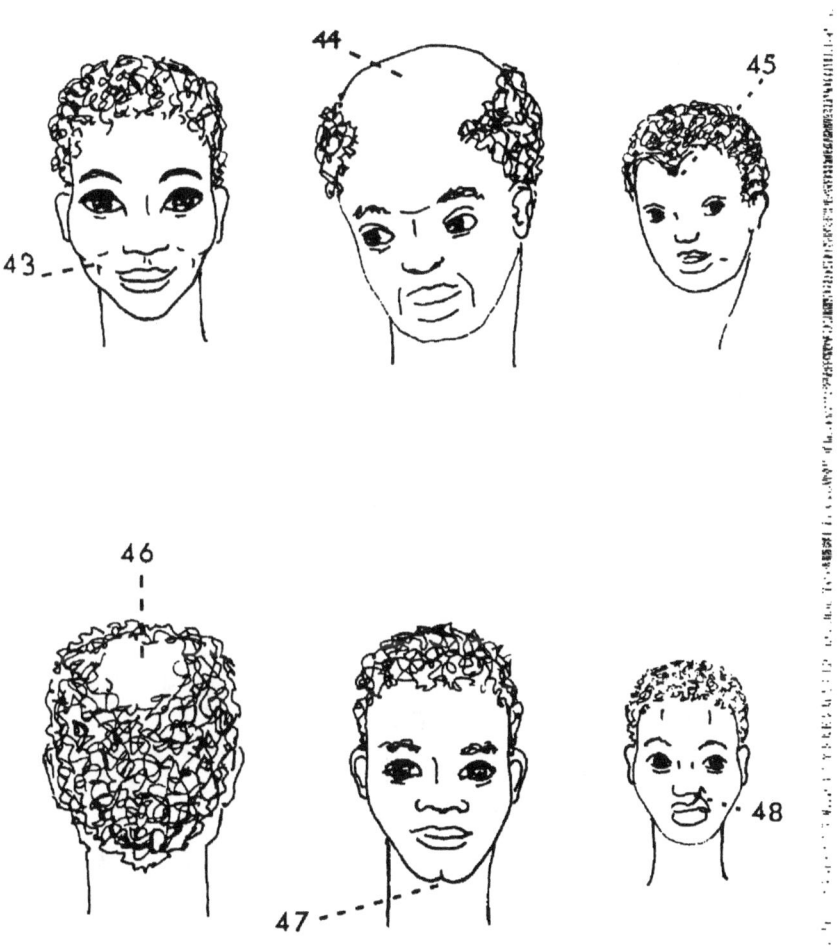

Fig. 4 The Head

External Anatomy

Fig. 5, 6
The Mouth

The Mouth

1. set of teeth
2. gum
3. teeth
   I. incisor
   II. canine, eye tooth
   III. premolar
   IV. molar
   V. baby or milk tooth
4. cavity
5. crown
6. root
7. cross-section of a tooth
   a. enamel
   b. dentin, ivory
   c. pulp
   d. nerves
8. filed teeth (ask names for the different shapes)
9. crack
10. chipped tooth
11. missing tooth: gap-toothed
12. tooth socket, alveolus

The Tongue

13. upper surface of tongue
14. palate
15. uvula
16. tonsils (palatal)
17. epiglottis
18. anterior pillar
19. lingual tonsil
20. V of the tongue
21. medial groove
22. papilla, taste buds
23. tip of the tongue

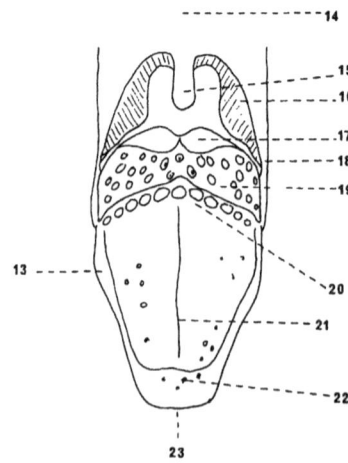

Fig. 5 The Mouth

Anatomy and Physiology/Animals and Plants 565

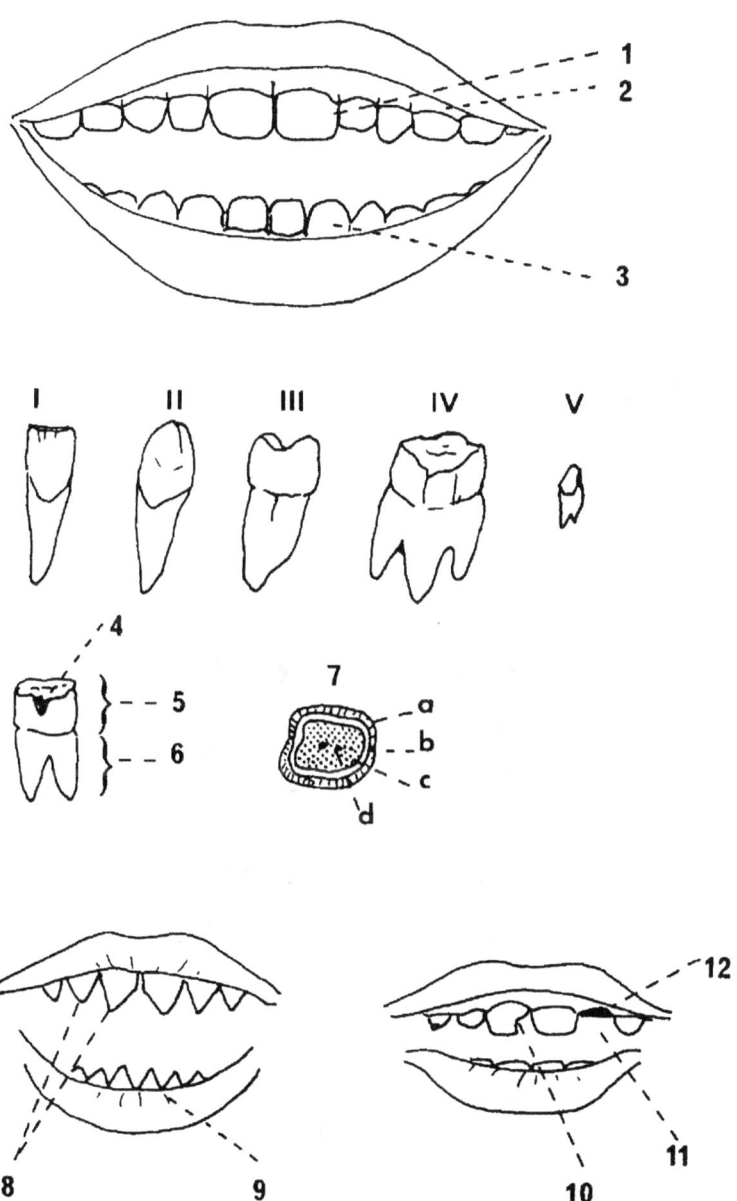

Fig. 6 The Mouth

External Anatomy

Fig. 7, 8
Physical Traits

Physical Traits

1. snub or flat nose
   large mouth
   thick lips
   drooping eyes
2. aquiline nose
   slanted eyes
   jutting chin
3. narrow temples
   jug ears
   round eyes
4. turned-up nose
   thick lower lip
   prominent cheekbones

Expressions

5. laughing, hilarity
6. weeping, peevish
   disposition,
   sobbing tears
7. smiling
   gaiety
   equanimity

Characteristics

9. moustache
10. necklace
11. goatee
12. sideburns

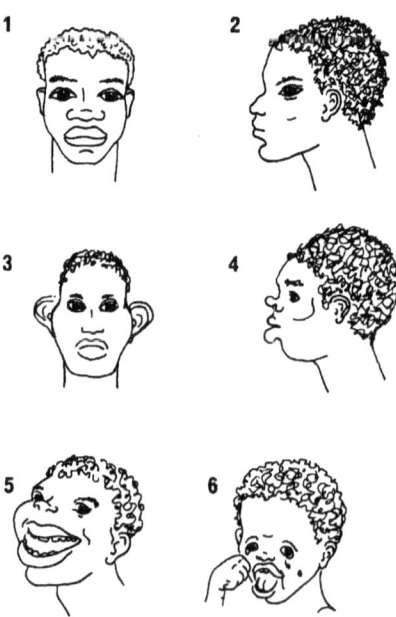

Fig. 7 Physical Traits

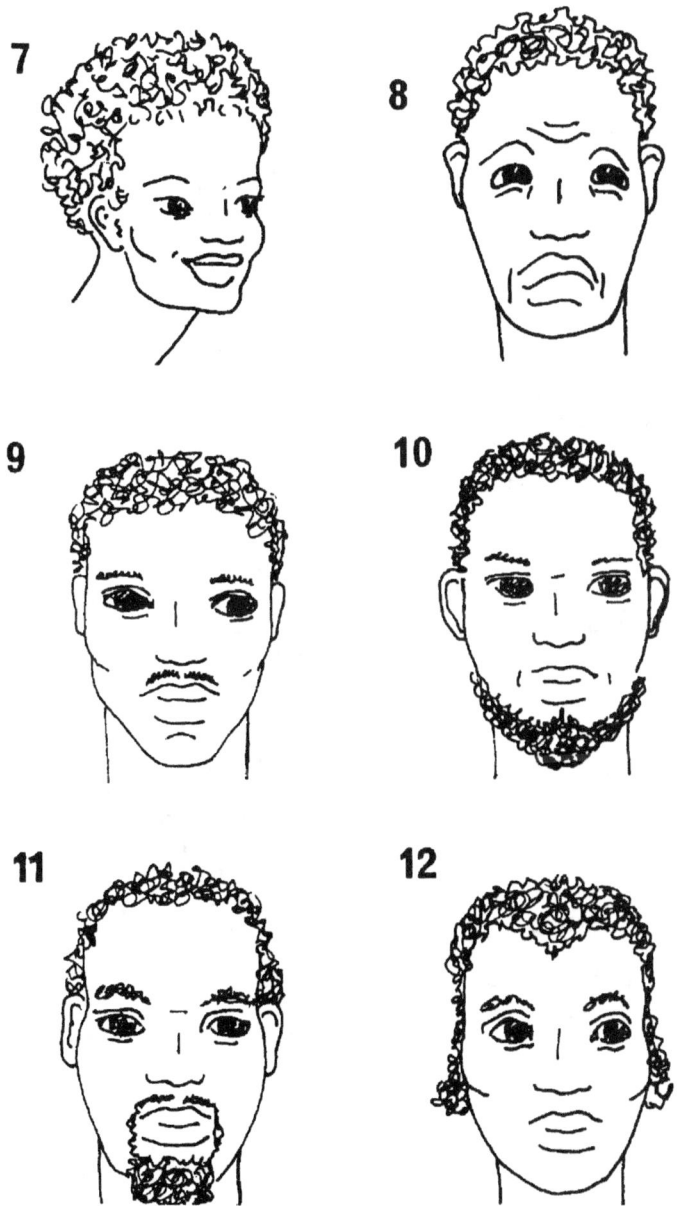

Fig. 8 Physical Traits

External Anatomy

Fig. 9, 10, 11
Foot and Hand

The Foot

A. Top of the foot
  1. little toe
  2. toes
  3. big toe

B. Sole of the foot
  4. toes
  5. ball of the foot, calloused part (forward callouses)
  6. arch, instep
  7. outer part of foot, calloused part (outer callouses)

C. Foot
  8. leg
  9. bump above the heel
  10. ankle
  11. heel
  12. instep
  13. top of big toe

D. Growths on the foot
  14. bunion
  15. corns, callouses

The Hand

E. Hand and back of the hand
  16. nail of little finger
  17. nail of little finger
  18. ring finger
  19. middle finger
  20. index finger
  21. thumb
  22. joint, knuckle
  23. knuckle
  24 a. fingernail
      b. half-moon, lunula
  25. tendon
  26. vein
  27. wrist
  28. wrist bone projection
  29. edge of the hand

F. Palm of the hand
  30. fingertip
      a. tactile part of the finger
  31. phalanges
      a. first phalanx
      b. second phalanx
      c. third phalanx
  32. ball of the thumb (thenareminence)
  33. crotch of the fingers
  34. membrane between fingers
  35. lines of the hand
      a. heart line
      b. head line
      c. life line
      d. fate line
  36. fingerprint
  37. fist
  38. sixth finger

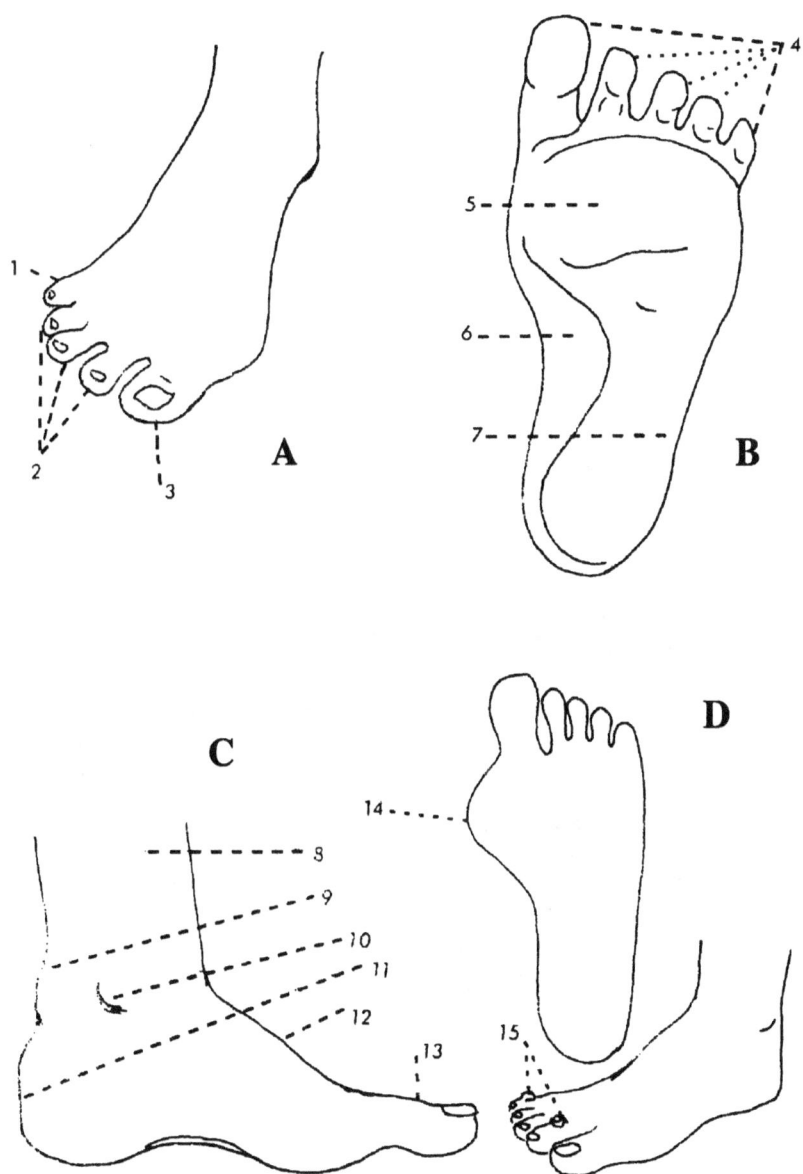

Fig. 9 The Foot

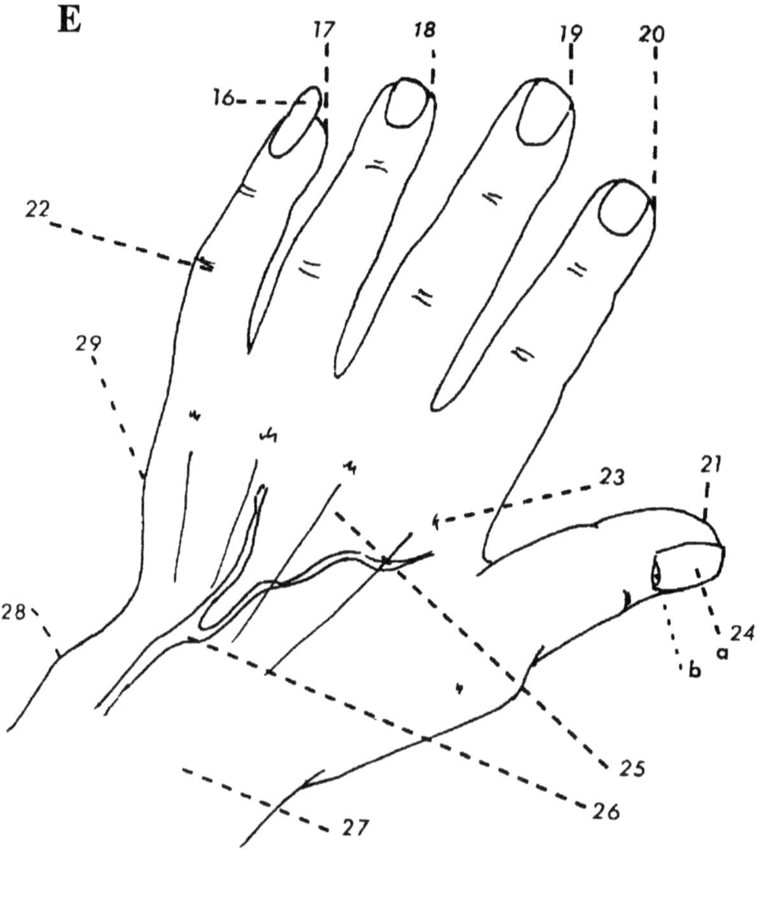

Fig. 10 The Hand

Anatomy and Physiology/Animals and Plants 571

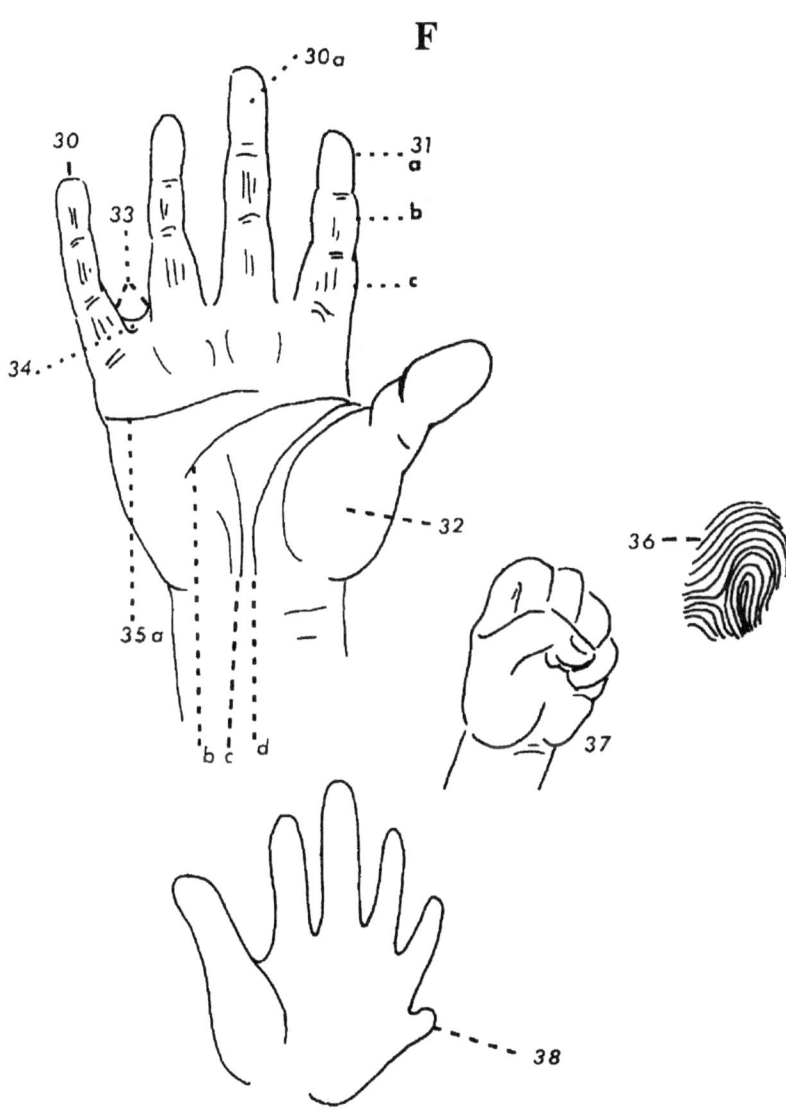

Fig. 11 The Hand

External Anatomy

Fig. 12
Conformations,
Deformities, Infirmities

A. short and skinny

B. short and fat

C. big and fat

D. tall and thin, slender

E. broad-shouldered, hefty

F. hunchbacked

G. hunchbacked and misshapen

H. giant

I. dwarf

J. bow-legged, bandy-legged

K. knock-kneed, wobbly-legged

L. lame

M. one-legged (one leg shorter than the other)

N. atrophied arm

O. dropped shoulder, lop-sided shoulders

P. armless from birth

Anatomy and Physiology/Animals and Plants 573

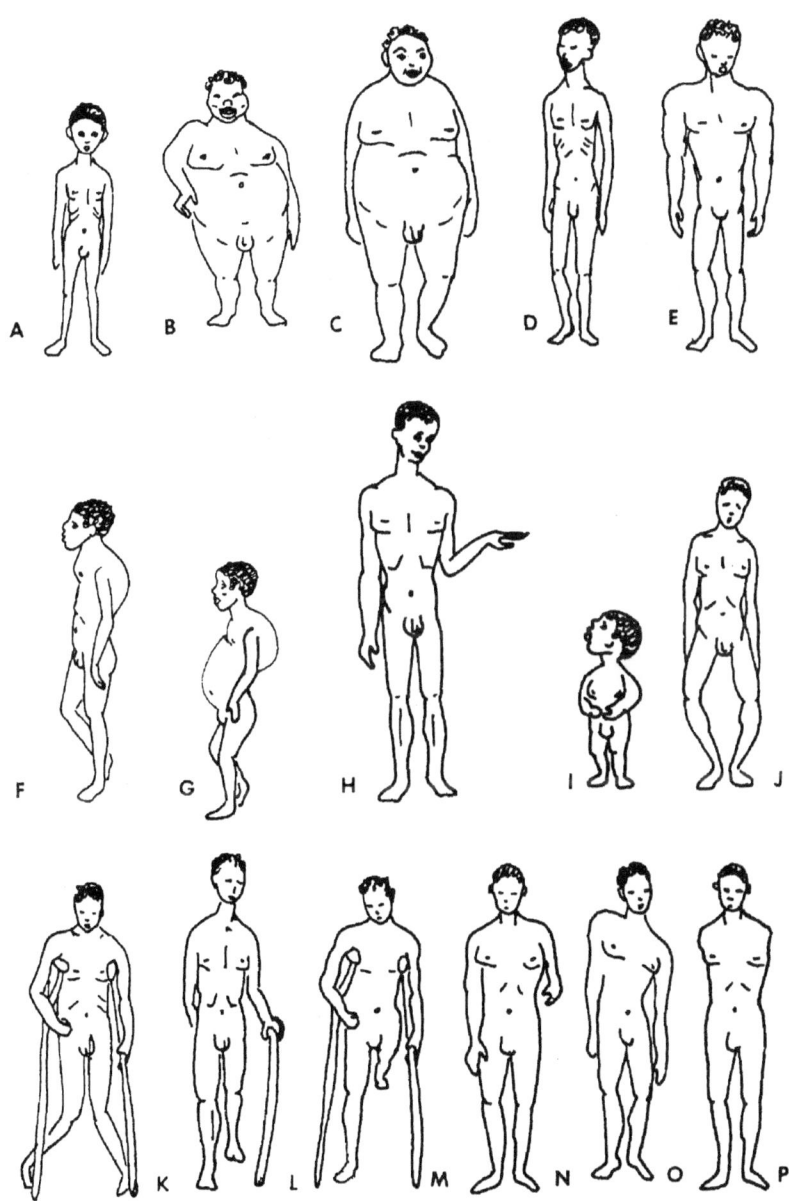

Fig. 12 Conformations and Deformities

External Anatomy

Fig. 13
Deformities or Accidental
Infirmities

1. polio of the leg
2. polio of the arm
3. elephantiasis of the leg
4. elephantiasis of the genitals
5. unilateral goiter
6. bilateral goiter
7. one-eyed (blind in one eye)
8. blind
9. legless
10. one-legged
11. varicose (veins)
12. one-armed
13. armless

Anatomy and Physiology

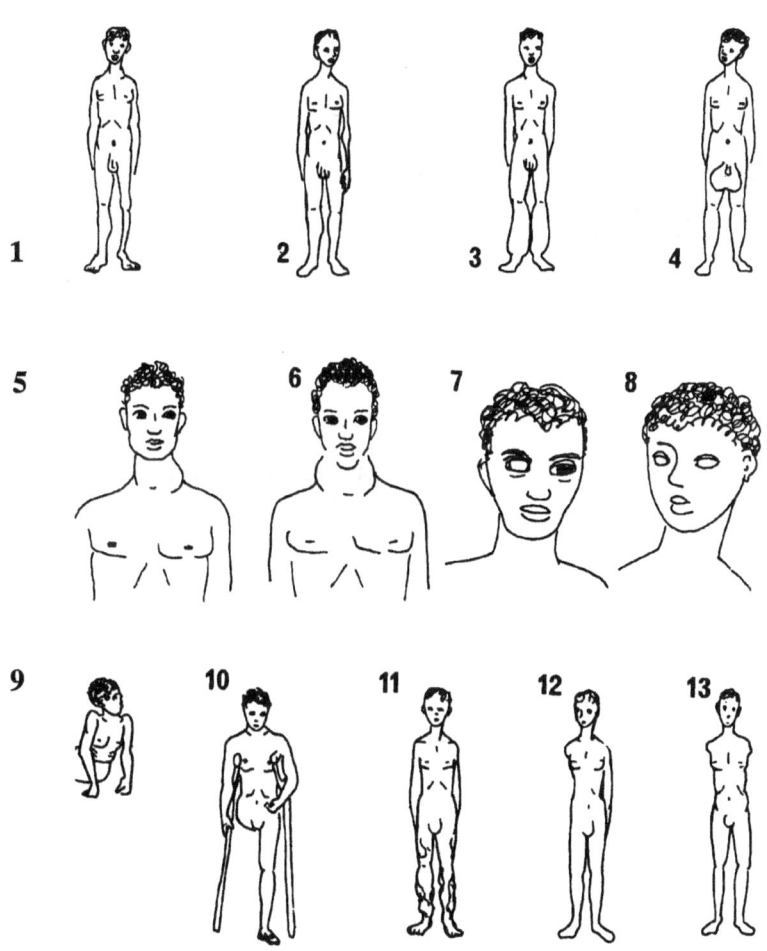

Fig. 13 Deformities

Internal Anatomy

Fig. 14
The Skeleton

A. Principle bones of the skeleton
  1. cranium (skull)
  2. mandible (lower jawbone)
  3. clavicle (collarbone)
  4. scapula (shoulder blade)
  5. manubrium (upper part of breastbone)
  6. sternum (breastbone)
  7. xiphoid process (lower part of breastbone)
  8. humerus
  9. radius
  10. ulna
  11. rib
  12. cost (rib) cartilage
  13. floating rib
  14. vertebral column
  15. pelvic bone
  16. iliac bone
  17. sacrum
  18. coccyx
  19. pubis
  20. ischium
  21. carpals
  22. metacarpals
  23. first phalanx
  24. second phalanx
  25. third phalanx
  26. femur (thighbone)
  27. head of femur
  28. patella (kneecap)
  29. tibia
  30. fibula
  31. tarsals
  32. metatarsals
  33. talus (ankle bone)
  34. calcaneus (heel bone)
  35. phalanges

Anatomy and Physiology

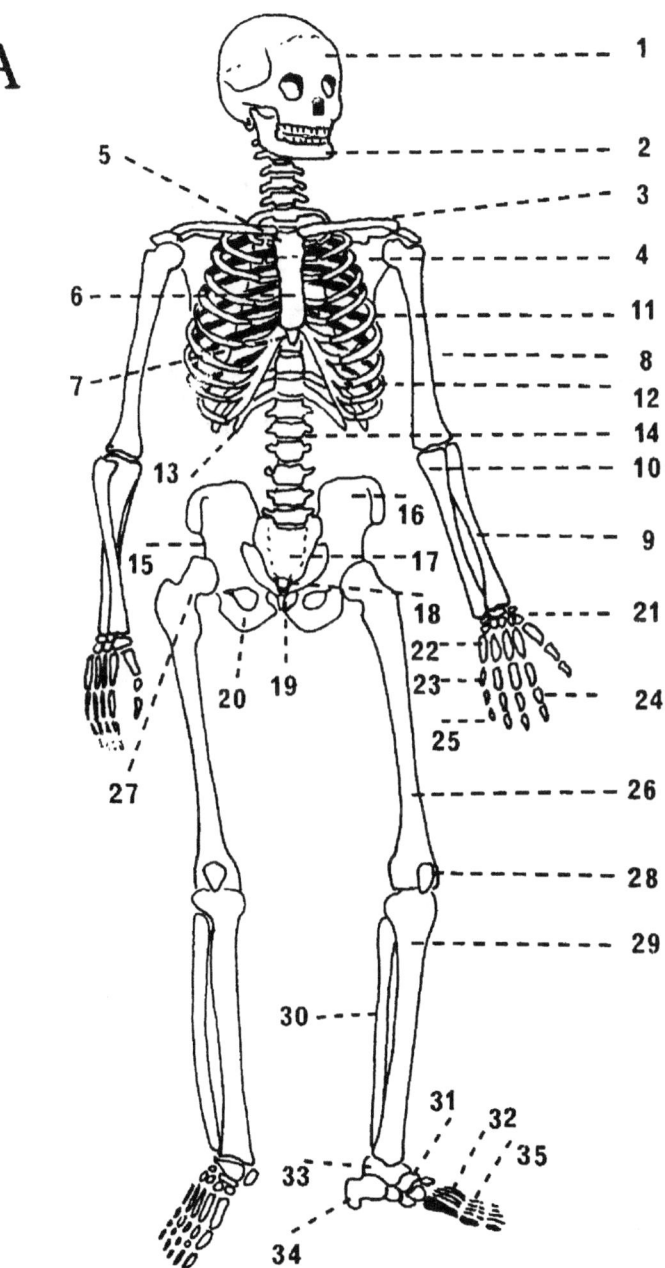

Fig. 14 The Skeleton

Internal Anatomy

Fig. 15
Bones of the Head

B. Bones of the skull and head

   1. frontal bone
   2. parietal bone (x2)
   3. temporal bone (x2)
   4. occipital bone
   5. mastoid process
   6. sphenoid bone
   7. malar bone
   8. maxilla
   9. mandible
  10. zygomatic process, arch
  11. articulating condyle
  12. suture line
  13. nose bones
  14. orbit

C. Articulation of the head with the vertebral column

   1. occipital bone
   2. condyle
   3. atlas
   4. axis (second vertebra)
   5. odontoid process

Anatomy and Physiology 579

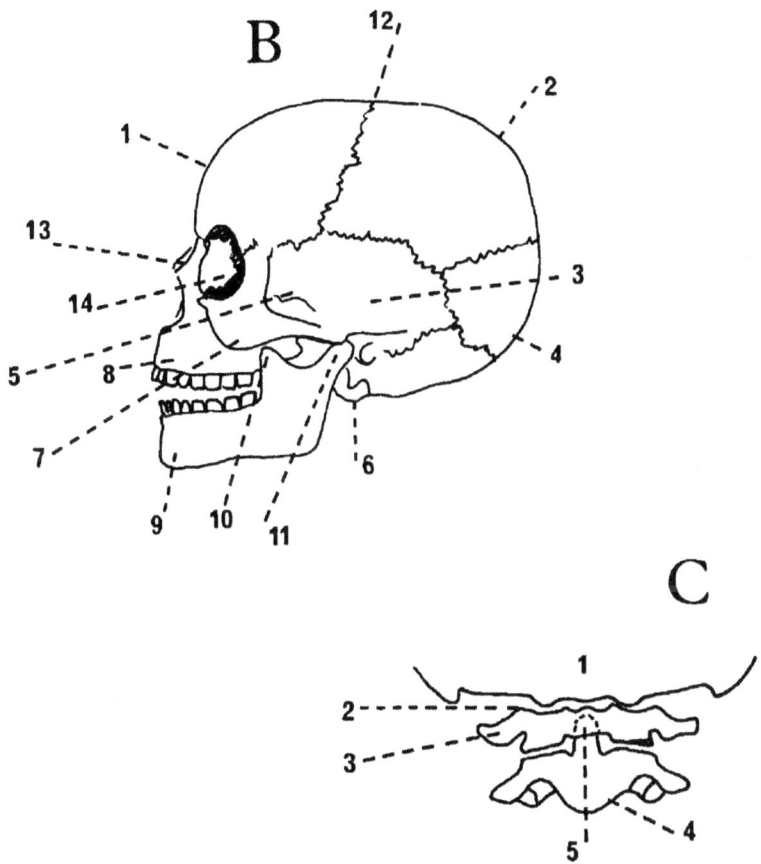

Fig. 15 Bones of the Head

Internal Anatomy

Fig. 16
Bones

D. Backbone

1. 7 cervical vertebrae
2. 12 thoracic vertebrae
3. 5 lumbar vertebrae
4. 5 sacral vertebrae, sacrum
5. 3 coccygeal vertebrae
6. coccyx

E. Detail of the vertebrae

1. spiny process of the vertebra
2. transverse process
3. articulating process
4. cerebral body
5. spinal canal
6. location of the spinal marrow
7. disc (elastic)

F. Parts of a bone

1. epiphysis
2. diaphysis
3. epiphysis
4-5. articulating surfaces

Anatomy and Physiology

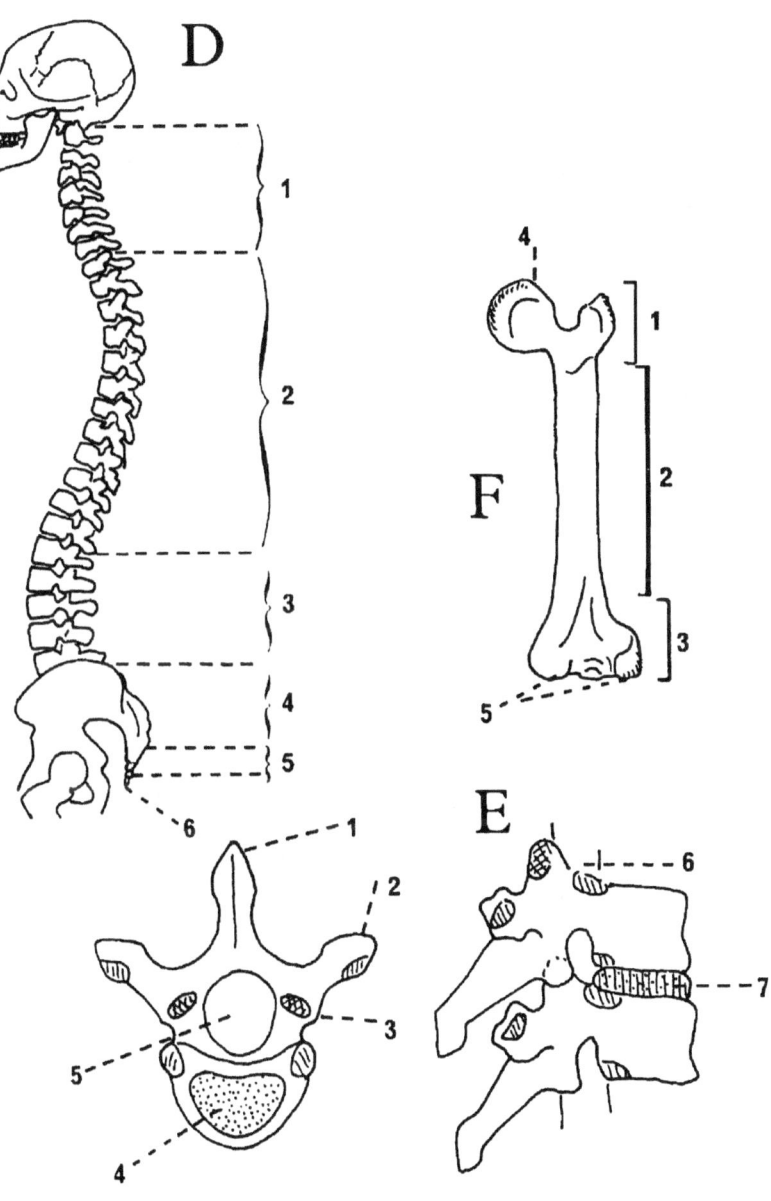

Fig. 16 Bones

Internal Anatomy

Fig. 17
The Digestive System

A. Digestive system

1. parotid gland, salivary glands
2. submaxillary and sublingual glands
3. esophagus
4. liver
5. gall bladder
6. cardia (opening of esophagus into stomach)
7. stomach
8. gastric juice
9. duodenum
10. pylorus (opening of stomach into intestine)
11. pancreas
12. large intestine
13. small intestine
14. appendix
15. rectum
16. anus

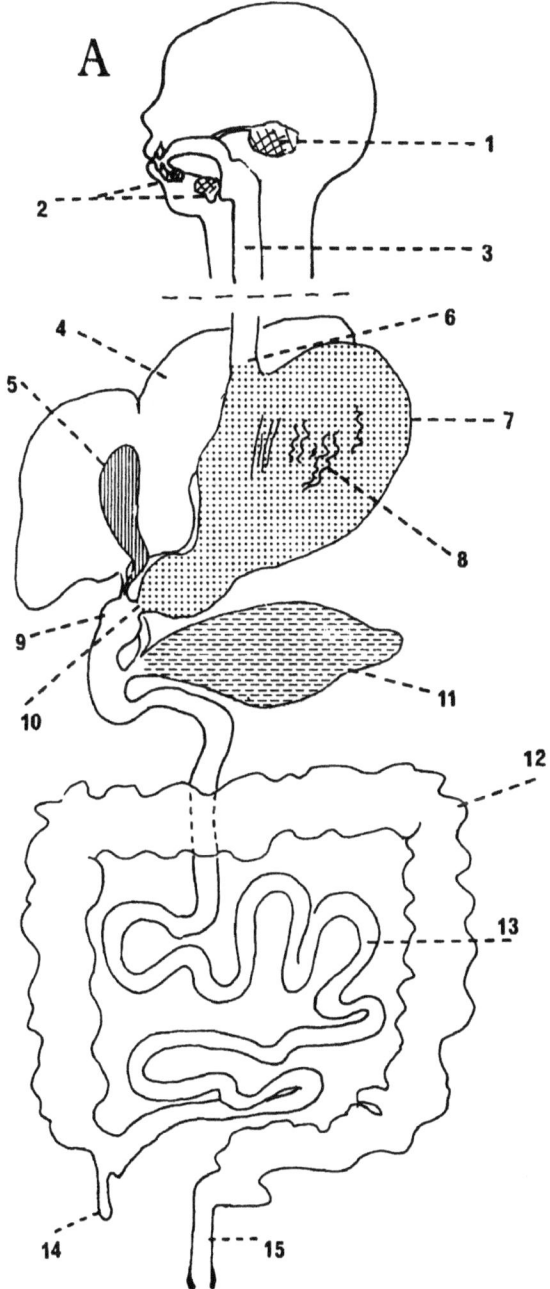

Fig. 17 The Digestive System

Internal Anatomy

Fig. 18
The Respiratory and Urinary Systems

B. Respiratory system

1. nasal cavity
2. pharynx
3. larynx
4. trachea, windpipe
5. aorta
6. pulmonary artery
7. pulmonary vein
8. rib (cross-section)
9. right lung (3 lobes)
10. left lung (2 lobes)
11. bronchiole
12. pulmonary alveoli
13. pleura
14. heart
15. diaphragm

C. Urinary system

1. diaphragm
2. adrenal glands
3. lower vena cava
4. right kidney
5. left kidney
6. right ureter
7. left ureter
8. aorta
9. bladder
10. urethra

Anatomy and Physiology

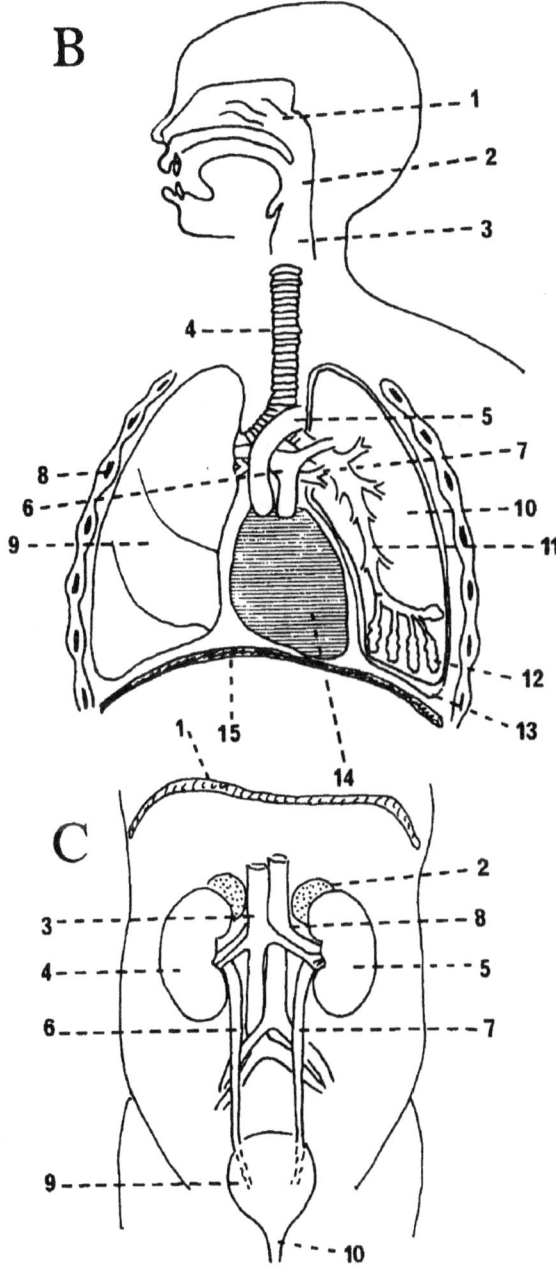

Fig. 18 The Respiratory and Urinary Systems

Internal Anatomy

Fig. 19
Internal Organs

A. The brain

1. cerebral hemispheres (left and right)
2. frontal lobe
3. parietal lobe
4. occipital lobe
5. interhemispheric fissure
6. cerebellum
7. spinal bulb
8. spinal cord

B. The heart

1. aorta
2. pulmonary artery
3. right auricle/atrium
4. fatty mass
5. right ventricle
6. left ventricle
7. left auricle/atrium
8. ventral fissure and coronary vessels

C. Female reproductive organs

1. ovaries
2. Fallopian tube
3. uterus
4. vagina
5. vulva

Anatomy and Physiology 587

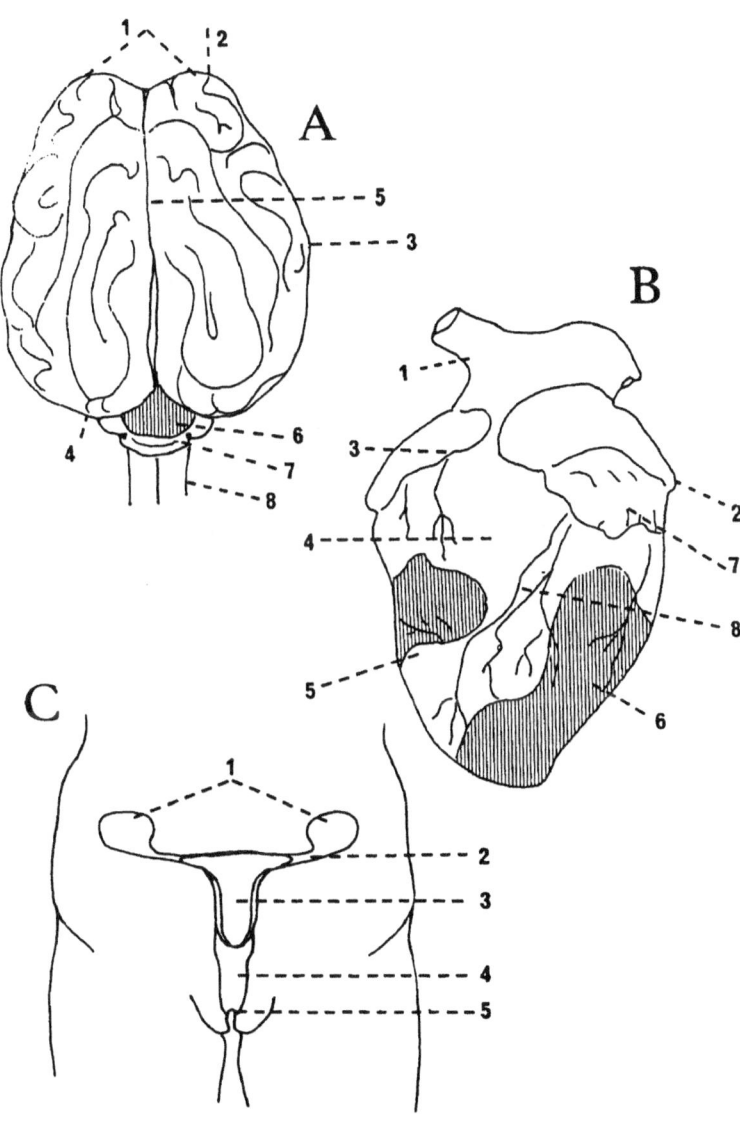

Fig. 19 Internal Organs

Internal Anatomy

Fig. 20
Internal Organs

D. The fetus in the uterus
   1. placenta
   2. amniotic fluid
   3. umbilical cord
   4. fetus
   5. bladder
   6. pubis
   7. backbone, vertebral column
   8. sacrum
   9. rectum
   10. coccyx
   11. cervical opening

E. Female genitals
   1. clitoris
   2. labia minora (small)
   3. urinary opening
   4. vestibule
   5. hymen
   6. labia majora (large)
   7. anus

F. Male genitals
   1. penis
   2. foreskin (prepuce)
   3. glans
   4. scrotum
   5. testicle
   6. seminal canal

Anatomy and Physiology

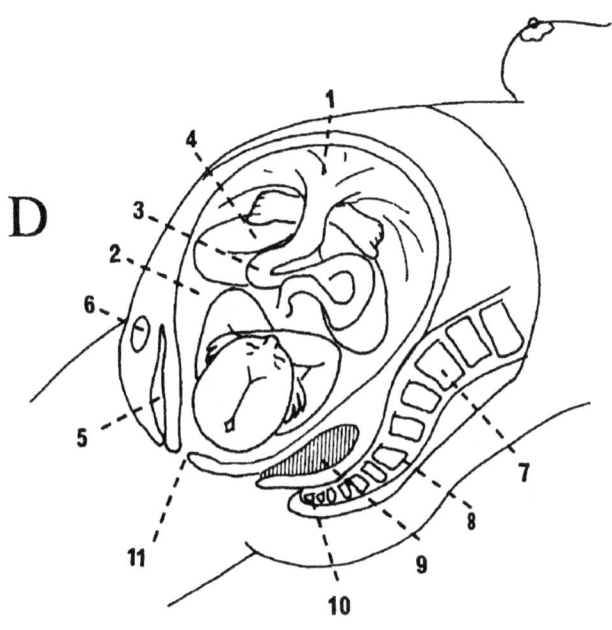

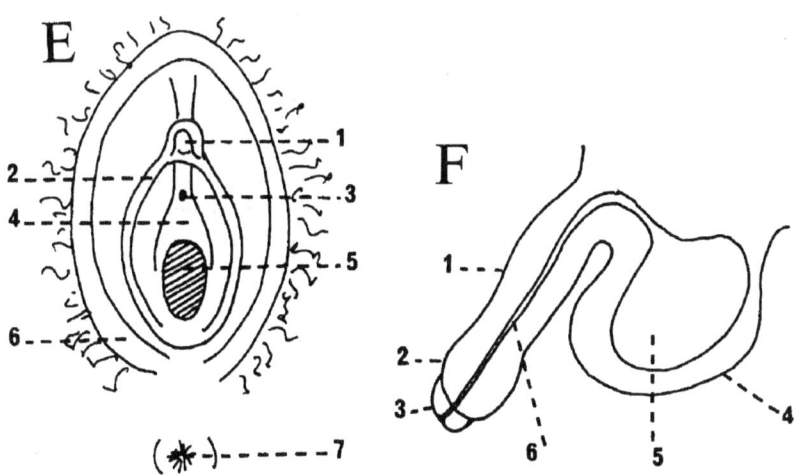

Fig. 20 Internal Organs

External and Internal Anatomy

Fig. 21
Mammals

External Anatomy

A. Herbivore

1. hollow horns
2. ear
3. forehead
4. bridge of the nose
5. tip of the nose
6. mouth
7. nostril
8. chin
9. cheek
10. lower jaw, jowl
11. neck
12. breast
13. shoulder
14. front leg
15. foreleg
16. knee
17. cannon bone
18. fetlock, pastern joint
19. hoof
20. side
21. belly
22. flank
23. stifle joint
24. leg (hind leg)
25. hock
26. tendon
27. wall of foot, pastern
28. pastern (joint), fetlock
29. tail
30. thigh
31. buttock
32. haunch
33. croup, rump, hindquarters
34. loin (small of the back)
35. back
36. withers
37. neck and shoulders / crest
38. axis, nape

F. Foot of herbivore with solid hoof: one digit–one hoof

1. underside of hoof
2. front view of hoof
3. side view of hoof

G. Foot of herbivore with cloven hoof: two digits–two hoofs

1. side view of hoof
2. front view of hoof
3. underside of hoof

Internal Anatomy

B. Stomach of ruminant

1. esophagus
2. rumen (1st stomach)
3. reticulum (2nd stomach)
4. omasum (3rd stomach)
5. abomasum, rennet stomach (4th stomach)
6. intestine

Anatomy and Physiology 591

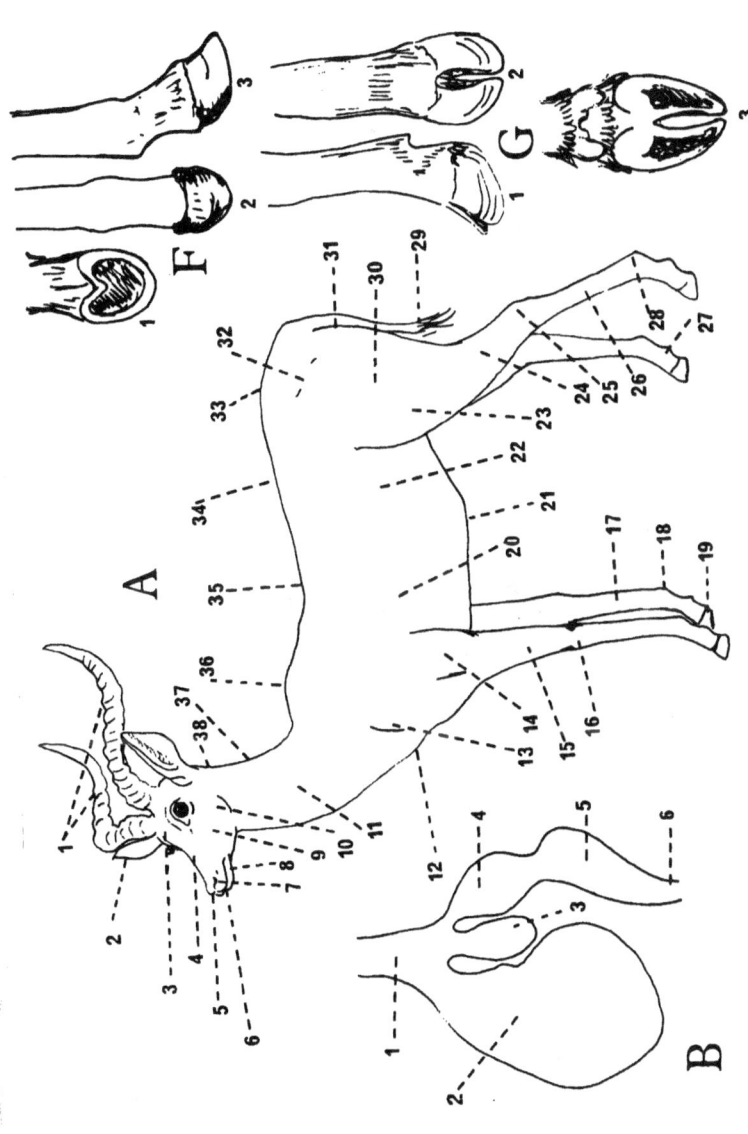

Fig. 21 Mammals

External Anatomy

Fig. 22
Mammals

C. Carnivore

1. spine
2. teats
3. whiskers

D. Paws of cat

1. pads on underside
2. retractable claws, extended

E. Hand and foot of monkey

1. 5 digits: 4 opposite the thumb
2. palm of hand
3. sole of foot

Fig. 22 Mammals

Anatomy and Physiology

External Anatomy

Fig. 23
Mammals

H. Female ruminant
  1. tail with switch (tuft)
  2. udder
  3. teat
  4. dewlap
  5. muzzle
  6. (hollow) horns
  7. cross section of hollow horn
  8. horn
  9. core of horn

I. Rhinoceros
  1. solid horns

J. Giraffe
  1. solid horns

K. Elephant
  1. trunk
  2. tusks

L. Warthog
  1. tusks
  2. warts

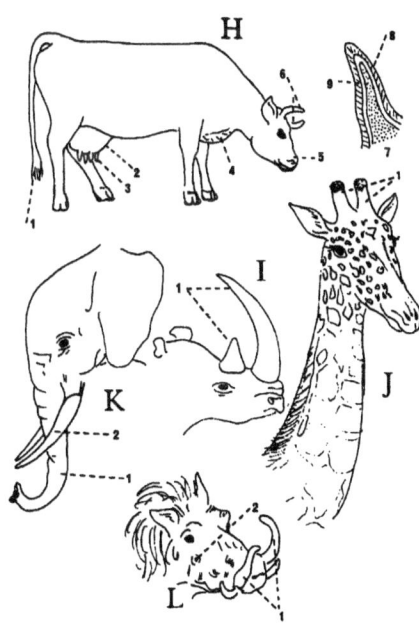

Fig. 23 Mammals

External Anatomy

Fig. 24
Mammals

M. Wild ass / donkey
1. mane
2. muzzle

N. Lion
1. mane
2. fang (canine tooth)
3. mouth

O. River hog
1. muzzle
2. snout

P. Dog
1. muzzle

2. nose
3. chops

Q. Mouse
1. hairless tail

R. Bat
1. wings
2. membranes

S. Monkey
1. hand
2. mantle (or cape) of hair
3. foot
4. side whiskers
5. buttock callouses

Anatomy and Physiology

Fig. 24 Mammals

External Anatomy

Fig. 25
Birds

A. Parts of the body

1. head
2. eye
3. circular eyelids
4. beak, bill
5. cere
6. nostril
7. chin
8. moustache
9. cheek
10. pteryla, feather tracts (head streaks)
11. nape (of neck)
12. back
13. breast
14. wing
15. coverts
16. breast
17. wing feathers, quill feathers
18. underside of tail
19. tail
20. tail feathers
21. upper tail-coverts
22. rump
23. hollow shaft
24. feather
25. filaments and barbules
26. down

B. Special features of the head

1. comb
2. earlet
3. wattle
4. aigrette or crest, tuft

Anatomy and Physiology

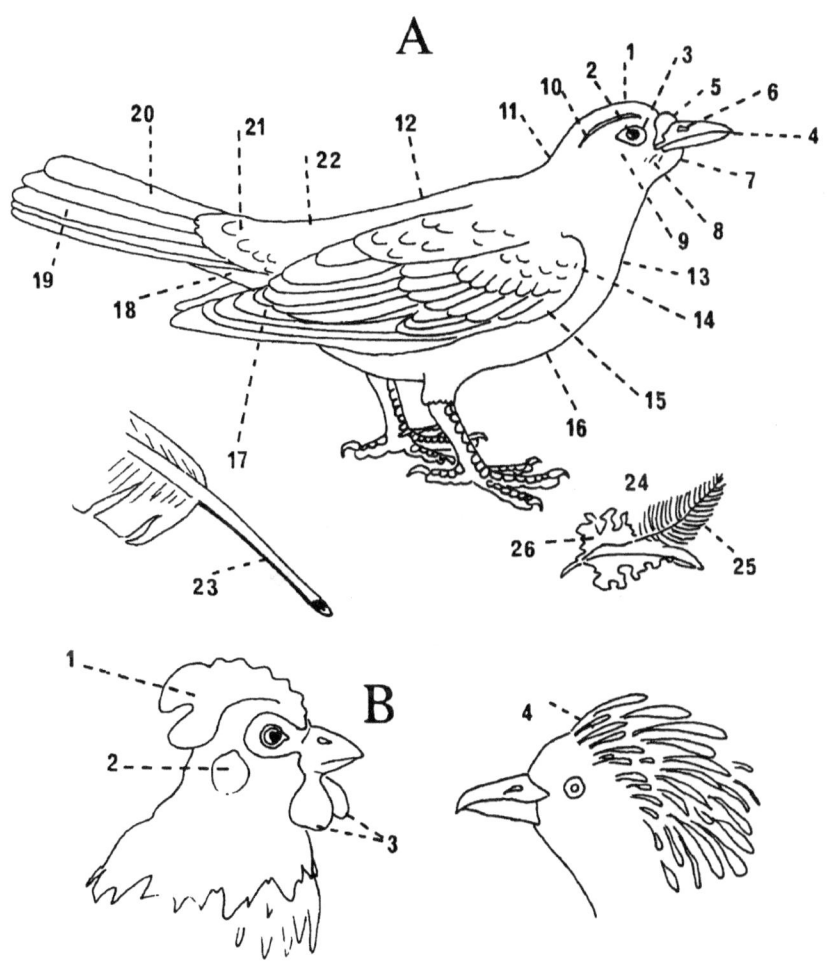

Fig. 25 Birds

External Anatomy

Fig. 26
Birds

C. Feet
1. spur
2. claws
3. scales
4. toes
5. long claw
6. webbed foot
7. foot of wading bird
8. lobate or leaflife foot (grebe)
9. sparrow's foot or foot of perching bird
10. talons
11. scalloped foot
12. foot of running bird

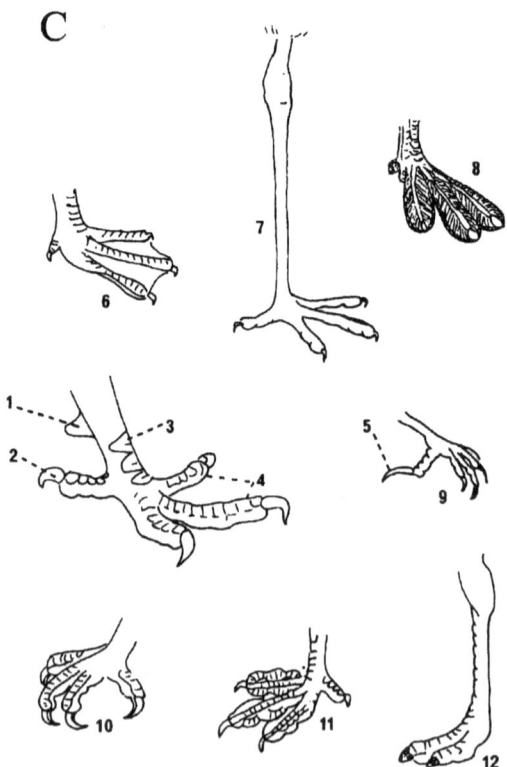

Fig. 26 Birds

Anatomy and Physiology

Internal Anatomy

Fig. 27
Birds

D. Female bird
  1. brain
  2. spinal cord
  3. sebaceous gland
  4. nostril
  5. trachea, windpipe
  6. lungs
  7. tongue
  8. esophagus
  9. crop
  10. supplementary ventricle (gastric stomach)
  11. gizzard (masticatory stomach)
  12. pancreas
  13. gall bladder
  14. liver
  15. intestine
  16. ovary
  17. egg in formation
  18. cloaca
  19. heart

E. Egg
  1. small end
  2. large end
  3. hard shell
  4. shell membrane
  5. egg white or albumen
  6. yolk
  7. germinal disc
  8. chalaza, treadle
  9. air chamber

F. (Air) Lungs
  1. trachea
  2. lung
  3. bronchi
  4. air sac

G. Skeleton
  1. forked clavicle (or collar bone)
  2. sternum (breastbone) with 'wishbone'
  3. fused vertebrae, 'carcass'
  4. digits

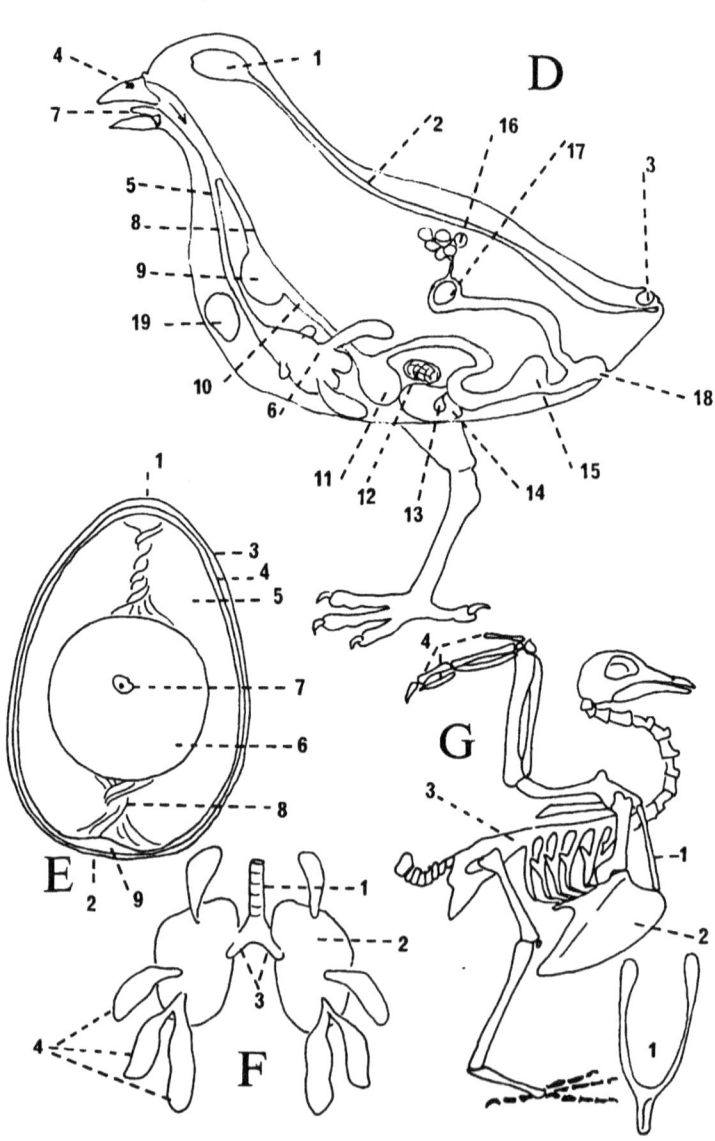

Fig. 27 Birds

Anatomy and Physiology

External Anatomy

Fig. 28
Amphibians and Fish

A. Fish
1. dorsal fin
2. lateral line
3. eye
4. nostril
5. mouth
6. barbels, whiskers
7. gills
8. pectoral fin
9. pelvic fin
10. anus
11. anal fin
12. scale
13. caudal fin

B. Young fish (fry)

C. Amphibian
1. gill
2. voice pouch
3. front leg
4. hind leg
5. wart (pustule)

D. Tadpole

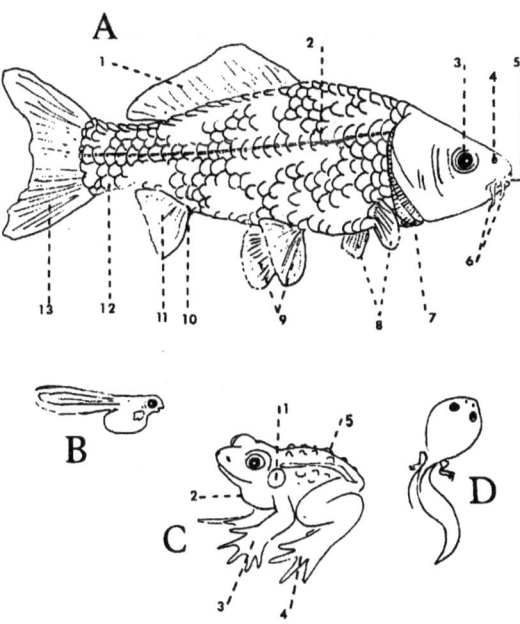

Fig. 28 Amphibians and Fish

External Anatomy

Fig. 29
Amphibians and Reptiles

E. Snake

F. Venom apparatus
  1. venom sac gland
  2. slit pupil
  3. fang
  4. venom
  5. forked tongue
  6. muscles

G. Turtle
  1. shell, carapace
  2. scale

H. Crocodile
  1. scale

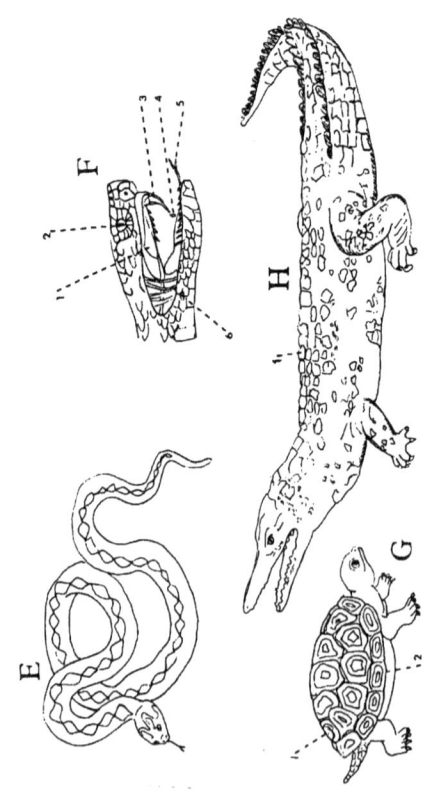

Fig. 29 Amphibians and Reptiles

Anatomy and Physiology

External Anatomy

Fig. 30
Invertebrataes

A. Centipedes *(Chilopoda: scolopendra)*
B. Worms
C. (Bivalve) mollusks
   (Lamellibranchia)
D. Spiders *(Arachnida)*
E. Spider's web

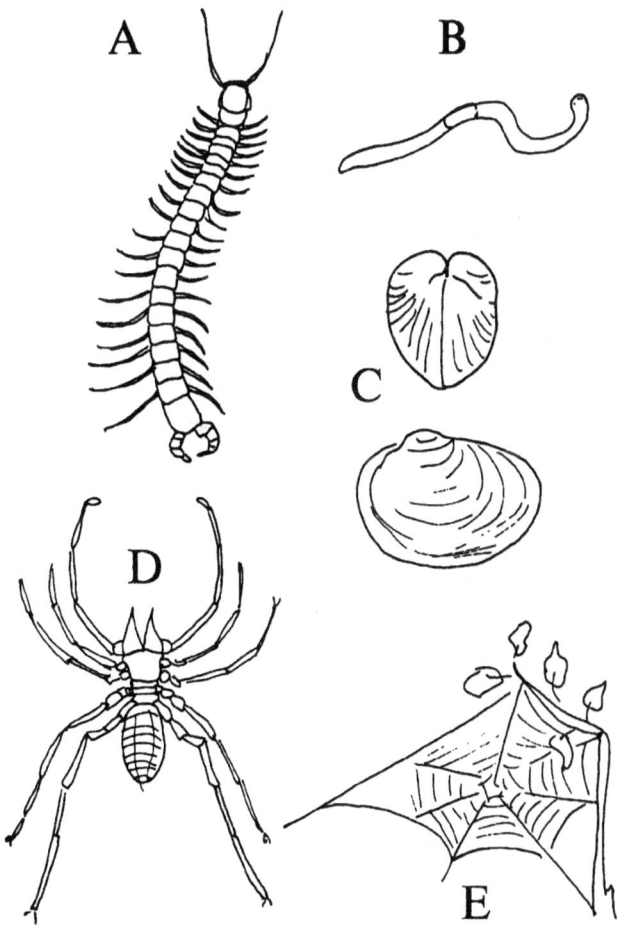

Fig. 30 Invertebrates

External Anatomy

Fig. 31
Invertebrates

F. Millipedes (Diplopods: galley slugs)
G. Crustaceans
H. Scorpions *(Arachnida)*
I. (Univalve) mollusks (Gastropods)
  1. shell
  2. anus
3. spiracle, air hole
4. foot
5. mantle
6. eye
7. eyestalk
8. feeler
9. mouth
10. operculum

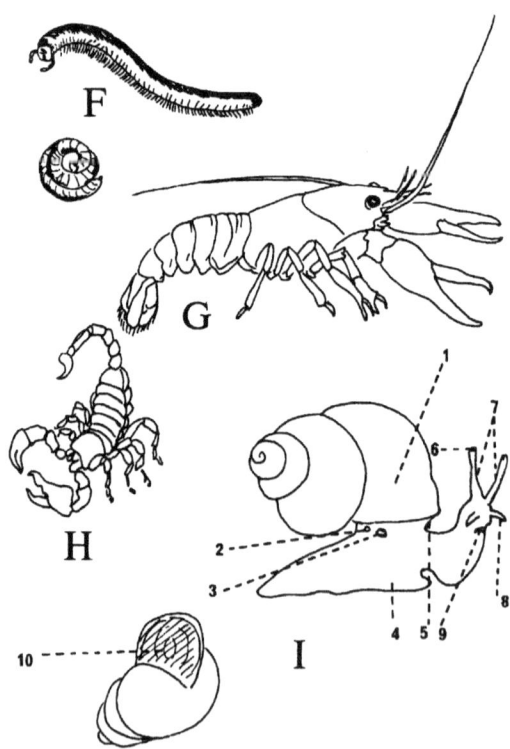

Fig. 31 Invertebrates

Anatomy and Physiology

External Anatomy

Fig. 32
Insects

A. External morphology (Bee type)

1. head
2. thorax
3. abdomen
4. leg
5. antenna (bent/elbowed)
6. compound eye (faceted)
7. ocelli (simple eyes)
8. sucking mouth parts
9. labrum (upper lip)
10. mandible
11. maxilla
12. tongue
13. labium (lower lip)
14. anterior wing
15. vein
16. posterior wing
17. sting(er)
18. spiracles, air holes
19. tarsus
20. tibia
21. femur
22. trochanter
23. anterior, front coxa (procoxa)
24. middle coxa (mesocoxa)
25. posterior, hind coxa (metacoxa)
26. claws
27. pollen brush
28. empty pollen basket

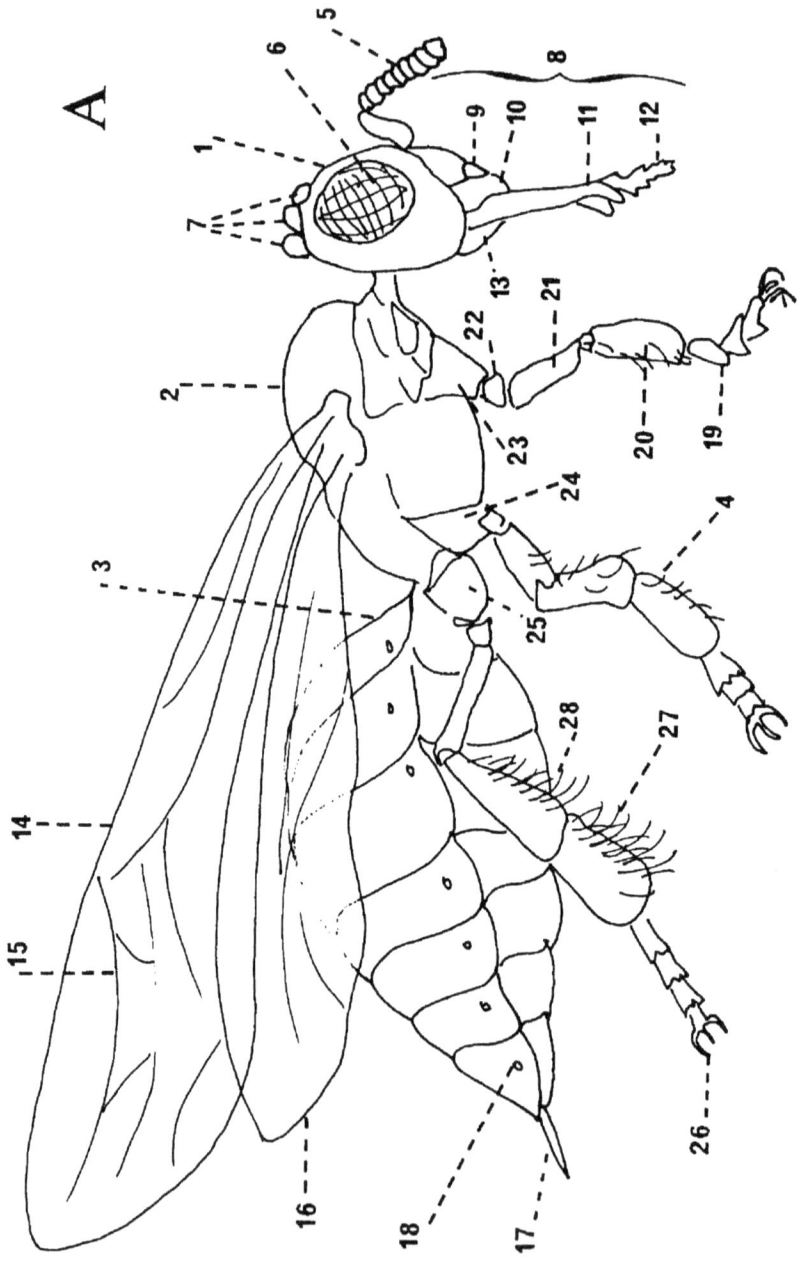

Fig. 32 Insects

Anatomy and Physiology

External Anatomy

Fig. 33
Insects

B. Another example: Beetle
(*Histeridae*)(dorsal view)

1. prothorax
2. scutellum
3. elytral joint
4. wing cover
5. propygidium
6. pygidium

C. Piercing mouth parts
(Mosquito)

1. palpus
2. piercing stylets
3. labium

D. Chewing mouth parts–Scarab beetle
(*Scarabaeidae*)

1. palpus
2. grinding mandibles
3. labrum (lip)

E-F. Grasshoppers
(*Orthoptera*)-male and female

1. drill or ovipositor

G. Life stages of certain
lepidopterans

1. caterpillar
2. cocoon
3. pupa
4. adult butterfly

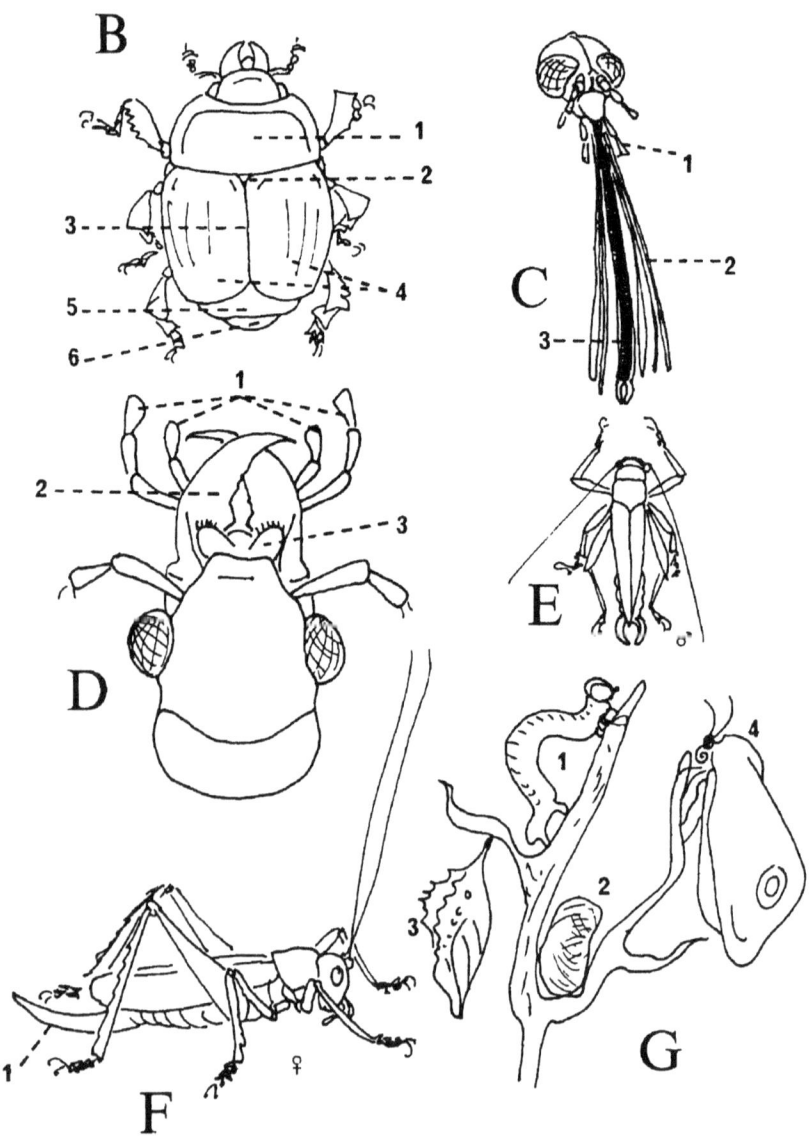

Fig. 33 Insects

Anatomy and Physiology 609

Seed-bearing plants

Fig. 34
Principal types of Leaves

Structure

1. simple leaf
2. composite leaf
3. needle (leaf)
4. scale leaf

Position on the stem

5. opposite leaves
6. alternate leaves

Base

7. tapered
8. rounded
9. truncate

Tip

10. pointed
11. mucronate
12. obtuse
13. truncate

Edge, margin

14. smooth
15. wavy
16. ciliated
17. scalloped, notched
18. sawtooth
19. sinuate
20. toothed

Shape

21. pinnate
22. even pinnate
23. odd-pinnate
24. bipinnate
25. palmate
26. digitate
27. lanceolate
28. ovate, oval
29. elliptic
30. oblong
31. obovate
32. oblanceolate

Peduncle

33. long peduncle
34. short peduncle
35. sessile
36. amplexicaul
37. decurrent, enveloped (sheathed)
38. perfoliate

Structure of the leaf

a. central vein
b. secondary vein
c. blade, limb
d. leafstalk, petiole, peduncle

**Principal types of inflorescence
(flower arrangement)**

39. cyme
40. raceme, cluster
41. panicle
42. umbel
43. corymb
44. spike

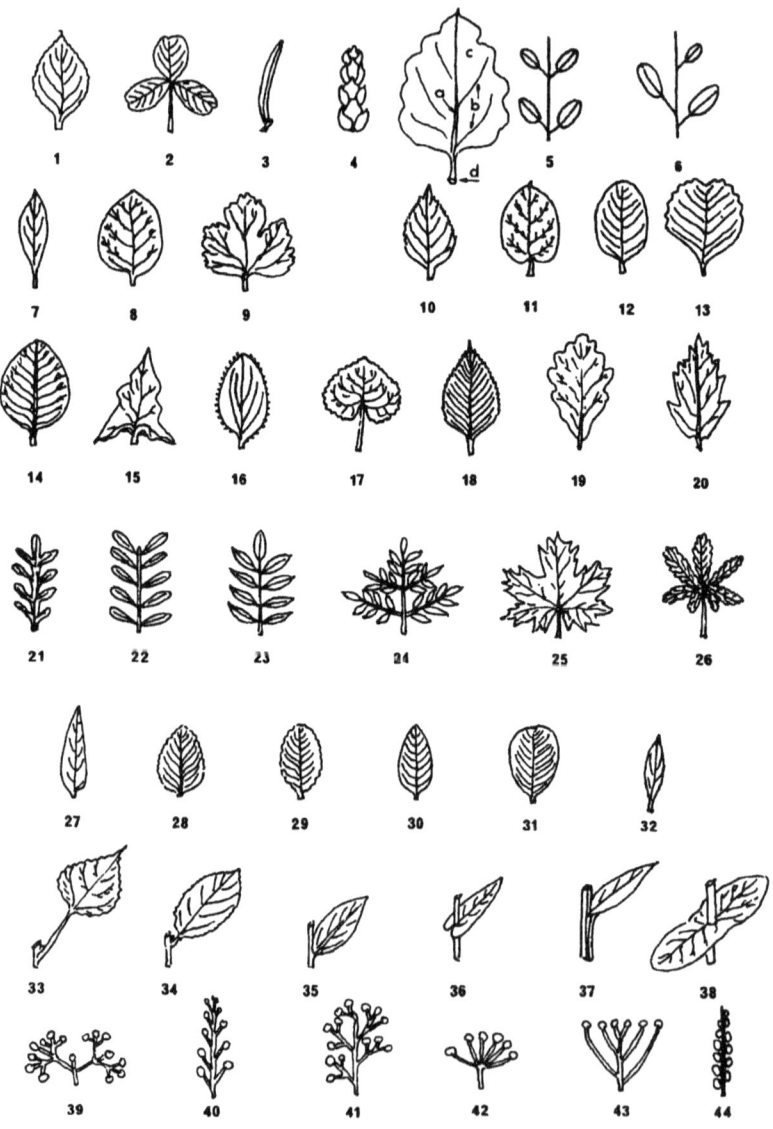

Fig. 34 Leaves

Anatomy and Physiology

Seed-bearing plants

Fig. 35
Flower

Reproductive organs

A. Cross-section of a flower

1. pistil
2. pollen grain
3. stigma
4. style
5. pollen tube (connected to the oosphere)
6. ovary
7. oosphere
8. ovule
9. secondary nucleus
10. chalaza
11. filament
12. casing pod, anther
13. pollen grains
14. stamen
15. petal
16. sepal
17. bud
18. fully open flower

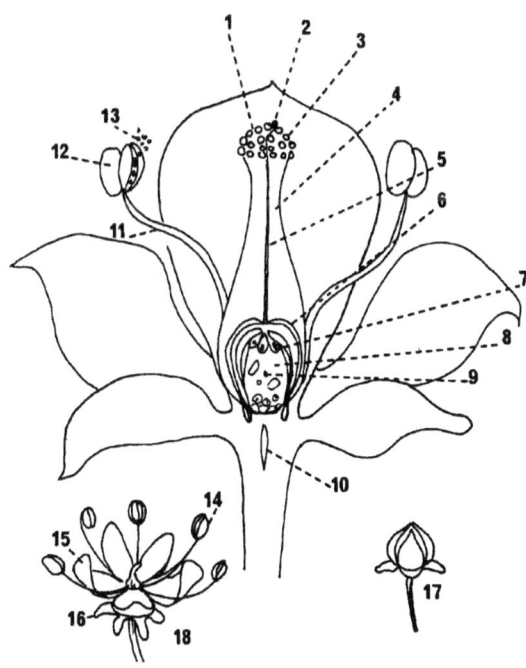

Fig. 35 Flower

Seed-bearing plants

Fig. 36
Diagram of a Plant

B. Stem, stalk

    1. terminal bud
    2. axillary bud
    3. (small) branch
    4. stipules
    5. composite leaf
    6. internode
    7. simple leaf
    8. node
    9. stem
    10. neck, annulus / (growth) ring

C. Root

    11. main root
    12. secondary roots
    13. cap (of hairs)
    14. absorptive hairs

Germination

D. Two types of seeds germinating = two types of sprouts

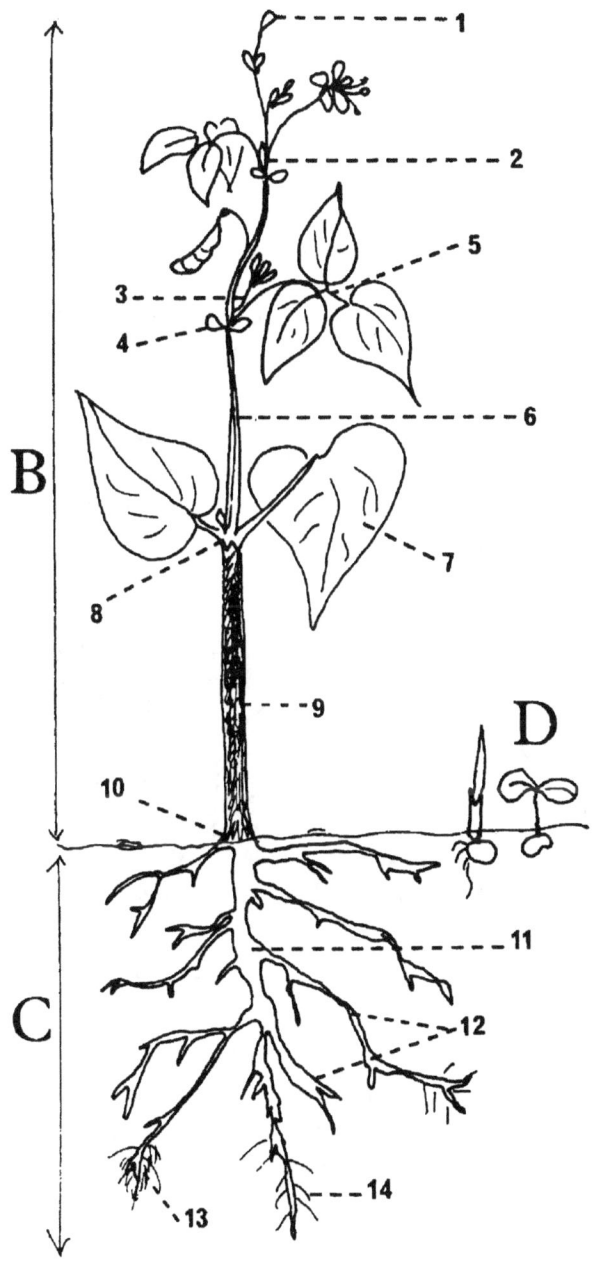

Fig. 36 Diagram of a Plant

Seed-bearing plants

Fig. 37
Types of Roots

1. tuber (manioc)
2. tuber (potato)
3. bulb (amaryllis)

4. tap-root (carrot)
5. stolons, runners (sweet potato)

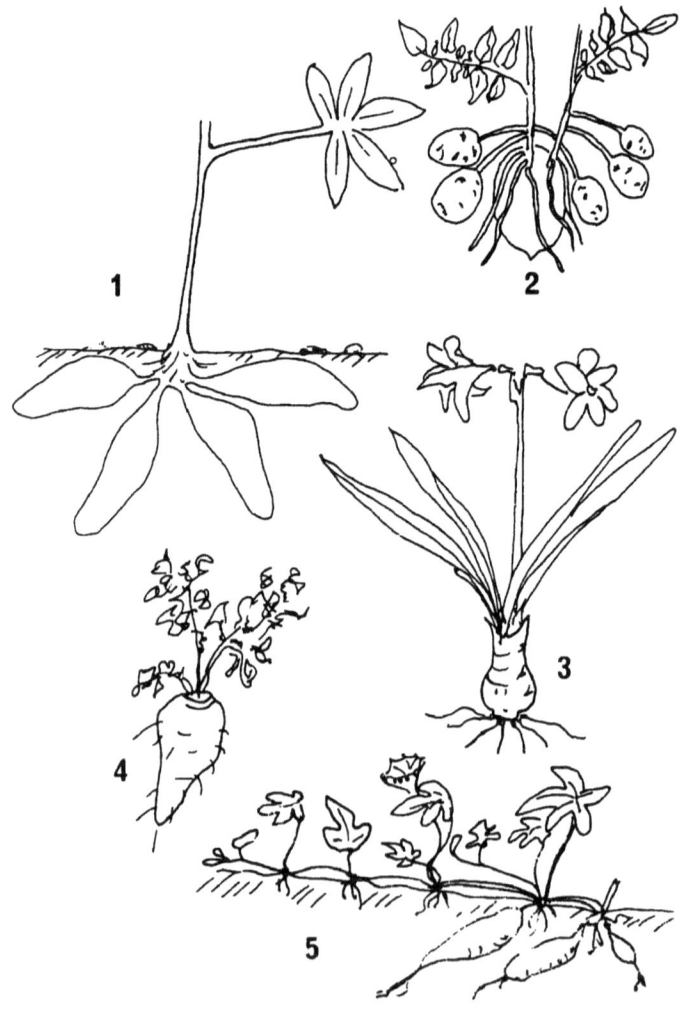

Fig. 37 Roots

Anatomy and Physiology

Seed-bearing plants

Fig. 38
Seed-bearing Plants

6. rhizome
7. aerial roots of climbing plants
8. grasses (gramineous, rye or barley type): root and stem
8.1 node
8.2 internode
8.3 leaf blade
8.4 ribbon leaf
8.5 ears (spikes)
8.6 spikelet
8.7 hair
9. Araceous plants (flower)
9.1 spatha
9.2 spadix
10. Araceous plants (arrow-shaped or lanceolate leaves and tubers)

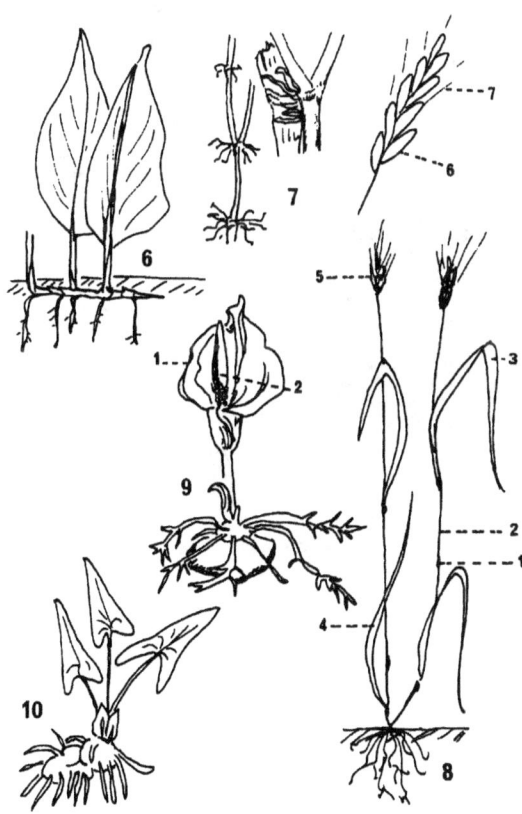

Fig. 38 Seed-bearing Plants

Seed-bearing plants

Fig. 39
Types of Fruits

A. Different types of fruit

1. seedy fruit contained in a pod
2. fleshy fruit with small seeds (pits)
3. capsule fruit: seedy fruit contained in a shell
4. cluster of fruits
5. three types of winged fruits
6. parachute seed or tuft

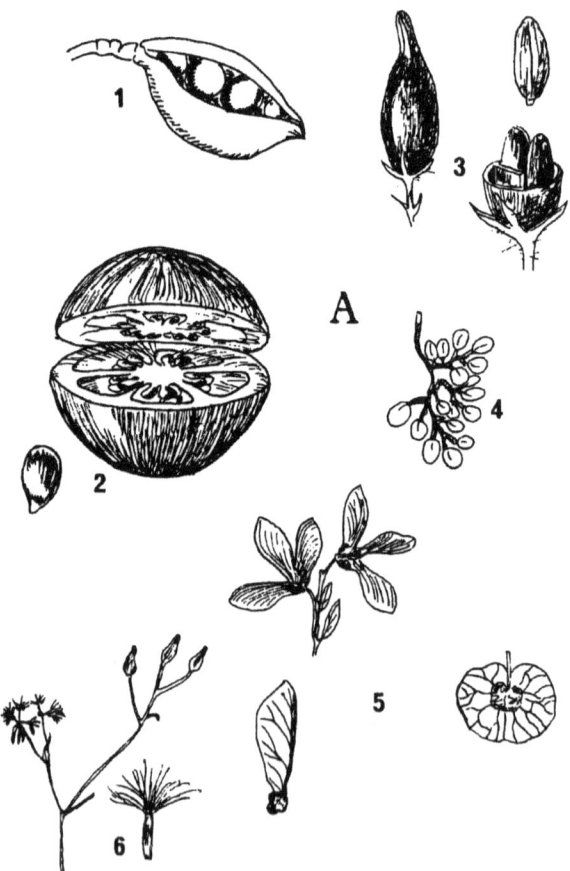

Fig. 39 Fruits

Anatomy and Physiology

Seed-bearing plants

Fig. 40
Supported Plants

B. Parasitic plant (lives at the expense of a tree)

C. Epiphytic plant (lives on a tree without doing it harm)

D. Climbing plant (around the trunk)

E. Tendrils

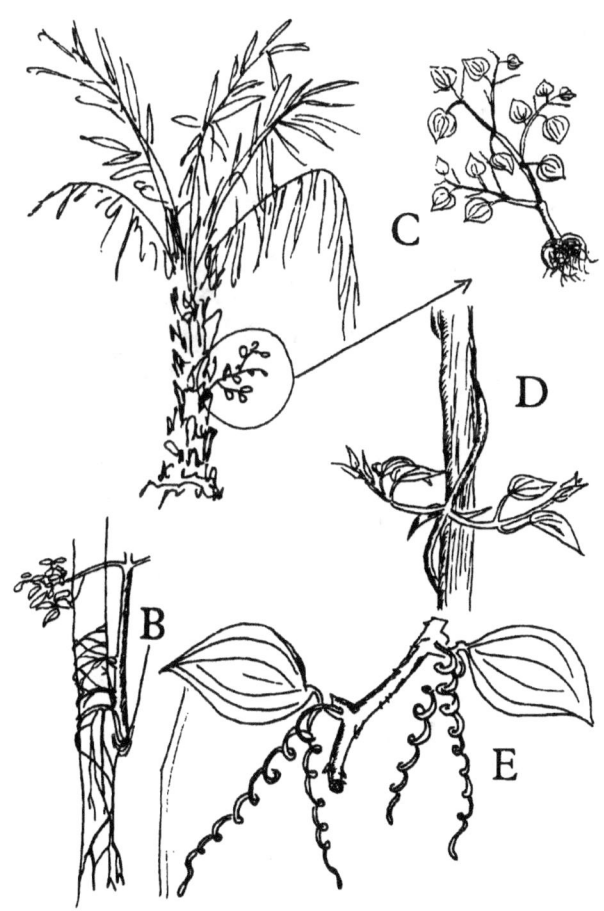

Fig. 40 Supported Plants

Seed-bearing plants

Fig. 41
Trees

A. General diagram of a tree

1. treetop
2. high branches
3. low branches
4. trunk or bole
5. foot: roots forming buttresses
6. healthy branches
7. dead branches
8. foliage

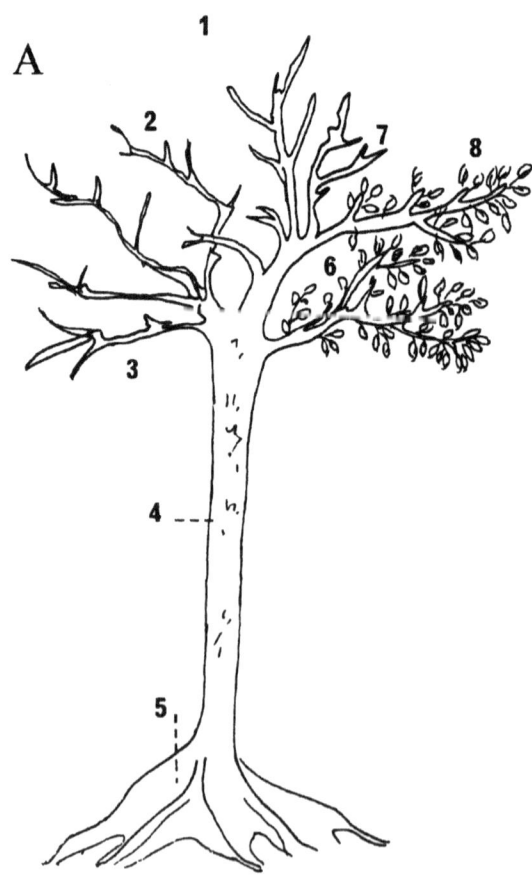

Fig. 41 Tree

Anatomy and Physiology

Seed-bearing plants

Fig. 42
Trees

B. Aerial roots

C. Transverse cross-section of the trunk

   1. bark
   2. liber, bast
   3. sapwood
   4. heartwood
   5. pith, core

D. Lengthwise cross-section of the trunk

   1. knot in the wood

Widely-used trees

E. Banana tree (whole plant)

   1. bulb
   2. sheath
   3. stipe
   4. spine
   5. jagged leaf
   6. new leaf
   7. young shoot
   8. leaf still rolled up
   9. dry leaf

F. Banana tree (flower and fruits)

   1. flower stem
   2. hand of bananas
   3. inflorescence
   4. bracts
   5. male bud

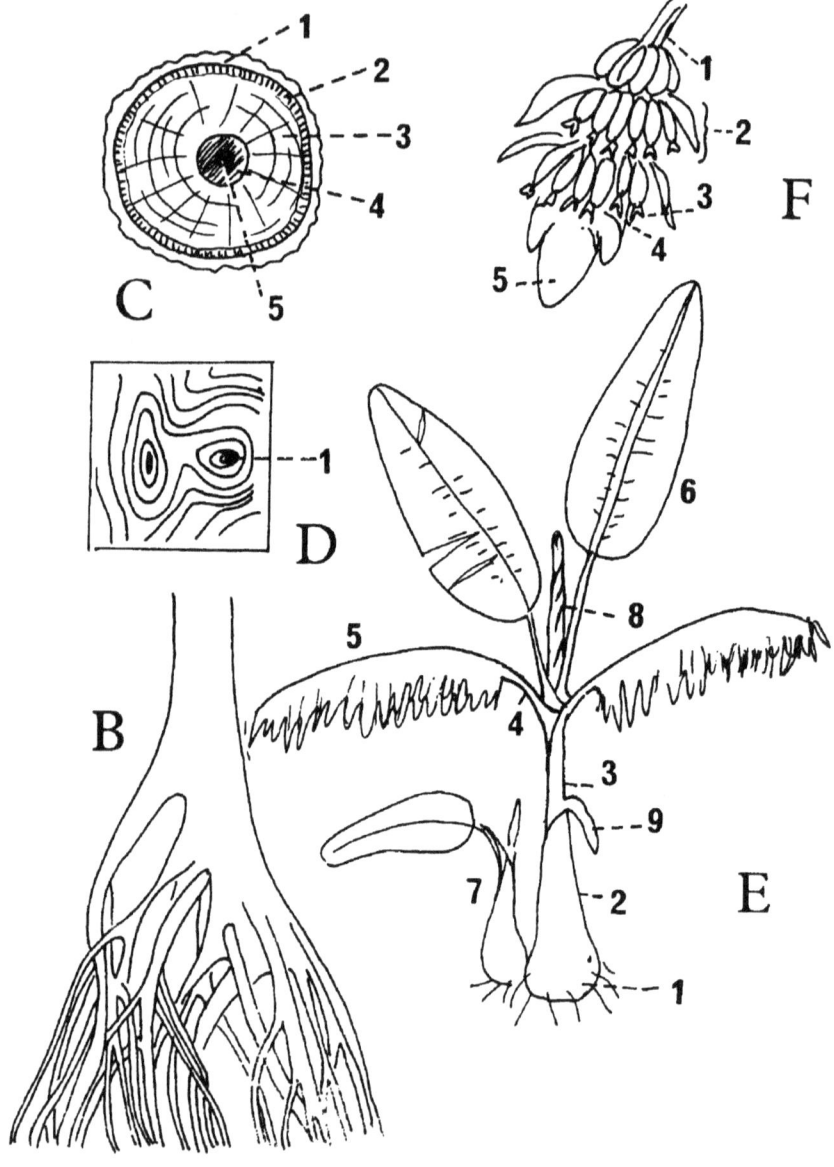

Fig. 42 Trees

Anatomy and Physiology

Seed-bearing plants

Fig. 43
Widely-used trees: Oil palm

M. External morphology
(the oil palm is monoecious: male and female flowers grow on the same tree, but rarely at the same time)

1. frond
2. flower bud
3. palm (live / dead)
   a. spine
   b. folioles
4. petioles
5. stickers, thorns of the petiole
6. stalk of palm nuts
7. male inflorescence
8. stipe or pseudo-trunk
9. stub (base of the petioles of fallen leaves)
10. roots
11. bulb
12. fibers surrounding the base of the palm

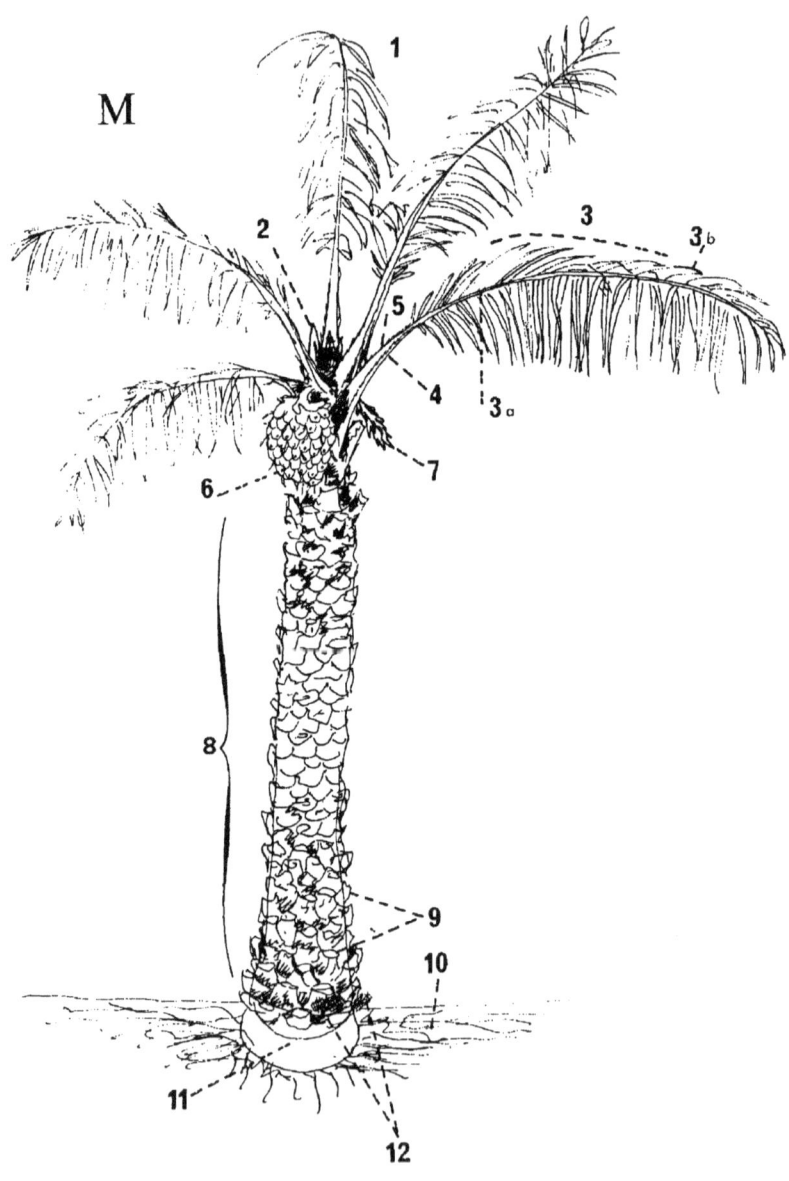

Fig. 43 Oil Palm

Seed-bearing plants

Fig. 44
Fruit

N. The fruit stalk: female inflorescence (detail)
  1. fruit: palm nut
  2. stalk thorn
  3. separate fruit: green palm nut / ripe palm nut / oily nut
  4. withered flower
  5. stone of the palm nut
  6. kernel: palmetto

O. Male inflorescence
  1. detail of the branch of male inflorescence

P. Cross-section of a palm nut
  1. drupe
  2. pulp
  3. shell, stone, pit
  4. kernel

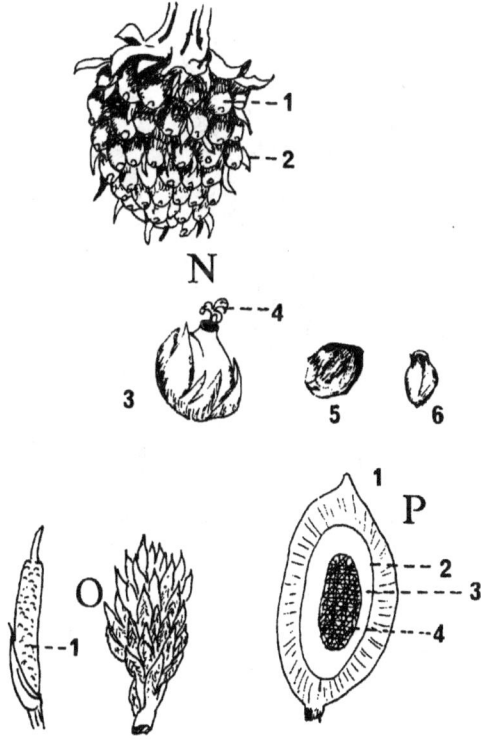

Fig. 44 Fruit

Seed-bearing plants

Fig. 45
Widely-used trees and plants: Papaya tree

M. Female papaya tree
  1. fruits: papayas
  2. female flower
  3. cut fruit showing its seeds

4. foliage
5. trunk

N. Male papaya tree
  1. cluster of male flowers

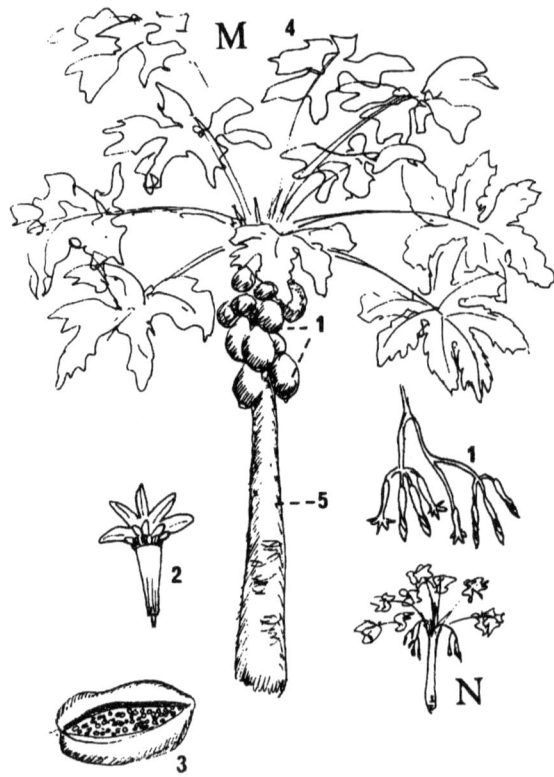

Fig. 45 Papaya

Anatomy and Physiology

Seed-bearing plants

Fig. 46
Widely-used trees and plants: Gourds

O. Utilitarian shapes

   1. cylindrical, no neck
   2. club-shaped
   3. spherical
   4. long-necked
   5. spherical, no neck
   6. crook-necked

O

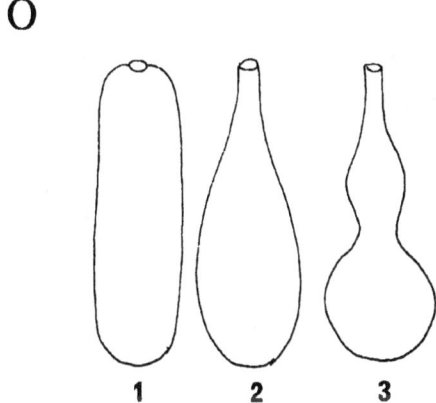

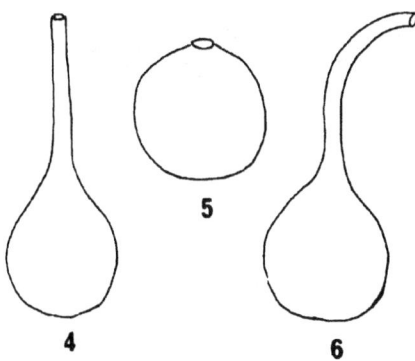

Fig. 46 Gourds

Spore-bearing plants

Fig. 47
Spore-bearing Plants

A. Lichen

B. Moss

C. Seaweed or thallophytes

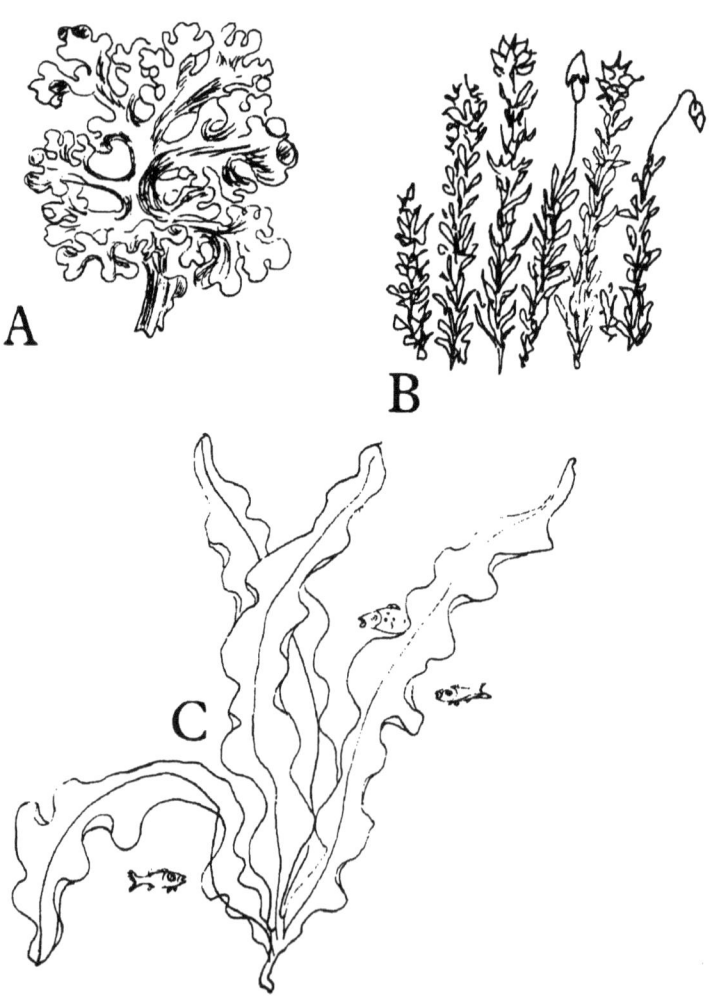

Fig. 47 Spore-bearing Plants

Anatomy and Physiology

Spore-bearing plants

Fig. 48
Spore-bearing Plants

D. Mushroom

1. cap / pileus
2. gill
3. annulus / ring
4. stem / stalk / stipe
5. volva

6. universal veil
7. yolk

E. Fern

1. underside of the leaf
2. detail showing spore cases
3. crook-shaped bud

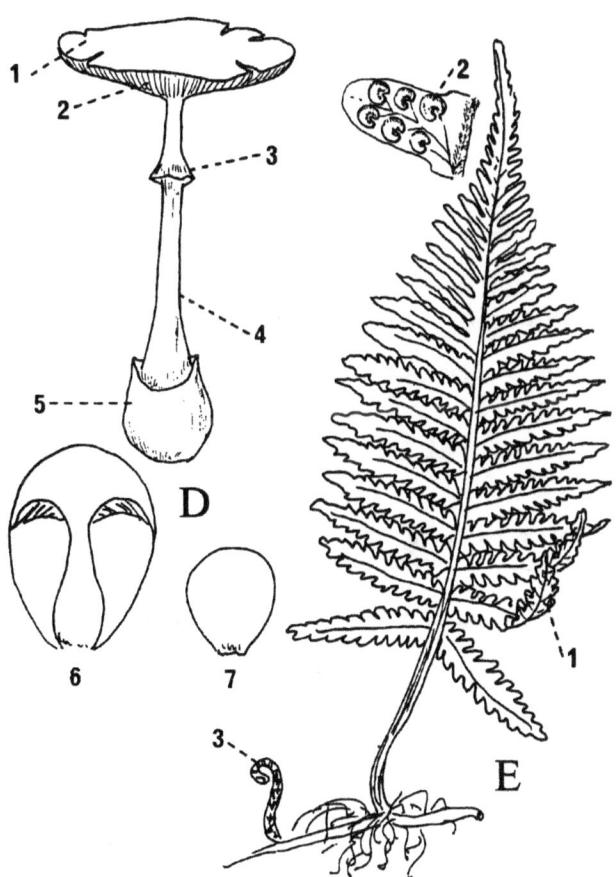

Fig. 48 Spore-bearing Plants

2 Physiology and Pathology
by Jacqueline M. C. Thomas

This questionnaire is accompanied by a series of sketches which make collecting anatomical vocabulary easier than with a word list. Here we include only words designating various conditions of existence, physiological and pathological phenomena, and body movements which can not be better expressed by a drawing.

1 Humans

Words designating respectively: humans / animals / plants

1.1 Conditions of existence

General terms
- species, race, family, humanity
- man / woman / child–old person / adult / young person (♂ or ♀) / boy ~ girl / child ~ little one / etc.

Growth and external appearance
- birth, to be born / to live, life / awakening, to wake up / to grow, to develop, growth / to get bigger, tall ~ to get fat, fat ~ to thin down, thin / to get old, old / to get wrinkled, wrinkled / to be dying, dying / to die, dying, dead, corpse / to come back to life, etc.
- tall, fat, short, slim, thin, huge, bloated, weak, strong, sickly, puny, spindly, doddering, infantile // size, weight, smallness, slimness, thinness, strength, weakness, etc.
- dark-haired, redhead, blond, white-haired // black, brown, red, white (-skinned) // hairy, bald (bald spot ~ receding hairline)

1.2 Reproductive functions

Conception
- mating, to couple / erection, to get an erection / to have relations, cohabit, coitus / to ejaculate, ejaculation, sperm / orgasm (♂ ~ ♀) / etc.
- conception, to conceive, to be pregnant / stopping of periods / early stages of pregnancy / nausea, vomitings at the beginning of pregnancy / etc.

Gestation
- pregnancy, gestation / cravings during pregnancy / fetus / first movements of the baby
- accidents of gestation: miscarriage, abortion / expelled fetus / etc.

Giving birth
- labor pains / delivery, to deliver / to give birth to twins / confinement / etc.
- water, to break one's water / placenta, to expel the placenta / care for the mother
- newborn / umbilical cord, to cut the cord / care for the newborn, etc.
- to beget (♂ ~ ♀), to multiply, etc.

Anatomy and Physiology 629

1.3 Bodily functions

Excretions (different ways of ...)
- excrement, to excrete, to defecate / urine, to urinate / sweat, to sweat / mucus / earwax / fart, to fart / belch, to belch / vomit, to vomit / spit, to spit / dribble, to drool / odor, to stink, to smell good / tears / etc.
- yawn, to yawn / sneeze, to sneeze / snore, to snore / breath, to breathe / cry, to cry out / hiccough, to hiccough / etc.

Ingestions
- hunger, hunger for meat, appetite, to eat / thirst, dehydration, to drink / etc.

Various functions
- sleep, to sleep / dream, to dream / nightmare, dream / tears, to weep / to laugh / groan, to moan, to groan / suffering, to suffer / thought, to think / speech, voice, to speak / etc.

1.4 Pathology

General terms
- sickness (general term) / pain, suffering, to suffer / groan, to groan / to bother / to move about restlessly, restlessness (of the sick person) / to shake a limb (as a result of pain) / loss of weight, to lose weight / weakening, to get weaker / poisoning, poisoned / to be failing, to fail / trembling, to tremble / healing, to heal / worsening, to get worse / to regain strength, convalescence / tiredness, to be tired / etc.

Various symptoms
- headaches, to have a headache / nose bleed, to have a nosebleed / fainting, to faint / fever, to have a fever / dizziness, to be dizzy / swelling, to swell / pus, to make pus / etc. // to flow, to ooze, oozing / to swell up, puffing up / bloating / to go down / etc.

Dermatological ailments
- wound / infection / ulcer / sore / boil / abscess / cyst / wart / recurring wounds / burns / spots without pigment / pruritis, itching, to itch / graze, to graze / scratch, to scratch / scar, to heal over / to coagulate, clot / to spurt (blood) / to dry, form a scab / etc.
- ailments with skin parasites: scabies, lump on the cheek, threadworm, fungal infections (mycoses), etc.

Endemic and contagious diseases
- smallpox, leprosy, yaws, malaria, sleeping sickness, elephantiasis, measles, chickenpox, whooping cough, rabies, typhoid fever, typhus, etc.

Ear, nose, throat, and lung ailments
- earaches, ear infection, mastoiditis, etc.
- cough, to cough / hoarseness, to be hoarse / cold, to have a cold / cold in the head / sinusitis / tonsillitis, sore throats / lung diseases, bronchitis, tuberculosis, pneumonia, congestion of the lungs, pleurisy / etc.

Eye ailments
- conjunctivitis, sticky matter in the eye, pus (purulence), blepharitis, . . .
- strabismus (convergent, divergent, etc.), near-sightedness, far-sightedness, . . .

Digestive system ailments
- odontology: tooth decay, abscessed tooth, cyst, grating the teeth, gingivitis, etc.
- gastroenterological ailments: dysentery, diarrhea, colic, vomitings, various stomach aches, distensions, hernias (umbilical, inguinal, etc.)
- liver disorders: jaundice, liver pains, etc.
- spleen pains
- intestinal parasites: tapeworm, worms (pinworms, roundworms, etc.)

Cardiovascular ailments
- heart diseases, hemorrhoids, varicose veins, stroke, paralysis of one side, paraplegia, cramps, blackout, etc.

Gyneco-urinary, venereal, and glandular diseases
- menstrual pains, sterility, cyst ~ abscess on the breast, abortion, etc.
- gonorrhea, syphilis, etc. / vaginal discharge, etc.
- goiter, ganglions (in the groin, armpit, neck, etc.)

Children's diseases
- rickets, distended stomach, various stomach aches, convulsions, various skin diseases, etc.

Mental and nervous diseases
- insanity, mild mental disorder, cretinism, epilepsy, Parkinson's disease, senility, tics, stuttering, to stutter, etc.

Osteology
- fracture, sprain, fallen arches, crooked legs

Various infirmities
- dwarf, dwarfism / nasal sound, nasal voice, to speak with a nasal voice / cripple, disability / blind, blind in one eye, deaf, dumb / hunchbacked, bow-legged / one-armed, one-legged / lame / giant / paralyzed / etc.

1.5 Medicine and hygiene

Medical treatments and practices
- to strike with a disease, to catch a disease
- to make an incision, to lance, to squeeze, to drain (an abscess) / to massage / to smear, to anoint, to rub / to peel off, to wash, to clean (a wound) / to scarify, scarification / to pour out (powder medicine ~ liquid medicine) / to bandage, to dress / to prepare (a powder ~ liquid ~ ointment remedy, etc.) / to give an injection / etc.
- to give an enema, to inject / to sprinkle, to spit often
- to treat, to treat in vain, to heal, cure
- various medical practices (to be observed)

Anatomy and Physiology

Givers of treatment
- traditional: medicine man, witch doctor, healer, etc.
- introduced: doctor, nurse (male or female)

Medications
- remedy, medicine (generic / used with magical practices / plant / compound (mixture) / poison / etc.)
- drunk or eaten remedy / powder for external use / shavings / on a string to be worn (around the neck, on the arm (biceps or wrist), around the waist, on the leg or ankle, around the chest, etc.), bells, seeds, etc.

Hygienic care
- soap, anointing oil, combs, hairdressing needles, mirror, razor, toothpicks, earpicks, etc.
- to wash, to bathe, to blow one's nose, to anoint oneself, to massage, to comb one's hair, to braid (the hair), to arrange the hair, to shave (the head), to shave (the beard), to scrub, to rub, to clean out (teeth, ears, nails), to file (nails, teeth) / etc.
- cleanliness, beauty, health / to be clean, beautiful, healthy, etc.

1.6 Body movements

General body activities
- walking, to walk, to go / stroll, to take a walk / to zigzag / to follow, to chase, to catch up, to rejoin (by walking, running) / to run, running / to dance, dance / to stamp, to trample, to stamp one's feet / to stumble, to stagger, to trip, to tumble / to pass, to enter, to go out / to hurry, to hasten / to turn, to turn away, to turn around, to go back, return / to run away, to escape / etc.
- climbing, to climb, to scale, to ascend, to move ahead by jerks, to come back down to the ground, to climb down / etc.
- swimming, to swim, to bathe, to dive, to drown, to splash oneself, etc.
- weight, to push, to shove / to hang behind oneself, to carry (in the arm, on the hip, at arm's length, on the shoulder, on the back, on the head, etc.), to lift, to weigh in one's hand, to carry, to transport, to hand, to hang up, to pull out, ... to lean, to drive in, to break, to break off, to bend, to lower, to bend out of shape, etc. / to drag, to cart along, to move with effort, to struggle, struggle, strength, effort, to roll, to hold, to grip, etc.
- jump, to jump, to jump up, to jump on / to cling onto, to hang onto / to fall / to squat down, crouching / to jump back, to bounce / to hop, to jump with the feet together, to jump over / to collapse, to flop, etc.
- to throw, to hurl, to swing, to hit, to strike, to beat, blow, to slap, to catch in the air, to catch, to let slip, to let go, etc.

Movements of parts of the body
- head: to lower, to bow, to turn, to nod forward, to nod (up and down, back and forth), to crease (the forehead), to wrinkle up (the nose), to quiver (nostrils), to sniff, to grimace, to wiggle (the ears, scalp), etc.
- eyes: to close, to look out of the corner of one's eye, to blink, to raise heavenward, to stare, to bulge out, to frown, to stare wide-eyed

- mouth: to kiss (kissing noise), to give a kiss (breath), kiss, to kiss on the mouth, to bite, to lick, to suck (by breathing in dissolving), to chew, to masticate, to swallow, to choke, to yawn, to spit, etc. // to blow, to whistle (with the teeth, lips, etc.), to cry out, to howl, to growl, to sing, to screech, to whisper, to stammer, to pout, to purse the lips, etc. / to stick out the tongue, to grind the teeth, etc.
- arms: to hold, to clasp, to slip (out of the hands), to hit with the flat of the hand, the fist, to grab, to take into the arm, to make a sign with the hand, to grasp, to take by the handful, to knead (by hand), to roll (between the hand as support), to rub (with the hand), etc. // to fold (the arms), to stick in, to rest (the hand), to stretch (out) (the arm), to shake (the hand), to pinch, to tickle, to stroke, to cradle, to embrace (hug) / right, left hand / hold the hands up in the air, to hold out the hand, to feel, to grope, to close the fist / fist, etc.
- lower limbs: to trip (with the foot), to limp, to stamp, to trample, to stride (over), to draw (with the foot on the ground), to trample, to press (on the ground with the feet), to crouch, to kneel, squatting, to sit, to get up, to stand up, to stand (without moving), to rock (back and forth) on the feet, to sway, to stretch out (the leg) / standing, upright / to stamp one's feet / to trip someone / etc.
- movements of upper and lower limbs and/or the trunk: to turn , to lean over (forward, backward, to the side), to fall (forward, backward, with arms and legs outspread, head over heels, ...), to crawl, to slip, to bow, to bend down, to get up, to lie down, to curl up (from cold, from pain, to sleep curled up), to stretch, to toss and turn (in bed), to turn around (on oneself), to lean on, to lean one's back on, to rest against, to keep in background, to rest, to shudder, to shiver, to tremble, to shake, to contort oneself, etc.

2 Animals

For each section under the heading 1. Humans, we must check if the words collected apply to animals, and ask also for the words specific to animals.

2.1 Existence

General terms
- wild animal / domestic animal
- species ~ race / animality / main families of animals:
  mammals (carnivores, herbivores, rodents, ...) / birds, snakes, fish, etc. // horde, flock, pack, band, etc.
- male / female / little one ~ old one / solitary / adult / young ($\male$ ~ $\female$) / female

Growth and external appearance
- to be born, birth / to grow, to get big, growth / etc.
- big (for a rat ~ for an elephant) / small (for a rat ~ for an elephant), etc. // spotted, striped, streaked // the largest animal of the flock (elephant, buffalo, etc.), the oldest, etc.

2.2 Reproduction

Conception
- mating, to mate / spawning, to spawn / nest, to nest / etc.

Anatomy and Physiology

- conception, to conceive / to be pregnant, egg-laying, to lay / egg (of different kinds of animals: birds, snakes, turtles, crocodiles, frogs, etc.)

Gestation
- pregnancy, gestation / fetus / to sit on (eggs), brooding / brooded egg, etc.
- gestation accidents: abortion / still-born young / clear egg, etc.

Giving birth
- giving birth, to give birth / hatching, to hatch / etc.
- newborn young (mammals), chicks, tadpoles, young fish, larvae, caterpillars, etc.
- to beget (♂ ~ ♀), to multiply / to swarm, swarm / etc.

2.3 General physiology

Excretions
- excrements (droppings, dung, manure, bird-droppings, . . .), slobber / odor, scent, musk, to give off musk (civet, mongoose . . .) / to regurgitate, pellets or balls thrown up / honey, to make honey / venom, etc.

Ingestion
- to eat, to graze, to browse, to gnaw, to nibble, to devour, to tear to shreds, to crunch, etc. / to drink, to sniff, to lap up, to chew the cud / etc.

Various functions
- to sleep, to hibernate / to roar, to growl, to grunt, to snort, to low, to meow, to bark, to bleat, to trumpet, to giggle, to cluck, to hoot / to migrate (to leave, to return), / to open out (natural opening) / to sting, to bite, . . .

2.4 Anatomy

Certain parts of the body are specific to a given species, or are common to several species, genera, families, orders, or classes. From the beginning, check which vocabulary terms from human anatomy are also used for animals. Beyond that, ask about:

Head: horns, tusks, mane, crest, muffle, muzzle, nostrils, snout, trunk, teeth, etc. / comb, crest, wattle, beak (straight, hooked), fangs, etc. / gills, etc. / antennae, . . .

Limbs: paws, legs, birds'-feet (with no calf) , hoofs, claws, talons, fins, etc. / wings, (hard) outer wings, etc.

Body: moulting, to moult or shed (snakes, birds) / saddle, rump, neck, hindquarters / hairs, scales, feather, down, large ornamental feathers on the wings and tail, shell, carapace, skin, hide / tail, stinger /etc.

Skeleton: bone, backbone, fishbones, shell (monovalve, bivalve) / breastbone / etc.

Internal organs: stomach, paunch, reticulum, omasum, rennet stomach; crop, gizzard, cloaca; swim bladder; venom sac, gall bladder (gall); kidney, etc.

2.5 Body movements

General body activities
- gait, to walk, to amble, trot, to trot, to jog along, to run, gallop, to gallop, ... / to fly, to fly away, to soar, to circle around (while soaring), to fly in formation, to swoop (toward the ground), to dive, to spiral, to swoop down in a swarm, ... / to creep, to slither, to wind along, to ripple, ... / to swim (fish and aquatic animals)
- climbing (different ways that climbing animals have to climb)
- jumping, to jump, leap, to leap up, to crouch for springing, to take wing (different ways depending on the case and the animal), to catch in midair), to carry off in the air, to take away, ...

Movements of body parts
- head: to rock, to swing the trunk, to sniff, to peck, to stake out, to burrow, ...
- eyes: to close the third eyelid (birds), ...
- mouth: to peck, to peck at, to gather nectar, ... / to cry, to trumpet, to giggle, to scold, to roar, to sing (rooster, birds, ...), to hoot, to whistle, ...
- limbs and body: to wriggle (worm, snake), ...

2.6 Other terms from the zoological vocabulary

Habitat
- burrow, den, home, nest (birds and insects, specific term for different species), ant-hill, termitary, apiary, tunnels, ...

Movements
- trail, animal tracks, ...

Specific grammatical determiners
- Are there special determiners, numerators, or ways of counting animals or specific kinds of animals (birds, fish; e.g., pigeons are counted by the pair, eggs by the dozen, etc.)

3 Plants

3.1 Existence

General terms
- species, subspecies, family / plant ...
- tree, bush, thick vine, creeper, grass (high / low), oil plant, epiphyte, parasite, fern mushroom, algae, ...
- male plant, female plant, shoot, ...

Growth and external appearance
- sprout, to germinate, shoot, to grow / growth, to grow / to grow thickly, to grow sparsely / to be green (fruit), to be ripe (soft, colored) / to be young, full-grown, old (tree) / to wither / to fade, wilt / to die / to dry up, to dry out, to parch / to

rot, to spoil, to get moldy, worm-eaten, to decompose / to split / to dry out without rotting (fallen tree) / ...
- big, tall, small, thick, slender, huge, spindly / leafy, bushy, dense, leafless / ...

Reproduction
- fertilization, bearing fruit, to bear fruit / fruit / flower, pollen / cluster / spores ...

3.2 Anatomy

Lower: root, stump, foot, rhizome, tuber, ...

Trunk: wood, bark, stem, trunk, stipe, ...

Top: branches, leaves, top, *cime*, flowering branch, fruit-bearing branch, thorn, ... / tree fruit ~ bush, herbaceous fruit, seed, pod, ear, bunch, drupe, kapok, ... / bud (flower), bud (leaf) / ... hooks, barb, stinging hairs, tendrils, breathing holes, bulbils, ... / veins, corolla, ...

Liquids and exhalations: sap, latex, glue, mucus, gum, resin, ... / fragrance, perfume, ...

3.3 Other terms from the botanical vocabulary

Mobility
- to uproot, to wrap around, to sway, to rustle, to bend, to crash down

Types of vegetation
- primary forest (deep forest), domestic forest (around the village), small forested zone (in the savannah), forest gallery, clearing (savannah in the forest), new forest growth (after cultivation), wooded savannah, grassy savannah, dry savannah, dry forest, steppe, etc. / desert, barren land, sparse vegetation, etc. / natural formations or groups of plants: palm tree–palm grove

Specific determiners (cf. 2. Animals; e.g., 'a pair of yams')

3 Information Grid for Ethnopharmacology
by Pierre Boiteau

N.B. Prepare two types of files:
a) by medicinal substance (one for each substance)
b) by method of prevention, diagnosis, or treatment

1 Scientific and English terminology

1. Name of the medicinal substance (English name and Latin name in the case of plant products) or name of the method (make one up if necessary)
2. Common names if they exist

   Identification number (assigned by a conventional system)

2 Vernacular terminology

1. Name of the medicinal substance or method (in the vernacular language)
2. Name of the vernacular language
3. Terms in adjacent dialects or languages (specify the name of these dialects in each case)
4. Terms in the trade language
5. Name of the trade language used
6. Vernacular term indicating its principal function or the special name given to the substance when used for therapeutic purposes.
7. Vernacular terms (a, b, c, ...) indicating secondary functions or names employed for uses other than therapeutic.

3 Geographic, ethnic, and localization

1. Geographic localization: there may be only one, or we may have to distinguish:

   A. where are the raw materials produced, starting with the technique
   B. where are mixtures prepared, etc.
   C. where is it marketed (possibly), etc.

2. Name of the ethnic group or the people involved (for A, B, C, ...)
3. Source of the information (for A, B, C)

   Name of researcher, subject and date of the mission
   Bibliographic references when using material already published, etc.

4. Lifestyle of those involved

   Type of town
   Number of inhabitants
   Communication routes
   Distance from an important city
   Means of access to the village

Factors of seasonal isolation
Presence or absence of recent migrations
Situation characteristic of recent acculturation, etc.

5. Relative abundance of the raw material

   Where can it be procured: place, phytogeographical formation, nature of the terrain, habitat, required ecological conditions.

4 Macro-environment, natural context, local pathology

1. General conditions of use of the medicinal substance or of the method described:

   Where are the necessary products found?
   How are they obtained?

2. Parts of the plant or animal used:

   How are they isolated?
   Do they have to be prepared?

3. How are they administered to the sick person?

   Approximate dosage (in local measurements), according to those involved.

4. In what circumstances is the remedy administered or is the method practiced?

   Can those involved give specific names for the diseases being treated? (cite the vernacular names)

5. Does the method entail any contra-indications? Of what nature?

6. What are the most widespread diseases in the district under consideration? (possibly ask the doctors in the nearest medical districts)

7. What are the symptomatic signs of the diseases most frequently found in the district?

5 Concrete description of the method (from a case observed)

1. Complete list of raw materials and techniques used (Number them a, b, c, d, ...).
   A file for each raw material is opened at the same time.

2. Place of preparation

   Description (with drawing if possible).
   Vernacular names (possibly English, too) of the materials used and the techniques brought into play.
   Weighing of the ingredients: local units of measurement may be used (vernacular terms with their quantified equivalents in the international system of weights and measures).
   Do not attempt a greater degree of precision than that usually used by those involved; such precision is misleading.

3. List of qualities (qualifiers) associated with the method or material used

   What properties are attributed to it?
   How is its effect on the body of the sick person explained?

4. Do those involved have an idea of the antiquity of the method?

   Who taught it to them?
   If it is their innovation, how did they find out the properties attributed to the various materials used?
   Why are these materials associated?

6 Micro-environment

(Here we want to have those involved describe a specific case of treatment through their eyes, or else to get from them the possibility of observing the treatment firsthand)

1. Who was sick? age, sex.
2. On what date did the event occur?
3. What was the state of the sick person?

   What visible signs of the disease did he evidence?
   Note all vernacular names of the pathological states described.
4. What medications were administered to him? At what point? How many times? How long did the treatment last?
5. What effect did the witnesses report?
6. Collect afterward, if possible, the testimony of the sick person himself.
7. Through the sick person, attempt to contact the empiric who gave the treatment.

7 Dynamic description

(gestures of the healer); (in the case that we get him to give the treatment in our presence)

1. Objective signs displayed by the sick person.
2. Questions for the sick person: how long has he been sick?; what does he complain of?–subjective signs.
3. The healer's evaluation of the state of the sick person, possibly.
4. Description of the gestures: if the healer consents, ask him to describe his operation himself; write down the description in as much detail as he gives, specifying especially the predicational terms relative to the successive techniques he employs.
5. Cross-cultural description: objective description of all that the healer does, by notes, sketches, drawings, symbolic notations, etc. For each phase of the treatment, note the attitude of the patient and of the treater, the time devoted to each operation, etc.

8 Cultural context

at the various phases (A, B, C, ...) of the operation, possibly, if it seems useful to study them separately.

1. Economic components

   Is the medicinal substance or the technique under consideration marketed?
   Exactly when is it traded? in what place?
   Is the exchange limited to within the village community or to wider groupings?
   Is it of mutual benefit, or does it have a market value (what is it?)
   Possible price of the medicinal substance under consideration in the nearest markets.
   Write down the names of these markets and the dates.

2. Social components

   Social and possibly political role of the practice under consideration.
   Is its use connected with a particular social stratum or class?
   Is it a mark of prestige?
   Who may use the substance or the method? (do age or sex enter into its use or social function?)
   Are there ritual taboos that bar certain individuals from using the method?
   Why is this treatment used rather than resorting to health training: reasons cited by those involved; other probable reasons (investigator's opinion).

3. Religious components

   Does the method or material have a religious significance?
   Are there beliefs related to its use? which ones?
   Is it used in certain ceremonies: circumcision, etc.
   Has the plant been used in the past for ordeals or other practices of this type, to lift evil spells, etc.?

4. Other cultural components

   Popular proverbs or sayings alluding to the material or method under consideration; related folk legends, stories, and texts; do figurative representations of it exist? Have there been in the past taboos on this material or method?

9 Diachronic comparisons

1. Distribution through space of the medicinal substance or of the method: countries where it is used, etc.

2. Modifications and innovations: examples: vernacular name changes; reasons cited for these changes.

3. Antiquity of its use (opinion of those involved).

   Cross-checking to account for its ancient or recent character (investigator's opinion).

4. Evolution of the technique: by what process? (One method may be replaced by another because the materials are easier to procure, because they turn out to be more effective, etc.).

10 Additional documentation; collected material

1. Existing illustrations: drawings, photos, etc.

Catalogue
Where are they?

2. Specimens

    Scientific specimens (herbarium for plants, with name of collector, No., collection where they are kept, etc.)
    Drug samples (part used, reference, place kept)
    Possible collections for chemical and pharmacological study (name of collector, No., laboratory that received the shipment, etc.)

3. Scientific bibliography

    References to the Latin diagnosis, to the principal authors that have described the species: synonyms, etc.
    References to chemical, pharmacological studies.
    Works dealing with the therapeutic use of the isolated constituents.

4. Problems raised by the author of the file

    Underline the gaps that remain to be filled, points which should be the object of an additional investigation, etc.

Questionnaire 14
Instructions for Collecting Zoological and Botanical Specimens

by Jacqueline M. C. Thomas

On the field the linguist does not usually have available the collaboration of one or several naturalists. Thus he must put together a collection of specimens himself, which will be handed over to specialists for identification when he returns.

1 Zoological collection

1.1 Dried insects (not fleshy)

Material
 - butterfly net used for all sorts of insects (flies, wasps, grasshoppers, etc.)
 - one or two cyanide jars (dangerous to handle)
 - several small jars with cotton or sawdust saturated with acetic ether
 - wooden boxes (interior size 125 x 200) fit out with shelves (see description below)
 - tweezers
 - crystal paper papillotes

Making the insect layers
 - From thick and slightly absorbent white paper, cut pouches as shown in figure 1.
 - Line the bottom with a thin layer of combed cotton and make it stick with four dots of glue (Limpidol).
 - Provide a white sheet of the same size (125 x 200) to cover the layer when filled.

Use
 - Capture: kill the insects caught in the acetic ether jars (several hours in one day)

- Preparation: take them out and line them up on the cotton layers with the tweezers.
- Labelling: write on the white covering sheet the number of the wooden box that contains the tray (for example A), the number of the tray (for example, II), and the number given to each in the tray represented roughly on this covering sheet (cf. fig. 2).
- Arrangement: place the covering sheet on top of the insects, turn down the four sides of the pouch in order (1, 2, 3, then 4). On the outside of this last flap, write the number of the box and of the tray (e.g., A II); put the tray in place in the box, which is also marked with its number (A).
- Preservation: cover the bottom of the box with paradichlorobenzene or naphthalene (mothballs)

Papillotes
- Construction: cut sheets of (crystal paper) to the size 125 x 200 (approximately half of a 8 1/2" x 11" typing paper sheet).
    fold as indicated in fig. 3, i.e., fold 1 onto 2, 3 tucked behind 2, and 4 folded over 1 (fig. 3B).
- Use: the butterfly is placed between 1 and 2 (fig. 3C) after being killed with cyanide. After killing the butterfly with cyanide, place it between 1 and 2 (fig. 3C).
    papillotes marked with a reference label (letter B – referring to butterflies – plus the number of the papillote) are piled up in a box like the other insects and protected with naphthalene

Reference number. Record the identification number either on a file card (by filling out questionnaire 12.1 Animal names, in the place reserved for it), or else in a collection notebook devoted to insects, where the following are indicated:
- reference number
- vernacular name
- common English name
- information collected

Example: A.II.5 *bɔ́tɔ́* : solitary forest wasp; considered the incarnation of small forest demons, sometimes friendly, and sometimes unfriendly; they may even kill.

1.2 Fleshy insects, caterpillars and spiders, worms, mollusks

These specimens spoil very quickly and cannot be preserved dry; they must be preserved in alcohol.

Material
- the same as in 1.1, but replace the wooden boxes with:
    test tubes or small jars (like for baby food)
    absorbent cotton and methylated spirits
    cloth-backed adhesive tape (not plastic)

Use
- Preparation: place a layer of cotton at the bottom of the jar, saturate with alcohol. Lay down a single specimen, put a round piece of paper on top, then another layer of cotton, saturate with alcohol, put down another specimen, etc.

Collecting Specimens

- Labelling: indicate the number of the specimen (1, 2, 3, 4, etc.) on each round piece of paper, starting at the bottom of the jar (fig. 4); wrap a strip of adhesive tape completely around the jar, so that the two ends overlap; mark with a soft lead pencil (not a ball-point pen, nor a marker with alcohol-soluble ink) the reference number of jar–use a two-letter sequence to avoid confusion with the boxes (e.g., AA, AB, AC, etc.)–see fig. 5.
- Preservation: the test tubes or jars should be hermetically sealed; to do this, after putting on the top, possibly soak it in paraffin.

Reference number
- Proceed as in 1.1.

1.3 Small animals (small fish, snakes, frogs, and mammals)

Materials
- a large glass or plastic container (of milk-jar size)
- scalpel or very sharp knife
- plastic bags (two-types: small and thin / large and very thick)
- absorbent cotton
- formaldehyde
- labels of permanent material (food labels), 15 x 25 mm (at least one side unpolished to write on with a soft lead pencil), with a hole at one end to pass a string through (fig. 6)

Use
- Preserving liquid: fill the large container halfway with one part formaldehyde and nine parts water (fig. 7)
- Preparing the specimen: clean out the specimen (especially the intestines); put a numbered label on its leg, neck, or the middle of its body (at a constricted place where it cannot slip, attaching it with a slip knot)–cf. fig. 8. Leave the prepared specimen to macerate 8 days in the large container
- Storing and preserving: take out the specimen and put it alone in a little plastic bag containing large pieces of absorbent cotton saturated with pure formaldehyde, and close the bag with a rubber band (fig. 8); then put the small bag into a large thick bag or large jar with a large piece of cotton saturated with pure formaldehyde in the bottom (snakes all together, rats all together, birds all together, etc.)–cf. fig. 9.
- seal the large bag or jar for transporting.

Identification. Number all specimens of whatever kind in the order collected (1, 2, 3, ...), and write the number on the label; the letter Z should appear on all labels, indicating that it is a zoological specimen.

Copy the identification number onto the file card or into the notebook as in 1.1.

1.4 Large animals

The collections obviously cannot include (very) large items. For these, collect only elements of identification such as skins and antlers. Complement these with a series of color slides of the whole animal before cutting it up. Several precautions are necessary for preserving skins. If alum is not available for a careful preparation, they can be dried out, which will keep them for some time.

Materials
- one scraper or knife
- about 50 wooden pegs (15–20 cm long)
- wood ashes

Use
- Scrape the inside of the skin so that no particles of flesh remain.
- Spread out the skin on a very dry and well-cleaned floor, the underside turned up (hairs, if any, toward the floor); stretch the skin out tight and fasten it with the wooden pegs (fig. 10)
- Rub the part exposed to the sun with the wood ashes, repeat until completely dry.
- Keep it hung in a sheltered, airy place until the moment of departure.

Identification numbers. Write the identification number (use the same numbering system as for small animals) directly on the skin with an indelible marker (ONYX Pocket, Baignol, and Farjon). Copy the identification number onto the file card or into the notebook as in 1.1.

The same procedure can be used for medium-sized or small animals (rats, squirrels, snakes), but be careful to keep the skull with the teeth in a small plastic bag for scientific identifications. Don't forget to put the identification number on the skull, too.

1.5 Photography

In all cases, identification will be greatly facilitated if one or several good color slides are made for each specimen, notably of insects with unstable colors, like grasshoppers; of all specimens preserved in alcohol or formaldehyde which distort the colors, especially of birds and fish; and finally, of animals for which only the skins are kept.

Materials
- camera 24 x 36
- 30–40 rolls of film of 36 exposures each
- extension rings and wide angle lens
- ruler, pins, board (100 x 100 cm) covered with plastic
- labels of several sizes (15 x 25 mm, 30 x 50 mm, 75 x 125 mm, 125 x 200 mm) or four pieces of slate of these dimensions and white chalk

Use. For small animals, especially insects, using rings is essential.

Several photos of each animal should be taken: profile, top and bottom or front and back; in addition, a close-up of the head or interesting features (fleshy outgrowths, tufts of hair, etc.). For birds, be sure to highlight large feathers on the wings and tail by spreading them out (fasten them onto the board with pins); similarly for fish, spread open all the fins so that the number of bones is visible (fig. 11).
- Arrange the animal on the board; fasten the parts to be highlighted with pins.
- Place the ruler at the bottom of the board (close enough to the animal so that it appears in the picture).

Collecting Specimens

- Put the label with the identification number of the specimen in an empty space (that will show up on the picture).
- Take the photograph, including the specimen, ruler, and label.

To avoid changing the lens, and setting up and taking off the rings too often, we recommend arranging the samples by size as much as possible.

2 Botanical collections

2.1 Collecting specimens

Materials
- clippers, and if possible pruning shears (clippers at the end of a long handle for gathering small branches of trees)
- large plastic bags for keeping specimens fresh for the whole length of the collection.
- well-equipped camera (24 x 36 color slides, rings)
- labels and identification notebook

Collection. Collect one or several specimens, including:
- stem with leaves, showing on the one hand the shape of the leaf (fig. 12: a – simple, b – composite, c – dentate, etc.), on the other hand the arrangement on the stem (fig. 12a,b – alternate, c – opposite, etc.)
- a flowering branch
- a branch bearing fruit (when flowers and fruits occur together, don't separate them)
- leaves from the top and bottom of the plant if they are different, which is often the case
- roots (possibly for herbaceous plants)
- tubers (for cultivated plants such as taro, yams, etc.)

2.2 Putting them in the herbarium

Materials
- unglossy newsprint for blotting (in quantity)
- press with straps
- methylated spirits
- labels (cf. 1.3 and fig. 6)

Press: simple presses can be made on the spot with strips of nailed or tied wood (fig. 13)

Steam oven: an automobile cab right in the sun will do nicely for this purpose; otherwise a drying system over a wood fire can be set up (fig. 14).

Use
- Prepare the specimen by taking off the excess foliage (i.e., leave only two or three representative samples of each type of leaf), a flower-bearing branch, and fruit-bearing branch (cf. fig. 15).
- Attach a label to the stem.
- Place the fresh plant, completely flat, between two sheets of newsprint.

- Pile several specimens (five or six) prepared in this way and put them into the press, i.e., between two small grids (fig. 13) tied very tight, either by a network of strings or with two straps.

From this point we proceed in two different ways, depending on whether we are making a dry herbarium or a moist herbarium. The latter type gives excellent results when carefully done, and is far simpler to make than a dry herbarium; specimens can be kept moist for several weeks, even three or four months. The first type, when carried through to the end, allows a permanent preservation, but is much more troublesome to carry out.

Moist collection:
- leave the plants in the press about 24 hours.
- put all the specimens contained in the press into a thick plastic bag of adequate size (about 35 x 65 cm)
- spray with methylated spirits (or even 1/2 alcohol, 1/2 water) so that the paper is soaked, but not so that the contents of the bag is swimming in alcohol.
- fold over the top of the bag and close it with a very tight rubber band, or if possible, seal the bag.
- big fleshy fruits require more alcohol or a preparation like the animals; when a specimen includes a big fruit, put only one specimen in a bag.

Dry herbarium:
- Put the press into the oven or set it up to dry out hung over a wood fire attended constantly (cf. fig. 14).
- Every 24 hours, undo the press to change the newsprint and replace it with dry paper; put it back in the press and into the oven (or back out to dry over the fire), until the specimen is completely dried out.
- Until returning from the field, the layers of the herbarium must be kept in a dry place protected from insects (paradichlorobenzene).

2.3 Photography

The color of flowers, fruits, and certain parts of plants (bracts, etc.) is unstable and fades, whatever means of preservation is used (moist or dry). Besides, the bearing of the plant, whether the fruits and flowers stick out or hang down, and other morphological characteristics, which are important for its identification, are recorded by a photograph much better than by the best description.

Materials
- 24 x 36 camera
- rings and wide angle
- 24 x 36 color slide film
- ruler (or metal tape measure with a ring or fastener)
- labels of several sizes or pieces of slate (cf. 1.5)
- nails and hammer

Use. Rings will have to be used for the very small plants and for detailed views (flower or fruits). The wide angle lens is indispensable for overall views of large trees whose bearing is often a characteristic feature.

Collecting Specimens

- Set up the ruler in a prominent place: for a bush, hang it from a branch (fig. 16a); for a grassy plant, hang it from a stake stuck in the ground (fig. 16c); for a tree, hammer in a yard-long stake or make a white mark on the trunk one yard from the ground.
- Set up the reference label in a prominent place, the same way as with the ruler; for a tree, the reference label can serve as an indicator or its size.
- Take overview photographs and detailed photographs (for flowers and fruits), fig. 16a,b.

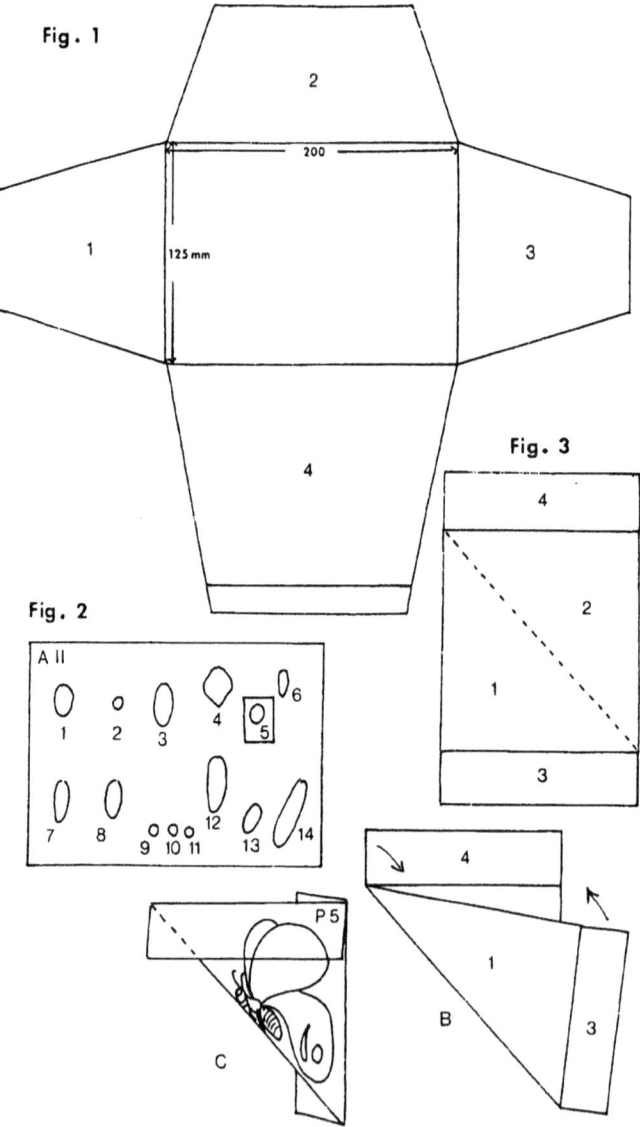

Zoological collection

Collecting Specimens

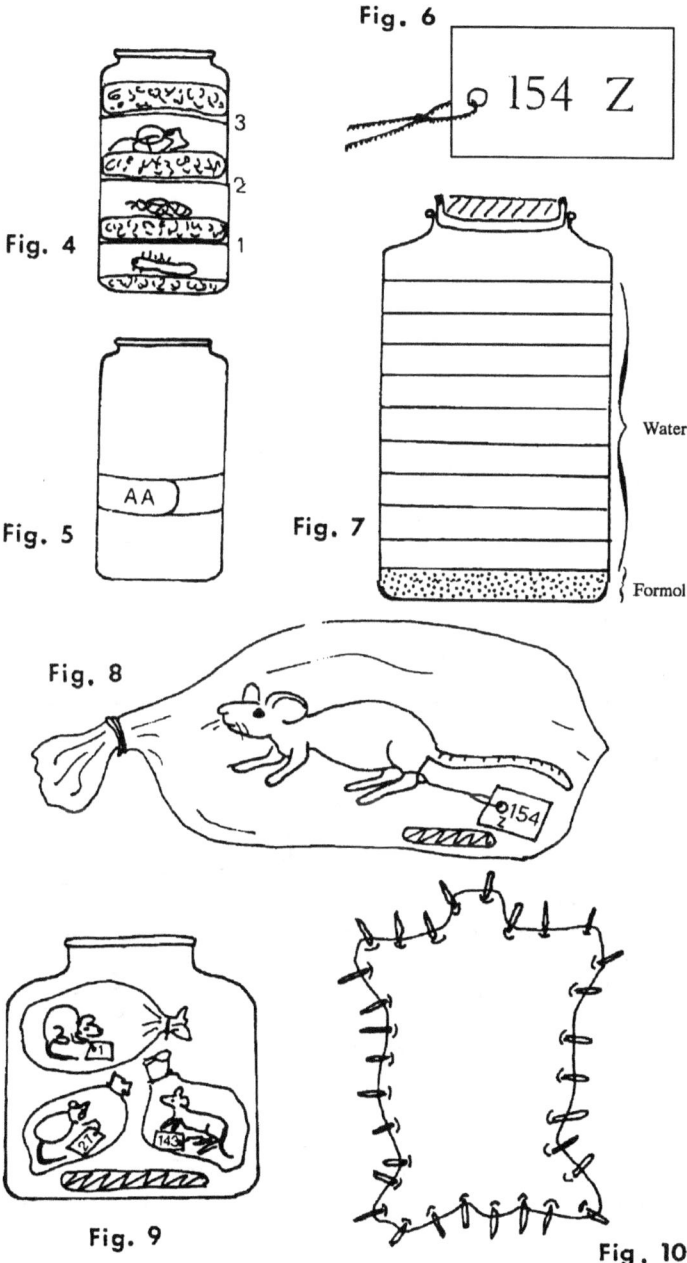

Zoological collection

Fig. 11

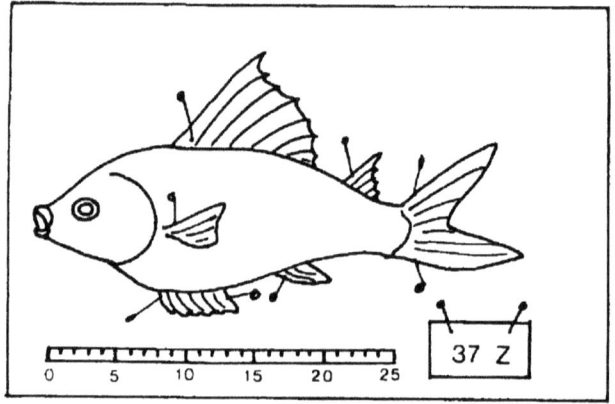

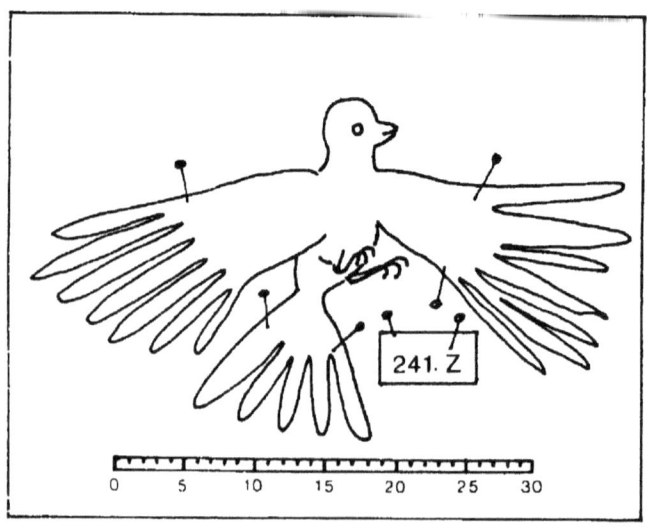

Zoological collection

Collecting Specimens

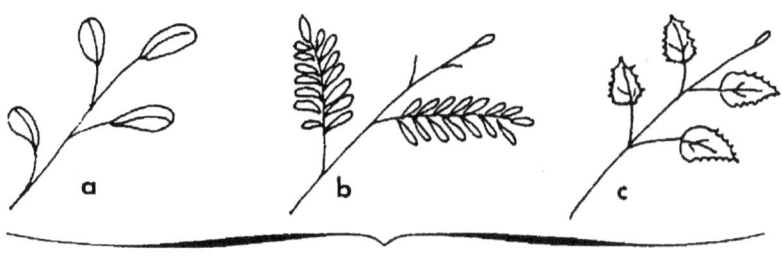

Fig. 12

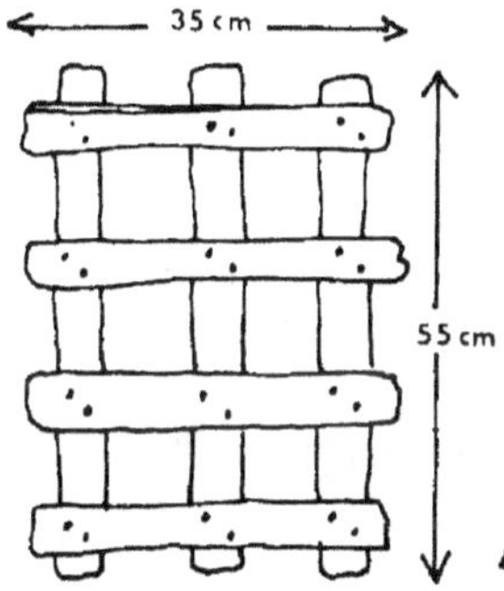

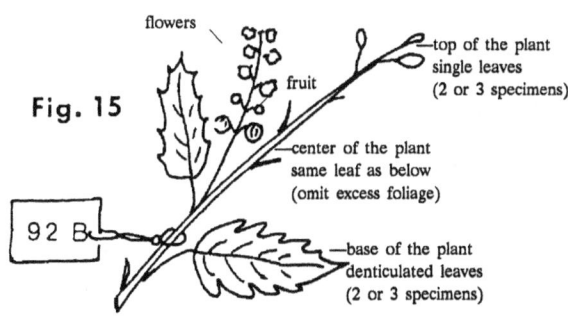

Fig. 13

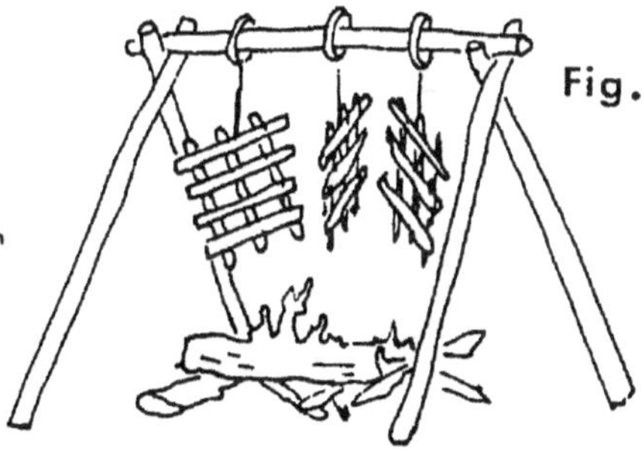

Fig. 14

Fig. 15 — flowers, fruit, top of the plant single leaves (2 or 3 specimens), center of the plant same leaf as below (omit excess foliage), base of the plant denticulated leaves (2 or 3 specimens), 92 B

Botanical collection

Fig. 16

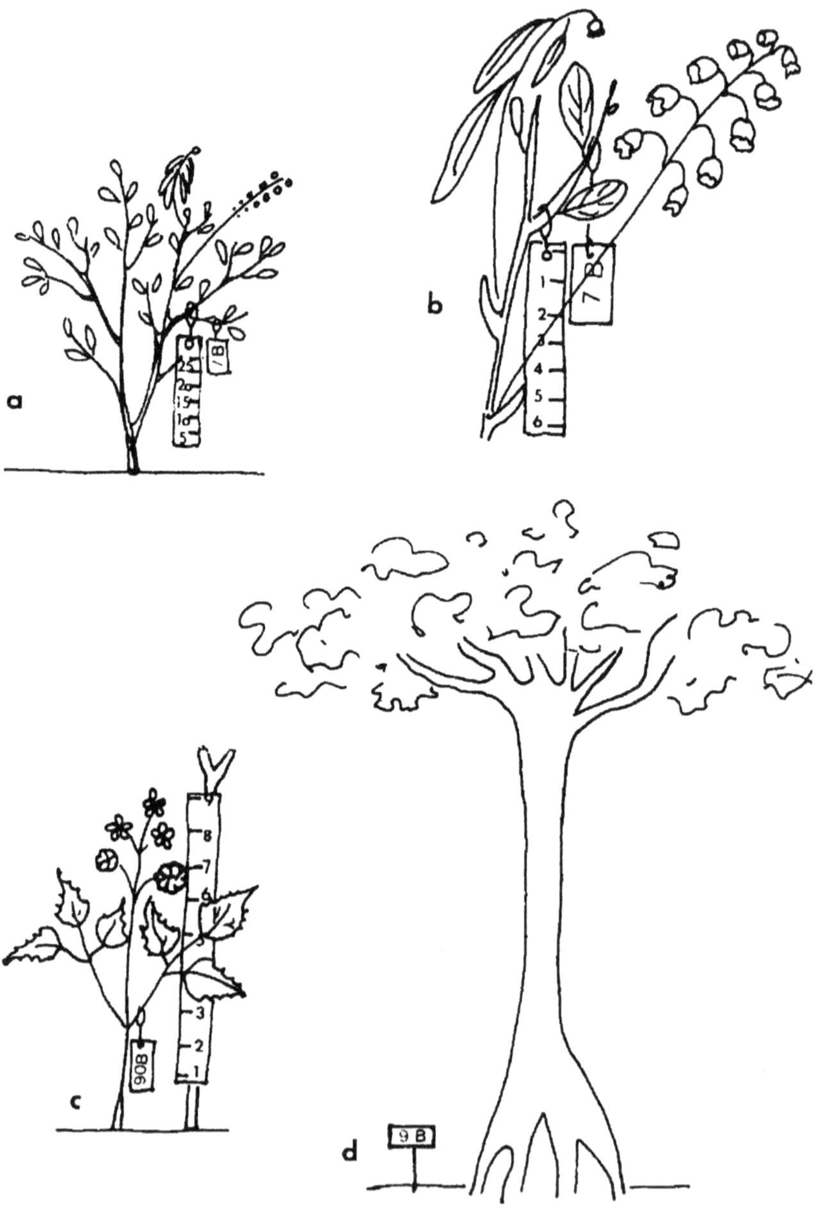

Botanical collection

Questionnaire 15
Sociological Phenomena

by Jacqueline M. C. Thomas

The aim of this questionnaire is to broaden and deepen the lexicon. Therefore, for each heading given, look for the terms which represent the different grammatical categories of the lexicon: *nouns and nominals* (terms which designate institutions / agents or patients / states or actions / processes or results / etc.), *verbs and verbals* (terms which express a process), *modifiers* of various categories (terms which modify nouns and nominals).

Family, political and social organization

1 Family organization

1.1 Filial kinsmen (Blood kinsmen)

1.1.1. Kinship terms (cf. tables of kinship terms)

Terms of address / terms of reference
E.g., Father! Where are you going? / My father came, your father came, his father ....
Mother! Go see the sick person / My mother is sick, your mother is sick, her mother ....
Brother! You are naughty / My brother is tall, your brother is tall, his brother ....
Sister! I came to see you / My sister came, your sister came, her sister ....
Uncle! You are sick / My uncle eats, your uncle eats, his uncle ....
etc., with different kinship terms and different possessives.

Generic terms which designate filial kinsmen
> paternal (father / father's father / father's father's father / etc.)
> paternal through the women (father's mother and her lineage / paternal grandfather's mother and her lineage / paternal grandfather's father's mother and her lineage, etc.)
> maternal (mother / mother's mother / mother's maternal grandmother, etc.)
> maternal through the women (mother's mother and her lineage, maternal grandmother's mother and her lineage, etc.)

Terms which designate: participants (members of ...)
> hierarchy (head of ...)
> the entire lineage of the clan / sub-lineage / the nuclear family (parents-children / family group)
> a group of related lineages / tribe
> ethnic group
> indefinite relationship

(Ask for the generic terms and proper names given to the lineages / tribe / race / etc.)

Parallel kinsmen: generic terms which designate father's brother and his children / mother's sister and her children–how are their respective spouses addressed?

Cross kinsmen: generic terms which designate mother's brother and his children / father's sister and her children–how are their respective spouses addressed?

Older and younger siblings: Terms which designate (generally and particularly) all the cases considered thus far (brother / sister / father's brother and sister / mother's brother and sister / etc.) and for the parents / for the brothers and sisters, etc.
> Verify the possibilities and impossibilities of marriage (cf. 1.2) in terms of the relations of the older and younger siblings; e.g., is marriage with older or younger sister of the wife forbidden or preferred?
> Term which designates the youngest child (M or F) (last of the family or of the wife: none born afterward).

1.1.2. Special cases of kinship

Adopted child (M or F): Term which designates the child in relation to the adopting parents (father / mother / paternal and maternal grandparents / brother / sister / etc.) and terms he uses to refer to them
> according to the lineage he comes from (is there adoption from another lineage?)
> adoption / recognition / disowning // to adopt / to recognize / to disown

Twins (2 M or 2 F or M+F):
> is there a separate word to designate them at the moment of birth or of death / at all times // children / adults // when both live (survive) / when only one lives)
> terms which designate the first born of the two / the second born (is there one or more traditional proper names)

terms which designate the child born after the (living or dead) twins and the following child
terms which designate their qualities (benevolent or malevolent) // birth rituals / death rituals / religious rituals
twin birth / to bear twins // death of twins / to die (as) twins / burial of twins / to bury twins // etc.

Terms which designate children born in special circumstances: (children born with a caul / with teeth / the umbilical cord around the neck / pulled out by the hips or by the feet / etc.) and their birth methods

Terms which designate ordinary births and the rituals of birth

Terms which designate natural children: born of adultery / of a parallel marriage / of a concubine / etc.

Passing on a name: (method of) naming the child

1.1.3. Family living patterns

Generic terms which designate the group living together
household / compound / neighborhood / village / estate / etc.
terms which designate the hierarchy (head of ... the household / etc.)

1.2 Direct alliance (Marriage)

1.2.1. Kinship by marriage

Terms which designate kinship by marriage
on the side of the wife
on the side of the husband

1.2.2. Contracting marriage

Terms which designate the kinsmen whom an individual is forbidden to marry (for M and for F).
On the charts, place an X by the women whom EGO M may not marry and by the men whom EGO F may not marry

Terms which designate relatives who are preferred marriage partners (for M and for F)
On the charts, place a = by the preferred prospective wives for EGO M and the preferred prospective husbands for EGO F
terms which designate these kinsmen

Terms which designate the breaking of the marriage ban (different types of incest according to the closeness of the relationship) and the marriage ban itself. Is there a sanction? Terms which designate it.

Terms which designate the marriage contract
> marriage (for M, for F) / remarriage (after divorce or widowhood) / polygamy // sororate (marrying one's sister's widower) / levirate (marrying one's brother's widow) // celibacy (for M or for F)

E.g., 'My brother is getting married tomorrow' or 'My brother married a pretty girl' ... 'My sister is getting married tomorrow' or 'My sister married a nice boy' or ....

> the different types of marriage: official (traditional, Christian, Moslem, or civil marriage, etc.); tolerated (parallel marriage, etc.); unofficial (concubinage, etc.)

E.g., 'My brother is getting married tomorrow (he is Moslem or Christian, etc.)'

> the stages and rituals of marriage: request for marriage (who does it?), engagement, courtship, conclusion of the alliance, ceremony, where will the couple live?, etc. / dowry (dowry currency), gifts, work obligation, fight for possession, beauty contest, involvement of the girl to be married, etc.
> the persons involved during these periods: intermediaries (for the marriage proposal), suitor, fiance(e), wife/husband (+ groomsman or bridesmaid, witnesses, those who officiate, etc.) / first spouse, second spouse, etc. (is there a collective term which designates the spouses irrespective of sex?) / concubine (M or F), parallel husband or wife, etc. // bachelor or spinster

Terms which designate the dissolution of marriage and the parties concerned
> divorce: divorce(e) (M or F), repudiated spouse (M or F), separated spouse (M or F), etc. / stages and rituals of divorce (reimbursement of the dowry, divorce ceremony, etc.), situation of the children (whom do the children go with, can they be gotten back, etc.)
> adultery: lover, mistress, illegitimate child (M or F), seducer, prostitute, etc. / consequences (for M or F): sanctions
> widowhood: widower or widow / orphans (of the father or the mother or both) / levirate / etc. // stages and rituals of widowhood (for M, for F): beginning of mourning, end of mourning period (ceremony, behavior, etc.)
> separation of the family, of the lineage, etc. / exile, etc. / separated, exiled, ... lineage // stages and rituals

Terms which designate the attitudes, behavior, ceremonies, rituals of each type of kinsman at the moment of the death and funeral

Terms which designate the participants
> M dies: situation of the survivor / of the children // new marriage (with whom?) / etc.
> F dies: situation of the survivor / of the children // new marriage (with whom?) / etc.
> situation of the children: when father and mother are deceased (father first or mother first) / adoption (by whom?) / etc.

beginning and ending of mourning period (preparation / ceremony / between the two: length of the mourning period // funeral (public ceremony, various public or private rituals, dances, songs, etc.) // nutisl (preparation of the body: removal of the internal organs, embalming, exhibition (showing) of the body (M or F) / placing in a coffin or under a shroud, etc. / placing in the grave (where / when / by whom–terms which designate them): tomb(stone), grave, cave, cemetery, etc. / embalmer, grave digger, (hired) mourners, etc.

Terms which designate forbidden behavior (with respect to a certain 'kinsman' by blood tie or by marriage, for example with respect to the uterine uncle or the parents-in-law)
> terms which designate: the violation of this prohibition / the sanction of this violation / the guilty person / etc.

Terms which designate obligatory behavior (with respect to a given kinsman)
> terms which designate the nonobservance of these obligations / the sanction of this nonobservance / the guilty person / etc.

2 Political and social organization

2.1 Different or social alliance

Terms which designate different types of alliance (in each case ask for terms which designate: the institution / the participants / the corresponding places / the corresponding periods (times, stages, ceremonies, etc.) / the measures taken (rituals, objects, etc.)
> *age classes*: individuals of the same age class (M or F) / initiation, neophytes, initiates, initiators ... / initiation camp / etc.
> *joking relationship*: joking relations (M or F), etc.
> *exchange system without price increase* relative in this system (M or F), etc.
> *exchange system with price increase* relative in this system (M or F), etc.
> *peace treaty*

2.2 Social relationships and their hierarchy

Terms which designate members of the hierarchy of political and social organization (in each case, ask for terms which designate: the superiors / the inferiors / the equals)
> *political and administrative authority*

-superiors: king, prince, chief (head of the family, of the lineage, chief of the tribe, the village, the estate, etc.), master, governor, prefect, etc.
-inferiors: subject, clients, administree, house slave, etc.
-equals: companion, close friend, friend, namesake, etc.
> *military and civil authority*

-general, commander, war chief, leader (in hunting, fishing, planting), etc.
-warrior, soldier, commando, etc. / slave or prisoner of war / enemy, foreigner, farmer, etc.
> *judicial authority*

-judge, lawyer, prosecutor, etc.

-defendant, opposing parties, condemned person, prisoner, hostage (debtor) / plaintiff, etc.
-witness (for the prosecution / for the defense)
> *religious authority*

-religious leader, priest, deacon, wise man, fetish priest, diviner, etc.
-faithful, believer, heretic, consultant, etc.
> *financial authority*

-financier, treasurer (paymaster), etc.
-taxpayer, someone liable to forced labor, etc.

Terms which designate:
> *the institutions and their respective actions*

-royalty, district office, clientele, etc.
-command, slavery, etc.
-justice, prosecution, charging, conviction/sentencing, testimony, defense speech, etc.
-church, priesthood, magic, divination, worship of ancestors (or of certain spirits . . .), etc.
-treasury, contributions, tax, statute labor, etc.
> *the corresponding places and means of actions* (their possible characteristics and distinguishing marks)

-district, kingdom, province, prefecture, estate, tribe, etc. / scepter, chief's staff, etc.
-army, regiment, battalion, combat, battle, commando, etc. / command's staff, war chief's headdress, etc.
-tribunal, jury, etc. / judgment, sentence, etc.
-church, altar, sacrifices, prayers, incantations, victims, offerings, *etc.*
-revenue office, cashier's desk, etc.

2.3 Life style

Terms which designate the different stages of the yearly cycle (period of sedentary life / of nomadism // period when the flocks are moved // hunting, fishing, food-gathering season // growing season // period of living scattered, grouped together // etc.

> *Terms which designate the structure of daily life*
>> occupations: work, division of tasks, etc.
>> leisure: rest, gatherings, conversations, chats, games, etc.

> *Terms which designate attitudes and behavior*
>> greeting, to greet / respect, to respect / obedience, to obey / applause, to applaud / pride, haughtiness / etc.
>> insult, to insult / mockery, to mock / palaver, to palaver / threat, to threaten / etc.

Sociological Phenomena

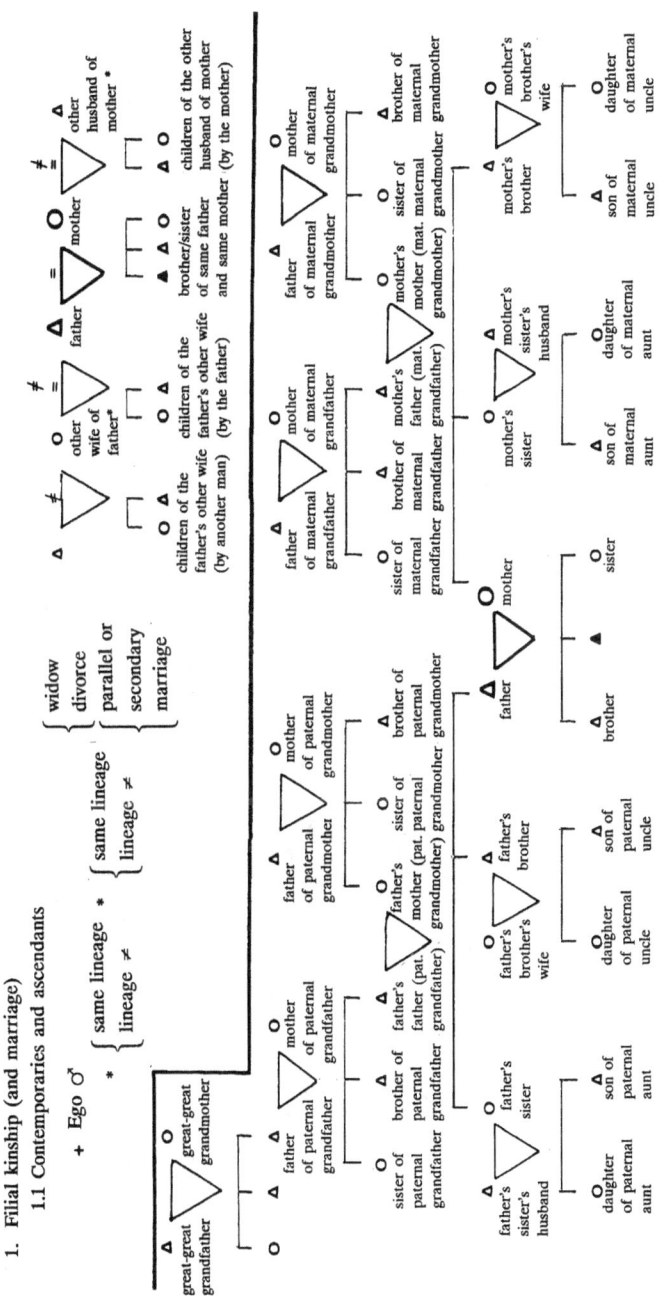

Kinship Table

660 Questionnaire 15

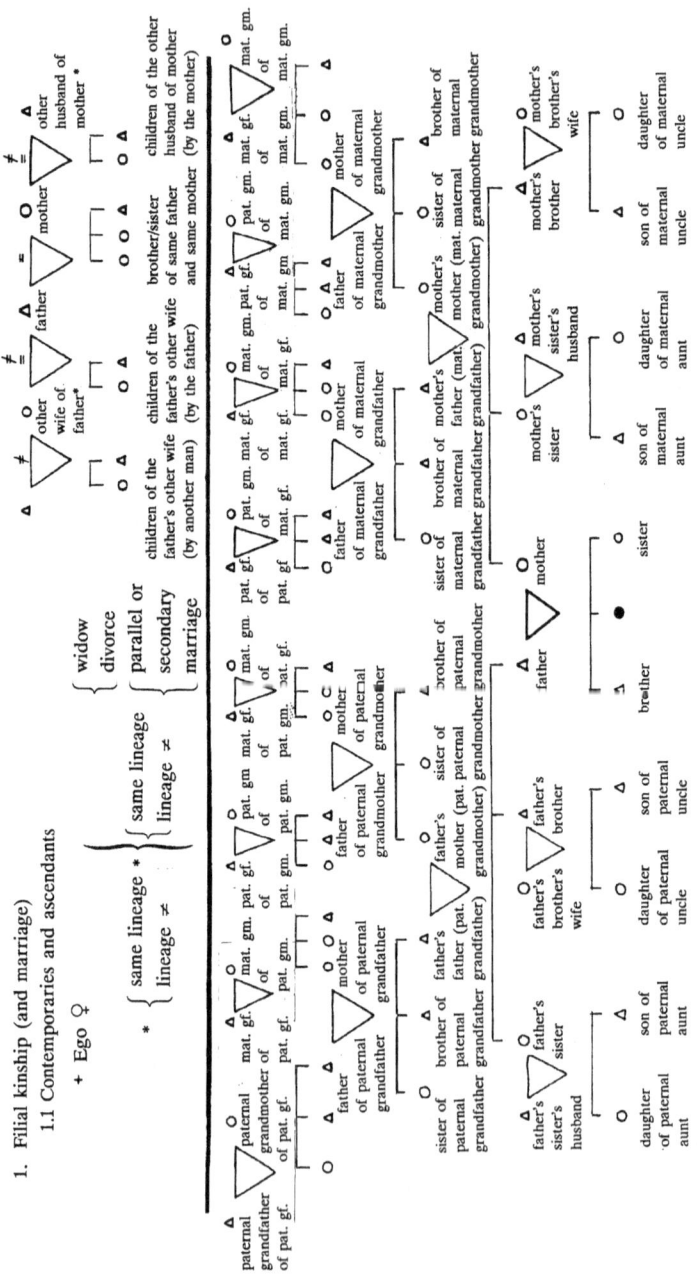

Kinship Table

Sociological Phenomena

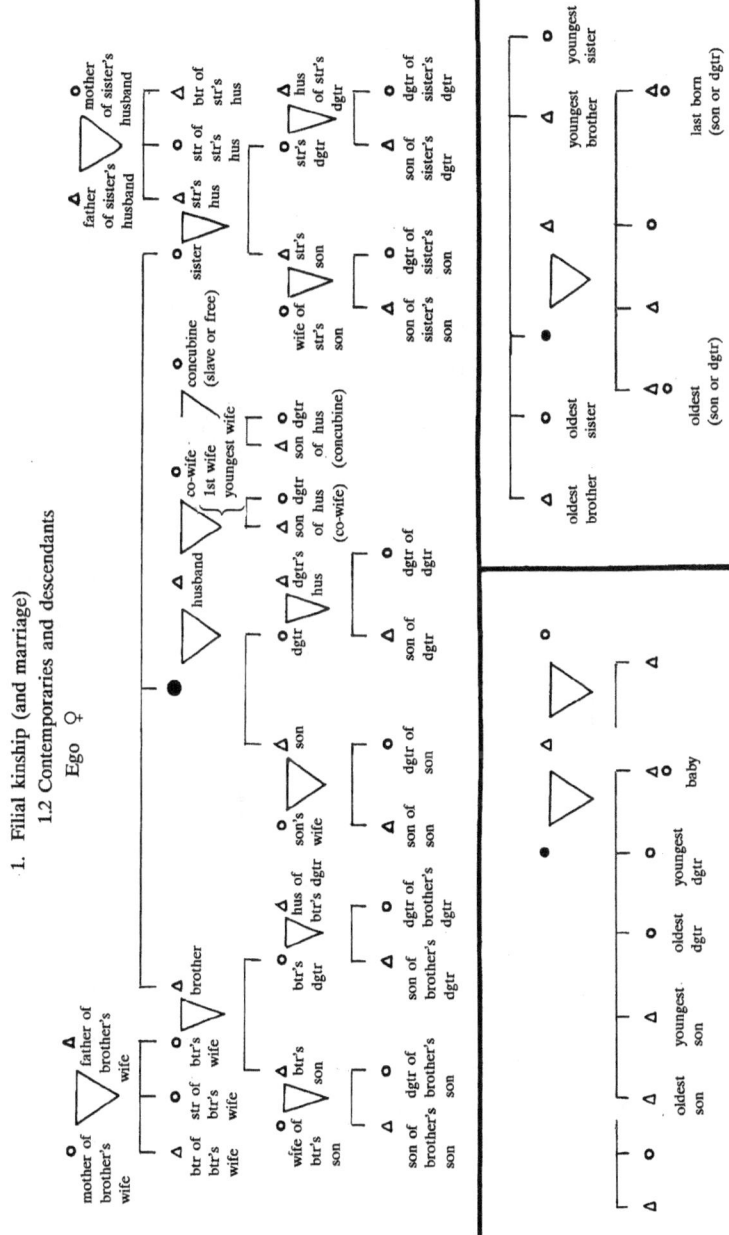

Kinship Table

Kinship Table

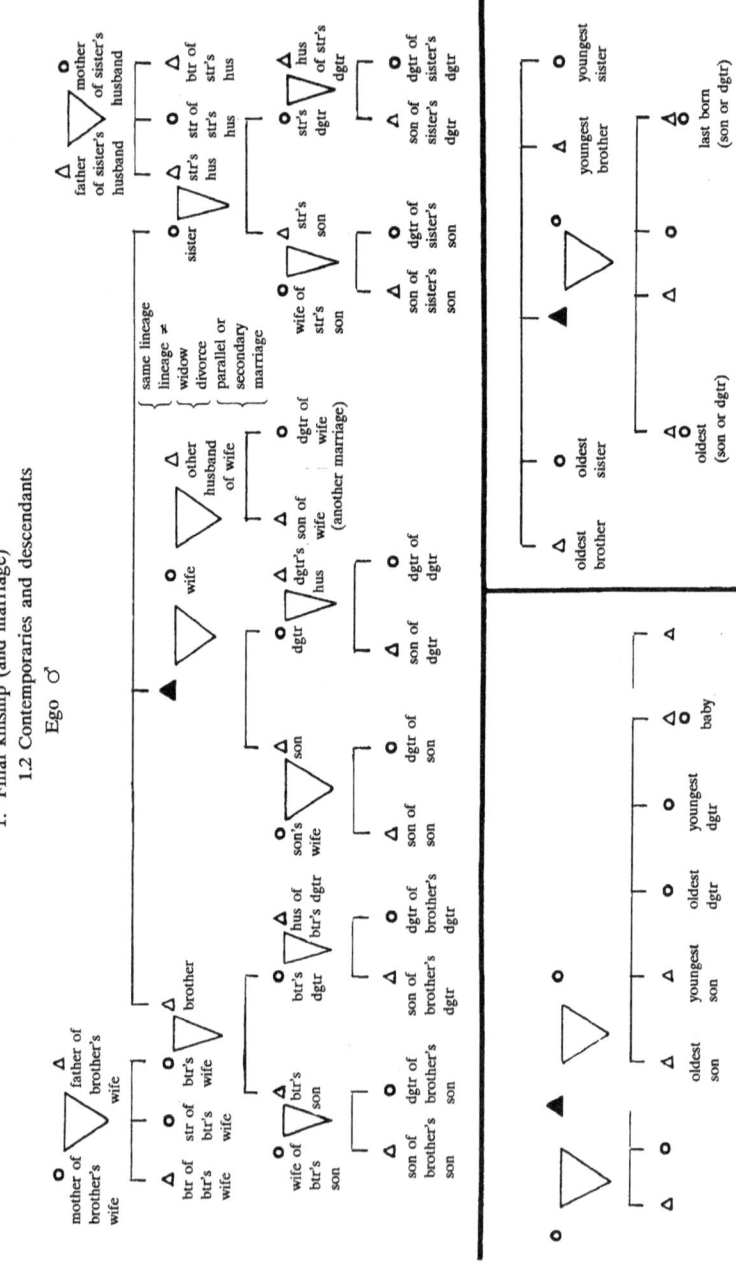

1. Filial kinship (and marriage)
1.2 Contemporaries and descendants

Sociological Phenomena

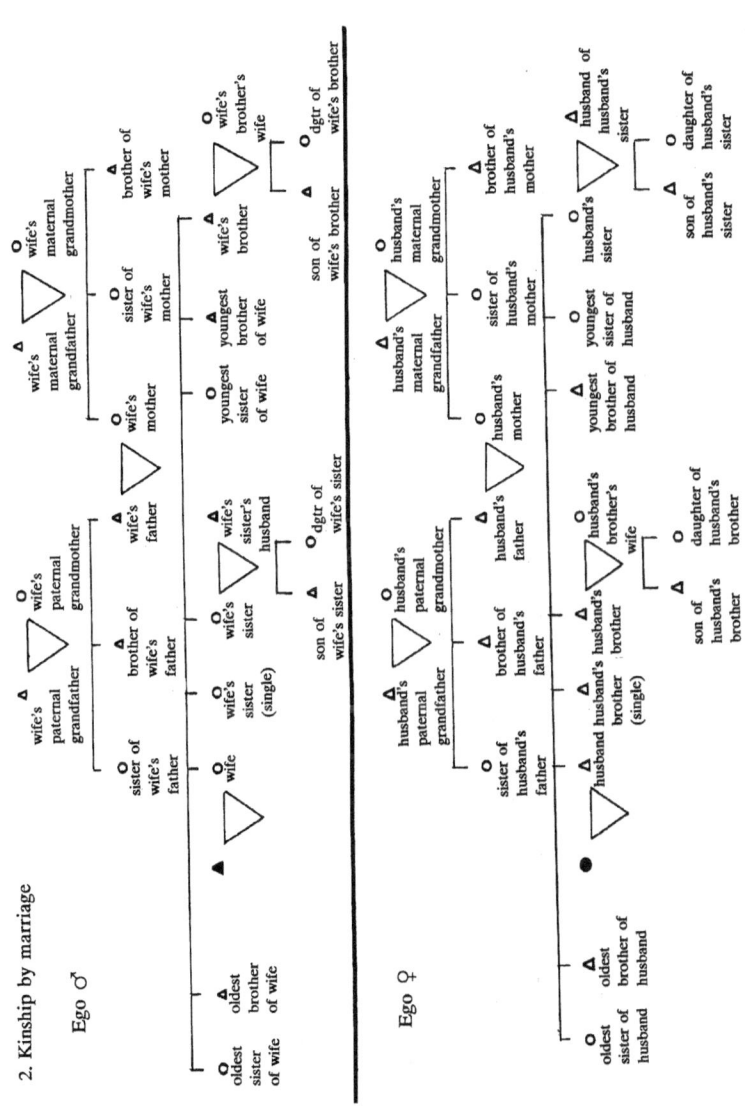

Kinship Table

Questionnaire 16
Psychological Phenomena

by Aurore Monod and Suzanne Platiel

Most of the headings in this questionnaire are intended principally to direct the research. The examples (that are) given cover most English categories, and offer possible guidelines for research to bring out the categories of the language under study. Try to discover the categories without straining to get a word-for-word translation of the illustrative terms cited.

1 The senses

1 Sight

1.1 Modes of perception
duration
ex., glimpse, see, look, stare, examine, contemplate, ...
acuity
ex., glance, distinguish, observe, look over, examine, ... near-sightedness, far-sightedness, piercing look, vague look, troubled look, ...

1.2 Categorization / Aspect
distance
ex., far, near, ...
form
ex., tall, fat, small, short, ...
colors: establish lists by distinguishing the abstract notion of colors in relation to objects, people, sky, earth, ...

1.3 Sensation
ex., glitter, shine, sparkle, gleam, dazzle, blinding, shimmering, ...

2 Hearing

2.1 Modes of perception
duration
ex., hear, listen, listen attentively, ...
acuteness
ex., deaf, keen of hearing; to shout, yell, whisper, murmur, mumble ...

2.2 Categorization
list of animal cries with corresponding verb
ex., coo (dove, pigeon), low, bleat, bark, ...
list of expressions that imitate sounds
ex., boom, splash, ...
list of expressions describing the sounds made by:
ex., rain (pitter-patter); thunder (rumble, boom); the sea; dragged, rolled, or falling objects; specific activities: pounding, hammering, ...

2.3 Sensation
ex., deep, melodious, high-pitched, discordant, nasal, loud, faint, grating, hissing, shrill, to groan, speech defect, to stutter, accent, ...

3 Smell

3.1 Modes of perception
ex., to smell, inhale, sniff, ...

3.2 Categorization
nomenclature of scents and odors of plants, prepared foods, animals, earth (dry and wet), corpses, ...

3.3 Sensation
ex., sweet-smelling, fragrant, sweet, sour, heady, nauseating, ... Note: The vocabulary of smell is very limited in English, but it is often very rich in many non-Indo-European languages.

4 Taste

4.1 Mode of perception
ex., chew, lick, crunch, suck, ...

4.2 Sensation
ex., salty, sour, acrid, bitter, hot (piquant), astringent, strong, mild, spicy, palatable, savory, bland, rotten, (sugary) sweet, ... (try each terms with different types of food, because a single English word may be translated differently according to the food it describes)

5 Touch

5.1 Modes of perception
without intermediary instrument between the object and the hand
ex., take, pinch, caress, feel, squeeze, massage, scratch, lift, release, knead, ...

with an instrument
ex., beat, grate, scrape, cut, crush

5.2 Tactile sensation
temperature
ex., burn, hot, cold, burning, lukewarm, ...
consistency
ex., smooth, coarse, rough, sharp (prickly), uneven, soft, firm, ... (see if the terms used are the same for: skin, fur, foods (fruits), different materials (wood, iron, ...), cloth.
weight
ex., load, burden, heavy, massive, weighty, light

2 Emotions and feelings (value judgments)

1 In relation to self

1.1 Nomenclature
terms
ex., love, hate, contempt, obedience, jealousy, envy, pride, indifference, ... disdain, fear, sadness, friendship, camaraderie, will, respect, ...
determine the parts of the body that are considered the seat of these emotions and feelings

1.2 External manifestations
ex., tears, groans, cries (of fear, joy, sadness), ...
to laugh, lament, ...
morose, gay, sad, ...

2 In relation to the outside world

2.1 With respect to humans
2.1.1. Moral qualities
ex., faithful, boastful, parasitic, proud, ignorant, good, wicked, violent, rude, taciturn, jovial, envious, confident, fair, sensible, dignified, lying, impartial, ...

2.1.2 Physical qualities
ask systematically for all body parts (nose, arms, breasts, ...) and terms which qualify them as beautiful or ugly
ex., handsome, ugly, weak, strong, ...

2.2 With respect to animals
systematic questionnaire for determining the physical and moral qualities and defects that may be attributed to animals. If so, which ones?

2.3 With respect to things
systematic questionnaire on nature, matter, objects, plants, ...
ex., beautiful, ugly, repulsive, ...

3 Language and thought

1 Language

1.1 Mode of speech
ex., say, speak, narrate, recount, joke, chant, ...
bad, soothing, angry, heated, cool speech, ...

1.2 Mode of narration
direct, indirect discourse, reported discourse, ...
testimony, hearsay, ...

1.3 Modes of address
inventory of greetings, formulas of politeness, terms of address, ...

2 Thought

2.1 Modes of thought
ex., think, calculate, reflect, analyze, judge, reason, forget, remember, dream, imagine, ...
logic, synthesis, mind, thought, criticism, ...
quick-witted, just, intelligent, stupid, ... (and give the adjectives which characterize thought and the mind)

2.2 Nomenclature for categories of thought
ex., intellect, spirit, soul, ...

4 Perception, organization, and relations with the social world

1 Space

1.1 Objective organization
linear
ex., straight, curved, winding, oblique, ...
planar
ex., rectangle, square, triangle, round, surface, ...
three-dimensional
ex., volume, sphere, cube, cylinder, ...

1.2 Cultural organization
earth
ex., terrain, hill, mountain, hillock, plain, plateau, valley, cape, island, peninsula, ...
water
ex., river, stream, sea, lake, brook, pond, pool, lagoon, intermittent or permanent waterway, ...
air
ex., sky, air, atmosphere, ...
division into layers, spheres, ...

Psychological Phenomena

1.3 Organization of social space: survey of socially important space
secular space
ex., marketplace, neighborhood, street, alley, walkways, parks, gardens, fields, clearings, forests, woods, playing fields, dancing area, ...
plantation, brush, village, courtyard, cultivated land, fallow land, virgin land, ...
religious space
ex., isolated area for initiates, men's house, women's house, young girls' house, house for storing masks, sacred rocks, sacred wells, ...
toponomy: list of the names of places in the village, around the village and outside of the territory that carry a specific name in history, legend, geography, as a place of pilgrimage, ...

1.4 Objective perception
size
ex., large, small, wide, narrow, immense, endless (determine if the same terms apply to an animal, a person, a plot of land, a village)
qualities
ex., fertile, rich, sterile, belonging to ... , specifically for ...

1.5 Space in relation to the speaker
position
ex., in front of, behind, towards (me, you, him, ... ; the village, the bush ...), moving away from, across from, around, beside, in back, ...
distance
ex., far, near, out of sight, out of reach, ...

2 Time

2.1 Cultural organization
punctiliar segments
ex., second, minute, hour, day (24 hr.), week, month and year (solar, lunar, other criteria), century, ...
periodic segments
- in relation to the sun
ex., day, night, dawn, daybreak, morning, noon, twilight, dusk, evening, morning, afternoon, evening, sunrise, sunset, spring, summer, autumn, winter, name of the longest day, the shortest day, solstice, eclipse, ...
- in relation to the temperature and/or activities
for a day's time
ex., shepherds' hour, milking time, nightfall, time for returning from the fields, nap time, nomenclature of the names of the days, ...
for a longer period of time (week or month)
nomenclature of the names of the weeks, of months, ...
ex., dry season, wet season, cold season, rainy season, ...
growing season, working season, calendar, epoch, period, ...

2.2 Organization of social time
Nomenclature of moments, times, seasons, socially important periods used to mark time
secular

- clans, within the family: anniversary, birthday, golden or silver wedding anniversary, ...
- clans, within the group

in relation to history: holidays (the equivalents of our independence day, armistice day, etc.)
ex., ancestral times, mythical times, history, antiquity, ...
in relation to work
ex., growing season, harvest time, sowing time, time for gathering in crops, for moving herds, for hunting, for setting brush fires
religious
- within the family
ex., initiation, circumcision, excision, engagement, wedding, funeral, ...
- within the group
ex., all religious festivals, times of sacrifices, for bringing out masks, ... (equivalents for Christmas, Ascension, ...)

2.3 Objective perception
duration
ex., as long as, during, for a long time, always, still, now in the process of, ...
brief, long, prolonged, rapid, ...
wait, cycle
verbal aspect markers

2.4 Time in relation to the speaker
punctiliar
ex., before, after, simultaneously, when, then, next, immediately, present, past, future, ...
verbal tense markers

3 Symbolic Systems

3.1 Music
instrumentology: names of musical instruments, of their component parts, notes (do, re, ...), octave, ...
typology of songs, rhythms, musical subjects
- generic terms
- names of specific songs

3.2 Painting, decoration, scarifications
materials used
- instruments
colorings
typology of forms, motifs, combinations
(note the symbolic significance of each):
- decorative
- representative
ex., frets, scrolls, angles, circles
colors with possible significance: go over the words for each category: house, fabric, ritual objects, utilitarian objects, jewelry, scarifications, body painting or tattooing

Psychological Phenomena

3.3 Dance
figures, steps, rhythms
nomenclature of dances
- generic terms
- proper names of dances

3.4 Plastics
vocabulary of volume
vocabulary of plastic objects: symbolism of shapes

3.5 Games
educational games
entertaining games
ex., round dance, hide and seek, ...

3.6 Divination
nomenclature of different types of divination
ex., consultation of the earth, geomancy, (foot)prints, ...
list of figures and representations with their significance

3.7 Means of classification
animal taxonomy (cf. zoology questionnaire)
plant taxonomy (cf. botany questionnaire)
linguistic taxonomy
- lexical categorizations
ex., type, kind, ...
    masculine, feminine, neuter
    singular, dual, plural
    exclusive, inclusive
heated speech, cool speech
- grammatical categories
ex., noun, verb, adjective

3.8 Measurement and calculation
measures of volume
ex., liter, ...
measures of weight
ex., kilogram, gram, ...
measures of distance
ex., meter (check if the same terms apply to all things measured linearly, such as land, cloth, ...)
measures of area
ex., hectare
measures for exchange
- nomenclature of coins or any other system used
ex., cowries, woven bands, etc.
- sample scale of values
ex., price of a chicken, an ox, a hoe, a wife, ...
calculating
ex., to count, to calculate, to add up, to add, subtract, multiply, divide, ...
- expensive, inexpensive

4 Behavior and social attitudes

4.1 Nomenclature of terms
kinship (cf. questionnaire on sociological phenomena 1. Family organization)
social and political (cf. questionnaire on sociological phenomena 2. Political and social organization
supernatural world
- gods: great, small, important, secondary, ...
- spirits: phantoms, doubles, fetishes, ...
- nature spirits: of water, earth, the bush, trees, forest, ...

4.2 Social relations
authority, joking, respect, vexation, tribe, allegiance, ...
attitudes that are prescribed, forbidden (with ensuing sanctions), tolerated, ...
- go over all the terms from 4.1 systematically and determine the relationships and the attitudes within a given category and between categories, in the domain of feelings and behavior (father/son; adult/chief; chief/sorceror; sorceror/spirit; ...)

prescribed rituals and objects
- by social classes: griots, blacksmiths, clan, ...
- by activity: hunting, fishing, farming, ...
  sports, festivals
- in relation to religion: ceremony, rites (masks, loincloths, ...), sacrifice, ...
- in relation to health: illness, healing, medicine (talisman, belt, bracelets)
- in relation to sorcery: magic, fetishes, devourer of souls, sacrifice, ...

Questionnaire 17
Names, Measurement, and Time

A. Names
by Jacqueline M. C. Thomas

1 Names of people (anthroponyms)

At least one hundred copies of this questionnaire should be made. The principal language speaker can assist with this questionnaire, so its importance and use should be explained to him. He must be from the same ethnic and language group as the people being studied. Give basic information about the principal speaker at the beginning (family name, personal name, ethnic group, language).

1. Name of the person interviewed Age:
   Meaning or translation of name. Sex:
2. When did he receive this name? Ethnic group:
3. Who gave it to him? Place of birth:
4. Why is he called by this name?
5. What is the function of the name (for protection, to bring good luck, etc.)
6. Who calls him by this name?
   - father   - mother   - brothers   - sisters
   - paternal uncle - maternal uncle
   - paternal aunt   - maternal aunt
   - son   - daughter   - wife or husband
   - father-in-law   - mother-in-law   - others:
   - friends of the same age - younger   - older   - others:

   Who may not call him by this name?
   - father   - mother   - brothers   - sisters

- paternal uncle   - maternal uncle
- paternal aunt   - maternal aunt
- son   - daughter   - wife or husband
- father-in-law   - mother-in-law   - others:
- friends of the same age   - younger   - older   - others:

What must they call him?

7. Does he have a namesake? What do they call each other?

8. Does he also have a Christian or Muslim name? Why?
   Has he changed this name?

9. What other names has the person had?
   Meaning or translation
   When and why did he receive them?
   Who gave them to him?
   What was the function of these names (for protection, good luck, etc.)?
   Who could call him by these names?
   Who could not? What did they have to call him?

10. Surname(s) of the person interviewed
    Meaning or translation
    Why and when did he receive them?
    Who gave them to him?
    What is their function?
    Who can call him by these names, and when?
    Who cannot (must not)? What must they call him?

11. Is there a food or other taboo connected with the name or surname?
    What is it? Does the person have personal taboo(s)? What are they?

12. Does the person have family taboo(s)? What are they?
    Does he have lineage or clan taboo(s)? What are they?

2 Names of lineages and/or clans

Approximately one hundred copies of this questionnaire should be made. The principal language speaker can assist with this questionnaire, so its importance and use should be explained to him. He must come from the same ethnic and language group as the people being studied. Give basic information about the principal speaker at the beginning (family name, personal name, ethnic group, language).

1. Name of lineage (or clan)
   Meaning or translation.

2. Why does it have this name (history)?

3. Are there sub-divisions (sub-lineages or sub-clans)?
   Does each one have a name? What is it? Why?
   When was the separation (made) and why?

4. Do the neighboring lineages call them by this name, or do they use another name? What is it? Why?

Names, Measurement, and Time

5. Has the lineage always had its present name?
   If not, what name did it have before?
   Why was it changed?
6. Has the lineage always lived at its present location?
   If not, where did it come from?
   Why did it leave there, and when?
7. Does part of this lineage still live there?
   Do those here see the others periodically?
   Is there a marriage taboo with them?
8. Does the lineage have food or other taboos? What are they?
   Why (history)?
9. Is there another lineage with the same name?
   If so, are they related and how?
   Why don't they live together?
   Do they have the same taboos?
   Is there a marriage taboo between the two?
10. Is the name the beginning of a motto?
    Does it have a musical expression?

3 Names of domestic animals
(dogs, cattle, camels, etc.)

This questionnaire was partly inspired by the one developed by Anne Retel-Laurentin for the names of dogs; it was enlarged and clarified, particularly for linguistic purposes. At least one hundred copies of the questionnaire should be made. The principal speaker can assist with this questionnaire, so its importance and use should be explained to him. It is strongly advised that he be from the same ethnic group and language as the people being studied.

> Informant (name, ethnic group, language):
> Village where he is working (name, ethnic group, language):

1. Proper name of the animal
   Translation or meaning
   species, sex, and age (possibly breed)
2. Why was it given the name?
   Did its present owner give the name? If not, who did?
   Has the name been changed? Why? When?
3. Does the animal also have a surname? What is it?
   Meaning?
   Why was it given the surname? Who gave it? When?
4. Name of present master of the animal
   Ethnic group–lineage and language

Name(s) of previous master(s), if any.
5. How did the present master obtain the animal?
   Did he buy it? for how much?
   Was it given to him? Why?
6. Was the animal given in exchange (with / without markup), as a dowry?
7. What is the animal used for (this specific animal)?
8. Can it be eaten?
   Will it be?
9. What will the owner do with it after its death (discard the carcass, bury it, use part or all of it, etc.)?
10. If the owner dies, to whom will the animal belong?

B. Measurement
by Pierre-Francis Lacroix–ERA 246

4 Investigation of measuring and accounting systems

This article is designed to facilitate an investigation of the systems of measurement and accounting used in the societies of West Africa. We did not feel it possible to draw up a questionnaire because of extreme diversity of objects to be measured and counted, and because of the great variety of the systems in use.

The aim of the investigation is to obtain historical, ethnological, and linguistic information. For the latter purposes, the investigator must have some linguistic knowledge. For the collection of terms of measurements and accounts, including those which describe the various processes involved in related operations, accurate transcription is essential. If the phonology of the language has been worked out, this transcription can be phonological; otherwise it should be phonetic. The official orthography of the language could also be used if it exists. The nouns obtained should be recorded at least in the singular and plural forms, unless they belong to a unique class of collective nouns. The simplest handling of verbs is to give the equivalent of the imperative form of English or French. The ethnological information should be precise, making extensive use of drawings and photographs.

For measurement and accounting systems in economic usage, give the buying or selling prices for each at the time of the study. Try to obtain information about:

a) possible seasonal variations in price;
b) historical information, such as the comparable price at the time of independence; in 1939; between the two world wars (using a point of reference, e.g., the famine of 1930–31); before the arrival of Europeans or the introduction of their monetary systems.

The metric equivalent for each unit of measure (and counting system, when possible) should be given. The following materials will be needed for this:
- level scales with weights (or any other simple, sturdy, and light weighing apparatus);
- a two-meter measuring tape or dressmaker's tape measure;

- a graduated half-liter glass or a glass liter container (not a bottle with a vaguely defined capacity).

Remember that the same term may designate considerably different measures of capacity in different places, even within a small ethnolinguistic zone (e.g., the various *azzaka / azzakka / azakka* of Aïr). Moreover, in a single place there may be measures of differing amounts or values which have the same name, followed by a qualification of some sort (moud, Sultan X's moud, German moud, etc.). Finally, there may be intentionally altered units of measure. All must be catalogued and described. Do not forget that the body or parts of the body are often used as standards of measurement, and that counting often makes reference to special number systems (e.g., with base five).

Information on various ways of regulating the accuracy of transactions should also be included in a study of this type:
- Who regulates them and in what way? Under what authority?
- What are the penalties in case of fraud? Who enforces them? (today or in precolonial days)

1 Measurement of space

Four categories are included here, based on the measurement of distance (relationships between space and time are often found in this category), of surfaces, of height/depth, and of the dimensions of a building.

A. Distance
- Names of the various possible stages of a journey and estimation of distances (normal distance covered by an animal, heavily loaded or not, in one day; distance covered by someone on foot between two times of day; etc.)
- Names given to relatively short distances (stone's throw, arrow's range, etc.)
- More precise measures of length: pace, foot, etc.; measures of thickness.

B. Surface
- Is there a unit of land measure or several? Is it determined by dimensions or by criteria of average productivity (e.g., the number of sheaves harvested)? What is its name?

C. Height / depth
- Names and description of units used to measure the depth of a river or well, the height of a tree, etc.

D. Architect's measurements
- Names and description of units used to measure the foundations of a house and its various dimensions;
- Terminology and procedures for estimating the size of a building (e.g., capacity of a loft).

2 Measurement of materials

A. Grain

1. What measures exist for grain (calabashes, baskets, metal containers, bushels, bags? What were they called? Description (shape, size, materials, capacity, etc.).

2. Other possible measures: e.g., the palm or both palms, a sheaf, ears, criteria for measuring sheaves. Names of these measures.

3. Possible bonus with a purchase (institutionalized or not, measured or not); e.g., a 'hatful' added to the measure, or an extra handful for every X handfuls. Names given to the various sorts of possible bonuses.

4. Various verbs (if their form is different from the nouns) used to express the process of measuring in this way.

B. Liquids

The principal liquids involved in transactions and measurements are: milk and milk products, oils, melted butter, alcoholic beverages, honey, water.

For each of these liquids, ask the questions of A1, A3, and A4 above if appropriate.

C. Various materials

In a comprehensive list, this section could include various flours and powders (gold dust, gunpowder, etc.), granulated salt, powdered sugar, etc., as well as measures used for cotton fiber, and wool and goat's hair.

3 Counting goods

A. Textiles

1. Unit used in the sale of cotton thread–its name and nature.

2. Cloth: does the counting system change according to the fabric (e.g., strips of cotton and manufactured cloth in pieces); or between traditionally made loincloths and those produced industrially; or according to the use to be made of it?

   Units used, with their names.

   Does the width enter into consideration? If so, give the terminology used. Give also verbs describing the different phases of the measurement, and the operation as a whole.

B. Products counted by the piece or by the set

Guidelines for counting by the unit vs. counting by the set, for various products: vegetables, onions, dates, peppers, fruits, cola nuts, soap, salt in chunks, cheese, fresh butter, tobacco (leaves, powder), tea, dried fish, porridge, firewood, etc.

Nature and composition of various groupings (pile, handful, ladleful–cf. 2B) with their names.

4 Products sold by volume / weight

A. Fresh meat and fish

1. Sale by piles vs. sale by the piece. Consider the distinction between meat and offal, cheaper and higher-quality cuts; sale of cooked meat (kebabs, grilled poultry, etc.). Give the various terms used and describe them.

2. In what ways is fresh fish sold (whole, by the cut, etc.)?

B. Prepared dishes
What are they? Give terminology and description (identify the ingredients used with their names); nature and names of the units of measure.

C. Rock salt and natron
Slabs of salt and natron and their smaller units; the various cakes of salt (description, names, sizes, weights).

D. Sugar
By loaves or lumps.

E. Metals (other than gold)
Iron; copper; silver; aluminum.
Consider the ways in which it is sold, various qualities and origins (for silver, note particularly the trade in coins withdrawn from circulation for the making of jewelry; for iron, scrap metal that competes with or replaces products extracted in traditional ways).

5 Questionnaire on money systems

1. Do we still know what the ancestors used to trade with? Is there a currency represented by strips of cloth, iron objects or iron symbols of objects, etc.?

   Is there a tradition on this matter?

2. Were cowrie shells used? Can we determine when this usage started? Did they replace an older monetary system (strips of cloth, for example)?

   Do we know through whom they knew about cowries?

   Name of the cowrie in the group concerned (singular and plural, or collective forms).

   Determine the semantic areas of this term (e.g., is it identical to the name for a shell in general, or a stone, or another variety of shell, etc.)

   Ancient value of the cowrie: Can the value in cowries of a goat (or some other object or animal) be remembered, at some datable points in the history of the region under consideration?

   How were cowries counted?

   How were they transported? Was there only one type of cowrie? How were they obtained?

Try to find out if other varieties of shells have been used for monetary purposes.

3. Have silver coins (e.g., Maria Theresa dollar, or others) been used as currency? At what period? What was their value and its fluctuations?

4. When did the various types of currency disappear in the face of modern European currencies? Did they persist for some time after the establishment of the colonial system? For what purposes? Are they still used for certain symbolic or ritual payments?

   What is the present value of cowries and silver coins of various types used for adornment?

5. European currencies: terminology–what names are given to the various coins and bills now in circulation? Is there possibly competition between two or more money systems?

C. Expression of time
by Pierre-Francis Lacroix–ERA 246

6 Linguistic questionnaire on the expression of time

Introduction. The aim of this questionnaire is to facilitate the study of the conception of time through its linguistic expression. The questionnaire was developed for use in West African societies (the Sudano-Sahelian peoples, in particular), but with some modifications it can be used in other geographical areas as well.

Various approaches are possible for a study of the conception of time in a culture. Reference will be made to existing works, for example the psychological study of L. V. Thomas among the Diolas, and the sociological study made of the societies of Côte d'Ivoire by a group of authors (see bibliography). Our approach will be strictly ethnolinguistic.

The application of this questionnaire requires a good grasp of the language and culture in no case should it be used at the beginning of an investigation. For obvious reasons, we will have to refer to English words here, and multiple meanings of a number of English words (e.g., time) will have to be distinguished in the investigation.

Remember that nouns must be obtained in at least two forms, singular and plural, and verbs in the imperative singular if possible. The transcription can be phonemic, if the phonology of the language has already been analyzed, or else phonetic. The official orthography can be used when this exists. Ethnological comments must be as precise as possible. The procurement of a star chart for the relevant latitudes is also recommended.

Language speakers should be chosen carefully. Older people will probably be the best qualified for this type of study. In societies with co-existing lifestyles (e.g., herders and farmers), and different registers of language (e.g., among literates; town and country dwellers; Muslims, Christians, animists; ...), one speaker is not enough. The choice will also depend on the person's sphere of knowledge and the type of expression desired.

Keep in mind that one goal of the investigation is to determine the *frame of reference* used by the people in dividing time (whether the day, the year, or any other time period). Possible reference systems are varied; for example:

- basic economic activity (agriculture, animal husbandry, fishing, ...):

> E.g., for the Dogon people, the names of most of the months are related to agricultural activities.
> 'the *Parkia biglobosa* is flowering' (third month)
> 'the *Lannea acida* is in flower' (fourth month)
> 'the time when one strikes (the fruit of) the kapok tree (to make it fall)' (sixth month)
> 'month of the feast of sowing' (seventh month)
> 'month of sowing' (eighth month)
> 'month of cultivating' (ninth month)
> 'second weeding' (tenth month)
> 'month when one chases the birds (who eat the millet)' or 'month of cutting down the *Digitaria exilis*' (eleventh month)
> month of the harvest' (twelfth month)

- religious life

> E.g., in Fulani, there are three systems for dividing the day. One of these belongs to Moslem culture and the Arabic language, and plays an important role in the daily prayers:
> subaka 'morning, sunrise' (time of the first prayer)
> juura 'noon' (time of the second prayer)
> laasara 'late afternoon' (time of the third prayer)
> futuroo during Ramadan, the time when one can begin to eat food, i.e., sunset

- observation of the stars (phases of the moon, positions of the sun, moon, and stars); astrology

- atmospheric phenomena (rain, wind, drought, cold, ...)

- observation of nature (plants, animals, ...)

> E.g., the four seasons of the Diola year are defined in this way:
> 'the dry season' begins when the leaves of the kapok tree fall, and when a certain species of *Acacia* comes into leaf.
> 'the period before the rains' is indicated by the appearance of leaves on the kapok tree, then the baobab and then the bastard mahogany. When the latter has come into leaf, a long-tailed bird begins to sing.
> 'the rainy season' is announced several days in advance by the singing of a species of small kingfisher.

The last season starts when the early rice and first groundnuts ripen.

Often, several systems of reference are superimposed. This situation may result in the use of several calendars, or it may be evidenced within a single calendar.

E.g., the months of the Mbum-Tiba calendar are named after all of these: atmospheric phenomena, observation of the vegetation, agricultural activities, and physical sensations.

1st month 'it is scorching a little'
2nd month 'it is scorching, the rain is coming'
3rd month 'the grass hides the stumps'
4th month 'grass covers the valleys'
5th month 'dizziness (from hunger)'
6th month 'flooding'
7th month 'rotting (of corn stalks)'
8th month 'formation of the ears of millet'
9th month 'now the morning (famine is past)'
10th month 'only the repletion'
11th month 'we no longer go to the fields'
12th month 'we no longer go into the water (because of the cold)'

N.B. The human lifetime and its stages provide an important system of reference, but it is seen more on the social level, and not directly in relation to the divisions of time.

1 Divisions of time

A. General comments

- Terms expressing notions of: time (in the sense of the period as a whole), of a particular moment within it, of a point which can be isolated from a sequence); duration; past, present, future.
- Is the name of the weather condition related to that which expresses a length or division of time (e.g., a day)?
E.g., in Dogon, the weather and the day are expressed by the same word.
- Terms expressing the divisions of human life: age, generation, age groups, different stages of life.
- How does one speak of the beginning and ending with respect to time periods?
- Study the verbs of movement (in general) in their use as related to time: come, go, do, etc.

B. Counting time

1. The year
- What name is used for the year (i.e., the revolution of the earth around the sun)? How many days, weeks, months, seasons make it up?
- Is the term used for counting years the same as for the year itself?
E.g., in Fulani, 'he lived for ten years' and 'he died in that year' are not expressed in the same way.

2. Seasons
- How many are there? When do they begin and end? Give their names; features serving as reference points; subdivisions and overlaps (periods straddling two seasons).

3. The month
- How many months? Give their names. Are they lunar or solar? Are the two superimposed? Give the names of the quarters of the moon. How is the discrepancy of the lunar months made up for? Which is the first month of the year? What determines this choice?

4. The week
- What is its name? Possible superimposition of the European or Arabic week (7 days) on the traditional week (e.g., 5 days). Give the names of the days of the week. When does it begin? Is one day more important than the others?

5. Day and night
- Names of: 24-hour day; daytime (sun up); work day; night (from sunset to sunrise); nighttime
- Are the names for day and night used to indicate light and darkness?
- Is counting done in days or nights?
- Divisions of the day and night
- Are there other concepts of day and night in addition to the basic ones and contrasting with them such as French jour/journée, matin/matinée, nuit/nuitée?

a) Are the names given related to human activities or to real time periods?

Which times of day and night have both a name referring to a specific astrological phenomenon and a name related to a human activity?

b) See whether the formulation of the greetings and the changes of greetings are related to the divisions of the day.

c) To obtain the names, start with a precise moment (in time) and progress very slowly (through the day), trying to think of all details. Noon and midnight are convenient reference points. Distinctions such as morning/afternoon/evening seem rather common; there may be major distinctions within these categories.

E.g., the Moors distinguish between the 'first part', the 'middle', and the 'remainder' of the night.

d) For finer distinctions, it may be useful to begin with the night, when the 'day' begins with the preceding evening (check on this first). The Mauritanean divisions could be used as terms of reference, as it may be difficult to make a more detailed breakdown.

E.g., divisions of the night as expressed by the Moors
- the moment following sunset
- two hours of twilight (dusk), subdivided into red-hued and white-hued reflections
- evening
- milking time for different animals (there are four)
- middle of the night
- last third
- two hours of twilight (transition from night to day), subdivided into: cock's crowing, small remainder of the night, dawn, between dawn and sunrise.

- for sunrise, distinction is made of the moment when the sun is one cubit above the horizon, two cubits, etc.

During the daytime the Moors measure time by the length of the shadow, which varies with the season (they have mnemonic poems to help make the application).

e) Note names which are expressive or use imagery.

E.g., certain names of the times of day may include annotations such as 'the little ... ,' 'the big ... ,' 'the cool ... ,' etc.

Special expressions may indicate uncertainty in certain transition periods; for example, the Moors say of the sun that 'it has fallen, it has not fallen'; the Dogon speak of twilight as 'heavy eyes' (the moment when one can no longer clearly distinguish). Other expressions may show the intensity at certain times: when the sun is at its zenith, the Moors use the expression 'hot on top, hot underneath.'

f) How does one say: one hour, one minute (superimposition of the European system)? A moment, a little while, an instant (all distinctions)?

6. For all the time divisions (year, month, day, ...)
Note these relative terms:
- last year, this year, next year, ...
- last month, this month, next month, ...
- yesterday, today, the day before yesterday, three days ago; tomorrow, the day after tomorrow, the third day, ...
- Is 'yesterday' distinguished from the preceding day, and 'tomorrow' from the following day?

C. Historical time

- Is there a separate term to distinguish mythical time from historical time?
- Does the concept of time extend beyond the year? Give the extent of time (human generation?). Are there notions such as 'epoch, era' ... ?
- Dating of certain outstanding years after notable events—historical, astronomical (eclipses, comets, ...), meteorological, zoological (locusts), botanical; famines and epidemics, ... Are these terms adopted generally, or simply individual points of reference?
- Is each year distinguished by a notable event?
- Epoch: Is the epoch of the introduction of an institution (currency, etc.) distinguished?
- Period: e.g., the time of the Fulani, of the French, ..., the reign of king X; the period separating successive celebrations of periodic ceremonies (e.g., the period of sixty years separating two *sigi* ceremonies among the Dogon. The period may be broken down into years. Material means for calculating the periods (knots in a string, notches in a stick, etc.
- When did meticulous attention to (the passage of) time begin? When did historical precision commence?

D. Rituals and time/rhythm of ceremonies

- Which days or periods of the year, month, week, ... are set aside for rest, and if possible, by whom? Names and meanings of feast days. Is a religious

Names, Measurement, and Time

year distinguished from an agricultural year? Are certain days or periods or times considered unlucky? Are they designated by euphemisms?
- Note songs, riddles, proverbs related to the stars and the counting of time; didactic poems or songs concerning time.
- See whether all levels of society use the same terms, or whether different usages exist for nomads or farmers, for city-dwellers, for strict Muslims, etc. Make comparison within the same linguistic community (some divisions may not coincide).
- Note the expression of time in traditional literature, the frequency of references to time, and the perspectives in which these are cited.

2 Perception of time

A. Morphemes and/or derivational markers. Ideophones

1 Specific time value

yesterday	in my time
today	a short while ago
tomorrow etc. (see 1.B.6)	long ago
tonight	in times past / in days of old
this morning, etc.	(all the nuances)
now	very long ago
immediately	a moment ago
presently	recently
in our days / life	days, months, years ago
in our time	days, months, years from now

2. Aspectual value

often	still
for a long time	not yet
already	a long time after
finally	during that time
soon	now and then
henceforth	on time
suddenly	at the same time
again	in the end
always	successively
never	progressively (as soon as)
quickly	firstly
slowly	lastly
Yearly	once
late	several times
a long time before	

- Expressions of repetition (e.g., the prefix *re-* in English)
- Negation as related to time (no longer, not yet, ...)

B. Terms indicating action
   (but not necessarily expressed by a verbal root)

to be in a hurry to
to hurry
to have time
to be late
to be early
to spend much time,
to last (African sense)
spend all one's time in
to spend the night in
to take one's time (to)
the time spent
to have a long time to live
to leave in the morning
to greet someone in the morning

to spend the rainy season (dry season ...)
to finish
to rise, set (stars)
to be a long time doing (without doing) something
it is time that
what time is it?
what day is it?
what year is it?

to do something late
to do something early
to delay, to be slow
to arrive too early
to do something at an opportune / inopportune time
to spend so much time in
to spend the day (in)
to waste one's time (in)
time passes
to have much time before one
to leave early
to do something before day
to return home in the evening (in the afternoon)
to begin
to remain
to be a long time with
it is time to

it is time
it is ... o'clock
what month is it?
it is ... (day, month, year)

C. Syntactic expressions of time

1. When (possibly associated with adverbs to indicate different nuances; cf. English 'when finally,' 'when suddenly).'

2. *simultaneity:* as (associated with a causal meaning in English), while, meanwhile, at the moment when,

   equivalent time duration: as long as, for as long as;

   joint progression: as, as fast as;

   accompanying repetition: each time that

3. *rapid succession:* only just ... when,

   just about to ... when,

   no sooner ... than,

   hardly had ... when.

4. *preceding, following:* before, after;

   action that continues until the next begins: until, in the meantime;

immediately following: as soon as, immediately after, once;

point of departure: now that, since.

Note: This list is not exhaustive and should be expanded. Certain ideas specific to the English means of expression (which has served as the basis here) will not necessarily have equivalents in the language being studied, and vice versa.

D. Proverbs and expressions

Look for proverbs and expressions concerning the perception of time. Certain examples (such as, in English, 'time is money,' 'time and tide wait for no man') can be suggested to the speaker; equivalent proverbs will usually be found readily if they exist. Once one proverb has been found, it will bring others to mind.

E. Verbal aspects

For this part of the questionnaire, refer to the study of aspects in the thematic verbal questionnaire by F. Cloarec-Heiss and C. Hagège (Vol. 2, Questionnaire 6A).

Bibliography

1. The *Sciences humains* series of the *Cahiers de l'Orstom* devoted a special issue (vol. V, no. 3, 1968) to the concept of time in several African societies: 'Temps et développement: Quatre sociétés en Côte d'Ivoire.' Articles by M. Augé (Alladian), J. L. Boutillier (Koulango), P. Etienne (Baoulé), and A. Schwartz (Guéré). These studies are complemented by an annotated bibliography by M. Le Pape, to which we will refer later.

2. The examples cited in this questionnaire are taken either from the works above or from the following:

P. Dubie. Mesures de temps en Mauritanie. Comptes rendus de la Première Conférence Internationale des Africanistes de l'Ouest, vol. II, IFAN 1951, pp. 242–57.

A. Leriche. Mesures maures. Notes préliminaires. BIFAN, 13, 4, Dakar, Oct. 1951, pp. 1227–56.

L. V. Thomas and D. Sapir. Le Diola et le temps. Bulletin de l'IFAN xxix, series B, no. 1–2, 1967, pp. 331–424.

Questionnaire 18
Oral Tradition

1 Text collection

*by Jean-Pierre Caprile,
Jean-Claude Rivierre,
and Jacqueline M. C. Thomas*

This questionnaire, when filled out, should accompany each recording of a text, as a form for identification and classification.

1 Informants

+ Narrator
Family name, given name:
Ethnic group:
Village:
Language(s):
Age and sex:
Social position:

+ Interpreter / Performer

2 Recording

Number:
Date:
Tape (quality):
Length (from counter):
Recorder (make and model):
Other technical characteristics:

Title:
Location:
Track:

3 Genre of text

Vernacular name of the genre:
Identification of the genre by the researcher:

Elicited text (technical narration, explanation, definition, commentary; anecdotal, autobiographical, descriptive, narration, etc.)

Spontaneous, nontraditional text (speech, conversation, palaver, pleading speech, etc.)

Traditional text in everyday language

- principal genres (historical narrative, myth, legend, story, fable, ballad, etc.)
- minor genres (mottos, proverbs, adages, sayings, precepts, riddles puzzles, short stories, counting-rhymes, ritornellos, lullabies, satirical songs, amusing stories, obscene stories, scatological jokes, ritual jokes, insults, etc.

Traditional text in special types of language

- poetry
- song
- other special usages (drumbeat messages, whistled messages, etc.)

4 Résumé

Give a brief résumé or the main thread of the story.
Indicate the names and possibly the characteristics of the main characters.

5 Characteristics of the text

(Typical, and not accidental to the conditions of the study)

Circumstances of the telling

Place (where is it told?)
E.g., in the bush / in the forest / in the village // in front of the house / inside the house // under a tree / under the open sky / etc.

Time (when is it told?)
E.g., daytime / nighttime // morning / afternoon / evening // at the close of day / etc.

Occasion (why, in what circumstances is it told?)
- daily life: work (while working in the field, while hunting, fishing, while paddling, etc.) / rest (evening gatherings, siesta time, break time, etc.)
- ceremonial:
  * fixed: firstfruits (of the harvests, hunting, fishing, etc.), commemorative feasts, religious meetings, etc.
  * variable: marriage, birth, mourning, funeral ceremony, etc.

Teller (who, what category of individuals may or must tell it): sex, age, social position, etc.

Audience (who, what category / categories of individuals listen?)

Ways and means of telling (traditional, and not accidental)

Oral Tradition 691

Mode of expression: recounted, spoken, mimed, sung, chanted, declaimed, etc. (Take note, if possible, of gesticulations, postures, voices, and the points at which they are used.)

Type of accompaniment
- without accompaniment
- with accompaniment: answering back, musical accompaniment, choir (spoken / sung), rhythmic accompaniment (by instrument—which one?) / by response, etc. Note the bearing and reactions of those who assist.

Special expressions
- introductory word or sentence / stereotyped closing of a narrative // stereotyped punctuation of the different sentences of the narrative / etc.
- archaisms, loanwords, etc.
- esoteric sentences or secret language; special social language (of one caste, sex, etc.)

Rituals of the telling (taboos, obligations, special rites that precede, accompany, or follow the telling, etc.) concerning the place, time, occasion, teller, audience, as for the ways and means of expression

6 Transcription of the text (by numbered sentences)

Phonological or phonetic transcription, carefully handwritten

Interlinear word-for-word translation

Free translation

Notes and explanatory comments

2 Ethnomusicology
by Simha Arom and Geneviève Dournon-Taurelle

I Musical instruments

1 Naming

    1.1 Name of the instrument in the vernacular
        Literal translation

    1.2 Synonym or onomatopoetic name
        Literal translation

    1.3 Name in the trade language or a widely-used local language
        Literal translation

2 Location

    2.1 Geographical
      - place or area where the instrument is used

- place or area where the instrument is made
- if appropriate, how the instrument was brought in and established (barter, exchange, purchase)

2.2 Ethnic group
- ethnic group and/or subgroup using it
- ethnic group and/or subgroup making it

3 Category of instrument and manner of producing sound

3.1 Membrane instrument
- the sound is produced by striking or rubbing a membrane (e.g., friction drums)

3.2 Stringed instrument
- the sound is produced by drawing a bow across the string, by plucking with fingers or a pick, or by striking

3.3 Wind instrument
- the sound is produced by the breath of the musician (e.g., flutes, whistles, conch shells) or by the surrounding air

3.4 Idiophone: (the body of the instrument itself is the resonating material)
- If the instrument does not fit into one of the preceding categories, it belongs here: the sound is produced percussively (knocking two or more objects together, beating, pounding), or by shaking, scraping, plucking

4 Physical description

4.1 Autonomy of the instrument
- the instrument is autonomous, i.e., it is moveable, physically transportable
- the instrument is fixed: to assemble it requires nontransportable, fixed, immovable materials (such as for the zither on the ground, or the xylophone on the pit)
- the instrument is unstable, short-lived, or temporary: it is put together on the spot with various materials, often ordinary objects which are returned to their original function after their musical use

4.2 Components of the instrument
- nomenclature of the different parts of the instrument in the vernacular language, with a literal translation
- note, depending on the category of the instrument, the number of membranes, strings, playing holes, the type of mouthpiece (at the end or along the side), etc.
- give the size (measurements) of the instrument and of its respective parts

4.3 Accessories
- nomenclature of sound-making accessories (round bells, cowbells, etc.), conspicuous or not, in the vernacular language with literal translation

4.4 Materials
- nomenclature of the different materials, conspicuous or not, which make up the instrument and its accessories: wood, bamboo, metal, skins, or animal

parts (bones, skulls, wings, entrails), latex, resin, etc.; in the vernacular with literal translation
- are there objects such as charms, talismans, etc., inside the body of the instrument? Give their vernacular names with literal translation
- is the decoration of the instrument: permanent (sculptured, engraved, painted) or temporary (for certain occasions only–which ones? drawings in porcelain, clay, red paint, etc.)
- is the function of the decorative elements purely esthetic or is it symbolic? if the latter, what is the meaning?
- size and bulkiness of the instrument and its respective parts

5 Manufacture and preservation

5.1 Instrument maker
- family and given names- ethnic group
- sex- village
- approximate age
- social position
- are there any others in the area who make the same type of instrument?
- are they still making them? where? who are they (name, age, etc.)?

5.2 Technique of production
- place of manufacture
- materials used (are they local or imported from where, how, by whom?)
- technique of manufacture (describe the different stages and procedures in production)
- tools used—vernacular names with literal translation

5.3 Ritual
- note the ritual observances related to the instrument maker and the making of the instrument as such

5.4 Keeping care
- is there a particular place where the instrument is kept between periods of use? if so, whose responsibility is it?
- if the instrument is not kept, is it abandoned or destroyed after being used? where, how, by whom, why?

6 Use

6.1 Function
- is the instrument for making music or for making noise (e.g., noisemaker, toy, etc.)

6.2 Distribution and use
- in the local area, is it widespread, rare, or about to disappear?
- is it currently used in neighboring ethnic groups?

6.3 How is it used

    6.3.1 where and during which events
- is the place of use unspecified (specify if there are preferred places) or regulated (specify where: inside or outside, village or bush; specify for what occasions: ceremonies, commemorative festivals, nighttime gatherings, etc.)

    6.3.2 para-musical use
- is it used to transmit linguistic messages, calls, encoded signals, warnings
- does it suggest or evoke the voice of the ancestors: is it used to communicate with the supernatural world (ancestors, spirits, etc.)

    6.3.3 extra-musical use
- apart from making sound, is the instrument used as a measuring instrument or receptacle (calabashes), as exchange currency or dowry (bells), or as a domestic object (pottery)

6.4 Times of use

    6.4.1 frequency
- is it unspecified or regulated (if so, specify: seasons, agricultural cycles, religious calendar, births, etc.)

    6.4.2 times of use
- is the instrument played during the day or night / in the morning or evening / at an unspecified time; exclusively, preferably, or usually at this time

6.5 Ownership
- is the ownership of the instrument individual (indicate social position and status of owner) or collective (village, lineage, initiation society, age group)

7 Playing the instrument

7.1 Ways of playing
- is the instrument *played by itself* exclusively or preferably; or is it used to accompany the singing voice (solo and/or chorus), the speaking voice (oral literature—stories, legends, myths), the spoken and singing voice (chantefable—in this case, is the instrumentalist also the storyteller-singer?), or dancing?
- is the instrument used *with similar instruments,* e.g., a band of horns, whistle ensemble, battery of drums of the same category: if so, what is the specific name of the instrument within the ensemble? what is its comparative size in relation to the other instruments (in the ensemble)? give the names of the other instruments in the family or in the ensemble
- is the instrument usually used *with instruments of a different kind* (i.e., orchestra)? What are these instruments? Give nomenclature in the vernacular with literal translation. Does the instrument have a special or preferential relationship with some other instrument (e.g., always played together)? What is it? Why?
- is there a notion of incompatibility (musical or other) between this instrument and certain others? Which ones? Why?

7.2 Playing techniques
- is the instrument played by one or several musicians (certain large instruments, such as drums, xylophones, or percussion logs, can be struck simultaneously by several players)
- describe the playing posture of the musician and the position of the instrument
- describe briefly the distinctive characteristics of the playing technique; use of the different parts of the body (hands, legs, etc.); as well as the manner of striking, plucking, rubbing, blowing, etc.; the way in which the accessories are used, etc.

7.3 Teaching how to play
- how is the skill of playing passed on? by simple imitation or by teaching (individually with a master, or collectively in a specific setting, e.g., during initiation rites)

7.4 Instrumentalist
- family and personal names
- approximate age
- ethnic group and subgroup
- sex
- village
- social position
- where, at what age, and how did he learn to play the instrument?
- has he lived outside his native ethnic group? where? when? for how long?

8 Sociocultural function of the instrument and its repertoire

8.1 Repertoire
- if a specific repertoire is associated with the instrument, specify the name of the repertoire (in the vernacular, with literal translation), its function, and its socio-cultural context

8.2 Type of function

8.2.1 Secular
- if it has only secular functions, is it usually used for work, for relaxation, for the personal pleasure of the player, as a children's game, for walking, etc.

8.2.2 Secular and ritual
- if it may be used for secular and ritual purposes, its use is differentiated as to its repertoire; specify.

8.2.3 Magico-religious
- if it has a magico-religious function, the instrument may be associated with rites and/or ceremonies (for twins, passage to a new age class, fertility, planting agriculture, healing, hunting, funerals, etc.). Is this usage associated with only one function?
- in the course of the ritual, is the instrument used continuously or intermittently (if the latter, note the number of times it comes in).
- is the instrument identified with a supernatural being, such as a spirit or demon, etc.?
- does it represent the voice of the ancestors?

- is it the object of worship or of a particular veneration? more generally speaking, does it have a nonmusical, ceremonial function?

8.3 Change of function
- the present function is the same as the original one
- the original function has gone through some changes: what are they? Certain instruments originally meant for magico-religious usage are today used differently and have fallen into a sort of public domain. What are these changes?

8.4 Literature and history
- do chronicles, epics, tales, legends, myths, etc., exist in which the instrument is mentioned?
- are there narratives which allude to the origin of the instrument or how it was introduced into the cultural group now using it?

8.5 Symbolism
- is there a symbolic meaning attached to the instrument? in its entirety, only certain parts, certain materials used to make it? take down the symbolic expressions in the vernacular with literal translation.
- are there symbolic relationships (e.g., of kinship) between the instrument and other similar ones, such as among trumpets, whistles, drums in addition to a generic name does it have a distinctive name expressing this type of relationship (cf. 7.1)
- is there a symbolism concerning the role of each of the hands of the player, e.g., male and female?

9 Gathering data

9.1 Collecting sound documents

9.1.1 Record the ritual words which accompany the different phases of the making of the instrument and, where applicable, those pronounced during its consecration

9.1.2 Record the ritual words which may precede the playing of certain kinds of music

9.1.3 Record one or several pieces characteristic of the instrument and (of) its traditional repertoire

9.1.4 Record separately, one after the other, all the sounds which the instrument can produce. Indicate orally on the tape the order in which they have been recorded (e.g., from the musician's left to right, while facing the instrument) and also, where appropriate, the names of these sounds in the vernacular

9.2 Transcription of the texts

All sound recordings that include words should be immediately transcribed and translated, as indicated previously for all the other areas of field research (cf. Introduction). Therefore, each text recorded should be accompanied by:
- phonetic or phonological transcription
- word-for-word translation
- idiomatic translation
- explanatory notes

Oral Tradition

9.3 Collecting photographic documents
- in black-and-white and in color; black-and-white is preferable if the researcher has only one camera
- instrumentalist in the process of playing: a) front view, b) in profile, c) 3/4 view
- close-up of the instrument in playing position: a) front view, b) profile, c) 3/4 view
- the instrument at rest: a) front view, b) profile, c) 3/4 view
- photograph as much as possible all the pictorial representations in the local art where the instrument is depicted (e.g., paintings, mural, bas-reliefs, etc.)

II Vocal music

1 Identification

1.1 Title of the song or distinctive opening line

1.2 Genre: if the song belongs to a definite genre (musical, poetic, or choreographic), indicate which one

1.3 Language of the text

1.4 Type and/or function of the song: work, diversion, children's magico-religious; incantation, exorcism

1.5 Circumstances of the performance: see list of circumstances and functions below

2 Ownership

2.1 Is the song considered as "belonging" to an ethnic group, an ethnic subgroup, a village, a lineage, a family, an age group, an initiation society (for males or females), an individual (what is his social status), a supernatural being (a divinity, a spirit, guardian spirit, soul of an ancestor, etc.)

2.2 Is its use by anyone other than the rightful owner(s) considered as a hostile act, or a usurpation, etc?

2.3 Is there a "copyright"? Is it possible to acquire the right to use (appropriate) a song? by what means? (purchase, exchange, etc.)

3 Informers

3.1 Singer
- family name and personal name
- ethnic group and subgroup
- village
- approximate age
- sex
- social position and status
- where, at what age, and from whom did he learn the song being recorded?
- has he lived outside of his native ethnic group? Where? when? for how long?

- is he familiar with a musical repertoire other than that of his own ethnic group (that of neighboring ethnic groups, Western music, indigenous church music, etc.)?
- has he had musical training in his ethnic group, or outside of his group (in another one, in state schools, from missionaries, etc.)?
- does he compose songs himself (writing new words for existing melodies, composing new melodies for traditional texts, or composing both words and music)?

3.2 Translator
- family name and person name
- ethnic group and subgroup
- village
- language(s) spoken
- approximate age
- sex
- social position and status
- amount of formal education
- has he lived outside of his native ethnic group? where? when? for how long?

4 Characteristics of the song

4.1 Musical characteristics
- is the song basically monosyllabic (one note for each syllable) or melismatic (sequence of different notes for a single syllable)?
- does the melody proceed by fixed intervals, by continuous slurring from one note to the next, or a combination of the two?
- is the song sung, spoken rhythmically (declamation), on the border between spoken and sung (parlando), or alternately sung and spoken, etc.?
- is there, traditionally, a purely instrumental version of this song?

4.2 Characteristics of the vocal performance

4.2.1 Techniques and special effects
- the voice is normal-sounding, the tone is forced, falsetto voice, guttural voice, yelling, murmuring, whispering, yodeling (Tyrolean), mouth closed, cooing (warbling), hissing, clucking, nasal sound obtained by pinching the nose, rattling, sobbing, trembling or quavering voice (vibrato), clicking the tongue, smacking the lips, laughing, inarticulate sounds, growling, cries, repeated whistling and hissing by successively breathing in and out, trilling with the tongue, striking the hand against the throat (Adam's apple) to produce a tremolo effect, other effects...

4.2.2 Amplifying and disguising the voice
- the singer uses his hands as a megaphone or uses a prepared megaphone (state material and size)
- the singer disguises his voice by using a reed pipe, a mask, or a mask with a reed pipe inside, etc.

4.2.3 Intention to imitate
- does the vocal performance intend to imitate (a certain character, the sounds of a musical instrument, a bird's song, the gait and/or cry of an animal, etc.)?

Oral Tradition 699

4.3 Linguistic characteristics

4.3.1 Characteristics of the text
- is the text in the vernacular, in the trade language, or in a language with specialized usage (for secret societies, etc.)?
- is the text sprinkled with terms in a foreign language, meaningless syllable, onomatopoetic and/or ideophone syllables?
- is the text rigidly fixed and cannot be varied in any way, fixed but with a certain margin of improvisation left to the singer, a "canvas" around which the performer embroiders/embellishes, a stereotyped phrase serving as a point of departure for improvisation; is the text historical, recurring, autobiographical, political, etc.?

4.3.2 Transcription of the text
- phonetic or phonological transcription, with sentences numbered
- word-for-word interlinear translation
- idiomatic or free translation
- notes and explanatory comments

5 Circumstances of the performance

5.1 Place and time
- if it is an everyday secular song, is it preferably performed in the village, in the bush, in the forest, or is this unspecified?
- if it is a ceremonial or ritual song, the place will be predetermined; specify where it is.
- are there taboos concerning the place(s)?
- is the song sung (preferably or obligatorily) during the day or at night, in the morning or evening, at sunrise or nightfall, at full moon of half moon, etc.?
- are there taboos concerning the time?
- is it used periodically? what is its use associated with?

5.2 Constituent part of the performance

5.2.1 Manner of performance
- in general, is the song sung by one soloist, by two soloists taking turns, by two groups taking turn, by a soloist alternating with a choir, by a choir, etc.?

5.2.2 Vocalists
- soloist: male, female, child, unspecified
- choir: men, women, adults (mixed), children (boys, girls, or mixed), adults and children (mixed), etc.

5.2.3 Rhythmic "body" accompaniment
- clapping hands, snapping fingers, hitting a part of the body with the hands (arms, thighs, chest, stomach), tapping on the ground with the feet, hitting water with the hands (fingers held together to form a sort of inverted spoon), etc.

5.2.4 Instrumental accompaniment
- list all the instruments which take part in the performance of the song: include strictly rhythmic instruments (rattles, spherical bells, cowbells,

drums, etc. or improvised instruments) as well as melodic instruments (harps, flutes, xylophones, etc.); give the vernacular name of each one, with the literal translation (see I. above for the investigation of the instruments)
- note the composition of the ensemble which participates in the performance, singers and instrumentalists: number of participants broken down by function (x soloists, choir made up of x persons, orchestra composed of such and such instruments).
- if appropriate, not the particulars concerning the position and/or movements of the singer's (or singers') body during the performance (standing, seated, or crouching; walking, turning, or dancing; arms raised, two performers hitting each other, etc.)

5.3 Teaching the songs
- how are the songs passed on? By simple imitation, by individual teaching (from a master, an elder, an initiate, the "owner", etc.), or by collective teaching (in initiation hideaway, musical societies, etc.)

5.4 Context

5.4.1 The song stands alone
- is it part of a ceremony (public or secret, familial or individual, etc.), or is it part of a ceremony (fixed, according to the religious calendar, agricultural cycles, etc.; or variable, for birth, healing, divination, engagement, wedding, funeral, etc.)
- give a succinct description of the ceremony or rite of which the song is a part

5.4.2 The song is part of a literary form
- is it part of a story, legend, epic, myth, ballad, chronicle, poem, etc.

5.4.3 The song is part of a musical form
- is the musical form a larger or more developed one? Is it made up of several (vocal and/or instrumental) pieces?
- do these pieces always follow in a specific (determined order, or is the sequential order unspecified? In the latter case, is the total number of pieces fixed (definite)?

6 Sociocultural functions

6.1 Social occasions

The circumstances and social occasions for singing are many and varied, and depend on the peoples and cultural groups. Although they may overlap and may be a bit arbitrary, the circumstances can be grouped into several large categories. Within these categories, the song may be performed, in its turn or in any order, by an individual or in a group, and by professional, nonprofessional, or semi-professional musicians.
- women's songs: for facilitating a delivery, for rocking a child, for nursing, for carry a child on the back, for fetching water, for grinding or pounding (millet, manioc, coffee), for gathering food, for fishing, for agricultural work, for driving birds toward traps, etc.
- children's songs: counting songs, singing or rhythmic games, rounds, singing games of skill (boys), etc.

- work songs: for slaughtering, paddling, ferrying on the river, clearing brush, sowing, harvesting and other agricultural work, or carrying; craftsmen's songs (basketmakers, weavers, smiths), herders' and shepherds' songs, etc.
- songs of amusement: for diversion, relaxation, dancing, satirical, anecdotal songs; drinking songs; racy or licentious songs; love songs; etc.
- songs for different occasions: for praising, for welcoming. for collecting (by children, beggars, blind people); songs of escape or fear, etc.
- ceremonial songs: of betrothal, marriage, initiation (boys or girls), secret societies, leaving for and returning from the hunt, war (encouraging the warriors), victory, etc.
- didactic songs: precepts, rules of conduct, etc.
- mourning songs: of lamentation, mourning, funeral; to celebrate the exploits of the dead person, to close the period of mourning, to be sung at the burial site, etc.
- religious songs: for twins, ancestors, incantations (for hunting, fishing, to ask for rain, etc.) sung invocations (to dead hunters, to spirits of the forest, of the bush, of the river), sung or chanted magical formulas, sons of possession (to obtain the healing of a sick person), songs for sacrifice, exorcism, masks, etc.; miscellaneous ceremonial and ritual songs (for the launching of a new canoe, for consecrating or initiating a new house, for bringing rain, for divination, for agricultural cycles, or the religious calendar, etc.)
- songs for the investiture of a king, chief, prince, etc.
- songs of the court
- sung greetings, mottoes, genealogies
- advertising songs to attract customers at the market
- songs of lament (by orphans, widows, invalids)
- sung narratives (tales, legends, myths, epics, etc.)
- songs appearing in ballads
- songs which are essentially improvised by the musician: poet-musicians, songwriters, etc.

6.2 Major themes
- stages of life: birth, twins, lullabies, children's songs and games, adolescence, initiation (circumcision or excision), love songs, betrothal and marriage songs, songs of mourning
- work: professional and guild, hunting, fishing, farming
- social occasions: for praising, welcoming, secular ceremonies and celebrations, court songs, etc.
- religious: religious ceremonies and celebrations, rituals, etc.
- knowledge and beliefs: are certain plants (sacred, medicinal, magical, etc.) or animals (taboo, sacred, protector of certain lineages) the subjects or songs? Are certain songs attributed to animals, or do certain objects have a song (bell song, drum song, etc.)?

6.3 Cultural ownership

6.3.1 Ownership
- is the song considered as originally belonging to the ethnic group which uses it; was it introduced from another ethnic group? If so, what was the group and what place does it come from? When was it adopted (number of generations back, in the time of a certain chief, before or after the

arrival of the Europeans, at the time of some other important event in the life of the group)?

6.3.2 Age and distribution
- is the song considered old or recent?
- is it locally widespread (known and sung by a large number of people), rare, or about to disappear?
- is it sung by neighboring ethnic groups or not?

6.3.3 Origin
- natural origin: known, anonymous, or collective authorship
- supernatural origin: from a spirit, genius, or ancestral spirit

6.4 Role and change of style
- does the song have an exclusive function or is it part of an exclusive repertoire (therapeutic, propitiatory, dedicated to a guardian spirit, etc.)? If so, specify which and give the vernacular name with literal translation
- has the song retained its original function? Some songs which formerly had a magico-religious role have lost their religious character for secular purposes (working, dancing for entertainment, etc.)

6.5 Conventions

6.5.1 Concerning the song
- ritual observances (such as taboos, words or gestures) concerning the place, time, length of time, the occasion, the audience (may it include anyone, or only the men / women / certain initiates / etc.)

6.5.2 Concerning the performers
- who is entitled to perform the song: men, women, adults, children, or anyone; only the member of a certain social class or those with a special status (chief, priest, healer, soothsayer, initiate, mother of twins, etc.)
- what obligations do the performers have before and/or after the performance? (taboos relative to age, sex, social position or status, lineage, caste; rituals which must be observed, etc.)

7 Recording

7.1 Identification
- number of the tape
- village where recorded
- ethnic group
- single or double track
- date of recording
- taped recorder (make and model)
- speed (15/16, 1-7/8)
- length
- recording made inside, outside, in an open area, under a tree, under a canopy
- recording requested or in natural setting, etc.

7.2 Instructions for recording

7.2.1 Independent songs
- record the song as sung spontaneously, in its original version
- record one or several other versions of the same song

Oral Tradition

- record the ritual words that precede or follow the song in its immediate context, i.e., including the sounds (words, noises, instrumental music) which precede and follow it
- if the song is part of a larger literary form (tale, legend, myth, ballad, etc.), record the song separately, then the whole of the form, including the song
- if the song is part of a larger musical form which includes other songs or instrumental music, record the song separately, then the whole

7.2.2 Song with an instrumental version
- if the song (of whatever category) has given rise to a purely instrumental (orchestral) version, record it.

7.3 Transcription of the words of the song

Each recorded song should be transcribed and translated immediately (word-for-word and idiomatic translations) just as is done for oral literature texts.

3 Investigating the oral style of traditional storytellers
by Geneviève Calame-Griaule

Words without gestures are empty
(J. Vendryes)

The importance of paralinguistic means of expression which accompany or replace the spoken word has long been recognized, especially for gesture systems. Several theoretical works have been written on the subject, but there are very few precise descriptions, and true corpuses are fewer still. The expressive style used by traditional storytellers is practically unexplored, even though ethnologists and linguists alike who collect oral literature texts lament the fact that the published form lacks the charm and life of the oral delivery.

Our purpose here is to respond to the wishes of these researchers. We aim to provide, not a questionnaire as such, but a research guide to facilitate the observation and description of what we call the oral style (or dramatization). By oral style we mean the set of expressive techniques implemented during a performance by a particular individual who uses the resources of his body and voice: gestures, mimicry, facial expressions, sound effects, intonations, etc. The *oral* style is to be distinguished from the *literary* style, a term which indicates the use of expressive techniques on the linguistic level.

Oral style establishes a direct relationship between the *narrator and the text* through the medium of a *language* and with reference to a *culture*. These four pillars of oral literature must always be kept in mind during the investigation. The relationship between a particular technique of oral style and the linguistic expression that it accompanies, emphasizes, or even replaces is constantly evident, as is also the cultural context which conditions expressivity, especially gestural language, as well as linguistic expressivity. Reference will constantly be made to the level of current social communication; this permits us to separate from the storyteller's oral style what is part of the everyday expressivity throughout the culture, what belongs to the literary level, and possibly what is traced to personal creativity. The researcher must always keep from interpreting his observations with respect to his own cultural code.

The oral style, like speech, must originate from a code common to the narrator and the listener. Stylistic techniques resulting from personal creativity must fall within this code, and include a minimum of common elements to remain comprehensible. It would also be of interest to discover the boundaries of noncomprehension, and also which categories of gestures (in the wider sense) lend themselves to innovation. The possibility of integrating (temporarily) a renowned storyteller's gesture should also be considered (cf. the success in our society of certain gestures or intonations of professional comedians or well-known actors).

This paper is designed principally for the study of narrative genres: stories, legends, mythical tales (insofar as they are narrated like stories), anecdotes, and narratives in everyday conversation. We have systematically avoided anything concerning poetic texts which are sung or declaimed in a special way, or accompanied by an instrument, for these require a study of their own. Besides, we must point out that this work is based on experience in Africa. It does not claim to be universal nor exhaustive, but is simply a preliminary basis for research. It can be adapted and supplemented by any researcher interested in trying this type of study.

Because such an investigation requires constant reference to the language and cultural context, it is preferable to undertake it only in a society which is already well known.

In this study we have grouped together a number of methodological instructions, specific points to be observed carefully, and classification categories for orientation in the study. Of course, the order of our comments does not imply a course to follow; the investigation should proceed in all areas concurrently.

1. Optimal conditions for the study
2. Social significance of the oral style
3. Techniques of the oral style
4. Relationship between the language and oral style
5. Relationship between the culture and oral style: interpretation
6. Methods of observation and description

1 Optimal conditions for the study

In order to study a storyteller's oral style in its most accomplished form, we must observe him in his most customary context, surrounded by a traditional audience. In meetings or evening gatherings, in the village or the city, in the family or in public. By attending these events, we observe the social context of the oral literature and find out the rules which govern it (cf. the general study of oral literature), as well as observing the storyteller and the reactions of the audience. The performance should be tape recorded as long as it does not disturb the story's progress or the behavior of those present.

Additional working sessions should be held with the speaker by himself or before a small audience. Here we go over and annotate the texts, sentence by sentence, with the speaker, recalling the gestures observed during the performance. Such work requires much patience and understanding on the part of the speaker, but experience shows that it is easy to interest a storyteller in this type of study.

As for the *speakers,* all the usual information will be taken down: name, age, sex, ethnic group, place of origin, tribe and subgrouping, social position, languages he speaks or understands. Make special note of the talents of the storyteller and how he learned the craft.

Oral Tradition

1) Is this an amateur or a professional storyteller?
2) Is he known as a storyteller (in his family, in his village, outside his village)? Do others come from far away to hear him?
3) From whom did he learn: a) to tell stories; b) the text in question:
   - from a relative: mother, grandmother, father, grandfather, maternal uncle, ...; from hearing another amateur storyteller; from a master or professional storyteller
4) Is he attempting to reproduce a model or to improvise in his own oral style? (ask the opinion of other people present)
5) If he is a well-known star, observe his demeanor (confident, coquettish, refusing requests in order to solicit more, etc.)

   As much as possible, try to diversify variables of the storytelling situation as follows:
   - have the same story told by different storytellers; male and female (repertoires often differ, so choice of story needs care), skilled and average storytellers, etc.
   - have the same story told by the same storyteller some time apart.
   - have the same storyteller tell stories of different genres, (e.g., magical, comic, war, love stories, etc.)
   - have the same storyteller perform before different audiences, to see if that changes his style.

2 Social significance of the oral style

The following series of questions will help determine whether the society under consideration is conscious of the importance of expressivity in the oral tradition:

1) Is the speaker aware that he is making certain gestures and facial expressions when he tells a story?
2) Is he aware of such expressiveness in other storytellers?
3) Is he aware that the audience's reactions (e.g., laughing) can be intensified or even sparked by gestures, mimicking, or an expressive intonation? Does he exploit these consciously?
4) Does he sometimes purposely replace words with gestures? In what situations?
5) By what criteria is an oral style judged good or bad? For example, are there storytellers who lay it on thick, or, on the other hand, are too sparing of gestures to suit most people? Do others try to imitate them?
6) Do men make different gestures from women? Is there a term which expresses the difference in code or style?
7) Will the gestures be the same if the audience is different? Does the speaker feel it necessary to have a traditional audience to give free rein to his gesticulations? Does he feel that the investigation creates an artificial situation for him?
8) Is he conscious of using the same gestures in storytelling as in everyday communication? Is he aware of using a different style?

9) What are the words in the speaker's language (and in other languages he knows) for the gestures and facial expressions which accompany the words? Are there special terms to designate those of the storyteller? What is the linguistic origin of these terms?

10) Are there sayings, proverbs, or popular expressions which highlight the importance of gestures which accompany (or possibly replace) the spoken language? Are there metaphorical formulas such as, gestures which accompany words are like ... ; to speak (narrate) without gestures is like ....

3 Techniques of the oral style

3.1 Gestures

Careful observation must be made of the items below. Of course, in listing the parts of the body that are involved, we cannot list the movements of these body parts which constitute gestures, because the possibilities are infinite.

1) initial spatial orientation of the storyteller: standing, squatting, sitting (on the ground or on a seat), placement of the legs, orientation with respect to the audience, placement with respect to an important person or someone chosen as respondent . . . . If he is a professional, note his characteristic stance and accessories (e.g., stick).

2) Use of space during the narration:
   - changing orientation (to show change of characters in a dialogue, or to face someone in the audience)
   - change of location while standing
   - change of position (lying down, kneeling, getting up (again), etc.
   - use of dance steps
   - use of the ground: hitting or beating, drumming, pointing to, or drawing on the ground
   - use of objects or people round about (e.g., including them in the story by pointing them out)

3) parts of the body involved in a gesture:
   - hands (right, left, or both), fingers, wrist
   - arm, forearm
   - chest
   - head, neck
   - entire body (e.g., halfway or completely raised up, etc.)
   - legs, feet

4) accessories:
   - clothing or parts of clothing, headgear, veil
   - jewelry
   - props: rod, stick, weapon, satchel, stone, object picked up off the ground or borrowed from someone, ...

5) nature of gesture, i.e., simple or complex:

- linked to other gestures
- combined with one or more of the other techniques mentioned below

6) is the gesture more or less quick?
- define the criteria for quickness

3.2 Facial expressions

Facial expressions are even more fleeting and difficult to observe and describe than gestures. The observer cannot help but be subjective in his own interpretations. Thus, he must always check them with the interpretations of the speakers and audience. Certain expressions, such as mean looking or suspicious, which are actually interpretations rather than descriptions, will always be difficult to avoid. A term such as grimace, for example, is equally insufficient; it is necessary to indicate what in the face is distorted to produce a given type of grimace. The parts of the face which are the most mobile and contribute the most to expressivity, i.e., the eyes and mouth, should be closely observed:

1) the eyes
- opening and closing the eyes
- fluttering the eyelashes
- looking sideways
- knitting one's brows
- raising and lowering the eyes
- glancing quickly
- following something with the eyes
- squinting, looking cross-eyed
- looking or staring wide-eyed, etc.

2) the mouth
- smiling
- grinning
- pouting
- raising or lowering the corners of the mouth
- sticking out the tongue
- pursing or rounding the lips
- showing teeth
- swallowing, etc.

Note that if the mouth is veiled, as is the case with certain nomads, the eyes assume expressive intensity.

3.3 Resources of the voice

Here again it is difficult to avoid some subjectivity in observation. For example, how does one objectively describe an irritated voice or a pleading tone? Errors in interpretation can be avoided by checking and rechecking with the text and with speakers' comments. Note the following elements:

1) intensity
- increasing or decreasing, by degrees
- whispering

- murmuring
- speaking at the top of one's voice

2) intonation
    - rising
    - falling
    - intonation patterns (not to be confused with linguistic tones)

3) delivery
    - slowing down or speeding up, by degrees
    - drawling
    - expressive lengthening of certain syllables
    - distinct or indistinct pronunciation
    - stammering, quavering voice, etc.

4) timbre
    - changes in register (low-pitched, high-pitched)
    - nasalization

5) changes in breathing
    - panting
    - breathing in
    - sighing

Several of these techniques may be used in combination to make a stereotyped imitation of certain character types: the old woman, the little child, the ogre, the hyena, etc. A certain voice may even identify them without naming them.

Considering vocal techniques raises the general question of the manner of the delivery, which concerns both oral and literary style. The rhythm of the narration, its speeding up or slowing down, is meant to evoke certain reactions from the audience (i.e., laughing, fear, suspense, surprise, ...) Furthermore, even though this consideration is limited to narrative genres, stories which incorporate sung sections should not be neglected. In such cases, which are common in Africa, attention should be paid to the transition from narrative to song and what effects this has on the oral style. We reiterate, however, that the whole question of the relationship between music and oral literature should be the subject of a special study.

3.4 Additional techniques

A number of techniques are grouped together here which are neither purely gesticulatory nor linguistic, but which contribute to oral expressiveness, often in an important way. It goes without saying that this list is not exhaustive.

1) laughing and crying: crying can be simulated by various groanings; for laughing, distinguish between the storyteller's spontaneous laugh when he is amused by a funny passage (sometimes before telling it, because he knows the text in advance), and the laugh which he attributes to one of his characters (nuances of laughing).

2) clicks: sounds produced without opening the mouth and with air passing through the nose (difficult to transcribe; be aware of their possible linguistic value); other noises made with the mouth.

3) whistling, sniffling, snoring, puffing out the cheeks, etc.

4) groanings, grunts, cries (of pain, joy, surprise, etc.); cries of animals; distinguish these from onomatopoeia that has a linguistic value.

5) pauses, silence, suspense-producing effects

6) sound effects: a) without props (snapping the fingers, clapping the hands, applauding); b) with props (jangling jewelry, rhythmic hitting to imitate a drum or forge).

4 Relationship between the language and the oral style

In this part of the investigation, we analyze the relationships between the expressive technique and the linguistic utterance that it accompanies, emphasizes, or sometimes replaces. The goal is to discover whether these relationships are constant or accidental. Insofar as they are constant, a lexicon of gestures, related to the lexicon of the language, can be compiled. A single gesture could thus correspond to several different linguistic utterances, and vice versa.

Try then to pinpoint any utterances generally accompanied by a specific gesture or expressive technique. If appropriate, distinguish the level of everyday communication and the literary style, where gesticulatory clichés may be discovered associated with the conventional clichés or motifs of the narrative.

Listed below are a number of suggested lexical categories, for the analysis must be based on specific linguistic structures. These suggested categories match up for the most part with the more detailed classification of gestures below in §5:

1) onomatopoeia and interjections

2) affirmative and negative adverbs

3) ideophones

4) deictics

5) adverbs and adjectives describing concrete qualities (shape, size, distance ...) or abstract qualities (beauty, madness . . .); intensifiers.

6) nouns and verbs describing postures, movements, technique; some languages are rich in verbal roots which express types of an action (walking, for example); look for gestures corresponding to nuances.

7) nouns and verbs describing psychological states

8) nouns designating characteristic beings or objects: proper nouns (heroes, animal characters, supernatural beings) that appear in a story along with a particular gesture or other expressive technique

9) words under linguistic 'taboo': sexual terms, scatological terms, etc.; possibly, euphemisms to replace them, or silence accompanied by an expressive technique.

10) conventional formulas (of politeness), insults, etc.

11) terms designating social institutions (religious, judicial, etc.); remember that the noun which designates them sometimes originated with a ritual gesture.

12) similes, metaphors

Note: Observe whether the particular expressive technique is associated with a single word, a phrase, or an entire sentence (in which case there may be a sequence of techniques that form the whole).

5 Relationship between the culture and oral style: Interpretation

In order to interpret these stylistic techniques, some classification system (at least tentative) is necessary. The one suggested here is meant only as a point of departure; it should be revised, based on research results and based on the particular ethnic group.

For convenience, we use the term gesture in the wide sense, including all techniques of the oral style considered above. We divide them into two major categories corresponding to two different types of symbolization. The category corresponding to the first type includes all properly *descriptive gestures,* whose purpose is to imitate, show, or indicate objects or phenomena perceivable to the senses. Although social conventions play a part in the manner of symbolization, they are more important in the second category; the relationship between signifier and signified is never completely arbitrary. This type will prove to be rich for oral narration. We call the second category *social gestures,* for lack of a better term, for they depend solely on social conventions and institutions. These pertain to a second level of symbolization, in that the signifier has only an arbitrary relationship with the signified.

For each of the two categories, note whether the gestures are specific to the literary style or if they are used in everyday communication. There will likely be more relationships with the social context in the second category, though this is not proven.

5.1 Descriptive gestures

1) in relation to position or movement in space
   a) posture or assumed pose: movement on the spot (lying down, kneeling, getting up, ...)
   b) change of location (leaving, fleeing, arriving, running, ...)
   c) climbing up, going down
2) as movements required in specific activities
   a) miscellaneous activities such as cutting, hitting, beating, feeling, opening, closing, pouring; and the various shades of meaning implied (e.g., cutting with a knife, axe, the teeth, etc.)
   b) bodily activities: walking, running, swimming, wrestling, dancing, grooming, putting on make-up
   c) activities of consumption: drinking, eating, tasting, feeding, nursing, ...
   d) trades and activities: blacksmithing, weaving, pottery-making, leatherworking, hunting, fishing, farming, sewing, spinning, cooking, buying and selling; medicine; music; war ... ; how is the use of the tool or instrument imitated?
3) suggesting qualities
   a) concrete qualities
      - shape: round, spherical, spiral, pointed ...
      - size: largeness, smallness, height, width, length, depth, enormity, vastness, ...

- distance: far away, close ...
- heaviness, lightness
- cold, heat
- taste: salty, sweet, bitter, good, bad, ...

b) abstract qualities
- beauty, ugliness
- strength, weakness; authority, power
- wisdom, insanity, stubbornness
- kindness, maliciousness

Note: Ask if there are differences or variants of the gesture depending on the intensity of qualifier used: very large, terribly heavy, ...

4) deictic gestures
- this one here, that one down there, the others, the one who left, etc.
- possible nuances: scorn, admiration, mockery (see next category)

5) psychological attitudes

This category of gestures is included here, even though they are related to the second group too. They are descriptive in that their purpose is to let the audience perceive know the psychological state of the characters. This list is in no way exhaustive:

a) joy, sadness, love, hate, disgust, disappointment, suffering

b) admiration, scorn, approval, disapproval

c) impatience, anger, intimidation / threat, mockery, aggression

d) shame, remorse, modesty, flirtatiousness

e) ignorance, doubt, incredulity, indifference, powerlessness

f) fatigue, weariness; hunger, thirst

g) anxiety, fear

h) humility, entreaty, asking forgiveness

Note the intensity of the feelings expressed. Distinguish also whether the gesture expresses a genuine or feigned psychological attitude for the character in the story.

6) gestures which personalize the protagonists of the story
   a) change of place or orientation to show the passage from one character to another (in dialogues); changes of tone, register, timbre, etc.
   b) symbolic gestures to typify a character by alluding to a distinctive physical characteristic or character trait. The gesture may even indicate the character's stage entrance without naming him. Animals, supernatural beings, comic heroes, etc., may also be characterized in this way.

7) obscene gestures

5.2 Social gestures

1) related to manners
   a) proprieties
   b) greetings, politeness, etiquette
   c) agreement, disagreement, questioning

2) related to institutions
    a) religious: prayer, exorcism, possession, cursing, invoking or calling up supernatural beings, death, funerals
    b) magic, sorcery
    c) legal: oathtaking, ordeal, contract
3) related to the unfolding of the discourse
    a) oratorical gestures
    b) phatic gestures: these have no particular meaning, but accompany or underline the discourse, revive the attention of the audience, etc. They may be individual in nature, but are related to the cultural context nonetheless.
    c) the absence of gestures, immobility: the deliberate absence of expressive gestures may be ritualistic, may be a question of propriety, etc.; expressive intensity is then carried by the voice.

Note: Certain gestures are especially important; the whole meaning of the story rests on them, and without them it would be incomprehensible. Even though such gestures may belong to either of our two categories, we will call them causal gestures in that they are given to justify an episode of the story or a personality trait of one of the characters.

It seems that all the gestures mentioned in the preceding categories may take on a comical meaning when they are diverted from their primary meaning (i.e., misunderstood), or magnified or exaggerated, or repeated several times, or done hesitatingly, etc. They may be studied from this perspective, which leads us to wonder whether gestures exist which are comical in themselves.

6 Methods of observation and description

To describe the techniques of oral style as defined here requires long, meticulous research. A great deal of data must be collected to constitute a corpus. Since all collected texts must be transcribed, translated, and annotated before the oral style can be analyzed, quality is to be preferred to quantity. Several stories studied in depth may yield a wealth of valuable information already. Research into the oral style will necessarily be linked to the role of oral literature in the society on the one hand, and to the nature of literary style on the other.

Because gestures and expressive techniques are usually executed rapidly, it is difficult to break them down into their component parts. The cooperation of the speaker is very important, for he must be willing to repeat the same gesture a number of times. It is difficult to observe everything at once, so we recommend the presence of another researcher or collaborator from the same ethnic group as the storyteller. This person will be able to complete the observations, and draw the attention of the researcher to significant details he had overlooked.

Different methods may be used in conjunction:

1) Tape recording will naturally be the basis for the study. The recording must be of good quality, so that nuances and intonations of the voice can be heard. The machine used must be sturdy enough to withstand the continual rewinding required by a systematic listening to the text bit by bit (see the general study of oral literature).

2) Description in the researcher's language of the expressive techniques observed, in great detail. Although it may seem crude, this part is indispensable. Objectivity without some element of interpretation is difficult at this stage. We may not say, for example, that the storyteller is raising his hand in greeting; we must simply note the movement of the arm, its direction, the height to which it is raised, the way the hand appears; at the same time, the expression of the face, the direction of the look. Interpreting the gesture as a greeting comes later. Record as much as possible right away; do not depend too heavily on memory for reproducing the gesture. Other methods will compensate for the mistakes and gaps inevitable in this description.

3) A system of symbolic notation would be desirable. None has yet been proposed for this area, although one already exists for choreography. Meanwhile, the researcher can perfect his own system with symbols to represent the hands, head; arrows to indicate movements; etc.

4) Photographs are invaluable for capturing certain stages of the gesture and certain expressions. Two methods are possible: a) snapping shots continuously during the narration (experience shows that this method is especially useful for phatic gestures); and b) asking the speaker to repeat the gestures corresponding to different parts of the text (this method is much better for isolating truly significant gestures). In any case, photography should not be used until after the gestural techniques have been thoroughly analyzed.

5) Quick sketches may be of great help, and show details not visible in photographs.

6) Movies are considered by many to be the ideal method of observation, since they recreate the performance in their totality and allow frame-by-frame analysis. These are disadvantages, however. The principal one is the cost. To make up a corpus for analyzing styles, a large number of documents must be gathered; it is physically impossible to film them all. Besides, filming requires meticulous preparation and cannot always be used when it is needed. This is the best means of observation, but it does not do away with other methods. Widespread use of videotape recorders is clearly desirable.

All observations should be organized in a single *gesture* file, classified according to a system of headings. Each file card should include:
- at the top of the card, an indication of the category (and subcategory, possibly) under which the gesture is classified
- a list of the body parts and accessories involved
- a precise and objective description of the gesture
- its association with other expressive techniques (facial expressions, intonations, additional techniques, etc.)
- the linguistic utterance which the gesture accompanies
- its interpretation related to the text and reference to the social context
- at the bottom of the card, the information concerning the speaker, language, ethnic group, and place of observation; this information can be succinct and refer to a file on the storytellers.

Note: A file of this type is based on the *gesture* per se, but could be organized in some other manner.

A separate *lexical* file should also be set up which shows correspondences between the language and expressive techniques. For each linguistic entry, give the techniques associated with it. Specify also whether the technique is purely narrative, or whether it is used for social communication too.

By putting together these corpuses and files, we can study the type of expressivity used by a particular ethnic group and language; then, we can make comparisons, first with neighboring or related ethnic groups, and finally on a wider scale.

Researchers are encouraged to publish texts collected in this way, accompanied by all notes they can make about the expressive techniques, presented perhaps like stage directions in a play. We hope in this way to reconstruct the living qualities of oral literature.

Bibliography

Calamé-Griaule, G. 1970. Pour une étude ethnolinguistique des littératures orales africaines. Langages 18:22–47.
———. 1971. Etude stylistique d'un conte dogon. Afrikanische Sprachen und Kulturen-Ein Querschnitt. Hamburg. pp. 266–78.
———. 1977. Pour une étude des gestes narratifs. Langage et cultures africaines, Essais d'ethnolinguistique. Paris.
Conté, P. 1957. Ecriture de la danse. Le système Conté. Cahiers de la danse. Paris.
Efron, D. 1941. Gesture, race and culture. Reissued 1971, Paris: Mouton.
Firth, R. 1970. Postures and gestures of respect. Echanges et communications 1:188–209.
Greimas, A. J., ed. 1968. Pratiques et langage gestuels. Langage 10
Hall, E.T. 1963. A system for the notation of proxemic behavior. American Anthropologist, 65(5):239–45.
Koechlin, B. 1971. Pour une ethno-technologie. Eléments d'un manuel de technologie culturelle (un prototype de grille documentaire). Bulletin du CEDRASEMI 2(3).
Leroi-Gourhan, A. 1964–65. Le geste et la parole. Paris.
Mathon–Baduel, C. 1969. Pour une sémiologie du geste en Afrique occidentale. Semiotica 1(3):245–55.
———. 1971. Le langage gestuel en Afrique Occidentale: Recherches bibliographiques. Journal de la Société des Africanistes 41(2):203–49.
Mauss, M. 1960. Les techniques du corps. Sociologie et anthropologie. Paris. pp. 363–86.
Metz, C. 1968. Langage gestuel. Supplément scientifique à la Grande Encyclopédie Larousse.
Sandor, I. 1967. Dramaturgy of tale-telling. Acta Ethnographica Academiae Scientiarum Hungaricae 16(3-4):305–38.

Questionnaire 19
Language Contact

by Jean-Pierre Caprile and Jacqueline M. C. Thomas

1 Survey Questionnaire

At least one hundred copies of this questionnaire should be made. The principal speaker can help with it, so its use and importance should be explained to him.

To facilitate its use in survey and analysis, obtain as many yes/no and coded answers as possible; then, the survey forms can be arranged as a two-column matrix, especially for the questions in §§7 and 8.

1 Civil status

Surname(s):   Given name(s):
Age: Sex:

2 Ethnic group

Ethnic group of the speaker
Ethnic group of his father:
Ethnic group of his mother:
Ethnic group(s) of spouse(s): 1.   2.   3.
marriage(s) with / without children)
- If his mother or spouse(s) is from a different ethnic group, does the speaker speak the language of the mother or spouse? Where and with whom did he learn it? When?

3 Residence history

Place of birth (within the ethnic group, or outside of it? (in which group?)):
Place(s) of residence from 1–15 years of age (indicate age ranges for each place):
Other places of residence (from age 15 to present):

4 Length of residence in a town

If the survey is conducted in a town of some importance where populations are intermixed:
- How long has the speaker been living in the town?
- Does he live in a district with his native ethnic group?
- or in the district of a different group (which one)?
- or in a district of mixed ethnic groups?

If the survey is not conducted in a town, has the speaker lived in a town?
- which one? (specify the district, as above)
- when? for how long? (specify dates and length of different stays)

5 Education

Total length of schooling (how many years of school?)
Highest level of schooling (what was the last class in school that the speaker attended?)
- Primary (specify class)
- Secondary (specify class)
- Superior (specify diploma or degree obtained and in what subject area(s)—(arts / sciences / law / medicine)
- Professional training

Diplomas received

6 Profession

Present profession (practiced for how long?)
Previous (other professions practiced before: which (in order after leaving school)? for how long? where?

Knowledge of languages

7 Which languages does he speak?

Which was the first language spoken (the mother tongue, learned from the mother and/or father)?
Which local (African) languages does he know?
    1.   2.   3.   4.   etc.
Which other languages (European, Arabic, etc.) does he know?
    1.   2.   3.   4.   etc.

(For each language, indicate the level of fluency: S (=speaking), C (=comprehension) // VG (=very good ability, as for a native speaker), G (=good, capable of holding or following a sustained conversation on most

Language Contact   717

subjects), FG (=fairly good, a level of everyday conversation), L (=low level, some words and phrases only)

8 Where and how did he learn the different languages?

Local vernacular languages:
    1. mother tongue 2.   3.   4.   etc.
Local trade languages:
    1.   2.   3.   4.   etc.
European or international languages (English, French, etc.)
    1.   2.   3.   4.   etc.

(For each language mentioned, state whether it was learned: at home (with the father/ mother/ grandparents—maternal or paternal/ spouse); from friends (playmates, friends at school, work); at a mission station (Catholic, Protestant); at school (government, mission, Koranic); at work; from living in an area where it was spoken)

(For each language, state at what age it was learned.)

Language use

9 Where, when and with whom does he speak

his native language? where? when? with whom?
trade language? where? when? with whom?
European language? where? when? with whom?
Other local language(s) where? when? with whom?
Other language(s) of wider communication where? when? with whom?

10 Which language is used

At home with relatives?
    In what language do the following speak to him?
 - his father - his mother - his grandparents - paternal, maternal
 - spouse(s) - his brothers and sisters - his children
    In what language do his relatives speak to each other?
    In what language does he speak to:
 - his father - his mother- his grandparents - paternal, maternal
 - spouse(s) - his brothers and sisters- his children
with relatives or friends in the bush:
with friends:
  - when walking   - when playing (cards, dice)
  - in meetings   - in other situations
with people of the village or district (in town)
at work
  - with friends   - with the employer
  - with clients   - with employees (for an employer)
at the market
in the shops

with government officials
- in government departments — with the police
  and offices
- at the post office — with others

in court
- customary village court
- customary district court (in town)

with foreigners
- with strangers (local people) — with strangers from the same country
- with those from other countries
- with Europeans

Attitude toward different languages

11 Languages most preferred

Which language does he prefer to speak? Why?
Which language does he like most? Why?
Which language does he speak best? Why?

12 Languages least preferred

Which language does he least like to speak?
Which language does he like least?
Which language does he speak least well?

13 Language of neighbors

Cite the languages of his neighbors (surrounding ethnic groups)?
Does he consider them to be related to his mother tongue? which ones?
Does he speak these languages? Does he understand them? Which ones?

14 Language center

Where is his mother tongue spoken best? (in which town, village, region)

The preceding information will provide the basis for very interesting (semi-intensive) sociolinguistic study of language contact, and the questionnaire could be terminated at this point. However, this study may be pursued in greater depth by means of the following questionnaire, which constitutes a valuable follow-up.

The specifically linguistic aspects of the problem must be studied from a sampling of texts collected in the different languages spoken (cf. Introduction).

2 Intensive questionnaire

1 Means of communication and culture

A. Audio-visual means

1. *Do you listen to the radio?*
   often / fairly often / rarely / never
   In which language(s) are the radio programs to which you listen?
   Which language do you prefer for radio programs?
   Would you prefer more time to be given to a certain language?
   Is there a language not used on the radio in which you would like to hear programs?

2. *Do you go to the cinema?*
   often / fairly often / rarely / never
   Which language(s) is/are spoken in the films you go to see?
   Which language would you prefer to have used in the cinema?
   Would you like films in an African language?
   a) which language?
   b) why?

3. *Can you read?*
   Which languages can you read?
   Do you read often / fairly often / rarely /never?
   Which types of books do you read (school books, religious books, novels, illustrated magazines, etc.)
   Give titles and authors.
   Do you read one or several newspapers? Which? (give the titles and frequency of publication: daily, weekly, monthly, etc.)

4. *Which language(s) do you write?*
   In which circumstances do you use the language(s) which you write? (at school, letters to friends or family, work, official correspondence, etc.)

5. *Which language(s) would you like to learn to read and write? Why?*

6. *Would you like to be able to read newspapers and magazines in an African language? Which language? Why?*

B. Traditional oral means

1. *Do you know any **proverbs**?*
   - in your native language: many / a few / none
   - in another African language? which? many / a few / none

2. *Do you know any **riddles**?*
   - in your native language: many / a few / none
   - in another African language and which? many / a few / none

3. *Do you find proverbs and riddles?*
    a. amusing and entertaining?
    b. instructive (teaching wisdom and prudence)?
    c. useless and uninteresting?

4. *Have you heard stories and tales?*
    a. in your native language: often / sometimes / never
    b. in other language(s), and which one(s): often / sometimes / never
    c. where did you hear them?
    d. when did you hear them?
    e. who was telling them? (a storyteller, relative, etc.)
   Do you tell stories and tales in an African language?
    a. often / sometimes / never
    b. in which language(s)?
    c. where do you tell them?
    d. when do you tell them?
    e. to whom do you tell them?
   What do these stories and tales mean to you?
   What do you think of their usefulness? Give reasons for your answer.

5. *Do you know any songs in an African language?*
    a. many / a few / none?
    b. in which language do you know them?
    c. when do you sing them?
    d. where do you sing them?
    e. with whom do you sing them?
   Do you enjoy singing in an African language? Which one? Why?

6. *Can you play an African musical instrument?* drum / flute / balaphon / African guitar (zither, harp) / other instruments (which ones?) Would you like to learn to play an African musical instrument?
    a. Which one?
    b. Why?
    c. Would you like to learn to play a European musical instrument?

7. *Have you been initiated?*
   In which language was the initiation performed?
   Is there a special language for initiation, different from the ordinary language?
   What is it called?
   Do you know it?

2 Religion

1. *Do you have a religion? What is it?*
   Do you have or do you know other religions?
   Do you have a village religion?

2. *Which language are religious activities conducted in?*
   prayer / singing / mass or services / catechism / other activities?

3. Which language are the religious texts that you use written in?

4. Can you read them: easily / fairly easily / with difficulty / not at all?
Why?

5. Which language do you prefer or would you prefer to speak in your religious activities?
   Which language do you prefer or would you prefer for reading and writing religious texts?

3 Military service

1. Have you completed military service? in a colonial army (French, English, German, etc.)? In the national army?

2. Which language(s) did you use with: the officers / other soldiers / the peoples of the places where you were garrisoned?

3. Which language(s) did you learn while in the army?

4 Study and use of English / French / Spanish . . .

1. Have you attended school? What class are you in now? At what level did you stop school?

2. Have you taken a professional training course (indicate type and duration)?
   - at which institution or establishment?
   - in which locality?
      Which language did you use during this course?
      Would you have liked to use a different language for the course? Which one? Why?

3. Where did you attend school before coming to town (name the town)?

4. How long have you attended school in town (name the town)?

5. What was your living situation / accommodation (with a family / with a guardian / at a mission or school boarding house / living alone)

6. Which language(s) do you speak at school:
   a. in class?
   b. during recreation?

7. Do you speak English (French, etc.) outside school: always / fairly often / never?
   a. where?
   b. with whom?
   c. why?

8. Does your family speak English (French, etc.):
   - father   - mother   - brothers and sisters

- grandparents   - spouse   - children
Who speaks English (French, etc.) in your family?
Does your guardian know English (French, etc.)? Does his wife know English (French, etc.)?

9. How many years of schooling have you had in English (French, etc.)?

10. Did you start to learn and speak English (French, etc.) before going to school? How and at what age? With whom?

11. Do you listen to radio broadcasts in English (French, etc.)? often / fairly often / sometimes / never?

12. Do you read books in English (French, etc.) apart from school books: often / fairly often / sometimes / never?
    Which books do you read? (novels / religious books / illustrated magazines / etc.) Give authors and titles.
    Do you read one or more English (French, etc.) newspapers? Which one(s)?

13. Why did you learn or are you learning English (French, etc.)? What does the English (French, etc.) language mean for you?

Questionnaire 20
Sociolinguistic Questionnaire

Study of multilingualism
by Michel Dieu

1 African languages

No. of investigator
No. of checker

Date:
Location— Province
Subdivision
District
Village/neighborhood
Original nationality of
person interviewed:

1.1 Languages spoken

List all the African languages (vernacular or trade), including pidgin, spoken or understood by the person being interviewed, in descending order (from the one spoken best to poorest).
1. Gbanzili
2. Sango
3. Ngbaka
4. Manza
5. Isongo
   etc.

1.2 Mother tongue

or language of his community of origin, even if no longer used or forgotten

1.3 Degree of fluency

Name of language	spoken completely fluently, without any difficulty	spoken fluently	spoken fairly well understood well	understood but spoken only a little	a few words only
Example:					
Gbanzili	x				
'Bolaka	x				
Sango	x				
Ngbaka		x			
Isongo			x		
Manza				x	
Banda					x

For each language spoken, indicate how well the interviewee considers that he speaks it (place an x in the appropriate column[18])

Place an x in this box if the mother tongue is not spoken ☐

2 Languages of wider communication

2.1 Languages known

Give any European languages spoken or understood: French, English, (Arabic), or others.
1.   2.   3.   4.   etc.

2.2 Degree of fluency

a. For English (and/or French, Arabic, etc.), can the person interviewed:
   1. ask directions, or give directions to a stranger? yes/no
   2. discuss a matter with a teacher or explain a situation to a civil servant (e.g., at the municipal offices) in English (or French / Arabic)? yes/no
   3. count in English (French / Arabic)? yes/no
   4. hold a conversation with an English (French, Arabic) speaker? yes/no

---

[18]Question 3 permits correction of the order given spontaneously in Question 1.

b. In the following cases, would he need to ask the assistance of a friend? yes/no
   1. to fill out an administrative form? yes/no
   2. to file a complaint? yes/no
   3. to make out application for a job, or write an important letter? yes/no
c. Does he write letters to his friends in English (and/or French, and/or Arabic)? yes/no
d. Do relatives or neighbors ask him to write letters for them? yes/no
e. Has he written, or does he write poems, stories, or plays in English (and/or French, and/or Arabic)? yes/no

www.ingramcontent.com/pod-product-compliance
Lightning Source LLC
Chambersburg PA
CBHW052037290426
44111CB00011B/1537